The Ultimate Training Workshop Handbook

The Ultimate Training Workshop Handbook

A Comprehensive Guide to Leading Successful Workshops & Training Programs

Bruce Klatt

McGraw-Hill

New York San Francisco Washington, D.C. Auckland Bogotá
Caracas Lisbon London Madrid Mexico City Milan
Montreal New Delhi San Juan Singapore
Sydney Tokyo Toronto

McGraw-Hill

A Division of The McGraw-Hill Companies

10 11 12 13 14 15 EDW/EDW 0 10 9 8 7

ISBN 0-07-913699-0 (hc)
0-07-038201-8 (pbk)

The sponsoring editor for this book was Richard Narramore, the editing supervisor was Scott Amerman, and the production supervisor was Tina Cameron. It was set in Goudy by Mosaic Studios in Calgary, Canada.

Printed and bound by Edwards Brothers.

This book is printed on recycled, acid-free paper containing a minimum of 50% recycled, de-inked fiber.

Dedication

To my mentors.

Over the years these people believed in me, challenged and supported me, and seemed to make it their job to help me succeed. Not surprisingly, these are the people I learned the most from.

George Campbell

Dick Duczek

Murray Hiebert

David Irvine

Shaun Murphy

Mogans Piepgrass

Denny Thomas

Peter Zakreski

and

John E. Jones
for his example and inspiration of powerful workshop and training-program leadership

Contents

Part 5 - Getting It Done: Leading a Workshop 378

Appendixes 549

Acknowledgments

Who achieves anything noteworthy without the help of others? Not me, that's for sure.

I'm grateful to my friends and colleagues from the old Vector Consulting Associates organization. They were like a second family to me. I respect and value every one of them. They trusted and believed in me, shared their work and gave me the support and challenge I needed to succeed. Included in this group are George Campbell, Nadine Ryan-Bannerman, Laurel McLean, Murray Hiebert, Dave Irvine, Shaun Murphy, Carla Dzurman, and Sydnie Waring.

I owe a special debt to those who suffered through an early draft of this book and provided thoughtful criticisms and support. Thanks to John Jones, Diane MacDonald, Shirley Bond, Laurel McLean, Dave Irvine, and Murray Hiebert.

Next, I'd like to thank my family. My wife, Cathy, proofread several drafts, but more than this, she gave me space and understanding through the last several months of writing this book, during which time she only saw the back of my head as I worked at my computer. My sons, Bryan and Jeff, both university students, also provided a lot of help and support. Bryan, an honors student in political science, worked an entire summer vacation proofreading, doing research, and helping me with drafts. Jeff, a computer science major, provided administrative support and made sure my many computer problems were fixed without delay. Working with my sons on this project has once again helped me realize how proud I am of both of them.

Finally, I'm grateful to the following people, each of whom sponsored one or several workshops and training programs that I led during the past few years that this book evolved. These include Larry Renooy, Judy Aikenhead, Daniel Briére, Gail Harrison, Cherry Davies, Jane Lackner, Darcy Verhun, Barb Daigle, Ron Smith, Dick Duczek, Laurel McLean, Jodie Winquist, Randy Findlay, Pete deBeer, Joanne Stalinski, John Eddy, Albert Elliott, Bob Redgate, Bill Douglas, Dean Fixen, John Henry, Hal Irvine, Brad Jackson, Jack Kapiczowski, Roger Kohut, Michele Luit, Peggy McLennan, Kim Frache, Stuart McKinnon, Garry Melrose, Jim Davis, Pat Breen, Ed Dyck, Mike Langley, Wes Omilusik, Don Petrie, Jennifer White, Marlene Raasok, Greer Black, Scott Richardson, Paul Rushforth, Paul Schoenhals, Doug Smith, Murray Todd, Ora Zabloski, Frank Johnston, Gene Syvenky, Bruno Friesen, Rick Smith, Ken Bailie, Bill McCracken, Cheryl King, Doug Beagrie, Nancy Newcommon, Shirley Bond, Fran Reiss, John Watson, Steve Baldick, Denise Burzminski, Jennifer Yip Choy, Joan McGregor, Brenda Kustra, Bob Kinasewich, Greg Hnatuk, Peter Arnold, Keith Winter, Marnie Schaetti, Kirby Kendrick, Gord Casperd, George Linder, Robin Glass, Marnie Virtue, and Laurie Anderson.

Foreword

Adults learn best when they have some control over how, when, where, and how much they will explore new knowledge and skills. Treating them respectfully means taking their needs and learning preferences into account in preparing for and conducting learning activities. Workshops are a time-honored way of capitalizing on common needs and wants, and setting up environments in which adults can grow purposefully.

Having designed and led hundreds of workshops over the past thirty years, I might have dismissed a book such as this as too elementary for my learning level. Fortunately, I consider myself to be a lifelong learner, and I opened this book expecting to find fresh insights and methods that I can use in my ongoing work with helping people learn. I was not disappointed. Bruce Klatt has put together a set of invaluable strategies, tactics, and techniques for both beginning and advanced seminar leaders.

Being a workshop leader is a position of trust. Participants are presumably drawn to the subject and to our claimed expertise in it. They deserve the best that we can deliver. This book helps us to explore how we prepare *ourselves* before presuming to prepare others. Although modern methods of facilitating adult learning emphasize the need to avoid overusing the lecture method, nevertheless we need to be fully prepared in both the content and the processes of learning.

Some wag asked me, “How do you make God laugh?” When I said that I didn’t know, he replied, “Make a plan.” The serious truth behind that joke is this: Plans are made on “sunny days.” During their implementation we must deal with unforeseen events. Planning a workshop is no exception. We must anticipate what might go wrong, and we need to plan for learning to take place as efficiently and effectively as possible. This book gives us practical “nuts and bolts” advice on how to carry out this vital task.

An old adage goes, “You never get a second chance to make a good first impression.” Getting a workshop started well is critical, and this book offers a number of useful hints and procedures for ensuring that workshops get off to a good start. Working through the designed plan requires considerable sensitivity and resourcefulness. Timing of learning activities is almost more an art than a science, and workshop leaders need to develop effective ways of deciding when to cut off activities and when to stretch them out for additional learning. All of this takes place while interacting with participants. For a new workshop leader the scene can resemble a class in beginning juggling, but “seasoned veterans” can lose focus as well. The keys to effectiveness are commitment to clear learning outcomes and the ability to adjust the activities to fit the readiness level of participants.

This book lays out a doable strategy in a way that any workshop leader can use immediately. For the new workshop leader, the book is a guide to effective practice; for the more experienced leader, it is both a review of needed basics and a compendium of seldom seen tidbits of useful method. I conducted a number of workshops for Bruce Klatt when he was Human Resources manager in a large company. He watched me extremely closely. In the intervening years he has carried what he learned in those sessions quite a bit further. I feel proud of being a part of his initial learning about learning theory and practice, and I am instructed by his additions to this literature.

John E. Jones, Ph.D.
Organizational Universe Systems
San Diego, California

Introduction

The Questions This Book Addresses

Anyone who plans and conducts workshops or training programs will want to know:[1]

1) *How can I conduct workshops and training programs that support participants' learning naturally, spontaneously, and at deep levels?*

   Learning in formal or structured situations (e.g., a classroom) often seems like such a struggle compared to how we naturally learn every day. Too often formal training seems academic and removed from the practical reality of our lives. The material presented seems only loosely connected with what we need to do in the "real world." Learning in these situations becomes a duty. It involves memorizing steps, remembering proper names for processes, and struggling to understand how what's being taught might be of value on the job. Yet, outside the classroom people seem to learn rather naturally and without much effort. And learning spontaneously and by experience provides knowledge that is richer, contains more associations, is integrated with previous ways of knowing, and is more accessible and usable. Thus, knowledge is deeper and more practical.

2) *How can I ensure that the workshops I lead help groups achieve significant tangible and critical intangible results?*

   Tangible results are outcomes that are easily observed or measured, for example, agreements, product designs, strategies, and action plans. Critical intangible results relate to human emotions. Without these *intangibles* there is little likelihood of meaningful follow-through on promises made, or responsibilities accepted, at the workshop. Intangibles include things like a new team perspective, a new sense of understanding, commitment to do what it takes to make something happen, and a new sense of hope and optimism for a given project.

3) *How can I succeed personally as a workshop or training-program leader?*

   Every time you work in front of a group they make a lot of assumptions based on how you handle situations (e.g., how you field difficult questions, how you lead subgroup exercises, how you deal with overly aggressive participation). A workshop leader's job is done in "real time" with people watching, ideas diverging, expectations varying, judgments forming, valuable time passing, demands pressing, and ideas about what to do next racing through your head.

This book is a "how to" manual for helping workshop participants achieve and learn, and for succeeding as a workshop and training-program leader. It's "one stop shopping" for leaders who want to do more than just get by. It's for those who want to lead extraordinary workshops and continuously develop themselves and their leadership skills. It's a resource book bringing twenty five years of diverse experience, education, reading, and learning about operating workshops into one comprehensive package of information. It's packed with a breadth of approaches, models, insights, how to's, and a wide range of powerful and practical "application" tools for succeeding as both a workshop and as a training-program leader.

The Focus of This Book

Workshops and training programs are just a couple of tools, albeit rather sophisticated tools with lots of bells and whistles, something like modern word-processing or spreadsheet packages. They're tools that are often used in conjunction with other efforts and aimed at achieving a purpose much broader than themselves (e.g., designing a product, planning or preparing to implement an organizational change, planning a business unit strategy, helping a group of people improve their performance on the job).

For some, workshops and training programs are used often and are a major part of their work. For others, they are used only occasionally. Some will want to know how to use all or most of the options these tools offer (e.g., how to contract with sponsor clients, how to use all four levels of evaluation); others will only want to know the basic features in order to do what they want to do (e.g., how to facilitate group discussion, how to lead small group exercises). This book is organized to appeal to both extremes and to those in-between. The first half, chapters one through nine, focuses on preparing to use workshops and training programs, specifically getting yourself ready, getting your clients ready, and getting the workshop or training program, itself, ready. The second half, chapters ten through sixteen, focuses on delivery, that is, starting up and leading a workshop or training program.

As a whole this book focuses on things you need to do to succeed in front of a group, taking workshops and training programs from the initial request and contracting stage, through planning, design, organizing, and delivery. It's comprehensive and practical, and organized as a quick reference guide. It also has considerable depth and should even be of value to experienced workshop and training-program leaders looking for new ideas, approaches, and models. It talks not just about theory, but about what actually works - the subtleties, the key tips and techniques, and the major principles of leading workshops and training programs.

The philosophy of this book matches that of today's continuously changing, learning, and highly results oriented workplace. The advice offered here will help workshop and training-program leaders succeed amid rising and changing expectations from participants and sponsor clients.

The Target Audience for This Book

This book is targeted at a wide range of professionals. It's for those of you who are experienced within your own area of technical or administrative expertise and who want to get better at designing and leading workshops, instructing in training programs, and teaching your expertise to others. (The terms *workshop* and *training program* are defined in chapter one.)

More specifically, this book is for people who lead workshops and training programs for organizations, be they in private industry, the public sector, or for professional associations. These include,

- External consultants who lead workshops and training programs.
- Human-resources (HR) and organization-effectiveness (OE) professionals working as employees in organizations, and operating workshops as part of their internal consulting practice.
- Technical and administrative professionals working as employees in organizations and leading workshops as a sideline (i.e., as a result of a personal interest, or because it's expected by their manager or others in their profession).
- Professionals who conduct workshops for their associations (e.g., geologists, systems analysts, purchasing coordinators, lawyers, engineers and accountants who lead workshops at professional conferences, or as part of professional designation programs).
- Professionals who have never led a workshop or training program before, but have considerable organizational background, know their technology well, and want to begin developing their workshop or training-program leadership skills. For example, someone who has recently left regular employment in a large organization and is now finding work - as opposed to looking for a "job" - helping others learn his or her *know-how*.[2]
- Professionals who want to help others learn how to lead workshops and training programs.

The secondary audience for this book includes,

- Educators and other professionals who conduct courses at colleges and other educational institutions. Because this book focuses on workshops for organizations, you won't find information here about grading exams or teaching concepts in the abstract.

What You'll Get from This Book

A book on leading workshops and training programs, on its own, won't produce effective workshop leaders, just as coaching, on its own, won't create good athletes. But it will help by giving you models and benchmarks for assessing what you're already doing well and for zeroing in on areas you want to improve. In addition to practical tools, it provides a framework to help you organize your own common sense and intuition, and to continuously learn from your experience. So, with determination and practice, this book will help you develop your confidence, knowledge, and skill as a workshop leader, and as a trainer of your technical or administrative expertise.

A workshop leader needs a full tool kit of models and methods, and that's just what this book provides. Abraham Maslow's "law of the hammer" suggests the problem with having a shortage of tools.[3] It goes like this: *If the only tool you have is a hammer, then everything you come across looks like a nail.* For workshop leaders this means that if you're particularly good at presenting information (i.e., lecturing) then you'll lecture, even when you should be facilitating a discussion and helping participants explore an issue on their own.

There will also be some important spin-off benefits from reading and studying this book. Although all the material here is tailored to operating workshops and training programs, topics such as leadership, writing outcome statements, negotiating differences, and giving and receiving feedback have wide application. For example, more and more managers and supervisors in organizations are being asked to lead, facilitate, and coach, in addition to their more traditional roles of planning, organizing, delegating, and controlling. These new, or more enlightened, approaches to managing are in many ways similar to leading a group in a workshop or training program. This book is also a useful reference for other "nonworkshop" tasks, such as running a meeting, setting objectives, or dealing with resistance from a co-worker. Not only will you become a better *workshop* leader by studying and practicing the models, strategies, and tools provided here, you will also become a better all round *leader* in your organization and community.

Why I've Written This Book

Philosophers say that nobody does anything from just one motive. That certainly applies to why I wrote this book. I have both selfish and unselfish reasons.

My Unselfish Reasons

1) When I first started leading workshops, I looked around for a book such as this. I found good books on the theory of "adult learning" but a dearth of information on how to actually stand up at the front of a room and lead workshops. Now twenty-five years later, I have the chance to rectify this

situation. I'm able to pass on to you not just theory, but everything from the major principles right on down to the subtleties of what works.

2) More and more, technical and administrative professionals working both inside organizations and as external consultants to organizations are being asked to teach some aspect of their expertise or "know-how." Too often, these people are taught "what" to instruct, but not "how" to instruct or lead a workshop.

3) In today's workplace, people in the HR, OE, and training fields are having difficulty obtaining substantial organizational experience. Organizations just aren't hiring and retaining people that provide these support functions as much as they once did. Yet, it's in these organizations that HR, OE, and training professionals learn and sharpen their skills as workshop and training-program leaders. Hopefully this book will help fill this void just a little.

4) Today, a lot of professionals who lead workshops and training programs work as independent consultants, in their own "one person" businesses. In some ways it's a rather solitary practice in that many don't get to regularly share their ideas, methods, successes, and so on with other professionals doing similar work. This makes it a little more difficult to continuously learn and develop in their profession. Hopefully this book will help fill this void just a little as well.

5) I'd like to help people grow and find "life value" in their work. This book explores not just the developmental possibilities of leading workshops but also the excitement, energy, and fun of succeeding in organizations. Although often maligned, organizations are central to our lives. They are, and likely will remain for many years to come, how we support our growing economy and ourselves as a society.

6) Ongoing development is today's new form of job security. People need to learn continuously and help others learn as well. By developing, stretching, and continually challenging ourselves we build a skill base, reputation, and a network of contacts that help us stay "employAble."[4] This book is aimed at helping you to help yourself grow as a workshop leader.

7) Too many workshops in organizations are dry, subject oriented, and abstract. I want to help workshop leaders make their workshops more practical, participant oriented, and energizing. I bring an operating manager's perspective. I think in terms of outcomes, results, and efficiencies for participants and for the organization.

8) I've been told many times by my clients that I lead workshops and facilitate groups particularly well. I believe I can help others do this too. This book is a product of that belief and my desire to help you and others learn. It was developed through practice. During its many drafts, its process and advice were

constantly tested in workshops and training programs that I conducted. It offers a thorough review of what I have learned about planning and operating training programs and workshops.

Thinking turns perceptions into words.
- Genie Laborde

My Selfish Reasons

1) As I struggled to write this book, I realized I was discovering what I had learned by putting it into words. I was capturing my intuition about leading workshops and training programs and making it explicit. Warren Bennis (1993) talks about this type of discovery in his book, *An Invented Life*.[5] It's a wonderful type of discovery, like realizing you know more than you thought you did, or that you have more to offer than might otherwise be seen on the surface.

Kasparov defeats Deep Blue. Score one for intuition!

It's quite a job trying to make explicit those things that you do intuitively every day. Here's an analogy that seems to fit. In February, 1996, Garry Kasparov defeated IBM's "Deep Blue" in a six game, half million dollar, winner take all chess match. What was amazing, and what captured so much attention over the period of the match, was that Deep Blue won the first game. Everyone was shocked. Had it finally happened? Had a computer, or in this case a series of six computers hooked up in parallel processing, finally been able to beat Kasparov, perhaps the best "human" chess player to ever live?

Deep Blue was able to calculate more than two hundred million chess moves per second, yet it was so stupid it didn't even know enough to be afraid of playing Kasparov. Thank goodness Kasparov won. He saved the dignity of the human race! Kasparov, after all, had a quality Deep Blue lacked. He could think strategically, not just tactically. Kasparov could use vision and intuition, and this proved superior to being able to explicitly calculate more than two hundred million chess moves per second.

However, could Garry Kasparov write a book logically outlining precisely how he defeated Deep Blue? That is, could he describe his thought processes, strategies, tactics, and so on in a way that would help his readers play chess as well as he does? The answer is "no"; that would be impossible. There's more to Kasparov's intuition than could possibly be set out logically in a book. However, Kasparov could likely write a book, or a series of books, if he so chose, helping us lesser mortals understand and play chess a little better.

I'm not for a minute saying that I'm the Kasparov of workshop leaders (although my mentor, John Jones, probably is). What I am saying is that workshop leaders work with a ton of intuition as well. Indeed, I know of many workshop leaders, even junior ones, who can probably operate a workshop better than Deep Blue, inspite of its ability to calculate over two hundred million moves per second!

My first job in writing this book was to capture, and make explicit, as much as I could about what I have learned, and what has become my intuition, about leading workshops and training programs. My second job was to set this information out in logical order. Only in this way can I help the reader get better at leading workshops and training programs.

End

2) I wanted to prove to myself that I could work as hard as it takes to get a worthwhile book published. I once heard Will McWhinney, the founder of the Fielding Institute in Santa Barbara, say that it was important to finish your thesis before you got over your neurosis. Writing this book was like that for me. I found I had to be almost obsessive at times in order to get it done. When I went running I'd think about changes and additions, when I went to bed at night I'd get ideas for making it better, and when I woke up in the morning I'd have reworked a couple of problem sections in my head. I had to be like a dog with a bone, and just refuse to let go of anything short of having it in the best shape possible, and hoping some "unsuspecting publisher" would take a chance on it. There were times when I asked myself, "Why am I working so hard on this?" "What if it never gets published?" " What if someone, somewhere across the world, is about to publish a similar book and beats me to it?" I just kept telling myself, "Come hell or high water, this book is going to be published!" Whatever it takes, that's the effort I would put in. And I did, or you wouldn't be reading this now.

3) Let's be honest. People write books for instrumental reasons. I'm no different. Having this book published will help my consulting practice. (I just don't want you to think this is my only reason for writing this book.) And, strangely enough, I also wrote this book to help myself, so I can have one, comprehensive, easy to carry around, and organized source of advice, as a reference for when I'm preparing and leading workshop or training programs.

4) Finally, I once heard Peter Block say that he wrote the book *Flawless Consulting* to finish that part of his life and his work, and move on to other parts of his consulting practice. His later books focused on different topics (e.g., *The Empowered Manager, Stewardship*).[6] Incidentally, I very much admire his perspective, and recommend all three of these books. His words have stuck with me. I think the reason I've written this book is so that I can move on as well.

How to Use This Book

The chapters in this book are set out in brief sections, many in point form. Examples and checklists are also provided. It's organized for busy people and it avoids academic jargon and detailed footnotes. It's not set out to be read chapter by chapter, or to entertain, although it can be read sequentially, and there are a few quips here and there. Rather, it's meant to help you get a job done: the job of leading extraordinary workshops and training programs.

> *The man who doesn't read good books has no advantage over the man who can't read them.*
> *- Mark Twain*

> *Employ your time in improving yourself by other people's writings, so you shall come easily by what others have labored hard for.*
> *- Socrates*

Despite the fact that people rarely take a book off the shelf after they've read it once, this book is meant to be reused. Use it in the following ways.

1) First, quickly scan the entire book to get a feel for what's offered and where.

2) Next, read the entire book once, from beginning to end, studying, marking, highlighting, and making notes in the margins. Organize the book as an ongoing reference. This way you'll be able to find things quickly later on. You may even want to mark an "S" or "DN" in the margins as you read to indicate a certain *strength* or *development need* you have as a workshop leader.

3) Use this book as an ongoing guide to help you contract, plan, and design your training programs and workshops, and to help you improve your workshop and training-program leadership.

4) Refer to this book when a specific problem arises, for example, help in reorganizing a poorly designed training-program *start-up* or help in learning how to handle overly aggressive participation in a workshop.

5) Keep this book nearby and refer to it randomly whenever you have a few minutes. For example, on the plane on your way to leading a workshop in another city, you may want to check out a particular method or approach for leading, facilitating, or presenting.

6) Quickly scan your highlighted parts and notes throughout this book once every few months, looking for ways to continuously improve your workshops and leadership style.

7) Set a goal for yourself to improve two specific things about your workshops, and your leadership, every time you lead a workshop. For example, a day or two

before a workshop, scan through the book and find a couple of areas you want to hold yourself accountable for improving. Then make explicit plans to improve your workshop in these given areas (e.g., giving better directions when setting up small group exercises, incorporating more variety into the workshop design to ensure participants are active and involved, asking more open-ended questions to draw out participants' issues and concerns during group discussions).

8) Make this book and the ideas in it your own, but don't adopt its style carte blanche. Integrate the concepts and tools with your own, practice them "under fire" in your workshops, then revisit this material and continually adapt and expand it, as needed, to suit your unique workshop situation and your leadership style. Experienced workshop leaders likely don't need to be told this. They'll get the ideas they want, then do their own thing anyway. But it's good advice for relatively new workshop leaders. You have to bring who you are to what you do, so by all means learn from others, but don't *adopt* someone else's methods or style. Rather, integrate and *adapt* what you learn to your own unique way of leading.

The Structure of This Book

Part One - Getting Yourself Ready: Preparing to Lead

Part One sets a context for leading workshops and training programs in organizations. Two chapters provide basic theory and models for working with participants and for understanding the learning process. The "how to" emphasis of this book is reserved for chapters three through sixteen.

Chapter One, *Building a Foundation for Leading*, highlights the essential qualifications, relationships, and knowledge required for leading workshops and training programs. Workshops and training programs are defined and compared, as are leadership and facilitation. The importance of trust and rapport in a workshop is examined, along with the key elements of trustworthiness.

Chapter Two, *Learning, Habits, and Levels of Knowledge*, focuses on "learning," the common denominator and primary outcome of workshops and training programs. Discussed are natural learning, deep learning, the principles of adult learning, learning styles, single-loop and double-loop learning, levels of knowledge, and the nature of habits.

Part Two - Getting Your Clients Ready: Defining Success

Part Two emphasizes the importance of pre-workshop contracting and focuses on your clients, their needs, and their preferences. Specific strategies are provided for identifying learning and business "needs," for planning purpose and outcomes, and for planning to evaluate the workshop or training program.

Chapter Three, *Investigating Needs and Planning a Workshop*, begins with strategies for identifying and assessing learning and workshop needs. Attention is then focused on determining a workshop's or training program's purpose, outcomes, and major steps.

You need to decide now, in the planning stage, how a workshop or training program will be evaluated. Chapter Four, *Planning to Evaluate a Workshop*, looks at why it's necessary to evaluate and the four levels for evaluating workshops, training programs, and your effectiveness as a leader. Specific guidelines for evaluating are provided.

Chapter Five, *Contracting Outcomes and Marketing Prior to Start-Up*, looks at the different clients you need to contract with (sponsor clients, administrative clients, end-user clients, yourself), and how to contract with each type of client.

Part Three - Getting the Workshop Ready: Planning to Achieve

Part Three explores the full range of workshop and training-program preparation including design, the agenda, marketing, materials presentation, and a valuable little ditty called the "activity smorgasbord."

Chapter Six, *Designing a Workshop*, sets out key principles of design. Kolb's learning styles are used as an organizing framework. A range of information is provided for each design option to help you choose a mix of methods appropriate to your particular workshop or training program.

Chapter Seven looks at *Organizing a Workshop*. Suggestions, diagrams, and checklists are provided for marketing, coordinating, and organizing workshops and training programs.

Much of the information and many of the examples in Chapter Eight, *Preparing and Using Visual Aids*, will be familiar to experienced workshop leaders. Nonetheless, these should be reviewed as useful insights are provided for the full range of visual aids in use today.

Chapter Nine, *Conditions for Workshop Success*, takes a close look at the importance and interconnectedness of learning and workshop climate, learning readiness, and participation readiness. Steps are discussed for getting participants involved and for maintaining an effective learning climate.

Part Four - Getting Underway: Starting-Up a Workshop

The importance of the start-up can't be overestimated; it sets the tone for everything that follows. Two chapters guide workshop leaders in starting-up, warming-up, and revving-up a workshop.

Chapter Ten, *First Steps in Starting-Up a Workshop*, explains how to get a workshop off to a flying start. The focus is on leader readiness, and warming-up and creating group interest in the purpose and outcomes of the workshop or training program.

Chapter Eleven, *Contracting Group Process During Start-Up*, provides detailed strategies for contracting how participants are going to work together.

Part Five - Getting It Done: Leading a Workshop

Part Five deals with the "nuts and bolts" of actually standing at the front of the room and leading a workshop. Five chapters cover moving, everything you need to keep participants involved, focused, achieving, and enjoying the workshop.

Chapter Twelve, *Moving, Adapting, and Ending a Workshop*, looks at how to move a workshop forward, changing direction and pace as needed, but always maintaining participants' interest and energy. Discussion centers on reviewing and summarizing, using feedback, and a range of strategies for staying on track.

Chapter Thirteen, *Working with Questions*, examines one of a workshop leader's most relied upon skills. Questions focus participants' attention and reinforce learning. The structure and multiple purpose of questions are highlighted to help you use this tool proficiently.

Chapter Fourteen, *Involving, Motivating, and Maintaining Interest*, shows how to keep participants enthusiastic and focused. Step by step guidance is provided for leading small group exercises. And because the ability to make people laugh provides a great advantage to a workshop or training-program leader, the principles, "do's" and "don'ts," and examples of humor are provided.

The first part of Chapter Fifteen, *Presenting, Facilitating, and Leading*, explores one of the most common methods of providing information to participants, the lecture or presentation. The subtleties of facilitating and leading are then reviewed, along with the advantages and disadvantages of co-leading a workshop or training program.

Participation is a prerequisite for any successful workshop but it must be managed. Chapter Sixteen, *Managing Participation in a Workshop*, starts off looking at that touchy subject of "control." Approaches for managing workshop time and for providing participant reinforcement are then described. Detailed strategies for dealing with participation problems are outlined.

A Bright Future for Workshop and Training-Program Leaders

If you're a baby boomer (i.e., born between 1948 and 1964), your parents probably kept the same career from the time they entered the workforce until their retirement.[7] Your mother likely worked in the home, and likely worked very hard. Your father, like mine, may have changed careers once or twice but within the same company. If you're a baby buster (i.e., born after 1964), this situation may have applied to your grandparents. However, in today's rapidly transforming business climate most of us will switch careers and organizations several times, including moving back and forth between self-employment and working for others, and even between full-time and part-time employment.[8]

No one is immune to change today. The truth is no one has ever been immune to change, even in the past. We sometimes polish our own egos by talking about the fast pace of change in our times, but change has always been difficult for people. How easy could it have been for pioneers in North America traveling by covered wagon across a vast uncharted land? How easy could it have been for North American native people as their traditional way of live was constantly encroached upon, and eventually, for all practical purposes, eliminated?

How extreme our present climate of change will get is uncertain, but it's clear that those who don't adapt will go the way of the dinosaur. My point? The need for those with expertise in helping others learn and adapt has reached unparalleled proportions. From small businesses right up to multi-national corporations, business leaders are realizing the value and necessity of training, learning, working together in teams, and adapting to changing circumstances. The future of workshop and training-program leaders has never been brighter.

I hope you will be conducting workshops and training others for many years, and that you will consult this book frequently for guidance, examples, and tips. But this book is not a panacea for curing any malady that may be afflicting a workshop. It contains no magic, only experience. It's not a substitute, but an adjunct for hard work and the guidance of an effective mentor or coach. Following its suggestions won't always be easy, just fulfilling.

Extraordinary leadership skills are developed. So never say, "I'm just not cut out to lead workshops." Your ability and corresponding success as a workshop leader are a function of your desire to learn and to constantly improve. Too often, people quit just before they succeed. Only with discipline and desire will the information presented in this book help you achieve your potential. I wish you all the best in your workshop leadership.

Notes

[1]Both the terms "workshops" and "training programs" are used often throughout this book. However, using these terms together, all the time, tends to make sentences run on, and seem a little *wordy*. Something like always having to write "he/she," "herself/himself," and so on. Therefore, in some instances the term "workshop" is intended to refer to both workshops and training programs; for example, only "workshop" is used in several chapter titles.

[2]Bill Bridges talks about how it's a world of markets as opposed to a world of jobs in the economy today. Thus the need to find "work" rather than a "job." See: Bridges, W. (1994). JobShift: How to prosper in a workplace without jobs. Reading, MA: Addison-Wesley.

[3]Kaplan also talks about the "law of the instrument," suggesting that if you give a child a hammer, he/she will find that everything in sight needs to be pounded. See: Kaplan, A. (1964). The conduct of inquiry. San Francisco, CA: Chandler, p. 28.

[4] I believe the term *employAbility* was first coined by Kanter, R.M. (1989). When giants learn to dance: Mastering the challenges of strategy, management, and careers in the 1990's. New York, NY: Simon & Schuster.

[5]Bennis, W. (1993). An invented life: Reflections on leadership and change. Reading, MA: Addison-Wesley, p. 35.

[6]1) Block, P. (1978). Flawless consulting: A guide to getting your expertise used. San Diego, CA: University Associates. 2) Block, P. (1987). The empowered manager: Positive political skills at work. San Francisco, CA: Jossey-Bass. 3) Block, P. (1993). Stewardship: Choosing service over self-interest. San Francisco, CA: Berrett-Koehler.

[7]The years 1948 to 1964 are used to define the baby boom period in Leinberger, P., & Tucker, B. (1991). The new individualists: The generation after the organization man. New York, NY: HarperCollins.

[8]Five excellent works that are well worth reading on the topic of the changing nature of work and jobs are: 1) Handy, C. (1989). The age of unreason. Boston, MA: Harvard Business School Press. 2) Bridges, W. (1994). JobShift: How to prosper in a workplace without jobs. Reading, MA: Addison-Wesley. 3) Toffler, A. (1991). Power shift. New York, NY: Bantam Books. 4) Reich, R.B. (1991).The work of nations: Preparing ourselves for 21st century capitalism. New York, NY: Vintage Books. And 5) Kanter, R.M. (1989). When giants learn to dance: Mastering the challenges of strategy, management, and careers in the 1990's. New York, NY: Simon & Schuster.

Part 1

Getting Yourself Ready: Preparing to Lead

Building a Foundation for Leading

INTRODUCTION

Leading workshops is a job requiring technical competence, interpersonal skill, and a knowledge of group process. Your antennae are always up scanning for problems, constantly assessing the needs of the group, and thinking through possible directions for the workshop. Most of the time the direction of the workshop is fairly predictable, but there are times when you're not quite sure what to do next, or just exactly where things are going at the moment. And there's always risk involved when you operate in front of a group. There's always the potential for success or disaster.

Your role as a workshop leader is to create an environment where participants have every opportunity to participate, learn, and produce. You want participants leaving your workshops and training programs energized and eager to try out their new plans, products, ideas, and learning "on the job." While techniques and tools like presentation methods, or feedback models, aid your cause considerably, there are a few basics or fundamental principles that workshop leaders need to succeed.

This chapter focuses on these basics, including:

- Understanding and comparing workshops and training programs.
- The basics of leading workshops and training programs.
- The basics of workshop leader success.
- The benefits of leading workshops and training programs.
- Understanding the importance of trust and rapport in workshops.

UNDERSTANDING AND COMPARING WORKSHOPS AND TRAINING PROGRAMS

What's the difference between a workshop and a training program? How are they similar?

Comparing How Workshops and Training Programs Make Change Happen

Workshops and training programs seek different types of *outcomes*, and thus take a different approach to supporting change and improvements in organizations. (The term "outcome(s)" is used throughout this book to refer to the goals or objectives set for a workshop or training program.)

Training seeks improvement in "individual performance." Schermerhorn, Hunt, and Osborn (1988) talk about individual performance as a function of *willingness*, *ability*, and *opportunity*.[1] Willingness relates to motivation and attitude. Willingness to contribute, to exert extra effort, to use sound judgment, and so on is an individual prerogative, hence the saying, "The best employees are volunteers." Ability relates to knowledge, skill, and confidence.[2] Opportunity concerns organizational supports and barriers. Examples of supports are authority to decide, sufficient time to perform, and state of the art equipment. Examples of barriers are insufficient resources, inflexible procedures, and inadequate information.

> ***If a person can't do something (it's) a training problem. If a person won't do something (it's) an attitude problem.***
> ***- Blanchard and Lorber***

Workshops focus on opportunity and willingness. Ability is a prerequisite. Training focuses on ability and willingness. It has little effect on opportunity. That is, the focus of training programs isn't redesigning the workplace and changing supports and barriers to performance.

Thus, change supported by workshops focuses on factors that support or block willingness and opportunity. For example, a workshop on goal setting would consider the resources needed, and the barriers that must be overcome in the organization, to accomplish agreed upon goals.

In general, workshops focus on specific work or organizational issues such as solving a problem; making a decision or recommendation; designing a system, plan, process, product, or program; directing people on projects; improving teamwork and group communication; creating a strategy for introducing a new product or service. Thus, a group might hold a workshop on goal setting, strategic planning, project implementation, or team building.

Change supported by training comes via learning new knowledge, developing skills, improving confidence, and/or by "reframing" how one looks at things in the workplace (e.g., problems, issues, procedures). Reframing, more properly referred to as "cognitive reframing," affects willingness to perform, in that it involves stepping back and looking at things differently. An example is seeing a demand from your boss as a requirement from a customer or as necessary to ensure high quality, as opposed to an arbitrary command just to exercise power over others. (Note: To some extent training influences *willingness* from an emotional perspective, but training is *not* therapy. Training is not about changing people at an emotional level.)

In general, training programs focus on ability issues and are conducted to help employees improve in areas such as negotiation skills, problem solving and decision making, interviewing skills, technical report writing, and even to improve their skills at leading workshops and training programs.

In summary, workshops focus on group and organizational change (e.g., working more effectively with another department, or implementing a new process or structure), while training programs focus on individual change and behavior. In this sense training programs are more basic to individual performance and effectiveness on the job, whereas workshops are more directly concerned with group and organizational effectiveness.

Comparing Workshops and Training Programs Logistically

Workshops are usually brief (i.e., a few days at the most) and focused on specific work and organizational issues. They're often conducted for work groups and teams, including the group's supervisor or manager, whereas training programs are conducted for individual employees in an organization. But on occasion employees may attend a training program as an intact work group, and on occasion the group's manager may even participate along with his/her work group.

In addition to seeking different types of outcomes, training programs also differ from workshops in duration and group mix. Training programs may or may not be brief. They might be an evening or half day in duration, but they could also be five consecutive days, one day every two weeks for six months, full time for six months, and so on.

The Training-Consulting Continuum

The distinction between training programs and workshops might best be understood by reflecting on a "training-consulting" continuum. Training, being relatively structured, content focused, solution oriented, and directed at the individual, can be contrasted with consulting that is spontaneous, business focused, problem and opportunity oriented, and directed at the group or organization. Workshops lie somewhere in-between these two extremes. In some cases workshops are almost pure consulting. At other times they have a strong training orientation.

Note: Appendix A provides a detailed comparison of workshops and training programs along the dimensions of purpose, outcomes being sought, steps involved, and capabilities required of the group and the leader.

The Training-Consulting Continuum

training	leading workshops	consulting

Training	Consulting
Relatively set, structured, and linear agenda	Flexible game plan, work on issues as they surface
Learning and participant focused	Business outcome and organization focused
The aim is to cover the material	The aim is for meaningful progress in reasonable time
The issue is assumed and solutions applied	The issue is defined or framed and solutions sought
Assumed participants need direction	Assumed participants will solve problems for themselves

The Bottom Line

Learning is always a starting point for organizational improvement but it's rarely the ultimate goal. That is, learning, for its own sake, doesn't "pay the bills" in organizations. Here's a "BGO" for you (i.e., a blinding glimpse of the obvious): *Knowing* is not the same as *doing*, just as *planning* is not the same as *accomplishing*. While training programs lead to new knowledge and skill, and workshops lead to new processes, programs, and plans, the bottom line is that both are means to achieve learning followed by behavior change on the job. And behavior change is a means for achieving better organizational results (e.g., reduced waste, increased production, improved product quality, increased market share).

> *Training teaches us the rules, experience teaches us the exceptions.*
> *- Henry Boettinger*

> ***Knowing and doing are not the same thing***
>
> Learning is the mental process that leads to new knowledge and skills. But in organizations new knowledge and skills are not an end in themselves. Take, for instance, the story of this little boy's encounter with a man out walking his dog.
>
> "Hey Mister," inquired the boy, "does your dog know any tricks?" "Sure, he knows hundreds of them," replied the man. "Really!" asked the boy, his voice betraying his excitement, "Can I see one?" "Look, I said he *knows* tricks, not that he *does* tricks," retorted the man with a wry smile.

What Workshops and Training Programs Have in Common

Workshops and training programs have many things in common. Both

- are focused on defined outcomes and conducted for the purpose of improving how people think about, organize, and perform work in organizations.

- have group sizes typically ranging from six to twenty participants, although they sometimes range as low as three or four and as high as thirty participants. Anything higher than thirty participants gets a little unwieldy. Note: There are a number of methods or approaches for handling groups of a hundred or even larger, for example, "search conference technology" outlined by Weisbord (1989) or "open space technology" outlined by Owen (1991). However, this type of meeting is not the focus of this book.[3]
- are highly participative, hard working, educational, and emphasize application.
- involve introducing new theory, models, tools, and techniques.
- are usually conducted away from the work site.
- require participants to work together as colleagues and share responsibility with the leader for the success of the event.
- require the leader to facilitate, lead, instruct, present, organize, redirect, coordinate, manage, and act as a resource for participants.
- require follow-up and reinforcement, after the event, to ensure change and improvement are occurring in the workplace. (Better results are achieved when the workshop or training *event* is considered to be part of a wider *process* of learning and action.)

Comparing trainers and workshop leaders

Sometimes experienced trainers make lousy consultants and workshop leaders, and sometimes senior consultants make terrible trainers. That is, some senior consultants are just too unstructured to be effective trainers, and some trainers are too narrowly focused to be effective consultants or workshop leaders. A couple of examples follow.

The senior consultant who has difficulty training

Some consultants, especially senior consultants, are often unaccustomed to the structure and tight timelines needed for training. They may well have an agenda, but, most of the time, are prepared just to "go with the flow." For example, a senior consultant might advertise a one day training program, and set out an agenda with ten key learning points. He/she starts off the training program as planned but by the third overhead transparency is off on a tangent. Four hours pass and the consultant has only covered the first and the fifth learning points, having skipped points two, three, and four for the time being. Indeed, as the day winds down, the consultant realizes he/she has only covered three or four of the learning points that were advertised. He/she now finds it necessary to quickly scramble through the last six or seven in under half an hour.

Some in the group are "put off" because they were expecting a quicker pace. The senior consultant/would-be trainer, however, is saying to himself/herself, "Boy, the group is really into this. What a great conversation!" He/she has been following the lead of a few "eager beavers" in the room, focusing on the complexity of the issue and on how it ties in with the unique needs of the group's business. Some will see the consultant's digressions as helpful, flexible, and relevant.

Meanwhile others in the group, often the more analytical and linear thinking members, of which there are many particularly in technically oriented organizations, are expecting him/her to follow the agenda and cover *all* ten learning points. They are worried about learning a skill, a new model, or new way of approaching their work. They want a narrow focus, a fast pace, and few, if any, digressions. These members of the group will be frustrated and feel cheated if all ten learning points are not given roughly equal time. Some will even feel the training program was hard to follow if learning points are not covered in the order set out in the agenda.

The experienced trainer who has difficulty leading workshops

An experienced trainer might try to a operate workshop as if it were a training event. As a result he/she might show little appreciation for the flexibility and outcomes, as opposed to process or agenda focus, needed to help groups solve complex, troublesome, and unique problems.

The experienced trainer organizes and structures the workshop as if the business issue were self-evident, and the solutions within the grasp of anyone willing to listen, learn, and practice his/her six step model for making change happen. He/she sticks with the agenda, fearing any digression would mean losing control of the workshop. He/she covers each and every one of the six steps with precision and skill, but ignores much of the complexity and multi-dimensional nature of the business issue in question. Some participants are quite happy, having received the "answers" in an organized and lock-step fashion. Others are more skeptical and resent being taught, when what they really needed was to dialogue about, define, and delineate the business issue.

(Note: Appendix B outlines the group's concerns when a leader is either training or consulting but should be doing the other.)

End

THE BASICS OF LEADING WORKSHOPS AND TRAINING PROGRAMS

Now it's time to distinguish between leading and facilitating a workshop. What's the right word for what you do when conducting a workshop or training program? Facilitating? Moderating? Instructing? Teaching?[4] Presenting? Directing? Delivering? Midwifery? Why not *leading*? But isn't a "leader" a manager? That is, someone with formal authority. Maybe. It depends how you define "leadership."

The words "authority" and "influence" seem to be at the forefront of most definitions of leadership. For example, Webster's dictionary (1981) defines a leader as a person that leads, guides, or conducts. It then goes on to distinguish two characteristics of a leader: *authority* and *influence*.[5] James Chaplin (1985) also includes both these characteristics in his definition. He writes that leadership is "the exercise of authority; the control, guidance, and direction of the conduct of others."[6] The definition of leadership use in this book does not include authority. A workshop or training-program leader rarely has organizational authority over the group he/she is leading. A workshop or training-program leader fails, however, if he/she carries no influence with the group. Influence and the ability to help a group

learn and achieve results are the essence of what is meant by leadership in this book. Given this, two complementary definitions of workshop and training-program leadership follow. The first looks at leadership in terms of outcomes and process; the second in terms of the leader's impact on learning and action.

Leadership Definition #1

The bias of this book is that both *results* and *democratic process* are essential. Achieving results in a workshop (e.g., clearly written goals, a completed project plan) without open dialogue, active and spontaneous participation, or honest emotional expression is a hollow victory. Results achieved without involvement, influence, and struggle may have little emotional support, and as such are unlikely to hold much sway with participants as they encounter the normal and predictable barriers to implementation following a workshop. Thus, "follow-up" may be without real conviction. This is what Karl Weick (1979) was talking about in his insightful book *The Social Psychology of Organizing*, when he said that "action without commitment is seldom effective."[7] If, in the planning stages, either *results* or *democratic process* seems unattainable, that may be the surest sign you can obtain to either seek change or to withdraw from leading this particular workshop or training program.

Leadership is liberating people to do what is required of them in the most effective and the most human way possible.
- Max DePree

I must follow the people. Am I not their leader?
- Benjamin Disraeli

In the past leaders have been trained to exercise leadership; they will now be trained to participate in leadership.
- Wilfred Drath and Charles Palus

Given this values base, effective workshop and training-program leaders are defined as men and women who achieve meaningful and lasting results through the use of democratic processes. That is,

leadership = democratic process + results

More specifically, effective workshop and training-program leaders get three results.

- Group agreement on workshop or training-program outcomes.
- Group achievement of these outcomes.
- Group commit to "follow up" based on these outcomes.[8]

And in achieving these three results, their behavior is guided by values such as

- open communication regardless of roles and ranks
- reliance on dialogue and consensus rather than coercion or compromise
- influence based on competence rather than on organizational power
- an atmosphere that supports emotional expression and task accomplishment
- a willingness to acknowledge and deal with conflict on rational grounds

What is intended here is focused and democratic leadership similar to that defined by Warren Bennis (1985).[9] This type of leadership is not to be confused with permissiveness or laissez faire. Rather, it is constantly focused on results, challenging, supportive, and damn tough when need be. It is also humanistic and underpinned by a strong belief in the value of people and of the importance of finding fun, accomplishment, and "life value" in work.

Workshop Leadership

The *workshop leader's* job is to help the group use their collective experience to organize and accomplish a specific and agreed task, leading to further action and results. Thus, *leading* a workshop involves helping a group do or create something neither they, nor you, know exactly how to do just yet. In this respect, leading is a learning process for both the workshop leader and for participants. Neither the group nor the workshop leader has all the answers or a surefire, step by step game plan, for accomplishing the designated task (i.e., the workshop outcomes). What they do have is confidence that together they can get the job done.

A leader can create an encouraging environment, but there has to be something inside the people as well.
- Michael Walsh

Training-Program Leadership

In contrast to a workshop leader, a *training-program leader* has clear answers, or at least "a set of answers" (*truth* is not the issue here). The training-program leader also has a fairly predictable "game plan" and structure for providing new information to a group and for helping them develop new skills. (As mentioned above, in training, the leader's job is to motivate and help individuals gain new knowledge, and develop skills, that will be used later on the job.)

Essential Qualifications for Leaders

Both workshop and training-program leaders must have knowledge of group process and a desire to help. In addition, what makes you capable of leading is that you have *technical expertise*. Thus, for example, if the workshop in question is for the purpose of developing accountability statements within a work group, you would be expected to have expertise in this area. Without this expertise you cannot lead. You can facilitate group discussion, act as a scribe, administrator, coordinator, or objective third party, but you cannot lead!

What Leaders Require from Participants

Needless to say, for democratic leadership to be possible, the assumption must be made that participants will be motivated to learn, think, contribute, and act appropriately, if they understand the importance and relevance of the outcomes being sought for themselves and their organizations. Thus, leadership is associated with democratic values, not with dominance or superiority (e.g., superior intelligence, a strong physical presence, charisma, associations with people in power).

The group must be willing to work and learn together to achieve a given outcome (e.g., solve a problem, plan a program, initiate a project). In a workshop setting this means the group must have and bring to bear their experience and expertise, for example, a thorough understanding of their business operations or knowledge of their industry and technical fields. In a training program the group must be willing to learn, experiment, practice, and commit to using new knowledge and skills "on the job." (See Appendix A for an overview of the capabilities required of workshop and training-program participants.)

Given the choice of influencing you through your heart or your head, I will pick the heart. It's your head that sends you off to check Consumer Reports when you are thinking of purchasing a car. It's your heart that buys the Jaguar, or the Porsche. ... People are persuaded by reason, but moved by emotion.
- Jeffrey Pferrer

Leadership Definition #2

Now it's time to look at a second definition of workshop and training-program leadership. Whereas the definition above focused on the products and process of leadership, this second definition is more psychological and centered on the effect the leader has on participants and on the group as a whole.

Definition #1: leadership = democratic process + results

Definition #2: leadership = social influence + meaning making[10]

Note that these two definitions are listed in order of priority. Thus, for example, social influence need be exercised democratically; otherwise it is not acceptable.

Workshop and training-program leadership is not pre-ordained. Rather, the leader emerges as a consequence of a process and his/her role in that process. For example, the leader might help a group gain a common intellectual and emotional understanding of what it means to be a "team" in their unique situation. Another example would be helping a group connect their plans and programs to their organization's wider vision. In the final analysis, leadership is the ability to *influence* participants and to help them create, discover, name, or in some way arrive at their own *personal meaning* of a situation, method, project, skill, organization, team, and so on.

Democratic workshop leadership, therefore, is the ability to participate in a group and help that group create or discover personal and shared meaning for themselves. A workshop leader helps a group reframe a problem, opportunity, initiative, or threat in a way that's significant; generates involvement, enthusiasm, learning, and commitment; and provides options and choices for action.

Leadership Is More Than Facilitation

To paraphrase Geoffrey Bellman (1990), a workshop leader is more than a facilitator, more than a kind of WD-40, or organizational butler, whose only role is to help the feature players move smoothly through their lines.[11] Pure facilitation is of minimum value. It's a basic skill, like dribbling is for a basketball player. But knowing how to dribble isn't enough to make you a basketball player, and knowing how to facilitate, on its own, doesn't make you a workshop leader.

Remember the difference between a boss and a leader: a boss says, "Go!" - a leader says "Let's go!"
- E.M. Kelly

You might compare workshop leadership with being a harbor or river boat pilot. Because of his/her experience and knowledge of a given terrain, a harbor pilot temporarily takes the helm and steers a ship through foreign waters. And because of his/her experience and knowledge of a given business terrain such as strategic planning, goal setting, team building, or project planning, the workshop leader temporarily takes the helm and guides a group during the duration of the workshop. A harbor pilot knows where the sandbars are; a workshop leader knows where a group is likely to run aground. He/she helps the group move safely and productively through a workshop to accomplish their desired outcomes.

The group's "real leader" or manager, having confidence in you, the workshop leader, works as a "first among equals" during the workshop. Needless to say this manager, the full-time captain of the ship, always has the option of stepping forward and taking back control. You have the helm only for a specific purpose (i.e., to help the group achieve agreed outcomes), and only as long as the group's manager, and the group as a whole, have confidence in your ability to steer them in the right direction.

One person with a belief is equal to a force of ninety-nine who only have an interest.
- John Stuart Mill

Leaders Declare Their Beliefs and Offer Substance

As a workshop or training-program leader you need to move beyond simple process intervention to saying what you know. You need to add to the content and share the facilitation role. (With experience you learn how to be both a process observer and an active player in the content of a workshop.)

More specifically, as a workshop leader you need to:

- Comment on whether a given piece of work should be done, not just on how the group is going about it.
- Offer substance and content. That is, you need to offer alternatives, options, and recommendations for action.

- Add content related to changes. You may not be able to add content related to your client's technology (e.g., how to audit a manufacturing business, how to organize a trucking distribution system, or how to design a health care system for the elderly), but depending on your experience, you can add content relating to such areas as planning, strategy, management systems, and change management.
- Stick to your values and declare your beliefs. This helps groups avoid action that seems expedient today, but adds to their long-term problems.

Thus, as a workshop leader, it's OK to have your own agenda; just keep it flexible and make it visible and discussible. Be up front and don't play games. Declare your biases and beliefs. It's OK to be invested in something specific getting done, even when that goes beyond helping the group do what they initially intended to do. This might involve helping a group reframe or redefine a problem, issue, or opportunity. Be willing to tactfully express what you think is important, and to act on your values. That's how you make a difference. That's how you *lead* as opposed to simply *facilitate*.

Needless to say, if you're not successful in helping a group reframe a given piece of work, or if you're not able to convince them to work toward a different outcome, then you either need to help them work the issue as they've agreed to define it, or you need to "fess up" and admit you're not able to help. In the final analysis, the group decides. You're a leader, not a dictator or a missionary. Remember that dictators are eventually deposed and missionaries end up in pots!

In summary, as a workshop leader, you are accountable for *an effective learning and working climate*. An effective learning climate is one of colleagues working together, where traditional management tasks are shared by the group (e.g., planning, organizing, controlling, delegating). You are but one of the leaders in the group. Each participant is also accountable for leadership and for the success of the workshop. The group as a whole, yourself included, is accountable for achieving the workshop's explicit and agreed outcomes. Ultimately the group fails or succeeds together. In this sense, workshops, during the duration of their existence, are what Katzenbach and Smith (1993) would call a *real team*.[12]

An example of reframing and workshop leadership

I was co-leading a two day workshop on board governance with the board of directors of a public sector organization. A friend and colleague, Dave Irvine, an expert in the field of personal growth and relationships, was co-leading with me. Dave and I had worked with this same board for a day about six months earlier on an unrelated matter, so although we didn't know them and their organization well, we were at least acquainted with the group and some of their issues. This is an important point, because had this been our first meeting with the group, we wouldn't have had enough "on deposit in the relationship bank" to challenge in such a major way and even before the workshop got started.[13]

As we were waiting for a few stragglers to arrive the first morning of the workshop we became engaged in casual conversation about actions taken by a board of directors of another public sector organization. I'll call this organization XYZ. The mandates of organization XYZ and of the organization we were working with at this workshop were distinct but nonetheless closely related. As a matter of fact, their mandates were so closely related that one director had been elected to sit on both boards to help improve coordination between the two organizations. Both organizations were in public sector education and they had many of the same customers or students.

As we talked, the group was complaining about a recent decision taken by the board of organization XYZ. They described it as a "betrayal" and were quite concerned it would negatively affect the ability of the two organizations to work together. I listened attentively but also challenged their interpretation of the other board's decision because it seemed like they were overreacting to it. It also seemed like they were seeing this decision as isolated and related solely to a given individual, and not seeing it was really just a "wake-up call" in a long-running pattern of problems related to how the two boards were structured and coordinated with each other.

In my challenge I mentioned how this didn't seem like betrayal but rather a natural consequence of how the two organizations, and the two boards of directors, were organized, structured, and coordinating their efforts. I gave a few examples using information that had surfaced during the conversation. By this time we had been talking about twenty minutes and all board members had arrived. I then recommended that they consider merging the two organizations into one and forming one board of directors accordingly. A few immediately picked up on the possibility. Others were skeptical. One or two might have even been offended.

We continued the discussion for another fifteen minutes at which time we decided to completely change the purpose of the workshop (we had yet to begin the planned workshop agenda of developing a governance model for the board). The new focus would be on exploring and deciding whether to approach the board of organization XYZ for the purpose of discussing a possible merger. I quickly worked up a strategy for doing this and reviewed it with the board. They liked it and that's how we spent the two days.

We didn't even look at the governance issue for which I had planned the workshop. All my overheads, process planning, and work targets went out the window. Instead of doing *things right* (the planned board governance agenda), we did *the right things* (working on the possibility of a merger with organization XYZ). The refocused workshop went well and the board made a decision to approach the board of organization XYZ to discuss the possibility of a merger. (Incidentally, the chairman of the board we had worked with these two days called me a couple of weeks later, thanked me again for reframing the workshop, and said they had approached the board of organization XYZ and found they quite receptive to discussing the possibility of merger of their two organizations. This work is now being planned.)

In hindsight, it was not my intention to refocus the workshop at the time this casual discussion with the group began, but as the discussion progressed I saw the suggestion of refocusing needed to be made. Making this suggestion was a little risky, and I was not at all certain how people would react. I was a little concerned some would even be insulted at the suggestion of merging with organization XYZ. And at the time I made the suggestion, neither Dave nor I had worked up any process ideas for leading the refocused workshop. I do however have a lot of background in organizations and knowledge of how boards function. And I was fairly confident, given the discussion in the group, that the question of merging with organization XYZ was at least a valid question.

The point of this story is that workshop leadership is far more than just facilitation. It's far more than just being a "pair of hands" to help the group accomplish its goals. Workshop leadership is using all you experience, knowledge, beliefs, and process skills to help the group deal with difficult issues, sometimes even issues the group can't see initially or would rather ignore.

End

THE BASICS OF WORKSHOP LEADER SUCCESS

When people think about instructing or leading a workshop, they often immediately focus on "delivery skills" such as presenting, facilitating, or leading. These skills are important, but in the long run, they're not nearly as important as the four basics outlined below. These basics cover a leader's background, experience, attitude, and development.

This book won't help you with the first basic, "being technically competent." It will, however, help you a great deal with the others, both in terms of understanding and in terms of guiding your practice of these fundamentals as a workshop leader. The basics of workshop leader success are:

> *Success is a matter of luck; just ask any failure.*
> *- Anonymous*

1) Be technically competent in your field

2) Bring who you are to what you do as a workshop leader

3) Be informed and care about your participants

4) Continuously develop yourself and your workshop or training program

1) Be Technically Competent in Your Field

It's vital to have solid, current, and even advanced technical competence in your field, be that engineering, accounting, geology, information systems, human resources, or any other technical or administrative field, in order to succeed as a training program or workshop leader (i.e., in order to help others learn and use your expertise). Understanding the discrete steps in workshop and training-program leadership comes later. Technical competence is demonstrated by your highly flexible use of the technology in question, especially in unusual situations. And you should have extensive experience using your technology "on the job."

> *Growth can take place with or without development (and vice versa). For example, a cemetery can grow without development; so can a rubbish heap. (Development) is an increased capacity and potential, not an increase in attainment. ... It has less to do with how much one has than with how much one can do with whatever one has.*
> *- Russell Ackoff*

I'd rather take a training program from a person who drools but knows their stuff *technically*, than from a leader who is polished and charming, but not highly skilled technically. It's not difficult to learn how to lead workshops and training programs. It takes a little practice, but it's doable. Thus, I would hire an experienced engineer who has never led a workshop and help him/her learn how to lead a workshop on engineering, but I would never hire an experienced workshop leader and attempt to teach him/her engineering for the same purpose. It takes a long time to become technically competent in most fields. However, with initiative, a little support, and a little guidance (e.g., this book), most people can become competent at leading workshops or training programs fairly quickly. Becoming proficient or highly skilled as a workshop or training-program leader takes a little longer, but even this, with practice, is an attainable goal for most professionals.

There's an old saying that "we teach what we need to learn." It sounds a little ironic, something like working your way through medical school by being a doctor. Maybe it goes back to George Bernard Shaw's quip that, "Those who can, do. Those who can't, teach." And the more recent version, "Those who can't teach, teach gym." Anyway, here's the point. If you're lacking a little confidence, that's OK, as long as you have practical experience and are competent in your technical or administrative field. This being the case, then leading workshops is a legitimate way to challenge yourself and to continuously learn and develop. However, if you really are not competent in your field, then you're not ready to lead a workshop or training program in this field. Don't set yourself up for failure. It's not fair to those who would be participating in the workshop (the participants), and it's certainly not fair to you.

Thus, if you're helping participants learn effective supervisory practices, you should at least have had experience, and success, supervising others. Or, if you're helping participants learn how to conduct a financial audit, you should have had extensive experience with financial audits yourself. Although this may seem a little obvious, it needs to be said. However, none of the above means you have to be an expert in, say, *WordPerfect*, just to help others learn a few simple features of that program. If you know these few features well, then you're "technically competent" to help others learn them.

The most important thought that you can ever hold is: Your life matters.
- David McNally

John Jones, a co-founder of University Associates and a long-time mentor of mine says, "You can only teach 10% of what you know." That is, you must know a great deal more about a topic than you intend to teach. Depth of knowledge is crucial for being able to discuss a topic using your own words and experiences, and in order to communicate in simple, understandable language. Whenever someone has difficulty making a point, seems to be using highly technical language, takes a half hour and three thousand words to explain a concept that should take two minutes and a couple of sentences, or seems to be repeating themselves endlessly, it's usually because they just don't know their technology "in depth."

2) Bring Who You Are to What You Do As a Workshop Leader

A workshop leader's attitude is infectious; if you're focused, interested, and enjoying your work, participants will likely do the same. Successful workshop leaders enjoy being a workshop leader and have a strong sense of themselves, their values, and their moral standards.

Enjoy Being a Workshop Leader[14]

It's important to enjoy the adventure of learning and discovery that each new workshop or training program brings, accept the accountability and even the anxiety that comes with the leadership role, and be comfortable relying on others and trusting the group.

Have a Strong Sense of Yourself, Your Values, and Your Moral Standards

If you're a good supervisor or manager, a good project leader, a good parent, or good at any of the other leadership roles in life, then you likely have what it takes to be a good workshop leader as well. The qualities of leadership are universal. They start with self-awareness. Socrates's injunction "know thyself" is still great advice. You need to be in touch with your own feelings, know what you want, be conscious of how your actions affect other people, and be "quietly confident" in your abilities. Or, as Weeks and James (1995) put it, you need to be at ease with who you are, and evidence a "shining sense of positivism and buoyant self-confidence that comes from being comfortable in one's own skin."[15]

The more I learn about myself, the more I become a different self.
- Ashleigh Brilliant

There's only one corner of the universe you can be certain of improving, and that's your own self.
- Aldous Huxley

In addition, you must be guided by a strong set of values which enable you to act and stand alone, and to decide and tell others what to do (when this is appropriate), in spite of not having the legitimacy of organizational authority. You must also be willing to learn from others, admit personal deficiencies, and benefit from criticism no matter how poorly it's given.

3) Be Informed and Care about Your Clients

Successful workshop and training-program leaders are informed about the group and care about participants, their learning, and their success.

Understand the Group's Unique Situation

Every group thinks their situation is unique, unlike any other you could imagine. And at one level this is true, although after you've done a hundred or so workshops, you realize these "unique situations" have more in common than what sets them apart. Nonetheless it's important to value and appreciate what is unique about each participant and group you work with. Successful workshop and training-program leaders dig for this information. You need to take the time, either before the workshop or during the workshop start-up, to learn about participants, their concerns, interests, hopes, and fears, as well as their background, experience, and work environments. The more you understand, the better prepared you are to help groups succeed.

Care about Participants, Their Learning, and Their Success

An effective workshop leader's first concern is with participants' learning and success, and with their readiness to use the products from the workshop "on the job." Don't measure your success only by the evaluation form at the end of the workshop. Factor in participant involvement, application during the workshop, and participants' use of workshop materials in the days and weeks after the workshop. And follow up with participants after the workshop. This might be as simple as a quick phone call or encouraging participants to call you if they need additional coaching.

Be kind, for everyone you meet is fighting a hard battle.
- Philos, Greek philosopher

Care more about participant success and learning than about your own performance. Be a guide on the side, not a sage on the stage. While you want your performance to contribute value to participants, and you want to be recognized for your contribution, you also want the group's focus to be on the workshop's stated purpose and outcomes. So don't overuse your strengths (e.g., questioning skills, knowledge of a given technical area, oration or presenting abilities, colorful computer graphics). Remember, any strength taken too far becomes a weakness. You need to facilitate, lead, challenge, and support. Aim at being a coach, not a boss, not an assistant, not a guru, and certainly not a "star on the training stage."

Foster an Abundance Attitude

An *abundance attitude* is one of sharing, giving, listening, and mutual success.[16] A "scarcity attitude" means you see things as win-lose and as a competition. A person with a scarcity attitude feels that helping someone else and making them look good will somehow diminish his/her own success. Their sense is one of *scarce resources,* like there's only so much recognition, appreciation, interesting work, or reward to go around. It's sometimes called the *fixed pie* syndrome. That is, by giving someone a piece of your pie you now have less for yourself. Thus, a person with a scarcity attitude wants to be right, wants to win, and wants to convince the other person of his/her position. He/she sells, advocates, and defends his/her position unquestioningly, whereas a person with an abundance attitude wants to learn, and so balances promotion and advocacy with inquiry, listening, and a willingness to hear contrary perspectives.

An abundance attitude leads one to see more beneficence and plenty in the world. There's lots of recognition to go around, and no need to hoard the limelight and seek credit only for oneself. Having an abundance attitude allows you to mentor, coach, and lead others, and to find value in and share their success. Your approach is no longer *we-they* but more community oriented. You're willing to *give your stuff away*, knowing that most people will appreciate and reward you for your help in due course. Sure, there are always a few who take advantage of those with abundance attitudes, but you soon get to know who these people are and can behave accordingly around them. But that doesn't stop you from starting with trust and being willing to share with others. Nor does it blind you to people's dark side. Rather you focus more on the value of each individual and are quick to believe each is motivated to learn and develop. You start by giving people the benefit of the doubt.

Encourage Teamwork in the Group

You don't have to blow out the other person's light to let your own shine.
- Bernard M. Baruch

As mentioned above, a group of participants in a workshop or training program is very much a "real team" for the duration of the event, in that they rely on and benefit from each other's contributions and share accountability for the success of the workshop. An effective workshop leader thinks and acts in the best interests of the group, including correcting participant mistakes personally, tactfully, and immediately. He/she cares about helping participants succeed and learn from each other and gains satisfaction from their individual and team success.

4) Continuously Develop Yourself and Your Workshop or Training Program

The Japanese Zen concept of learning has a lot of merit. Emphasizing continuous development, it goes something like this, "A person learns in order to do better what he/she already knows how to do well." Workshop and training-program leaders need to be lifelong learners.

It takes twenty years to make an overnight success.
- Eddie Cantor

If you deliberately set out to be less than you are capable, you'll be unhappy for the rest of your life.
- Abraham Maslow

Develop Your People and Relationship Skills

Training has a lot to do with relationships.
In an interview with Bill Moyers (1990), Mike Rose talks of training and education as attempts to bring people "in."[17] He suggests that, in this sense, they are automatically relationships. And like all relationships they are by invitation only. You can't subpoena people to like each other, and you can't subpoena people to learn.

The ability to deal with people is as purchasable a commodity as sugar and coffee. And I pay more for that ability than for any other under the sun.
- John Davison Rockefeller

Relationship skills such as the ability to relate to people who think differently than you do, the ability to pick up tacit messages, and so on are critical to success as a workshop or training-program leader. E.L. Thorndike called this "social intelligence," and defined it as the "ability to understand others and act wisely in human relations."[18] In a similar vein Coleman (1995) summarizes Salovey's five domains of "personal intelligence."[19] These include both interpersonal and intrapersonal skills. A more concise review of "people skills" would be hard to find. They are:

1) Recognizing your feelings as they happen. (People with this ability are better pilots of their lives.)
2) Managing your feelings so they are appropriate (e.g., the ability to shake off anxiety).
3) Self-motivation (e.g., the ability to invest emotions in a goal, to delay emotional gratification, to get into a "flow state" where things get accomplished).
4) Recognizing emotions in others (e.g., being able to tune into the subtle signals that indicate what others want).
5) Handling relationships well (e.g., influencing, supporting).

I find the great thing in this world is not so much where we stand, as ...(the) direction we are moving. To reach the port of heaven, we must sail sometimes with the wind and sometimes against it - but we must sail and not drift, nor lie at anchor.
- Oliver Wendell Holmes

Develop Your Leadership Skills

A study by Lowy, Kelleher, and Finestone (1986) correlated a number of variables with high learning managers.[20] Not surprisingly, these variables are practically identical to those associated with successful workshop leaders. Among other things, these included plenty of contact with other people, opportunity to influence, freedom to operate and to express one's own style, pressure for results, and constantly questioning and improving existing practices. The surprising variables in this study are goal ambiguity and the absence of regular feedback. That is, despite pressure for results, high learning managers were often not given specific goals or targets. Rather, they had to create these for themselves. Same thing with feedback. High learning managers were not offered regular or structured feedback (e.g., performance evaluation). If they wanted feedback, they had to go out and get it for themselves. It wasn't handed to them on a silver platter. As with high learning managers, both the need to create your own goals or workshop outcomes and the need to seek feedback are cornerstones of workshop leader success.

If you want to double your success rate, just double your failure rate.
- Tom Watson

You can't live without an eraser.
- Gregory Bateson

Value Mistakes

Making mistakes is OK. Admitting them is even better. John Ralston Saul (1994) makes a key point about mistakes and error. He says, "In science, error is still recognized as a permanent characteristic of progress."[21] So, why do workshop and training-program leaders sometimes deny or downplay their mistakes? It's because where mistakes are punished, responsibility is discouraged. Our fear of error stems from our specialist approach to work. We come to see ourselves as experts and feel our expertise depends on being seen as right in all matters related to our "expertise." Ralston Saul argues that we need to reexamine this severe attitude toward competence. It's tremendously freeing once you learn that it's OK to make and admit you made a mistake. Being a workshop leader often means giving things your best shot, floating trail balloons, and taking risks. If you don't make a few mistakes, you're just not trying hard enough!

> ***Whatever thy hand findeth to do, do it with thy might.***
> ***- Ecclesiastes 9:10***

Know Your Limitations

Workshop leaders don't have to be saints but they must be devoted to their own development. (Anyway, being a saint is a pretty tough job while you're still alive!) Be conscious of your limitations and what you still have to learn. Find ways to compensate for your limitations, for example, you may chose to co-lead a particular workshop, rehearse a particular leadership method ahead of time, or carry detailed notes for leading a particular session of a workshop.The bottom line with being a workshop or training-program leader is this: Don't accept work you are not qualified to perform (regardless of how hungry you are). This doesn't mean you have to be an outstanding facilitator or the best in your technical field. It does mean you have to be competent in the technical focus of the workshop or training program, be it environmental assessment, organizational design, or drill stem testing. It also means you need some basic skills in leading workshops or training programs.

> ***Progress and growth are impossible if you always do things the way you've always done things.***
> ***- Wayne Dyer***

Continuously Develop Your Workshop or Training Program

Aim for each workshop to be different and better than the previous one. This way you'll collect experience conducting fifty workshops, instead of conducting five workshops ten times. Ask a trusted colleague to "sit in" on a workshop you lead, make notes on where the workshop can be improved, and give you honest, direct feedback, along with suggestions for improvement. And as part of your preparation for each workshop, read over evaluations from your previous workshops. Choose two areas you want to improve,

> ***Seek out the struggle that will toughen you up. Negativism is a sin; so is self indulgence. Bad times, such as depression or a state of war, should be a challenging test. Real men (and women) tighten their belts, throw full weight into the harness of their daily activities, and pull with all their might and main.***
> ***- J.C. Penney***

then set a couple of learning outcomes for yourself in these areas. Take a few risks. *Never lead a workshop without a strategy for improving at least two things about the workshop design and about how you lead the workshop.*

Build a Repertoire of Practical Models, Methods, and Theory

Have a "pocket full of models" relating to everything from leading workshops to learning, change, and motivation (e.g., Bennis' "force field analysis," Lewin's "action research," McWhinney's "four boards of play," Block's views on empowerment). And though it's a lot of work, keep up with new developments, tools, and models as they arise. This means staying on top of the current literature and developments in your technical field and in fields relevant to leading workshops or training programs (e.g., team theory, adult education, group process techniques).

The Benefits of Leading Workshops and Training Programs[22]

Why would anyone want to lead workshops or training programs? What's in it for you? This section looks at three levels of benefits for workshop leaders - personal, professional, and organizational.

a) Personal Benefits

Workshop leaders benefit in direct personal ways. For one, there's personal growth associated with the demanding role of helping others learn, produce a product, or solve a problem. Speaking in public, organizing training, and dealing with the many situations that arise in workshops challenge and develop one's leadership and organizing abilities. Interpersonal skills are also challenged, and a new role is experienced that is very different from most daily technical or administrative responsibilities.

Workshop leaders develop "contacts" throughout an organization. That is, depending on the workshop or training program being led, workshop leaders get significant personal and professional exposure to people from across the organization, and from many different professions, and levels of responsibility within the organization. When you spend a day or two leading a workshop, people remember you, the help you provided, and your technical expertise. Today, when job security seems to be a thing of the past, increasing your personal contacts and reputation, while it doesn't guarantee employment, nonetheless enhances job security.

Being a workshop leader also looks good on a resume. After all, in addition to contacts and professional reputation, job security is also very much a function of continually developing one's skills. As well, workshop leaders often have opportunities to visit and learn from parts of their organizations (e.g., field locations) that they otherwise might not have seen.

b) Professional Benefits

Professionally, many things happen as a result of leading successful workshops and training programs. It's a great way to shake yourself up professionally; to get out of a rut. Taking responsibility for leading a group always involves risk and new skill development, but it also involves surfacing and questioning many of the assumptions that guide your technical or administrative practice. Continuous professional challenge is demanded when leading workshops; you're required to stay current and even ahead of technical developments in your field. Thus, workshop leaders learn their technical or administrative areas in-depth. *We learn best by helping others learn.*

> ***The practice of intellectual rigor in the classroom requires an ethos of trust and acceptance. Intellectual rigor depends on things like honest dissent and the willingness to change our minds, things that will not happen if the soft values of community are lacking. In the absence of communal values, intellectual rigor too easily turns into intellectual rigor mortis.***
> ***- Parker Palmer***
>
> ***Communication is more a function of trust than of technique.***
> ***- Stephen Covey***

In addition, leading workshops or training programs expands what Covey (1989) calls your "circle of influence" in an organization.[23] You become a credible resource, and people from different parts of the organization approach you for your help in a range of areas. There is something of a "halo effect" that takes hold if you have impressed people, and oddly enough they begin approaching you for help even in areas outside your particular expertise. Needless to say it's important to recognize your limitations when accepting these invitations to help.

c) Organizational Benefits

Organizationally there are many winners from successful workshops and training programs. The organization gets problems solved, products developed, and better trained employees. The employees receiving training improve their professional skills and increase their value to their organization. Even more benefits result where the workshop leader is also an employee in the organization. In these cases, the workshop leader understands the company's unique situation and can tailor training very specifically to individual and organizational needs. Finally, as workshop leaders continue to develop their skills and their approach to leading, many reach a point in their careers where they begin to contribute to the technical and administrative advancement of their profession.

Trust and Rapport

Just as belief and hope are essential to change, risk is essential to learning, especially to double-loop learning. (Double-loop learning is discussed in chapter two. For now it's important to know that it involves challenging one's own assumptions, beliefs, and habits.) Without trust, participants are unlikely to risk differing with established practices, standards, or approaches to problems. They are unlikely to experiment or to leave the security of their present ways of knowing and acting.

I've learned that trust is the single most important factor in both personal and professional relationships.
- H. Jackson Brown, Jr.

Successful workshop and training-program leaders hold themselves accountable for earning participants' trust. And as a "trusted source," having earned the group's respect and confidence, your invitations to participants to risk, to share their perspectives, and to challenge their past ways of thinking and acting are much more likely to be accepted and acted upon. You are much more able to influence participants' learning, and your ability to facilitate and lead the workshop is greatly enhanced once participants believe that you know what you're talking about, that you want to be helpful, and that you're open and honest.

A) Without Trust Workshops and Training Programs Fail

Once participants are learning ready, and once trust is established with yourself, and preferably among participants as well, participants are much more predisposed to listen, experiment with, challenge, and integrate new information. Certainly the opposite holds as well. If participants don't trust you, then you and your words have very little credibility. Needless to say, this greatly limits your ability to influence participants' learning and workshop results. The bottom line here is that relationships are built on trust, and any relationship, including that between yourself and participants, is doomed to failure if trust is not established or if it is later lost.

B) How We Think of Trust

In business today, we use the word "trust" in highly imprecise ways. Lacking an actionable definition, we think of trust either as encompassing all aspects of a relationship, or as nothing very tangible at all. It's everything because it's the "oil in the machine of relationships." It's nothing because "it's too intangible and amorphous to work with." We chalk *trust* up to personal chemistry or personality, and having framed it in this way we make it inactionable. It's now outside of our "circle of influence." "If only we had more trust," people say, like somehow it depends on fate. It doesn't. That's not to say trust can be controlled, only that it is actionable, it can be influenced, and given integrity and sincerity, it can be built with a group. This section provides essential "how to's" for developing trust with participants.[24]

Two stories about trust

1) The importance of being a "trusted source"

No matter how good the information you provide to the group, it will be viewed skeptically, if not totally discounted, unless and until you become a "trusted source" with them. The O.J. Simpson acquittal is a case in point. Rightly or wrongly, the jury didn't trust the Los Angles police, their lab techniques, their racial impartiality, or their investigation procedures. (This "lack of trust" became clear in televised interviews with jury members after the trail.) So, no matter how overwhelming the evidence presented over the nine month trail (e.g., DNA, the glove, the limo driver, the blood stained carpet in O.J.'s residence, Simpson's history of being abusive), it was not enough. And ten times more evidence wouldn't have been enough either. No trust, no influence, no conviction.

2) The power of being a "trusted source"

Once I got some good, hard feedback that I needed to stop writing on a flipchart, and stop scribbling notes to myself, while participants were talking. I realized there was value in this feedback, but, looking back, I largely ignore it. The person who gave me this feedback was bright, and well intentioned, but I just didn't have that much respect for his opinion. This isn't an excuse; it's just a fact. I should have paid attention, and changed my behavior, but I didn't. About a year later, Shaun Murphy, a trusted colleague, gave me this same feedback. Shaun and I had just finished a workshop for a group of managers, and as part of our debriefing I asked him if he had any feedback for me so I can continue to learn. He said, "Yes, there is one thing. At times today you wrote notes to yourself, or scribbled on the flipchart, when people were talking. This gives the impression that you aren't listening." To quote Yogi Berra, "It was like déjà vu, all over again." Only this time, the moment Shaun said this, I realized this problem was solved. Instantly, I made a decision to change this behavior. It hasn't been a problem since. Why did I take so long to fix up this little quirk? And, why did I resolve it so quickly based on Shaun's feedback? Likely the fact that I had heard it before helped, but a large part of my decision to improve was based on my trust and respect for Shaun. For me, and for many others, Shaun Murphy is a "trusted source."

C) Guidelines for Understanding Trust

Trust presents a paradox in that it needs to be earned, but in order to be earned, it first has to be given. Yet trusting someone without the facts to base it on is naive. That's why trust is often given in small amounts over time. As we experience success trusting an individual, we are more and more willing to trust further. And trust isn't binary. It's not "on" or "off," but rather it's a matter of degree. Overall, the following ten guidelines help us understand the nature of trust.

1) Trust is a rather delicate flower. Especially if we trust someone and this trust is broken, it's hard and sometimes impossible to repair. The message here is simple. Don't do anything to break or betray trust with the group. It's just too hard to win back. That's not to say that, given the right circumstances, it's impossible to win back. Just that it takes a lot of work. (Given that there is a basic respect and goodwill between people, and a willingness to work on relationships, forgiveness and relationship renewal are possible in workshops, even following disappointment and betrayal. Without these circumstances, however, trying to win back trust is like pushing on a rope! It just doesn't work real well.)

   Critical behaviors as a workshop leader: Don't to anything to break trust with the group. Keep your promises, take responsibility for your own actions, and don't exaggerate, fabricate, fake answers, or BS your way through a conversation. Fess up when you don't have the answer.

2) Sometimes it takes courage to trust, especially if you've experienced betrayal in your life. And strangely enough, those who have never experienced a good, hard betrayal may not have yet learned to trust wisely. It doesn't take courage to trust naively, in an unquestioning, unconditionally accepting or Pollyanna sort of way. Children trust this way but most adults don't, thank goodness.

   > ***Never trusting and always trusting are inappropriate.***
   > ***- David W. Johnson***

   Questions participants might be asking themselves: Will confidences be kept? Will what is said in the workshop or training room stay in the room? Will the training-program leader keep his/her word and not talk to my boss about my progress?

3) If you want to be trusted as a workshop leader, you must first give participants evidence that you're trustworthy. Trust isn't based on your credentials (i.e., your experience, education, research); it's based on your relationships and what

you're doing at the moment. This includes demonstrating competence and being sincere, honest, reliable, and caring.

Questions participants might be asking themselves: Are there hidden agendas here? Can I trust the other participants and the workshop leader? Does the leader know what he/she is talking about?

4) Accept that trust cannot be controlled, legislated, or forced. That doesn't mean, however, that you can't at least *influence* trust. What it does mean is that you need to do your best, and then "let go" if your best isn't good enough. Nobody is trusted by everybody, some people aren't capable of trusting anyone, and with the possible exception of those closest to us, trusting completely and unconditionally is probably naive.

   Questions participants might be asking themselves: Is the leader trying to control the outcome? Is he/she merely engineering consent? Is he/she too rigid or pushing his/her own agenda?

5) Trust has to be constantly earned. Like relationships, trust either grows or it stagnates, but it cannot be held constant. You simply can't put trust or relationships on auto-pilot. Like the old saying in professional sports, "What have you done for me lately?" Trust needs to be demonstrated and reinforced or it slowly loses strength.

   Questions participants might be asking themselves: Why should I trust the leader? Has he/she gotten to know me and my concerns? What do I know about him/her?

> ***Trust, unfortunately, is not a state of mind that can be established once and for all. Trust must be established with each individual, over and over again.***
> ***- Egon Guba and Yvonna Lincoln***

6) Trusting others predisposes them to trusting you. We know that behavior begets behavior. Listening to someone helps ready them to later listening to you, and supporting someone often means they'll support you in return. The corollary holds as well. If you want someone to level with you, start by leveling with them; if you want someone to share information with you, start by sharing your information with them. It doesn't always work. Nothing, where people are involved, always works. But it is, nonetheless, a useful guideline.

   Questions participants might be asking themselves: Does the leader trust the group? Has he/she shown confidence that we know what we're doing, or does he/she seem reluctant to trust our suggestions? Has the leader leveled with us about his/her own biases and beliefs?

7) Trust can only grow in an environment of goodwill, respect, and a willingness to work on your relationship with another person. Without these elements in place, trust entropies and conflict resolution strategies either make things

worse, or have only minimal impact, as they must ignore the relationship and operate exclusively on a rational and objective level.

Questions participants might be asking themselves: Does the leader seem interested in us as a group, in our issues, or is this just another "gig" for him/her? What's the leader's emotional investment in this workshop and this group?

We are born princes (and princesses) and the civilizing process makes us frogs.
- Eric Berne

8) We trust people who are self-aware and loyal to the truth as they see it. Charlotte Roberts writes that conflicts arise between honesty and loyalty, and that "the only sustainable loyalty is loyalty to the truth."[25] Honesty, she maintains, has its "pinch points," and sometimes these demand a frustrating compromise among loyalties - to the truth, to a relationship (e.g., a boss or former boss, a friend or co-worker), to a position, to an organization, to a program, to the peace, to longstanding attitudes, to self-interests, and so on. These compromises can mean denying our own perceptions and leave us standing in the middle, trying to balance loyalties without conflict, and taking the burden of a problem on our own shoulders while doing what we can to fix it covertly. And even in those situations where you'd cause yourself or someone else undue hardship by sticking to the letter of the truth, you can at least remain loyal to the spirit of the truth. For example, suppose you have to ask a participant to leave a training program because he/she isn't meeting the standards demanded for completion. You might, given the circumstances, simply tell those remaining that you and the participant in question came to a mutual agreement that he/she wasn't ready for this training at this time. You might also voice support for this person's future development and express your commitment to helping him/her qualify for the program at a later date.

Questions participants might be asking themselves: Does this leader call a spade a spade or is he/she just giving us a very safe and "political" perspective? Is there a conflict of interest at play here?

9) You don't have to be perfect to be trustworthy. We all fall a little short of other people's expectations, and even our own expectations, every now and then. So, if you're a perfectionist, "let go" of this need. See your mistakes, and those of others, as learning opportunities, as temporary, and as isolated, not as permanent, pervasive, and proof that there's an inherent flaw in your character! Learn and move on. Don't bring yourself down by what Martin Seligman (1990) calls "a tyranny of *should's*," that is, constantly reliving your past mistakes and current shortcomings (e.g., "I should have done this," "I shouldn't have done that"). Seligman puts it succinctly, if not a little tongue in cheek, "stop 'should-ing' on yourself."[26]

Questions participants might be asking themselves: Is the workshop leader fair? Does he/she have a balanced perspective? Does he/she have a positive outlook? Does he/she make me hopeful? Is he/she informal and fun to be around? Can I be myself around him/her?

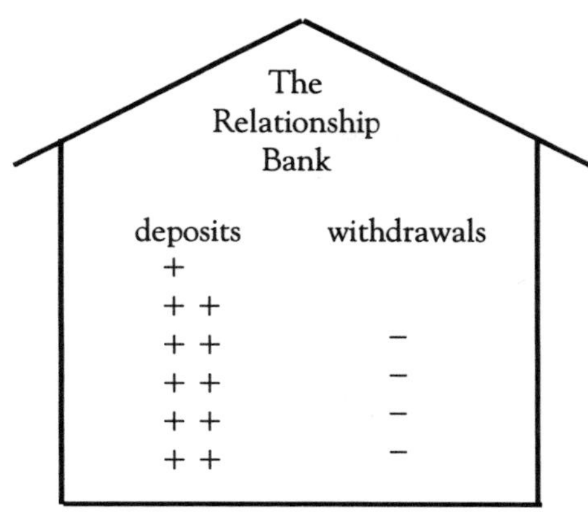

10) We tend to trust people who have a positive balance in the relationship bank. That is, building trust in any relationship, including that between a workshop leader and a group of participants, is a matter of demonstrating more strengths than weaknesses, more support than challenge, more caring than confrontation, more consideration than irritation, and so on. Think of Covey's (1989) metaphor of a relationship bank.[27] If you make enough deposits in the relationship with participants by being open, supportive, reliable, and listening, then it won't hurt quite as much when you make a withdrawal. A withdrawal could be on purpose, by challenging or confronting, or by carelessness, such as not following through on a promise. Without something in the bank, however, a withdrawal puts the relationship into bankruptcy. Trust is damaged. Having a lot of *positives on deposit* doesn't mean participants won't still get upset, irritated, and angry at you, but it does mean they will also likely listen and give you the benefit of the doubt.

Questions participants might be asking themselves: All things considered, does this leader deserve the benefit of my doubt? Is he/she worth challenging? Can I be honest with him/her? Is this a risk worth taking? Can I show my ignorance in front of this leader without fear of being evaluated harshly, written-off, or stereotyped?

D) Trustworthiness

What makes you worthy of someone's trust or confidence? And what makes you willing to put your trust in others? How can you, as a workshop leader, go about building trust with a group? How can you tell that there's a high level of trust in a group? These questions and others are answered in the following three sections.

a) The four elements of trustworthiness

b) Questions for assessing trust

c) Tools for building trust

a) The Elements of Trustworthiness

The bottom line for workshop leaders is, "How can I influence trust?" So let's avoid the detail and look at a general framework for demonstrating trustworthiness. It's a framework for making trust *actionable*. We tend to trust people who provide the following four elements in a relationship. So if you want to be trustworthy, here's a list to examine your own behavior.

An important caveat: Treat the following as principles, not techniques. You must be sincere in your intentions and behavior. Trying to "technique" someone using these four elements may work with some people in the short run, but over time trust will be damaged. As Abraham Lincoln once said, "You can fool all of the people some of the time, and some of the people all of the time, but you can't fool all of the people all of the time." Although what people don't realize is that Lincoln was fooling when he said this![28] Joking aside, the following advice only has value when practiced with integrity and sincerity.

Be Open We tend to trust people who are open about their *thoughts* and *feelings*, people who say what's on their mind, and tell others what they're feeling. Sharing what you're feeling usually means you're "self-aware" and that you have enough self-esteem to accept your feelings as legitimate. You don't withhold information. You don't play games. This doesn't mean you always act on your feelings, but it likely means you rarely, if ever, act on anger. Anger is the only emotion you should not "act out." Saying you're mad is OK. Acting out your anger by yelling and kicking garbage cans in front of workshop participants isn't OK.

Examples

A participant asks a question you just can't understand. Solution: Fess up. Say, "I just don't get your point, and I know I'm missing something. Can someone help me on this one?"

You get confused or lose your place in your workshop leader's guide. One possible solution: Again, just fess up. Say, "I'm temporarily lost, and it's got me kind of frustrated. Let's take a ten minute break while I find my place in the leader's guide. Can everyone be back at 10:15 sharp?"

Be Congruent Related to being open about your feelings but distinctly different is being *congruent*. We tend to trust people who give us a consistent message, that is, they don't give us "double messages." You know these people because "they walk their talk." They likely have strongly held values, and they live by them. When people aren't congruent, their tone and nonverbals simply don't match their words. It takes courage to be congruent and to live by your values. Not everyone can do this, and none of us can do it perfectly. Anyway, when we do manage to pull it off, and live according to our values, our self-esteem as well as our relationships are enhanced. And, although it's not always the case in the short term, in the long run it's a lot less stressful to live according to your values.

Example

Two participants are constantly taking "pot shots" at you. Don't act as if it doesn't matter, or as if you don't really notice. You need to acknowledge what is happening in a nonblaming way. One possible solution: Follow the advice provided in chapter sixteen, in particular the 5C model, and the strategy of giving two good faith replies, then naming and dealing with the resistance directly.

Be Supportive We tend to trust people who support us, people who see that we are deserving of recognition and have worth as individuals. This doesn't mean they don't challenge us, or "call us" on our behavior every now and then. It does mean that they don't just look for the negatives. They also look and find the value in our suggestions, and in us as individuals.

Example

A participant seems way off track, but trying. One possible solution: Encourage, support, and find value in whatever the participant does right, or even approximately right. For example, build on their contributions and relate them to the purpose of the workshop. Find ways to provide extra coaching (e.g., at a break or between sessions).

Be Reliable We tend to trust people who do what they say they are going to do and who take responsibility for their own actions. We value predictability in relationships, provided of course that the predictable behavior is positive.

Example

While doing an "end of day review," the group requests that you "pick up the pace" a lot on day two. One possible solution: Even though you feel defensive and want to argue back with a few "yeah buts," you need to listen, understand, and then say what you will do differently. That evening revise your game plan, and the next day follow through. Then check with the group to ensure the pace has improved.

b) Questions for Assessing Trust

Three critical questions for assessing whether to trust a person, and for assessing your own trustworthiness vis-à-vis that person, follow from the above four elements of trustworthiness.

Open and congruent

1) Does he tell me the truth? (Do I tell him the truth?)

Supportive

2) Does she stand by me under pressure? (Do I stand by her under pressure?)

Reliable

3) Does he follow through on promises to me? (Do I keep my promises to him?)

c) Tools for Building Trust

How can you begin to build trust with a group or with an individual workshop participant? Dave Irvine offers this perspective.[29] Start by assessing the level of goodwill and respect. Is there a desire to work through differences? Is there a desire to invest in the emotional bank account? Come clean with where you stand with this participant or group in your own mind. Are you prepared to make the investment? Next, assess the level of your emotional bank account with a participant or group. Assuming that there is a desire to make deposits, the following is a list of guidelines for doing so.

Open

- *Seek first to understand, then to be understood*[30]
  Trust takes time and requires genuine concern and caring for others. Listen to participants and be patient.

- *Share your thoughts, hopes, and concerns*
  Being open with your opinions, your uncertainties, and your biases offers a rich sense of involvement, but it also implies vulnerability. Needless to say, discretion is also required. Being open doesn't mean unloading your burdens on the group or sharing all your concerns about the workshop. That is, being honest and blurting out anything that runs through your mind are not the same thing. Timing, sensitivity, tact, and discretion are important.

Congruent
- *Stick to your values*
  Be clear on and don't compromise your values and integrity. Trust requires self-respect.

Supportive
- *Accept participants and groups as they are*
  Trust requires respect for differences and openness to feelings. Don't get *ego invested* in changing or controlling participants or groups. Pain (i.e., disappointment, frustration, anger) is proportionate to our investment in expecting others to be different than they are. Three strategies are important here, 1) change the changeable, 2) accept the unchangeable, and 3) remove yourself from the unacceptable.
- *Build on participants' strengths*
  You might provide difficult feedback or "constructive criticism" later, but initially, as trust is in the early stages of developing, avoid criticism.

> ***The major reason capable people fail ... is that they don't work well with their colleagues. The statement, "He's good, but he has trouble getting along with other people," is the kiss of death.***
> ***- Lee Iacocca***

Reliable
- *Allow room for participants to make mistakes*
  Both trust and learning require risk. Don't be too quick to jump on mistakes (e.g., a participant failing to follow through on a promise). Find out what's behind the problem. Ask, "How can I help?" (For more on this approach see the section titled "Two good faith replies ... " in chapter sixteen.)

E) Rapport

Whereas trust is a belief in the honesty and integrity of another person, rapport is the establishment of a relationship characterized by trust, harmony, understanding, and mutual respect between people. Thus, trust is essential to rapport. As a workshop leader, you need to see building and maintaining rapport with the group as one of your key responsibilities. Although rapport is a shared responsibility with participants, you must see it as firmly within your "circle of influence," that is, as something you can affect, as opposed to something that concerns you, but over which you have no control.

Following *the basics of workshop leader success* (discussed above) goes a long way toward building rapport with a group. And once you've established rapport, the workshop takes on a climate of colleagues working and learning together. Participation flows naturally, people take risks, they give each other and you the benefit of the doubt, and they challenge each other without becoming defensive. They support and build on each other's comments, there's energy in the room, and people have fun.

Two sure signs of being in rapport with a group are lots of eye contact and a running joke. The latter is when the group good naturedly jokes or teases you, or each other, about a habit, phrase, or process that keeps recurring in the workshop. It's usually something simple, and the sort of thing that's not very funny outside of the workshop or training program.

Reeeeeeeno - An example of a running joke

I was reading aloud through a number of flipchart pages as the group was following along. It was a "first pass" at the information generated in several subgroups, and I was wanting to ensure everyone in the whole group understood what was meant by each item on these pages. As is often the case, the pages were full of abbreviations and technical terms that were common "shorthand" in the group. This particular group was a home manufacturing company. I came to the term "Reno" and pronounced "Reeno," as in Reno, Nevada. The group look perplexed. I could just see them all silently asking, "Reno!" "What's that?" After a brief pause someone laughed and said that's "reno"; it stands for "renovation." This was followed by laughter and a few other good natured comments, implying a person would have to be newly arrived from Mars not to know the "Reno" meant "renovation." To them is was only common sense.

Over the next two days the term "reno" must have come up a dozen times or more. Every time someone in the group would pronounce it by exaggerating "reeeeeeeeeeno," just to jazz me a bit. Everyone would chuckle. It was all in good fun.

Running jokes can be a lot of fun, although, like I said above, they don't seem funny when they're retold. It's the kind of joke where someone would say, "You just had to be there."

Think of being in rapport with a group as having a large positive balance in the "relationship bank." There is so much goodwill and mutual respect deposited that even if you make a withdrawal (e.g., you do or say something stupid), the group just laughs it off. Not only that, but you can turn a mistake into a learning experience for the whole group. Without rapport, however, participants may simply "tune out" and write you and the workshop off as a lost cause.

Resonance in the physical world is the way to get maximum transfer of energy. In the world of the mind, it is the way to get a maximum transfer of idea content. ... It has its roots in sympathy. The word "sympathy" is derived from two Greek roots - syn, meaning "together"; and pathos meaning "feeling" ... feeling together.
- Henry Boettinger

CONCLUSION

Summary

This chapter contrasts and compares workshops and training programs and defines workshop and training-program leadership. In addition it highlights the basic requirements of being a successful workshop leader and the importance of trust and rapport in workshop relationships. Understanding these principles is critical to effective use of the theory, methods, and techniques covered later in this book.

Comparing and Contrasting Workshops and Training Programs

In terms of process and the leader's role, workshops and training programs have more in common than separates them. The chief difference is in the type of outcomes being sought. Whereas workshops seek outcomes closely related to work group, business, and operating issues, training programs focus one level down, on individual learning and behavior change on the job. Thus, workshops seek to help a group think, learn, gather information, prepare for a task, decide, plan action, solve problems, produce a product, or perform a task, while training programs seek to help participants gain new knowledge and develop skills.

The Basics of Leading Workshops and Training Programs

As a workshop leader, you are accountable for an effective "learning climate" (i.e., relationships, context, structure, and process). This means you are responsible for playing a central role in the process of cultivating and maintaining a climate of colleagues working, learning, and accomplishing together.

Leading a workshop is a step above *facilitating*. Facilitating requires knowledge of group process. Leading requires facilitation skills, relevant technical know-how, and a focus on accomplishing a meaningful result. The terms "workshop leader" and "training-program leader" have been chosen over other options such as facilitator, instructor, or presenter to describe the role of operating or conducting workshops and training programs. Leadership, as it's operationally defined here, has two complementary definitions. First, it has to do with accepting and sharing accountability for workshop or training-program results and for an involving and participative process. Second, it has to do with influencing and helping individual participants, and the group as a whole, discover common language and common meanings (i.e., to help a group create and discover personal and shared meaning for themselves) and commit to following through on workshop or training-program results.

The Basics of Workshop and Training-Program Leader Success

It's hard to be perfect in an imperfect world. The good news is, you don't need to be perfect as a workshop leader, but you do need to be technically competent, have an attitude of abundance and caring, be informed about your clients (the workshop participants), and invest in your own development.

First, you need to know, in depth, the technical material you're helping others learn. This doesn't mean you have to be a basketball star to coach high school basketball. It does mean you have playing experience and that you understand the intricacies of the game.

Second, you need to enjoy being a workshop leader; have a strong sense of yourself, your values, and your standards; care about participants, their learning, and their success; and trust the group. An effective workshop leader is a team player who cares about helping others succeed and learn, and gains satisfaction from the success of others.

Third, you need to care and be informed about the group. Know their unique situation and understand how best you can help them achieve the outcomes being sought from the workshop or training program.

Fourth, you need to continuously develop yourself, your leadership abilities, and your leadership tools, always striving to run each workshop better than the last, learning as you go.

The Benefits of Leading Workshops and Training Programs

There are personal, professional, and organizational benefits to leading workshops and training programs. Personally, you develop confidence, as well as pubic speaking and interpersonal skills. With experience, you learn how to handle almost any situation that might arise in a group of adults. Professionally, you develop contacts and your reputation as a leader. The challenge of leading workshops shakes you up and gets you out of your rut. It helps you surface and reevaluate many of the assumptions that guide your technical or administrative practice, and it requires you to stay current and even ahead of technical developments in your field. Finally, organizational benefits include solving problems and developing products in workshops, as well as more informed, capable, and confident employees.

Trust and Rapport

Without rapport any workshop is an uphill battle. With rapport a workshop flows smoothly, taking on the atmosphere of colleagues working and learning together. Trust is essential to rapport. Participants are more open to learning from a "trusted source," someone they believe is credible and authentic. Yet trust has to be earned and given freely; it cannot be forced. Assess your relationship with the group using the four elements of trustworthiness - openness, congruency, support, and reliability.

Checklist

Basics of Workshop Leader Success	*Four Elements of Trustworthiness*
1) *Be Technically Competent in Your Field* 2) *Bring Who You Are to What You Do As a Workshop Leader* • Enjoy being a workshop leader • Have a strong sense of yourself, your values, and your moral standards 3) *Be Informed and Care about Your Clients* • Understand the group's unique situation • Care about participants, their learning, and their success • Foster an abundance attitude • Encourage teamwork in the group 4) *Continuously Develop Yourself and Your Workshop or Training Program* • Develop your people skills • Develop your leadership skills • Value mistakes • Know your limitations • Continuously develop your workshop or training program • Build a repertoire of practical models, methods, and theory	1) Be open 2) Be congruent 3) Be supportive 4) Be reliable *Guidelines for Understanding Trust* 1) Trust is a rather delicate flower 2) It takes courage to trust 3) Give participants evidence that you're trustworthy 4) Trust cannot be controlled, legislated, or forced 5) Trust has to be constantly earned 6) Trusting others predisposes them to trusting you 7) Trust can only grow in an environment of goodwill, respect, and a willingness to work on your relationship 8) We trust people who are self-aware and loyal to the truth 9) You don't have to be perfect to be trustworthy 10) We tend to trust people who have a positive balance in the relationship bank

Exercise

Indicators of Trust

Here are a couple of questions to get you thinking about trust in a group. Jot down a few responses before moving on.

1) What are the indicators that there's a high level of trust in a group?

Examples

- There's a high level of energy and focus.
- There's an open flow of information.
- Participants don't talk about the need for more trust.
- Subgroups get on with their tasks (e.g., brainstorming, role playing).
-
-
-

2) What are the indicators that there might be a lack of trust in a group?

Examples

- Participants seem to analyze things to death ("ready, aim, aim, aim, aim ...).
- Participants talk about the need for more structure, clearer rules, more guidelines about process, and so on.
- Participants talk only to you, the workshop leader, as opposed to speaking directly to each other.
- Things being said outside the workshop (e.g., the hallways, the washroom) are different from what is being said in the workshop room.
-
-
-

Exercise

Your Strengths and Limitations As a Workshop and Training-Program Leader

1) Of the four basics of workshop leader success outlined above, what are your strengths as a workshop leader? (Be as specific as possible.)

2) What are your strengths as a training-program leader?

3) What are your limitations, or areas where you would like to be more effective as a workshop leader?

4) What are your limitations as a training-program leader?

5) What two things will you do to build on your strengths, and what two things will you do to overcome or lessen your limitations as a workshop and training-program leader? (Be as specific as possible.)

Notes

[1]The performance equation is discussed in: Schermerhorn, J.R., Hunt, J.G., & Osborn, R.N. (1988). Managing organizational behavior (3rd ed.). New York, NY: John Wiley & Sons, pp. 69-72.

[2]Hersey and Blanchard define ability as competence and confidence. Carrying this one step down, competence would equate with knowledge and skill. See: Hersey, P., & Blanchard, K.H. (1982). Management of organizational behavior. Englewood Cliffs, NJ: Prentice-Hall.

[3]For information on search conference technology see Weisbord, M.R. (1989). Productive workplaces: Organizing and managing for dignity, meaning, and community. San Francisco, CA: Jossey-Bass, pp. 284-292. For information on open space technology see Owen, H. (1991). Riding the tiger: Doing business in a transforming world. Potomac, MD: Abbott Publishing, pp. 182-206.

[4]Norman Cousins (1981) notes that: "Socrates had no particular liking for the term 'teacher' when it applied to himself; he preferred to think of himself as an intellectual midwife. What is most valuable in the Socratic method is the painstaking and systematic development of thought from its earliest beginnings to its full-bodied state. The mind was fully engaged; this was what was most vital to the process. See: Cousins, N. (1981). Human options. New York, NY: Berkeley Books, p. 29.

[5]Webster's new collegiate dictionary (1981). Toronto, Ont: Thomas Allen & Sons, p. 647.

[6]Chaplin, J.P. (1985). Dictionary of psychology (2nd ed.). New York, NY: Laurel, p. 253.

[7]Weick, K.E. (1969). The social psychology of organizing. New York, NY: Random House.

[8]The term "follow up" is commonly used in training and consulting circles to mean following through on promises or commitments to take action, following a workshop or training program.

[9]Bennis, W., & Nanus, B. (1985). Leaders: The strategies for taking charge. New York, NY: Harper & Row.

[10]The idea that leaders are involved in "meaning making" is from: Drath, W.H., & Palus, C.H. (1994). Making common sense: Leadership as meaning-making in a community of practice. Greensboro, NC: Center for Creative Leadership.

[11]Bellman, G.M. (1990). The consultant's calling: Bringing what you are to what you do. San Francisco, CA: Jossey-Bass.

[12]The term "real team" was coined by Katzenbach, J.R., & Smith, D.S. (1993). The wisdom of teams: Creating the high-performance organization. New York, NY. HarperBusiness. "Real teams" are distinguished from working groups. "Real teams" have a shared purpose, joint accountability, do "hands on" work together, and produce a specific team product.

[13]The concept of the relationship bank is from Covey, S.R. (1989). The 7 habits of highly effective people: Powerful lessons in personal change. New York, NY: Simon & Schuster.

[14] This and the following point were inspired by: Martin, K.P. (1990). Discovering the what of management. Flemington, NJ: Renaissance Educational Services.

[15]Weeks, D., & James, J. (1995). Eccentrics: A study of sanity and strangeness. New York, NY: Villard, p. 39.

[16]I learned the phase "abundance attitude" and learned what it really means through years of working with a friend and colleague, Murray Hiebert. He's a senior consultant who "gives his stuff away," who trusts and cares about his clients, and who's been a great mentor and friend to me over many years.

[17]Moyers, B. (1990). A world of ideas II: Public opinions from private citizens. In A. Tucker (Ed.). New York, NY: Doubleday, pp. 218-226.

[18]E.L. Thorndike, an eminent psychologist in his time, popularized the notion of IQ in the 1920's and 1930's. Taken from: Goleman, D. (1995). Emotional intelligence. New York, NY: Bantam, p. 42.

[19]This model was first presented in Salovey, P., & Mayer, J.D. (1990). Emotional intelligence: Imagination, cognition, and personality, Vol. 9. p. 189. Taken from: Goleman, D. (1995). Emotional intelligence. New York, NY: Bantam, p. 43.

[20]Lowy, A., Kelleher, D., & Finestone, P. (1986). Management learning: beyond program design. *Training and Development Journal*, 1986, 40 (6), pp. 34-37. Quoted in: Brookfield, S.D. (1987).

Developing critical thinkers: Challenging adults to explore alternative ways of thinking and acting. San Francisco, CA: Jossey-Bass.

[21]Ralston Saul, J. (1994). The doubter's companion: A dictionary of aggressive common sense. Toronto, Ont: Viking, p. 120.

[22]Diane MacDonald, a friend and colleague, developed the first draft of these benefits during the 1980's when we worked together at Dome Petroleum. Dome Petroleum was a large oil and gas company in Calgary, Alberta, Canada.

[23]"Circle of influence" is a term borrowed from Covey, S.R. (1989). The 7 habits of highly effective people: Powerful lessons in personal change. New York, NY: Simon & Schuster.

[24]Chapter fifteen provides concrete strategies for building trust with a group through methods of presenting, facilitating, and leading.

[25]Senge, P., Ross, R., Smith, B., Roberts, C., & Kleiner, A. (1994). The fifth discipline fieldbook: Strategies and tools for building a learning organization. New York, NY: Currency Doubleday, pp. 213-215.

[26]Seligman, M.E.P. (1990). Learned optimism: How to change your mind and your life. New York, NY: Pocket Books, p. 72.

[27]Covey, S.R. (1989). The 7 habits of highly effective people: Powerful lessons in personal change. New York, NY: Simon & Schuster.

[28]It may have been P.T. Barnum who first fired this quip.

[29]I'd like to thank Dave Irvine, a good friend and colleague, for this perspective.

[30]This phrase if borrowed from: Covey, S.R. (1989). The 7 habits of highly effective people: Powerful lessons in personal change. New York, NY: Simon & Schuster.

Chapter 2

Learning, Habits, and Levels of Knowledge

INTRODUCTION

Travel back to your teenage years. It's a beautiful sunny day, the birds are singing, and the swimming hole beckons with its cool, clear promise of a spring afternoon's merriment. But you're stuck inside a musty old classroom listening to Mr. Fooglehorn drone on about the evolution of Chinese offshore fishing policy or some other equally useful piece of information. Sounds like fun, right? Unfortunately, this is how some workshop leaders run workshops, emphasizing boring facts at the expense of the adventure in learning.

Second only to freedom, learning is the most precious option on earth.
- Norman Cousins

The illiterate of the future are not those who can't read and write but those that cannot learn, unlearn, and relearn.
- Alvin Toffler

Learning is the most important common denominator in workshops and training programs but we sometimes confuse it with formal instruction. How do people learn? What is our natural way of learning? These are simple questions but their answers are far from simple. A sophisticated and detailed look at learning and all its complexity is beyond the scope of this book, however it's important to understand the basics. Understanding learning - the adventure and spontaneity of learning, the difference between double-loop learning and learning within a given goal or perspective - provides a foundation for leading workshops and training programs in organizations.

This chapter examines:

- Learning, teaching, and the natural learning cycle.
- Andragogy (adult learning) and pedagogy.
- Learning styles.
- Single-loop and double-loop learning.
- Understanding, forming, and changing habits.
- Levels of knowledge.

LEARNING

Workshop leaders need to understand how people learn in order to fully appreciate and apply the models and methods provided later in this book. Understanding the differences between conventional teaching, natural learning, and deep learning is a good starting place. This leads to a discussion of the natural learning cycle.

The dog too old to learn new tricks always has been.
- Anonymous

A) Learning, Teaching, and Facilitating

How we learn often determines the quality and usefulness of the knowledge gained. Some argue that only learning from experience leads to usable knowledge. However, learning only by experience, without the benefit of structured education or training, is a slow "hit and miss" process. Without the structure and direction of workshops and formal training programs, there's no way to be sure experience is providing all the important learning we need. And, of course, there's the matter of efficiency. Learning only by experience is often slow and time consuming. While workshops and training programs are a poor substitute for learning by experience, they do, however, when combined with learning on the job, help speed up the learning process. They do this by guiding learning through a controlled and "safe" environment, and by providing immediate feedback to participants (e.g., when learning on the job, we're not always sure which of several actions we have taken have led to success, whereas in a workshop this feedback is direct, immediate, and descriptive).

Klas Mellander (1993) says that "the purpose of (leading) is to make learning possible."[1] That is, it creates conditions that encourage and support learning as opposed to simply conveying information. This definition holds workshop leaders and trainers accountable for high quality inputs (e.g., a supportive and challenging learning climate, relevant examples, quality learning materials) as opposed to simply being responsible for activity (e.g., lecturing, handing out materials, controlling side conversations). It also recognizes that learning involves choice. As a workshop or training-program leader, you can make learning *possible*, but you can't make learning *happen*.

Traditional Teaching, Natural Learning, and Deep Learning

Inescapably, the following distinctions are generalized and a little arbitrary. However, they make a point. This is that workshop and training-program leaders should seek to avoid traditional teaching and the *grade school* approach. *Natural learning* leads to the best results. When *deep learning* occurs - and it does sometimes - it's a bonus. Aiming for deep learning as it's operationally defined here is unrealistic for most workshops and training programs.

Traditional teaching is "jug and mug," with the big jug (the teacher) filling up the little mugs (the students). It's Moses coming down from the mountain; telling and selling. It worked for Moses, but thanks to traditional teaching today, many graduates of North American high schools are functionally illiterate. Some can't even read their own diploma! Traditional teaching pays little attention to learning readiness and learning climate. It speeds along delivering material no matter what color the light; red, yellow, or green. Traditional teachers deliver the material and hope for the best, finishing the class regardless of whether students do or not!

If teaching is transformed in our time, it will not be the result of snappier teaching techniques. It will happen because we are in the midst of a far reaching intellectual and spiritual revisioning of reality and how we know it.
- Parker Palmer

In traditional teaching, sometimes referred to as pedagogy, the teacher explains the meaning of each term separately, in a linear fashion. Students are asked to "pay attention" and have few opportunities to make use of their own experience. Learning gained in this way is fragmented, hard to recall, and hard to use. Knowledge is seen as a quantity that can be measured, even though it's the qualitative aspects of knowledge that determine its value. Further, measuring encourages memorization instead of natural learning. Memorizing is superficial; it doesn't entail acquiring the underlying experience, understanding, or insight needed to apply learning in creative ways. And one of the biggest problems with memorizing is that we think we understand, even when we don't.

Grade School	*Natural Learning*	*Deep Learning*
Traditional North American grade schools (particularly in the '50s and '60s).	Highly effective workshops and training programs.	Exceptional therapy groups that promote intellectual as well as emotional learning.
Traditional teaching. Teachers tell. Students are expected to "pay attention."	Leaders guide, coach, and facilitate (e.g., challenge, support).	The group is coached but basically self-directed. Participants may take turns facilitating.
Students constitute a captive and passive audience. Learning readiness is incidental to the teacher's role and actions.	Participants are volunteers and anxious to learn and accomplish the outcomes being sought.	Participants come prepared for the pain, hard work, and risk of sharing their feelings and thoughts at a deep and intimate level.
Students have very few opportunities to make use of their own experience.	Participants learn by doing. They are active, involved, and draw their own conclusions.	Participants engage in open and nonjudgmental communication with healthy boundaries.

Grade School	*Natural Learning*	*Deep Learning*
Memorizing meets most requirements for learning.	Participants develop intellectual and instrumental meanings and connections (e.g., new ways of understanding problems).	Profound personal (intellectual and emotional) truths are realized, providing the opportunity for deep personal change.
Learning is linear, fragmented, and abstract. From the student's perspective there is little immediate or practical value.	A bird's-eye view, gestalt, or overall context for learning is developed. Emphasis is on the practical and the "here and now."	Learning is emotional and intellectual, and because it is connected with theory, it is also transferable.
Coercion is employed (e.g., grades and punishment).	Sharing takes place in an atmosphere of common goals, respect, and mutual support.	Learning requires the absence of coercion and power.
Knowledge is seen as a quantity that can be measured.	Learning is related to experience, thus the quality of knowledge increases. Change on the job is expected.	Learning is deeply personal, and change is completely voluntary.
Students are often bored, watching the clock, and dreaming of recess.	Participants are involved, committed, learning, and achieving results.	Participants are renewed and energized.

Lasting improvement does not take place by pronouncements or official programs. Change takes place slowly inside each of us and by the choices we think through in quiet wakeful moments lying in bed just before dawn.
- Peter Block

Coercion is employed in traditional teaching. In grade school it works to a degree because of the power of the carrot and the stick (also known as the great jackass theory of motivation). In traditional schools it's grades and punishment. In organizations it's much different. Although there are always a few adults who will do as they're told, most will resist. If the organization's culture supports choice and honest communication, resistance in response to traditional teaching will be direct. If it doesn't, resistance will go underground. That is, participants will "role play" the workshop, fight back where it seems safe to do so, and resent the leader, the process, and likely everything else associated with the workshop.

At the other extreme, deep learning involves both intellectual and emotional understanding. Valerie Malhotra Bentz (1991) describes it as a "communicative process whereby profound truths are realized emotionally and intellectually."[2] She goes on to say that these truths are "socially created in an atmosphere of trust, (and that) when such shared moments are achieved, those present feel renewed and energized. Deep learning, Malhotra Bentz maintains, leads to deep personal change among participants. That's not to say that change is immediate, but rather that the process leading to change has begun.

Natural learning, on the other hand, is learning by doing. It's reflecting on what you've done and its consequences, assessing how this fits with what you already know, and how it might be relevant in the future. Natural learning creates a bird's-eye view; a gestalt. It provides an overall context in which participants perceive relationships. New learning is related to existing knowledge, and thus the quality and value of knowledge increase.

Workshop leaders practicing natural learning are guides, coaches, facilitators, and leaders as opposed to traditional teachers. Rather than simply presenting material to a captive and passive audience, you deal with participants who are active, involved, and draw their own conclusions. You assist participants to create and discover their own opinions and insights, rather than believing that your personal conclusions, even when based on years of experience, can become participants' conclusions just because you say so. You encourage participants to find words for things that they already understand intuitively. You provide for experimentation and discovery, rather than turning participants into walking reference books and champions of total recall.

B) The Natural Learning Cycle

Learning progresses as a cycle; when we act we generate consequences that provide us with feedback. Now we learn about our actions. What we learn may change our thinking and so we act differently next time. By acting differently we generate new consequences that provide us with additional feedback, and on and on. This cycle of acting, learning, and acting differently has been called "action learning." A simple and powerful concept, action learning can be traced back to Kurt Lewin's work in the 1940's. As Weisbord (1987) explains, the term was intended to embrace "enhanced problem-solving, ... preserve democratic values, build commitment to act, and motivate learning - all at once."[3] The term is insightful because it's really the only way we can learn where any level of complexity is involved. It's our natural way of learning.

In *the natural learning cycle* experience is interpreted and transformed to create knowledge. This process starts with an interest in doing something (focus), collecting data and organizing this into useful information (search), making decisions on how to proceed (integrate), fitting these decisions to the situations you intend to act on (generalize), then taking action (act).

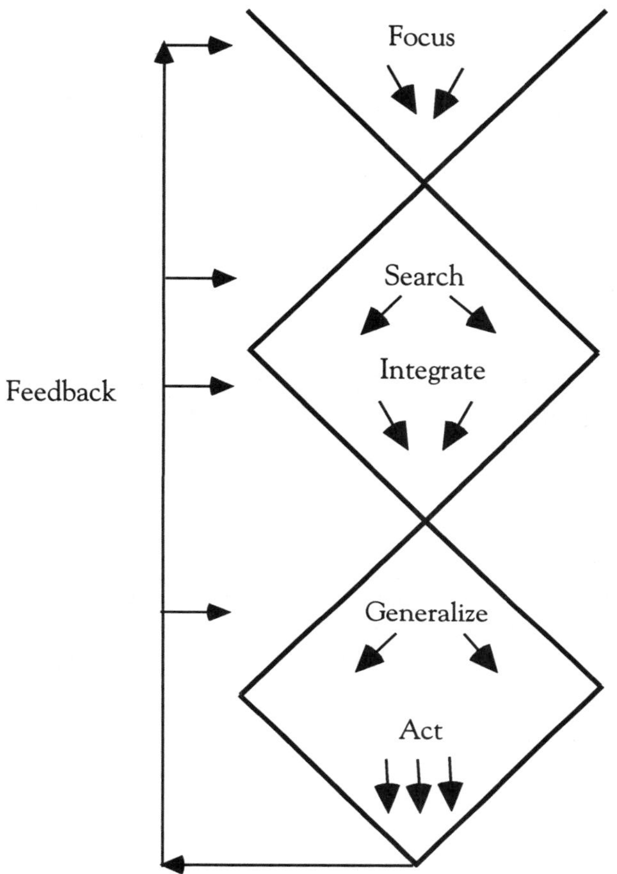

The Natural Learning Cycle

Creating knowledge through the interpretation of experience.

1) Focus
2) Search
3) Integrate
4) Generalize
5) Act

You might think of this diagram as a rope. With only one twist it would easily fall apart. But the more twists and strands in a rope (i.e., the more one focuses, searches, integrates, generalizes, and acts), the stronger it will be. Hence, the greater the depth, assessibility, and strength of one's learning.

Due to the limitations of language, the natural learning cycle is described here in a linear, step-by-step fashion. In practice, this is far from the case. Within seconds we might cycle between two steps, jump to the next step, cycle back to step one, jump to action, and so on. (The arrows on the left hand side of the diagram above are intended to show how we can recycle back to any step, from any step, in the natural learning cycle.) Natural learning can be a rather clumsy "two steps forward, one step back" kind of activity, as we use analysis and intuition, interpreting experience and making meaning in our own very personal ways.

1) Focus

***Speculation leads to learning, just as theory leads to science.* - William Hazlitt**

Learning starts with speculation and focus, a need and a desire to learn. Something happens and we awaken inside. Something shakes us up. Maybe we see an opportunity, or maybe it's just our natural curiosity. Maybe we become aware of something we might lose if we don't begin to think and act differently. At any rate our attention is focused, our curiosity aroused, our interest heightened. Our mind becomes open to change and this experience leads us to act. We are *learning ready.*

The term "learning readiness" is elegantly described by Gary Zukav (1979) in his book *The Dancing Wu Li Masters.* "A Master teaches the essence," Zukav writes. "When the essence is perceived, the Master teaches what is necessary to expand the perception. Thus, the Wu Li Master does not speak of gravity until the student stands in wonder at the flower petal falling to the ground."[4]

Examples of focusing

- You buy a VCR. You don't have a teenager in the house, so you must learn how to operate it on your own. Sure, the sixty page operating manual is a little intimidating, but you really want to record your favorite show this evening while you're away coaching your son's soccer team. You experience the need and desire to learn how to operate your new VCR. You are "learning ready." This is focus.
- Learning readiness is a powerful thing. Einstein was learning ready when he dreamt of riding on a light wave. From this, he arrived at his special theory of relativity. Most of us, when really focused and fired up about something in our lives, have experienced "waking up" in a similar way. Suddenly we have this idea or solution relating to work we've been doing during the preceding days. This is also focus.

2) Search

You're now focused and learning ready. You have purpose and energy. The next step is to collect data and organize it into usable information. Asking questions, exploring, researching, and observing, you document or make a mental note of what's interesting and relevant. You challenge the data and search for contrary information as a way of checking your assumptions and ensuring you're looking in the right "ball park."

Your motivation varies as a function of your *focus* (i.e., your interest and need for the information). If you have a burning need for learning, your search will know few limits. For a workshop leader, working with a group of participants who are really fired up is pure magic. They ask questions, challenge, dialogue, and debate in a way that makes the workshop come alive. Time flies, everyone has fun - and the fun is "on topic" - and almost everything you do as a workshop leader yields a high return. The very opposite is true where participants are just "not much interested" in the learning content. Leading now is like pulling teeth; every minute is either boring or painful. When a group isn't learning ready, it feels like anything you do falls flat. Most of the fun in the workshop, if there is any, is off topic, and leading the workshop is hard work.

Examples of searching

- Going back to the VCR example discussed above, now that you're focused and learning ready it's time to search for answers. Rolling up your sleeves, you venture into the operating manual, first reading about some of the more common functions such as how to set the timer and how to play rented movies. You read a little and tinker a little. You understand what you read by how your VCR reacts to your tinkering. You are learning by experiencing and experimenting. Spontaneously, you start playing around with other features, some of which you haven't even found in the operating manual yet. You try things and watch what happens. This fiddling leads you back into the relevant parts of the operating manual. You learn by doing and unless you're a VCR repairman, you're unlikely to read the entire operating manual from one glorious cover to the other. That would be about as exciting as reading the phone book. Instead, like a phone book, you use the operating manual only to look up what you need to know when you need to know it.
- You decide to write an article on a certain topic (e.g., inventory control). Deciding on a focus for the article (e.g., using XYZ software to lower inventory costs), you develop a few key questions to aid your search (e.g., How and under what conditions does XYZ software improve inventory turnover and reordering schedules?) Using your questions as guides you review recent literature on the topic, then meet and discuss inventory control with experts in the field.

3) Integrate

At this point you're armed with focus, motivation, and information. Now what? Now you turn data into information as you organize your findings into categories that are relevant and meaningful to you. You contemplate and struggle with how your findings fit together, how they meet your needs, and how they fit with your previous experience. You might share and compare your data, observations, responses, and ideas with others, or you might think quietly on your own. You ask yourself, "What messages are here?" "How do they relate to what I want to do?"

Without checking the validity and relevance of what you've learned, the new information isn't worth much. You need to confirm new learning with past experience. In this way new information acquires additional associations that reinforce it. Thus, you replace or update old information with new, and integrate new learning with existing knowledge. This becomes what you *know* and *believe*. The more information you have about a given topic, the more refined brain cell connections become, and the easier it becomes to access this information. When you've converted the new information into experience and insight, drawn conclusions, and arrived at some "personal truths," you've internalized and integrated the new learning.

There's an old saying, "People who think learning is fun have either never learned or never had fun." Learning isn't always easy; it's not enough for someone to give us the answers. We have to think through problems for ourselves if we want to arrive at our own understanding. Only in this way do we gain usable knowledge. Natural learning requires an effort to achieve understanding. It demands thinking. If you are going to learn anything, you must draw your own conclusions based on your own experience. In other words, to learn you need to struggle. You need to be involved.

An example of integrating

- Let's suppose you're still struggling with your new VCR. You've read part of the instruction manual and experimented a little bit, and while you're catching on, you're still not sure how to record from the TV. That's when you notice a little button that says "record" on the face of the VCR's remote control. You realize that pushing this button must be at least one of the steps necessary to tape from the TV. Looking it up in the instruction manual, the technical mumbo jumbo now takes on a new meaning as you incorporate it with your knowledge of the existence, and location, of the "record" button.

4) Generalize

You've integrated past experience and new learnings, and arrived at a new level of knowledge. But, as yet, this new way of knowing only applies to the very specific situation in which you've just developed it. It's quite limited. Now you have to generalize it to other situations, and discover other uses, in order to increase the value and application of your new knowledge. That is, you need to formulate and develop strategies and principles to guide when, how, where, under what conditions, and for what purposes you will apply your new knowledge. Often decisions to generalize are made intuitively and at the moment, but they're guided by experience, preparation, conscious thought, and practice.

In the moment, in the heat of a situation, you reach for a theory of approach. What makes sense here? How should I proceed? You recall past learning and ways of knowing. You generalize from these to the present situation, converting this prior learning and experience into "usable" knowledge. Fitting past learning into a new situation helps to further define and clarify your knowledge.

Examples of generalizing

- Now that you've conquered the heights of VCR operation, you venture one step further. You buy a video camera. Learning to operate your new electronic toy is made easier by existing knowledge of how your VCR works. You guess that many of the same principles apply, much the way learning a second word processing or spreadsheet program is easier once you've learned the basics by struggling with your first such program.

- After studying this book on leading workshops and incorporating this information with your experience and previous knowledge, you decide on a theory of approach for leading workshops. Generalizing, you decide how to apply your learning. From now on you will always do something to help participants become learning ready before introducing new learning content. Further, you decide never to introduce new learning content "unless and until" participants are learning ready. This approach is also based on your belief that external motivators are generally too limiting and insignificant to cause participants to be actively involved and motivated in a workshop. External rewards and pressures to learn (grades, recognition, threats, orders from the boss) are just not as powerful as being learning ready and focused internally. It's not that external motivators don't have value, it's just that information acquired because of them is generally more superficial, less integrated, and less useful than information obtained when highly motivated and learning ready. And, the learning process itself is a lot less fun. The necessity for learning readiness in a group becomes one of your beliefs or "personal truths."

5) Act

Now you act on your belief or generalization. The consequences of your actions provide more data for learning. Focusing on this new data the natural learning cycle begins anew. That is, by field testing your generalizations you get "real-world" consequences. This provides data for modifying your beliefs. Thus, acting on your beliefs and paying attention to the consequences of your actions, you get even more data for learning.

Examples of acting

- You program your VCR to record at the desired times and leave to coach your daughter's soccer team. All the time you're hoping the TV listing is accurate, and you don't inadvertently end up taping some "made for TV movie," requiring an audience IQ roughly equivalent to that of your average rock star! (By the way, while we're on the subject of TV, which did come first, the couch or the potato?)

- You lead a workshop following your new beliefs and "theory of approach." You assess results. How useful was this new approach? Was it easy? Hard? What additional modifications are needed? Your experience gives you new information from which you may either adapt, discard, or further commit to your beliefs.

ADULT-LEARNING PRINCIPLES

Whether you call it "natural learning" as above, organic learning, or experiential learning, it's all the same thing. It's learning by doing. Learning by being involved, by struggling, by experimenting, by trying, by discovering, by creating.

Adult-learning principles are almost the opposite of traditional teaching, at least in the sense of traditional teaching as it's presented above. These principles support and encourage natural learning. Malcolm Knowles, considered the father of adult-learning theory, coined the term *andragogy* to distinguish adult learning from *pedagogy*, the teaching of children.[5] Understanding the logic behind these distinctions, and the following three principles of adult learning, will help you facilitate and lead in a way that's "in sync" with and supports the needs of adults in your workshops and training programs.

> ***However much respect (participants) may have for the superior learning of their teachers, they believe they themselves have something of value to offer. ... They see themselves not just as receptacles for instruction but as essential participants in the educational experience. They mirror the central tendency of the age - which is the quest for individual respect.***
> ***- Norman Cousins***

A) Three Powerful Principles of Adult Learning

The following three principles of adult learning support and encourage the natural learning process. Use these as a guide when you lead workshops and training programs.

1) Adults bring a lot of experience with them to workshops, and therefore have something to contribute and something to lose.

2) Adults want workshops that focus on real-life *here and now* problems and tasks, rather than on academic situations.

3) Adults are accustomed to being active and self-directing.

Although these principles are related, they're also distinct. Assumptions and practices that follow from each are set out below, in point form, for ease of comparison and review.

1) Adults Bring a Lot of Experience with Them to Workshops, and Therefore Have Something to Contribute and Something to Lose

Assumptions behind this principle

- Adult learning is unique to each individual. Every person learns at their own pace and in their own way.

- Adults have a lot invested in their experience.

- Very few adults want, or expect, to change their self-concept. If they are to change at some deep personal level, it must be of their own volition. It's not a workshop leader's role to *force* personal change.

Practices suggested by this principle

- Adults want to test a workshop's learning content against what they already know. Encourage them to answer questions from their own experience.

- For learning to occur, workshop leaders need to encourage questioning and value difference. Adults won't buy *your* answer; they need to discover answers for themselves. Presenting information as "truth" is usually met with skepticism.

- Adults don't want to risk looking stupid or being shown up in any way. It's critical to maintain their self-esteem, at all times, during the workshop. In the words of the poet Alexander Pope, "men must be taught as if you taught them not, and things unknown posed as things forgot."

- Provide a supportive and challenging workshop climate. Overlook mistakes and do away with any sort of punishment. Learning can only be encouraged, not coerced. Indeed, in adult learning mistakes are sometimes forced, not just allowed to happen. Mistakes create differences, and differences enable learning. However, while adults need to struggle to learn at a significant level, they also need to be supported, respected, and accepted. They become engaged and focused when workshop conditions are supportive. They resist and defend themselves when conditions are threatening.

- For learning to occur, material has to be provided in manageable steps. In this way adults understand as they learn, and gradually come to master the complete task.

- Adults want feedback, for example, on how they're progressing in a workshop, and on how they can improve. Positive reinforcement is also needed when adults first practice a new skill.[6]

2) Adults Want Workshops That Focus on Real-Life "Here and Now" Problems and Tasks, Rather Than on Academic Situations

Consider this story

Klas Mellander (1993) tells a story something like this.[7] You don't know me. You're standing in a hallway talking to friends and I saunter up to you and say, "To get to the washroom, go down two floors, take the third door on the left, then the first right after you get past the blue gym." Then I turn and walk away, leaving you scratching your head and wondering why the company hasn't instituted mandatory drug testing. Two hours later you need to use a washroom. You start looking for me because no one you ask seems to know where the washroom is. Finally you find me and ask, "Listen, where did you say that washroom was again?" I reply, "The washroom? Did you know that even the ancient Greeks had special washrooms for men? They handed it down to the Romans, who improved the design ..." and on and on. You'd have an accident before I got to the Middle Ages! Yet, this is what some workshop and training-program leaders do. They either tell us things we don't need to know, or, when we do need to know them, they tell us something else.

Assumptions behind this principle

- Adults see learning as a means to an end, rather than as an end in itself.
- Learning is voluntary. It must have personal meaning and it must be of direct and immediate value, or adults just won't be interested. Adults only learn what they want to learn; to do what they want to do.

Practices suggested by this principle

- Ensure that your workshops provide useful information relevant to participants' immediate needs. Adults have a "here and now" perspective and want to focus on current issues, rather than on material that may be useful in the distant future.
- Tell adults about the purpose and benefits of the workshop, and about the process you intend to follow. Adults become restless if they feel their time is being wasted. They must know what's in it for them.
- Summarize and review often, and do progress reviews. Adults like to see that progress is being made.

3) Adults Are Accustomed to Being Active and Self-Directing

Assumptions behind this principle

- The best learning is based on experience.

- Most adults like to work with others. Aim for a cooperative and collaborative process that supports participants sharing their experiences.

Practices suggested by this principle

> ***The way we teach depends on the way we think people know; we cannot amend our pedagogy until our epistemology is transformed.***
> ***- Parker Palmer***

- Adults should be given more than just the opportunity for active participation. Participation needs to be encouraged, supported, expected, and even demanded (albeit gently), particularly when adults are being paid to be in a workshop. Don't embarrass them, but don't let them hide either. Expect and act as if *active participation* is the norm. Sometimes this is difficult, especially early in a workshop. After a few hours of "not giving in" however, adults usually come around and participate actively.[8] The end result is that everyone learns and enjoys the workshop more. (Note: Language is powerful. This book refers to adult learners as "participants." I suggest you use the same language in your workshops.)

- For learning to occur, adults have to *do* things. They must get involved and work at tasks and exercises. Adults need to learn by doing, and making mistakes. They need to discover solutions on their own. It's not enough to have adults just read, listen, or watch a film.

- Adults want to be consulted and listened to. Although workshop leaders need to be directive at times, directing should be the exception rather than the rule.

B) Comparing Andragogy and Pedagogy

The following comparison of andragogy and pedagogy is intended to get you thinking about the way you want, and don't want, to conduct your workshops. (Hint: Choose andragogy.) Use it occasionally to check your leadership practices and habits.

The pedagogy side of this comparison may dredge up old memories of your school days with its deep seated concern for straight lines; absolute control over when you stand, how you sit, and who you talk with; and the rush of energy you felt when it was time for recess. Talk about motivation to learn!

Pedagogy is associated with traditional teaching, a field that has grown little in the last one hundred years. It's been said that if Rip van Winkle were to awaken today, aside from the fact that buildings are much larger, schools would be the only institution he would recognize! I need to end this little tirade by adding balance to my perspective on the North American school system. Although only recently, things seem to be improving in isolated pockets of this system. Examples of innovative change in education are described by Goleman (1995) and Osborne and Gaebler (1992).[9]

	Pedagogy	*Andragogy*
The concept of the learner[10]	Students are fully dependent on the teacher.	Participants are "self-directing" and not dependent on the workshop leader.
The role of the learner's experience	Students have little experience related to the learning content. Thus, teaching is straight *transmission* from the teacher to the student.	Participants have a great volume, quality, and variety of relevant experience. This experience is a primary source of participants' identities. In addition, participants come to workshops with many preoccupations and prejudices gained through years of experience.
The learner's readiness to learn	Students learn what and when they're told to learn.	Participants only learn when they experience a need to know or do something. Their readiness to learn is often triggered by a change in their situation.
The learner's orientation to learning	Students are subject centered.	Participants are life, task, and problem centered.
The learner's motivation to learn	Students are motivated to learn by external pressures.	Participants are only motivated to learn primarily by internal pressures such as self-esteem, recognition, quality of life, and greater self-confidence.

Myths about Andragogy

Adult-learning principles make a lot of sense, but like any guideline they need to be practiced with common sense and flexibility. For example, adults are not always self-directing. Groups of adults can use a little direction, and a little external control, from time to time.

I contradict myself. I am large. I contain multitudes.
- Walt Whitman

Stephen Brookfield, a leading adult educator, suggests we need to challenge a number of widely held beliefs about andragogy.[11] Brookfield's andragogic myths (May, 1989), outlined below, are a counterbalance to Knowles' theory of andragogy (1984). It's not that Brookfield feels andragogy is away off base. Rather, he's making the point that adult-learning theory can be interpreted in extreme ways, almost as a religion. When this happens, adult learning or andragogy is no longer practiced flexibly and with common sense. For example, although adults are expected to be self-directed in their learning (one of Knowles' principles), there are times when they need a little push and a little direction from a workshop or training-program leader.

Exploring these myths in detail would be a considerable digression from the purpose of this book. They're presented here merely as food for thought, and as a contrary perspective to help balance the information that's presented above. (Note: Here's a tough but accurate statement. If you can't handle contrary perspectives, then leading workshops and training programs, for adults, might not be the right line of work for you.)

Brookfield's andragogic myths

- Learning is a joyous activity. (In other words, sometimes learning is a struggle, even painful.)
- Adults are innately self-directed. (Sometimes adults need to be directed, pushed, and challenged. Of course, all the while, they need to be supported.)
- The best adult-learning experiences are based on the "felt needs" of the learners. (Sometimes adults are not aware of their own learning needs.)
- There is a unique adult-learning style. (Adult learners are no more homogeneous than are any other group of learners.)
- There is a unique adult-teaching style. (Many teaching, facilitating, and leadership approaches work, given the right circumstances.)

LEARNING STYLES

Roger Smith (1982) defines learning style as "a person's highly individualized preferences and tendencies that influence his or her learning."[12] Notwithstanding that learning styles are "highly individualized," the following four-box model provides an overview of what David Kolb (1984) sees as the basic or critical distinctions of learning styles.[13] (Note: Even if it were possible, presenting a model of learning styles that is as complex as reality itself would also be as immobilizing as reality itself. That is, it would not provide a clear framework for decision making.) Kolb's model is a distant cousin of the many social typologies that have been popular over the years (e.g., Myers Briggs). Its roots trace back to Dewey, Piaget, and Jung. Kolb's model is provided here for a couple of reasons.

> *"Everything, men, animals, trees, stars, we are all one substance involved in the same terrible struggle. What struggle? ... Turning matter into spirit." Zorba scratched his head (and said) "I've got a thick skull boss, I don't grasp these things easily. Ah, if only you could dance all that you've just said, then I'd understand. ... Or if you could tell me all that in a story, boss."*
> *- Nikos Kazantzakis, Zorba the Greek*

First, although like any social typology this model is an oversimplification of reality (e.g., it doesn't consider natural or deep learning where a person might access two, three, or all four learning styles at once), it is nonetheless instructive. It makes the point that people prefer to learn, deal with new ideas, and solve problems in different ways. The big message is - to borrow an old phrase from transactional analysis - "different strokes for different folks."[14] It's a good message for workshop leaders to keep in mind. You need to understand and adapt your material and delivery to participants' preferences for reality. To help you do this, Kolb's model is used as a sorting tool for the workshop design options provided in chapter six.

Second, discussing this model with participants will help them understand their own learning needs and habits. A self-scoring inventory and interpretation booklet is published by McBer and Company (1985) to accompany this model.[15] This booklet, only fourteen pages, is concise and well written. It provides an excellent overview of Kolb's model along with scoring, graphing, and interpretation tools. (Keep in mind this model is self-diagnostic and descriptive, as opposed to predictive. That is, it clarifies and provides insight about one's own learning preferences, but is not valuable as a predictor of other people's preferences or behavior.)

A) Four Learning Styles

The ***accommodator*** style is based on feeling and doing. Accommodators prefer "hands on" work, carrying out plans, experimenting, new experiences, trusting their "gut" instincts versus using logic, and relying on people versus technical analysis for implementing solutions.

The ***diverger*** style is based on feeling and watching. Divergers are good at seeing many points of view. Other strengths are gathering information and identifying differences and problems.

The ***assimilator*** style is based on thinking and watching. Assimilators prefer conciseness, ideas versus people, and logical versus practical values.

The ***converger*** style is based on thinking and doing. Convergers prefer practical uses for ideas, finding solutions, and technical tasks versus interpersonal tasks.

B) A Four-Box Model of Learning Styles

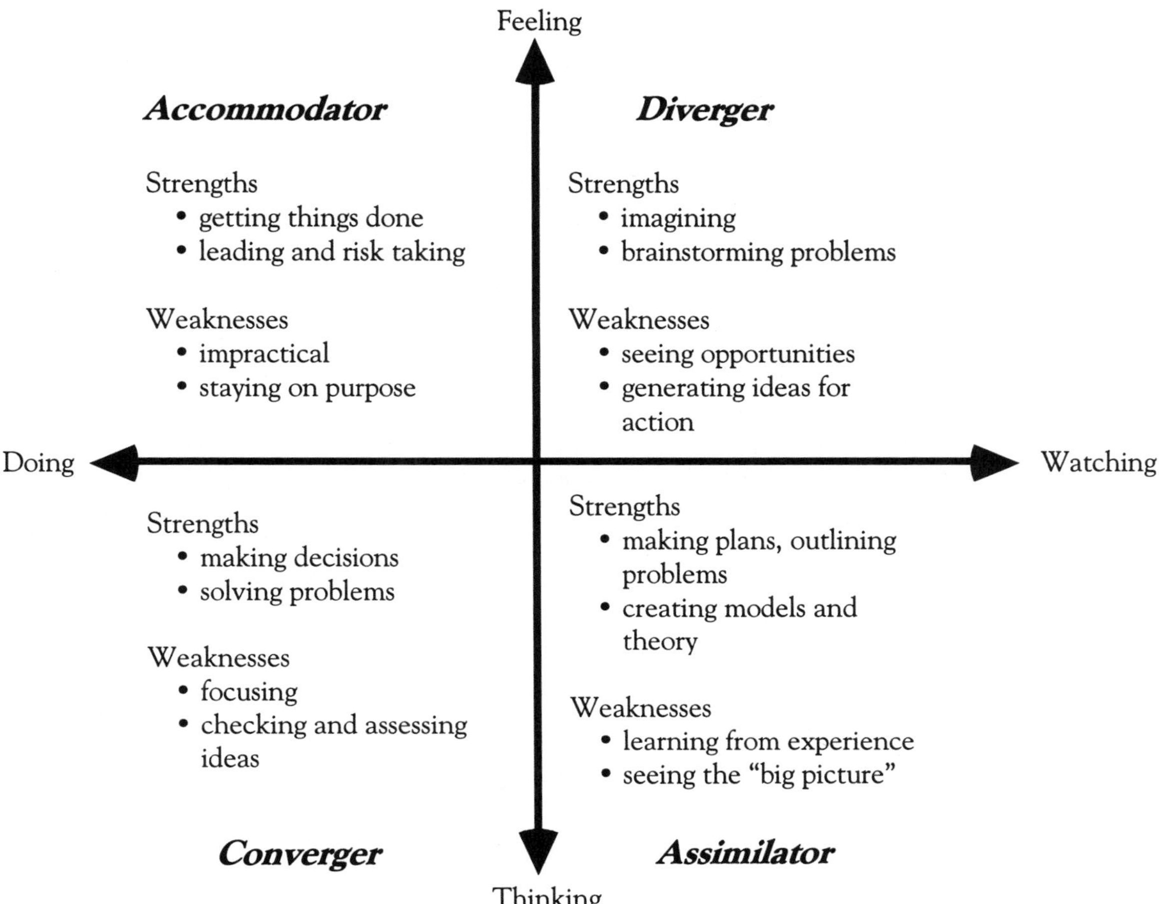

SINGLE-LOOP AND DOUBLE-LOOP LEARNING

How do workshop participants come to believe that it's possible to change their ways of knowing, habits, assumptions, or objectives? How do they learn to create enhanced objectives for learning, work, and relationships? Chris Argyris and Donald Schon (1974, 1978) answer these questions using the concepts of single-loop and double-loop learning.[16] These are concepts that every workshop and training-program leader should be familiar with. Use them as tools to challenge participants to think "outside their box," that is, outside the assumptions and limitations they've, perhaps unconsciously, constructed for themselves.

Single-loop learning involves changing methods and improving efficiency to obtain established objectives (i.e., "doing things right"). Double-loop learning concerns changing the objectives themselves (i.e., "doing the right things").

Single-loop and double-loop learning are easily understood using the analogy of a household thermostat. Single-loop learning compares with a given temperature setting (i.e., the objective) on the thermostat. A feedback loop connects the household temperature, as sensed by a thermometer, with the controlling mechanisms which generate or shut off the flow of hot air in the house. As the temperature oscillates around a static setting, the system is engaged in single-loop learning, accomplishing a set objective.

Double-loop learning - sometimes called generative learning - involves changing the setting on the thermostat (i.e., changing the objective of the system). Double-loop learning involves challenging established assumptions, objectives, and ways of working and discovering, inventing, and producing new options, objectives, perceptions, assumptions, and ways of approaching problems. Thus, double-loop learning is learning how to challenge one's own habits, assumptions, and ways of thinking.

Single-Loop Learning

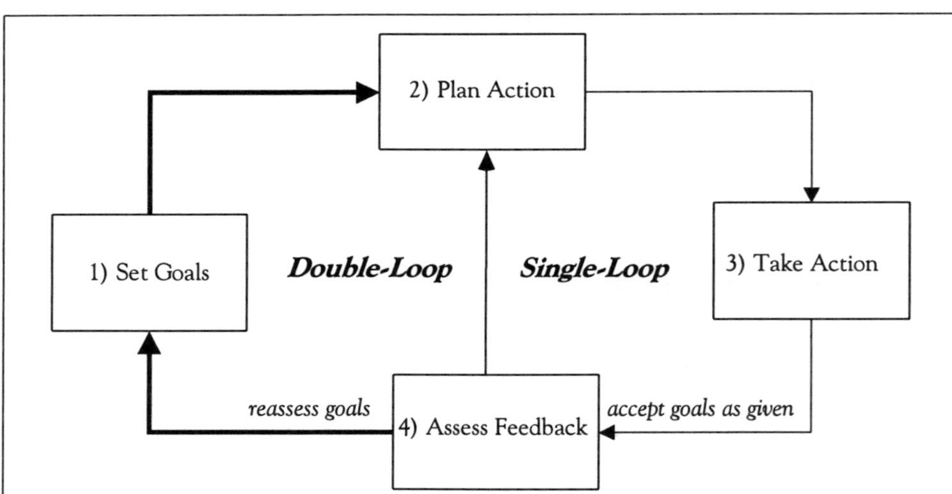

Both single-loop and double-loop learning start with step 1) set goals. Thereafter, single-loop learning assumes the established goals are correct and cycles within steps 2, 3, and 4 in order to achieve these goals. Efficiency becomes the concern.

Double-loop learning does not assume the established goals cannot be changed. It cycles back to step 1) and reassesses goals in light of feedback. Based on revised goals, new action plans are made, and different actions are taken. Effectiveness becomes the concern.

Single-loop learning enables us to avoid continuing investment in the highly predictable activities that make up the bulk of our lives (e.g., driving a car, dealing with customers). It is sufficient where errors can be corrected within our existing ways of knowing (i.e., our habits, norms, standard practices, customs, traditions, ways of approaching problems). However, it also keeps us stuck within this framework. Single-loop learning is comfortable; we don't question our practices, assumptions, or everyday habits.

A little learning is a dangerous thing.
- Alexander Pope

Faced with having to change our views or prove that there is no need to do so, most of us immediately get busy on the proof.
- John Kenneth Galbraith

Double-Loop Learning

Double-loop learning is dynamic and upsetting in that it involves a change in established objectives. It's essential when we can no longer correct or improve something (e.g., how we deal with conflict, how we supervise employees) simply by doing better what we already know how to do. Thus, double-loop learning is hard work. It means we must change habits, challenge and restructure deeply held assumptions, and act in new and unfamiliar ways.

Participants who are defensive and afraid for whatever reason, lack self-awareness, or aren't particularly interested in improving the results they are already getting will rarely allow questions, even from themselves, about their assumptions and habits. They may be open to learning as long as their established ways of thinking about and seeing the world are not questioned. That is, they may be open to single-loop learning but not double-loop learning. Thus, they may be open to learning a new analytical technique for managing people but not in learning an entirely new approach to managing people, which would require them to change their basic assumptions about human motivation.

The significant problems we face today cannot be solved at the same level of thinking we were at when we created them.
- Albert Einstein

I've been in this business 36 years, I've learned a lot -- and most of it doesn't apply anymore.
- Charles Exley

The only man who is educated is the man who has learned how to learn.
- Carl Rogers

Some men see things as they are and ask, "Why?" I see them as they have never been and ask, "Why not?"
- George Bernard Shaw

Double-loop learning depends on awareness. Participants must be open to recognizing the existence of error or opportunity. It's impossible when people are defensive or unwilling to discuss their assumptions because this inhibits awareness.

An example of double-loop learning

Jane Jacobs (1992) has a great analogy. She remarks how it's unfortunate that very few of us are like Isaac Newton, who said to himself, "Why is that?" when he saw an apple fall instead of float away from a tree. For most people, finding an answer depends on first recognizing that a valid question exists. Unlike Newton, most of us, most of the time, are not receptive to anomalies around us, to questioning our own assumptions. We just "assume" and leave it at that. We force the world into our foregone conclusions and tailor our beliefs to fit these conclusions.[17]

The bottom line is you can't force people to single-loop let alone double-loop learn. And although there are ways to influence and encourage openness to learning, the best you can do as a workshop leader is to take people to "the dawn of their own awareness."[18] That is, you can encourage them to become aware of a given situation and its implications. You can help them understand the need to rethink how they operate. You can also provide suggestions and strategies for change. In the end, however, if they chose to downplay, deny, or ignore their situation, or if they acknowledge their situation yet choose not to act, then that's it. Unless you have formal authority in the organization, or can influence those who have this authority, there's nothing further you can do.[19]

> ***The teacher, if indeed wise, does not bid you to enter the house of their wisdom, but leads you to the threshold of your own mind.***
> ***- Kahlil Gibran***

An example of how tough double-loop learning can be in organizations

Henry Mintzberg (1994) says, "Every manager has a mental model of the world in which he or she acts based on experience and knowledge. When a manager must make a decision, he or she thinks of behavior alternatives within their mental model."[20] This is single-loop learning.

Now, say you're conducting a workshop for a group of managers on "high involvement management," and you're doing this in a bureaucratic and hierarchical organization. One thing you need to acknowledge to yourself, and to your sponsor clients, is that managers who have worked their entire careers in organizations such as this have likely been institutionalized into an analytical, linear, and somewhat "nonlearning" mindset.[21] It's at least a "non-double-loop learning" mindset. They may be open to learning new methods or techniques that support their present management practices (i.e., single-loop learning), but they are likely to become defensive if questioned about the assumptions that lie beneath their current practices. That is, they're not likely open to double-loop learning.

To be open to double-loop learning these managers must first recognize that it's legitimate to challenge how they've operated all these years. For example, in order to change habits in organizations that have a long history of command and control style management versus participation by employees in problem solving and decision making, managers must first recognize that the question, "*How can we support a high level of employee initiative?*" is a valid question. But by doing this they are also allowing their assumptions and beliefs to be challenged. For example, one of these beliefs may well be that involving employees in problem solving and decision making is neither necessary nor worthwhile. They may even believe it's potentially limiting, in that it may slow down, or corrupt, existing and reasonably successful management processes.

Thus, before these managers are open to learning about possible options for improving employee initiative, they must first be prepared to double-loop learn. But unless and until they see practical solutions to accomplish this goal, they're unlikely to see the question, "*How can we support a high level of employee initiative?*" as legitimate. That's where expressions like "let's get back to reality" come in. If an idea doesn't fit within a manager's present frame of reference, then it's labeled as "unrealistic" and summarily dismissed.[22] It becomes a standoff. Without practical solutions, inquiry is not legitimate. But without inquiry, practical solutions are hard to invent or discover.

End

HOW THEY FIT TOGETHER - TRADITIONAL TEACHING, NATURAL LEARNING, DEEP LEARNING, SINGLE- AND DOUBLE-LOOP LEARNING

Deep learning, as it's defined above, always entails double-loop learning; however, it would also be possible to double-loop learn as part of the natural learning cycle. That is, a degree of rethinking one's initial objectives, and ways of acting, is involved as participants gain new information, develop plans, reach agreements, and learn in a way that changes how they frame or see things.

Learning in grade schools, at least in the grade schools of the past, is completely distinct from how we learn naturally. Thus, grade schools are not shown on the continuum below. Deep learning, however, can be thought of as being at the extreme end of the natural learning continuum. Single-loop and double-loop can also be thought of as being on a continuum. Thus, it can be difficult at times to agree on whether learning has involved a change in perspective, and if so, how significant a change.

Training programs usually involve giving participants new information and helping them learn within what Thomas Kuhn (1970) calls a paradigm, which is an existing way of seeing and understanding the world.[23] Thus, while training programs can involve a degree of double-loop learning, they most often entail single-loop learning, that is, learning how to do something that one already knows they need to do, but learning how to do this better and more efficiently.

Habits grow from deep roots that go down into the culture and the social psyche.
- Bill Bridges, JobShift

Habit is habit, and not to be flung out of the window by any man, but to be coaxed down the stairs one step at a time.
- Mark Twain

Workshops also require single-loop learning; however, because they often deal with sensitive team and goal issues, they usually involve a higher degree of emotional and double-loop learning than do training programs. Therefore, workshops are shown to the right of training programs on the continuum below.

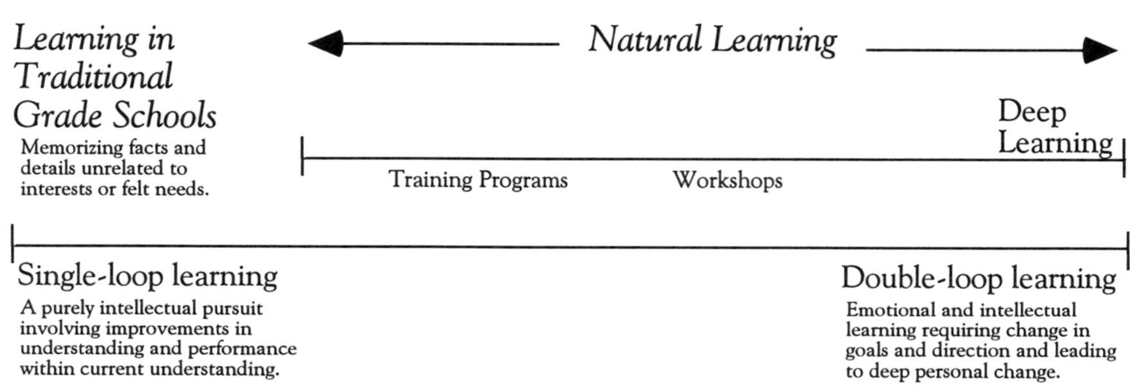

HABITS AND EMOTIONS

Habits and emotions are cousins. Daniel Goleman (1995), for example, doesn't make much of a practical distinction between the two. He writes, "All emotions are, in essence, impulses to act, the instant plans for handling life that evolution has instilled in us. The very root of the word *emotion* is *motere*, the Latin verb 'to move'..."[24] Habits, our emotions to act, are initially developed in a given circumstance. And initially these habits were likely appropriate, if not necessary, given circumstances at the time. The problem is that these "knee jerk" reactions to what *feels right* don't change as circumstances change. Once established, habits operate quickly, without the benefit of our intellect and ability to reason, and outside of consciousness. Thus, the same habits that were once highly functional and led to success can, given a change in circumstances, become highly dysfunctional and lead to failure (e.g., poor work or study habits, poor eating habits, poor supervisory and relationship habits).

Habits develop in small, inconspicuous steps over time, but once developed, they are very powerful! Consequently, you need to know a little about helping participants understand, challenge, and change or accept their habits. You also need to understand your own struggle with habits, and how these support or limit your effectiveness as a workshop leader.

Helping participants acquire and integrate new information and develop new skills is challenging enough, but having them do this while changing old assumptions and habits is the ultimate challenge for a workshop leader. This is asking them to double-loop learn, to question and possibly discard familiar and perhaps comfortable ways of thinking, feeling, and acting. It's no small task.

> ***The fact that an opinion has been widely held is no evidence whatever that it is not entirely absurd; indeed in view of the silliness of the majority of mankind, a widespread belief is more likely to be foolish than sensible.***
> ***- Bertrand Russell***

How difficult is it to change habits? To make a major change in your lifestyle? Have you ever quit an addiction (e.g., smoking, eating French fries) or changed an ingrained habit (e.g., saying "ah" when you speak in public)? It's not just individuals, but groups, organizations, and entire societies that struggle with habits. Organization and societal habits are often referred to as policy or culture. And traditions are simply habits formed by societies over years of practice.

Habits limit what we consider and what we do. In this way they keep us stuck. Research suggests that 70% to 90% of our behavior is habitual. Indeed, some authors suggest this figure is even higher. Earnie Larson (1985), for example, suggests that "as much as 98% of what we do is the result of habit, not choice."[25] (Larson maintains that thinking and action based on habit are not choice, because habits operate outside our consciousness.) Other research suggests that as long as we keep an open mind, our beliefs and values remain dynamic, and we continue to learn. Daniel Golden, writing in *Life* magazine (July 1994), talks about how "evidence is accumulating that the brain works a lot like a muscle - the harder you use it, the more it grows."[26] With the right "mental exercise" it seems we're capable of learning effectively well into our senior years.

Some people, however, choose to stop learning. They take the easy "downhill" road and coast. Strangely enough, this happens at any age. When it does, their beliefs and values "lock in" based on their maturity and needs at that time. These people suffer from "hardening of the categories." Their beliefs, values, and thinking become rigid and stuck in "the good old days." But as Casey Stengel once said, "Déjà vu ain't what it used to be." The good old days are gone. We need to function in the present and prepare for the future. We need to get into the habit of challenging our own habits.

Following are just a few examples of habits workshop leaders need to avoid.

- Taking yourself too seriously, usually by becoming "ego invested" in participants learning a particular concept or skill; or taking your stories as fact, and not staying open to other perspectives, interpretations, and contrary evidence.
- Acting defensively when challenged.
- Answering a participant's questions before allowing other participants to respond.
- Lecturing, particularly lecturing too long (i.e., more than fifteen or twenty minutes).
- Asking closed ended questions even though more group input is needed.

A) The Positive Side of Habits

Many habits and traditions are useful and positive, for example, seeing Christmas as family time, effective study habits, or the habit of telling the truth. Habits are also efficient. They're a shortcut for getting things done. For example, you don't need to occupy your mind when opening a door. You stay focused on a conversation, or on other thoughts, because it's habit to simply turn the doorknob clockwise. Like operating on auto-pilot, habits free us up to think about and do other things. We can walk and chew gum at the same time. We can drive a car in heavy traffic while carrying on a conversation. The only problem is that when circumstances change we need to change habits. But unlike an auto-pilot, changing habits is more difficult than simply readjusting the dials. Human auto-pilots often get stuck in the wrong direction.

> ***For better or worse, intelligence can come to nothing when emotions hold sway.***
> ***- Daniel Coleman***

B) The Dark Side of Habits

Over time, as circumstances change, habitual ways of thinking and acting limit our progress and success. For example,

- Many managers in the early 1980's unwilling to change from the old "command and control" style of management to the more participative and "commitment based" approaches for supervising employees.[27]
- Many employees in large organizations in North America in the late 1970's and early 1980's unwilling to recognize that job security is a thing of the past.[28]

- GM's much documented practice of ignoring or downplaying the significance of foreign competition, particularly Japanese competition, in the automotive industry in the 1970's.[29]

Just as they keep individuals and organizations stuck, habits can also keep entire societies stuck, eventually leading to failure. For example, Paul Kennedy argues the tradition based Bourbons in eighteenth century France failed because "they never learned anything and never forgot anything."[30]

C) Changing Habits

Habits don't change with wishes, hopes, desires, pain, thoughts, logic, "I shoulds," "I should nots," the best laid plans, or any other sort of intention, feeling, or scheme. They change as a result of courage, a good game plan, a few first steps, and consistent action. This requires discipline. You have to wage a war against habits. Making a change, particularly a major change in yourself, is no small task.

Emotions and beliefs are masters, reason their servant. Ignore emotion, and reason slumbers; trigger emotion, and reason comes rushing out to help. At the least, reason excuses; at the most, it restrains its master.
- Henry Boettinger

Habits develop gradually over long periods of time and are replaced with better habits the same way. Thus, we must break habits the same way we formed them: one drink, one cigarette, or one Twinkie at a time. We vow that we won't drink the *next* cocktail, smoke the *next* cigarette, miss the *next* chemistry class, eat the *next* bag of potato chips, or that we will study one hour a night, exercise four times a week, and so on. We know we can avoid one destructive behavior and make one positive step at a time. Beyond that, we're not sure.[31] Like the old joke, "How do you eat an elephant?" "One bite at a time." So, don't expect to go from stumbling aimlessly along to leaping tall buildings in a single bound. Change habits a step at a time.

It is not our willingness to do something that makes a difference; it is our willingness to do what it takes.
- Earnie Larson

There's no easy way to develop personal discipline or change ingrained and well-practiced habits. There's no easy way to take the initiative to accomplish something when you'd much rather be doing something else. Changing habits doesn't usually lead to instant gratification, making personal discipline all the more difficult. In fact, the first feedback you get is likely negative, as others try to persuade you to forget your studies and do something that's more fun, or as you practice your golf swing the way the golf pro suggested, and it just doesn't seem as comfortable as your old way.

Personal discipline allows you to ignore the criticism of others and to stop blaming your heritage, your environment, bad luck, or other people for your situation. You realize you are the only person who is ultimately responsible for your success, your failure, and your happiness.[32]

Man stand for long time with mouth open before roast duck fly in.
- Chinese proverb

Samuel Cypert wrote a great little book titled, *The Power of Self-Esteem.*[33] He tells the following story.

> *A man went running up to a famous pianist after a concert. "I'd give anything to be able to play the piano like that," he shouted enthusiastically to the pianist. "No you wouldn't," the pianist answered. "People always tell me that, but how many are willing to spend twenty years practicing as I have, four to six hours a day? Not many!"*

Any positive change in our lives usually involves a great deal of time and persistence. Few of us make these changes well. Most of us compromise. Most of us are unwilling to pay the price success demands. Many of us likely quit just before we're successful.[34]

Forming Habits

> *The predominant models among cognitive scientists of how the mind processes information have lacked an acknowledgement that rationality is guided by - and can be swamped by - feeling.*
>
> \- Daniel Goleman

What starts as need or function eventually becomes our belief, and what becomes our belief eventually gets codified as a value. In practice, our values always involve tradeoffs and sacrifice. Thus, values only have meaning when they are in conflict (e.g., honesty and income).

Our thinking is based on our values, and how we think or approach a given subject influences how we feel about that subject. For the most part we fool ourselves when we claim to act on our thinking. In truth most action is habitual, based on feelings. Advertisers know this. They sell the sizzle and not the steak. They sell soft drinks with music that helps us feel young and alive. They advertise cars by showing how they give us power, class, or sex appeal. Why did you get married? Because it was the rational thing to do! Why did you buy a certain house or car? Sure logic is involved, but feelings dominate most of our decisions.

So if you want people to "act" a certain way, first you've got to help them "feel" a certain way. And to help them feel differently, you've got to get them thinking differently.

Changing Habits

As circumstances around you change, your needs change, and so too do your beliefs and values. This in turn changes how you think, feel, and act. (Note: I recognize that many view values as essentially stable after childhood. My view is that significant change and turmoil can cause one to reexamine his/her values, and that changing or modifying values after childhood is not only possible, it's actually quite common.)

To change a habit insert a new level of thinking, then act on this "rethinking," not on the old "feeling." For a while this will feel uncomfortable. Over time, with discipline and consistent action, the new way of acting will come to "feel" right. It will become our new habit. Feelings can ignore our rethinking, but they do respond to consistent action. Thus the phrase, "Fake it till you make it."

It helps to replace a negative habit with a positive one. For example, acting decisively is the first step toward overcoming indecisiveness. Studying one hour a night is the first step toward overcoming worrying about grades.

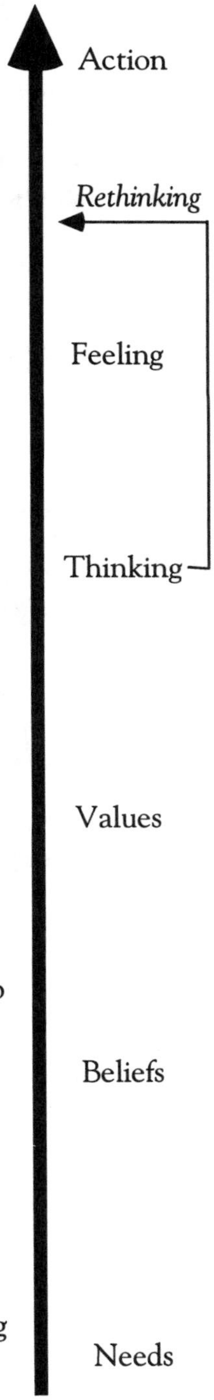

If, after hearing about how much work it takes to change a habit, you're still interested in doing so, here are five steps. Use these as a guideline.

1) Acknowledge that certain behaviors and ways of thinking are indeed habits, and that these are more limiting than helpful.

2) Assess how these habits are limiting your success and also how they're helpful. Use the chart immediately below.

3) Identify desirable habits, ones that would help to achieve your goals. Use the chart below to assess how these are likely to be helpful and limiting.

4) With full knowledge of the advantages and disadvantages of both the old and the new, develop an action plan for practicing your new way of thinking and acting.

5) Accept that, for a while, the old habits will still have a hold on you. You'll feel like going back even though your plan and your thinking says "hang in there." Stick to your plan, a step at a time, a day at a time, until new habits form. If you fall back into the old habits, as we all do from time to time, don't say, "Now I've blown it. Why keep trying?" Rather, acknowledge you've slipped and commit once again to your plan. If you slip back fifteen times, still keep trying. You've only failed when you've decided it's too hard and you've given up trying.

Articulating the Advantages and Disadvantages of a Habit

	The old habit	The new/desired habit
Advantages		
Disadvantages		

How I changed my driving habits

In addition to courage, willpower, and discipline, changing habits requires a game plan or strategy. A couple of years ago, for instance, I decided to change my driving habits. I'd been a little too aggressive behind the wheel and was starting to "earn" a few traffic tickets. In addition my driving was causing me stress and developing poor relations with my primary passenger (my wife). My best intentions always let me down. Then I decided on two clear "first steps," and my driving improved almost immediately. These steps were simple. First, I decided not to run yellow lights. Second, I decided that whenever someone signals to move into the lane ahead of me, I would let them in. I no longer sped up and acted like they were robbing me of my rights to the road. (If someone doesn't signal, however, they're still fair game. After all, you can't take all the fun out of driving!) Anyway, with these simple first steps, I call them my "lite rules," and a little practice, my driving habits improved considerably, although there's always room for more improvement.

LEVELS OF KNOWLEDGE

The following distinctions will help you think more specifically about the value and purpose of learning. For example, when combined with the evaluation methods described in chapter four, they will help you target your workshop and training-program materials, design, and delivery.

Six Levels of Knowledge

In their taxonomy of educational objectives in the cognitive domain, Krathwohl, Bloom, and Masia (1964) identify six levels of knowledge.[35]

1) Awareness - to recall, recognize.

2) Understanding - to translate from one form to another.

3) Application - to apply or use information in a new situation.

4) Analysis - to examine a situation and break it down into parts.

5) Synthesis - to put together information in a new way.

6) Evaluation - to judge based on explicit criteria.

Being *aware* that people use personal computers is certainly a lower level of knowledge than *understanding* how they use them and what they use them for. Knowing how to use a personal computer yourself (*application*) is at a higher level than understanding their purpose. Being able to *analyze* and take a software program apart is yet a higher level of knowledge about personal computers. Being able to construct a software program (*synthesis*) takes even more background and knowledge.

The highest level of knowledge is *evaluation*, the ability to draw conclusions and make decisions based on established criteria. This requires wisdom and intuition. These qualities come to the prepared mind. The confusing part about evaluation is that it's so complex almost anyone can claim expertise at this level. For example, we often evaluate others without really knowing them, or we evaluate a management decision without really having inside knowledge of the criteria or options this decision was based on. When it comes to evaluation it's sometimes hard to tell the experts from the ordinary "Joes."

CONCLUSION

Summary

A workshop leader's role is to help participants learn as deeply and accomplish as quickly as possible. Understanding how we learn naturally, the principles for working with adult learners, and how habits are formed and changed provide a foundation for helping participants learn and accomplish. Having distinctions for "levels of knowledge" will help you be specific about the focus of learning.

Learning, Teaching, and Facilitating

Traditional teaching emphasizes the teacher's role as "information giver" and downplays accountability for motivating those doing the learning. It relies on rote mechanisms and produces memorization more than in-depth understanding. In contrast, the natural learning process requires participants to be involved, to struggle with learning materials, and to arrive at their own answers. Here, the teacher - now more properly called a facilitator or leader - doesn't just provide information to be memorized, but helps participants to create and discover their own insights and conclusions.

The Natural Learning Cycle

Learning from experience involves a five step *natural learning cycle*. The first step is *focus*. Usually some change in our life causes us to focus on a new way of understanding or acting. Focus provides the motivation and desire to set foot on the path to learning. Being focused is synonymous with being learning ready. The second step is *search*. Data is sought out and organized into useful information. In the third step, *integration*, collected information is consolidated with previous learning. Information is digested and its validity is checked against the learner's beliefs and previous knowledge. The fourth step is *generalizing*. Newly acquired knowledge is formed into theories or concepts that have practical value. Generalizing leads to *acting*. Here newly formed theories and concepts are applied and their usefulness again assessed. By applying new learning and assessing the consequences of our actions, we gain additional insights and continue the learning process.

Principles of Adult Learning

Three principles of adult learning are particularly relevant for workshop and training-program leaders.

First, adults bring a lot of experience with them to workshops, and therefore they have something to contribute and something to lose. In addition to having a breadth and depth of experience, adults have a lot invested in their experience. Therefore, new learning that contradicts any part of their experience must be understood, accepted, and integrated with previous knowledge. New learning can't be forced on adults. They must decide for themselves and arrive at their own conclusions.

Second, adults want workshops and training programs that focus on real-life "here and now" problems and tasks, rather than on academic situations. They want relevant and useful knowledge that can be implemented more or less immediately.

Third, adults are accustomed to being active and self-directing. They don't respond well to long lectures or being "force fed" information. They need to be supported, challenged, and guided to discover things for themselves.

Andragogy and Pedagogy

Andragogy is the term applied to adult learning in contrast to pedagogy or teaching children. Adult learning is self-directed, problem centered, motivated by a desire to learn, and enhanced by an adult's experience. Children, on the other hand, bring little or no experience into the learning process, are dependent on the teacher, motivated externally (e.g., coercion), and subject centered. However, applying adult-learning principles too religiously can cause as much trouble as ignoring them. Brookfield explains that adults don't always see learning as a joyous activity and aren't always learning ready and self-directed.

Learning Styles

Kolb's model of learning styles (accommodator, diverger, assimilator, converger) is provided here simply to make the point that adult learners are not a homogeneous group. They prefer to learn, deal with new ideas, and solve problems in different ways. Reviewing this model with workshop participants will help them understand their own learning needs, habits, strengths, and limitations. This, in turn, encourages them to either change, accept, or compensate for their learning preferences.

Single-Loop and Double-Loop Learning

Use the concepts of single-loop and double-loop learning to challenge your own and participants' thinking. Single-loop learning involves improving efficiency to obtain established objectives. It works fine where errors can be corrected within your existing norms, practices, and traditions. However, recognize that your solutions are restricted within your established ways of knowing and thinking. Double-loop learning involves revisiting original objectives as opposed to assuming these are undiscussable and can't be altered. It's learning how to invent and discover new options for action. Double-loop learning is essential when we can no longer achieve or improve results simply by doing better what we already know how to do.

Habits and Emotions

Our habits, whether strengths or limitations, are entrenched and difficult to break. They save time and energy, sparing us from thinking through routine matters, but they are also limiting. Some habits in particular, such as acting defensively, asking closed ended questions, or taking oneself too seriously, impair a workshop leader's effectiveness. Any habit can be changed, but they must be changed the same way they developed: one thought, one step, one day at a time. This requires personal discipline and a clear plan of action.

Levels of Knowledge

Having distinctions for levels of knowledge (awareness, understanding, application, analysis, synthesis, evaluation) will help you think more specifically about the value and purpose of learning. This in turn will help you focus your workshop and training-program materials, design, and delivery.

Checklist

Learning, Teaching, and Facilitating	*Andragogy*
• Learning is the mental process that leads to new knowledge and skills • Traditional teaching is linear (i.e., the teacher explains the meaning of each term separately) • Experiential learning is organic and provides an overall context in which learners can perceive relationships *The Natural Learning Cycle* • Focus • Search • Integrate • Generalize • Act *Adult-Learning Principles* • Adults bring a lot of experience with them and therefore have something to contribute and something to lose • Adults want workshops that focus on real-life problems and tasks • Adults are accustomed to being active and self-directing *Pedagogy* • The student is fully dependent on the teacher • The student has very little experience that is of much value or is related to the learning content • Students learn what and when they're told to learn • The student is subject centered • Students are motivated to learn by external pressures	• Participants want to be "self-directing" • The participant has a greater volume, quality, and variety of experience • A participant's willingness to learn is triggered by a change in their situation • Participants are life, task, or problem centered • Participants are motivated by internal pressures *Brookfield's Andragogic Myths* • Learning is a joyous activity • Adults are innately self-directed • The best adult-learning experiences are based on the "felt needs" of the learners • There is a unique adult-learning style *Learning Styles* • Accommodator • Diverger • Assimilator • Converger *Single-Loop and Double-Loop Learning* • Single-loop learning involves changing methods and improving efficiency to obtain established objectives • Double-loop learning concerns changing the objectives themselves *Changing a Habit* 1) Acknowledge that the habit exists 2) Assess how the habit is limiting you 3) Identify desirable habits 4) Develop an action plan 5) Accept that it'll be a struggle

Exercise

Single-Loop and Double-Loop Learning

1) Describe a couple of examples where you have single-loop learned.

Examples

- I'm already quite good at using Microsoft Word, but recently I've just learned how to use the indexing and table of contents features of this program.
- I've rethought my career over the past year and have strongly committed to publishing two or three books over the next five years. (Note: This is single-loop learning. My career goals haven't changed.)

2) What are a couple of examples where you have double-loop learned? (This doesn't have to be a big deal, although it may have involved strong emotions and the pain of "letting go" of old ways of thinking and acting.)

Examples

- There was a time when I managed more than led workshops and training programs. I was too much in control, too concerned with the agenda, and too concerned with getting my material to the group. Some time ago, I completely rethought this goal. Now I keep my eye on *outcomes*. I still have my views and learning materials (e.g., models), but I only introduce them when they are needed to achieve the outcomes being sought.
- I've developed a new attitude about exercise. At one time I had unrealistic expectations about running. I trained like I was going to be in the Olympics or something. It's beside the point that I ran slow. So slow, in fact, that I was the only person who could tell I was running! I now exercise regularly just like before, but I have a new goal. I just want to keep fit. Now incidentally, I enjoy exercise a lot more.

Exercise

Understanding Adult-Learning Principles[36]

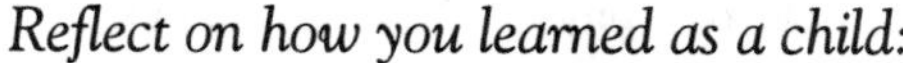
Reflect on how you learned as a child:

1) How do you remember learning as a child?

2) What do you remember thinking about your teachers?

3) How do you like to learn now?

Consider the adult-learning principles discussed in this chapter.

- Adults bring a lot of experience with them to workshops, and therefore have something to contribute and something to lose.
- Adults want workshops that focus on real-life "here and now" problems and tasks, rather than on academic situations.
- Adults are accustomed to being active and self-directing.

4) What are some of the workshop and training-program leadership practices that flow out of these assumptions?

5) How are these practices different than those you experienced as a child in grade school?

Notes

[1]Mellander, K. (1993). The power of learning: Fostering employee growth. Alexandria, VA: The American Society for Training and Development.
[2]Malhotra Bentz, V. (Winter, 1991). Deep learning and group process. *Fielding Magazine*, pp. 16-19.
[3]Weisbord, M.R. (1989). Productive workplaces: Organizing and managing for dignity, meaning, and community. San Francisco, CA: Jossey-Bass, p. 187.
[4]Zukav, G. (1979). The dancing wu li masters: An overview of the new physics. New York, NY: Quill William Morrow.
[5]Knowles, M.S., & Associates. (1980). Andragogy in action. San Francisco, CA: Jossey-Bass.
[6]More is said about positive reinforcement in chapter fourteen.
[7]Mellander, K. (1993). The power of learning: Fostering employee growth. Homewood, IL: Business One Irwin.
[8]Chapter ten provides strategies for getting participants involved and active.
[9]See "Project Spectrum" described by: Goleman, D. (1995). Emotional intelligence. New York, NY: Bantam, p. 37. A few such examples are also described in: Osborne, D., & Gaebler, T. (1992). Reinventing government: How the entrepreneurial spirit is transforming the public sector. Toronto, Ont: Plume.
[10]The five categories used here are from Knowles, M.S., & Associates. (1980). Andragogy in action. San Francisco, CA: Jossey-Bass.
[11] This information is adapted from a presentation by Stephen Brookfield in May 1989. The occasion was the Visions Conference for Adult Educators in Calgary, Alberta, Canada.
[12]Smith, R.M. (1982). Learning how to learn: Applied theory for adults. Chicago, IL: Follett, p. 17.
[13]Kolb, D.A. (1984). Experiential learning: Experience as the source of learning and development. Englewood Cliffs, NJ: Prentice-Hall.
[14]Harris, T.A. (1967). I'm OK - you're OK. New York, NY: Avon Books.
[15] Kolb, D.A. (1985). Learning-style inventory: Self scoring inventory and interpretation booklet. Boston, MA: McBer & Company.
[16] This section was inspired by the following two books: 1) Argyris, C., & Schon, D.A. (1974). Theory in practice: Increasing professional effectiveness. San Francisco, CA: Jossey-Bass. 2) Argyris, C., & Schon, D.A. (1978). Organizational learning: A theory of action perspective. Reading, MA: Addison-Wesley.
[17] This story has been adapted from: Jacobs, J. (1992). Systems of survival: A dialogue on the moral foundations of commerce and politics. New York, NY: Random House.
[18]I learned this phrase from John E. Jones. He used it often in referring to Gibran's famous quote referenced immediately above. John, a co-founder of University Associates, now heads up his own consulting practice, Organizational Universe Systems, out of San Diego, California.
[19]Argyris and Schon (1974, 1978) also talk about deutero learning. This is outside the scope of this book so only a brief explanation is provided here. It involves being aware of how we double-loop learn and reflecting on the processes by which we inhibit our ability to double-loop learn. That is, challenging how we ignore, downplay, or deny, rather than support inquiry into our own assumptions, habits, objectives, traditions, and so on. Thus, deutero learning also involves looking at previous learning situations (e.g., a previous job, organization, city, marriage, school) from the perspective of a new learning situation or context. As you learn to deal with the new situation, you learn by contrast about the previous context for learning. Thus, as a member of one organization you may have worked for years not realizing that your learning was being restrained, until you next experienced a more enlightened learning environment. Your conclusion about the previous organization (i.e., that your learning had been restrained) is based on contrasting it with your new environment. Once the contrasting experience is understood, the former, and in this case deficient, context for learning is recognized immediately.
[20]Mintzberg, H. (1994). The rise and fall of strategic planning: Reconceiving roles for planning, plans, and planners. New York, NY: The Free Press, p. 368.
[21]The terms "sponsor client," "administrative client," "contact client," and "end-user client" are used throughout this book. Simply put, the sponsor client is the person, or group of people,

responsible for approving and sponsoring the workshop or training program. The sponsor picks up the tab, and needless to say expects something in return for his/her investment. Administrative clients look after administrative arrangements (e.g., arrangements for facilities and equipment, coordination with workshop participants). Contact clients introduce you to key people in an organization. They can help you navigate an unfamiliar organization and put you in touch with decision makers. Finally, end-user clients are the workshop or training program participants. These are the people who attend, participate, and learn during the workshop and then apply the workshop outcomes on the job (e.g., decisions, programs, products, skills).

[22] For an insightful discussion of double-loop learning see: Argyris, C. (May-June, 1991). Teaching smart people how to learn. *Harvard Business Review*, pp. 99-109.

[23]Kuhn, T.S. (1970). The structure of scientific revolutions (2nd ed.). Vol. 2. No. 2. International encyclopedia of unified science. Chicago, IL: The University of Chicago Press.

[24]Goleman, D. (1995). Emotional intelligence. New York, NY: Bantam, p. 6.

[25]Larson, E. (1985). Stage II recovery: Life beyond addiction. San Francisco, CA: Harper & Row, p. 34.

[26] Golden, D. (July, 1994). Building a better brain. *Life*, pp. 63-70.

[27]For an excellent overview of this change in management approach see: Walton, R.E. (March-April 1985). From control to commitment in the workplace. Harvard Business Review, pp. 77-84.

[28]Bill Bridges talks about the need for this shift in thinking from "jobs" to "work." See: Bridges, W. (1994). JobShift: How to prosper in a workplace without jobs. Reading, MA: Addison-Wesley.

[29]Mitroff says the couple of years with high earnings that General Motors had in the 1970's was the worst thing that could have happened to them. They took these earnings as a sign that they didn't have to worry about Japanese competition. See: Mitroff, I.I. (1988). Business not as usual: Rethinking our individual, corporate, and industrial strategies for global competition. San Francisco, CA: Jossey-Bass. In addition, Daniel Burrus (1993) has a similar view. He says, "The Japanese did U.S. business a favor by coming on as strong as they did in the 1980's. If they had continued to tiptoe around those slumbering giants, many of them would have died in their sleep." See: Burrus, D. (1993). Technotrends: How to use technology to go beyond your competition. New York, NY: HarperBusiness, p. 39.

[30] Kennedy, P. (1993). Preparing for the twenty first century. Toronto, Ont: HarperCollins.

[31] Cypert, S.A. (1994). The power of self esteem. New York: AMACOM, p. 25.

[32]This is not to say that success is easily defined or that factors outside oneself aren't important. Howard Gardner is quoted as saying that, "there are hundreds and hundreds of ways to succeed, and many, many different abilities that help you get there." Taken from Daniel Goleman's interview with Howard Gardner about his theory on multiple intelligences. Goleman, D. (1986, November 3). Rethinking the value of intelligence tests. Education suppl. *The New York Times*. From: Goleman, D. (1995). Emotional intelligence. New York, NY: Bantam, p. 37.

[33]Cypert, S.A. (1994). The power of self esteem. New York: AMACOM, p. 98.

[34]For the purposes of understanding habits, and helping others change habits as a workshop or training-program leader, the relationship between thinking and feelings is shown here to be simple and linear. While this works fine for purposes of this book and its message, it is of course a gross oversimplification. The relationship between thinking and feelings is believed to be highly complex and interdependent. Daniel Goleman talks about the complex interplay between our thinking and our emotions. He writes, "Indeed, intellect cannot work at its best without emotional intelligence. Ordinarily the complementarity of limbic system and neocortex, amygdala and prefrontal lobes, means each is a full partner in mental life. ... This turns the old understanding of the tension between reason and feeling on its head: it is not that we want to do away with emotion and put reason in its place, as Erasmus had it, but instead find intelligent balance of the two. The old paradigm held an ideal of reason freed of the pull of emotion. The new paradigm urges us to harmonize head and heart." From: Goleman, D. (1995). Emotional intelligence. New York, NY: Bantam, pp. 28-29.

[35]Krathwohl, D.R., Bloom, B.S., & Masia, B.B. (1964). A taxonomy of educational objectives. New York, NY: David McKay Co.
[36]I would like to thank Nadine Ryan-Bannerman for the original draft of these questions. Nadine is a friend and colleague, and a consultant in Calgary, Alberta, Canada.

Part 2

Getting Your Clients Ready: Defining Success

Chapter 3

Investigating Needs and Planning a Workshop

Few of the things we want most are attainable by means that appear possible. It is the function of planning to make the impossible possible.
- Russell Ackoff

INTRODUCTION

Workshops and training programs need direction and design to be successful, but first they must have a destination. That's why this chapter is important. It takes planning from investigating and assessing workshop and learning needs through to writing purpose and outcome statements. Once these statements are in place it's time to look at workshop and training-program design. This is the focus of chapter six, *Designing a Workshop*.

This chapter covers:

- The elements of planning and how they fit together.
- Investigating workshop and learning needs.
- Planning workshops and training programs.

THE ELEMENTS OF PLANNING AND HOW THEY FIT TOGETHER

The Elements of Planning

Nine terms or elements of planning are discussed in this chapter and throughout this book. These are: needs, agenda, purpose, outcomes, content, group process, design, capability, and feedback.

Workshop Needs, Learning Needs

Workshop needs or *learning needs* relate to problems or opportunities. There is something participants need to learn or do differently in order to solve, resolve, or dissolve a problem or to plan for and take advantage of an opportunity. An example of a learning need is a participant's need to learn a given method or skill, and as a result do something differently on the job. An example of a workshop need is a group's needs to design and commit to implementing a new business unit strategy.

Agenda, Purpose, Outcomes

An *agenda* is an activity plan (e.g., steps, sequence, and timelines). Don't confuse it with the *purpose* of a workshop, which is the aim, intention, or raison d' être of a workshop (e.g., to meet certain workshop or learning needs), or with *outcomes* or *outcome statements,* which describe what success looks like, that is, what specifically the workshop or training program is aiming to achieve in measurable or observable terms.

Content, Process

Content or *learning content* is the material (e.g., theory, models, ideas, information, new ways of thinking) that you provide to participants, and that you hope and expect participants will learn and apply. *Group process* concerns how a group works together (behaviors such as, how decisions are made, how sensitive issues are discussed, how ideas are challenged). Doyle and Straus (1976) make the distinction this way: "If you are chewing gum," they quip, "the chewing is the process and the gum is the content."[1]

Design

Workshop or training-program *design* focuses on delivery methods and strategies, that is, how, or in what ways, participants are involved in achieving stated outcomes (e.g., exercises, activities, processes).

Capability

Capability refers to the skills, abilities, and attitude of those with a stake in the workshop or training program (e.g., sponsor clients, participants). These include being willing to challenge, the ability to articulate an interest or a given position, knowledge of a certain product or service, being open to new ideas and new ways of thinking, the ability to "let go" of old biases and ways of working.

Feedback

Feedback is what you hear, see, or feel following an action. It is used to evaluate a workshop or training program, and your leadership of same. Feedback can be internal (i.e., self-feedback) or from others. It can also be evaluative or descriptive, general or specific, and immediate or delayed. How you receive feedback and what you do with it are quite another matter. Examples of feedback from others are participants working enthusiastically in subgroups (lots of noise, focusing on the assignment or exercise), written comments on an evaluation form, and a participant's supervisor saying that the participant's performance has improved since a given training program. Examples of feedback to yourself are a feeling of success and confidence following a workshop or training program and telling yourself a couple of things you will do differently next time.

How the Elements of Planning Fit Together

Here's how these nine elements fit together. Use this sequence as a guideline when planning a workshop or training program.

1) Get clear on workshop or learning *needs*.

2) Clarify the *purpose* of the workshop or training program based on the needs you are seeking to fulfill.

3) Develop *outcome statements* based on this purpose.

4) Determine what *capabilities* are required for the workshop or training program to be successful.

5) Decide what *feedback* you want during and following completion of the workshop or training program, and how the workshop or training program will be evaluated.

6) Decide on learning *content* or material. What do you want participants to learn or achieve?

7) Select *design* options based on the outcomes being sought, workshop or learning content, and time and resources available.

8) Develop the *agenda* (steps, sequence, timing).

9) Contract *group process* with participants during the workshop or training program start-up.

INVESTIGATING WORKSHOP AND LEARNING NEEDS

Organizations expect workshops and training programs to contribute to substantial and specific changes in what and how people do things. So, before the workshop or training program begins, you need to know exactly what you're trying to achieve and what success will look like (i.e., what changes are expected and how you'll know when they have been achieved).

This section covers:

a) Critical questions for assessing workshop and learning needs

b) The "felt needs trap"

c) A model for understanding learning needs

d) Distinct approaches for investigating workshop and learning needs

e) A technique for probing workshop and learning needs

a) Critical Questions for Assessing Workshop and Learning Needs

Perhaps the best known gurus of needs assessment are Robert Mager and Peter Pipe. Their 1984 book, *Analyzing Performance Problems*, is required reading if you intend on spending any kind of time in workshop and learning needs analysis.[2] The following list is at least partly inspired by their work. Use these questions to guide your needs assessment process.

1) What's the problem or opportunity? What organizational changes are needed? (e.g., resource use, customer relations, budget follow-up)

2) What's the value and likelihood of achieving these changes? (e.g., Who benefits, and by how much, if these changes are made? What barriers and supports will influence our ability to accomplish these changes?)

3) How much of these needed changes involve employees' willingness to do the job, opportunity to do the job, and ability to do the job?

4) What behavior changes will most support the desired organizational changes? (e.g., how people deal with the new budgeting process, specific approaches to managing staff)

5) What external factors control or influence these behaviors? What incentive is there for employees to perform or not to perform? What obstacles in the organization may be preventing employees from performing as required? (e.g., accessibility of a given system, leadership style)

6) What information would help employees perform better? What knowledge, skill, or insights are needed to achieve these behavior changes? (e.g., using a computer ordering system, understanding the company's approach to quality)

7) Who can most influence needed organizational changes? Which participants need to be involved in the workshop? (e.g., first line supervisors, budget analysts)

8) What workshop process and learning materials will provide this knowledge, skill, or insight to participants?

b) The "Felt Needs Trap"

If you want to know what a person's learning needs are, you ask him/her, right? Well, maybe. If you ask a drunk what he needs, what's he going to say? "A drink!" If you ask a poor leader what her workshop needs are, what's she going to say? "Better followers!" She would likely say something like, "These people need to learn to be team players." So you'd train her employees to listen better and support their boss, right? Of course not! But all too often workshop leaders end up with the wrong focus because they fall into the *felt needs trap*.

Asking people is still the easiest way of finding out their learning needs and interests. You'll get a reasonably useful answer, as long as you are not asking about their "blind spots" (i.e., areas where they are unaware of their incompetence). Now, here's the *real* problem. Guess where people likely, maybe desperately, need help? If you said, "their blind spots," you're right!

People who are aware of their incompetence are likely to do something about it. They may get help, or they may compensate in some way for this weakness or development need. It's the people who are *unconsciously incompetent* who really need to attend workshops, but you can't start with these people by offering training. They're unaware they need it. You first must help them become "learning ready."

c) A Model for Understanding Learning Needs

Here's a model for understanding terms and phrases like blind spots, the felt needs trap, learning readiness, common sense, and habits. This model explains why these concepts are important, practical, and necessary, and provides invaluable wisdom for assessing learning needs in organizations.[3] It serves to keep you "on your toes" when interpreting data collected from *sponsor* and *end-user* clients. It alerts you to the fact that sometimes, even most times, clients don't know what they need. So, what they ask for doesn't matter. (This, in spite of the fact that clients often present their needs for a workshop or training program in the form of a solution; for example, "We need a team building session.") The reality is that some of their needs - often the critical needs - are usually in their blind spot.

What clients ask for is the *presenting problem*. It's a starting point, not a final destination. Your job is to dig deeper and discover the real learning and workshop needs of your clients.

	The client is not competent	***The client is competent***
The client is conscious of this situation	*Things I know I don't know* (*conscious incompetence*) You recognize your learning needs (e.g., you've tried to ride a bike and fallen on your face).	*Things I know I know* (*conscious competence*) You're keenly aware of each step required to perform (e.g., the first few times you successfully rode a bike).
The client is not conscious of this situation	*Things I don't know I don't know* (*unconscious incompetence*) Your blind spot. Your incompetence has become a bad habit (e.g., you've been riding a bike for years, ignoring most traffic signs and safety practices, and blaming others for your accidents).	*Things I don't know I know* (*unconscious competence*) Your competence has become a good habit (e.g., you've been riding a bike for years in a courteous and law abiding manner, and without incident).

You can also think of this model as steps or stairs. As you move along the stairs you progress from lacking awareness of you inability, being mindful or conscious of your inability, being conscious of you ability, and finally, to being unaware or unconscious of what you do that makes you capable and proficient.

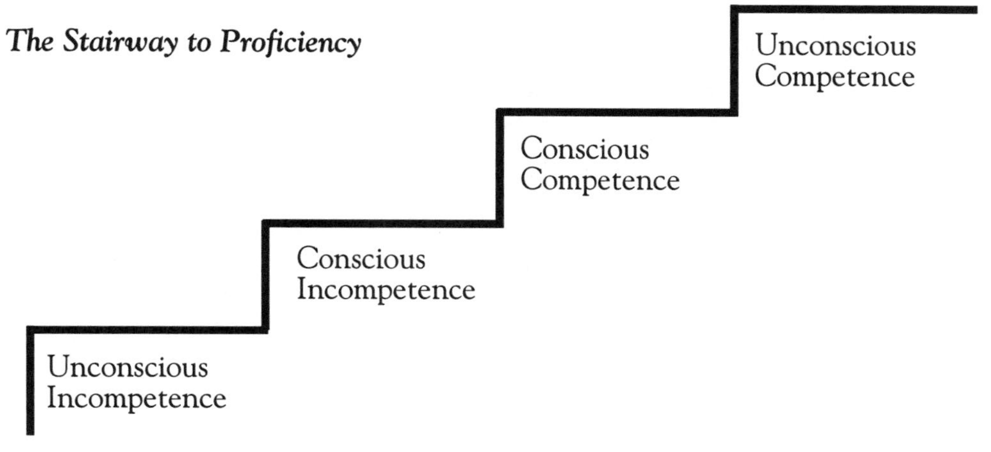

We all have learning needs we're aware of, and others where we have no idea we need help. The big benefit to workshop and training-program leaders working with people who are conscious of their incompetence is that at least these people are aware of their learning needs. This doesn't necessarily mean they're *learning ready*, but it's a good first step.

You don't have to waste anyone's time working with people who are consciously competent, because these people know that they know.

Being *unconsciously incompetent* is the home of the felt needs trap. Trying to help these people learn is futile. Don't introduce new learning material until you've first helped them become learning ready (i.e., conscious of their need for learning).[4]

To the expert (i.e., the person who is *unconsciously competent*), describing his or her performance to others is difficult. It just seems like second nature or common sense. Thus, "an expert," Henry Mintzberg (1994) quips, "has been defined as someone with no elementary knowledge."[5] To help others learn, these people first need to "go back in time" and remember the basics.

d) Distinct Approaches for Investigating Workshop and Learning Needs

Some learning and workshop needs are more stable, less complex, and easier to define and categorize than others. Learning how to interpret a set of administrative policies, or how to use a word processing program, for example, as opposed to learning how to supervise in a technical environment, how to lead workshops, or how to write creatively. Planning and analysis systematically favor the former kinds of learning, while intuition and synthesis favor the latter. Thus, the necessity for having two significantly different, if not diametrically opposed, approaches to assessing workshop and learning needs. Hiebert and Smallwood (1987) have labeled these the *objectivist* and *interpretative* approaches to investigating and defining workshop and training needs.[6]

The Objectivist Approach

The objectivist approach is based on determining objective "realities" in the environment. It works best when learning needs can be clearly defined in behavioral terms, and when they remain stable over time. These conditions are most often met with training for production workers. For example, there is an established and behaviorally proper way to repack gas valves at a gas plant, or fry burgers at a fast-food restaurant. The objectivist approach is of less value when the environment is dynamic or

learning needs can't be described in behaviorally subdivided terms, for example, knowledge work such as mediating a conflict, developing a corporate strategy, or leading a project team.

Knowledge workers (e.g., systems analysts, human resources advisors, geologists) work with information, use judgment and discretion on the job, and are expected to demonstrate expertise, creativity, and commitment to results. Production workers (e.g., auto mechanics, building cleaners, "roughnecks" on oil rigs), on the other hand, are expected to comply with fairly routine and established practices. Their work is straightforward, outputs are easy to measure, and consequences are easy to apply.

The Interpretative Approach

The interpretative approach assumes there are many complex and changing variables that need to be considered when investigating the learning needs of an individual or group. For example, assessing the learning and development needs of a group of senior managers in a large manufacturing business necessitates organizing an infinite amount of data into "points of view" requiring interpretation. Leadership problems among this group of managers (e.g., they don't keep each other informed, they don't coordinate well with each other on key projects, their subordinates feel like they are being "micro-managed") simply can't be seen as "objective measures of reality." Thus, a workshop for these senior managers would then be based on alternative choices for action, informed and sufficient knowledge, and reasonable theories of approach, rather than on complete knowledge, predictability, and a "one best way" method or process.

The interpretative approach requires conceptual and perspective abilities. Hiebert and Smallwood compare this to "a parent looking up into the sky with a young child and saying, 'There's the Big Dipper.' The youngster at first takes it literally and looks for a dipper. But only after some explanation, and use of imagination, can the child connect the stars mentally to form a dipper."[7] Pattern recognition such as this is an exercise in synthesis rather than analysis. The interpretative approach is used in a similar way to connect pieces of information into a pattern. The key questions are, "Is this pattern useful?" "Does it provide you with a reasonable place to start a workshop or training program?" "Is there agreement on and commitment to beginning the workshop based on this interpretation?"

Contrasting the Objectivist and Interpretative Approaches

Roger Sperry (1974) argues that intuition exists as a distinct process, different from rational analysis. It follows that the interpretative and objectivist approaches don't blend into one another, nor are they easily substituted for one another.[8] You could equate the objectivist approach with single-loop learning and the interpretative approach with double-loop learning. Whereas the objectivist approach can be made explicit, can be decomposed and analyzed, and is based on established goals the interpretative approach is often implicit, based on reassessing goals, and concerns inferences, synthesis, and the conception of something new, such as a unique way of framing or describing a situation.

The objectivist approach assumes workshop and learning needs can be chunked, and that these parts are unmistakable, indisputable, unambiguous, and relatively unchanging. All one has to do is discover and define them. The interpretative approach assumes just the opposite, that workshop and learning needs are indeterminate, ambiguous, fluid, and even a little paradoxical. Thus, one can only collect "data points," because the environment is constantly changing, and the data is inevitably open to many interpretations.

Difficulties Describing the Interpretative Approach

A couple of difficulties accompany describing steps in the interpretative approach. The first is that this approach in intuitive and steps are fluid, changing as the situation changes. The second is that, in describing these steps, one is forced to use objectivist language to explain interpretative processes. Thus, one is forced to describe impressions in rational terms and feelings in terms of behaviors. In Henry Mintzberg's words (1994), "'Proof' ... loads the dice in favor of ... programmability." That is, the need for programmability forces you into explaining and justifying interpretations much like "trying to explain color using black-and-white photography."[9] (Incidentally, this also relates to why some clients, particularly those indentured in linear thinking and seeking "the answers," seem so impressed with a well written workshop agenda, and seem so unimpressed when an agenda is not clearly set out in detail. It's like the agenda, the epitome of programmability, is itself the "objective truth." Agendas are discussed in chapter six.)

Steps in the Objectivist and Interpretative Approaches

Both the interpretative and objectivist approaches use the same investigative techniques (e.g., interviews, surveys, observations), and each starts and ends with a common step: gathering data to begin (e.g., interview key managers about their goals and strategies) and workshop evaluation to end. In-between, they take entirely different paths. Steps in each approach are outlined below.

Steps in the Objectivist Approach	***Steps in the Interpretative Approach***
1) *Gather Data*	1) *Gather Data*
2) *Analyze the Data* The data is straightforward and requires no interpretation. Outcomes needed from the workshop are obvious.	2) *Analyze the Data* The data is complex and requires interpretation. Organize and reorganize the data, interpret and reinterpret, until you're able to create a reasonable and agreed interpretation of the situation. Agree on workshop outcomes based on this interpretation of the data.
3) *Write Workshop Outcomes* These aren't expected to change (i.e., single-loop learning).	3) *Write Workshop Outcomes* Agree that these may need to change as new data or interpretations surface (i.e., double-loop learning).
4) *Design and Conduct the Workshop to Meet Outcomes*	4) *Design and Conduct the Workshop to Meet Outcomes* Keep these flexible. Changes may be needed as new data and new interpretations surface during the workshop.
5) *Supervisors Support and Reinforce Participants' New Behaviors on the Job*	5) *Supervisors Support and Reinforce Participants' New Behaviors on the Job* As this happens everyone learns. That is, the process of using new skills on the job provides feedback, which leads to creating new interpretations and new plans for action. New action is taken as needed (e.g., a follow-up workshop, new incentives, additional supervisory support).
6) *Evaluate the Workshop*	6) *Evaluate the Workshop*

In practice you'll often need to mix the objectivist and interpretative approaches. Some of the data you collect will be straightforward and obvious, while other data will be complex and require a good deal of interpretation. Thus, some outcomes sought from a workshop or training program may be "taken for granted," while others will need to be kept flexible and adapted as new information surfaces.

Workshop and learning needs - When to act and when to analyze

It's simplistic to say that action is better than analysis or that long, detailed learning-needs assessments are never appropriate. Yet these statements capture one aspect of the bias of this book. Perhaps, Karl Weick's words fit best (1969). He says "chaotic action is better than orderly inaction."[10] That hits the nail right on the head. Taking action to solve a problem, or to seize an opportunity, albeit only a first step (e.g., leading a workshop to help managers improve their leadership practices), beats surveying, and studying, and analyzing, and studying some more, and attempting the perfect needs analysis before taking any action within an organization. The following is an example of deciding action in under an hour. It's about doing a learning-needs assessment, doing it quickly, and keeping it simple.

Three senior managers, working as a senior management team and supervising a group of middle managers, asked me to help them assess their Division's learning needs. They were clear on their Division's strategy, but wanted to make a wide range of other improvements (e.g., morale, communication, role definition, leadership style), and seemed a little immobilized by the breadth of their task. I had been coaching this senior management team for about six months, so I knew a little about them, their Division, and the middle managers who reported to them.

In an hour-long meeting with three managers from this Division (one of which was a member of the senior management team) we wrote out a number of assumptions and decided on the approach listed below. The next step would be to present these assumptions, and this approach, to the middle management group to gain their support. The middle management group would be the "end-user clients," the people expected to make improvements in their personal leadership styles. We needed their commitment to changing their leadership practices, to the approach we were suggesting, and to the assumptions this approach was based upon.

If the middle managers couldn't see value in this approach, or if they couldn't agree with these assumptions, then we would have to find another way to get this work done. We didn't want to take the position that we had the "one best way." We were fully prepared to have our assumptions challenged, our suggested approach criticized, and to hear alternative approaches. What we were firm on, however, was our goal of improving leadership practices in the Division.

In wanting to stay flexible on process we were keeping Ludwig von Bertalanffy's term "equifinality" in mind (1950).[11] It means there are many ways to accomplish an outcome. A related term, also from the biological sciences, is "requisite variety." It refers to the fact that in any ecosystem, the organism with the greatest repertoire of responses has the highest probability of survival. Both "equifinality" and "requisite variety" are useful perspectives for workshop or training-program leaders. Don't fall in love with just one way of doing things! Don't become process bound!

Our Assumptions

We agreed it was important to make our assumptions explicit. This way they would be challengeable. In no time at all we had developed the following five generic assumptions about helping middle managers improve their leadership practices, and six assumptions specific to this particular group of middle managers.

Generic assumptions

1) Developing your leadership skills and practices is part of every manager's job.

2) "Action learning" is usually better than a detailed needs analysis. That is, collecting a data sample, acting on this data, learning from the result, making adjustments, and trying again is better than gathering detailed data and analyzing it to death, the latter being what Peters and Waterman (1981) call "ready, aim, aim, aim, aim ... ," but never firing.[12] However, gathering a little data before acting is better than acting without any input from key stakeholders whatsoever. This is known in the trade as "ready, *fire*, aim!"

3) Attitude follows behavior. As managers improve how they do a few things (e.g., involving their subordinates in decision making), over time, their attitudes will follow, as they begin to see the value of working in new ways.

4) Most managers know more about being good leaders than they actually practice. Thus, in many instances, helping managers become better leaders isn't so much a training need as a need for clear goals, clear first steps, the desire and self-discipline to make needed changes, and follow-up by senior managers to ensure progress is being made.

5) Starting change at the top in an organization (i.e., with the senior management team) models development for those in the middle. Thus, senior managers need to be "first out of the chute," or at least part of the initial change effort along with middle managers. That is, senior managers need to be prepared to hear criticisms of their leadership practices without acting defensively, and to make meaningful and observable improvements in their leadership style.

Specific assumptions (based on knowledge of this group of middle managers)

1) Although the leadership style in this Division is already fairly enlightened, making significant improvement in leadership practices won't happen overnight. Thus, the need to start with small, practical steps, and achieve early success (quick wins). As employees see improvement in leadership practices, morale may improve. (Many other factors, besides leadership, are affecting morale in this Division, not the least of which is ongoing pressure to do more with less, a pressure not unfamiliar in many organizations today.)

2) The Division had recently moved from a longstanding tradition of bureaucracy and rigid hierarchy to team-based structures, participative management, and a renewed emphasis on customer service. This was fundamental change, and middle managers who were unable to adjust their leadership practices accordingly would be risking loss of employment. And there had been pain along the way (e.g., layoffs, cutbacks).

3) Many in the middle management ranks, being human, had simply gotten themselves into sloppy leadership habits over the years, and these needed to change for their leadership practices to improve.

Many of these sloppy leadership habits were "blind spots" for the middle managers. However, it is believed that they are fairly open to learning, and so will be willing to accept the pain that comes from receiving feedback about one's "blind spots." (Frederick Nickoli, the voice of the German enlightenment, spoke eloquently of this pain when he said that "criticism is the only help mate we have which, while disclosing our inadequacies can, at the same time, awake us to the desire for greater improvement."[13])

4) This group of middle managers has a number of learning needs in common. Thus, working on their individual leadership development needs, as a team, makes good sense.

5) This group of middle managers will be willing to learn in front of each other and in front of the three members of the senior management team. Further, they will find learning from each other to be worthwhile and helpful. (Having worked with this group of managers on a couple of previous occasions, I knew them to be a fairly open-minded and effective team.)

6) Working on their individual leadership learning needs together, in the group, will also help this group of managers become an even better team. As a result of this work they should have a better understanding of each other's styles, preferences, and leadership practices.

The Approach That Would Be Suggested to Middle Managers

Based on the assumptions outlined above we developed the following *outcomes* and *steps* for helping the three members of the senior management team, and the middle managers who reported to them, to improve their leadership practices.

Outcomes Being Sought

We would start with a one day workshop focused on leadership practices and aimed at achieving the following outcomes.

1) Improved self-awareness of leadership strengths and areas needing development within the middle management ranks.

2) Improved understanding within the management team of each other's perspectives and leadership style.

3) Early improvements in leadership practices that are noticeable to employees within the division.

Steps - Prior to, During, and Following the Workshop

Prior to the workshop

- We would start with very basic and simple benchmarking. Each middle manager would collect questionnaire responses from a representational group of his/her employees. The questionnaire would be brief and seek information about the manager's leadership practices.

At the workshop

- All managers would bring their questionnaire results to the workshop.

- Taking one manager at a time, we would discuss his/her questionnaire results and seek input from the other managers in the group. In this way we would help each manager verify and prioritize his/her questionnaire results and decide on areas for action.

- Next, each manager would identify two or three areas for improving his/her management practices. Following this, goals and a "game plan" for making improvements would be developed by each manager with coaching and support from others in the group.

- Throughout this day long workshop I would sprinkle the odd sermonette on leadership as it seemed appropriate. This information would only be provided, however, where it could be grounded in the discussion of the group or in the feedback they had received through their questionnaire results.

Follow-up session

- A follow-up session will be held at a later date (to be decided) to coach, challenge, and support each manager and to ensure each is making meaningful progress in reasonable time.

End

e) A Technique for Probing Workshop and Learning Needs

An old technique known as "asking why five times" can be useful for investigating workshop and learning needs. It's a cute but annoying process and simply involves asking "why" over and over, until the person you're asking (sometimes yourself) either goes nuts or coughs up the answers. In theory this is supposed to "peel the onion," getting to the core of "why" a person is doing something or thinking a certain way. It has some merit, but only use it with even-tempered people!

Example: Asking "why" five times

Why should we conduct a training program on interviewing skills?

Answer: To help participants (who will be interviewing candidates for hire) learn and practice behavioral-analysis interviewing techniques.

Why do we want participants to learn behavioral-analysis interviewing techniques?

Answer: So they'll investigate their hunches by getting examples of behavior, instead of just settling for attitudinal statements from interviewees.

Why do we want participants to investigate their hunches?

Answer: So they can support their recommendations to hire or reject with examples of the candidate's behavior. This will make recommendations for hire more objective.

Why do we want interviewer's recommendations to be more objective?

Answer: It'll provide the managers, who will be making the final hiring decisions, with additional and more explicit data for deciding.

Why do the hiring managers need more explicit data?

Answer: It'll give them more confidence in their hiring decisions. This should lead to the hiring managers being more willing to accept responsibility for their hiring decisions versus giving this responsibility over to the interviewers.

End

PLANNING WORKSHOPS AND TRAINING PROGRAMS

Having clear and agreed *purpose* and *outcome statements* gives a workshop or training program an essential foundation. Everything else you do as a leader is based on this planning (e.g., selecting design options, evaluating the workshop).

a) The Process Cycle

The process cycle is magic for planning a workshop or training program. Leaders usually plan *content* but seldom plan *process*. The process cycle will help you plan both. It's a method for involving stakeholders in planning a workshop or training program from scratch, that is, even before *purpose* is defined. (Stakeholders include potential participants, their supervisors, managers sponsoring the workshop or training program, and yourself.)

The secret of success is constancy of purpose.
- Benjamin Disraeli

The process cycle

1) Purpose (is, is not)
2) Outcomes (workshop, leadership)
3) Steps (before, during, after)
4) Capabilities (stakeholders, resources)
5) Feedback (stakeholders, evaluation)

"Would you tell me, please, which way I ought to go from here?"
"That depends a good deal on where you want to get."
"I don't much care where."
"Then it doesn't matter which way you go."
- Lewis Carroll

Agreement on the five sections of the process cycle constitutes a pretty good contract with clients. It can be used to define outcomes, roles, accountabilities, and even how the workshop will be evaluated.

Purpose (is, is not)

- The intention and focus of a workshop or training program.

- Ensure purposes are attainable and not in conflict. Get agreement on what purpose "is" and "is not." The former specifies what you want to happen. Agreeing on the latter helps dispel false expectations.

Success ... My nomination for the single most important ingredient is energy well directed.
- Louis B. Lundborg

- Once a list of possible purposes has been brainstormed, agree on the one or two most important purposes for a workshop or training program. (Brainstorming is defined in chapter six.)

Outcomes (workshop, leadership)

- The measurable or observable results expected and sought from the workshop or training program.

- Develop clear outcomes for the top one or two workshop or training-program purposes. This will help you focus the workshop or training program and meet timelines. It will also provide a basis for evaluating. (You can think of *outcomes* as objectives or goals if you wish. In this book, for the sake of consistent terminology, they're called *outcomes*.)

- Two types of outcomes need to be explicit, *workshop or training-program outcomes* and *leadership outcomes*. Confusing the two leads to chaos. Both are valuable, but because they focus on participants, *workshop or training-program outcomes* are more important.

- *Workshop outcomes* identify the benefits participants and the organization will receive as a result of the workshop. They focus on what participants will achieve (e.g., a draft of team goals for the coming six months).

- *Training-program outcomes* identify what participants will learn (e.g., the four principles in the Harvard Negotiation Technique).

- *Leadership outcomes* support *workshop and training-program outcomes*, but are set to help you grow and develop as a workshop or training-program leader. They focus on workshop process and on the leader's actions before, during, and after the workshop (e.g., contracting roles during workshop start-up, asking open questions, involving participants in small group exercises).

- You need to discuss, negotiate, and agree with the group on the *workshop and training-program outcomes*. Whether you choose to share your *leadership outcomes* with the group is up to you.

Steps (before, during, after)

- Brainstorm the things that need to happen before, during, and after the workshop or training program to achieve the desired outcomes. Don't worry about sequence initially. Steps can be organized later.

- Defining steps gives you a track to follow (e.g., in preparing an agenda). After all, as George Campbell, a friend and colleague says, "It's hard to keep people on track if there is no track!"[14]

Capabilities (stakeholders, resources)

- Who needs to be present? What attitudes and behaviors do they need to exhibit (e.g., willing to share information and maintain confidences, willing to take reasonable risks)? Who should *not* be present?

- Will participants be willing and able to participate (e.g., ability to clearly articulate the existing business unit strategy)? Will there be opportunity to participate (e.g., opportunity to hear from everyone in the group)?

- What resources are required (e.g., flipcharts, facility, pre-work)?

Feedback (stakeholders, evaluation)

- What will the sponsor client say if the workshop goes well, surpassing everyone's expectations? What will participants say? What will you say to yourself?

- How will the workshop be evaluated? At what levels (e.g., reaction, learning, behavior, organizational results)? How will evaluation results be used?

A partial example of a process cycle for a training program (in this case, a training program titled "Train the Trainer")

Purpose - is

- Provide opportunities to learn and practice group facilitation skills.
- Provide a "toolbox" of concepts, methods, and models for facilitating and leading workshops and training programs.

Purpose - is not

- A presentations training program.

Workshop Outcomes

- Participants can use a variety of questioning methods while facilitating groups.
- Participants can evaluate and compare approaches for handling under, over, and aggressive participation in a group.

Leadership Outcomes

- Participants are involved quickly at the beginning of the training program.
- Subgroup exercises are noisy, highly involving, and fun.

Steps (before, during, after)

- Agree on outcomes, roles, and the agenda during the start-up.
- Review ways that participants can use the workbook as an ongoing resource.

Capabilities (stakeholders, resources)

- Participants are willing to give and receive feedback on their practice sessions.
- Participants are willing to experiment with new and unfamiliar approaches to leading workshops and training programs.

Feedback (stakeholders, evaluation)

- Participants say that the training program provided them with useful concepts, methods, and models.
- Participants rate the workshop an eight or higher using the Company's evaluation form.

A partial example of a process cycle for leading a training program

Purpose - is

To improve the clarity of my directions for small group exercises.

Purpose - is not

A focus on oration or form.

Outcomes

Participants follow my directions for operating small group exercises with a minimum of clarification needed. (There may be the odd exception. There's always someone in a group who needs reassurance, or who doesn't understand clearly, no matter how well you provide directions.)

Steps

Use the steps provided for giving directions in the section titled "Leading Exercises, Simulations, and Subgroup Activities" in chapter fourteen.

End

(Note: Appendix C provides examples of training-program outcomes.)

b) Gathering Information in a Group - Putting the Process Cycle to Work

Typically the process cycle begins with brainstorming the workshop's purpose. Brainstorm what purpose "is" and what it "is not." Next, select the top two or three purpose statements. Outcomes are then developed for these high priority purposes, and steps are developed for achieving each outcome. Next, the capabilities and resources needed to achieve the outcomes and steps are identified. Finally, discussion moves to how the workshop will be evaluated, and what feedback can be expected from stakeholders.

When using the process cycle, focus most on *purpose* and *outcomes*. Both need to be worked down to simple, clear language, and *outcomes* need to be in some way measurable or observable.

There's no ideal "group size" for completing a process cycle. It depends on who needs to be involved and committed to the success of the workshop or training program. It usually takes anywhere from one and a half to two hours to do a rough "first pass" when five to ten people are involved. With more people it takes a little longer, simply because it takes more time for everyone to contribute.

Once drafted, you can use the process cycle in a number of ways. It's an excellent guide for selecting workshop and training-program designs, for preparing an agenda, and for preparing marketing notices or other communications about a workshop or training program. It also provides a foundation for contracting with workshop stakeholders (e.g., sponsor clients, participants).[15]

(Note: Appendix D provides an assortment of alternative approaches for deciding and defining outcomes.)

CONCLUSION

Summary

It's not just throwing a football that a quarterback gets paid for. It's knowing what a play is meant to accomplish, knowing where the defensive backfield is likely to be positioned, knowing where his receivers are going to be at a given moment, and so on. All this knowledge comes from planning. Preparation and planning aren't the most absorbing parts of being a quarterback or a workshop leader, but they're often where leaders fail. This work needs to be done well.

Planning in Perspective - How the Pieces Fit Together

Have clear distinctions for workshop and learning needs, purpose, outcomes, agenda, design, content, group process, capabilities, and feedback. Confusion results and planning suffers when these are muddled together.

Assessing Workshop and Learning Needs

You need some definition of what success looks like for your workshops and training programs. Are you working on ability, willingness, or opportunity? Training programs focus primarily on *ability*, participants' knowledge, and skill. Workshops focus on all three. *Willingness* relates to motivation, attitude, job satisfaction, and consequences on the job. Many factors in the organization's environment provide or block *opportunity*, such as, time and resources, systems, demands made by others, and so on.

Investigate a range of factors when assessing workshop and learning needs, including the problem or opportunity a workshop or training program is expected to address, the value being sought from a workshop or training program and the likelihood of achieving this value, which performance factors need attention (e.g., willingness, ability, opportunity), what behavior changes are needed, external factors influencing performance and results, what information is needed and by whom, and who can most influence results.

The "Felt Needs Trap"

Not infrequently people are unconscious of their learning needs. They simply have a "blind spot," although asking them about these needs isn't always a waste of time. Sometimes just the action of asking helps them surface or become conscious of these needs. The 80/20 rule applies here as well. Eighty percent of people generally have a pretty good idea of their learning needs, whereas the other twenty percent have quite a few "blind spots." The bottom line is, unless and until people become aware or conscious of the knowledge they lack, and the skills they need to develop, they won't see much value in participating in a training program.

A Model for Considering Learning Needs

Clients often present their workshop and training needs in the form of an explicit or implied solution (e.g., these guys need to learn how to work together). Often, however, clients don't know exactly what they need help with. If they did, they would probably have taken appropriate action long before calling you. When you do get called in, keep in mind that learning needs could fall into one of the following four categories. These relate to end-user clients' awareness and ability.

Unconscious Incompetence

This is the worst possible combination. These clients have blind spots. They're unaware and appear not to care. In fact they may care a great deal, should their learning needs become known to them, but asking them about learning needs that they are completely unaware of will either cause them to reflect seriously on the issue or think you're from another planet.

Conscious Incompetence

Clients who are aware that they lack certain knowledge and skills aren't necessarily learning ready, or even willing to discuss their learning needs. But at least when you raise the question, they won't think you're from Mars.

Conscious Competence

Being fully aware or conscious of your competence usually indicates you're fairly new to a given profession or type of work. Each step you take is thoughtful and purposeful. You work hard to demonstrate the common sense of those who are expert in the field, despite lacking their common experience.

Unconscious Competence

Experts are unconsciously competent. They perform on "auto-pilot." It's difficult for them to help others learn their secrets, because much of their information and many of their skills are so integrated with who they are, and with what seems to them like "common sense." Thus, experts can sometimes have a great deal of difficulty explaining the subtleties of their thinking and acting, so that others can benefit from their experience and wisdom.

Two Distinct Approaches for Investigating Workshop and Learning Needs

The objectivist and interpretative approaches to investigating workshop and learning needs are presented as extremes to make a point. This is that on some occasions workshop and learning needs can be considered in rational and certain terms, as if they were part of an unchanging and defined universe. On most occasions, however, this is far from the case. Most often workshop and learning needs are dynamic, complex, and can be interpreted in a variety of ways depending on one's assumptions and perspective.

The objectivist approach is best when assessing production and some technical training needs, as it assumes concrete training realities, for example, that there's one "right way" to perform a task. The interpretative approach, on the other hand, assumes no "objective reality," only points of view requiring interpretation, for example, the assessing interpersonal or relationship skills needed to work with employees, whose organization is being restructured as part of a hostile takeover.

The Process Cycle - Planning Workshops and Training Programs

The process cycle is a five step method (purpose, outcomes, steps, capabilities, feedback) for involving participants and sponsor clients in planning a workshop or training program. The magic in the process cycle is that it separates logical types of information. Thus, a *purpose* statement is not confused with *outcomes*, and they in turn are not confused with the *steps* needed to accomplish these outcomes. This results in clear, unpretentious, and easily understood *purpose* and *outcome* statements.

Distinguish between a focus on the *workshop* or *training program* and a focus on *leadership* when writing outcome statements. And ensure they are measurable or in some way observable. Other than that, keep them simple and flexible with the minimum amount of detail necessary to satisfy you and your client's needs for focus and clarity.

Checklist

Planning in Perspective • *Needs* (problem or opportunity) • *Purpose* (why we're here) • *Outcomes* (what specifically we're aiming to achieve) • *Agenda* (activity plan) • *Learning Content* (what you want participants to learn) • *Group Process* (how we intend to work together) • *Design* (strategies) • *Capabilities* (willingness, ability) • *Feedback* (what you see, hear, feel) *Questions for Assessing Workshop and Learning Needs* • Is there a problem or opportunity? • What is the value and likelihood of success? • Do needs relate to willingness, opportunity, or ability? • What behavior changes are needed? • What external factors are influencing behaviors? • What information is needed by employees? • Who can influence the needed changes? • What workshop process and learning materials are required?	*Factors in Performance* • Willingness • Opportunity • Ability *A Model of Learning Needs* • Unconscious incompetence • Conscious incompetence • Conscious competence • Unconscious competence *Approaches for Investigating Workshop and Learning Needs* • Objectivist • Interpretative *The Process Cycle* • Purpose (is, is not) • Outcomes (workshop, leadership) • Steps (before, during, after) • Capabilities (stakeholders, resources) • Feedback (stakeholders, evaluation)

Exercise

Your Blind Spots

It's not all that difficult to see other people's blind spots, but what are yours? What ways of thinking or working hold you back or limit your potential? Just thinking about these won't likely provide the best answers. You can't see the back of your own head. You need feedback from other people you trust, but who have different ways of looking at things.

1) Name two of your blind spots related to leading workshops or training programs.

2) What are you going to do to overcome these? List two specific actions to overcome each blind spot.

Notes

[1]Doyle, M., & Straus, D. (1976). How to make meetings work. New York, NY: Jove, p. 25.

[2]Mager, R.F., & Pipe, P. (1984). Analyzing performance problems: Or you really oughta wanna (2nd ed.). Belmont, CA: David S. Lake Publishers.

[3]The idea of this model isn't mine. Trouble is, it's been around so long I forget where it came from. Anyway, these words are mine, so my "plagiarism conscience" is relatively clear.

[4]For ideas on how to help groups become "learning ready" see chapter nine.

[5]Mintzberg, H. (1994). The rise and fall of strategic planning: Reconceiving roles for planning, plans, and planners. New York, NY: The Free Press, p. 327.

[6] The following section was inspired by an article by a friend and colleague, Murray Hiebert. I highly recommend this article. It contains subtleties, nuances, and examples that really bring the interpretative approach to life. It's also great advice for consultants, internal or external. The objectivist and interpretative approaches form a continuum of problem solving strategies often used by workshop leaders. See: Hiebert, M.B., & Smallwood, W.N. (May, 1987). Now for a completely different look at needs analysis: Discover the pragmatic alternatives to traditional methods. *Training and Development Journal*, p. 77.

[7]Hiebert, M.B., & Smallwood, W.N. (May, 1987). Now for a completely different look at needs analysis: Discover the pragmatic alternatives to traditional methods. *Training and Development Journal*, p. 77.

[8]Sperry, R. (1974). Messages from the laboratory. *Engineering and Science*, pp. 29-32. Taken from: Mintzberg, H. (1994). The rise and fall of strategic planning: Reconceiving roles for planning, plans, and planners. New York, NY: The Free Press, pp. 303-304. Mintzberg also talks about how Herbert Simon would disagree. Simon would see these two approaches as related, arguing that intuition and judgment are nothing more than "analysis frozen into habit," p. 311.

[9]Mintzberg, H. (1994). The rise and fall of strategic planning: Reconceiving roles for planning, plans, and planners. New York, NY: The Free Press, p. 304.

[10]Weick, K.E. (1969). The social psychology of organizing. New York, NY: Random House.

[11] Weisbord references the term "equifinality" and notes that "nature arrives at the same place from many directions." He sites Trist's and Emery's work with mining teams in the 1950's. Each team worked in its own way and achieved roughly the same results. "This scientific observation never occurred to Taylor who was convinced that only 'one best way' existed to do anything." From: Weisbord, M.R. (1989). Productive workplaces: Organizing and managing for dignity, meaning, and community. San Francisco, CA. Jossey-Bass, pp. 159-160. Offering another but compatible perspective Irene and Herbert Goldenberg note that Ludwig von Bertalanffy's general systems theory "presents an epistemology in which it is not the structure that defines an object but its organization as defined by the interactive pattern of its parts. That is, the component parts of a system are less important than their interrelations." From Goldenberg, I., & Goldenberg, H. (1985). Family therapy: an overview (2nd ed.). Pacific Grove, CA: Brooks/Cole, p. 96.

[12]Peters, T.J., & Waterman, R.H. Jr. (1981). In search of excellence: Lessons from America's best-run companies. New York, NY: Harper & Row.

[13]Saul, J. R. (1995). The unconscious civilization. Concord, Ont: Anansi.

[14]This expression is borrowed from a friend and colleague, George Campbell, Calgary, Alberta, Canada.

[15]These terms are described in chapter five.

Planning to Evaluate a Workshop

INTRODUCTION

Being committed to making each and every workshop better than the last is essential to being a long-term success as a workshop leader. What keeps lesser workshop leaders mediocre is their complacency with the status quo. To succeed and grow as a workshop leader you need to be self-aware and open to feedback. This means you must *evaluate*. You need to hear from your customers, the workshop participants and your sponsor clients (the senior managers who pay the bills for the workshop). Like everyone, you have "blind spots," places where feedback from others is needed. As I've heard John Jones says from time to time, "You can't see the back of your own head."[1]

Now, in the planning phase, is the time to decide on evaluation. Two areas for evaluation need to be considered (the workshop and your leadership), along with four levels of evaluation (reaction, learning, behavior, and results).

This chapter provides powerful tools for evaluating. It covers:

- Why it's necessary to evaluate.
- What to evaluate.
- Four levels of evaluation.
- A closer look at the four levels.
- Evaluation in perspective.

Personally I liked the university. They gave us money and facilities and we didn't have to produce anything. You've never been out of college. You don't know what it's like out there. I've worked in the private sector. They expect results!
- Dr. Ray Stantz, played by Dan Aykrod, in the movie Ghostbusters

WHY IT'S NECESSARY TO EVALUATE

Why do you want feedback from your clients (e.g., participants, sponsor clients) about your workshops and training programs? Or, as a friend of mine says, "Why add to your problems by facing reality?" Workshops and training programs need to be viewed like any other investment. That's why. They need to make good business sense by contributing to production, sales, and business income.

Both you and your clients need to find out if the workshop or training program is "paying off," if you should invest further, or if you should bail out now and cut your losses. You want some idea of the value that the workshop or training program is providing vis-à-vis the outcomes being sought. And you want to find out if, by modifying the workshop or work environment in some way, you can increase this value (e.g., changing the work environment to improve participants' opportunity to practice newly acquired skills on the job).

Evaluation meets short-term and long-term objectives. First, it's an organized way of demonstrating to your sponsor client that the workshop or training program was successful. Second, it's a way for you to collect much needed feedback on specific aspects of the workshop and your leadership. Your goal is continuous improvement of the workshop in question and your own development as a leader. Not to mention, in the long term, the best employment security you have is your own knowledge, skill, and "track record" (i.e., your contacts, reputation, history of success).

What to Evaluate

First, you evaluate *the value of the workshop or training program to participants and to the organization*. That is, you evaluate "to what degree" the workshop or training program has met the explicit outcomes being sought. (Chapter three defines outcomes and provides guidance in developing outcome statements.) The bottom line for workshop evaluation is: "Are participants using their new knowledge to create value for themselves and their organizations?"

If we choose to evaluate, it must be because the potential good outweighs the harm, not because evaluation is scientific ... - G.V. Glass

Second, you evaluate *your performance as the workshop or training-program leader*. Leadership outcomes are what you want to accomplish as a workshop leader. To learn from each workshop and continuously improve as a leader, it's necessary to define specific leadership outcomes to focus your development. For example, you may want to engage participants in deeper levels of dialogue during your workshops. You decide one way to make this happen is to improve your questioning skills. To this end you develop a leadership outcome to challenge you to ask more *open ended questions*. An accompanying outcome might focus your attention on *listening actively* as each participant speaks or on *redirecting* participant comments and questions within the group.

FOUR LEVELS OF EVALUATION

Donald Kirkpatrick (1975) identifies four levels of evaluation.[2]

Level-1, Reaction	(Did they like it?)
Level-2, Learning	(Did they learn?)
Level-3, Behavior	(Did they use it?)
Level-4, Results	(Did it make a difference?)

There's a simple logic to these four levels. They are in hierarchy and increasing complexity. For example, it's assumed a participant wouldn't have learned well if he/she didn't like a training program. Also, it follows a participant can't use something that they haven't learned.

Level-1 Reaction	*Workshop or training-program evaluation* This level of evaluation focuses on participants' *reactions* to the workshop, indicating how well they're accepting the process and learning material. It asks, for example, "Do you feel the workshop has helped you understand and use the computer bulletin board?" Any number of stakeholders might be asked, for example, workshop participants, their supervisors, or sponsor clients. *Example* • Evaluation forms. Usually participants are asked to complete these before leaving the workshop. They might also be asked to complete these after they've had a chance to apply their new learning (e.g., a week or two after the workshop). Examples of level-1 evaluation forms are provided in Appendix E. *Workshop-leader evaluation* Asking participants to evaluate your effectiveness as a leader. *Example* • Evaluation forms asking questions such as, "Did the leader allow time for participation?" "Was the leader supportive of different views?" "Did the leader make the learning material relevant and interesting?"

<table>
<tr>
<td>Level-2 Learning</td>
<td>
Workshop or training-program evaluation
Have participants learned the workshop content? Can they demonstrate this in some way? This level of evaluation focuses on awareness and understanding. For example, you might ask a participant to “list the steps in teaching a new employee how to use the computer bulletin board.”
Examples
<ul>
<li>An oral or written test that covers the material presented in a workshop.</li>
<li>A quiz or interview a month after the workshop to assess learning retention.</li>
<li>Pre- and post-testing (i.e., testing participant knowledge both before and after a training program).</li>
</ul>
Workshop-leader evaluation
Have you learned about designing and leading workshops?
Example
<ul>
<li>Reflecting on what you have learned about leadership during a particular workshop and changes you will make as a result of this learning.</li>
</ul>
</td>
</tr>
</table>

Level-3 Behavior Change	*Workshop or training-program evaluation* Are participants doing things differently in the workshop or on the job? Are they practicing new skills effectively? Are these changes visible or in some way measurable? This level focuses on assessing change in participants' behavior as a result of a workshop or training program. An example is observing a participant using a computer bulletin board after participating in a workshop on this topic. *Examples* • Observations of participant performance during the workshop. • Demonstrations of skills in a workshop or on the job. • A supervisor completing a "descriptive based" performance assessment. This could be done both before and after a workshop for purposes of comparison. *Workshop-leader evaluation* Assessing how well you accomplished your leadership outcomes or goals. Did you do what you wanted to do, and act the way you wanted to act, as the workshop leader? *Example* • You could do this on your own, ask participants, or have an experienced workshop leader audit your workshop and give you feedback. (Leadership outcomes might focus on things like handling underparticipation, having a smooth and energizing workshop start-up, asking open ended questions, or not acting defensively when being challenged by the group.)

Level-4 Results	*Workshop or training-program evaluation* Measuring or in some way observing "bottom line" organizational results following a workshop or training program. Assessing if behavior changes made by participants improved results for the organization, and whether these behavior changes were made as a result of what participants learned in a particular workshop. The tricky, if not impossible, task is tracking and attributing these improvements back to the workshop. (More is said about this below.) Thus this level of evaluation focuses on the desired product or benefit to the organization. An example is observing a new employee who has just been trained to use a computer bulletin board do this in a way that benefits the organization. *Examples* • Reductions in costs, lost time accidents, turnover, grievances, absenteeism, customer complaints. • Increases in quality, speed, morale, sales, number of claims processed, number of projects accepted, or number of suggestions submitted. • Increased capacity for organizational improvement. *Workshop-leader evaluation* Assessing "bottom line" results for the leader and for the workshop itself. *Examples* • Was the workshop highly rated? • Did the sponsor client offer repeat business? • Are former participants recommending the workshop to others? • Have you noticeably improved your workshop leadership abilities? • Have you developed and successfully tested new approaches or designs for the workshop? • Has conducting the workshop provided data for completing an article you were writing? • Were participants active and involved during small group exercises?

A CLOSER LOOK AT THE FOUR LEVELS

The focus of the following discussion is on *workshop or training-program evaluation* rather than *workshop leader evaluation*. However, many of the points made below apply to both.

Level-1 Evaluation - Reaction

Level-1 measures feelings such as attitude, energy, enthusiasm, interest, and support. However, what shows up on evaluation forms are words, not deeds. There's often a dissonance between what people espouse and what they actually do, particularly when it involves changing long-established habits. And sometimes learning isn't fun. Natural learning can sometimes be painful, and deep learning almost always involves some pain. What are participants going to say on the evaluation forms when this happens?

The evaluation forms that leaders pass out at the end of a workshop or training program are the most common method of level-1 evaluation. John Jones (1990) calls these "smile sheets."[3] The questions asked are often only a little more sophisticated than, "Did you like me?" "Did you like the workshop?" "Are you happy now?" These forms have a positive bias requiring them to be interpreted cautiously and relative to other workshop evaluations. Thus, a workshop rated only average might well be a problem. Yet these forms have their value. Besides being easy to use, they are at least a crude indicator of workshop success. One thing's for sure. If a lot of people say "the workshop was a waste of time," you can be fairly sure they won't be using much of it on the job. If most say "it was fantastic," this at least *indicates* they may have learned something. Whether they learned what you intended them to learn, or whether they change their behavior on the job, is another matter.

The best level-1 evaluation is face-to-face discussion with either a group or with individuals. For example, use a simple "T chart" technique with a group to evaluate a workshop. ("T" charts are explained in chapter eleven.) On one side of the "T" chart put, "What went well?" On the other side put, "What could we have done differently?" The group brainstorms, lists a few compliments, and decides on a few improvements. This usually takes five minutes. During this time you're collecting the data using a common text (e.g., flipchart), asking questions to clarify and keep the dialogue going, and listening actively. Later you must respond to suggestions the group has made. "Responding" may mean changing a process or a piece of learning content as requested by the group, or it may simply mean explaining the importance of these.

One thing seems clear; some evaluation is better than no evaluation. Even simple evaluation forms are better than no feedback whatsoever. The "bottom line" advice for level-1 evaluation: Do it, but be careful about drawing conclusions from the data (e.g., deciding a process such as role playing is too stressful for a particular group). Rather, use the data to help you focus further inquiry (e.g., under what conditions would role playing be acceptable, or what alternative approaches to role playing would help participants practice a given skill).

Asking the group to complete level-1 evaluation forms

(Note: The following example concerns asking participants to complete "level-1" evaluation forms at the end of a workshop. Chapter twelve reviews approaches to getting feedback during a workshop.)

Formal "level-1" evaluations are usually the very last thing you do in a workshop. You've just completed the workshop wrap up and participants are often in a hurry to get going. The last thing they want to do is spend another five or ten minutes completing a form. Yet, you need this feedback from them. You need to know what people felt and what they will be saying about the workshop. After all, sponsor clients (i.e., top management) often make decisions about a workshop based on two or three casual comments from people they trust. In addition, other employees in the organization are likely to decide whether a given training program will be helpful to them based on a few casual comments from one or two employees who have already taken this training.

Make sure you leave five or ten minutes before the contracted ending time for participants to complete the evaluation forms. Asking them to take extra time for evaluations is a tougher sell. Next, recognize that participants are in a hurry and empathize with them. Say something like, "You've worked hard and you're probably in a hurry to get going, and you will be out of here at 4 PM as agreed. We need just one last thing from you. It's important. It helps us improve the workshop for others, and it provides feedback for the workshop sponsor. So please spend at least five, and no more than ten, minutes giving us this feedback. Be specific. And writing your name on the form will help us follow up for clarification or additional information."

A little humor softens resistance to completing evaluation forms. Ask something like, "Who hates completing these forms?" Raise your hand to show the group you're polling. A few participants usually respond by raising their hands. Then add with a serious face, "OK then, here's the deal. Just sign your name and hand it in. I'll complete the rest for you."

Next, recognize that people will be leaving at different times as they complete their evaluation forms. Say something like, "You'll probably be completing this evaluation at different times, so once it's done you're free to leave. Let me say now that I've enjoyed working with each of you, and I wish you every success practicing these new skills on the job." (Your appreciations need to be specific and sincere.)

Now, pass out the evaluation forms and don't interrupt the group as they complete these. Watch to make sure participants don't forget to hand them in as they leave. The need for participants to hand in their completed evaluation forms may seem obvious, but strangely enough, some will unintentionally leave with these, if you haven't explicitly asked that they be handed in before they leave the room!

End

Guidelines for Conducting Level-1 Evaluation

- Decide what information you're seeking and what parts of the workshop you want to evaluate (e.g., workshop objectives, materials, process, techniques, and so on). Do the same for evaluation around your performance as the workshop leader.

- Tailor the evaluation form to the purpose of your workshop.

- Design a form that *quantifies* reactions and has space for written comments, including suggestions for improving the workshop. Quantitative data is easily summarized. Qualitative data helps you interpret quantitative data. In the example below, comments in the "why" section help clarify the rating that is circled.

> 3. I received useful feedback following my practice sessions.
>
> Not at all 1 2 3 (4) 5 Very much
>
> Why: *The feedback was thorough and helpful. It recognized my strengths and pointed to areas I need to improve. It was also given in a very supportive manner.*

- Make sure the form can be completed in five or ten minutes. Any longer discourages this type of feedback.

- Ask workshop participants to take at least five minutes when completing the form. If you don't make this request, some participants will just "tick the boxes" or "circle the numbers" and be done inside of thirty seconds.

- Encourage participants to complete the form honestly. Letting them know their honesty is a gift and is appreciated improves the quality of feedback you will receive.

- Except in rare cases where trust is nonexistent, ask participants to identify themselves on the form, or at the very least make this optional. More is said about this below.

- Sometimes delayed reactions (e.g., one or two weeks after the workshop) are best, but your "return rate" will decrease substantially. If you want feedback from everyone, have participants complete the form before they leave the workshop.

- Develop a standard for each rating category for a given workshop and use it to compare ratings over time.

- The last step for each level of evaluation is the same, that is, listen to the group's feedback and take decisive action based on this feedback. It's important to make visible adjustments in content or process when suggested by participant feedback, or failing this, to discuss with participants why these changes are not possible.

What You Can Expect from Level-1 Evaluation Forms

I've learned that if you depend on others to make you happy, you'll be endlessly disappointed.
- H. Jackson Brown, Jr.

What sort of evaluations should a workshop leader or trainer expect to receive? Use the old 80/20 rule as a guide (the Pareto principle).[4] A useful, worthwhile, and enjoyable workshop usually has 80% of its evaluations rated above average, if not in the top quartile. The other 20% are only average, and one or two, at the most, may be below average.

You can expect three different types of feedback on evaluation forms, particularly on level-1 evaluation forms. You'll get

- feedback that's nice to hear.
- feedback that stings a little.
- cheap shots.

There are a few specific and "always nice to hear" compliments from participants who got something special, and even something unexpected, from the workshop. Next, there's often specific and constructive feedback that "stings a little." This is information you can learn from. It stings because it's "on target," but that's also why it's useful. Pay attention to this feedback and use it to improve the workshop and your leadership. Finally, although it's rare, every now and then you'll get a "cheap shot" on the evaluation form. "Cheap shots" aren't intended to be constructive. They're about anger, and you're the "target for today." Usually these evaluation forms are left unsigned so the "shooter" doesn't have to be accountable for what he/she says. Cheap shots are an example of what Brickell (1974) calls "the instinctive ability of ... (an) evaluator to bite the hand that feeds you while seeming only to be licking it."[5]

An example of a cheap shot

I was once leading a workshop for a university faculty and decided to joke with a participant about their accent. This person was from Liverpool in the UK and had this great English accent. I asked, tongue in cheek, "Where did you learn to talk?" It seemed like fun and the person being teased laughed along with the group. But someone else, for some reason, was quite "put off." On the evaluation form, he or she made the comment, "The workshop leader should know better than to single someone out and ridicule how they talk."

What do you do with "cheap shots"?

First, realize they say more about the person who "took the shot" than they say about you.

Second, don't take them to heart. Depersonalize the rejection in order to learn. It's no big deal; *shit happens* (a technical term spawned from the wisdom of Forest Gump).

Third, always check to ensure you have a good rapport with a group before using the sort of "put-down" humor I've described here. On hindsight I had only been working with this group for a couple of hours. This type of humor works best after a day or so with a group. Strangely enough, "put-down" humor doesn't usually offend the person you're teasing, likely because you're looking right at them and they can tell you're joking. When someone does get upset, it's often another person in the group who missed the subtlety involved, or who doesn't understand the relationship you have with the person you're teasing.

Fourth, find the kernel of truth in "cheap shots" and consider whether you want to adjust your approach. Seek solutions not excuses. For example, I now preface any teasing about accents by saying, "I like your accent." Then I ask, "Where did you learn how to talk?"

Asking Participants to Identify Themselves on Evaluation Forms

End each evaluation form with a request that participants identify themselves (e.g., "Participant Name: ____________"). There are two reasons for doing this. First, it requires participants to take responsibility for their own comments. These are adult participants after all. Second, it allows you to follow up with a given participant for clarification or to provide additional coaching where this seems needed.

There may be a few participants that "hold back" on their criticisms because they're asked to identify themselves or who choose not to provide their name on the form even though it's requested. Other than setting and maintaining an effective workshop learning climate - one that gives participants permission to be honest and direct - there's not much you can do about this. Some participants will always provide more honest and direct feedback than others.

If you feel strongly that participants should have the right to remain anonymous on evaluation forms, then rather than eliminating the requirement for them to identify themselves altogether, consider making *name* optional. For example, place the following request at the end of the evaluation form, "Participant Name (optional): ________________."

Rate everything a perfect ten!

On a couple of occasions I've participated in workshops lead by Ken Blanchard. Famous for his "one minute manager books" and his earlier work with Paul Hersey on situational leadership, Blanchard is a master workshop leader.[6] Among his unique approaches is how he handles the evaluation form. He passes out his "level-1" evaluation form, first thing in the day, and asks everyone to rate the workshop a ten (the highest possible rating). Next he has everyone write out what they need to do to contribute to the workshop being worthy of this rating. For example, people need to participate, challenge, share their stories, relate what's being discussed to their own situation, be open to new ideas, and so on. Blanchard does this good naturedly and with a lot of humor.

Needless to say Blanchard's workshops are rated highly, but his approach to evaluation isn't the only reason. This approach isn't about manipulating a high rating. Someone of Ken Blanchard's stature isn't likely to lead an unsuccessful workshop. Rather, it's about calling attention to each participant's role in the success of a workshop. Blanchard does this masterfully.

Level-2 Evaluation - Learning

It's relatively easy to measure learning when skills are taught. The most practical method is simply having participants demonstrate a skill using a simulation, role play, or in a number of other ways. What's more difficult is assessing learning where principles and facts are taught. Here you're pretty much restricted to using either oral or "paper and pencil" tests. However, exercises involving participants in practical situations (e.g., problem solving simulations) are a better way of evaluating knowledge than are oral or written tests.

Problems with paper and pencil tests are well known. We all have years of experience with these, going back to the days when we were "institutionalized" in schools. For starters, written tests must accurately cover the material presented for the evaluation to be effective. Another problem is that some people are good at taking tests, while others suffer performance anxiety when a test is handed out. Finally, there's a big difference between an "application level of knowledge" and simple awareness or understanding. Paper and pencil tests measure understanding, at best. Success on tests doesn't always translate into success on the job.

Guidelines for Conducting Level-2 Evaluation

- Assess attitudes, knowledge, and skills, both before and after the workshop. Analyze the data statistically. For example, compare the mean of a test given to a group before the workshop to the mean of the same test given after the workshop.

- Use an *objective* measure such as a paper and pencil test for assessing knowledge and attitude.

- Use performance tests for assessing skills (e.g., simulations).

Level-3 Evaluation - Behavior

Although levels 3 and 4 evaluations endeavor to assess "on the job" results, they also rely on indirect and subjective measurements. And because many uncontrollable variables are at play, cause and effect relationships are difficult to determine.

Measuring behavior change is simple and straightforward with production work, but complex and difficult with knowledge work. The power of *habits* also needs to be considered when assessing behavior change. Behavior change is always easier to achieve when it asks people to work in new ways, but doesn't require them to change long-established habits. Work group and organization habits (i.e., norms and organization culture) are especially difficult to change. They operate within a closed system that rewards and reinforces old behaviors. Dr. W.E. Deming (1982) talks about this difficulty.[7] Deming maintains that employees' influence on norms and culture is somewhere around 6% and that the influence exerted by an organization's systems and processes accounts for the other 94%. Thus, when it comes to improving norms and cultures, the leverage for such action lies with changing the nonhuman aspects of organizations such as structures, systems, processes, strategies, and so on. To paraphrase Deming, "pit a well trained person against a poor system, and the system wins every time."

Guidelines for Conducting Level-3 Evaluation

Discussion of level-3 guidelines is combined with that of level-4 (see below).

Level-4 Evaluation - Results

Two key benefits result from doing levels 3 and 4 evaluation. The first is management education. Managers learn more about what's going on in their work areas by going through the process of observing and surveying. Second, as a result of doing evaluation at these levels, those involved see the workshop's function as a process benefiting the organization, not merely as a classroom activity.

Level-4 evaluation seeks to answer important and complex questions. Have organizational results improved because of behavioral changes workshop participants have made? Have these behavioral changes resulted from new knowledge and skills that the workshop participants received in a given workshop or training program?

With knowledge work, in particular, measuring workshop results is not as simple as "connecting the dots." Even if people liked the workshop (level-1), learned the content (level-2), made behavior changes on the job (level-3), and organizational results were achieved (level-4), this still doesn't necessarily mean these organizational results were caused by the behavior changes or that behavior changes can be attributed directly to learning in the workshop.

Level-4, and to a lesser extent level-3, evaluation involves dealing with many uncontrollable and complex variables. Known as the "third variable" or the "separation of variables" problem, this leads to an inability to distinguish causation from association. Russell Ackoff (1981) has an analogy that makes sense here. He asks, "Does an acorn produce an oak tree?"[8] The answer is that an acorn is necessary but not sufficient to produce an oak tree.

Sometimes training may be as necessary, although also as insufficient, as an acorn. Other times training is just like an extra three days of sunlight or rain. Both may help but it's tough to argue they were necessary. Would the oak tree have died without these three days? Would it have been as strong as it is today? For example, does supervisory training produce good supervisors? Maybe! Like the acorn, training may be needed. However, just as the acorn needs water, soil, and sunlight to produce an oak tree, so too does training need an adequate environment to produce organizational results. This might include effective production methods and policies, supportive organizational systems, opportunities for participants to practice, and a challenging work environment complete with reinforcement and coaching.

That's why level-4 results are so hard to measure. You have to consider the influence of an organization's water, soil, and sunlight. Not to mention the squirrels running all over the place and those rare collections of *nuts* in various departments of the organization!

Critical Considerations Before Doing Levels 3 or 4 Evaluation

Levels 3 and 4 evaluation require a systematic, statistical, and consulting orientation. Thus, the following factors need to be considered before beginning these levels of assessment. *Note*: Jim and Dana Gaines Robinson (1987) have done some outstanding work in analyzing the critical considerations involved in levels 3 and 4 evaluation. They deserve credit for many of the following insights.[9]

- Recognize that only specific tasks and skills can be tracked at levels 3 and 4 such as handling customer complaints using a given method or asking open ended questions in a performance appraisal interview. Changes resulting from a workshop that are values, principles, or knowledge based can't be tracked at levels 3 and 4. Neither can skills covered in a workshop that are defined too generally, for example, providing more support to subordinates or communicating better with customers.

- Recognize that only some workshops, not all, can and should be tracked at levels 3 and 4. For example, you wouldn't likely invest in level 3 or 4 evaluation for a single training program. However, if you intend to offer a training program companywide, expecting several hundred employees to participate over the course of two or three years, then it makes sense to use level 3 or 4 evaluation. These levels of evaluation provide information about a training program's effectiveness. They also enable you to adjust the training to further improve results.

- Ensure your clients care about workshop impact and structured assessment. You need clients who believe in and care about the results of the evaluation.

- Make sure you have a good working relationship with clients(e.g., workshop participants, sponsor clients) before doing levels 3 and 4 evaluation. Clients need to provide you with access and support for conducting these levels of research. You need to count on them for help if you experience problems during the evaluation.

- Have a clear and explicit purpose for conducting levels 3 or 4 evaluation and be clear what skills you want to measure.

- Allow time for behavior change to take place on the job before conducting levels 3 or 4 evaluations. That is, allow time for workshop participants to practice and integrate new skills back on the job.

- Do a cost-benefit analysis before conducting these levels 3 and 4 evaluations, as these are expensive and time consuming. For example, it usually takes a minimum of ten working days to do level-4 evaluation, even though the workshop itself may take only two or three days to conduct.

- Only do level-3 evaluation once it's clear that behaviors on the job have changed, and only do level-4 evaluation if organizational results have improved. Level-4 evaluation then attempts to discover a relationship between the new behaviors and the improved results. For example, you might seek evidence suggesting employees are using a new sales approach and that more sales are being made. Then investigate the relation between the new sales approach and improved sales.

- Don't attempt to isolate or measure the amount of contribution a training program or workshop has independently made to organizational results. There are too many uncontrollable and interdependent factors at play in the work environment, for example, a new marketing program, a new sales policy, or changes in leadership. Any of these, in addition to the training program, may have contributed to improved results. Avoid the "land mine" of trying to "proportion out" credit.

Tools and Skills Needed to Conduct Levels 3 and 4 Evaluation

- Basic survey and questionnaire building skills are needed for collecting relevant, objective, and accurate data from the appropriate sources.

- Basic research, statistical, diagnostic, and interviewing skills are needed to assess the strengths of causal relationships between learning content, participant learning, new behaviors on the job, and organization results.

- It's best to share evaluation results with clients in an interactive meeting and to work in partnership with sponsor clients and participants. Thus, consulting, feedback, information handling, meeting, and management skills are also needed.

Guidelines for Conducting Levels 3 and 4 Evaluation

- Before and after, measurements and control groups are useful. For example, you could have supervisors or subordinates complete questionnaires on participants' behavior "on the job" before the workshop, and again a few weeks after the workshop.

- Seek information about the work environment. Is it supporting or preventing new skills from being used? Immediate supervisors, in particular, have a big impact on whether participants practice and use new skills on the job. How the supervisor models, coaches, supports, challenges, and reinforces the participant carries a great deal of influence. Of course there are many other factors at play as well, for example, peer pressure and changes in systems and programs.

- Survey or interview participants, their bosses, their subordinates, or others (e.g., peers) who know about workshop participant behavior on the job and about changes in organizational results. Repeat the survey or interviews at appropriate times.

- Protect individual identities when measuring group results. This will yield more accurate measures.

EVALUATION IN PERSPECTIVE

This section looks at the following aspects of evaluation.

A) The "inside stuff" on evaluation

B) The leader's role in evaluation

C) Client bashing

D) Attribution theory

E) Evaluating the performance of participants

A) The "Inside Stuff" on Evaluation

Written or statistical information is often sterile, providing description but not explanation, for example, revealing that participants were uninvolved and learned little during a particular exercise but not what prevented their active participation or learning. On the other hand, a single story from a disgruntled participant may be worth a whole stack of completed evaluation forms. While the latter may suggest a problem, the former can suggest a solution. That's why face-to-face evaluation is preferred by many workshop leaders. Only in this way can they "read" the subtleties and nuances in participants' evaluations.

> ***Qualitative course evaluations ... prove effective at gauging the sentiments of the class but are useless for understanding successes or diagnosing failures.... A conversation with a candid student or two can often supply the needed information.***
> ***- Henry Mintzberg***

Each of the four levels of evaluation comes with its own set of problems. Levels 1 and 2 are relatively easy and inexpensive to administer in a workshop or training program, but they don't tell you much about whether a workshop is adding to an organization's bottom line. Levels 3 and 4 are a different story. Level-4, in particular, requires working with clients at their work site. It measures improvements to organizational results (e.g., the cost of reworks has decreased 34%), but these are usually "all but impossible" to attribute back to a particular workshop. In addition, level-4 evaluation is costly and complex. Many variables are at play and a lot of time and resources are required to observe and measure.

In a way workshop evaluation is a "red herring" anyway, particularly for a workshop or training program that provides complex learning, such as leadership or supervisory skills. These types of training are so obviously needed, and so obviously of benefit to organizations, that one might ask, "Why bother evaluating when we know they're useful and worth the investment?" Staying a level-1 or level-2 evaluation is often better than attempting some "leap of faith" level-4 measurement and concluding that "the workshop resulted in reducing the organization's turnover rate by 3%." True believers will say it's conservative. Skeptics will say it's "smoke and mirrors." Nothing's been achieved. When it comes to level-4 evaluation it's possible to get precise far beyond one's ability to be accurate!

Yet, what's the alternative? You need to do some sort of formal evaluation, however difficult or uncertain. Neglecting evaluation leaves workshops and training programs as something of a philanthropic "classroom" activity. Also, managers love measures, and well they should. So don't let this section's skepticism over evaluation fool you. Evaluation, while not always easy or scientific, is usually well advised.

B) The Leader's Role in Evaluation

Potential problems abound around the leader's role in evaluation. These result from the fact that evaluation is not a simple matter of "cause and effect" but rather one of multiple processes affecting and being affected by each other. Guba and Lincoln (1981) provide a thorough look at these problems in all their complexity.[10] For our purposes, however, suffice it to say that workshop and training-program evaluation inescapably involves both judgment and description. Naturally, it's the *judgment*, on your part and on the part of your clients, that can be problematic, political, and anxiety creating.

Anxiety is a normal reaction to evaluation.
- Egon Guba and Yvonna Lincoln

Bateson's analogy of "billiard balls" and Hoffman's reference to "kicking a rock or a dog" help clarify the role of judgment in evaluation. Gregory Bateson (1972) states that it's sound judgment to think of cause and effect in the physical world,[11] that is, to think in linear terms such as A causes B, which then causes C, and so on, much as billiard balls affect each other. However, Bateson's "billiard ball" model makes little sense when applied to the complexities of organizations and interpersonal relationships. Lynn Hoffman (1981) carries this analysis a little further. Hoffman notes that there's a difference between kicking a rock and kicking a dog.[12] The rock goes where you kicked it, in accordance with the laws of physics. The dog, on the other hand, judges and reacts to your kick. The dog's reaction is based not just on how hard you kicked and where you kicked, but also on how it felt and its relationship with you.

Needless to say, evaluating workshops and training programs is a lot more like kicking a dog than like kicking a rock. And like it or not, how you go about evaluating and your relationship with your clients influence their behavior. As a result, in some way, unintentional though it may be, you can't help but contaminate your own evaluation. In living systems, and even more so in human systems, the very act of evaluating influences what is being evaluated. And, to quote Guba and Lincoln (1981) once again, "in all evaluations there are factors that militate against openness and candor..."[13] The following considerations apply most directly to collecting and interpreting "level-1, reaction" evaluation.

Distortions in Gathering Evaluation Data Can Arise From

- The level of trust between you and the group. (If participants don't trust you, they're unlikely to risk being specific in their feedback.)

- The manner in which the data-gathering techniques are employed. (An example is how evaluations are asked for. When handing out "level-1, reaction" evaluation forms at the end of a training program, a friend of mine says, "Be as tough as you want; just remember, I've got twelve kids at home to feed!" Sure, there's humor here, but there's also a message! Needless to say, you need to ask for level-1 evaluation in a neutral way. Just say something like, "I appreciate any feedback you're willing to provide, and the more specific the better.")

Distortions in Interpreting Evaluations Can Arise From

- What's at stake, and how you're feeling about yourself and about the group. Guba and Lincoln (1981) note that different interpretations are functions of different value positions.[14] For example, if you're feeling low self-esteem and high threat, this will likely influence what you pay attention to and how you interpret it. Argyris and Schon (1974) write that "at any moment, one variable many be more interesting than others and move to the foreground of our attention..."[15]

Actions to Help You Remain "Objective" When Interpreting Evaluations

- Allow your interpretations of workshop and training-program evaluations to be challenged by "objective third parties" (i.e., people who are willing to be honest and direct with you, and whose opinion you trust).

- Chinese mythology tells how it is not possible to cross the same river twice. In other words, each workshop is unique. Nonetheless, by comparing trends across a number of workshops and training programs you'll get an more accurate and realistic picture of the workshop's and your strengths and development needs.

C) Client Bashing - Not the Way to Go

If a workshop bombs, what might you say, at least to yourself? "What a bunch of turkeys! They were the worst group; only two had any interest in learning and even they weren't motivated to challenge at any significant level." "It's hard to soar like an eagle when you're working with a bunch of turkeys!"

I will always cherish the initial misconceptions I had about you.
- Anonymous

If a workshop is a big success, what might you say, at least to yourself? "I did a great job." "I really pulled that one out of a hat." "Boy, my skills as a workshop leader are really improving!"

My point is this. Share responsibility for workshops that fail *and* that succeed. Blaming the group only shields you from the difficult question, "How do I continue to learn and develop as a workshop leader?" Granted, sometimes participants may be passive and uninterested, but you won't grow if you take the "blaming route." Blaming leaves failure in your "circle of concern," and as such makes it inactionable, something that worries you, but over which you have no influence whatsoever, let alone control.

D) Attribution Theory

Attribution theory is an example of how trust and rapport, or the lack thereof, look in practice. It colors the lenses through which participants evaluate the success of the workshop and your contribution to that success as the workshop leader.

The only man I know who behaves sensibly is my tailor; he takes my measure anew each time he sees me. The rest go on with their old measurements and expect me to fit them.
- George Bernard Shaw

What (people) believe about each other may be more important than objective reality in influencing relationship satisfaction.
- Frederick Kanfer and Arnold Goldstein

Lord and Smith (1983) describe attribution theory as "a specific attempt to (1) understand the cause of a certain event, (2) assess responsibility for outcomes of the event, and (3) assess the personal qualities of people involved in an event."[16]

Here's how it works. If you like someone, you have a high level of trust and rapport with that person, and you're more likely to evaluate their performance through rose colored glasses. However, if someone constantly rubs you the wrong way, if you don't see him/her as credible or authentic, it's likely that you'll be more inclined to evaluate their performance harshly.

Peter Scholtes (1988) sees attributions as "a substitute for the hard work of seeking real explanations." He also comments that it creates resentment in that "it is perfectly normal to bristle when someone tells you they know what makes you tick or tries to explain your motives."[17] Nonetheless, attribution theory is very powerful and very much at play in workshops and organizations. It's just a fact of life. Once someone sees you a certain way, it can either be very advantageous or a tough rap to beat!

The following table shows the not uncommon, though extreme, attributions we make about others.

What participants are likely to say about you as their workshop leader	If you have a high degree of trust and rapport with the group	If you have very little or no trust and rapport with the group
If the workshop is seen as a success	• She's deserving • She's earned this success • She works hard and is very dedicated • She's smart • Only she could have pulled this workshop off so well	• He's lucky (e.g., he was in the right place at the right time) • Anyone could have led this workshop (he succeeded in spite of himself)
If the workshop is seen as below average and a waste of time	• He faced impossible circumstances (e.g., tough group, poor facility, constant interruptions) • Nobody could have made this workshop a success under the circumstances	• There's an inherent flaw in her character • She's unmotivated • Only a loser like her could have screwed this workshop up • She plays politics so she'll get away with it yet again (what a brown noser!)

Why this failure? A story of attribution theory at work

It's February 15, 1996, "Flag Day" in Canada, and the Prime Minister of Canada, Jean Chretien, wades through a crowd of protesters in Hull, Quebec. Suddenly Chretien grabs a man by the throat and pushes him to the ground. At that moment, the security force charged with protecting the Prime Minister remains safely behind! The man assaulted by Chretien, later identified as one of the protesters, hadn't moved to provoke Chretien. He had just stood there. Naturally the entire event was televised. It's a tense time in Canada as one of its provinces, Quebec, wants to secede and become a sovereign nation.

The next morning every caller to a radio phone-in program comments on this incident. Every caller saw exactly the same televised footage, yet their conclusions fell into two distinct camps. A classical case of attribution theory at work.

Some thought the Prime Minister was "losing it." They talked about flaws in Chretien's character and weakness in his emotional stability. They said he was irrational, out of control, and seemed stressed out. One man said his seven-year-old daughter turned to him and asked, "Daddy, why is the Prime Minister attacking that man?" Not surprisingly several of those callers sharing this perspective also took a moment to criticize Chretien's political agenda.

Others supported Chretien and blamed his security force or the protester. One caller said, "I don't care what the video showed; the Prime Minister was just defending himself." These callers also talked about the circumstances that preceded this event, saying that Chretien had reason to be anxious. These circumstances included a middle-of-the-night break-in at the Prime Minister's residence three months earlier, Yitzhak Rabin's assassination while walking through a crowd in Israel four months earlier, and about a year earlier the arrest of a woman as she attempted to enter a convention where the Prime Minister was about to speak. She had a crossbow.

Those supporting Chretien even blamed the protester. He was unemployed and protesting proposed cuts to unemployment insurance payments. Some callers said that instead of protesting he should have been out looking for work.

Even the press in Canada was split into two camps. The French press in Quebec focused on the brutality, and the English press in the other nine provinces focused on problems with the Prime Minister's security.

E) Evaluating the Performance of Participants

This chapter talks about evaluating workshops and training programs, not about evaluating individual workshop participants. It's necessary to grade *students*. That's how universities and professional organizations (e.g., management accountants) maintain their standards. But organizations rarely, if ever, grade individual participants in workshops. They're more concerned with employee behavior on the job (e.g. effective customer service) and organizational results (e.g., repeat business from customers) than with measuring and maintaining learning standards in company workshops. Besides, giving grades to individuals results in four particularly acute problems.

> ***The evaluator cannot maintain scientific objectivity; to imagine that one can do so is to pursue an unattainable Holy Grail.***
> ***- Egon Guba and Yvonna Lincoln***

First, participants tend to focus on getting the grade versus the quality of their learning. Thus, the focus of learning becomes quantitative versus qualitative in nature. Quantitative measures lead to shallow learning such as memorizing, driving qualitative, experiential, and natural learning into the background. Qualitative learning is now a by-product or a "nice to have." The *real* objective becomes getting good grades.

Is this going to be on the exam?

I've taught night classes at our local university and recall feeling frustrated when students would suddenly stop me and ask, "Is this on the exam?" Here I thought we were having this great discussion and they were only concerned with grades! But I was wrong to be frustrated. If you're going to grade individuals, accept that grades will become the primary focus for many participants. Grades are noticed. Employers, universities, and others pay attention to grades. What gets measured gets our attention.

This will definitely be on the exam!

Laurel McLean, a friend and colleague of mine, leads workshops inside organizations. Coming from her rather brassy sense of humor, she has turned *exam phobia* into a little "attention getting" statement. When she wants the group to pay particular attention to learning a given piece of information she exclaims, "This will definitely be on the exam!" Participants laugh. They know there isn't going to be a test. But, she says, they seem to pay closer attention for a while. Humor is almost always a great "attention getting" tool.

Second, evaluating individuals puts workshop leaders in a position of judging, grading, and approving. This interferes with being seen as a colleague, coach, and facilitator. The risk here is that you end up relating with participants through your role and authority rather than as the first among equals, as colleagues, and as members of the same team working toward a successful workshop.

Third, when participants are asked to compete for scarce resources called *grades*, the learning environment becomes more individual and competitive and less cooperative and communal. An ounce of competition drives a pound of cooperation away. Yet relationships, trust, and cooperation are essential ingredients in an effective learning climate. In Parker Palmer's words,

> *What scholars now say - and what good teachers have always known - is that real learning does not happen until students are brought into a relationship with the teacher, with each other, and with the subject.*[18]

The fourth critical problem with grading individual learning is that it puts participants under pressure, taking the fun out of learning. Participants learn substantially more when the process is enjoyable. ;

CONCLUSION

Summary

Why It's Necessary to Evaluate

On occasion evaluations are requested by the sponsor client and your reputation with that client hinges on the outcome. But even if an evaluation isn't requested, it's important that you receive organized information about the workshop and your leadership. The ongoing development of both the workshop and your leadership abilities is at stake.

What to Evaluate

You need to evaluate the workshop and your performance as the workshop leader. Both should be assessed based on explicit, specific, and agreed outcomes. These outcomes can be along four distinct levels of evaluation, 1) reaction, 2) learning, 3) behavior, or 4) results.

The Four Levels of Evaluation

With each successive level of evaluation, the information gained is more useful, but it also gets harder to determine cause/effect relationships. In addition, with each level the evaluation gets more complex, time consuming, and costly.

The first level looks at *reactions and feelings*. You're seeking opinions, usually from participants. This can be done verbally or with a simple evaluation form.

The second level concerns *learning*. Here you assess whether the training material has been understood and to what degree. For example, you might give participants a quiz to assess their understanding of key concepts.

The third level assesses *behavior* in the workshop and on the job. For instance, you might have participants demonstrate a task or skill in the workshop, or you might have participants' immediate supervisors evaluate participants behavior on the job, along specific parameters, both before and after the training program.

The fourth and most complex level measures *results*. It asks how the workshop or training program has benefited the organization. Results are often more associative than causal, but do provide a level of confidence when major decisions are needed around revising, cutting back, or expanding training in an organization.

Problems with Evaluation

Written or statistical evaluations are often sterile when compared to candid discussions with participants and sponsor clients. Written evaluations may suggest problems, whereas face-to-face discussions also generate solutions. In addition, each of the four levels of evaluation comes with its own set of problems. Level-4 results, in particular, are "all but impossible" to attribute back to a particular workshop. Finally, in a way, and for some workshops or training programs, evaluation is something of a "red herring." That is, some types of training are so obviously needed and so clearly of value (e.g., supervisory training) that evaluation is just for show. The decision to continue this training is never in question. Needless to say, that doesn't mean the evaluation can't be useful for improving the workshop.

The Leader's Role in Evaluation

You (the workshop or training-program leader) play a key role in helping to ensure that evaluations are open and direct. Distortions in gathering evaluation data can arise from the level of trust between you and the group and the manner in which you employ data-gathering techniques (e.g., what you say when you hand out level-1 evaluation forms). Distortions in interpreting evaluations can arise from what's at stake for you in how the workshop and your leadership is evaluated and how you're feeling about yourself and about the group. Finally, actions to help you remain "objective" when interpreting evaluations include allowing your interpretations to be challenged by others and comparing trends across a number of workshops and training programs.

Blaming and Client Bashing

It's important to look at yourself, your role, and your workshop design whenever you encounter problems or receive difficult workshop evaluations. This doesn't mean you don't share responsibility for workshops with participants, but only that, when something goes wrong, it's advisable to "look at yourself first." That's where you have the most ability to influence and make change happen. Although participants likely play a part in workshop problems, blaming them will only keep you stuck.

Attribution Theory

Attribution theory demonstrates the importance of having a high degree of trust and of being in rapport with the group. Participants give you the benefit of the doubt, laugh off mistakes, and share responsibility for problems if a strong rapport exists between you and the group. Without rapport, participants are more inclined to withhold support, blame you for mistakes, and doubt you, your methods, and your learning content.

Evaluating the Performance of Participants

This chapter is about evaluating a workshop or training program and its leadership. It is not about grading individual participants. Although sometimes required, grading participants has four unsavory side effects. First, participants tend to focus on the grade rather than on their learning. This leads to superficial learning such as memorization. Second, workshop leaders become judges versus colleagues, coaches, and facilitators. Third, the learning environment becomes more individual and competitive and less cooperative and communal. And finally, for many people grades take some, if not all, of the fun out of learning.

Checklist

What to Evaluate

- The workshop or training program
- Your leadership

The Four Levels of Evaluation

- Level-1, reaction
- Level-2, learning
- Level-3, behavior
- Level-4, results

Guidelines for Conducting Level-1 Evaluation

- Decide what information you're seeking
- Tailor the evaluation form
- Seek quantitative and qualitative information
- Make sure the form can be completed in five or ten minutes
- Ask participants to take at least five minutes when completing the form
- Encourage participants to complete the form honestly
- Ask participants to identify themselves on the form
- Consider collecting feedback one or two weeks after the workshop
- Develop a standard for each rating category for a given workshop
- Listen to the group's feedback and take decisive action

Guidelines for Conducting Levels 3 and 4 Evaluation

- Use before and after measurements and control groups
- Seek information about the work environment
- Survey or interview participants, their bosses, their subordinates, and others
- Protect individual identities when measuring group results

Critical Considerations Before Conducting Level 3 or 4 Evaluation

- Only specific tasks and skills can be tracked at levels 3 and 4
- Not all workshops can or should be tracked at levels 3 and 4
- Don't attempt to isolate the amount of contribution from a training program
- Before doing levels 3 or 4 evaluation
  - make sure you have a good working relationship with clients
  - ensure your clients care about these levels of structured assessment
  - have a clear and explicit purpose
  - ensure behaviors on the job have changed
  - ensure organizational results have improved
  - do a cost-benefit analysis

Guidelines for Conducting Level-2 Evaluation	*Problems with Evaluating Individuals*
• Assess attitudes, knowledge, and skills both before and after the workshop • Use an objective measure for assessing knowledge and attitudes • Use performance tests for assessing skills	• Participants focus on the grade versus the quality of their learning • Workshop leaders become judges versus colleagues, coaches, and facilitators • The learning environment becomes more individual and competitive and less cooperative and communal • Learning isn't as much fun *End*

Exercise

Using Evaluation Results to Make Improvements

Go over the evaluations from the last couple of workshops or training programs that you have led.

What two things does the group say you do particularly well?

What two areas are rated the lowest?

Write out two specific actions you will take to continue to build on your strengths and to overcome your lowest rated areas.

Notes

[1]John E. Jones heads up his own consulting practice, Organizational Universe Systems, San Diego, California.

[2] Kirkpatrick, D.L.(1975). Evaluating training programs. Washington, DC: American Society for Training and Development.

[3]Jones, J.E. (December, 1990). Don't smile about smile sheets. *Training & Development Journal.*

[4] The 80/20 rule is attributed to the economist, Vilfredo Pareto. It suggests a ratio of causes and consequences, for example, 80% of one's success comes from 20% of one's efforts; 80% of a workshop's problems come from 20% of participants or 20% of what the leader does. The 80/20 rule thus encourages working smarter and finding leverage in one's actions, that is, focusing on those vital few issues (the 20%) that will get you 80% of your success.

[5]Brickell, H.M. (1974). The influence of external political factors on the role and methodology of evaluation. A paper presented at the annual meeting of American Educational Research Association. Taken from Guba, E.G., & Lincoln, Y.S. (1987). Effective evaluation: Improving the usefulness of evaluation results through responsive and naturalistic approaches. San Francisco, CA: Jossey-Bass, p. 296.

[6]Situational leadership is described in: Hersey, P., & Blanchard, K.H. (1982). Management of organizational behavior. Englewood Cliffs, NJ: Prentice-Hall. Ken Blanchard's first two "one minute manager" books were, 1) Blanchard, K., & Johnson, S. (1982). The one minute manager. New York, NY: William Morrow. 2) Blanchard, K., & Lorber, R. (1984). Putting the one minute manager to work. New York, NY: William Morrow.

[7]Deming, W.E. (1982). Quality, productivity and competitive position. Cambridge, MA: MIT Press.

[8]Ackoff, R.L. (1981). Creating the corporate future. New York, NY: John Wiley & Sons.

[9] Some of these points have been inspired by an audiotape from: Robinson, J. & Gaines Robinson, D. (1987). Providing training. Training '86: HRD Masters. Minneapolis, MN: Lakewood Publications.

[10]Guba, E.G., & Lincoln, Y. S. (1987). Effective evaluation: Improving the usefulness of evaluation results through responsive and naturalistic approaches. San Francisco, CA: Jossey-Bass.

[11]Bateson, G. (1972). Steps to an ecology of mind. New York, NY: Ballantine. From Goldenberg, I., & Goldenberg, H. (1985). Family therapy: an overview (2nd ed.). Pacific Grove, CA: Brooks/Cole, p. 6.

[12]Hoffman, L. (1981). Foundations of family therapy. New York, NY: Basic Books. From Goldenberg, I., & Goldenberg, H. (1985). Family therapy: an overview (2nd ed.). Pacific Grove, CA: Brooks/Cole, p. 7.

[13]Guba, E.G., & Lincoln, Y.S. (1987). Effective evaluation: Improving the usefulness of evaluation results through responsive and naturalistic approaches. San Francisco, CA: Jossey-Bass, p. 294.

[14]Guba, E.G., & Lincoln, Y.S. (1987). Effective evaluation: Improving the usefulness of evaluation results through responsive and naturalistic approaches. San Francisco, CA: Jossey-Bass, p. 328.

[15]Argyris, C., & Schon, D.A. (1974). Theory in practice: Increasing professional effectiveness. San Francisco, CA: Jossey-Bass, p. 15.

[16]Lord, R.G., & Smith, J.E. (January, 1983). Theoretical, information processing and situational factors affecting attribution theory models of organizational behavior. *Academy of Management Review*, Vol. 8, pp. 50-60. Taken from: Schermerhorn, J.R., Hunt, J.G., & Osborn, R.N. (1988). Managing organizational behavior (3rd. ed.). New York, NY: John Wiley & Sons, p. 82.

[17]Scholtes, P. (1988). The team handbook: How to use teams to improve quality. Madison, WI: Joiner Associates, pp. 6-42.

[18]Palmer, P.J. (1993). To know as we are known: Education as a spiritual journey. San Francisco, CA: HarperCollins, p. xvi.

Chapter 5

Contracting Outcomes and Marketing Prior to Start-Up

Introduction

Contracting carries obligations and accountabilities. It involves gaining clarity and understanding and deciding and agreeing on who's doing what, why, and when in a workshop. Like positioning an aircraft on the runway, you need to line up straight for takeoff and coordinate with the tower on purpose, direction, and timing. But contracting is not just a time to clarify and agree on workshop outcomes; it's also a time to build rapport and trust with clients.

Contracting is fundamental to workshop and training-program success. If you don't contract with clients before the event begins, your ability to manage expectations, to target the workshop or training program to the most pressing needs of your clients, to develop clear and realistic outcome statements, and to prepare your design and materials is greatly reduced. Success then becomes a matter of "hit and miss" or lucky coincidence. More often than not, a negative workshop evaluation can be traced back to poor contracting.

This chapter provides detailed "how to" guidance for contracting before the workshop or training program begins, including:

- Deciding which client groups to contract with.
- How to contract with different client groups.
- Pre-workshop contracting with participants.
- Marketing with "one pagers."

Who You Need to Contract With

There are three clients you need to communicate with and have "on side" before the workshop or training program begins: the sponsor client, the administration or contact client, and end-user clients or participants. (If you're not familiar with these terms, and even if you are, they're described below.)

This section discusses contracting with

A) Sponsor, administrative, and end-user clients

B) Prisoners and vacationers (a subset of end-user clients)

C) Yourself

A) Sponsor, Administrative, and End-User Clients

First some definitions.

A *sponsor client* is the person or group of people responsible for sponsoring and approving the workshop or training program. The sponsor client gives the "go ahead" for the workshop or training program, pays the bills, and expects a return on the investment. Hopefully, your sponsor client will also be a champion for the workshop and the changes the workshop is aiming to support.[1]

An *administrative client* (sometimes called a *contact client*) looks after administrative arrangements. This person coordinates with participants, schedules meeting times, arranges for workshop facilities and equipment, and generally organizes what needs to be organized (e.g., refreshments, meals).

End-user clients are the workshop or training-program *participants*, the people who attend, participate, work hard, and learn during the workshop and then apply the workshop outcomes (e.g., decisions, programs, products, skills) on the job.

Sometimes your sponsor client is also your administrative client and also an end-user client or workshop participant. Other times these are three different people, perhaps even in different departments of an organization.

If participants are serious about their learning, they'll be looking for something specific from a workshop to fill a definite need. For example, they'll be wanting to develop a plan, to solve a problem, to design a system, to learn a procedure, or to get better at dealing with a specific issue or group of people. In addition to their contract with you (the workshop leader), participants will also have a contract with your and their sponsor client. This may be implicit or explicit, but participants will be expected to do something differently "on the job" as a result of the workshop or training program. The sponsor client will be looking for some sort of improvement resulting from changes that participants make on the job.

B) Prisoners and Vacationers - A Subset of End-User Clients

Two types of end-user clients spell potential trouble for workshop leaders. These are prisoners and vacationers. They come to workshops with "zero" or even negative expectations of learning and no thought of contributing. Fortunately, as today's organizations place more and more of an emphasis on training, both groups are seen less frequently in training rooms.

Prisoners are sent to workshops by their bosses to be "fixed." Naturally they resent this and are often a long way from being "learning ready." Unless you contract effectively with prisoners they will likely resist almost everything that goes on in the workshop. Don't take prisoners. If you find out before a workshop begins that someone is being "sent," talk with your sponsor or administrative client and try to avoid this situation.

Vacationers sign up for training programs just to get away from their job for a while. They come anticipating an easy time, and may be frustrated when you demand more than just passive learning. (Chapter eleven provides suggestions for dealing with prisoners and vacationers once the training program begins.)

We are all finite people with specific abilities, knowledge, experience, emotions, feelings, values, and expectations for ourselves and others. When we are unrealistic in our expectations for our performance, we set ourselves up for failure. Thus if you always aim too high you'll be disappointed by constantly failing. If you expect too little of yourself, however, your self esteem will suffer knowing that you could have done better.
- Samuel Cypert

C) Yourself (The Workshop Leader)

You need a contract with yourself to learn from your mistakes and to continuously develop and improve as a workshop leader. What do you expect to achieve personally by leading a given workshop? What do you expect to achieve professionally? What improvements do you want to make to the workshop or training program?

Given that striving for perfection is praiseworthy but futile, focus on improving just two specific things every time you lead a workshop or training program. These may have to do with your facilitation, preparation, or any aspect of your role as a leader. Examples are improving how you summarize and review at the end of each workshop session, how you bridge from one topic to another, or how you use open questions to expand and enrich dialogue in a group.

A story about multiple clients and breakdown

Several years ago I was doing a three day training program on problem solving and decision making with a senior technical group in the oil and gas industry. During the *start-up* I asked the group about their expectations and interests. The first comment was, "I don't want to be here." I remember saying to myself, "Oh oh, I hope this guy is the only resident *overaggressor.*" But the comments got worse after that, and, as it turned out, this first comment was the best I was going to get on this morning. Let me tell you what preceded this great start and how we later turned this training program into a workshop in order to make it work.

Prior to the workshop start-up, I had only contracted with the sponsor client. I hadn't met any of the training-program participants or "end-user clients." The sponsor client had been an absolute supporter. Indeed, he had shown unbridled enthusiasm for the training program and had talked about how important it was for the work his group was doing. He had even remarked that the training process that I had outlined seemed to fit perfectly with his group's style and method of working together. Looking back, I think I allowed his enthusiasm to lead me into a false sense of invulnerability. I think sometimes we ask fewer questions, make more assumptions, and do less "up front" work with those we deem to be *perfect* sponsor clients. This story confirms that the best sponsor clients can lead to the worst workshops and training programs. It also contradicts the myth that *if you get senior management to "buy in" everything will work as planned.*

After this rocky start, we soldiered through the first day, but it wasn't getting any better. I started day two with recontracting. As a result, we shifted gears and spent the next two days working leadership and team issues. Thus, a training program turned into a workshop. The group seemed satisfied in the end, but as I left the workshop room that last afternoon, I wondered how my perfect sponsor client was going to take this news!

Options available when a training program or workshop doesn't seem to be working

There are a number of variations but basically only three directions a workshop or training program can go following breakdown. You can,

1) continue on as best you can.
2) recontract with the group and change the focus.
3) end the training program or workshop with some agreed next steps.

Regardless of which of these options you and the group decide upon, it's important to "fess up" and discuss the breakdown openly and without blaming. Thus, you would start by admitting that the workshop isn't working. Give a couple of examples of what has occurred in the workshop so the group is clear about what you're seeing and why you feel this way. Next, ask a few open questions to get guidance from the group, for example, "What suggestions do you have at this point?" "How can we remedy this?" "What suggestions do you have for proceeding?"

Likely there will be differences in the group. You might even note these on a flipchart to keep suggestions visible and keep discussion moving. At some point you need to help the group decide on a course of action. First, outline the options clearly and get the group to agree on these options. Try to limit these to a reasonable number (e.g., three or four) for decision making. One option might include ending the workshop at this point and meeting with the workshop sponsor, as a group, to discuss next steps. Another option is continuing on, but with a new focus (e.g., leadership, goal setting). Second, clarify how the decision needs to be made, for example, by consensus, voting, unanimity, and so on.

Third, use the agree decision process and have the group select an option. Fourth, do what's necessary to implement the agreed option. The principle in all this is to "trust the group." They know what's needed most, what works, what they will support, and where their energy is for work. They need to make the decision and be committed to the result.

Who's the "real" client?

Sometimes the participants like the workshop, but your sponsor client (usually senior management) doesn't. Sometimes it's the other way around. Your job is to please both groups. No one said it would be easy!

The question, Who's the real client? is a trick question. Don't think in terms of *real* or primary and secondary clients. It's dysfunctional. They're all real! They're all important. You have to please your contact client (the person who recommended and introduced you into the organization), your administrative client (the person managing logistics and administrative issues such as communication and coordination with participants), your sponsor client (the person approving the workshop or training program and paying the bills), and your end-user clients (the workshop or training-program participants). Organizations are too complex to think in terms of pleasing just one or two types of clients and still being able to get the results you're looking for.

Sometimes, just to complicate things a little further, there's even a technical client. That's a person who gets to approve the process you're using and agree that it fits with other initiatives in the organization. Purchasing departments, for example, often play this role. You need to meet their standards or they reject the contract. Technical clients have the right of *disapproval*, even though they rarely have the right of *approval*. Internal training departments sometimes play the role of "technical client." That is, your workshop or training program must meet their standards, even though your sponsor client is in another part of the organization.

End

HOW TO CONTRACT WITH DIFFERENT CLIENTS

The first step in contracting is finding out what clients want. Second, compare this with what you're prepared to offer. Finally, form explicit, though not necessarily written, agreements with clients.

This section covers

A) Contracting with sponsor and administrative clients

B) Contracting with prisoners and vacationers

C) Contracting with participants

A) Contracting with Sponsor and Administrative Clients

If you don't take the time to communicate and contract properly with your sponsor and administrative clients, sooner or later you'll pay. This isn't a threat; it's a fact. With your sponsor client you'll pay in terms of poorly managed and unmet expectations. With your administrative client you'll pay in terms of coordination problems with participants or unsuitable facilities or equipment.

Your need to communicate and contract with sponsor and administrative clients will vary a lot depending on the industry you're working in and the policies of each particular organization. In some industries, "Oil & Gas" for example, a handshake is usually all that's required even though this is your first contract with a given client. In others, "Government" for example, even though you may be well known and have conducted many workshops within a given department, their procedures still require a formal proposal and written contract with all the standard escape clauses. After all, to use a phase from Osbome and Gaebler (1992), it's incumbent on public organizations to be able to demonstrate that they're "spending money wisely."[2] In order to satisfy audits, "wisely" is operationally defined to mean having pre-defined outcomes, roles, procedures, cancellation clauses, and so on. Thus the need for formal contracts.

Generally, however, contracting need not be particularly time consuming, complex, or onerous. Often it's as simple as a short meeting and a half page memo clarifying understanding, expectations, and agreement. And even when it's a formal contract with government, once you're used to how these contracts are written it's not a big deal to quickly review, sign, and have your signature witnessed.

Sometimes it's all too easy to give contracting with the sponsor client the short shift. Often sponsor clients even encourage this. They're busy people and just want you to get on with the workshop or training program. Don't fall into this trap. Meet with sponsor clients and ask them challenging questions to clarify purpose, outcomes, and roles. The process cycle is an excellent tool for this meeting.

Following are examples of the types of confirming memos and letters you might consider sending to your sponsor and administrative clients.

An Example of a Confirming Memo to Your Sponsor Client[3]

The key with this type of memo is to say just enough to cover your butt! (I hope you realize I'm only kidding.) Memos like the following don't have to be long winded and carefully researched. They only take a few minutes to write, and clients appreciate the clarity they provide. Also, if there has been a misunderstanding, a memo like the following should surface and help you clarify expectations. Finally, this type of memo confirms the "partnership" role of your sponsor client in the success of a workshop, along with the responsibilities for action and follow through.

- Internal Correspondence -

July 6, 1999

To: (Sponsor Client's name)

From: (Workshop Leader's name)

Re: Strategy Planning Workshop, August 27, 28, and 29, 1999

Thank you for this morning's meeting. Just to be sure I understand what we have agreed to, here are the major deliverables as I see them for this workshop.

Workshop Purpose

- Revisit, clarify, and revise the department's three year strategy

Expected Outcomes

- Consensus in the group that they have a common understanding of what *strategy making* and *strategic programming* are, how these are distinct, and how they are accomplished.
- A thorough review of current planning processes and results achieved.
- A good "first cut" at strategic programming for the department (i.e., articulating the strategy, elaborating substrategies, tying in goals developed at last May's planning meetings).

Page 1

- Internal Correspondence (continued) -

I will:

- Clear my schedule to make room for this workshop. If there are any difficulties, I will let you know by the end of the week.
- Spend two days gathering data about current planning processes in your department by interviewing several of your specialists and customers.
- Analyze the results of these interviews and compile a brief report with recommendations prior to August 8th.
- Advise Tom of my facilities and equipment requirements for the workshop.

You will:

- Notify the specialists and customers you want me to interview.
- Provide me with your department's current three year strategic plan.
- Get approvals for me to access data on your current planning processes and systems within your department.
- Be available for consultation if I run into any roadblocks that we haven't anticipated.

Tom will:

- Look after all administrative arrangements for both the workshop and the pre-meeting on August 8th, including coordinating with your staff about times, dates, places.

We'll meet again on August 8th, along with those who will be participating in this workshop, to review my interview findings and finalize the outcomes and agenda for this workshop. If I've missed any key points, or if you have any concerns about the above, please call me at extension 1070.

Page 2

An Example of a Confirming Letter to Your Administrative or Contact Client

You might use this example as a template for your confirming letters to "administrative clients." Delete or add information as necessary. For example, details not included in this example are cancellation notice and minimum and maximum number of participants.

March 14, 1999

Mr. (Administrative Client)
XYZ Company
119 11th Avenue S.W.
Boston, MA 03456

Dear (Administrative Client),

I wish to confirm your *Train the Trainer Workshop for Professionals* for:

Date:	Thursday and Friday, June 17 & 18, 1999
Time:	8:30 a.m. to 4:30 p.m.
Location:	31st Floor Training Rooms XYZ Company 110 4th Avenue
Workshop Leader:	Bruce Klatt

The following administration dates are suggested. Please let me know if these need to change.

- List of participant names to make up packages to me — May 25th
- Packages to your office for distribution — June 1st
- Participant questionnaires returned to me — June 11th

I ask that the XYZ Company supply the following:

- The workshop facility.
- Refreshments during breaks.
- Three flipcharts.
- An overhead projector and screen.
- Videotapes and equipment (for taping participant practice sessions).
- Workshop administration (e.g., internal coordination with participants).

Page 1

I will supply all workshop materials:

- Participant Workbooks
- Learning Style Inventories
- Pre-Workshop Participant Questionnaires

Enclosed is a diagram of the suggested room set-up. Please set the training room up in a U shape. Also, I'd like a large table in the front corner for training materials. I'd prefer a training room large enough for subgroups to work in the corners without disturbing each other. Alternatively, a smaller room with a couple of "break out" rooms would be fine.

The cost for this workshop is $5500.00. We also charge expenses when out of town.

If any of the above needs clarification or if additional information is needed, please call me at phone (403) 278-3821 or fax (403) 278-1403.

Yours truly,

Bruce Klatt

Page 2

Equipment and Room Set-Up

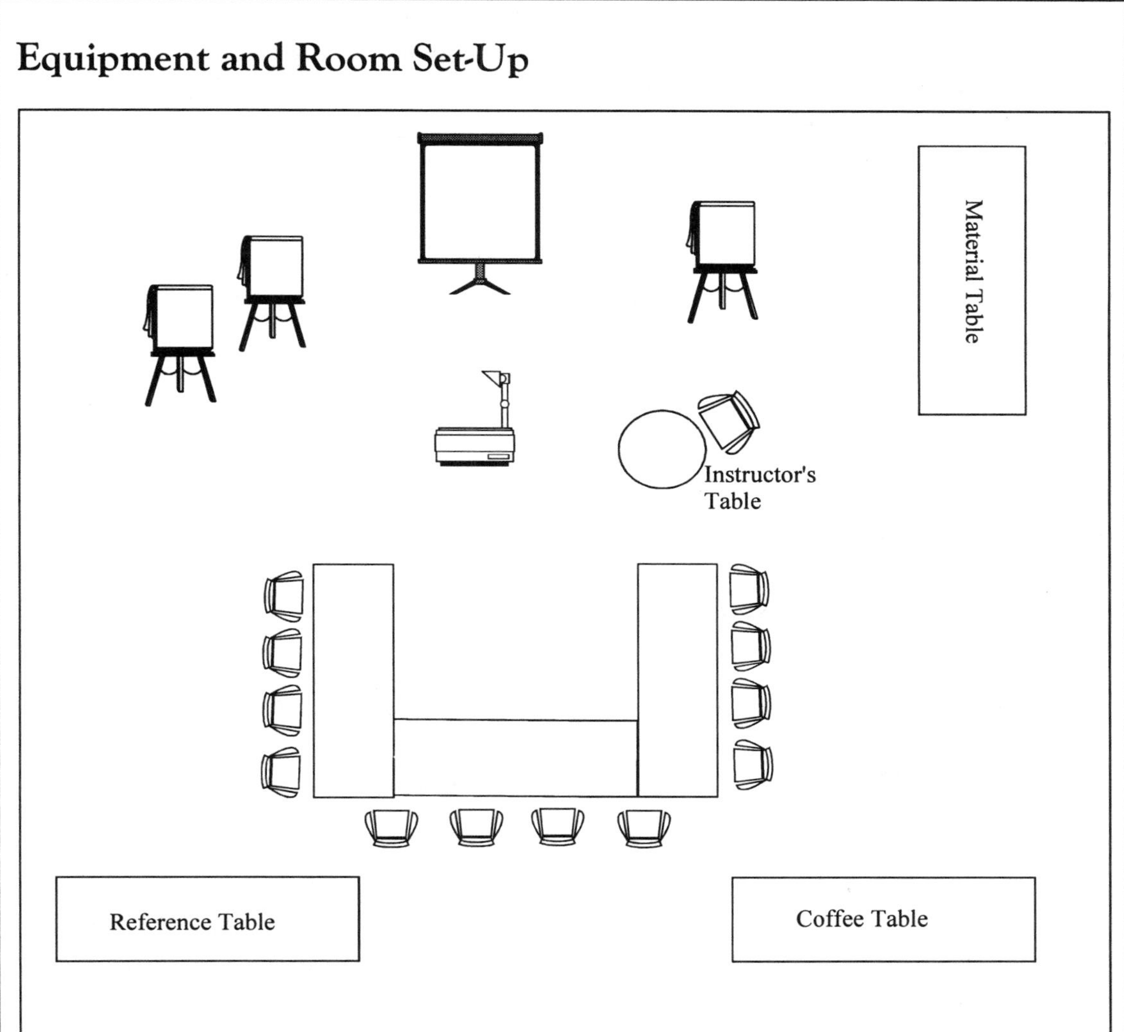

Room must be big enough for small groups of participants to meet in the corners without distracting each other.

Lots of wall space is required for hanging flipchart pages.

Page 3

B) Contracting with Participants (End-User Clients)

Contracting with participants is implied in the marketing materials you circulate encouraging people to "sign up." Your next opportunity to contract clear expectations with participants is during the pre-meeting, if there is one, or during the workshop start-up, if you don't hold a pre-meeting. The pre-meeting is discussed in the following section. Chapter eleven focuses on contracting with participants during the workshop start-up.

CONTRACTING WITH PARTICIPANTS DURING THE PRE-MEETING

If you have or can create the opportunity for a pre-meeting, do it. This meeting is invaluable. It allows you to communicate "face to face" with participants on several important aspects of the upcoming workshop or training program. In this way participants know what they're getting into, what's expected of them, and what they can expect from the workshop or training program.

A pre-meeting takes anywhere from one to two hours for a training program and two to four hours for a workshop. Pre-meetings for training programs take less time as *purpose* and *outcomes* are usually fairly well defined prior to pre-meeting. Usually, pre-meetings are held two or three weeks before a workshop or training program. This gives participants time to follow through on assignments and preparation agreed to at the pre-meeting.

A number of valuable, and even essential, steps can be taken a pre-meetings. These include:

- Introductions. Meeting participants and having participants meet each other.
- Constructing or reviewing workshop or training-program purpose and outcomes. (In some cases, a "first pass" of these may have already been developed with your sponsor client.)
- Discussing the benefits of the workshop or training program with participants.

- Developing and/or distributing pre-workshop assignments (e.g., reading, completing self-scoring inventories). Pre-workshop assignments represent participants' investment in the workshop. Stress the importance of these to workshop success.
- Distributing materials such as a pre-workshop questionnaire (example below), confirming letter to participants (example below), workbook, training-program overview, and suggested agenda.
- Gathering, discussing, and guiding participant expectations about the upcoming workshop or training program.
- Getting participants thinking about their learning needs before the workshop or training program begins.
- Reviewing administrative issues (e.g., start time, location).
- Setting the climate for the workshop or training program (e.g., involvement, hard work, informality, fun, challenge, risk taking).

Just by having a pre-meeting, you demonstrate to participants that you're organized and care about their interests and needs. This helps show that you're credible and authentic as a workshop leader and builds some early rapport between you and the group. Now, when you start the workshop or training program a couple of weeks later, having had a brief meeting with the group, you know names and a little about each participant. But what's even more important, you know exactly what the group expects because you've clarified *purpose* and *outcomes* at the pre-meeting.

Review and personalize the benefits of the workshop at the pre-meeting. Don't take it for granted that participants are fully aware of these benefits. Talk about the value previous groups have received from the training program or similar workshops and talk with people very specifically about why they want to attend, what they hope to learn and achieve, and how specifically the workshop or training program will be of value to them.

One way of getting participants thinking about what they would like to learn at an upcoming training program is by having them complete a pre-workshop questionnaire. It doesn't have to be elegant, just four or five questions asking about related experience and how they see themselves using new learning from the training program (see example below). Ask participants to return their completed questionnaires about a week before the workshop. Then analyze and organize their comments and present these back to the group during the workshop start-up. (An important note about pre-workshop assignments: Any pre-work you assign needs to be covered in the workshop. Participants resent it when they're asked to do something ahead of time, such as reading or completing a questionnaire, and then little or no attention is paid to this work during the workshop.)

In some cases a face-to-face meeting with participants prior to a workshop or training program just isn't possible. Nonetheless, you must do something to ensure that participants know about the purpose of the workshop and the benefits of participating. And you want to make sure they don't attend with false or unrealistic expectations. The easy way is to circulate an overview prior to the workshop or training program, outlining how participants will benefit, who should attend, what they will learn, and some logistical issues. In addition, regardless of whether you have a pre-meeting with participants or not, these issues need to be revisited, contracted, and confirmed during the workshop start-up.

An Example of a Confirming Letter to Workshop Participants

This letter would either be mailed to participants a few weeks before the workshop or handed out and discussed during the pre-meeting.

May 21, 1999

XYZ Company
P.O. Box 1000, Station M
Los Angeles, CA 0087067

Dear (Participant's Name):

Re: Train the Trainer Workshop for Professionals

This workshop is scheduled for:

Date:	Thursday and Friday, June 17 & 18, 1999
Time:	8:30 a.m. to 4:30 p.m.
Location:	31st Floor Training Rooms XYZ Company 111 5th Avenue S.W., Calgary
Dress:	Casual
Workshop Leader:	Bruce Klatt

==========================

This workshop requires approximately six hours pre-work. Please read below.

==========================

Welcome to the workshop! We have high expectations of assisting you to learn the models and skills necessary for helping others learn. This workshop is designed specifically to help professionals in organizations teach some aspect of their technical or administrative "know how."

Please do the following to prepare for this workshop:

1) Review the workbook in some detail and develop three questions or issues requiring clarification.
(Time estimate: two hours +.)

Read through most parts; skim others. Jump around from chapter to chapter and section to section. Get a good feel for the workbook, its contents, and how it's laid out. Highlight and mark it as you see fit; it's yours. Make a few notes about things from the workbook that you want to clarify or discuss at the workshop and write out at least three questions or issues for clarification. Bring this workbook and your questions with you to the workshop.

Page 1

2) Read and complete the Learning Style Inventory.
(Time estimate: one hour.)

Please read and complete this inventory and bring it with you to the workshop. Come prepared to discuss your results.

3) Complete and return the Participant Questionnaire.
(Time estimate: fifteen minutes.)

Complete and return this questionnaire by June 11th. More directions are provided on the questionnaire.

4) Dream a little about the training programs you will be leading.
(Time estimate: fifteen minutes during REM sleep!)

Just think a little and in general terms about the types of training you expect to be delivering within Company XYZ. No need to write any of this down.

5) Plan for two hours of take-home work the first evening of the workshop.

Your second practice session is on day two of the workshop and you need this first evening to prepare.

I look forward to working with you at the workshop. If you have any questions, don't hesitate to call me at phone (403) 278-3821. My fax number is (403) 278-1403.

Yours truly,

Bruce Klatt

Page 2

An Example of a Pre-Workshop Participant Questionnaire

Use the example of a "pre-workshop participant questionnaire" on pages 168-169 as a template for your own pre-workshop questionnaires. Information is gathered on participants' backgrounds, relevant experience, and specific training interests and concerns. Ask participants to complete a pre-workshop questionnaire and return it to you at least one week before the training program. (This particular example is from a training program titled *Train the Trainer Workshop for Professionals*.)

There are at least five reasons why you should use a pre-workshop questionnaire. First, it gets participants thinking about their training needs, interests, and goals. Second, it provides you with valuable information for tailoring the workshop. Third, it aids contracting and allows a faster workshop start-up. Fourth, this information helps you avoid making faulty assumptions about participant needs. Going into the workshop you'll already have a pretty good idea of what the group wants emphasized. Fifth, adult learners need to know that their experience and skills are recognized and that they're not being treated like "blank slates." To this end, prepare a flipchart summary of the key information from these questionnaires and review this with the group during start-up. This gives all participants a clear understanding of the group's training needs and interests.

Train the Trainer Workshop for Professionals

Pre-Workshop Participant Questionnaire

Your Name: ______________________________

Your Organization: ______________________________

Purpose of the Workshop

The *Train the Trainer Workshop for Professionals* is designed to help you improve your skills and confidence as a workshop and training-program leader.

Purpose of This Questionnaire

This questionnaire is designed to help target the content of the workshop to your specific needs as participants.

Instructions

Please complete the questionnaire and return it by *June 4th* to:

Bruce Klatt & Colleagues
119 Lake Mead Drive S.E.
Calgary, Alberta
T2J 4B2

Note: If you need any clarification on this questionnaire, how it will be used, or on any other matter related to the upcoming workshop, please do not hesitate to call me. My office phone is (403) 278-3821. My fax number is (403) 278-1403.

Page 1

1. Briefly describe your experience leading training programs.

2. List two or three specific outcomes you want from this workshop.

3. Summarize two or three strengths you presently have as a training-program leader.

4. List two or three areas you most want to improve as a training-program leader.

5. Describe a training situation you would most like to improve after this workshop.

6. Note any further comments, requests, or ideas your have for this workshop.

Page 2

MARKETING TRAINING PROGRAMS WITH "ONE PAGERS"

It's not enough to have a great training program; you want people to know about it, to feel it would be valuable for themselves or their employees, and to attend. Sometimes it's difficult reaching the right people with your marketing. *You need people to want what they need.* That is, you first need people to be aware of their learning needs. Second, you need them to want to learn, and of course third, you want them to attend your training program to do this learning.

While "word of mouth," particularly participant endorsements, is the best method of marketing a training program, marketing materials are also helpful. Often prospective participants want something to look at, something that gives them an overview of the training program and tells them "why" they should attend. Yet, people don't read long-winded marketing materials, so keep them to a page or less. That's where "one pagers" come in.

Below are two examples of "one pagers" - a training-program overview and a marketing circular. Both examples are from a *Train the Trainer Workshop* that I lead. It's based on the material in this book.

Example of a One Page Training-Program Overview

Remember the real estate agents' old maxim about buying a house. "The three most important things are location, location, and location." Well, it's something like that with marketing a training program. The three most important features are telling potential participants about the benefits, the benefits, and the benefits. You've got to tune into people's favorite radio station "WII - FM" (What's in it - for me?).

Notice on the following example that the first section is "How You Will Benefit" and the third section is "What You Will Learn." Both focus on benefits to participants. The only other two messages on this "one pager" are *who* should attend and *logistics*. Getting the right people, and the right mix of people in the training room, is of no small consequence. Participants often learn as much from each other as they do from the training materials and from you (the training-program leader).

TRAIN THE TRAINER WORKSHOP FOR PROFESSIONALS[4]

How You Will Benefit

Technical and administrative professionals are facing increasing demands to develop others within their companies. This workshop will give you skills in helping others learn your technical or administrative expertise, confidence as a workshop leader, and provide you with a comprehensive array of tools including:

- Models of workshop leader success, adult-learning principles, and change in organizations.
- Strategies for planning, designing, and organizing workshops and training programs.
- Hands-on experience leading workshop sessions.
- Feedback on your workshop and training delivery practices.
- A comprehensive workbook for your ongoing reference.

Who Should Attend

Professionals who will be leading workshops and training programs within their area of expertise and who will be helping others learn and apply new skills within their Companies.

What You Will Learn

- *Planning Training*: Assessing training needs, planning training process using adult-learning principles, writing outcome statements, and training evaluation and follow up.
- *Designing Training*: Designing training using Kolb's four learning styles and over forty design options.
- *Organizing Training*: Organizing for a workshop, writing an agenda, preparing materials, and communicating with your sponsor and end-user clients before the training program begins.
- *Delivering Training*: Creating a positive learning climate, managing participation, presentation and demonstration techniques, facilitation and questioning skills, managing workshop time, dealing with resistance, and most importantly, each participant will have two "practice delivery sessions," with feedback, during this two day workshop.

Logistics

Duration:	Two days.
Group Size:	Six to twelve participants.
Pre-Workshop Assignment:	Four hours. Reading, thinking, and completing two questionnaires.
Day 1 Evening Assignment:	Two to three hours. Preparation for practice delivery on day two.

An Example of a One Page Marketing Circular

This "one pager" anticipates and responds to questions potential participants may be asking themselves about a training program.

TRAIN THE TRAINER WORKSHOP[5]

I was amazed to find out how many different ways I could be presenting information in my sessions - and the workbook is a great resource. - Business Analyst

Training issues	*Participants will learn*
How do I improve my training and delivery skills?	• New methods of designing and delivering workshops and training programs. • Your personal strengths as a workshop leader and areas for improvement.
How do I keep people interested through the whole training program?	• Methods of designing, planning, and delivering workshops to keep participants involved, stimulated, and learning.
How do I deliver training that is effective?	• How to assess training needs and set learning outcomes. • How to plan for learning readiness. • Surfacing and dealing with resistance to learning. • How to check for the effectiveness of training through different methods and levels of evaluation.
What are the personal benefits of attending this workshop?	• Skills that are transferable to supervising, leading, presenting, facilitating, and planning. • Strengthen and refine existing skills. • How to identify and act on areas for improvement. • How to ask for and receive value-adding feedback to ensure continuous improvement.

Training issues	*Participants will learn*
What benefits does my organization get from holding this workshop?	• How to design and deliver in-house training programs that are tailored specifically to the organization's needs. • How to create the conditions for maximum learning. • How to use the workbook to streamline planning time. *End*

Ensure Your Marketing Materials Look "Professional"

Finally, a little sermonette about the quality of your marketing materials. You might compare these to a job application or resume. Often they are a potential client's introduction to you and your training program. You need to make a good "first impression." Write these in the active voice and pay attention to spelling, grammar, make sure copies are of a good quality, and so on. This seems obvious but you'd be amazed at some of the marketing and promotion materials that get circulated.

CONCLUSION

Summary

Contracting lays the groundwork for the workshop by clarifying roles, responsibilities, process, and most importantly, the workshop's purpose, outcomes, and content. There's no better guarantee of workshop success than having all stakeholders agree on what they're trying to learn and accomplish, what's expected of each of them, and what others have agreed to do and be accountable for, before, during, and after the workshop.

Clients You Need to Contract With

There are six different clients (including yourself as your own client) that you need to contract with.

1) Your sponsor client is the person who foots the bills and expects a return on his/her investment.

2) Your administrative client coordinates and administers the workshop.

3) End-user clients are those who will be participating in the workshop or training program.

4) Prisoners who are being sent to the workshop or training program to be "fixed."

5) Vacationers who intend to attend the workshop or training program to get "time off" from their jobs.

6) Yourself, the workshop leader. (Contract with yourself to continuously improve your workshop delivery, develop your leadership skills, develop your workshop design, and achieve a higher level of success with each workshop you conduct.)

How to Contract with Different Types of Clients

Contracting with sponsor and administrative clients usually involves little more than a brief meeting (an hour or two at the most), informal conversation, and a brief memo or letter.

Next, find out what potential participants expect from and are prepared to offer the workshop and then let them know what you are and aren't offering. Avoid taking prisoners, and if necessary, remind your sponsor client that people can't be forced to learn. If you have no choice but to accept prisoners into the workshop, let them know that while sympathizing with their situation, they have the same responsibilities as all other participants. Be firm with vacationers; they chose to attend. Expect them to participate actively.

Pre-Workshop Contracting with Participants

Establish yourself with the group by showing that you're competent, credible, authentic, and care about their learning. Review the benefits of the workshop or training program and involve participants in planning outcomes. Clarify administrative and logistical issues. Overall, aim for a shared responsibility in the upcoming workshop and have participants leave the pre-meeting eager for the workshop to begin.

Marketing with "One Pagers"

One page training-program overviews are no substitute for "word of mouth" marketing, but they're an additional support. They provide prospective participants with a synopsis of the training program and extol its benefits. In addition, you might consider distributing a "one page" marketing circular that anticipates and answers questions participants may have about the training program. Focus on the benefits to participants.

Checklist

Who You Need to Contract With	*One Page Training-Program Overview*
• Sponsor client • Administrative client • End-user clients • Yourself (the workshop leader) • Prisoners • Vacationers *The Pre-Meeting* • Introductions • Review/develop purpose, outcomes, benefits • Pass out materials • Discuss pre-workshop assignments • Gather, discuss, and guide participant expectations • Get participants thinking about their learning needs • Review administrative issues • Set the climate for the upcoming workshop or training program	• Workshop title • How you will benefit • Who should attend • What you will learn • Logistics

Exercise

Contracting Purpose and Outcomes with Clients

How well do you contract with clients prior to the workshop or training-program start-up?

What prevents you from doing better?

If you were given the time and resources, what two specific steps would you take to improve your contracting with sponsor and end-user clients?

Is there any way you could do this contracting with your present resources? If so, how?

Notes

[1]The term "champion," as in "change champion," is in common use in business and management books today. Championing change (e.g., a given program, a given approach) connotes speaking out for, defending, advocating, supporting, and so on. When the term "change champion" is used to refer to a senior manager in an organization, it also connotes a willingness to use his or her power and authority to ensure organizational supports are in place, and that organizational barriers are removed, to a given change process or program.

[2]Osbome, D., & Gaebler, T. (1992). Reinventing government: How the entrepreneurial spirit is transforming the public sector. Toronto, Ont: Plume.

[3]I would like to thank Murray Hiebert, a friend and colleague, for providing me with an example of a confirming memo to a sponsor client.

[4]I would like to thank Laurel McLean, Calgary, Alberta, Canada, for writing this "one page" marketing handout.

[5]I would like to thank Nadine Ryan-Bannerman, Calgary, Alberta, Canada, for writing this "one page" marketing handout.

Part 3

Getting the Workshop Ready: Planning to Achieve

Chapter 6

Designing a Workshop

INTRODUCTION

You're familiar with Lego, right? Those plastic building blocks that magically attract children and vacuum cleaners! As a toddler, my son Jeff could do anything with Legos. He was that creative and patient sort of kid that worked for hours constructing magnificent structures of spacecrafts, motor boats, and houses. Like Legos, workshop design options come in different shapes and sizes, but they must also fit together for a common purpose (e.g., to solve a problem, to learn a process). Just as you're constrained by the Legos available for the job, you're constrained by group size, facilities, time, and other resources when designing a workshop or training program. And just as a well-constructed Lego spacecraft, with a mix of creative options and colors, can open the eyes of any toddler, a well-constructed workshop or training program, using a variety of designs, will appeal to almost any workshop participant.

Now that you're clear on purpose and outcomes, it's time to design the workshop or training program. Below are forty-seven design options (Legos for workshop and training-program leaders). Don't be intimidated by the variety. You can usually use a dozen or more of these in every workshop or training program.

An organizing framework, based on Kolb's learning styles, is provided to help you select designs. Become proficient at mixing, matching, and adapting these designs because you'll need to do this often as group mix, workshop focus, and other circumstances change.

Finally, once you've settled on workshop design, it's time to draft an agenda. This chapter ends with suggestions for doing this in a way that communicates clearly, yet frees you from rigid timelines and from becoming "process bound" (i.e., becoming restricted to a given process, method, or activity).

This chapter covers

- Design is the leader's job.
- Design strategies.
- Design options sorted by learning style.

- Interpreting design options.
- Design options.
- Putting design options to work - An example.
- The workshop or training-program agendas.

Training should generally be designed so as to approximate as closely as possible the conditions under which what is being learned ... will be put to use.
- Roger Smith

DESIGN IS THE LEADER'S JOB

Participants need to be involved in contracting outcomes and process (i.e., how they work together); however, it would be unusual to involve them in a significant portion of designing a workshop or training program. Roger Smith (1982) puts this succinctly as follows

> *One trusted axiom of adult educators – "Involve the participant in the planning process" - is best forgotten when designing training activities. Training design is an exception. In this instance, the planning process is sufficiently complex - involving learning about learning - to preclude much useful input from the participant. ...The main reason participants should not be involved in training design is that few if any will feel at home with the kind of multilevel diagnosis that is usually required.* [1]

"Learning about learning" in the above quote refers to the need to understand "how" people learn, and not just "what" it is they need to, or are expected to, learn. Few participants would have knowledge in areas such as adult learning, double-loop learning, or training-program evaluation (e.g., few would read this or related books). Therefore, few would be able to help much with workshop or training-program design. By all means seek input from interested participants, sponsor clients, and other workshop leaders, but, in the final analysis, you are accountable for the success of your workshop or training-program design.

WORKSHOP AND TRAINING-PROGRAM DESIGN STRATEGIES

Keep the following strategies in mind as you select from the workshop design options provided in this chapter. These strategies are consistent with the adult-learning principles discussed in chapter two.

1) Keep Participants Involved and Active

Provide lots of opportunity for participants to express themselves, work together, and to be *active*. Use small group work frequently and inform participants what's going to happen next, how, and why.

2) Use Stories and Examples

Use relevant stories, examples, case studies, and metaphors. Sharing your own stories, and having participants' share their stories, is key to motivating the group. It helps to make complex concepts understandable by providing context and demonstrating value.

> ***There is at least as much satisfaction to be derived from the pursuit of solutions and ends as there is in attaining them.***
> ***- Russell Ackoff***

3) Employ All the Senses to Make Maximum Impact on Participants

Get participants using all their senses (e.g., hearing, seeing, touching). For example, don't just talk to participants about using new innovations in computer hardware. Show them diagrams, and let them handle and examine a piece of hardware. Passing around a new mouse for a computer, a valve from a pipeline, or a switching device from a robot involves participants, gets them asking questions, and makes for a more memorable learning experience.

4) Let Participants Collaborate and Share Information

Encourage and support interdependence among participants. Cooperation between students in grade school is called "cheating," but in adult education, cooperation is an important learning strategy. Minimize or eliminate competition among participants when you want them to learn and work interdependently. Human nature being what it is, an ounce of competition drives away a ton of cooperation.

5) Challenge and Support Participants

Ensure participants are successful and supported as well as challenged, especially when doing exercises or answering questions. Challenging participants is a balancing act; the more support you provide, the more challenge they are open to accepting. Too little challenge, and participants won't learn at a significant level. Too much and they burn out, switch off, blow up, or leave. Constantly monitor, adjust, and balance the level of challenge and support in the group to achieve an optimal level of "creative tension."

6) Keep the Structure Informal

Allow participants to call breaks, to stretch, and to move around as they please. Don't force them to sit there dreaming of recess! People are more creative and visionary when the structure is informal. Call "minibreaks" frequently (e.g., five minute breaks every hour). This gives people time to go to the washroom. We're not nearly as visionary when we need to pee!

7) Let Things Unfold

This strategy is especially directed at experienced workshop leaders. Those new to leading workshops will feel very uncomfortable with the level of ambiguity recommended here. Nonetheless, the following is "food for thought" for inexperienced workshop leaders.

Have some structure to start, but don't panic if this structure needs to change or if things get bogged down or derailed temporarily. Multiple and changing structures are characteristic of highly effective workshops. Sometimes the best answer is to let the group struggle for a while. In Harrison Owen's (1991) words, "structure happens."[2] When purpose and outcomes are clear, and the group is learning ready and focused, structure just happens as a natural expression of the group's needs and interests.

> *There is more to life than increasing its speed.*
> *- Mahatma Gandhi*

When structure doesn't happen, don't keep fussing with it. Go back to workshop purpose and outcomes first, or learning readiness second. Thus, as long as purpose and outcomes are clear, and the group is learning ready, sooner or later and with a little help from you (the workshop leader), participants self-organize to get what they want from a workshop.

8) Build Flexibility into the Agenda

Don't design the workshop agenda so tightly that you can't adjust for unforeseen circumstances or spend extra time on marginal or contradictory opinions. Allow for adjustment and adaptation. For example, often participants get highly involved in a discussion or activity, and you just know it is valuable. Now is not the time to say, "Sorry, but our schedule dictates we move on!" Rather, encourage and support their energy. Build on their input without dominating the discussion and recognize their contributions, summarizing and redirecting their questions as necessary.

Only a flexible schedule that works toward meaningful outcomes, rather than toward a timetable of activities, allows you to take advantage of these special learning and sharing moments.

9) Build Free Time into the Workshop Schedule

> *The world is ruled by letting things take their course.*
> *It cannot be ruled by interfering.*
> *- Lao Tsu*

Often it's the "open spaces" in workshops (e.g., the coffee breaks, lunch breaks, evening time together) that provide significant moments for people. A friend of mine says, tongue in cheek, that "workshops are stimulating conversations interrupted occasionally by leader led activity." So in addition to having a flexible agenda, build in ample free time, that is, time away from the meeting or training room. Participants need time to discuss the workshop casually.

Participants often use free time to compare learning, swap stories, discuss their role in the workshop, and discuss how new learning applies to their work. As a result, free time or social time often generates valuable insights, questions, stories, suggestions, analogies, and challenges that reinforce learning and add value to the next session of the workshop.

Finally, learning is exciting, but it's also tiring. People need time away just to relax, reflect, and recharge their batteries between sessions. In addition, free time is valuable for relationship building among participants. Often people share more of themselves during free time at workshops as they're away from their day to day pressures and their "taken for granted" work roles.

10) A Workshop Design Strategy to Avoid - Traditional Teaching

Traditional teaching or pedagogy was introduced in chapter two. Avoid this approach with adults. Contrast the leader or teacher centered assumptions underlying traditional teaching with the learner or participant centered assumptions underlying "adult learning" (the approach presented throughout this book). In the latter, a workshop leader does not begin until participants are learning ready. The message in the participant centered or adult-learning approach is simple. Design your workshops for participants, not for the leader (i.e., for participants' learning needs and learning styles). Do things to involve participants in a way that gets them excited and eager for learning. For example, involve them in diagnosing their own learning needs and in formulating learning outcomes. And although it's usually not possible to involve participants in the workshop design, at least try to put yourself in their place and develop a workshop that would inspire you to attend, participate, and learn.

DESIGN OPTIONS SORTED BY LEARNING STYLE

Accommodator (feeling and doing)	*Diverger (feeling and watching)*
• Appreciative inquiry • Behavior modeling • Coaching • Debate • Demonstration (being involved in) • Dialogue • Forum (asking questions) • Game • Open space technology • Panel (being on the panel) • Peer-assisted learning • Practice exercise • Question and answer • Role playing • Sensitivity training • Simulation • Skit • Story telling (telling a story) • Subgroups • Teleconferencing	• Demonstration (watching) • Field trip • Guided imagery • Panel (listening to a panel) • Story telling (listening to a story)
Converger (thinking and doing)	*Assimilator (thinking and watching)*
• Case study • Clinic • Discussion • Drill • In basket • Instruments • Job instruction training • Marathon • Programmed instruction • Project • Vestibule training	• Brainstorming • Contrasting perspectives • Forum (listening) • Lecture • Listening team • Matrix analysis • Mind mapping • Nominal group technique • Polarity • Quiz • Reading • Reflection • Story boarding • Study guide

Kolb's learning styles, discussed earlier, are used here as an organizing tool for the design options outlined in this chapter. Naturally you'll need to consider what resources are available when selecting design options (e.g., time, equipment, facilities, expertise). The key, however, is to select designs to suit your workshop purpose and outcomes, a variety of participant learning styles, and your personal leadership style (in that order). And beware of your learning-style bias. Take care not to overuse methods that match your style while underusing other learning styles. (*Note*: An example showing how design options can be put to work in designing a workshop or training program is provided near the end of this chapter. See the section titled, "Putting Design Options to Work - An Example.")

In chapter two it was noted that both natural and deep learning can involve accessing two, three, or all four learning styles at once. And indeed, many of the design options described below fit into two, three, or even all four learning styles. Nonetheless, with only a few exceptions, design options are sorted here into only one learning style. While this "sort" is accurate for some design options, for others it's only a "best fit." However, the result is a practical tool that leaders can use to guide their selection of design options as they develop their workshops and training programs.

INTERPRETING DESIGN OPTIONS

Design options are listed alphabetically and quite a bit of detail is provided with each. However, these are set out so that you only have to refer to this detail "if and when" needed. Even then, it's only a guideline.

Referring to the template on the following page, the box on the right has the important information, in particular, the first two categories *activity* and *use*. As you design a workshop or training program, use this information to make your "first pass" at selecting design options. Next, use the information from the box on the left to help check your picks and to ensure you're accessing all four learning styles in your workshop or training program.

Design Option Template - Interpretation Guide

Use this template to interpret the information provided for the forty-seven design options listed below.

Name of Design Option (Example - Role Playing)	
Relevance • Whether this design applies to training programs, workshops, or both. (Example - Workshops) ***Learning Style*** • Learning style this activity most appeals to. (Example - Converger) ***Administrative*** • ***Technical*** • ***Interpersonal*** • A guess at appropriateness of this design to these types of work and learning. (Example - Medium) ***Participant Risk*** • Estimate of the degree of risk participants might perceive. (Example - Low) ***Group Size*** • ***Subgroup Size*** • Group and subgroup size appropriate for this design. A best guess needs to be interpreted flexibly. (Example - 15 to 20) ***Contrast With*** Related or similar designs. (Example - Role Play, Behavior Modeling) ***Preparation*** What you need to do to prepare the group to succeed at this activity. (Example – Assign a facilitator) ***Other Requirements*** Time, space, and equipment requirements. (Example - 2 hours)	***Activity*** What participants will be doing Example • Each participant tells a story relevant to the topic, subject, theme, or issue in discussion. ***Use*** Why you might use this activity. What you are aiming to accomplish. Example • Exploring an issue ***Special or Critical Considerations*** Necessary conditions for this activity to be of value. Example • Problem must be clearly stated. ***Advantages*** The benefits, or the "upside," of this activity. Example • Linear thinkers favor this approach as it structures issues and reduces complexity. ***Disadvantages*** Drawbacks, or the "downside," of this activity. Example • Easily faked. ***Example*** An example of use in a workshop or training program. • A group of managers identifies communication concerns in their company and self-organize to simultaneously work solutions around a number of these issues.

Appreciative Inquiry[3]

Relevance
- Workshops
- Training Programs

Learning Style
- Accommodator (feeling/doing)

Administrative	• Medium
Technical	• Medium
Interpersonal	• High
Participant Risk	• Low
Group Size	• Any size
Subgroup Size	• 2 – 7

Contrast With
- Question and Answer
- Dialogue
- Brainstorming

Preparation
- Set workshop climate for seeking "the positive" rather than finding fault.
- Demonstrate the technique using a volunteer from the group.

Other Requirements

Time: 1 to 2 hours.
Space: Room for subgroups to talk without interrupting each other.
Equipment: A flipchart for each subgroup, markers, masking tape.

Activity
- Participants interview each other one on one or in small groups.
- Alternatively, this approach can be used by you to draw information from individual participants or from the group as a whole.
- A step up from "problem solving." The focus is on what's going well (e.g., looking for and valuing small pockets of success).

Use
- To develop a "possibility blueprint" (i.e., to decide what *might*, *should*, and *will* be).
- To gain new perspectives.
- To provide approval and resources.
- To remove roadblocks.

Comparing Problem Solving and Appreciative Inquiry

Problem Solving	*Appreciative Inquiry*
• gather information	• gather and value insight
• detached, objective, analyze causes	• involved, empathetic, factor in multiple inputs
• monitor other person's emotional response	• monitor own and other's emotional response
• rational, stay with facts, analyze options	• intuitive, imagination, consider values/feelings
• search for truth, plan action	• search for energy, envision possibilities

Advantages
- Surfaces the positives.
- Creates a climate of mutual inquiry (e.g., supports, energizes, encourages, provides recognition).
- Builds commitment and relationships.
- Overcomes problems with the problem solving approach where time is spent focusing on what's *not* working and when the only time people search for improvements is when a problem is defined.

Disadvantage
- Exclusive focus on the positive may miss developing a full understanding of problems or obstacles.

Examples
- Developing a list of accomplishments.
- Evaluating a project and planning improvements.

Behavior Modeling

Relevance
- Training Programs

Learning Style
- Accommodator (feeling/doing)

Administrative	• Medium
Technical	• Low
Interpersonal	• High
Participant Risk	• Medium
Group Size	• 12 - 25
Subgroup Size	• 2 - 4

Contrast With
- Role playing
- Practice exercise

Preparation
- Steps, demonstration, and materials prepared.

Other Requirements

Time: 1 hour +.
Space: Room for subgroups to practice.
Equipment: As required for the demonstration (e.g., TV and VCR).

Activity
- Participants practice a skill using a four step method.
  Step 1: Participants are shown the steps.
  Step 2: Effective behavior is demonstrated (live or on video).
  Step 3: Participants practice using the steps.
  Step 4: Participants are given feedback on their practice.

Use
- Teaching a specific skill.

Advantages
- The exercise is experiential.
- Simple, clear steps are provided.
- Feedback is immediate.

Disadvantages
- People resist role playing, at least initially.
- Participants may not fully understand the theory being applied.
- The steps oversimplify reality.
- Little attention is paid to participants' attitudes.

Example
- Teaching front line supervisory skills (e.g., giving feedback).

Brainstorming[4]

Relevance
- Training Programs
- Workshops

Learning Style
- Assimilator (thinking/watching)

Administrative	• High
Technical	• High
Interpersonal	• High
Participant Risk	• Low
Group Size	• Any size
Subgroup Size	• 2 - 7

Contrast With
- Dialogue
- Nominal group technique

Preparation
- Agree on a clear problem statement.
- Review the guidelines for brainstorming, emphasizing no evaluation on the first pass.
- Each subgroup will need to appoint a facilitator.

Other Requirements

Time: 15 to 30 minutes is usually enough time

Space: a large room or separate rooms so subgroups don't disturb each other

Equipment: a flipchart for each subgroup, markers, masking tape, pads of sticky notes (e.g., Post-its)

Activity
- Participants generate creative ideas ranging from the obvious, the interesting, and the absurd.
- Quantity is sought.
- During the initial "data dump," allow questions for clarification, but not evaluation.
- Once the data is on the wall, ideas are further clarified, evaluated, organized, combined, built on, and improved.

Sequence
Hold to this sequence. Take only one step at a time.
1) Data dump. Generate quantity and creative ideas.
2) Clarify. Ensure people understand the data.
3) Evaluate. Dialogue, discuss.
4) Prioritize. Decide what is most important.

Considerations
- Must be freewheeling (wild ideas, wishful thinking, and hitchhiking or building on other people's ideas are encouraged).
- Must use a common text (e.g., flipchart, yellow sticky notes on a wall).

Use
- Generating ideas and enthusiasm.

Advantages
- Encouraging creative thinking.
- Helping groups see the big picture.
- Participants are active and involved.

Disadvantages
- All too often groups evaluate ideas as they work rather than simply generating the data. This slows down the process and results in fewer creative ideas.
- Can be time consuming and difficult to manage. Lots of "half baked" or "top of mind" thoughts.

Examples
- Generating ideas for advertising a new product.
- "Taking stock" in a project team by brainstorming behaviors that members should *stop* doing, *start* doing, and *continue* doing.
- Generating a list of values that will become the foundation of a new compensation program.

Case Study	
Relevance • Training Programs ***Learning Style*** • Converger (thinking/doing) ***Administrative*** • High ***Technical*** • High ***Interpersonal*** • Medium ***Participant Risk*** • Medium ***Group Size*** • Any size ***Subgroup Size*** • 1 - 5 ***Contrast With*** • In basket • Clinic ***Preparation*** • The case and materials must be prepared ahead of time. ***Other Requirements*** *Time*: Time to get familiar with the case and for dialogue and analysis *Space*: Nothing special *Equipment*: Varies (may require AV equipment)	***Activity*** • Participants are given job-like problems in writing or verbally and asked to analyze and present recommendations. • Participants can work alone or in subgroups. • A variation is the *minicase*, where a brief situation is described to a group of five to fifteen participants who briefly discuss how the case should be handled, focusing only on key facts. ***Use*** • Testing. • Reviewing. • Giving examples of situations and procedures. ***Advantages*** • Develops problem solving skills. • Can be focused on specific learning objectives. • Participants are involved. • Systematic. • If a live or actual case is used, participants can get real work done while learning. • Participative. • Quick (minicase). • Useful for a variety of training areas. ***Disadvantages*** • Participants must complete the exercise before getting feedback. • Artificial. Learning may not be directly applied to the job (unless they are using a live case). • Without close supervision, participants could spend a lot of time working on a wrong or a low yield solution. • Assesses intention versus actual practice (i.e., espoused theory versus theory in action). • Time consuming. ***Example*** • Participants are given a case study of a communication breakdown between two executives. Their assignment is to develop strategies for overcoming the lack of cooperation and information sharing that has resulted between the two executives' departments.

Clinic

Relevance
- Training Programs
- Workshops

Learning Style
- Converger (thinking/doing)

Administrative	• High
Technical	• High
Interpersonal	• Medium
Participant Risk	• Medium
Group Size	• 2 - 12
Subgroup Size	• NA

Contrast With
- Project

Preparation
- Participants must be familiar with the problem under discussion

Other Requirements

Time: Varies
Space: Nothing special (a meeting room)
Equipment: Nothing special (e.g., a flipchart)

Activity
- Participants meet to analyze and resolve a specific problem they have encountered on the job.

Use
- Deciding options and dealing with a specific job issue.

Advantages
- Provides a sharp focus.
- Practical and relevant.

Disadvantage
- Learning may not be debriefed adequately or transferred to other job situations.

Examples
- A group of campaign managers meets to decide damage control measures needed as a result of their candidates latest public relations fiasco.
- A group of computer programmers discusses how to get rid of the bugs in their new software.

Coaching

Relevance
- Training Programs
- Workshops

Learning Style
- Accommodator (feeling/doing)

Administrative	• High
Technical	• High
Interpersonal	• High
Participant Risk	• Medium
Group Size	• 1 - 5
Subgroup Size	• NA

Contrast With
- Peer-assisted learning
- Job instruction training

Preparation
- Coaching works best when it's based on tangible data (e.g., survey benchmarking).

Other Requirements

Time: Usually a heavy time requirement (e.g., several hours per coachee)
Space: A place to talk privately
Equipment: Nothing special (e.g., a flipchart)

Activity
- Participants receive coaching from you, one-on-one, or in small groups.
- A variation on coaching is the *tutorial*. It's done on the job. You or an advanced participant demonstrates and assists others, providing guidance and feedback.

Use
- Helping others develop their potential.
- Helping others take advantage of opportunities.
- Helping others overcome performance deficiencies.

Advantages
- Learning is sharply focused and individualized.
- Feedback and support are immediate and specific.
- The process is active, engaging, and challenging.

Disadvantages
- Time consuming for coach.
- Requires the right chemistry between the participant and the workshop leader (i.e., an effective coaching relationship).

Example
- A workshop leader may coach a participant between workshop sessions in a particular area the participant is having difficulty with (e.g., dealing with conflict, facilitating a discussion group).

Contrasting Perspectives

Relevance
- Workshops

Learning Style
- Assimilator (thinking/watching)

Administrative	• High
Technical	• Medium
Interpersonal	• Varies
Participant Risk	• Low
Group Size	• Any size
Subgroup Size	• 2 - 7

Contrast With
- Brainstorming
- Appreciative inquiry
- Polarity

Preparation
- Set a clear focus and timelines for data collection.

Other Requirements

Time: 1 hour +.
Space: Lots of wall space to post completed flipchart pages.
Equipment: One flipchart for each subgroup. Lots of flipchart paper.

Activity
- Data is generated by participants and later prioritized or high graded for action planning.

Use
- Collecting data to assess a situation.
- Generating a balance in perspectives in a group.

Perspectives That Might Be Compared - Examples

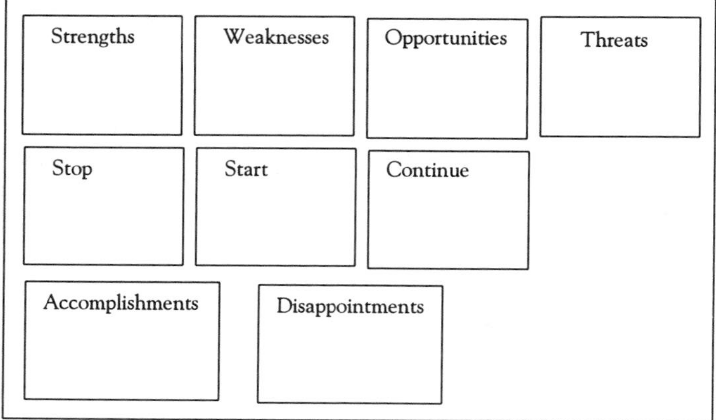

Special Considerations
- The *stop/start/continue* and the *accomplishments/ disappointments* dates must be written in behavioral terms (e.g., observable or measurable).
- The *SWOT* (strengths, weaknesses, opportunities, threats) must be as specific as possible.

Advantages
- Generating a lot of relevant data quickly.
- Getting a full and balanced picture of a situation.

Disadvantage
- Sometimes groups don't focus enough on the positive (e.g., the "continue" in the *stop/start/continue*).

Examples
- Outlining what a team needs to *stop/start/continue*.
- Listing accomplishments and disappointments while "taking stock" of a project.
- Environmental scanning in preparation for a strategic planning workshop (SWOT).

Debate

Relevance
- Training Programs
- Workshops

Learning Style
- Accommodator (feeling/doing)

Administrative	• Medium
Technical	• Medium
Interpersonal	• Medium
Participant Risk	• Medium
Group Size	• 15+
Panel Size	• 2 - 7

Contrast With
- Panel
- Extended panel
- Discussion

Preparation
- The question to be debated must be well thought out.

Other Requirements

Time: Varies (1/2 hour and up)
Space: Nothing special
Equipment: Nothing special

Activity
- Two teams of participants defend opposite sides of an issue.
- Participants take turns presenting their arguments, while the rest of the participants take notes and prepare questions to ask after the debate.

Use
- Explores all aspects of an issue.

Advantages
- Generates counterevidence.
- Generates emotion, energy, and often fun.

Disadvantages
- Emphasizes winning and encourages competition. This may lessen future cooperation within a group.
- May encourage and reward narrow perspectives.
- Participants not actively involved will be learning passively for a time.

Example
- Two teams of product development specialists debate the comparative merits of buying versus making a new product.

Demonstration

Relevance
- Training Programs
- Workshops

Learning Style
- Diverger - (watching) (feeling/watching)
- Accommodator - (being involved in) (feeling/doing)

Administrative	• High
Technical	• High
Interpersonal	• High
Participant Risk	• Low
Group Size	• 1 - 12
Subgroup Size	• NA

Contrast With
- Behavior modeling
- Coaching
- Role playing

Preparation
- The demonstration must be accurate, or you end up teaching the wrong thing.

Other Requirements

Time: Varies
Space: Varies
Equipment: TV and VCR if demo is on videotape

Activity
- Participants observe a task or procedure being performed correctly.
- The demonstration may be in person or on videotape.

Use
- Teaching a skill.
- Promoting interest and confidence in using a method or procedure.

Advantage
- Time and cost effective.

Disadvantages
- Recall may be limited.
- Debriefing is required to ensure participants understand why a procedure has been performed in a certain way and not in another way.

Examples
- A videotape demonstrating effective recruitment interview techniques.
- A live demonstration of the correct procedure for caulking a bathtub.
- A face-to-face demonstration between a coach and a performer (the person being coached) showing how to help surface and deal with indirect resistance.

Dialogue

Relevance
- Training Programs
- Workshops

Learning Style
- Accommodator (feeling/doing)

Administrative • High
Technical • High
Interpersonal • High

Participant Risk • Medium

Group Size • 6 - 20
Subgroup Size • NA

Contrast With
- Discussion
- Panel
- Expanded panel
- Demonstration

Preparation
- Preparing questions to stimulate dialogue.
- Ensuring those participating have an "open mind" and will allow themselves to be influenced.

Other Requirements

Time: One half hour plus
Space: Room for inner and outer group (fishbowl)
Equipment: Nothing special

Activity
- Two people (e.g., participants, resource people) hold a conversation while other participants observe. Alternatively, the conversation may be among yourself and all participants in the group, with or without resource people present.
- The key is that this conversation be an open exchange of ideas on a topic. *Advocacy* (telling and selling) needs to be minimized, while *inquiry* (listening and exploring with an open mind) needs to be maximized.
- Those participating may present opposing views or simply discuss the issue in an informed manner; however, to quote Senge (1990), "the purpose of dialogue is to go beyond any one individual's understanding."[5] Thus, no attempt is made to reach a solution or to win an argument. Rather, the focus in on sharing information and perspectives.
- Those participants observing the dialogue make notes and write questions to be asked later.
- A variation is the *fishbowl* design. An inner circle of participants dialogue while the outer circle observes. Following this, the group as a whole discusses its learning.

Use
- Exploring an issue.
- Developing perspectives.

Advantages
- Creating interest.
- Stimulating thinking.
- (fishbowl) Providing a relevant example or seeking meaningful feedback on *inner group* process.

Disadvantages
- Observers are passive.
- (fishbowl) The *inner group* may be intimidated (at least initially).

Examples
- While others watch and take notes, senior geologists exchange interpretations of specific geological data and its implications for the presence of fossil fuels.
- (fishbowl) An intact work group of professionals meets in the inner circle. They discuss the organization of their group, their successes and failures, and their need for continuing teamwork in the group. Other participants observe and make notes for later discussion in the group as a whole.

Discussion	
Relevance • Training Programs • Workshops ***Learning Style*** • Converger (thinking/doing) ***Administrative*** • High ***Technical*** • Low ***Interpersonal*** • Medium ***Participant Risk*** • High ***Group Size*** • 2 - 7 ***Subgroup Size*** • NA ***Contrast With*** • Dialogue • Panel • Extended panel ***Preparation*** • Clarity on the decision to be made. ***Other Requirements*** *Time*: Varies a great deal (usually at least a 1/2 hour and possibly as much as a day) *Space*: Nothing special *Equipment*: Nothing special	***Activity*** • A group of participants attempts to reach a conclusion (e.g., agree on a solution, agree on how a problem is to be framed). • Discussion can be leaderless or moderated, unstructured and spontaneous, or highly structured. ***Use*** • For decision making. ***Advantages*** • Encourages sharing of differences. • Encourages confrontation. ***Disadvantage*** • Conflict and emotions can rise. When not properly handled, winning can become more important than learning or arriving at the best overall solution. ***Example*** • A group of managers hold a discussion to decide whether to debt or equity finance a new acquisition.

Drill	
Relevance • Training Programs ***Learning Style*** • Converger (thinking/doing) ***Administrative*** • High ***Technical*** • Varies ***Interpersonal*** • Medium ***Participant Risk*** • Low ***Group Size*** • 1+ ***Subgroup Size*** • Varies ***Contrast With*** • Simulation • Role playing ***Preparation*** • Clear steps and procedures. ***Other Requirements*** *Time*: Minimal *Space*: Varies *Equipment*: Varies	***Activity*** • Participants repetitively practice a skill. ***Use*** • Learning a skill. • Increasing efficiency and improving the quality of performance. ***Advantages*** • Aiding retention. Learning is reinforced. • Performance is enhanced. ***Disadvantages*** • Can be boring or unchallenging. • Doesn't teach "why" a skill is important or needs to be performed in a certain way. ***Examples*** • A group of supervisors practices the four steps of giving feedback to a subordinate. • A group of technicians practices assembling and arming a given type of antiaircraft ordnance.

Field Trip	
Relevance • Training Programs ***Learning Style*** • Diverger (feeling/watching) ***Administrative*** • High ***Technical*** • High ***Interpersonal*** • Medium ***Participant Risk*** • Low ***Group Size*** • 1 - 12 ***Subgroup Size*** • NA ***Contrast With*** • Demonstration • Job instruction training ***Preparation*** • Usually plenty of pre-arranging and coordination required. ***Other Requirements*** *Time*: Usually at least a 1/2 day *Space*: Varies *Equipment*: Transportation	***Activity*** • A group of participants is taken to a location to observe specific tasks being performed. • The trip is carefully planned for learning through observation and analysis. It's not just a casual tour. ***Use*** • When applications of knowledge or principles are more easily shown than described. • When relationship building is important. ***Advantages*** • Creates relevance. • Generates interest. • Builds relationships. ***Disadvantages*** • Costly, time consuming. • Can become unfocused (a casual tour). • Key learning is sometimes missed (e.g., participants may get caught up in the dynamics of a given piece of the operation and miss the big picture of how the operation is organized). ***Examples*** • A group of branch managers visits their organization's head office to meet managers from other departments and discuss interdependencies. • A group of technical specialists from the head office goes on a tour of their company's new manufacturing plant.

<table>
<tr><td colspan="2">Forum</td></tr>
<tr><td>
Relevance
• Workshops

Learning Style
• Assimilator (thinking/watching)
• Accommodator (when challenging with questions) (feeling/doing)

Administrative • Medium
Technical • Low
Interpersonal • Low

Participant Risk • Low

Group Size • 100+
Subgroup Size • NA

Contrast With
• Panel

Preparation
• Prepared presentation.

Other Requirements

Time: Varies (usually a couple of hours)
Space: Space for a large audience/group
Equipment: Microphones in the audience for the question and answer period
</td><td>
Activity
• Following a formal presentation participants ask questions of the speaker. Questions may be submitted in writing or asked in person.

Use
• Informing and discussing an issue with a large group.
• Usually a forum is used at the beginning or end of a workshop. Presenters are often senior executives.

Advantage
• An efficient way of informing many people at once.

Disadvantages
• Presentations are sometimes superficial and leave many questions unanswered.
• Questions from the floor are generally guarded.
• For the most part, learning is passive.

Example
• A CEO informs a large group (e.g., a division or an entire company) of upcoming changes within the organization.
</td></tr>
</table>

Game	
Relevance • Training Programs • Workshops ***Learning Style*** • Accommodator (feeling/doing) ***Administrative*** • High ***Technical*** • Medium ***Interpersonal*** • High ***Participant Risk*** • Medium ***Group Size*** • 6 - 25 ***Subgroup Size*** • 2 - 7 ***Contrast With*** • Simulation • Role playing ***Preparation*** • The game must be fully planned beforehand. ***Other Requirements*** *Time*: Varies (usually at least an hour) *Space*: Varies *Equipment*: Varies	***Activity*** • Participants are involved in an exercise in which competition, cooperation, or both are used to practice previously learned principles. • Intended to be fun, energizing, and active. ***Use*** • Creating learning readiness. • Demonstrating applications for learning. ***Advantages*** • Experiential, active, fun • Done in "real time" ***Disadvantages*** • Game must be relevant to learning content and participants' context. • Must be effectively debriefed. ***Example*** • There are lots of examples of games in the University Associates annuals. An example is the game called Win As Much As You Can, which is aimed at having participants experience the conflict between competing and cooperating in groups that are interdependent.

Guided Imagery

Relevance
- Training Programs
- Workshops

Learning Style
- Diverger (feeling/watching)

Administrative	• Low
Technical	• Medium
Interpersonal	• High
Participant Risk	• Low
Group Size	• Any size
Subgroup Size	• 1

Contrast With
- Role playing
- Reflection

Preparation
- Focus the group on a topic, problem, or purpose for the guided imagery.
- Relax the group. Have them sit back, get comfortable, close their eyes, and prepare to daydream a little.

Other Requirements

Time: 15 minutes for the guided imagery and from 1/2 to 1 hour to record and harness the resulting ideas and energy
Space: A quiet nonoffice setting, away from interruptions
Equipment: Comfortable chairs, flipcharts for debriefing

Activity
- Take participants through a relaxation sequence (e.g., asking them to sit back, get comfortable, close their eyes, imagine themselves on a quiet sunny beach with a gentle breeze, and so on). Next, guide them through a process of "daydreaming" or imagining. For example, have them imagine themselves performing a task, confronting their boss, or working effectively in a argumentative group.

Use
- Strategic planning (e.g., visioning)
- Generating creativity, commitment, and energy for a given approach, product, idea, or strategy.
- Planning personal change.

Advantages
- Repeated mental rehearsal is a surprisingly effective supplement, although not a replacement, for actual practice.
- Focuses creativity.
- Helps create beliefs in and commitment to action.
- Taps into feelings in an otherwise rational environment. Beverly Byrum (1989) notes that "guided imagery works by allowing a person to release the analytical part of his mind to a guide who leads him to receive information from the intuitive part of his mind, which will then be helpful in problem solving."[6]

Disadvantages
- Some people find it awkward and unsettling.
- Easily faked.
- It doesn't work well if you try to control the outcome. That is, he/she tells participants what they're feeling, seeing, and doing in their "daydream," as opposed to just guiding their experience with open questions.

Examples
- Imagining yourself successfully working through conflict with a peer.
- Imagining shooting free throws in basketball.
- Imagining yourself selling a product or idea to a customer.
- The *expert within* exercise where participants are guided to create their own images of an expert, their own questions, and their own "expert" answers.

In Basket	
Relevance • Training Programs ***Learning Style*** • Converger (thinking/doing) ***Administrative*** • High ***Technical*** • Low ***Interpersonal*** • Low ***Participant Risk*** • High ***Group Size*** • 1 - 8 ***Subgroup Size*** • 1 ***Contrast With*** • Quiz • Simulation ***Preparation*** • Lots of preparation is required (e.g., the letters, requests, and information going into the in basket). ***Other Requirements*** *Time*: Usually at least an hour *Space*: Room for participants to work alone without disturbing each other *Equipment*: As found in average office (e.g., phone, fax)	***Activity*** • Prepared items are given to participants as if arriving in their in baskets. Participants prioritize, make decisions, handle difficulties, and respond to deadlines in order to complete their *in basket* workload. ***Use*** • Primarily for testing administrative, judgment, organizing, and decision making skills. • Assessing and comparing participants' abilities (e.g., management assessment centers). ***Advantage*** • Able to simulate on-the-job situations. ***Disadvantages*** • Loss of learning if not effectively debriefed and corrected. • A lot of work goes into preparing in-basket exercise materials. ***Example*** • Comparing how well a group of participants prioritizes and responds to a heavy workload of assignments, questions, and requests.

Instruments

Relevance
- Training Programs
- Workshops

Learning Style
- Converger (thinking/doing)

Administrative	• Medium
Technical	• Low
Interpersonal	• Medium
Participant Risk	• Low
Group Size	• 7 - 15
Subgroup Size	• 1

Contrast With
- Game

Preparation
- Prepared and tested instruments.
- Template of method for scoring the instrument.

Other Requirements

Time: Varies (usually at least a 1/2 hour)
Space: Nothing special
Equipment: Nothing special

Activity
- Participants complete questionnaires or checklists to gain insight about themselves or to explore a topic.

Use
- Self or team assessment.

Advantage
- Can be used to create relevance for theory and model, or to create *learning readiness* among participants.

Disadvantages
- Time consuming.
- Easily faked.
- Participants lacking self-awareness will not be able to accurately complete a self-assessment questionnaire.
- The instruments themselves (e.g., some psychometric instruments, some social styles inventories) are of questionable value. Often they are descriptive of the moment but not predictive of other times or other people's behavior.

Example
- Having participants complete a learning style inventory / questionnaire to give themselves a better grasp of their habits, interests, strengths, and limitations as a learner.

Job Instruction Training[7]	
Relevance • Training Programs ***Learning Style*** • Converger (thinking/doing) ***Administrative*** • High ***Technical*** • High ***Interpersonal*** • Medium ***Participant Risk*** • Medium ***Group Size*** • 1 - 5 ***Subgroup Size*** • NA ***Contrast With*** • Coaching • Programmed instruction • Practice exercise ***Preparation*** • Clear steps for performing a job. ***Other Requirements*** *Time*: Usually a couple of hours or more. *Space*: Similar to the work site. *Equipment*: Similar to equipment available at the work site.	***Activity*** • Participants are guided through a formal step-by-step procedure for performing a task "on the job." Also called *on-the-job training*. ***Use*** • On-the-job training and guidance. ***Advantages*** • Personalized. • Self-paced. • Practical. ***Disadvantages*** • Time consuming to develop and to implement. • Can get boring. ***Example*** • Training employees how to use new packaging equipment on the job.

Lecture

Relevance
- Training Programs
- Workshops

Learning Style
- Assimilator (thinking/watching)

Administrative	• Medium
Technical	• High
Interpersonal	• Medium
Participant Risk	• Low
Group Size	• 5+
Subgroup Size	• NA

Contrast With
- Forum

Preparation
- Prepared lecture or lecturette.

Other Requirements

Time: Lecturette, 5 to 10 minutes. Lecture, up to an hour.
Space: Nothing special.
Equipment: Varies (e.g., TV and VCR, overhead projector, flipchart).

Activity
- You deliver a prepared oral presentation to the group. This could take anywhere between fifteen minutes to an hour. Participants are expected to listen, make notes, and ask questions.
- A variation is the *lecturette*, a brief oral presentation lasting less than five minutes, followed by a brief discussion involving participants. Lecturettes are best interspersed throughout a workshop.

Use
- An expert informing an interested group.
- Presenting a particular point of view.
- Introducing a topic.
- Quickly reviewing bits of theory (lecturette).

Advantages
- Suitable for any size group, and acceptable in most training sessions, when combined with other methods.
- Presenting is a relatively easy skill to learn.
- Cost effective.
- Timing based on relevance, as the need arises (lecturette).
- Brief and interest grabbing (lecturette).
- Overcomes some of the weaknesses of formal lectures (lecturette).

Disadvantages
- Nonparticipative (i.e., puts participants into a trance if more than 20 minutes long).
- Does not allow for individual differences (i.e., it can't deal with values, beliefs, and attitudes, or teach specific skills).
- Participants might not take accurate notes (this problem can be partially solved by providing handouts).
- Participants must wait until they are tested to find out how they are doing.
- Leaves participants with only an overview of theory rather than in-depth understanding (lecturette).

Examples
- A math or management skills lecture at a university.
- A brief presentation introducing participants to a new topic or new material in a workshop (lecturette).

Listening Team	
Relevance • Training Programs ***Learning Style*** • Assimilator (thinking/watching) ***Administrative*** • Medium ***Technical*** • Low ***Interpersonal*** • Medium ***Participant Risk*** • Low ***Group Size*** • 30+ ***Team Size*** • 2 - 5 ***Contrast With*** • Lecture • Forum ***Preparation*** • A focus for listening. ***Other Requirements*** *Time*: Varies *Space*: Nothing special *Equipment*: Note pads, perhaps audiotaping equipment	***Activity*** • A group of participants is assigned to listen to a speaker, take notes, prepare questions, and summarize a presentation. • They then report their observations and conclusions. • Participants may also question the speaker. • Several listening teams can each focus on a different aspect of the presentation. • A variation is *reaction team*, where a group of participants is asked to react to a speaker's presentation by seeking clarification, asking questions, and making comments. ***Use*** • Capturing specific information from a lecture. ***Advantage*** • Provides multiple perspectives on lecture information. ***Disadvantages*** • Too sharp a focus may result in missing other related information in the lecture. • May result in overkill. • Not all participants are actively involved. ***Example*** • During the same lecture, one listening team focuses on what a speaker says about communication strategy and another focuses on what is said about organization systems.

Marathon	
Relevance • Workshops ***Learning Style*** • Converger (thinking/doing) ***Administrative*** • Medium ***Technical*** • Medium ***Interpersonal*** • High ***Participant Risk*** • Medium ***Group Size*** • 3 - 25 ***Subgroup Size*** • NA ***Preparation*** • Clear purpose and outcome statements for the workshop ***Other Requirements*** *Time*: Varies (usually two or three days, or more) *Space*: Residential (where participants can stay overnight) *Equipment*: Varies	***Activity*** • Participants stay in the learning environment for an extended time, usually in a secluded spot to minimize distractions and to allow intense concentration on the outcomes being sought from the session. ***Use*** • Completing a plan or developing a product. • Learning and practicing supervisory and management skills. ***Advantages*** • Allows a full-time focus on learning or producing a product. • Provides a supportive environment. • Well suited for interpersonal skills training. ***Disadvantagse*** • Takes people away from their jobs and homes for long periods of time (i.e., often considered an imposition by participants). • Expensive. ***Examples*** • A group of executives spends a full week at a mountain resort working on a new marketing plan. • A team of programmers that is behind schedule shuts themselves in their offices until they finish coding their new software upgrade.

Matrix Analysis

Relevance
- Workshops

Learning Style
- Assimilator (thinking/watching)

Administrative • High
Technical • High
Interpersonal • Low

Participant Risk • Low

Group Size • 6+
Subgroup Size • 2 - 5

Contrast With
- Story boarding
- Mind mapping
- Brainstorming

Preparation
- "Seed" an example or two to get the group started.

Other Requirements

Time: 1 hour +
Space: Lots of wall space to hang flipchart paper
Equipment: Flipchart pages taped together with matrix lines pre-drawn

Activity
- Participants scope out options for action on a project, problem, or opportunity. First they list all possible subfunctions (left-hand column). Second, they list all possible alternative means to accomplish each subfunction.

Use
- Encourage creative and systems thinking.
- To work toward agreement on the best overall combination of approaches.

Advantage
- Linear activities have an appeal for technically trained people.

Disadvantage
- Interrelationships among the *methods* are not shown.

An Example of a Matrix Analysis

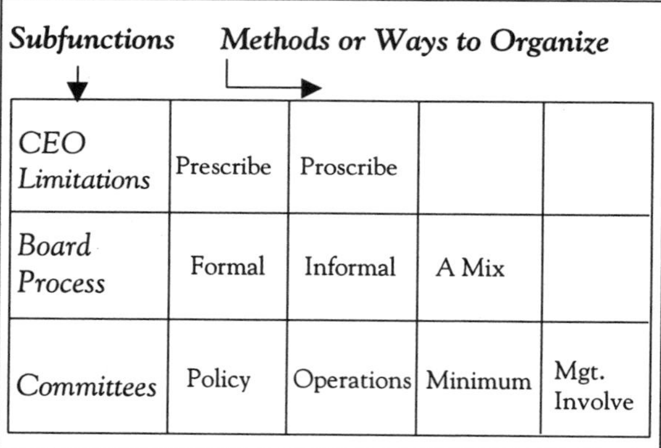

Subfunctions	*Methods or Ways to Organize*			
CEO *Limitations*	Prescribe	Proscribe		
Board Process	Formal	Informal	A Mix	
Committees	Policy	Operations	Minimum	Mgt. Involve

Examples
- Designing a governance model for a Board of Directors.
- Selecting designs for each section of a training program.
- Planning a conference.

Mind Mapping[8]

Relevance

- Workshops

Learning Style

- Assimilator (thinking/watching)

Administrative	• High
Technical	• High
Interpersonal	• High
Participant Risk	• Low
Group Size	• Any size
Subgroup Size	• 5 - 7

Contrast With

- Brainstorming

Preparation

- Set context for free association, nonevaluation, creative thinking.
- Show a simple picture of a mind map and "seed" a couple of examples of words or phrases.

Other Requirements

Time: about 1/2 to 1 hour for initial mind map. Additional 1 to 2 hour for dialogue, reorganizing, and redrafting.
Space: Away from interruptions.
Equipment: Variety of different colored highlighters, large sheets of paper (i.e., four flipchart pages taped together for a group of 5 to 7 people).

Activity

- Participants scope out a project, problem, or opportunity following the rules for brainstorming (i.e., free association, no evaluation initially, creative thinking). Starting at the center of the flipchart page, they write a word or phrase that accurately frames the topic or focal point of the mind map.
- Without worrying about logical level, order, or relationships, and using only single words or brief phrases, participants write all related information on the page.
- Participants draw connections between ideas as they are listed.
- Participants work until all possible elements or issues have been exhausted.
- Next, categories are color coded to show additional relationships.
- In all likelihood participants will need to redraw the mind map at least once in order to reorganize by categories and to improve the visual of relationships and connections among the elements.

Use

- Assessing or analyzing a complex problem or opportunity.
- Helping groups to organize their thoughts around a complex and multi-dimensional issue.
- Seeking a sense of the elements and their relationships within a topic (e.g., problem, opportunity).

An Example of a Mind Map

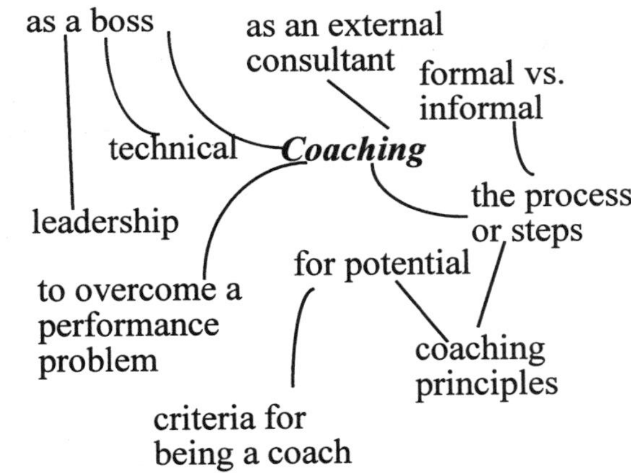

Mind Mapping (continued)	
	Lotus Blossom • A more formal variation of mind mapping shows information by level or logical type (e.g., chapters, sections, paragraphs). 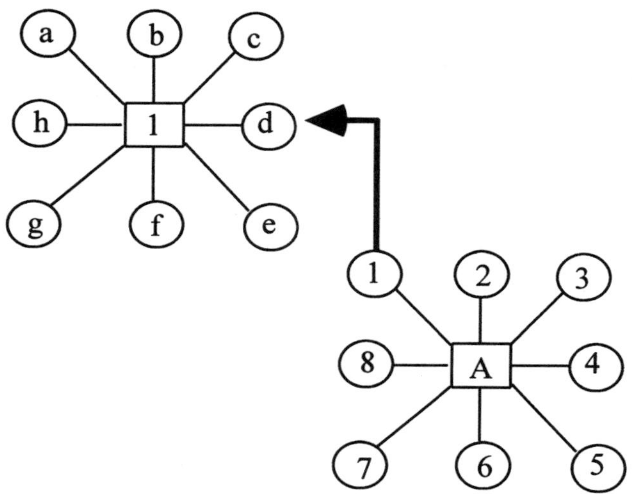 ***Advantages*** • Encourages intuitive and creative thinking. • Most people learn visually, and mind mapping results in a picture of a situation showing its complexity and interrelationships. • Provides confidence that all elements or factors of an issues (or at least all key factors) have been considered. ***Disadvantages*** • Without a clear "beginning frame" or topic you end up chasing after a lot of extraneous ideas or elements. • You must be willing to rethink, dialogue, reorganize, and reprioritize a few times, otherwise you'll overwhelm yourself with complexity. ***Examples*** • Designing a workshop. • Preparing a presentation. • Preparing to tackle a project or write a report, an article, or a book.

Nominal Group Technique[9]

Relevance
- Training Programs
- Workshops

Learning Style
- Assimilator (thinking/watching)

Administrative	• Medium
Technical	• Low
Interpersonal	• Medium
Participant Risk	• Medium
Group Size	• 10 - 25
Subgroup Size	• 1 (writing)

Contrast With
- Brainstorming

Preparation
- Provide a clear and specific definition of the problem to be worked.
- Agreement in the group that no one will attempt to identify who contributed a given piece of information or a question (i.e., input remains anonymous).

Other Requirements

Time: 10 to 20 minutes for each participant to write out his/her ideas and questions. An hour to organize, evaluate, and prioritize the data.

Space: Lots of wall space for flipchart pages.

Equipment: Flipcharts, yellow sticky notes, markers, masking tape.

Activity
- Participants work alone and respond anonymously in writing. Written responses are collected, read aloud, and recorded on flipcharts.
- Each idea is discussed in turn (as with brainstorming, questions of clarification are encouraged, and evaluation is temporarily suspended).
- A voting procedure may be used to rank or order ideas.
- A variation is *slip writing*. Participants write their input or questions on small slips of paper (e.g., Post-its). Slips are then collected and passed to you (the workshop leader). You then read these to the group. The group reacts, discusses, and builds on this anonymous input.

Use
- Helping groups to make decisions in spite of time pressures, low trust levels, and nonconfronting members.
- Overcoming political and status issues in a group.
- Getting input from a group while retaining authority to make the decision alone (e.g., polling members of a group without needing to include them in the decision).
- Helping participants ask questions anonymously.
- Getting problem solving ideas and generating a lot of ideas from a large group quickly.

Advantages
- Surfaces concerns while minimizing fear of retribution.
- Suitable for use in very large groups.
- More accurate information may be collected than might otherwise be the case, if input was not allowed to remain anonymous.
- A lot of data can be generated quickly.
- Participants can be in different locations.
- Every participant is given the opportunity to contribute.
- Useful in situations of low trust, high risk, or both.

Nominal Group Technique (continued)	
	Disadvantages • Questions have less impact when they can't be related to a specific context, and there can be no direct *follow up* because input was anonymous. • How the problem is stated has a big impact on the type of input received. • Discussing responses in the group may result in information being withheld or in the contributor being identified involuntarily. • People can take cheap shots and not be held personally accountable for their comments. ***Critical Consideration*** • Problem must be clearly stated. ***Example*** • Employee grievances about their boss are brought out in the open and discussed, while minimizing the fear of being personally identified with a given grievance or comment.

Open Space Technology	
Relevance • Workshops ***Learning Style*** • Accommodator (feeling/doing) ***Administrative*** • Low ***Technical*** • Low ***Interpersonal*** • Medium ***Participant Risk*** • Low ***Group Size*** • 30+ ***Subgroup Size*** • 3+ ***Preparation*** • Participants must be experienced in their field(s) and motivated to get something done. ***Other Requirements*** *Time*: At least a day. *Space*: Break-off rooms for concurrent sessions. *Equipment*: Varies. At least a flipchart in every break-off room.	***Activity*** • To paraphrase Harrison Owen (1991), a theme is decided upon and participants are asked to write issues related to this theme on flipchart paper. Each participant must be willing to facilitate a small group discussion on any issue they identify.[10] • Once everyone's issues (e.g., concerns, interests) are written on flipchart paper, participants sign up for discussions on those issues that interest them. They then self-organize and "work the issues" (i.e., frame the concern or opportunity, develop options and recommendations for action). ***Use*** • Having participants decide what issues should be discussed and then take responsibility for working these issues as they see fit. ***Advantages*** • Participants are responsible for raising any issues they want to be covered in the workshop. • Participants organize to deal with the issues that are of most interest to them. ***Disadvantage*** • There is little or no control over how many issues are raised. ***Example*** • A group of managers identify communication concerns in their company and self-organize to simultaneously work solutions around a number of these issues.

Panel	
Relevance • Training Programs • Workshops ***Learning Style*** • Diverger (listening to) (feeling/watching) • Accommodator (being on the panel) (feeling/doing) ***Administrative*** • Medium ***Technical*** • Medium ***Interpersonal*** • Medium ***Participant Risk*** • Low ***Group Size*** • 30+ ***Panel Size*** • 2 - 4 ***Expanded Panel*** • 4 - 8 ***Contrast With*** • Dialogue ***Preparation*** • Coordination with panel members. A clear focus of panel discussion. ***Other Requirements*** *Time*: Varies. At least an hour. *Space*: Nothing special. *Equipment*: As required by panel members.	***Activity*** • Experts take turns making brief presentations and then discuss an issue while participants observe. Participants ask questions after each panel member has spoken. A moderator directs discussion. • A variation is an *expanded panel* where participants can take turns joining the panel, and thereby participating actively in the discussion. • Another variation is a *colloquy*, a modified panel composed of half participant representatives and half content experts. Participants on the panel ask questions and raise issues with the experts. The questions asked by participants on the panel can first be chosen by the whole group. • Yet another variation is the *interview*, where participants interview a person, or panel of people, who are content experts. ***Use*** • Presenting and contrasting a number of views. • Encouraging active learning by sharing differences, participating, and challenging experts. • With large groups. • Understanding complex procedures or systems where there are many ways of accomplishing a task. ***Advantages*** • Gets at multiple perspectives. • Participants have a chance to get involved (expanded panel). • Places participants and experts on an even playing field (colloquy). • Little preparation required other than effective questioning skills. • Can bring out multiple competing perspectives (interview).

Panel (continued)	
	Disadvantages • Requires using experts' time. • Discussion with participants is somewhat formal and restricted. • Not all participants are involved. • Puts participants under some pressure (expanded panel). • In the case of interviewing a single expert, the group is only getting one person's perspective. • Experts may confuse their intent with their actual behavior (espoused theory versus theory in use). • Participants may not be aware of assumptions embedded in their questions. • Participants are passive when the interview is conducted by the workshop leader. • Difficult to control. ***Examples*** • At a workshop on coaching skills, participants ask questions of a panel of managers who have experienced formal coaching on the job. • A group of systems analysts interviews a panel of experts from Microsoft about the capabilities of a new operating system.

Peer-Assisted Learning	
Relevance • Training Programs • Workshops ***Learning Style*** • Accommodator (feeling/doing) ***Administrative*** • High ***Technical*** • High ***Interpersonal*** • Medium ***Participant Risk*** • Low ***Group Size*** • 6 - 20 ***Subgroup Size*** • 1 - 3 ***Contrast With*** • Coaching • Subgroups ***Preparation*** • Participants who are willing to experiment, challenge, and support each other. • There must be a good degree of trust and rapport among participants. ***Other Requirements*** *Time*: Extra time for peer meetings (e.g., up to an hour per workshop day). *Space*: A private place for subgroups to meet. *Equipment*: Usually a flipchart.	***Activity*** • Participants do exercises together and give each other feedback. They help each other learn under your guidance as a leader or coach. ***Use*** • Giving advanced participants an opportunity to help less advanced peers. ***Advantage*** • Junior people hear directly from experienced peers. ***Disadvantage*** • Senior technical people may teach shortcuts that are not supported by management. ***Example*** • A group of oil field workers try to figure out for themselves how to work a new oil pump, while an engineer from the oil pump company guides them along.

Polarity

Relevance
- Workshops
- Training Programs

Learning Style
- Assimilator (thinking/watching)

Administrative	• Low
Technical	• Medium
Interpersonal	• High
Participant Risk	• Medium
Group Size	• 15+
Subgroup Size	• 2 - 7

Contrast With
- Debate
- Discussion

Preparation
- Define polarities (interdependent dilemmas or paradoxes that won't go away).
- Be sure the situation is not a problem to be solved, but is rather a polarity to be managed.
- Ensure the group understands that managing polarities well means committing to an ongoing shift in emphasis (e.g., *both/and*, not *either/or*).
- Help the group use opposition as a resource.

Activity
- Do a lecturette on polarities and then ask participants to identify, name, and describe the polarity that's keeping them stuck. Johnson (1992) describes polarities as opposites that are also part of a whole (e.g., inhaling/exhaling, being decisive/being flexible, crusading/tradition bearing, team work/individual work).[11] This design is only needed as polarities arise in a workshop or training program and seem to be keeping participants stuck, usually because they are treating the *polarity* as if it were a *problem* and seeing only one pole as the solution. This in turn causes more problems.
- Develop guidelines for action (e.g., those crusading need to clarify what they value in the status quo, the downside of where they want to go, and what assurances they can give to tradition bearers).
- Plan to manage the dilemma (e.g., How will the organization be alerted when or before it slides into one of the downsides? What groups are most sensitive to each of the downsides?)

Problems Sometimes Confused with Polarities
- Either/or decisions (e.g., where to go for lunch, whether to hire Larry or Judy, what supplier to use, make or buy).
- Mysteries, for example, gravity (Newton), flight (Wright brothers), a who-done-it novel.
- Continuums (e.g., light vs. heavy cars, with light being desirable and constraints being safety and ride quality).

Use
- Maximize the upsides of each pole.

Advantages
- Expand and shift one's perception from a problem to be solved to a polarity to be managed.
- Allow other perspectives and not get stuck on one's own personal *truth*.
- Recognition that there's no such thing as victory over the other group or participant. Effective change requires being good at both crusading and tradition bearing (i.e., crusaders need to respect what others have built, tradition bearers need to be willing to risk).

Polarity (continued)	
Other Requirements *Time*: Depends on emotion. 3 hours to 1 day. *Space*: Room for subgroups to work without disturbing each other. *Equipment*: A flipchart for each subgroup.	***Disadvantages*** • Treating problems as polarities (e.g., either/or decisions, mysteries). • Avoiding issues by identifying them as polarities. ***Examples*** • Understanding a leader's style (e.g., the very same behavior employees call *rigid*, the leader calls being *clear*. But *flexibility* is not a solution and neither is *clarity*. Both are important.). • Working with a team on when to be *inclusive* (i.e., involving, consulting, conferring) and when to be *exclusive* (i.e., working on your own, focusing on a given task, not informing others).

Practice Exercise

Relevance
- Training Programs

Learning Style
- Accommodator (feeling/doing)

Administrative	• High
Technical	• High
Interpersonal	• High
Participant Risk	• Medium
Group Size	• 1 - 12
Subgroup Size	• 1 - 3

Contrast With
- Drill
- Job instruction training
- Programmed instruction

Preparation
- Clears steps and task process.

Other Requirements

Time: Varies.
Space: Varies (may need a place to practice without being observed by others).
Equipment: Varies.

Activity
- Participants practice performing a task.

Use
- Testing.
- Reviewing.
- Practicing.
- For any type of task.

Advantage
- Reinforces learning and gives participants a chance to apply their learning.

Disadvantages
- Feedback may not be given effectively.
- If the practice isn't set up properly, it may be seen as pretend versus real practice.

Example
- A group of technicians practice installing Ethernet cards in a personal computer.

Programmed Instruction

Relevance
- Training Programs

Learning Style
- Converger (thinking/doing)

Administrative	• High
Technical	• High
Interpersonal	• Low
Participant Risk	• Low
Group Size	• 1 - 2
Subgroup Size	• 1

Contrast With
- Game
- Practice exercise
- Simulation

Preparation
- Clear program outline. Clear directions. Coaching is often needed.

Other Requirements

Time: Ample time to complete program and to debrief
Space: Varies
Equipment: Varies

Activity
- Participants are presented specific steps to performing a task via computer or printed text. They respond to directions and move through the process until they know how to perform the skill.

Use
- Teaching intricate procedures.

Advantages
- Learning is self-paced and in small steps.
- Lots of time to practice.
- Immediate feedback.
- Minimal supervision needed.
- Every participant receives the same information.

Disadvantages
- Requires a lot of technical support.
- Standardized programs don't readjust themselves to the level of the participant.
- No human leader.
- Expensive to develop and maintain.
- Inflexible.
- Usually can't ask questions.
- Often doesn't anticipate unique situations.

Example
- Step-by-step instructions on video telling you how to install a 48 megabyte SIMM in your Macintosh computer.

Project

Relevance
- Training Programs
- Workshops

Learning Style
- Converger (thinking/doing)

Administrative	• High
Technical	• High
Interpersonal	• Medium
Participant Risk	• Medium
Group Size	• 3 - 7
Subgroup Size	• NA

Contrast With
- Case study
- Marathon
- Simulation

Preparation
- Definition of problem or opportunity. Clear guidelines or parameters for investigation (e.g., Is there room to redefine or reframe the?).

Other Requirements

Time: Varies with problem size
Space: Nothing special
Equipment: Varies

Activity
- A group investigates a problem or opportunity.

Use
- In-depth study and application of knowledge.

Advantage
- Focused and practical.

Disadvantage
- Theory may not be transferable to other job situations.

Example
- A purchasing group develops a new approach to tracking and controlling materials handling problems.

Question and Answer	
Relevance • Training Programs • Workshops ***Learning Style*** • Accommodator (feeling/doing) ***Administrative*** • Medium ***Technical*** • Medium ***Interpersonal*** • Medium ***Participant Risk*** • Medium ***Group Size*** • Any size ***Subgroup Size*** • NA ***Contrast With*** • Brainstorming • Dialogue ***Preparation*** • Participants who are interested and willing to challenge. ***Other Requirements*** *Time*: Varies *Space*: Nothing special *Equipment*: Varies (perhaps a flipchart or overhead)	***Activity*** • The leader covers learning content by asking participants a series of questions. This can be reversed with participants asking questions of the leader or of each other. ***Use*** • Advanced training with participants that are motivated and informed. ***Advantages*** • Informal. • Minimum preparation time. • Those who choose to participate are active and involved. ***Disadvantages*** • Lack of structure may lead to inefficient use of time or may frustrate participants. • Some participants may choose to listen passively. ***Example*** • The leader of a workshop starts out by asking participants to name what communication strategies they think are the most useful and why.

Quiz

Relevance • Training Programs ***Learning Style*** • Assimilator (thinking/watching) ***Administrative*** • High ***Technical*** • Medium ***Interpersonal*** • Medium ***Participant Risk*** • Medium ***Group Size*** • 1 - 40 ***Subgroup Size*** • 1 ***Contrast With*** • Practice exercise • Question and answer ***Preparation*** • Quiz must be prepared beforehand. Quick method for checking responses. ***Other Requirements*** *Time*: Time to discuss results *Space*: Nothing special *Equipment*: Nothing special	***Activity*** • A method of testing participants' knowledge or having them practice a skill. It usually involves having participants complete a questionnaire or test. • Can be written or oral. ***Use*** • Self-evaluation. • Review. ***Advantages*** • Quick. • Helps focus study. ***Disadvantages*** • Loss of usefulness if not adequately debriefed. • Some participants get performance anxiety around anything that sounds like a test. ***Examples*** • A verbal quiz on supervisory techniques during a workshop. • Students assessing their own learning by completing self-scoring quizzes in their study guide.

Reading	
Relevance • Training Programs • Workshops ***Learning Style*** • Assimilator (thinking/watching) ***Administrative*** • High ***Technical*** • High ***Interpersonal*** • High ***Participant Risk*** • Low ***Group Size*** • Any size ***Subgroup Size*** • 1 ***Contrast With*** • Study guide • Reflection ***Preparation*** • Quality and relevant articles or books selected for reading. • Ensure participants are motivated to do the assigned reading and learning. ***Other Requirements*** *Time*: Varies *Space*: Personal space to read and reflect at one's own pace *Equipment*: Nothing special	***Activity*** • Participants are assigned materials to read (e.g., selected articles or books). ***Use*** • Having participants examine theory in-depth. • Doing research. ***Advantages*** • Inexpensive. • Self-paced. ***Disadvantages*** • Passive. • Retention may be low. • Some people hate to read. They may not do assigned readings. ***Example*** • To provide participants with additional background on a subject or theory.

Reflection

Relevance
- Training Programs
- Workshops

Learning Style
- Assimilator (thinking/watching)

Administrative	• Low
Technical	• Low
Interpersonal	• High
Participant Risk	• Low
Group Size	• Any size
Subgroup Size	• 1

Contrast With
- Guided imagery
- Reading

Preparation
- Participants who are motivated to learn and willing to challenge their own assumptions (i.e., to double-loop learn).

Other Requirements

Time: Varies.
Space: Quiet place. Personal space.
Equipment: None, other than a good head on your shoulders!

Activity
- Participants are given time alone to review and think about what has been learned, discussed, or presented. They're asked to assess its applicability and think about how to make it work in their organizations.

Use
- When personal perspectives are required.
- When you want participants to integrate new learnings with old learnings.

Advantage
- Relates learning content to experience and beliefs.

Disadvantages
- Facing "unhappy truths" can be difficult.
- Tough to assess whether participants are taking part (i.e., it's easily faked).

Example
- Give participants fifteen minutes alone prior to the daily wrap up of the workshop to reflect on what they've found valuable in the day and how they might apply it on the job.

Role Playing	
Relevance • Training Programs • Workshops ***Learning Style*** • Accommodator (feeling/doing) ***Administrative*** • Low ***Technical*** • Low ***Interpersonal*** • High ***Participant Risk*** • High ***Group Size*** • Any size ***Subgroup Size*** • 2 - 4 ***Contrast With*** • Practice exercise • Simulation • Behavior modeling ***Preparation*** • Participants who are willing to risk and experiment. ***Other Requirements*** *Time*: Varies (usually less than an hour) *Space*: Nothing special *Equipment*: Varies	***Activity*** • Participants enact *job-like* situations in order to try out new skills. They then debrief what they said and did during role play. ***Variations*** • Confrontation (e.g., one participant is confronted by another and asked to answer questions, handle problems, or solve complaints). • Consultation (e.g., a participant tries to help a client solve a problem). • Court techniques (a situation or person is *tried* as participants work out the consequences of a mishandled task). ***Formats*** • *Doubling* (i.e., another participant stands behind the role player and acts as an alter ego to expand upon or reveal feelings not expressed by the role player). • *Monodrama* (i.e., there is only one role and the role player gives a monologue while other participants observe). • *Multiple* (i.e., a number of separate role plays occur at the same time). • *Role reversal* (i.e., participants assume the roles of others with whom they normally interact on the job). • *Role rotation* (i.e., the role play is stopped briefly so that participants can trade roles before continuing). • Soliloquy (i.e., the role play is stopped briefly so that one or more participants can be interviewed). ***Use*** • Situations where participants need face-to-face interaction (e.g., learning interpersonal skills). • Developing and changing attitudes. • Trying out sensitive or potentially controversial behaviors. • Training others in diagnosis and problem solving. • Portraying a problem involving feelings and attitudes. • Stimulating discussion.

Role Playing (continued)	
	Advantages • Emotions are "parked" because the situations being worked on are simulated, not real (i.e., participants are involved in specific, although contrived, job related experiences). • Participants are given immediate feedback on their performance. • Participants use each other as resources. • Participants are active and challenged. ***Disadvantages*** • Participants are often anxious about playing a role. • If not organized carefully, time can be used unproductively. • Success in a contrived environment can create a false sense of security. (Role playing results do not necessarily translate into success on the job.) ***Example*** • Two participants role play a subordinate-boss confrontation to develop their conflict resolution skills.

Sensitivity Training

Relevance
- Workshops

Learning Style
- Accommodator (feeling/doing)

Administrative	• Low
Technical	• Low
Interpersonal	• Medium
Participant Risk	• High
Group Size	• 5 - 25
Subgroup Size	• 3 - 5

Contrast With
- Nothing comparable

Preparation
- Participants who are prepared for this level of intimacy and for deep personal learning.

Other Requirements

Time: Usually at least two days, but the real answer is "as much time as it takes." (Once you open a can of worms, you have to deal with what crawls out.)
Space: Nothing special.
Equipment: Nothing special.

Activity
- Participants are involved in an intense interpersonal experience. They interact together and receive feedback from each other in order to learn about their own behavior and the effect they have on others.
- A mild form of group therapy, this design option needs to be facilitated by an experienced professional. (Sensitivity training was all the rage in the late 1960's and early 1970's. It is not widely used in organizations today.)

Use
- Getting specific, blunt, and even emotional feedback about how one is seen by others.

Advantage
- Can lead to personal change.

Disadvantages
- Threatening (feedback at this level of intimacy can be painful).
- The facilitator needs to be highly skilled at interpersonal relations (i.e., he/she almost needs training as a therapist).
- Can move a group too deep into sharing. If not facilitated well, a group can get into sharing at an intimate level that's not necessary for effective working relationships, and people can get hurt. Once said, some things are not easily forgotten. (You can't put the toothpaste back in the tube.) This can lead to permanent damage in relationships.

Examples
- The old T groups, that now defunct fad of the 60's where people were put in touch with their own feelings and asked to be brutally honest with each other.
- Some team-building workshops dabble with sensitivity training.

Simulation

Relevance
- Training Programs
- Workshops

Learning Styles
- Accommodator (feeling/doing)

Administrative • High
Technical • High
Interpersonal • High

Participant Risk • Medium

Group Size • 2 - 12
Subgroup Size • 1 - 3

Contrast With
- Role playing
- Practice session
- Behavior modeling
- Game

Preparation
- Varies from a little to a great deal.
- Clearly define the problems to be solved.
- Exercises must be developed ahead of time.

Other Requirements

Time: Varies from an hour to several days.
Space: Plenty of space to spread materials out.
Equipment: Can range for flipcharts for each subgroup to highly sophisticated simulation equipment.

Activity
- An equipment and situational training environment is set up allowing participants to practice a task under *job-like* conditions.
- A variation is the *laboratory*. A training site is set up to allow experimenting and testing by participants. This can be done for technical training, scientific training, or training in human relations.
- Another variation is the *action maze*. Participants solve a problem by making decisions. These decisions determine what participants will see next (i.e., branching).

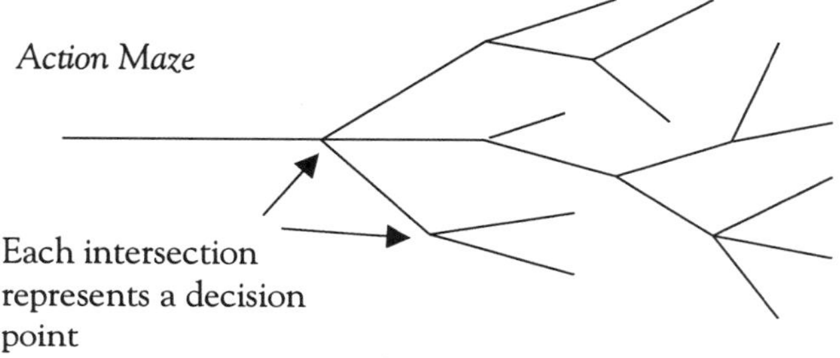

Use
- Complex skill training that would be costly, risky, or impossible to do on the job (e.g., landing an aircraft, handling a gas kick on a drilling rig)
- Review, testing, self-testing
- Practicing complex technical learning requiring skill, knowledge, and judgment.

Advantages
- Practice in a risk-free environment.
- The exercise is experiential.
- Consequences of decisions provide participants with feedback.
- A simulation creates a condition in which learners can learn more than they are taught.
- Improves problem solving abilities, for example, showing the dangers of relying on outdated assumptions.
- Helps teams realize the value of getting input from all team members. (Sometimes the most useful ideas come from the most unlikely sources.)
- Cost (e.g., it's much cheaper to train a pilot in a simulator than in an actual plane).

Simulation (continued)	
	Disadvantages • Simulations can be costly and time consuming to develop and maintain. • Participants may not fully understand why they got a certain result. • A lot of work goes into developing an *action maze* exercise. ***Examples*** • Managers learning in a communications lab. • A team-building simulation (e.g., surviving in the woods, constructing a model). • Flight simulator for training commercial pilots. • A drilling simulator for training rig supervisors how to anticipate and control "gas kicks."

Skit	
Relevance • Training Programs • Workshops ***Learning Style*** • Accommodator (feeling/doing) ***Administrative*** • Low ***Technical*** • Low ***Interpersonal*** • Medium ***Participant Risk*** • Medium ***Group Size*** • 5 - 25 ***Subgroup Size*** • 1 - 5 ***Contrast With*** • Role playing • Demonstration ***Preparation*** • Well-prepared presentation. ***Other Requirements*** *Time*: Varies. Usually brief (e.g., 5 to 15 minutes). *Space*: Nothing special. *Equipment*: Varies (e.g., props).	***Activity*** • Participants do a short, dramatic presentation that is rehearsed beforehand. ***Use*** • Demonstrating a skill. • Illustrating principles or providing material for analysis and discussion. ***Advantages*** • Quick. • Graphic. ***Disadvantages*** • Preparation time. • Not all participants are involved; some are just spectators. ***Example*** • A group of sales representatives demonstrates their sales technique by acting out a meeting with a client.

Story Boarding

Relevance
- Training Programs
- Workshops

Learning Style
- Assimilator (thinking/watching)

Administrative	• High
Technical	• High
Interpersonal	• Medium
Participant Risk	• Low
Group Size	• 5+
Subgroup Size	• 3 - 5

Contrast With
- Mind mapping
- Brainstorming

Preparation
- Ensure a sharp and clearly defined focus.
- Prepare the group to bring order and clarity to unstructured problems but not to solve these problems just yet.

Other Requirements

Time: 1/2 to 1 day.
Space: Lots of wall space and room to move around in subgroups.
Equipment: Lots of cards (e.g., approx. 3"×5") or similar size yellow stickies (i.e., Post-its), masking tape, markers.

Activity
- Having agreed on a focus participants identify the main categories, headings, subheadings, topics, and so on of a project, program, opportunity, etc.
- Next, the group or subgroups work either on the whole or on designated subtopics (e.g., parts of the story board).
- The process involves several levels of iteration as main heading cards and subtopic cards are reorganized, reworded, and shuffled around.
- Work progresses down to where there are no serious overlaps in categories.

Use
- Organizing complex situations.

Advantages
- Able to take big fuzzie problems, issues, programs, or projects and work these into a logical order.
- Linear thinkers favor this approach as it structures issues and reduced complexity.

Disadvantage
- Very time consuming and as such should be used only when an issue or problem is highly leveraged.

A Partial Example of a Story Board

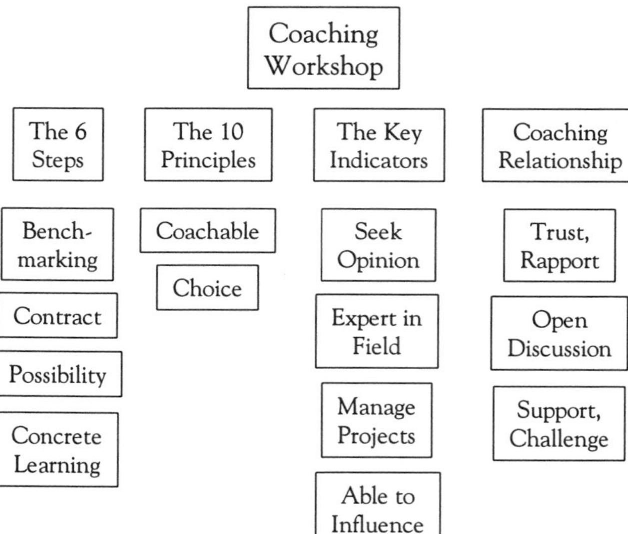

Story Boarding (continued)

A variation is the affinity diagram

- The goal is to discover patterns, categories, and insights in unstructured questions, agendas, or issues.
- Whereas story boarding starts with a "first cut" at headers or categories, affinity diagrams start more open ended. Data is recorded on cards or "sticky notes" and posted randomly on a wall. Without discussion, participants look for patterns and sort the sticky notes or cards into categories. Appropriate headers are then written for each category.

Example of an Affinity Diagram

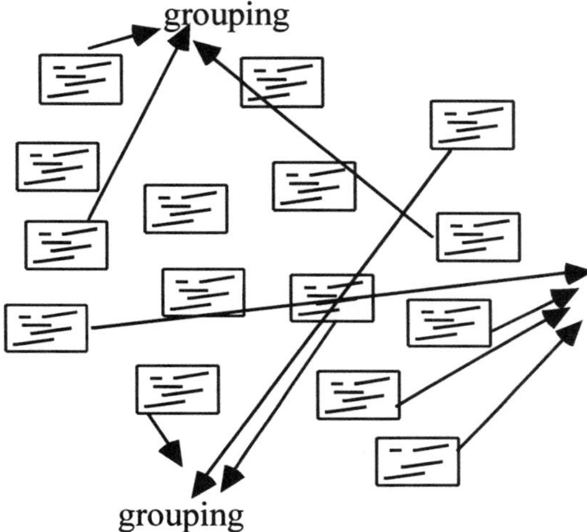

Examples

- Scoping out a project.
- Outlining a development plan for a Board of Directors.
- Outlining a book or project report.
- Developing an agenda for a workshop or training program.

Story Telling

Relevance
- Training Programs
- Workshops

Learning Style
- Diverger (listening to a story) (feeling/watching)
- Accommodator (telling a story) (feeling/doing)

Administrative • Low
Technical • Low
Interpersonal • High

Participant Risk • Medium

Group Size • 5+
Subgroup Size • 3 - 5

Contrast With
- Case study
- Guided imagery

Preparation
- Agree on the purpose, focus, or theme of stories.
- Form subgroups and set time limits.
- Set context for listening, sharing, understanding.
- (Option) tell a relevant story to "seed" or demonstrate the process.
- Participants must be prepared for a degree of sharing at an emotional level.

Other Requirements

Time: 20 to 30 minutes per participant
Space: nonoffice environment
Equipment: one flipchart per subgroup

Activity
- One or more or every participant tells a story relevant to the topic or theme in question. A brief discussion follows each story, and key points are noted on a flipchart.

Use
- Allowing participants to express their values, attitudes, beliefs, and personal priorities.
- Providing examples of experiences that demonstrates the value of learning material or emphasizes the importance of an issue or topic.
- Gaining new perspectives on one's own and on other participants, values, priorities, hopes, and concerns.
- McWhinney (1992) describes the use of stories and myths as "central elements in achieving resolutions." He goes on to say that stories are "a means of moving out of one's own construction of reality and entering into a dialogue with multiple realities to reframe one's own and others' experience in alternative frameworks."[12]

Advantages
- Participants can relate to each other based on similar past experiences.
- Provides examples of when and how to use learning on the job.
- Participants share an emotional part of themselves at their choosing and in a relatively safe and nonforced way.
- Stories provide data that is richer and has more connections to the human experience than does pure reason, logic, and analysis.

Disadvantages
- Some participants may choose to learn passively.
- Can be time consuming (e.g., each story along with questions could take up to half an hour).

Examples
- A group of experienced managers telling stories about how they successfully and unsuccessfully handled disciplinary action with marginal performers over their many years as managers in organizations.
- A newly formed work group (i.e., following a corporate merger, a new task force, project group) talking about their past experiences in new work groups, including their hopes, expectations, and concerns.

Study Guide

Relevance • Training Programs ***Learning Style*** • Assimilator (thinking/watching) ***Administrative*** • High ***Technical*** • Medium ***Interpersonal*** • Low ***Participant Risk*** • Low ***Group Size*** • 10+ ***Subgroup Size*** • 1 - 3 ***Contrast With*** • Reading • Tutorial ***Preparation*** • A well thought out study guide. ***Other Requirements*** *Time*: Study time varies. *Space*: Private space for individuals or subgroups. *Equipment*: Nothing special.	***Activity*** • A "road map" is provided for participants to follow in studying a subject. Often this includes a summary of key learning points. The road map or study guide can include many types of activities and materials and can be used individually or in groups. ***Use*** • Quick reference for students regarding what the workshop leader thinks is important. ***Advantages*** • Helps participants focus. • Valuable resource for self-evaluation. ***Disadvantage*** • Can result in "spoon-feeding" participants in that it tells participants what is important versus having them decide or discover this for themselves. ***Example*** • Participants using a study guide to decide which parts of a workbook they will read more carefully than others.

Subgroups	
Relevance • Training Programs • Workshops ***Learning Style*** • Accommodator (feeling/doing) ***Administrative*** • Medium ***Technical*** • High ***Interpersonal*** • High ***Participant Risk*** • Medium ***Group Size*** • Any size ***Subgroup Size*** • 2 - 7 ***Contrast With*** • Nominal group technique • Project ***Preparation*** • Clear directions to guide subgroup activity. ***Other Requirements*** *Time*: Varies widely (e.g., 15 min., an hour, longer). *Space*: Break-off rooms or a large enough training room so subgroups won't disturb each other. *Equipment*: Varies.	***Activity*** • A large group is subdivided into smaller groups to perform an assigned task. Subgroups meet at the same time. Following completion of the task, debriefing is done in subgroups and also usually in the group as a whole. • *Neighbor discussions* (sometimes called "buzz groups") are a subset of this design option. Participants turn to the person sitting on their left or right and discuss an issue, answer a question, or generate questions to ask within the group. Meetings are brief (e.g., five or ten minutes at the most). • *Syndicates* are a second subset of this design. Subgroups meet away from each other (e.g., in various corners of the room). Meetings vary from twenty minutes to an hour. • *Committees* are a third subset of this design. Subgroups are asked to handle a specific assignment. Each committee reports back to the whole group for direction and feedback. Committees may meet during a workshop session or between sessions. Depending on their assignment, meetings may be a half day or longer. • *Critique* is a fourth subset. Participants split into subgroups to analyze the strengths and weaknesses of a subject, system, approach, or proposal and suggest improvements. • *Critical incident* is a fifth subset. Participants are split into subgroups and given incomplete data about a problem. By analyzing the data and asking the right questions, participants are given the additional data needed to solve the problem. • *Pyramiding* is a sixth subset. It's useful for large groups. Participants start working on a problem by themselves and gradually form into larger groups (e.g., from two to four to eight).

Subgroups (continued)	
	Use • Reacting to a topic, reviewing previously presented material. • Problem solving, generating ideas or questions. • Discussing an issue or perspectives. • Getting participants active and working in teams. • Working toward consensus. • Involving participants in research and decision making (committee). • Isolating a specific recommendation, option, or method (critique). • Learning and testing application (critical incident). ***Advantages*** • Various points of view surface. • Quick (neighbor discussions). • Participative, a change of pace (i.e., gets participants talking to each other). • Creates teamwork and synergy in subgroups. • Provides a sharp focus for participants (critique). • Struggling in subgroups reinforces learning and integrates new learning with existing knowledge. • Participants are active and involved, and risk is low because the problem's solution is found with larger groups (pyramiding). ***Disadvantages*** • Unless properly debriefed, valuable information generated within a subgroup may not be shared with the whole group. • Without supervision and clear directions, groups can go off track (e.g., meetings may be poorly organized and facilitated, or the problem or option may not have been adequately defined). • While looking at efficiencies, participants may lose sight of initial assumptions (critique). • Can be overused, time consuming (committees).

Subgroups (continued)	
	Examples *Neighbor discussions* • Turning to their neighbor, participants take five minutes to discuss the learning points they are unclear on and generate questions to ask the workshop leader. *Syndicates* • Participants working in subgroups of four coach each other on developing measures for their individual "accountability statements." *Committees* • A committee of engineers is asked to recommend options for building a bridge across a specific location on a river. *Critique* • Senior executives form into subgroups to critique their companies long-term business strategy. *Critical incident* • Subgroups of middle managers work independently on a case study of an organization. Their task is to help solve a morale problem in this organization. By asking questions of the workshop leader, who is intricately familiar with the organization, they are able to hone in on the crux of the problem and recommend solutions. *Pyramiding* • A group of professionals develops team goals. First, working alone, they each draft out one goal for their team. They then pair up and help clarify and prioritize each other's goal. Another pair then joins them and they work on all the goals generated by the four people and put these in priority. Another foursome then joins them and so on.

Teleconferencing

Relevance
- Training Programs
- Workshops

Learning Style
- Accommodator (feeling/doing)

Administrative	• High
Technical	• Low
Interpersonal	• Medium
Participant Risk	• Low
Group Size	• Any size
Subgroup Size	• NA

Contrast With
- Dialogue
- Lecture

Preparation
- A great deal of coordination and scheduling is required.

Other Requirements

Time: Varies. Usually fairly brief (e.g., under an hour).
Space: A quiet place to talk on the phone.
Equipment: Usually speaker phones. Video conferencing requires sophisticated AV equipment and connections.

Activity
- Several participants talk with each other by telephone (usually long distance). An expert may begin with a brief lecture. This is followed by a question and answer session.
- A variation is *video conferencing*.

Use
- For meetings between people in a work group or project team that are separated geographically.
- For presenting to very large groups spread across an entire continent.
- Combining local initiatives with centralized expertise.

Advantages
- Cheaper than travel costs.
- Can be held more frequently than "in-person" meetings.
- Can include large numbers of participants.

Disadvantages
- Impersonal (i.e., there's really no substitute for meeting face to face).
- A great deal of coordination, equipment, and technical expertise is needed.
- Phone links can fail at critical times during a video or teleconference.

Examples
- Head office managers teleconferencing daily with remote manufacturing facilities.
- A teleconference to all hospitals in Canada helping professionals deal more effectively with change and transition in a chaotic workplace.

Vestibule Training	
Relevance • Training Programs ***Learning Style*** • Converger (thinking/doing) ***Administrative*** • High ***Technical*** • High ***Interpersonal*** • Low ***Participant Risk*** • Low ***Group Size*** • 1 ***Subgroup Size*** • NA ***Contrast With*** • Simulation • Quiz • Programmed instruction ***Preparation*** • Varies widely. ***Other Requirements*** *Time*: Varies *Space*: Break-off rooms or private space to work alone or in small subgroups *Equipment*: Varies	***Activity*** • A private place is set aside to allow participants to learn in an "off line," but realistic, environment. ***Use*** • Complex technical or administrative training. • A compromise between classroom and on-the-job training. ***Advantages*** • Self-paced, individualized learning. • Helps bring people up to standard quickly. ***Disadvantages*** • Costly. • Little human contact. • Inflexible (e.g., participants can only ask those questions that have been presupposed by the program). ***Examples*** • Often used with programmed instruction. An example is a person working alone at a computer, using a tutorial to learn a new software package. *End*

PUTTING DESIGN OPTIONS TO WORK - AN EXAMPLE

The following example shows how easy it is to use a variety of design options and access all four learning styles with participants. This particular example covers the pre-work assignment (prior to the training program start-up) and the first morning of a training program on "coaching skills." Don't struggle too hard to understand the activities described in the left-hand column. The example isn't intended to help you run this particular training program, but rather to show how a variety of design options and learning styles can be accessed in a short period of time.

Activity	*Time*	*Design Option*	*Learning Style*
Pre-work Assignment			
Reading an assigned article on coaching.	1 hour	Reading	Assimilator
Completing a questionnaire on one's coaching background and interests	1/2 hour	Reflection Instrument	Assimilator Converger
Training Program Start-Up			
"The Hook" Brief introductions followed by a panel. Experienced coaches discussing the benefits and value of coaching and reviewing some of their more memorable coaching contracts.	1 hour	Panel Q & A (question and answer) Story Telling	Diverger (listening) Accommodator Diverger (listening)
Review and finalize outcomes Review content, materials	10 min. 10 min.	Dialogue Discussion	Accommodator Converger
Expectations (hopes/concerns), Reviewing pre-workshop questionnaire	30 min.	Brainstorming Discussion	Assimilator Converger
Training Program - In Progress			
Brainstorm and dialogue "best / worst" experience as a coachee	30 min.	Brainstorming Dialogue	Assimilator Accommodator

Activity	*Time*	*Design Option*	*Learning Style*
Training Program - In Progress (continued)			
The principles of coaching - The 10 C's (reference reading pre-work)	30 min.	Lecture Dialogue Q & A	Assimilator Accommodator Accommodator
Demonstrate part of a benchmarking meeting (with volunteer from the group). Discuss in group.	15 min.	Demonstration Q & A Role Playing	Diverger (watching) Accommodator Accommodator
First round - Benchmarking meeting between coach and coachee	30 min.	Simulation Q & A	Accommodator Accommodator
Participants complete the self-diagnostic instrument - "Criteria for coaching success"	15 min.	Reflection Instrument	Assimilator Converger *End*

In this example, all four learning styles are accessed and thirteen design options are used. These are:

- brainstorming
- demonstration
- dialogue
- discussion
- instrument
- lecture
- panel
- question & answer
- reading
- reflection
- role playing
- simulation
- story telling

Many other design options would also work in the above example, for example, *appreciative inquiry* (asking participants about their strengths as coaches), *case study* (analyzing a specific coaching case, perhaps one involving a breakdown or conflict between the person being coached and the coach), *guided imagery* (having participants "daydream" about coaching successfully with a particular person, in a particular situation), and so on. Keep the term "equifinality" in mind. You can arrive at the same place from many directions.

When you set out a training program in this format, it's easy to evaluate how effectively you're accessing and sequencing learning styles. It also becomes easy to see if you're over or under using a particular learning style. Note in the above example that as training programs start-up they tend toward *watching* styles (diverger and assimilator). This is necessary but it is also dangerous. It stems from the need to dialogue, brainstorming, lecture/inform, and so on, while introducing the training program and contracting with participants. It's dangerous because it models a "watching" as opposed to a "doing" learning climate. As training programs progress, however, it gets easier to use the more active or *doing* styles (accommodator and converger), as you get participants involved in role playing, simulations, using instruments, and so on.

This is one of many arguments for keeping the "start-up" brief, tat is, because start-ups tend to be less involving and active for participants. It's also the key argument for having a "hook" right up-front in a workshop or training program.[13]

THE WORKSHOP OR TRAINING-PROGRAM AGENDAS

Here's another BGO (remember this stands for "a blinding glimpse of the obvious"). *Don't ever conduct a workshop or training program without an agenda.* People get frustrated if they don't know what steps are involved and what's coming when. For reasons outlined immediately below, agendas for training programs are usually more realistic than those for workshops.

> ***Humans are the most control-oriented animals on the planet. ... When we are unable to meet our control needs, we become disoriented.***
> ***- Daryl Conner***

Workshop Agendas

Recognize that workshop agendas are strange creatures, both necessary and at the same time something of a facade. (I'll talk more devoutly about training-program agendas in the following section.) Often, a workshop agenda isn't so much a game plan as it is a pretext for holding the workshop in the first place. Yet, agendas are so much a part of our habits and conventions it's considered unconscionable to begin a workshop without one.

Workshop agendas are often a facade because within an hour or so most workshops find their own rhythm and direction, at which point the "formal agenda" is either forgotten, or at most given only cursory attention thereafter. Perhaps what having a formal workshop agenda signifies more than anything is simply that you, the workshop leader, have given this thing a little forethought. It's proof that you have prepared.

Training-Program Agendas

Agendas for training programs are quite another matter and far from a facade. As mentioned in chapter one, training programs are more structured and predictable than workshops. It's not that training programs are rigid and unresponsive to participants' needs, but rather, relative to most workshops, their outcomes are more predetermined, and their timelines are more easily predicted. Training-program agendas are essential, valuable, and provide considerable guidance to training-program leaders and participants.

Writing an Agenda

Once purpose and outcomes are clear, and you've settled on design options, it's time to draft an agenda. Most workshop leaders prefer working toward useful and agreed upon outcomes, but without a rigorous, tightly organized agenda or timetable. An agenda that's too detailed boxes you in. Besides, who can make all those scheduling decisions ahead of time? (When it comes to workshop agendas, I believe *indecision is the key to flexibility*!) So, whether for workshops or training programs, use agendas as guidelines for organizing big chunks of time and for showing the "big picture" at a glance, but not for planning how each minute will be spent. Keep agendas flexible and keep them brief, for example, keep them to one page (see examples on pp. 246-248).

A skill testing question

For extra credit, what's the most common mistake made by new workshop or training-program leaders when writing an agenda?

Write your answer here: ________________________________

Answers:

They think everything will take half the time it usually takes! They fear running out of material, so they build everything into the agenda, including the kitchen sink. Like that old joke about having too much month left at the end of the money, they are worried about having to much workshop left at the end of the material. If this is your concern, the "activity smorgasbord" described in chapter seven is for you.

Poor contracting may be another reason for overloading an agenda. For example, a training-program leader may have unwittingly overcommitted to his/her sponsor client, promising to cover material at a hundred miles an hour, because "only the best and the brightest work here!"

If you've been guilty of overloading agendas, here's what you need to do. Stop it! Just say "no." You want a crisp pace to your workshops and training programs but you don't want to move the group so fast that all they have time to do is "role play" learning. Learning at the "application level" or above necessitates involvement, dialogue, practice, reflection, sharing contrary opinions, and so on. This takes time. Anticipate this, and build the time into your agendas.

Sample Agendas

Below are three examples of agendas. Two are from my "Train the Trainer" program. The third is from my "Coaching" workshop. The two from the "Train the Trainer" program are identical except that one is the "leader's agenda" and the other is the "workshop agenda" that participants would see. The leader's agenda has additional information to cue the leader at appropriate times. (For even more detailed reminders see the activity smorgasbord described in chapter seven.) As in the examples provided here, keep the workshop agenda, the one that you hand out to participants, simple and uncluttered.

The type of agenda shown here leaves you with plenty of room to maneuver. Simply move the horizontal lines around as needed to signify how much time has been scheduled for each part of the agenda. Notice these lines (or time allocations) don't tie you down to specific times, but do provide approximate guidelines. Notice also how easy it is to quickly assess what's being emphasized and what's not. In the first example, "delivery and practice" takes up part of the first day and all of the second day, while "planning training" is only given about an hour on the first day. Participants can see immediately that the focus of this workshop is on delivery and practice.

Train the Trainer - Agenda

Time	DAY 1	DAY 2
8:00	Introductions & Start-Up	2nd Practice Delivery
	Foundations for Training	Delivering Training
	Planning Training	2nd Practice Delivery
12:00	LUNCH	
1:00	Designing Training	2nd Practice Delivery
	Prep 1st Practice Delivery	Delivering Training (continued)
	1st Practice Delivery	2nd Practice Delivery
4:30	Prep Evening Assignment	Wrap Up

Train the Trainer - Leader's Agenda

	DAY 1	DAY 2
8:00	Introductions & Start-Up (Start-Up Content, Workshop Introduction, People Introductions, Objectives, Agenda, Expectations, Evaluation Form, Learning Contract, Workbook, Pre-Workshop Questionnaire, Evening Work)	2nd Practice Delivery (Three 10 min. Deliveries and Feedback)
	Foundations for Training (Workshop Climate, Adult Learning, Pre-Workshop Assignment, The Nature of Work and Change)	Delivering Training (Training Roles, Time, Facilitating, Presenting, Questioning, Nonverbals, Managing Participation, Dealing with Resistance, Negotiating, Visual Aids, Teaching a Job, Reinforcement, Feedback, Motivation)
	Planning Training (Training Needs Assessment, Marketing, Process Cycle, Planning Checklist, Evaluation, Setting Objectives, Organizing a Workshop, Writing an Agenda, Classroom Set-ups)	2nd Practice Delivery (Three 10 min. Deliveries and Feedback)
12:00	LUNCH	
1:00	Designing Training (The Experiential Learning Cycle, Learning Environment, Matching Learning Styles, Workshop Design Options)	2nd Practice Delivery (Three 10 min. Deliveries and Feedback)
	Prep 1st Practice Delivery	Delivering Training (continued)
	1st Practice Delivery (Using the "Heinz 57" - Twelve 5 min. Deliveries and Feedback)	2nd Practice Delivery (Three 10 min. Deliveries and Feedback)
4:30	Prep Evening Assignment	Wrap Up

Coaching Workshop - Agenda

8:00	Objectives/Climate Content/Materials
8:40	Introductions/Expectations
9:10	Best/Worst Experience As "Coachee"
10:00	*Break*
10:10	Exercise - Step 1: Benchmarking Demo, Practice
11:30	The Principles of Coaching - The 10 C's
12:00	*Lunch*
1:00	Step 3: Defining What's Possible Developing Learning Experiments
2:10	Steps 4 and 5: Taking Action and Staying on Track
3:00	*Break*
3:15	Comparing Internal Coaching, Mentoring, and External Coaching
3:45	Step 6: Ending the Coaching Contracts
4:00	Coaching Tools
4:30	Wrap Up
5:00	*End*

CONCLUSION

Summary

Design Is the Leader's Job

Selecting from the design options described in this chapter requires the type and range of information outlined throughout this book. Few participants will have knowledge of these areas. You may wish to seek help from other, perhaps more experienced, workshop leaders to select, adapt, or build appropriate designs for your workshop or training program.

Workshop Design Strategies

Keep the following strategies in mind as you select design options provided in this chapter.

1) Keep participants active and involved. Passive learning is *low yield*.

2) Use lots of relevant stories and examples. They ground learning by providing context.

3) Employ all the senses. Most of us are visual learners, but the more senses we use when learning (e.g., visual, auditory, kinesthetic), the more modes of recall we have available.[14]

4) Encourage participants to collaborate and share information. If later you want participants to work or learn on their own, just introduce a little competition.

5) Challenge and support participants. Don't spoon-feed, but don't introduce so much ambiguity you risk them becoming confused and disheartened.

6) Keep the structure informal. Encourage participants to raise questions, call "time out," and move around as they wish.

7) Let things unfold. It's important to have structure, but it's also important to be flexible. Change the agenda and workshop designs as needed.

8) Build flexibility into the workshop agenda. In this way, when a rich vein of learning is discovered (e.g., a participant introduces an idea for an exercise, or the group gets interested in a particular model) you are able to stay with this for a while, taking advantage of these "learning moments."

9) Build free time into the workshop agenda. Participants do some of their best learning when they discuss the workshop between sessions.

10) Avoid traditional teaching. Workshop leaders are not evaluated by whether they finished the curriculum, but by *results* (e.g., a product is developed, participants learned a new way of working on a project). Workshop and training-program leaders need to be concerned with learning readiness, learning climate, participation readiness, and with their own readiness to lead. (Each of these areas is discussed at length in this book.)

Workshop Design Options Sorted by Learning Style

Each design option is sorted into one of Kolb's four learning styles. Designing your workshops to appeal to a range of learning styles challenges participants who may normally only use one or two of these styles. In addition, it ensures your workshop process appeals to a mix of participants, favoring a variety of learning styles.

Workshop Design Options

Descriptions of workshop and training-program design options are provided in this chapter, along with the advantages and disadvantages of each and an example of each option in practice.

Developing a Workshop Agenda

Keep the agenda simple and flexible and based on clear outcome statements. It's sometimes tempting to skip having a written agenda, but this is almost always a mistake. First, participants need to see your game plan. Second, an agenda allows participants to see what's being emphasized and what preparation may be needed and when. If nothing else, a written agenda helps participants mentally prepare for each session of the workshop or training program. Avoid detail in your agenda. Leave room to maneuver and adjust as the workshop or training program develops. You need to be able to take advantage of unforeseen opportunities as they arise.

Putting Design Options to Work - An Example

An example is provided showing how easy it is to employ a number and variety of design options. The key here is selecting design options appropriate to the stated workshop or training-program outcomes, keeping participants involved and active, and accessing all four learning styles to hold participants' interest.

Checklist

Workshop Design Strategies

1) Keep participants involved and active
2) Use stories and examples
3) Employ all the senses to make maximum impact on participants
4) Let participants collaborate and share information
5) Challenge and support participants
6) Keep the structure informal
7) Let things unfold
8) Build flexibility into the workshop agenda
9) Build free time into the workshop schedule
10) Avoid traditional teaching

Kolb's Learning Styles

- Accommodator (feeling/doing)
- Diverger (feeling/watching)
- Assimilator (thinking/watching)
- Converger (thinking/doing)

Types of Workshop and Training-Program Agendas

- Workshop agenda (for participants)
- Leader's agenda (to cue the leader)

Workshop and Training-Program Design Options

- Appreciative Inquiry
- Behavior Modeling
- Brainstorming
- Case Study
- Clinic
- Coaching
- Contrasting Perspectives
- Debate
- Demonstration
- Dialogue
- Discussion
- Drill
- Field Trip
- Forum
- Game
- Guided Imagery
- In Basket
- Instruments
- Job Instruction Training
- Lecture
- Listening Team
- Marathon
- Matrix Analysis

Workshop and Training-Program Design Options (continued)

- Mindmapping
- Nominal Group Technique
- Open Space Technology
- Panel
- Peer-Assisted Learning
- Polarity
- Practice Exercise
- Programmed Instruction
- Project
- Question and Answer
- Quiz
- Reading
- Reflection
- Role Playing
- Sensitivity Training
- Simulation
- Skit
- Story Boarding
- Story Telling
- Study Guide
- Subgroups
- Teleconferencing
- Vestibule Training

Exercise

Workshop and Training-Program Design

What learning style do you personally prefer? What's your second preference? Just take a guess. Note: If you want something better than a guess, I recommend the learning style inventory published by McBer & Company (1985).[15]

1st preference: ____________________

2nd preference: ____________________

What five workshop or training-program design options do you use the most?

What five could you use a little more? Would using these add variety and interest to your workshops or training programs?

Notes

[1]Smith, R.M. (1982). Learning how to learn: Applied theory for adults. Chicago, IL: Follett, p. 140.

[2]Owen, H. (1991). Riding the tiger: Doing business in a transforming world. Potomac, MD: Abbott Publishing, pp. 140-141.

[3]From: Pitman, T., & Bushe, G. (September, 1991). Appreciative process: A method of transformational change. OD Practitioner.

[4]Osborn, A.F. (1963). Applied imagination (3rd ed.). New York, NY: Scribners.

[5]Senge, P.M. (1990). The fifth discipline: The art and practice of the learning organization. New York, NY: Doubleday, p. 241.

[6]Byrum, B. (1989). New age training technologies: The best and the safest. The 1989 Annual: Developing Human Resources. San Diego, CA: University Associates, p. 189.

[7]Related to job instruction training is the section titled "Teaching a Specific Job or Task" in chapter fifteen.

[8]Buzan, T. (1983). Using both sides of your brain. New York, NY: Dutton.

[9]Nominal group technique is sometimes referred to as the "Delbecq technique," after its original author. See: Delbecq, A.L., & Vande de Ven, A.H. (1971). A group process model for problem identification and program planning. *Journal of Applied Behavioral Science*, Vol. 7, pp. 466-492.

[10] Owen, H. (1991). Riding the tiger: Doing business in a transforming world. Potomac, MD: Abbott Publishing.

[11]Johnson, B. (1992). Polarity management: Identifying and managing unsolvable problems. Amherst: MA: HRD Press Inc.

[12]This quote adapted by Will McWhinney is from: Smith, K.K. (1982). Rabbits, lynxes, and organizational transitions. In J. Kimberly & R. Quinn (Eds.). New futures: The challenge of managing corporate transitions. Homewood: IL: Dow Jones-Irwin. p. 292. From: McWhinney, W. (1992). Paths of change: Strategic choices for organizations and society. Newbury Park: CA: Sage. p. 8.

[13]The "hook" is described in chapter ten.

[14]Genie Laborde outlines the NLP processes (neuro linguistic programming) known as representational systems. These are visual, auditory, kinesthetic, and cerebral. See: Laborde, G.Z. (1984). Influencing with integrity. Management skills for communication and negotiation. Palo Alto, CA: Syntony. pp. 58 - 67.

[15]Kolb, D.A. (1985). Learning-style inventory: Self scoring inventory and interpretation booklet. Boston, MA: McBer & Company.

Chapter 7

Organizing a Workshop

Introduction

This chapter provides a basic level of information on organizing a workshop. The concept of an activity smorgasbord is introduced, and practical examples of organizing checklists are provided (e.g., for communicating, scheduling, ensuring appropriate materials and equipment). Finally, ten alternative room set-ups are illustrated.

This chapter covers

- The activity smorgasbord.
- Organizing checklists.
- Room set-ups.

Activity Smorgasbord

What if you're instructing a workshop and you get stuck "big time"? You don't know what to do next. The group is waiting; your mind is racing; you start to panic. Or, what if the group wants to emphasize something you haven't prepared to discuss (e.g., you thought the group wanted to spend more time on strategy, but it turns out they want to focus instead on goal setting)? Or, what if you're just a neurotic person who can't sleep the night before the workshop unless all the bases are covered? Well, fear not; the *activity smorg* is here. It slices, dices, and purées any workshop. All you need to do is add a group and heat. Here's how it works.

The activity smorg is just a list of activities, models, and ideas you have in your toolbox for a given workshop. It's organized using the same structure as either the workbook or agenda. It's written in shorthand as a checklist for quick reference. Use whatever short forms, slang, or descriptive phrases make sense to you. And don't worry about sentence structure, grammar, punctuation, and so on. Your activity smorg will be unintelligible to participants or anyone else for that matter. That's OK. You're the only person who needs to use it. It only needs to make sense to you.

The activity smorg will help you respond to the group in a flexible and focused way. That is, it will help you organize and adapt a workshop based on changing group demands. It will also ensure you keep the group active and learning. The idea isn't just to pick any activity when things slow down in a workshop, but rather to select activities and models with a clear focus on the outcomes being sought from the workshop or training program.

A partial example of an activity smorg

The following is drawn from a more detailed "activity smorg" for a training program that I lead. It's included here only as an example. (The full activity smorg for this training program is five pages.) Quickly scan to get a feel for how it's set out. Warning, you'll drive yourself nuts trying to figure out what the following details mean (e.g., "nine dots" is a little game I play when discussing double-loop learning, the symbol "*" signifies an essential item, "H" reminds me of a joke I could tell related to a given exercise). The shorthand is only intelligible to me. It reminds me about activities, models, and ideas I might use at a given point in the workshop.

Activity Smorg

Introductions

* Self first. Then popcorn style. H - Don't be last! (1/2 hour)
- Workbook, process, philosophy. (15 min.)

Contracting

* Climate - informal, permission. OH cartoons.
- Review evaluation form. Contract roles, process, and outcomes.
- Flip: "What are the benefits of being an in-house workshop leader?" (What are your selfish reasons?) OR "What does it feel like to be a part-time workshop leader?" OR "What does it feel like to be a participant in an in-house workshop?"

* Review agenda.

Pre-workshop assignments

* Review summary of participant questionnaires.
* Review all pre-work (e.g., questions from workbook).

Adult learning

* * T chart learning readiness (is, is not). (1/2 hour)
* Flip best experience, worst experience, what did leader did, didn't do. Draw out principles. (situation, behavior, feelings) Debrief. (1/2 hour)
* Nine dots.

Implementation planning (1/2 hour)

* * Write two things you will do differently as a result of this workshop.
* Cartoon review. (1/2 hour)
* Challenge to group - every time out, work on two things to improve.

End

Organizing Checklists

Following are three checklists to help you organize. Use these as examples to develop checklists for your workshops and training programs.

A) Overall Organizing Checklist

Use this checklist to organize the overall project of planning, designing, developing, delivering, and following up on a workshop or training program.

1) Assess participants' workshop needs. Distinguish among participants where they have unique needs.

2) Decide on the levels of evaluation (reaction, learning, behavior, organizational results) that will be used.

3) Decide on and write *purposes* and *outcome* statements for the workshop or training program (e.g., the process cycle). (If applicable, revise purpose and outcomes based on evaluations from previous workshops.)

4) List and summarize key learning points (i.e., each major piece of the learning content) and briefly outline why each is important.

5) Decide on group size and develop the workshop smorgasbord (see above).

6) Outline what resources and time are needed to conduct the workshop, and decide and design specific activities participants will engage in (e.g., small

group exercises, simulations). Use your workshop smorgasbord and the options described in chapter six to design the workshop.

7) Plan the workshop start-up and check it using the principles of adult learning described in chapter two. Pay particular attention to learning climate, learning readiness, and participation readiness.

8) Plan the workshop's sequence (i.e., what will you present first, second, and so on) and draft the workshop agenda. You may want a more detailed agenda for yourself. (Examples of agendas are provided in chapter six.)

9) Produce workshop materials (e.g., flipcharts, handouts).

10) Create, develop, and/or locate lots of stories, examples, and metaphors to enhance the learning content. Ensure your examples are relevant and understandable. You may also want to prepare a leader's guide. The smorgasbord is helpful here.

11) Ensure administrative issues are covered (e.g., pre-work, facility and equipment requirements, correspondence with participants). See checklists below.

12) Practice leading the workshop; in particular practice your workshop start-up.

B) Schedule and Timetable Checklist

The following example is a timetable of events from a *Train the Trainer Workshop* that I lead. It clarifies steps and helps coordinate workshop preparation.

Participants Confirmed 1 Month Prior to Workshop	*Pre-Meeting with Participants* 3 Weeks Prior to Workshop	*Questionnaires Returned* 1 Week Prior to Workshop	*Workshop Conducted*	*Follow Up Meeting* 6 to 8 Months Following Workshop
Workshop facility booked Pre-meeting scheduled List of participant names to administrator (needed to prepare participant packages).	1/2 to 1 hour introductory meeting with participants. Participant packages passed out and discussed (e.g., workbook, pre-workshop assignments). Workshop purpose reviewed. Questions and concerns addressed.	Completed "pre-workshop participant questionnaires" returned to administrator.	Time left open for 2 to 3 hour evening assignment on day one.	Informal 1 to 2 hour "round table" meeting with participants. Those participants who attend are asked to come with 2 or 3 specific questions or issues they've had difficulty with since the workshop.
Target Date:	Target Date:	Target Date:	Target Date:	Target Date:

C) Communication, Materials, and Equipment Checklist

Below is an example of a preparation checklist for the *Train the Trainer Workshop*. Adapt it as needed to suit your own workshops and training programs.

Workshop Name: ____________	Client: ____________
Workshop Date(s): ____________	Leader(s): ____________
# of Participants: ____________	Client Contact: ____________
Client Phone #: ____________	Address: ____________
	____________

Check (☐) when complete. (To ensure you don't leave home without it.)

Communication	*Materials*	*Equipment, room set-up, and other materials*
• Workshop scheduled • Administrative arrangements made with client • Confirming memo sent to contact or sponsor client • Expectations clear (sponsor and end-user client) • Number of participants known • Correct spelling of participant names (to personalize materials) • Introductory meeting scheduled with participants approximately 3 weeks before the workshop • Covering letters, pre-workshop assignments, and workbooks given out or sent to participants	• Agenda • Handouts ready. Copies made and 3-hole punched. Flipcharts prepared. • Workbooks • Learning-style inventories • Participant pre-workshop questionnaires • Prepared overhead transparencies • Overhead cartoons organized • Door sign • Name tents • Copies of articles • Copies of participant list for each participant • Books for reference table • Copies of my papers, book summaries, and book reviews • Bio, brochure • Roll of quarters	• Facilities confirmed • Extra writing paper and pens • Post-its, dots (for voting) • Masking tape, pins • Markers (water based, dry erasable, overhead) • Overhear projector and screen • Materials and leader tables • Unused overhead transparencies • Flipcharts and flipchart paper • TV, VCR, videotape (for use as demo) • Video equipment and 1 tape per participant (filming practice sessions) • Desk clock • Refreshments ordered

ROOM SET-UPS

Set up the training room to maximize involvement and comfort. Seat participants so that eye contact among them is automatic. Don't overcrowd, but don't spread people too far apart either. That "long distance feeling" may lead to less discussion. Ensure there's plenty of table space for binders and other materials, even if participants won't be doing much writing. Place all equipment, materials, and aids in sequence for quick access.

Before the workshop begins, check ventilation, fan noise, temperature, lighting, and outside disturbances, particularly in hotels where noise from neighboring rooms can be very distracting.

The following diagrams provide examples of typical workshop and training room arrangements. Vary the room design based on a number of factors such as workshop purpose, group size, topic, relationships within the group (e.g., various departments or professional backgrounds). For example, use of the "U-shape with tables" for groups under twenty participants is quite common.

Use the "multiple round tables" design (although sometimes the tables are square) when group size ranges from thirty to about sixty participants. This design creates five to eight subgroups or "islands" of five to eight participants each and allows variations in prior knowledge to be absorbed and managed within the subgroups. That is, each participant has a "home base" where he/she can get help understanding learning material that may be unclear (e.g., participants can discuss a given concern at their table, even though they may not consider it significant enough to raise in the group as a whole). The "multiple round tables" design allows you to circulate easily and be near each subgroup.

The following options for workshop and training room set-up are diagrammed below.

- Traditional rows (classroom style)
- Three rectangular tables
- Circle
- One rectangular table
- One aisle
- Two aisles
- Open rectangle
- U-shape with tables
- U-shape without tables
- Multiple round tables

Workshop and Training Room Diagrams[1]

Traditional Rows

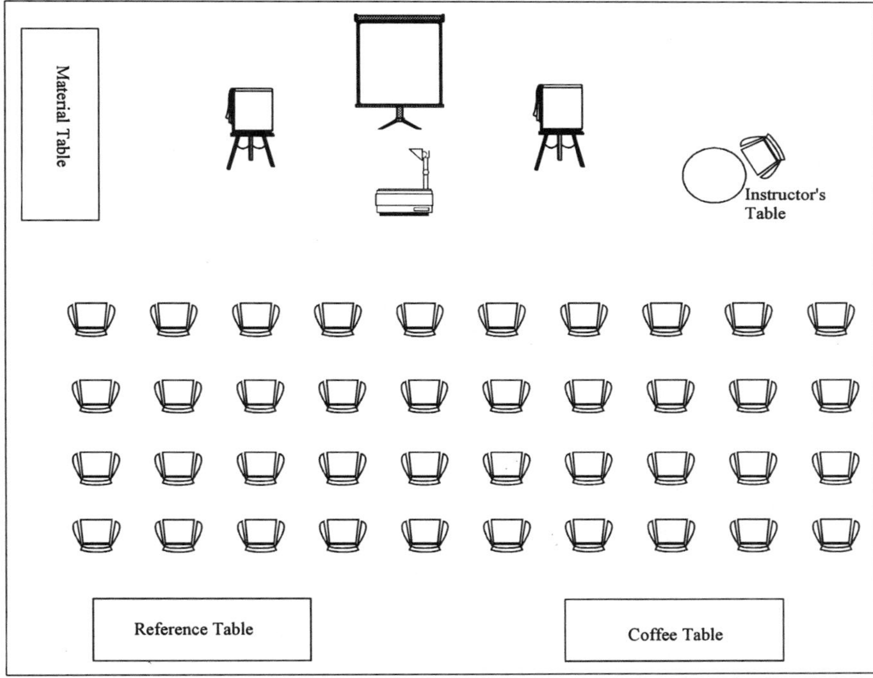

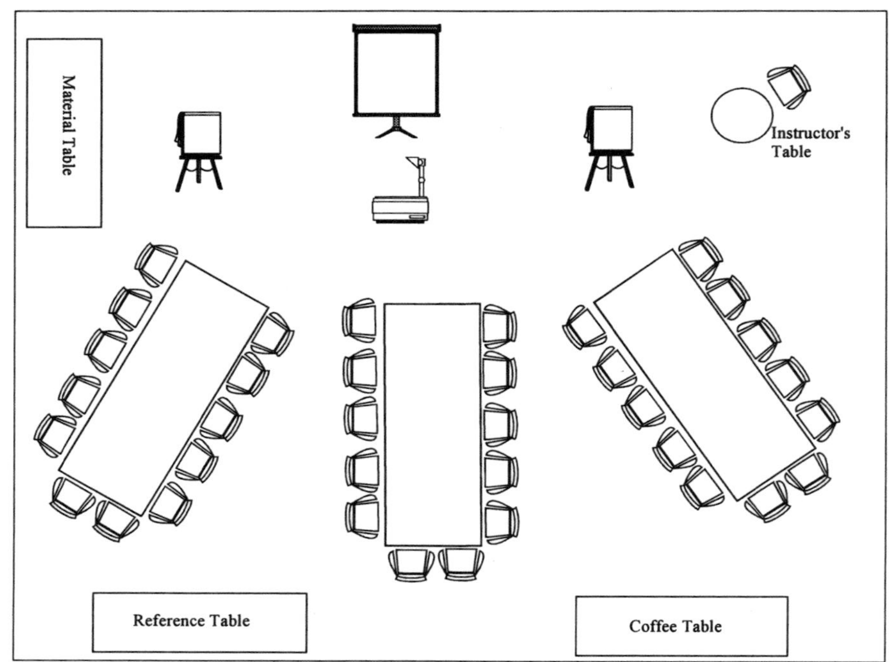

Three Rectangular Tables

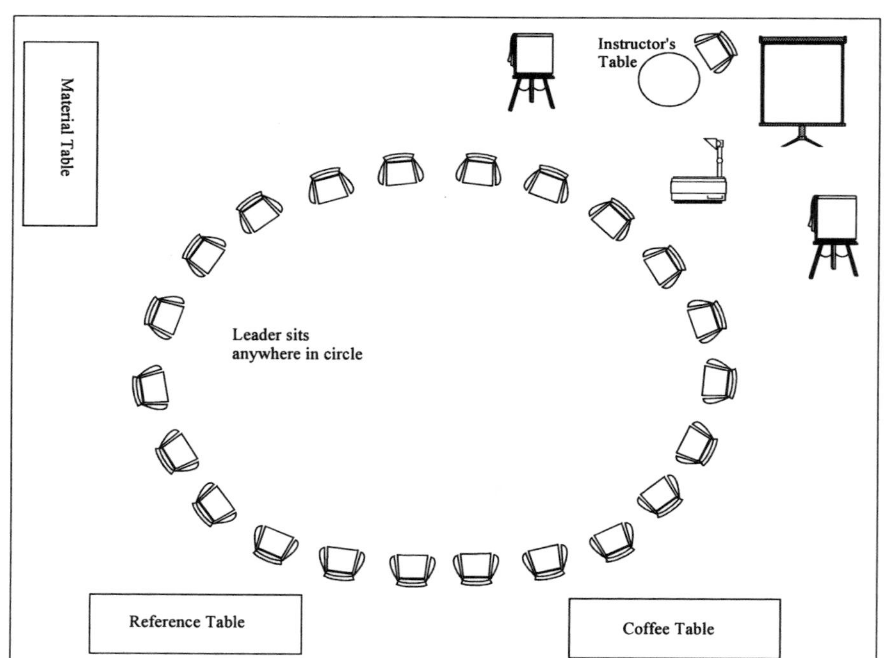

Circle

One Rectangular Table

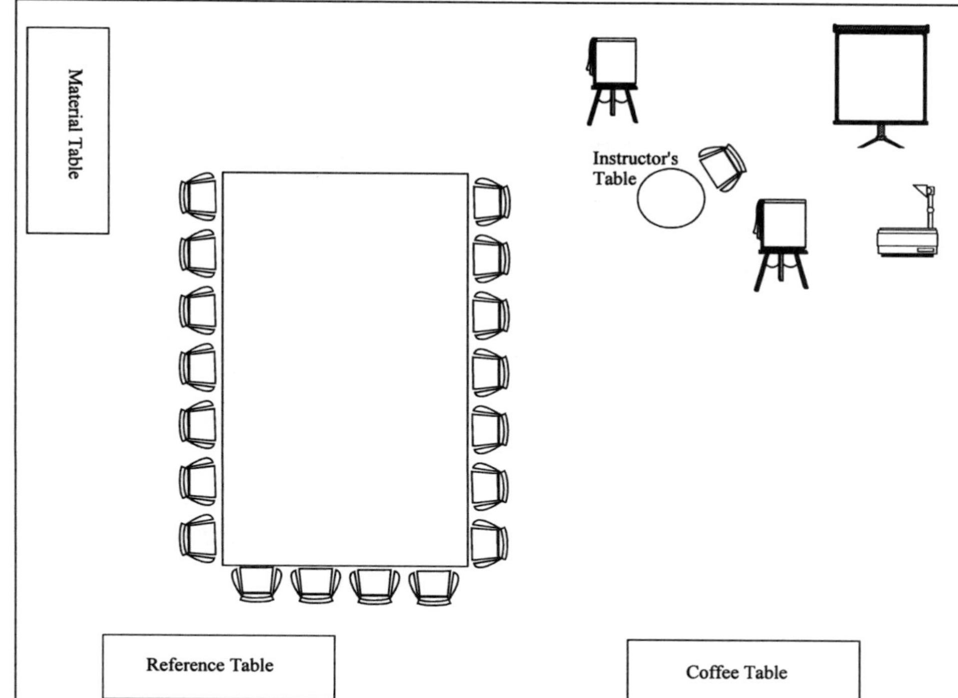

One Aisle

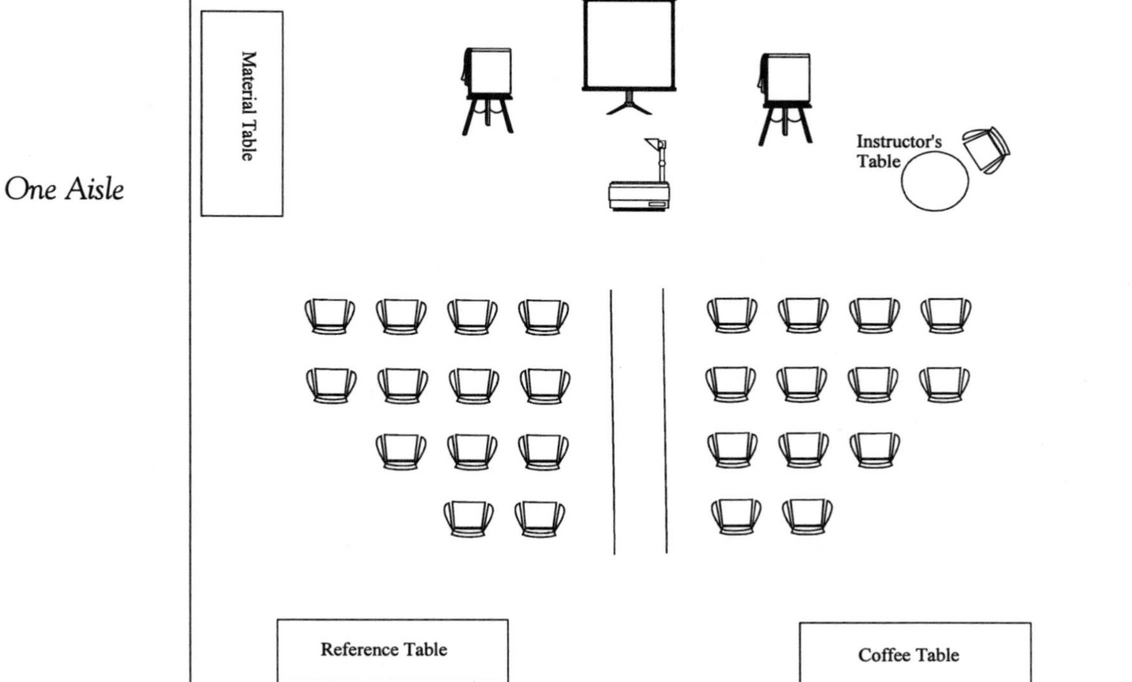

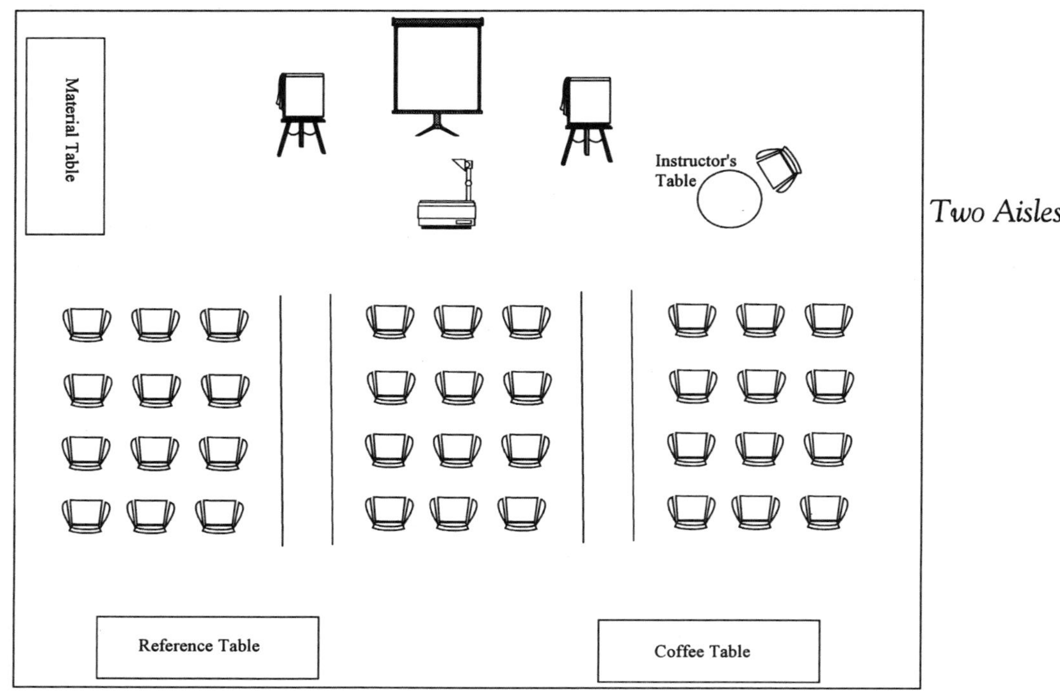

Two Aisles

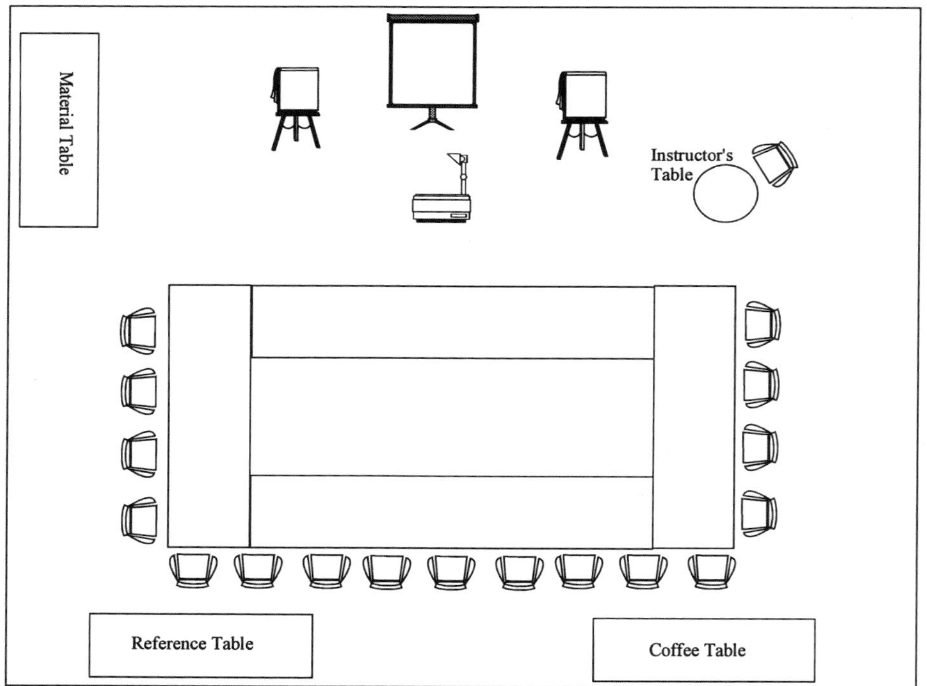

Open Rectangle

U-Shape with Tables

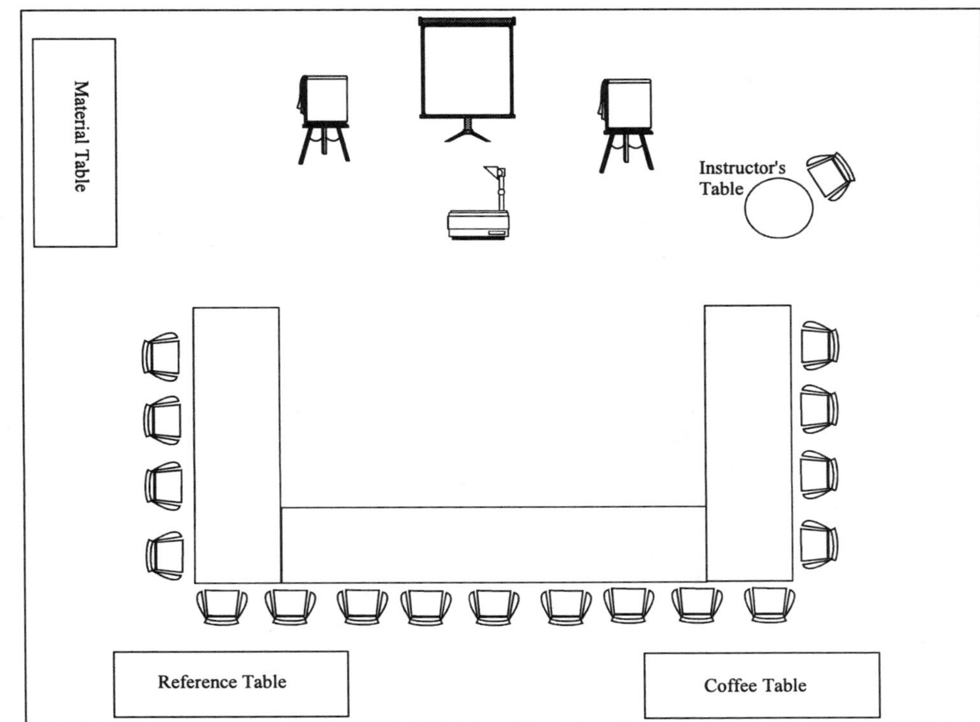

U-Shape Without Tables

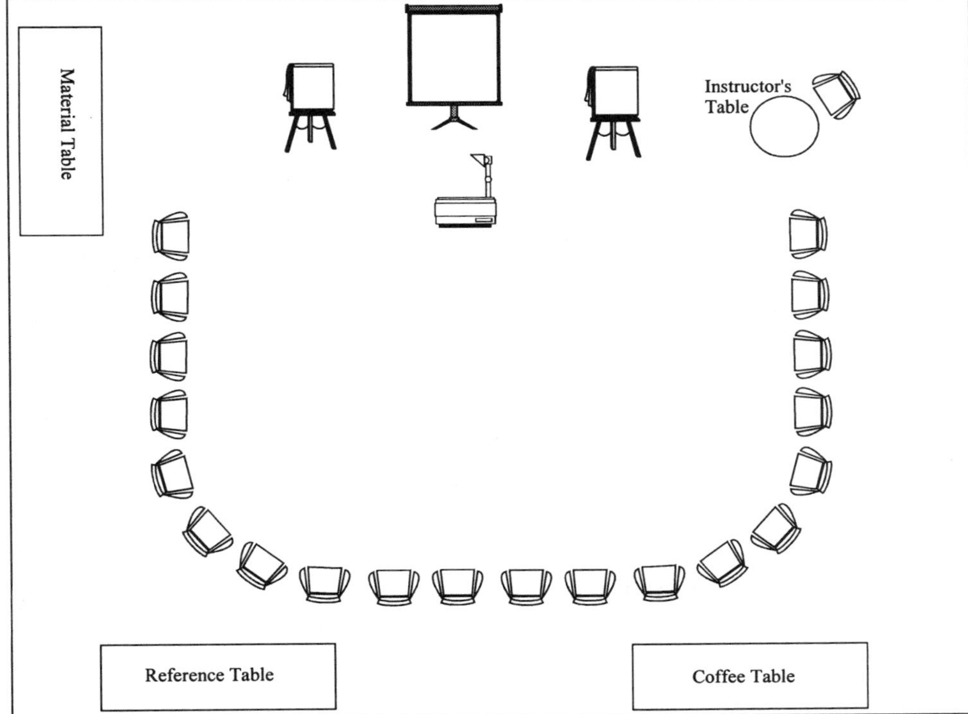

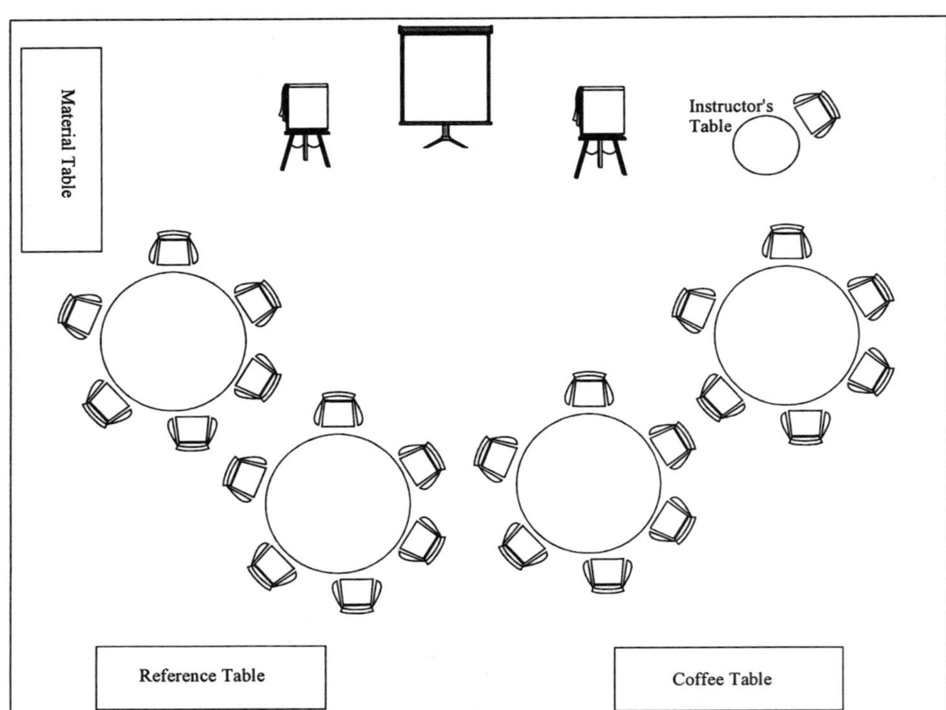

Multiple Round Tables

CONCLUSION

Summary

Activity Smorgasbord

An activity smorgasbord is just a "prompt list." It's a list of activities, models, and ideas that you're already familiar with. It's organized to correspond to your workshop or training-program agenda or workbook. These lists are written in shorthand and intended "for your eyes only." They are handy reminders of what you might want to do during each part or session of the workshop. One quick glance at your activity smorg, and "presto," you magically pull an activity or model out of your hat, and the workshop moves along, right on focus.

Preparation Checklist

Three preparation checklists are provided in this chapter. Use the *overall organizing checklist* to ensure that you cover "all the bases" when organizing a workshop or training program. Adapt the *schedule and timetable checklist* to your own workshops and training programs. Finally, the *communication, materials, and equipment checklist* will help you ensure you've got everything you need on hand at your workshop or training program. It'll help you to sleep a little better the night before.

Training Room Set-Ups

Diagrams of ten workshop and training-room designs are included in this chapter. How you choose to set-up your training room is a function of how many participants are taking part, the workshop's purpose and content, and the relationships you want to foster in the group.

Checklist

Overall Organizing Checklist	*Example of a Schedule and Timetable Checklist*
1) Assess workshop needs 2) Decide levels of evaluation 3) Write purpose and outcomes 4) Summarize key learning points 5) Develop smorgasbord 6) Design the workshop or training program 7) Plan start-up 8) Plan sequence 9) Produce materials 10) Develop stories, examples, and metaphors 11) Cover administrative issues 12) Practice	• Participants confirmed • Pre-meeting with participants • Questionnaires returned • Workshop conducted • Follow up meeting

Exercise

An Activity Smorgasbord for Your Workshop or Training Program

1) Brainstorm a list of activities, models, ideas, tools, gimmicks, phrases, tactics, exercises, and so on for your next workshop or training program, that is, elements that you might be able to use when you lead this particular workshop or training program. Don't worry about the order at this point. You can clean that up later. Keep descriptions brief.

-
-
-
-
-
-
-
-

2) Next, "high grade" this list and put it in some logical order.

3) Finally, meet for a half hour with a friend or colleague and see if he/she can help you add to this list.

Notes

[1]I would like to thank Sydnie Waring for developing these workshop and training-room diagrams.

Preparing and Using Visual Aids

INTRODUCTION

Visual aids are an important way for workshop and training-program leaders to add punch to their presentations and maintain interest. The following will get you thinking about what equipment and materials preparation you need to do prior to the workshop. It also covers the effective use of a wide range of learning and presenting aids.

This chapter is considerably different than others in this book; it doesn't deal with concepts, just with simple and straightforward procedures. Most of the information in this chapter will be considered "common sense" by experienced workshop and training-program leaders. They might just want to quickly skim this chapter, picking up a few pointers to polish their style. For those of you who don't have a lot of practice using visual aids, however, you'll find the following helpful. It may even spare you potential embarrassment at the hands of an acrobatic flipchart or a cold, vengeful VCR.

Bandler and Grinder (1975, 1979,1981) say that most people are visual learners.[1] That is, most of us learn more from seeing than from hearing or touching. Thus, visual aids are not just "nice to have," they're necessary. With the following tips and a little practice, you'll also find them easy to use.

This chapter covers:

- Overall guidelines for using visual aids.
- Visual and learning aids.
- Examples of prepared workshop and training-program materials.

OVERALL GUIDELINES FOR USING VISUAL AIDS

Rejeanne Taylor (1991), a presentations skills consultant, provides two clear guidelines for using visual aids. One, keep them simple. Two, ensure they are consistent with your verbal message. "To be effective," Taylor writes, "visuals must provide an almost 'instant' visual message which is in 'sync' with the spoken message."[2]

Ask yourself the following questions as you prepare visual aids for your workshop or training program.

Deciding the message

- What's the message I want participants to get? What do I what to emphasize? How can I say this so participants grasp the key points and don't get lost in the details?

Deciding when to use visual aids

- Does the message warrant a visual aid (i.e., is it complicated, is it numerical or statistical, does it require an explanation or outline, does it add humor)?

Selecting a visual aid

- How many people will be there? How will the room be organized? What equipment will be available?

Avoiding the don'ts

- Am I using a visual aid as a crutch or as an "add on"? Does it fit with the flow of my presentation/delivery?

Visual and Learning Aids

Flipcharts

It's almost impossible to use a flipchart so poorly that it doesn't add value to your work. The following tips will help you use this tool to great advantage.

Some things have got to be seen to be believed.
- Ralph Hodgson

Flipcharts are still the most convenient form of "common text" available today. Their biggest advantage is that they can be used for building ideas, lists, models, and what have you in real time or "on the spot" with a group (e.g., brainstorming lists). The biggest drawback is that they don't come with a "spell checker." There are three ways around this problem. First, tell people it takes very little imagination to go through life always spelling the same word the same way. Second, just say, "It's not that I'm a bad speller, but rather I simply prefer my own version of these words." Third, write so sloppily on the flipchart that people feel lucky just to be able to guess at the word, let alone be concerned with your spelling! But seriously, flipcharts greatly aid group understanding, reference, and recall.

Only record information on flipcharts that will be referred to again in the workshop. As a rule, if a flipchart isn't worth posting, then it's not worth writing in the first place. So use flipcharts in moderation. Overusing them slows conversation, causing the pace to drag.

When possible, prepare flipchart pages ahead of time and store them in a cardboard tube for transportation. Title them, use "masking tape tabs" for organizing them, and pencil in notes as personal reminders. Then immediately before the workshop, pre-tear pieces of masking tape for posting flipcharts on the walls. Stick these to the flipchart stand for easy access later on. One word of caution: Stick these pieces of masking tape on the flipchart stand where they won't tangle with flipchart page, as the pages are turned over to the back of the flipchart.

Place the flipchart easel close to participants. Most are not adjustable for height. When writing or speaking, stand to the side of the flipchart and face the group. Try not to speak while writing, although occasionally time pressures makes this necessary. Make these exceptions brief, and speak loudly.

When facilitating discussion, record participants' ideas and examples using their exact words. Ask them to paraphrase or summarize. If their points are too wordy, get permission from them before abbreviating their words (e.g., "How can I write that up here?"). Use multiple colors, arrows, circles, and underlining for emphasis. Put checkmarks beside ideas that are repeated.

Legibility is important when recording on flipcharts. So remind yourself to slow down in order to write neatly. Letters should be at least two inches high. Printed letters are easier to read than writing, although you won't always have time to print. Keep diagrams simple. Write in lists or bullets, with only the title and the first letter of each bullet capitalized. Aim for fewer than fifteen or twenty words per page. And although it's not always possible, try to avoid "squeezing in" information.

Use broad tipped markers, and try to alternate colors for each bullet. Dark colors such as black, green, and blue work best, but don't use any more than three different colors per page. Yellow and pink aren't visible, even from a short distance away. Red has too much of an evaluating or "teacher image," so avoid it, except for underlining or highlighting. Keep all your red markers in a separate bag and pass them out only for voting or prioritizing. When voting, ask participants to place a big red checkmark (✓) beside their choices.

Water-based markers won't soak through to other pages, can be washed out of clothing, and can be used even when writing on a page already posted on a wall. Alcohol-based markers, on the other hand, last longer but usually soak through to the following page. So when using alcohol-based markers, only use every second page of the flipchart pad.

If you make an error on a prepared flipchart that must be corrected, rather than rewrite the entire page, cover it with a "paper patch" using Scotch tape.

When removing flipchart pages from the pad, tear firmly while holding the bottom of the page. Post flipchart pages in some logical order. These will be useful later for summarizing and reviewing. Keep a clear stage. When moving to a new topic, reorganize and clean up flipcharts at the front of the room to avoid distracting or confusing participants. Among other things, this means posting or piling used flipchart pages neatly and out of the way.

Overall, flipcharts are familiar and accepted equipment in workshops. They can be used spontaneously and aren't expensive. The downside is that they are difficult to transport and are only useful with groups smaller than twenty-five or thirty. Needless to say, in very large groups (e.g., a hundred or more) flipcharts can still be used for subgroup work.

Static Pages

"Static pages" are flipchart sized pages that stick, or are supposed to stick, to the wall. Use a little masking tape when they don't stick as advertised. They're made of plastic and are reusable as long as you only use dry erasable (whiteboard) markers. They're inexpensive and usually sold in pads of five to twenty, and they're a lot easier to haul around than flipcharts. The disadvantage is that if you leave your markings on too long, they're toast.

Overhead Projectors

You don't need a darkened room to use an overhead projector. However, it's important that participants have a good view of the screen, without any glare. When using another visual aid, such as a flipchart, it's also important to have the overhead projector out of your way. To accomplish this, put the screen in a corner rather than at the center of the room. Set the overhead projector squarely in front of the screen to avoid distortion and have it on a low table so it doesn't block participants' views. Next, focus and check for readability from the farthest point of the room.

Murphy's law states that "if something can go wrong it will." So always keep a spare bulb handy, and know how to change it quickly. Remember, it only takes one psychiatrist to change a light bulb, but the light bulb really has to want to change! And carry an extension cord in your box of workshop materials. Hotels never have these when you need them.

If you need to move the overhead projector during the day, mark the floor with masking tape so that you can reposition it properly and with a minimum of effort.

Use large type and lists or "bullets" on transparencies. Each sheet should only have about six to eight short lines of information. Some workshop and training-program leaders suggest even less information. They talk about the "rule of four." That is, each overhead transparency should have only four lines with four or fewer words per line.

Avoid confusion by numbering your transparencies and use the transparency frame to make notes to yourself. When displaying the transparencies, position them on the projector before turning it on and stand in a position where you don't block participants' views. Also, position the transparency as high as possible on the overhead. This makes it easier to see for participants at the back of the room. Overlap transparencies as you move from one to the next to avoid subjecting participants to "white blasts of light." When finished, turn the projector off before removing the last transparency.

Some people have a personal aversion to "overhead striptease." This is where the workshop leader only shows one bit of the transparency at a time. As the workshop leader exposes the overhead ever so slowly, some feel overcontrolled and treated like inattentive children. Sometimes it may be necessary but it's annoying. If you must use this approach, tell people *why*. This way they'll give you the benefit of the doubt. One tip here: Place the masking or nontransparent page under, rather than on top, of the transparency. This way it won't fall off as you near the bottom of the transparency. Another tip is leaving the bottom third of the transparency blank.

When using an overhead, face the group rather than the screen when speaking and stay out of the projector's beam. Turn the overhead projector off temporarily when a participant asks a question or a discussion starts. This way there is less distraction and it shows you value participants' input. When you want to take back control of the discussion simply switch the projector back on, and you immediately have everyone's attention.

Point to the transparency rather than to the screen. If you are at all nervous, make sure to lay the pointer on the projector table. Otherwise what seems like just a little shaking will be magnified on the screen. On the screen it will seem like your hand is oscillating a couple of feet each way. This actually happened to a friend of mine but he made a great recovery. "Don't worry about the shaking," he said, "I shoot with my other hand." The group laughed and his presentation never missed a beat.

Another tip is to make sure your pointer is flat, otherwise it tends to roll around on the transparency table. A flat pencil or swizzle stick is best.

The overhead table is a magical place. Something happens that only a physicist could explain when an overhead projector has been turned on for a while. Transparencies take on a life of their own. They won't stay where you put them and seem to slide around telekinetically. Anyway, all this can be exorcised simply by using frames on your transparencies. Needless to say, the problem with transparency frames is that they won't fit into any file folder known to man. This makes them a real nuisance to carry around.

A good "rule of thumb" is to always have handouts of your overheads. This way people can review an overhead even after you've taken it off the projector table. Handouts also provide a convenient place for note taking.

In summary, overheads are familiar, accepted, and convenient. Transparencies are easy to transport and can be used spontaneously. Maybe the biggest plus with overheads is that they can be used with any size group. On the downside, overheads are a little more formal than flipcharts, and workshop leaders often use too many transparencies.

Having said all this about using overhead projectors I must "fess-up" and say that I rarely use them. It's not just that they are more formal than flipcharts, but that they also take flexibility away from how you're able to organize the training room. A flipchart can be moved easily. An overhead projector is more limiting. Overheads are also noisy, and the arm of the projector is usually obstructing somebody's line of sight. And, you can't post overhead transparencies like you can flipchart pages. Thus, you lose the easy reference capability for reviewing and summarizing when starting-up and wrapping-up workshop sessions.

Electronic Flipcharts

Electronic flipcharts are great but you don't find them in many companies. They work well but are expensive and difficult to transport. Their big advantage is that you can push a button and instantly photocopy a flipchart page. This copy is the size of a standard sheet of printer paper (i.e., 8 1/2 × 11 inches). Their disadvantage is that you can only show one flipchart page at a time.

Chalkboards

Chalkboards are cheap, messy, temporary, and associated with school. Workshop leaders only use them when they have no other choice, as in a university classroom for example. It helps a little if you use a chalk holder, and for lack of any other positive feature, at least you can correct mistakes easily on a chalkboard.

Whiteboards

It's easier to write neatly on whiteboards than on flipcharts or chalkboards, probably because of the smooth surface. Like chalkboards, the text is temporary so you can also correct mistakes. Their big drawback is their limited space and fixed position on the wall. Worse yet, whiteboards are easily ruined by using the wrong type of marker or the wrong kind of detergent to clean them. Only dry erasable markers should be used on whiteboards. The other downsides are that material can't be saved, and you need to turn your back to the group as you write.

Slides

Slides provide high-quality images and can be used with any size group. They have several drawbacks, however. These include their formality (i.e., lack of spontaneity, the need for a darkened room), cost, and time required to prepare. Slides are also easy to load upside down or backward and are often overused by workshop leaders. Finally, with slides as with overhead projectors, carry an extra bulb and extension cord and practice using the equipment ahead of time. In particular know how things hook together, switch on, and focus.

TV's and VCR's

There are some great business tapes available for workshops, the John Cleese series for example. And videos certainly do captivate an audience. The downside is that TV's and VCR's are expensive and need lots of cables and cords. It's also guaranteed this equipment will make you look like an idiot if you aren't prepared. So arrive early, set up, and test. Learn how to use the buttons, because no two TV's or VCR's anywhere in the world have the exact the same controls! Don't use tapes that are too long; something under fifteen or twenty minutes is about right. Preview the video ahead of time, set the tape to the spot you want, and you're ready to go. When presenting to large groups, use big screens or multiple TV sets hooked together.

Computers

I recently heard a long-time university professor bemoan the fact that student essays are getting worse, not better, since students began using computers. Before computers, he argues, student essays were more focused, more concise, and more organized. Without computers students had to sit down and figure out what they wanted to say beforehand. They had to develop structure and flow to their essays before they began typing. Computers, however, allow students to start writing without a plan. They just start dumping data into an essay without a clear purpose or structure. Thus, an effective tool is used improperly as a substitute for thinking, planning, and hard work, rather than as an aid and time saver. This probably isn't exactly what Marshall McLuhan (1995) had in mind when he wrote his paradox "the medium is the message," but it seems apropos nonetheless.[3]

Computers offer countless advantages, but they can also cause chaos for workshop leaders, particularly when you're using somebody else's equipment. Incompatibilities in operating systems and programs can surface, and you're constrained by where screens or projectors are located, where cords and cables will reach, and how the room is set up. Indeed, training rooms are arranged for discussion in small groups, and this is often incompatible with using computers and monitors. Invariably participants can't read what's projected from the computer because they're sitting too far away, the monitor has too much detail, or the information simply isn't left on the screen long enough.

As with the university professor bemoaning student essays since computers became commonplace, technology can actually detract from, rather than support, your message if you're not careful. It's also possible to hide behind technology. Rather than having to properly structure a presentation, a workshop leader can just throw tons of data, graphs, colors, charts, and pictures at participants from his/her computer. The workshop leader then becomes "data focused" rather than "participant focused." All his/her time goes into preparing "the show" versus thinking about and planning for participant interaction and learning. And because "the show" becomes the goal and demands so much attention to detail (e.g., preparing graphics), participants get turned into "an audience." As was said earlier, passive learning isn't very effective.

One Fortune 500 company has gone so far as to ban "high tech" presentations from some of its meetings. They noticed presentations were getting less concise and more time consuming with lots of pizzazz, lights, color, flashing screens, moving characters, graphs, charts, pictures, and more data. They also noticed presentations were taking more time and money to prepare. At the same time they discovered their meetings were less relevant. They were experiencing most of the downsides of "high-tech" presentations and few of the upsides.

Finally, I suggest having a backup strategy when using high-tech equipment, because all too often machines don't work as planned. This strategy might be as simple as carrying a set of "low-tech" overhead transparencies or some lecture notes, anything that could be used in a pinch should the equipment decide to be a little obstinate.

Articles and Objects

This is like adult "show and tell." Allowing participants to handle an object (e.g., a valve from a pipeline) helps them understand and make connections with the learning material. So pass objects around, let participants touch and examine them, then leave them on display for observation during breaks. Plan your presentation to allow for the distraction involved as the object moves from participant to participant.

Pointers

Pointers are helpful, just don't fidget with them; it's distracting to participants. Laser pointers have much greater range, but if your hand is shaking, it looks like a light show.

PREPARED WORKSHOP AND TRAINING-PROGRAM MATERIALS

You'll need to prepare flipchart pages, handouts, and overhead transparencies (perhaps even slides, computer graphics, and so on) prior to the workshop or training-program start-up. But, pre-writing flipchart pages for each workshop or training program is a hassle, especially if you use a lot of these. Reusing them isn't the answer either. They tend to get marked-up, curled at the corners, and look "used." Here's how to take the sting out of this process.

Assuming you're not a member of "The Lead Pencil Club" - members are known as "Leadites," not to be confused with Luddites - that is, assuming you have a computer, here's what you do. Start by typing and organizing prepared flipchart pages on your computer. Use the top right-hand corner to code an organizing system. This will later be "penciled in" on the top right-hand corner of the corresponding flipchart page (e.g., a number, a letter, or a comment) to help you sequence and organize your prepared flipchart pages. In the examples below, you'll find four different organizing systems.

1) The first simply provides directions. For example, in the top right-hand corner of the flipchart page titled "Parking Lot" you'll see the comment "Post." Thus, this page is to be left on the wall for use during the training program.

2) Another organizing system is numerical. These flipchart pages will be used in approximately this order during the workshop or training program.

3) The group marked "Not Ordered" will be used in any order, as needed, during the workshop or training program. The group marked "Start-Up" will be used during the workshop or training-program start-up. "HO" (for "handout") indicates this page will be copied and distributed to participants rather than written on a flipchart page.

4) Another group is ordered by task or exercise, for example, "PS 1," "PS 2," and so on. This indicates that these flipchart pages are for a "practice session."

Once you get your flipchart pages organized this way in your computer, you can take a copy and ask your assistant to "neatly" write out the flipchart pages. Ask him/her to refer to the guidelines above for writing flipcharts. Once written, flipchart pages can then be piled in their respective categories, rolled-up, and placed in a cylinder for transport to the workshop or training program.

Examples of Prepared Flipchart Pages and Handouts

The following are examples of prepared flipchart pages that I use in a training program titled *Train the Trainer*. These are shown here just to give you a sense of how they should be set-out and organized. Notice that you're able to get a lot more detail into handouts, as opposed to flipchart pages.

Post

Parking Lot

1

Three Tools for Working with Groups

- Making information visible
- Brainstorming
- Prioritizing

2

Adult Learning

Adults bring experience with them:

- They have something to lose and gain
- They want to be listened to
- They want to test new ideas and skills
- They expect to be able to answer questions from their own experience
- They get "ego invested" in what they do

3

Adult Learning

Adults want training to focus on "real life" issues:

- Deal with the here and now
- Learning as a means to an end
- Focus on *how to's*
- Be aware of gains and making visible progress

4

Learning Readiness

How can you tell when people are learning ready?

How can you tell when people are *not* learning ready?

Not Ordered

Process Cycle

Purpose

- What is?
- What is not?

Outcomes

- What outcomes are desired?

Steps

- What actions to produce results?

Capabilities

- Who's in the room?
- What do they need to bring/do?

Feedback

- Who needs to hear what during and after the workshop?

Not Ordered

How We Develop Competence

Unconscious Competence

Conscious Competence

Conscious Incompetence

Unconscious Incompetence

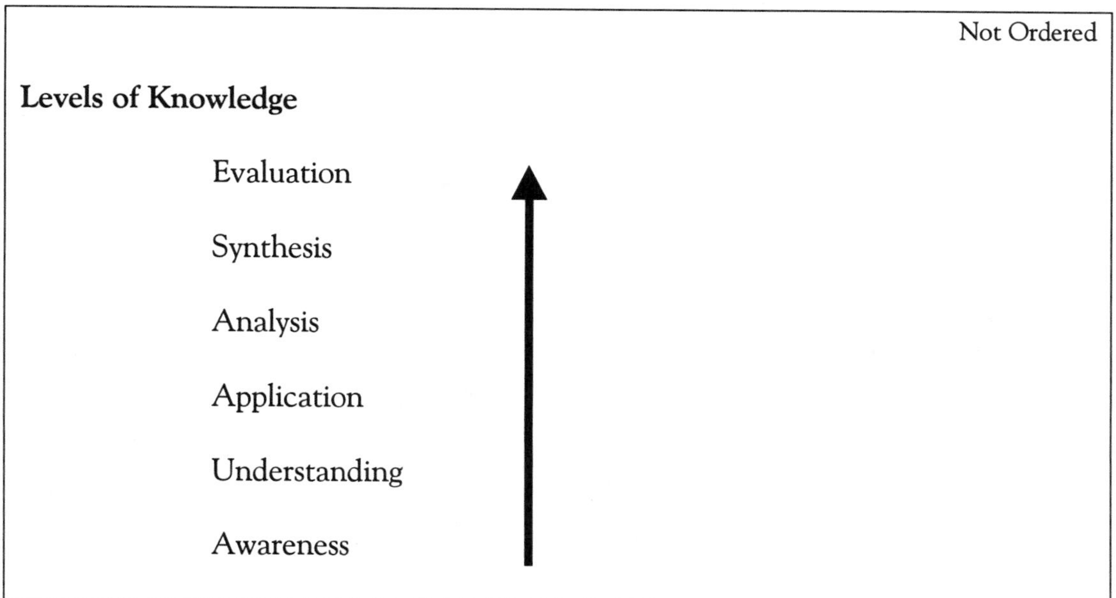

Not Ordered
Levels of Knowledge
Evaluation
Synthesis
Analysis
Application
Understanding
Awareness

PS 1

Practice Sessions - Guidelines for Selecting a Topic

- Existing or upcoming in-house training that you will be delivering
- Live, real (not hypothetical)
- Could be technical, administrative, operations, or interpersonal type training
- Something from the workbook (e.g., help the group use questioning skills)
- Select something that will challenge you a bit (i.e., not something that you can do on "automatic pilot")

HO

Practice Session - How Feedback Will Be Given

Duration: 10 minutes

Order of Giving Feedback

1) The practicer
   - What I did well ...
   - What I would do differently next time ...

2) The group
   - What the practicer did well ...
   - What the practicer might do differently next time ...

3) The observer (using notes)
   - What the practicer did well ...
   - What the practicer might do differently next time ...

4) The facilitator (providing only feedback that has not already been mentioned)
   - What the practicer did well ...
   - What the practicer might do differently next time ...

HO

1st Practice Session

Teaching the Design Options

Read assigned pages. 5 minutes

Pick one method to teach the group. 2 minutes
- A method you'll use sometime in the future.
- A method you want to learn.
- A method you are not presently good at using.

Jot down a few thoughts on how you can teach this method. 3 minutes

Meet with a coach to help you prepare. 8 minutes
- You coach for four min. You get coached for four min.

Prepare materials (if any), and rehearse or reflect on how you might teach this method. 4 minutes

Teach the method to the group. 5 minutes

Get feedback from the group on your instruction. 3 minutes

Total Time 30 minutes + 10 minutes per participant (delivery and feedback).

HO

2nd Practice Session

Practice Session - Observer's Role

Write

- Specific words and phrases.
- Suggestions for alternative approaches.

Feedback

- Give feedback verbally.
- Then give your notes to the practicer.

Suggestions

- Focus on the practicer's learning outcomes.
- Don't try to catch everything; just be clear on what you do give feedback on.
- Be descriptive, not evaluative (a gram of observation is worth a ton of evaluation).
- Don't participate in the practice session (you'll be too busy writing observations).
- Write neatly; don't rush.
- Don't write more than one page of feedback.

CONCLUSION

Summary

Visual aids spruce up a workshop and focus the group's attention. There is one caveat, however. Although you want participants to focus on your visual aids, don't let them become *your* focus of attention. Keep your attention on the group.

Flipcharts

Despite today's high-tech business climate, the flipchart is still one of the most widely used visual aids. They're portable, permanent, and easy to use. For maximum visibility use dark colored, broad tip markers. Write clearly and keep the flipchart close to participants. (Otherwise, distribute binoculars so they can read it!) Organize prepared flipchart pages with "masking tape tabs" and use "paper patches" to cover up mistakes. Posting pages in order during the workshop provides a great visual aid for summarizing and reviewing.

Overhead projectors

Overhead projectors are another common visual aid. When using overheads and slide projectors keep a spare bulb and extension cord handy, although chances are you won't need either until you forget them at the office! Hand out photocopies of your overhead transparencies to aid note taking.

Electronic flipcharts

Electronic flipcharts display only one page of text at a time, but instantly copy that text onto regular size paper. They're not very portable, but when you have one handy, they're a great time saver.

Slides

Slides aren't often used in workshops due to the time and expense required to produce them. Slides also require a darkened room. They're more common in formal presentations.

TV's and VCR's

There's a wealth of excellent business tapes available for workshops. Always do a dry run ahead of time, and set your tape to the spot needed, so you're ready to go.

Computers

Computers permit polished presentations, but they also test your technical expertise. Different software programs and operating systems are always looking for ways to disagree.

Checklist

Flipcharts

- For groups smaller than twenty-five or thirty
- Only record information that will be referred to again
- Post flipchart pages in some logical order
- Overusing flipcharts slows conversation
- Prepare pages ahead of time
- Use masking tape tabs
- Speak standing to the side of the flipchart and facing the group
- Record participants' exact words and phrases
- Write clearly
- Write in lists or bullets with fewer than fifteen or twenty words per page
- Use broad tipped markers and dark colors
- Water-based markers won't soak through
- Correct errors with paper patches
- Flipcharts can be used spontaneously

Static Pages

- Use masking tape when they don't stick to the wall
- Only use dry erasable markers

Electronic Flipcharts

- Can push a button and instantly photocopy the flipchart page
- Use only dry erasable markers
- Can correct mistakes easily

Chalkboards

- Use a chalk holder
- Can correct mistakes easily

Whiteboards

- Use only dry erasable markers
- Can correct mistakes easily

Slides

- Slides are easy to load upside down or backward
- Carry an extra bulb and extension cord
- Practice using the equipment

TV's and VCR's

- Excellent business tapes are available
- When presenting to large groups, use big screens or multiple TV's hooked together
- Arrive early, set up, and test (learn which buttons do what)
- Don't overuse
- Set the tape to the spot you want so you're ready to go

<table>
<tr>
<td>

Overhead Projectors

- Locate the overhead projector to the side
- Focus and check for readability
- Have a spare bulb and extension cord
- Use large type and lists or bullets (six to eight lines per transparency)
- Number transparencies
- Make notes to yourself on the transparency frame
- Avoid "overhead striptease"
- Point to the transparency rather than to the screen
- Leave the bottom third of the transparency blank
- Distribute handouts of your overheads
- Overhead projectors can be used with large groups (e.g., 200 or more)
- Avoid blinding the group between transparencies

</td>
<td>

Computers

- Check for incompatibilities in operating systems and programs and have a backup strategy in case the equipment fails
- Avoid having too much detail on the monitor
- Stay "participant focused" versus "data focused"

Articles and Objects

- Pass objects around and then leave them on display

Pointers

- Don't fidget with pointers

End

</td>
</tr>
</table>

Exercise

Working with Visual Aids

1) Which visual aids do you use best (e.g., flipchart, overhead projector)?

2) What are your strengths working with visual aids? How can you continue to develop these strengths?

3) Which visual aids do you use least well? Why?

4) Name two things that you will commit to doing better to improve your use of visual aids.

Notes

[1]1) Bandler, R., & Grinder, J. (1975). The structure of magic. A book about language and therapy. Palo Alto, CA: Science and Behavior Books. 2) Bandler, R., & Grinder, J. (1979). Frogs into princes: Neuro-linguistic programming. Ed. Stevens, J.O. Moab, UT: Real People Press. 3) Bandler, R., & Grinder, J. (1981). Trance-formations: Neuro-linguistic programming and the structure of hypnosis. Ed. Andreas, C. Moab, UT: Real People Press.

[2]Taylor, R. (1991). "Presenting ... you." Calgary, Alta: Infinite Scope. Unpublished manuscript, p 6-3.

[3]McLuhan, E., & Zingrone, F. (Eds.). (1995). Essential McLuhan. Concord, Ont: Anansi, p. 3.

Chapter 9

Conditions for Workshop Success

INTRODUCTION

Once the elements of learning climate, learning readiness, and participation readiness are in place, the success of a workshop or training program is practically assured. This chapter provides critical insight and practical advice for managing these elements.

It's possible to de-motivate participants. This can result from being manipulative, working with a hidden agenda, not following through on promises, being arbitrary and dictatorial, not telling the truth, acting defensively, and so on. It's *not* possible, however, to control, command, or insist that participants "be motivated." Nonetheless, there are things you can do to encourage participants feeling supported and challenged (learning climate), motivated to learn and to achieve meaningful results (learning ready), and willing to be active and involved (participation ready).

Conversely, there's no point delivering new learning content before participants are *learning ready*. And asking participants to be active and involved in discussions or small group exercises before they're *participation ready* usually leads to problems at worst or a poor product at best.

This chapter covers:

- Learning climate.
- Learning readiness.
- Participation readiness.
- How the three interrelate (learning climate, learning readiness, and participation readiness).

WORKSHOP AND LEARNING CLIMATE

Pilots pay a lot of attention to atmospheric conditions. For them, ignoring the weather could lead to disaster. It's not all that different for workshop leaders, except that their "weather" is the emotional environment in the workshop or training room, and when they "crash and burn" it's only metaphorical. But it still hurts.

George Bernard Shaw was wrong when he said that, "Everybody complains about the weather but nobody ever does anything about it." Successful workshop leaders do a lot of things to influence the "weather" or climate in their workshops. It starts with having a clear picture of what a positive and energized learning climate looks like.

An effective learning climate is a little paradoxical. You want participants to be comfortable yet struggle with ideas and perspectives. You want them to be reflective yet also active and vocal. You want them to feel supported but also challenged. The bottom line on learning climate is "energy." You want energy in the room. A workshop leader can work with both positive and negative energy, but not with apathy. Apathy means the workshop is dead in the water - there is no challenge, no involvement, and no caring. Apathy is anathema to workshop leaders.

This section covers:

A) Assumptions underlying workshop and learning climate

B) Effective and ineffective learning climates

C) Strategies for creating an effective learning climate - the short answer

D) Strategies for creating an effective learning climate - the long answer

A) Assumptions Underlying Workshop and Learning Climate - A Context for the Context

The term "workshop or learning climate" refers to the environment or context in which participants learn and accomplish workshop and training-program outcomes. But, what's the context for learning climate? What assumptions underlie learning climate? That is, what's the context for this context we call learning climate?

The focus of the assumptions underlying learning climate is on how to influence individual and group change in organizations, because after all, that's the raison d'être for workshops and training programs. Whereas workshops usually focus on group change, training programs focus on individual change, that is, change in terms of knowledge, skill, behavior, and even attitude and perspective.

The following three approaches (command, reason, and facilitate) to influencing groups and individuals to change their thinking and behavior provide a contrast for understanding learning climate. Each of these approaches results in different levels of commitment and action. All have their place, and depending on the situation, any one of these approaches might be the best way to influence change. These approaches can be used alone or in combination, but no matter how you use them, no single method or combination of methods works perfectly or all the time.

The *command* method involves demanding or ordering others to change their behaviors. Sometimes it works and sometimes it's necessary. Organizational authority is still very much needed on occasion. As the old saying goes, "It's difficult to rule with fear, but impossible to rule without it" (see the section below titled, "Demanding Learning Readiness"). Sometimes, however, the *command* method results in all kinds of problems. Force often leads to temporary compliance. This may continue as long as someone in authority is watching or as long as rewards and punishments exist. However, force often results in defensiveness, and even subtle forms of sabotage. Nonetheless, Al Capone, the Chicago gangster, preferred this method. He said, "You can get more done with a kind word and a gun, than you can with a kind word alone."

"Command" at its worst

Here's an example of the *command* method at its worst. About twenty years ago I was organizing a three day supervisory training program at the retail store in a small prairie city. The general manager of the store was a hard nosed, "get things done" kind of guy, and he usually got results. Never known as a participative manager, he sent the "invitation" letter to would-be participants. His letter had their names, the workshop title, the place, the starting time, and only one sentence, "Be there." Just guess how motivated these people were to learn and change, particularly during the first morning of this workshop!

The *reason* method involves persuading others through special knowledge and logical arguments. Closely associated with traditional teaching, this method assumes rational people are guided by reason and self-interest and relies on expert power to provide evidence, unbiased reason, and "truth." Usually, this method results in longer lasting and more internalized change than the command method. But it also results in lots of "yeah, buts." People don't always listen to reason and common sense. Anyway, it turns out that common sense isn't all that common, particularly when people don't have common experience. That is, we all see the world a little differently.

The *facilitate* method involves working with participants' values and assumptions. The goal is not just to change behavior, but also to change attitudes so that support for behavior change emerges naturally. Personal values, group norms, and shared goals are seen as the foundation for effective change. Thus, learning and change are given a personal reference, as workshop leaders invite resistance and challenge. Power is shared in the workshop, and participation and experimentation are encouraged. The *facilitate* method usually results in longer lasting and more internalized change. After all, would you rather be "sold" or "decide to buy" on your own? Would you rather be "taught" or "learn for yourself"? In each case the *facilitate* method aims at accomplishing the latter.

The *command* method is rarely effective in workshops or training programs, particularly if overused. However, on occasion it's used in combination with the *reason* method in training programs for production workers. Needless to say, you always want elements of the *reason* method in a workshop, but it's not the best driving force for generating an effective learning climate and encouraging learning readiness. The best workshops and training programs for any type of employee, but particularly for knowledge workers, are by far and away the *facilitate* method. This may be used in combination with the other methods, but *command* must always be a last resort.

B) Comparing Effective and Ineffective Learning Climates

What does an effective learning climate look like? What do you hear? What do you feel? The chart on the following pages contrasts what you see, hear, and feel in an outstanding and a poor learning climate.

C) Strategies for Creating an Effective Learning Climate - The Short Answer

A workshop is a lot like an airplane; it moves a group of people to a different place. But no one on board is just a passenger; everyone "works" the flight. Everyone has a role, and everyone is responsible for getting to their own destination. The group succeeds or fails as a team, and the workshop leader owns no less, or no more, responsibility for workshop success than does each and every participant in the workshop. Nonetheless, you need to focus on actions *you* can take in establishing an effective learning climate (i.e., actions within your "circle of influence"). So, how do you establish an effective learning climate?

The short answer is that it's a result of everything you do as a workshop leader. It's not a matter of a simple six-step model or a few basic "do's" and "don'ts." As a matter of fact, the list is never ending. For example, you can develop rapport, practice adult-learning principles, ensure your workshop process is understood, clarify participants' needs, review the benefits of the workshop, tie-in learning material using examples and stories that are relevant to the group's situation, and on and on. Therefore, strategies or "how to's" are provided throughout this book, particularly below and in chapters ten through sixteen.

	An Outstanding Learning Climate	*A Poor Learning Climate*
What you see	• Participants are active (e.g., they're working in small groups, moving around). • Participants are sitting up, leaning forward, and looking you in the eye. • Judging by facial expressions participants seem eager, learning ready, and glad to be involved. • Participants are taking notes and reading handouts. • Participants arrive on time at the beginning of the workshop and after breaks.	• One or two participants are into heavy duty doodling. • One or two participants can barely keep their eyes open after lunch. • Expressions on participants' faces say "we're tired, bored, and lost." • One or two participants drop out (i.e., they're suddenly "busy" and unable to attend the next session). • A few participants are slouched over in their chairs or leaning way back conducting a ceiling tile census.
What you hear	• Participants are constantly asking challenging questions and adding stories and examples to the workshop. • There's lots of involved discussion. • Participants talk about the workshop during breaks. • Participants come to you at the breaks with questions, ideas, and stories. • There's lots of noise during small group exercises. • There's laughter and "on-topic" humor. • You say to yourself, "This is going great!" • You hear comments from the group like, "We didn't know we could work this well together." "We're really making progress." "I'm getting a lot out of this."	• Participants say things like, "This doesn't relate to our situation." "This isn't new to us." "This isn't what I thought we'd be doing." • You're the only one asking questions. And for that matter, you're the only person answering them as well. • You have to call on participants by name to get a response to your questions. • Mostly you hear your own voice (i.e., you're doing most the talking). • The jokes are "off-topic." • You say to yourself, "What a bunch of turkeys." • Most of what you try with the group is met with outright resistance (e.g., skepticism) or what seems to be indirect resistance (e.g., questioning directions endlessly).

	An Outstanding Learning Climate	*A Poor Learning Climate*
What you feel	• The best of you is coming out, you're really "on," you're even surprising yourself (e.g., whenever you seem to need a model, idea, or method it comes out of your mouth). • The workshop is flowing like you've done it a hundred times before. • You're in rapport with the group (e.g., an ongoing joke has developed in the group). • You're taking risks and just about everything you try is working.	• You feel off balance and out of "sync" with the group. • You feel like you have so much more to offer but it just won't come out in this workshop climate and with this group. • Everything you try is an uphill battle. • One or two participants take shots at you hoping to catch you off guard. • You're on the defensive and decide to "play it safe." • You feel like you've got a slow leak! You just want to do your job and get out of there.

D) Strategies for Creating an Effective Learning Climate - The Long Answer

There are lots of ways of involving participants, establishing an effective learning climate, and sharing responsibility for the workshop. Each of the fifteen strategies presented below is well within every workshop leader's "circle of influence." They focus on sharing responsibility for workshop and training-program success. Use them to involve participants, to provide direction, and to stay on course.

1) Aim for a Strong Performance Ethic

Focus on learning and behavior change in the workshop and on providing knowledge and tools for helping participants improve their performance back "on the job." A strong performance ethic includes hard work, joint responsibility, risk taking, informality, and fun. But the focus is always on outcomes. Both you and participants need to constantly revisit the workshop's purpose and desired outcomes, keeping everyone working toward a meaningful and agreed upon target.

2) Motivate Participants and Practice Adult-Learning Principles

Practice adult-learning principles. It is not enough to facilitate and instruct; you must also create a motivating climate. Model a high-performance ethic. Your main motivation tool is enthusiasm for the subject, for being in the workshop, for working on participant issues, and for learning. And although it can be overdone, it's a good idea to share your stories (personal and professional) with the group. This adds context, life, and meaning to the learning content. Design the workshop with a variety of learning styles in mind, using different approaches, processes, activities, and ways of involving participants.

Emphasize fun that is "on-topic" and related to learning and performance. Keep in mind that informality, as well as humor, helps create readiness and openness to learning. Tell participants, "One of the things we learn in school is waiting for recess. You're adults now, so get up and move around as you see fit."

3) Establish Yourself Personally and Professionally with Participants

It's important that you make an initial deposit in the "relationship bank" with participants. Trust and goodwill between participants and yourself, like oil in an engine, reduce friction and help everything you do to flow with a lot less effort.

As early as possible in a workshop, you need to become a "trusted source" of learning for participants. Thus, participants need to see two things quickly. One, that you are credible and know your stuff. That is, you know your technology, and you have a process for running a workshop. Two, that you are authentic, you're open and honest, and work without hidden agendas. This latter point is related to giving participants "permission" to challenge (see below).

"Stay loose." Don't take yourself and your own stories too seriously. There are always other perspectives. You want to come across as being serious about the learning material and about your role as workshop leader, but not about yourself.

4) Clarify Purpose and Outcomes with Participants

Set clear expectations so that participants know what to expect, what material will be covered, and what is expected of them. Encourage caring by telling participants "why" learning a given method or approach is important, and work toward explicit outcomes.

Knowledge without values can be found in almanacs; information without motivation can be found in computers.
- Norman Cousins

A colleague of mine tells participants, "I could get you dancing on the table in front of the group, if I could just get you to understand why." Hearing this, people usually mumble and look doubtful. He then picks one participant and asks, "Would you do it for $500?" Of course he's only kidding, but he does have a point. Understanding the need, the importance, and the purpose of learning goes a long way toward becoming motivated to learn. As the old saying goes, "Where there's a will, there's a way."

5) Show Context

Showing context always helps. That is, show the "big picture," the framework, and how things fit together. It's easier to put a puzzle together if you assemble the outside pieces first. This gives shape and direction to your work and provides boundaries that guide your next steps. So too, participants will be more motivated to learn, and more able to understand new learning material, if they understand the *context*, that is, if they know how the new learning fits with what they already know and do.

The motivating value of understanding context is brought out in the old story about three bricklayers. When asked what he was doing, the first bricklayer replied, "I'm laying bricks." The second said, "I'm building a wall." The third announced, "I'm building a cathedral." Which bricklayer do you think was the most motivated?

6) Start with a Bang

Have the workshop start-up well planned not to bore participants. Set an informal climate of high energy, challenge, involvement, fun, and focus. Do something unexpected. Entertain participants and get their attention. Show context, then head right into a brief piece of learning content to "hook" participants. Show them value and get them excited about what's coming next.

Once you've got them "hooked" go back and do the necessary introductory and contracting work. This includes agreeing on things like ground rules, roles, the agenda, and ensuring everyone has a stake in the success of the workshop or training program.

7) Start Where There Is Energy

Start with what participants feel is most important for them to learn. This is where their energy is. Adults prioritize learning by asking themselves, "Will this help me do something that I want to do?" The law of conservation of energy applies here. It states that energy can neither be created nor destroyed; it's out there somewhere. It's the same thing with a group; the energy is either there, or if it isn't, you have to find it. Fortunately, apathy is rare. There's usually some energy present in the group.

During a start-up, successful workshop leaders identify the focus of participants' interest and energy. In doing so, they save the time and effort of trying to create new energy where energy already exists. Thus, where the group is motivated toward a specific piece of learning content, capitalize on their energy by using this content as your starting point. If the group wants to learn X, begin with X, and save Y for later. This necessitates maintaining a flexible agenda.

8) Begin at the Group's Level

Begin at the group's level of competence, and when you need to use technical jargon, take time to explain each term carefully. Even senior people sometimes interpret technical terms differently. Use simple, clear, and unpretentious language; avoiding "impressing them" with your vocabulary. Never use a ten dollar word when a ten cent word will do (or "propitiate," if you will!). For example, why do people say "utilize" when all they really mean is "use"?

Keep things simple at first. You can introduce complexity later. In some ways "training is a lie," because things are always more difficult in "real life." But for now, just take it one step at a time. Start by showing participants how the new learning material builds on what they already know. Demystify the learning content. Lead up to things. Show relevance and subtleties to gain interest. Use lots of stories and examples to "ground" learning content and to ensure that participants understand how *your* theory ties in with *their* practice.

9) Work with a Clear Agenda

Participants need to know the "game plan." So keep things simple, easy to follow, and uncomplicated. Don't overwhelm participants with all the detail at once. Build context and large frameworks as you go, helping participants understand and relate new learning to their own knowledge and experience.

10) Make Your Process Visible, Discussible, and Challengeable

Making your process visible on a flipchart or overhead helps participants follow your direction. Another big advantage is that a visible process is "challengeable." Thus, participants can surface issues and questions about the workshop process that they otherwise would not be informed enough to raise.

Ensure participants know what you're doing, why you're doing it, why at this time, and how an activity fits in with the overall purpose of the workshop. One way to do this is by using a lot of "what" and "why" "bridges."

Invite the group's input early and often in the workshop. For example, ask questions during the start-up, such as, "What would make you really satisfied with this workshop?"

Finally, keep administrative commitments. End the day when you say you will, or failing this, negotiate with the group to change the ending time.

11) Involve Participants in Operating the Workshop Early On

Assign workshop responsibilities to participants. For example, hold participants accountable for calling "time out," if and when they get lost. You might even go as far as setting up various workshop committees. A morale committee would take responsibility for helping people recharge their batteries from time to time. Whenever things seem to be dragging, just call on this committee to get people's energy up. A housekeeping committee would help keep the training room organized. A program committee might organize an evening's entertainment and so on.

12) Build Participant Confidence

This seems obvious but it needs to be said. Treat participants with respect and courtesy. In turn, you'll find participants will often treat each other the way you treat them. And open participants' eyes to their own worth and to what they already know. Show them how the workshop can build on their existing knowledge and how this will benefit them. For example, if you're teaching people how to use a word processor, let them know they already have the most important skills, these being language, grammar, writing, and communication skills. If you are teaching people how to be workshop leaders, remind them they already have 90% of the skills they need, these being technical, communication, and organization skills.

13) Lead by Example

Another way to build participant confidence is to lead by example. Model being relaxed, having fun, telling it like it is, being on time, working hard, taking risks, and so on.

Leading by example also means being willing, and prepared, to do anything you would ask the participants to do. Not only that, but you should "go first," particularly if some risk is involved. Putting yourself "on the line" demonstrates trust in your own process, courage, and a willingness to "learn in public" along with participants.

> ***The only completely consistent people are dead.***
> ***- Aldous Huxley***

Going first allows you to model how you want participants to respond. This adds clarity to your directions and expectations and helps participants be more confident about their role. An example would be introducing yourself first, as a way of demonstrating how you want the group to introduce themselves. Another example would be demonstrating an interview technique that you later want participants to practice during a small group exercise.

14) Establish a 50/50 Partnership with Participants

Responsibility for the workshop or training program needs to be shared. Tell participants, "The success of this workshop is completely dependent on how well we work together and on your willingness to be accountable for your own learning."

Although the workshop leader has information (e.g., learning material) that participants don't have, he/she must avoid being put into a "one up" position. Insist on a 50/50, or at the very least a 60/40, relationship between yourself (the workshop leader) and participants. This has several implications. For example, anyone can challenge anyone else, and anyone can call "time out" when they are lost. Thus, the workshop should feel like colleagues working together with you, the workshop leader, being merely the first among equals. (Although, as a comedian once quipped, "The trouble with treating people as equals is that they may want to do the same with you!")

Have participants think through and describe what they will do to ensure that they get what they need from the workshop. Two approaches work here, *pre-evaluation* and *flipcharting* responses. Pre-evaluation involves reviewing the evaluation form with the group during the workshop start-up and discussing how everyone can contribute to a successful workshop. Flipcharting involves a question like, "What can I (each participant) do to make this workshop a success?" Participants brainstorm this question. Their responses are then recorded on a flipchart and discussed within the group. Both of these approaches surface how participants can contribute to getting what they want from the workshop and to making the workshop successful.

15) Give Participants "Permission"

Remember, learning is a voluntary activity, and training is only an invitation. Give people permission "not to know all the answers" and "to make mistakes when practicing." Encourage mistakes and ask participants to give themselves permission to be "educated in public," that is, in the workshop, with others watching. Tell participants to experiment and "push the envelope" by testing the limits of their knowledge and skill. One way of knowing that you're pushing your limits is by making mistakes. Use a little humor by poking fun at the old cliché, "There are no dumb questions." Tell people, "There are no dumb questions, only dumb people."

Use constructs, such as Edward de Bono's six thinking hats, to give people "permission."[1] For example, ask participants to "put on your black hat and only think negative thoughts." At other times say, "Put on your yellow hat and see everything through rose colored glasses."

One of the very best ways to give permission is to "stroke the hell" out of any challenge that participants make. After dealing with a participant's challenge, talk with the group about what just happened, encouraging future participation. Say something like,

> *What Joe did just now is the kind of challenge I welcome from all of you. If you're willing to speak up and push a little, just like Joe did, then this workshop will be a success. We'll all learn more, and you'll get everything I can offer, because I'm at my best when challenged. By challenging, you'll be able to ensure the workshop material is making sense to you.*

One caveat when inviting challenge. Don't mistake an unconstructive objection for a challenge. There is challenge, there is pickiness, and there is something resembling sabotage.

Pickiness and sabotage

Pickiness

Some people are always looking for "nits to pick." For example, every now and then, you'll get a participant who can't deal with a spelling mistake on a flipchart. This person will usually say something like, "I can't focus on what we're doing until that spelling error is corrected." You might say "BHD" (big harry deal) to yourself. That's OK; just don't say it out loud. Deal with these people politely. They don't mean any harm.

Sabotage

It's very rare, but sooner or later you'll get a participant, or even a small group of participants, who are angry about something. Worse yet, this participant or group may not be very skilled at dealing with their anger. The worst case scenario is when the dissenting participant or small group carries considerable influence within the whole group.

My story of sabotage

In the following case, the primary saboteur was actually the group's manager. He was both the sponsor and a participant in the workshop, and he wasn't alone. Indeed, when it comes to finding others to support and agree with them, at least in their presence, managers are rarely alone. Two or three other participants were happy to provide "tactical support" for undermining the workshop.

This manager led the sabotage in a subtle and "businesslike" manner. Like any saboteur worth his salt, this participant was indirect and camouflaged his anger. The following paragraph describes one of the ways he seemed to be trying to sabotage the workshop. Notice how subtle, and even well intentioned, sabotage can be made to appear. Remember, any one act doesn't, in itself, constitute sabotage. Rather, it's a series of independent and sometimes coordinated maneuvers, each dedicated to the same purpose, that over time lead one to conclude "it's sabotage."

As I was introducing the second day of the workshop, this participant stopped me with the statement, "We need to rearrange the room." Curiously, he had been in the room with me for a few minutes before the workshop started and hadn't said a thing. I asked for permission to finish the introduction that I was presently doing (I was using the overhead at the time) and assured him we would rearrange the room within the next ten minutes. I then asked, "Is that OK?" He shrugged like it was, but didn't say anything one way or the other. He was being as indirect as possible.

Not a minute later, he interrupted me again, acting like he hadn't even heard my promise to rearrange the room. Now he took the position that I had simply ignored his request, claiming that I had lost his trust.

Five "rules of thumb" for dealing with sabotage

One, stay "tuned into" your feelings. Acknowledge that sabotage, or something that seems like sabotage, is going on, and that it's upsetting. Let yourself know that it's OK to feel defensive. Just don't act it. You have to model reason, calmness, and fairness for the group. You're not there to demonstrate how an angry leader "flies off the handle."

Two, act decisively, not punitively, just firmly, fairly, and immediately. Sometimes just recognizing and naming it helps. For example, you might say something like, "Tom, it feels like you want to say something that you're just not saying." "Would you be willing to talk about it in the group?" If Tom says "no," then you might ask, "Would you be willing to talk about it with me privately at the next break?" You can't afford to ignore, downplay, or deny that sabotage is happening. It's often subtle, but it's usually visible. You'll lose credibility with the group if you "just let it pass."

Three, don't attempt to read minds, assume motives, or play psychologist. Don't try to guess why this person is angry; just accept that they are. They may be frustrated by something in the workshop, or maybe there's just a lot of change going on in the organization and they're feeling the pressure. Your chances of winning a lottery are better than guessing what's really bugging them. Also, don't assume that they're a "no good complainer" either. Stereotyping is not only a waste of time, it's misleading. Many workshop leaders, myself included, have proven this several times by turning these enemies into allies during workshops.

Four, remember that "a workshop leader loses all arguments." Don't get sucked into arguing. Anyway when people get stressed or angry they get stupid, workshop and training-program leaders included. You need your best judgment in these situations. Now is not the time to let your emotions take over.

Five, "trust the group." Look for the kernel of truth in what the participant is saying. Ask yourself, "Is there anything here that I can build on?"

Back to my story of sabotage

Following these five "rules of thumb," at the participant's second interruption I simply stopped the introduction I was doing and had the group rearrange the room.

A couple of hours later, the same person was again working his "agenda." Again, I simply responded in good faith. By midafternoon of the second day, he "crossed the line." Making one of his objections to my behavior, he pushed to such an extreme that a few members of the group groaned in unison. I knew he heard this feedback, because at the next break he came to me and apologized. After that, he became my ally. Strange how things sometimes get resolved!

My reactions to this sabotage

Pickiness doesn't bother me a bit. I enjoy challenge - it spices up a workshop. But the sabotage in the case above was unrelenting and widespread. Coming from the group's leader, it put a pretty good sized dent in my motivation to work with this group. I still remember the group well. My motivation at the beginning of the workshop was to "win big." I thought the workshop would prove very valuable to the group, and I was eager to be involved.

After a day and a half of what seemed like unrelenting resistance, pickiness, and sabotage not just from the manager, but also from two or three others in the group, my motivation changed from "win big" to simply "don't lose." That is, I just wanted to get through the workshop without losing my temper, walking out, or giving up. I made it, and surprisingly, the workshop was rated fairly well on the evaluation forms.

Like most groups, this one had a silent majority. Several of them came up to me after the workshop, expressing the usual gratitude. Although it was the type of thing one hears after a "successful workshop," I wasn't happy. I knew the group got less than I had to offer. Although knowing how to act "nondefensively" (even when feeling defensive), there were times during this workshop when I simply "stayed in my foxhole." Even experienced workshop leaders aren't at their best when under constant fire.

What I learned

To start, let me state what I already knew. Don't blame the client! "Client bashing" keeps you stuck. You won't learn or grow as a workshop leader by blaming your clients.

I think when something goes wrong, as it did in this case, the workshop leader has to look inward. Ask yourself, "What could I have done differently that might have prevented these problems?" I'm not implying the workshop leader is always the only one who needs to learn something, but merely that you need to think first about what actions you can take, that is, what actions are within your circle of influence.

When I asked myself this question the answer wasn't all that difficult to discover. My problems went right back to contracting. I hadn't spent the usual time with my sponsor or end-user clients before the workshop. Even though there were special needs associated with this workshop, I only had a brief introductory interview with the sponsor client. I had no contact whatsoever with end-user clients before the workshop began.

Special needs associated with this workshop included

- The group had a history of discontent. Members joked that working in the group was like "herding cats."
- A steering committee for the group made attendance at the workshop mandatory. In other words, we took prisoners.
- The workshop was held on a weekend (i.e., we took their "family time"). During the workshop one participant actually said several times, and also noted on his evaluation form, that he was being forced to "jeopardize his family life!" (This was a middle aged, intelligent man, who held a responsible position in industry. It's amazing how, when we're angry and under stress, we can revert to talking and acting like dependent children.)
- Participants had to pay their own tuition. Thus, even though their organization mandated attendance on a weekend, without pay, participants had to pay their own tuition.

Taking prisoners is, and was then, very much against my beliefs. I could offer dozens of excuses for why I went along with this, but they'd all be rationalizations. The bottom line was that before the workshop began, a lot more time should have been spent "up-front" with my clients. I didn't take the time, and I paid the price. I no longer downplay the importance of contracting with clients before a workshop or overlook my own beliefs about how to contract for a workshop or training program.

Conclusion

I ran two workshops for this particular manager, himself a capable consultant and workshop leader. After these were complete, I spent an hour with him reviewing the situation. He was gracious and appreciative. Having a candid and friendly discussion, I gained a lot of respect for him. Funny isn't it. If only I'd taken the time to have this same conversation *before* the workshops!

End

LEARNING READINESS

Whereas "learning climate" refers to the atmosphere of a workshop, "learning readiness" relates to an individual's or group's need, desire, and motivation to learn.

When participants are learning ready the workshop progresses like magic. The learning climate becomes less important. That is, participants who are really energized and eager to learn won't be distracted if the room isn't organized exactly to their tastes. They won't allow themselves to be lost. If you forget to "bridge" from one topic to the next, or if you don't clearly explain an exercise, "learning ready" participants speak up. They ask for clarification and they challenge. They won't just sit there, bored and lost. ("What" and "why" bridges are discussed in chapter twelve.)

When the student is ready, the teacher will appear.
- old Chinese proverb

A person who has a "why" can deal with any "how."
- Friedrich Nietzsche

Question: How many psychologists does it take to change a light bulb? Answer: One, but the light bulb really has to want to change. This little joke, as corny as it is, still makes a important point. You can't make participants *feel* something, you can't *change* participants, and you can't *fix* them even if they want to be fixed. Ultimately learning readiness is an inside job. Each participant is responsible for being ready to learn. You can lead a horse to water, but you can't make him drink. Anyway, before you try to push him in, just stop and think about how bad a wet horse smells! (Maybe this smell is a good metaphor for the resistance we get when we try to force learning on others.)

This section covers:

A) The elements of learning readiness

B) Strategies for assessing learning readiness

C) Strategies for encouraging learning readiness

D) Demanding learning readiness

A) The Elements of Learning Readiness

Chapter two sets out five steps in the natural learning cycle (focus, search, integrate, generalize, act). The first step, *focus*, concerns one's need and motivation to learn. Being "focused," in the sense of how it's operationally defined in the "natural learning cycle," is being "learning ready." Now it's time to look even deeper at how one comes to be focused or learning ready.

The following six conditions are helpful if participants are to become open to learning and to changing their thinking and behavior on the job. These conditions form the elements of learning readiness.

1) *Awareness of problems or opportunities*. Participants need to be aware that the way they presently perform on the job either causes problems or misses opportunities. They need to know why a job needs to be done differently.

2) *Awareness of one's role in a situation and of the possibilities for improvement*. Participants need to understand how their thinking and acting contribute to a problem or the potential they have for influencing an opportunity. They also need to understand that to do the job differently their behavior has to change. Finally, they have to believe that this change is possible. Without belief or hope, change is unlikely.

A sower went out to sow his seed; and as he sowed, some fell along the path, and was trodden under foot, and the birds of the air devoured it. And some fell on the rock; and as it grew up, it withered away, because it had no moisture. And some fell among thorns; and the thorns grew with it and choked it. And some fell into good soil and grew, and yielded a hundredfold.
- Luke 8:4

3) *Awareness of personal and organizational benefits*. Participants need to understand how doing a job differently will be of value to themselves and their organization.

4) *Awareness of the need for learning in order to make improvements*. Participants need to recognize that in order to perform the job in a new way, they need new information and new skills.

5) *A desire and motivation to learn that exceeds the loss of old ways of knowing and working*. Participants must want to achieve, learn, and grow in order to improve how they perform on the job. The value they attribute to changing their behavior is weighted against the effort required to learn and practice new skills. They must perceive that "value" to be worth the effort. Otherwise, it's unlikely they will be motivated to understand the job in a new way, to perform in a new way, and certainly not to change old habits, if this is required.

   The old change formula comes to mind, this being $P \times V \times FS > R$. "P" represents the pain, discomfort, or disparity participants feel and that is motivating them to consider change. "V" stands for a vision of something better, in other words, some reason to hope. "FS" signifies the need for clear "first steps" or "how to's." Participants need "practical action" ideas to get them started. Finally, "R" stands for resistance. In other words, all three factors (P, V, FS) must multiply to be greater than the loss that participants perceive is involved in giving up their old ways of thinking and acting.

6) *A supportive and challenging work climate for learning*. Participants need a work climate conducive to learning, practicing, and experimenting. It's a climate where people aren't punished for making errors while trying to improve, where

coaching and recognition are provided, where change is supported, and where people are allowed to use judgment on the job.

A story about becoming "learning ready"

There are many things in life that I've learned only when I absolutely had to, and not a moment before. Learning how computers work is a case in point. At one time I had an office manager who handled all the technical details related to my computer. Her name is Syd Waring, and she is a genius. Syd knew how to troubleshoot software problems, get fax machines to actually fax things, and link computers together. Not only that, no matter what problem I asked her to solve, she was polite, cheerful, and enthusiastic (yes, this person really does exist!). Whether it was snail mail or e-mail, with Syd around, all I had to do was "lick and stick" or "point and click."

Then one day Syd was gone. She had a new baby and her other dependent, me, was left at the office to fend for himself. Finally, out of necessity, I was learning ready. (Actually, I was more like "learning desperate"!)

I spent two full days tinkering with the hardware and reading fax manuals, software manuals, computer manuals, answering machine manuals, and telephone manuals (even my phone system was complex). It wasn't pretty, but it worked. Now if something goes wrong with my electronic toys, I tackle it head on and learn. I can no longer yell down the hall to Syd for help. Necessity may be the mother of invention, but "learning readiness" is also one of her litter.

B) Strategies for Assessing Learning Readiness

A good rule of thumb is "don't talk to brick walls." This translates into not delivering training (e.g., materials, exercises) until participants see a need to learn what you're offering. And the degree of learning readiness, or motivation for learning, that participants experience determines how much they will benefit from the learning opportunities provided in a workshop.

In their article on organization development readiness Pfeiffer and Jones (1978) compare OD readiness to reading readiness in children.[2] They note that when a child is not yet ready to read, any method of teaching reading skills will fail. But, when a child is "reading ready," almost any method of teaching reading skills is effective. It's an interesting analogy for learning readiness and learning. Thus, although it's a generalization, you could say that when participants are learning ready, almost anything you do to facilitate learning in a workshop or training program seems to work. When the group is not learning ready, however, it's an uphill battle. Almost anything you do to introduce and facilitate new learning will yield poor results.

How can you tell if a group is learning ready? How can you be sure they are even aware of their own learning needs? Below are five approaches to assessing a group's learning readiness. Use these individually or in combination, but whatever you do, don't start into new learning material "unless and until" you're confident that the group is ready to learn. (*Note*: You need to periodically assess the group's learning readiness as a workshop or training program progresses and as you move from topic to topic.)

1) Explain and Discuss the Elements of "Learning Readiness" with the Group and Then Ask Directly

Explain the concept of "learning readiness" to the group and ask them directly, "Are you ready to learn this ... method, theory, technique?" Ask the group, "How do you know you're learning ready?" Get a few specifics. Trust the group unless you have clear contradictory evidence. If this is the case, present your evidence openly and directly, discussing it with the group. Don't be afraid to challenge the group to both understand and explain their motivation to learn.

2) Have Participants Talk While You Listen

There's an old joke that says, "A good listener is usually thinking about something else." Well, for a workshop leader, not listening *actively* leads to big problems, not the least of which is a loss of credibility with the group. So if you're not a good listener, then you'd better learn. There's no way anything in this book will help a poor listener become a good workshop or training-program leader.

Practice what Carl Rogers (1951, 1961, 1969, 1980) calls "active listening."[3] This goes beyond hearing the words participants are saying. It involves an effort to fully understand the participant's intended message and paying attention to the participant's nonverbal mannerisms. (Nonverbal messages, and a methodology for active listening, are discussed in chapter sixteen.)

Robert Smith (1982) offers workshop and training-program leaders what, on the surface, might seem like self-contradicting advice on listening. He says that the best leaders listen by being both empathetic and evaluative.[4] That is, on the one hand "the (leader) seeks to suspend negative attitudes and preconceptions and enter into dialogue with the (participant)." "At the same time the (leader) weighs what is being said in order to judge its relevance and see how it relates to previous experience and personal learning purposes." Thus, there's more to listening than meets the ear!

Don't assume you fully understand participants' learning needs or their readiness to learn. It's always possible they already know what you're planning to help them learn, and telling people what they already know is a mistake. So, the first step is to ensure participants need to know the material you're introducing. Let them talk while you listen. Devote most of the early discussion to what participants want to learn and "why."

3) Pay Attention to Tones, Nonverbals, and Indirect Communication

Groups of "nonverbals," in combination with other clues (e.g., tone, past experience, a little careful "reading between the lines"), can help you decide what questions to ask for further information. Indirect communication is hard to pinpoint. For example, a participant may be upset about one thing, but talk as if they're upset about something else entirely. Based on nonverbals and other clues you can, to use Peter Block's words (1981), "invite participants to be direct."[5]

4) Pay Attention to Rapport

Being in rapport with a group doesn't ensure they're learning ready, but it is a positive sign. Without rapport, participants might simply "tune you out." Once rapport is established, the group "helps themselves to learning," interrupting when they're lost or want more information. They challenge what you say till they know exactly what you mean and how it relates to their situation. They share responsibility with you for the success of the workshop, and almost anything you do as a leader works. For example, even if you ask closed questions when you should be asking open questions, if there is sufficient rapport, the group still responds, building a learning conversation.

5) Pay Attention to Little Words

Pay attention to little words like "why" and "how."[6] Participants asking "why" may not have "bought in," as yet, to the value of the learning content. So, deal more with the benefits of a given theory, model, process, or procedure. Participants asking "how" may indicate they're satisfied with the need for the new knowledge or skill and want to get on with learning. So, now it's time to stop talking benefits and needs and start helping the group learn and practice.

C) Strategies for Encouraging Learning Readiness

Naturally you want to get to new learning material as quickly as you can in a workshop, following start-up, contracting, and assessing learning readiness. However, if you're not convinced the group is learning ready, spend as much as 25% of workshop time to help them become learning ready. If, at the end of this amount of time, the group is clearly not "learning ready," then contract to delay, reschedule, or cancel the workshop. It doesn't make sense going ahead if participants have no interest in learning the material you're offering.

The bottom line on learning readiness is *you need participants to want the learning that they need.* And participants need workshop leaders to help them understand *why* the new learning is important and how they will benefit from the workshop. So, here's the all important question. How can workshop leaders engineer or facilitate the essential shift in consciousness that gets participants ready, willing, and keen to learn? That is, how do you first provide the experience that helps participants become learning ready, so that the learning experience that follows takes them somewhere? Below are ten options for doing just that.

1) Assess Learning Readiness

The process of assessing learning readiness (discussed above) itself helps create learning readiness by getting participants to make connections between what the workshop is offering and their interest and need for this learning.

2) State and Discuss the Benefits

State the benefits clearly; then discuss these with the group. Encourage the group to challenge. Have the group "T" chart how the workshop's learning content will help them and how it will hinder them in their job. Don't defend. Deal with each challenge on its merits. Don't represent the workshop as a panacea. You want participants to decide to "buy" for themselves. You don't want to have them feel like they've been manipulated.

3) Provide Expert Testimony, Senior Management Support, and/or Anecdotal Evidence from Previous Participants

The following suggestions are useful during the workshop start-up or during a pre-meeting with the group. Have a panel of previous participants come in and discuss the value they received from participating in the workshop. Have experts in the field speak on the importance of the information offered in the workshop. Have senior executives speak to the group and endorse the workshop. Another option is to have this support and testimonials in writing and use them as a handout during the workshop start-up.

4) Provide Hard Data

If available, provide data demonstrating the value of the workshop. This may be statistical data from a survey, data on production figures since the new way of working (taught in the workshop) was implemented, or data on what other companies have concluded about the method being taught in the workshop.

5) Show Relevance with Stories and Examples

Stories and examples are powerful. They help participants connect emotionally with learning content. They provide examples of when, and how, to use learning on the job.

6) Give Them a Taste

This is kind of like how cinnamon bun companies operate in shopping malls. You don't get a free cinnamon bun, but rather a small piece, just enough to leave you wanting more. Needless to say, you're offered this right beside the place where they sell the buns. Does this work? You bet! The workshop equivalent to a cinnamon bun is the "hook" in the workshop start-up.

7) Demonstrate the Need

Run an exercise to help demonstrate the value of the learning material being offered and the need for the group to learn this information or skill. For example, if your workshop aims at helping people deal better with conflict, run a simulation that helps participants self-assess their approach for handling conflict.

8) Model Confidence and Commitment

Don't ever run a workshop you don't believe in. Your attitude rubs off on participants, so you need to model confidence and commitment. Develop solid reasons why this workshop is valuable and test them from time to time. Don't get so comfortable with the workshop, or the materials, that you start to take them for granted, or worse yet, start to think they work all the time in every situation. Periodically question your approach to the workshop and the workshop purpose and materials. Be confident that what you're offering is top quality and relevant.

9) Ask Participants to Reserve Their Judgment for Now and Give the Workshop a Chance

This is kind of an "when all else fails" suggestion. That is, when nothing you do seems to help the group get learning ready, yet you feel ending the workshop is not a good option, then "push on." But do so with the full knowledge that the group is not learning ready. Contract with the group to check learning readiness after you've tried a few things to see if they have found them helpful. Ask them if they're willing to reserve judgment and give it a try. If they say "no," then end the workshop and deal with the consequences as needed.

10) Adapt the Workshop When Necessary to Help Participants Become "Learning Ready"

It's participants' interests and needs, not the workshop agenda, that are paramount. If changing the agenda or even some of the outcomes being sought from the workshop is what it takes to help participants become learning ready, then so be it.

A story about resisting learning

I once ran a two day *Train the Trainer* workshop with a group of senior administrative people. This group taught management theory to other administrative people and were all reasonably experienced workshop leaders. One member of the group, in particular, was very experienced. In some ways the others considered him to be their informal leader. In the past they had consulted him whenever they were uncertain about how to facilitate a workshop and on matters relating to the content of their workshops. His leadership in the group had never been formally recognized, however. Officially they were all considered peers.

Early on, it became clear he was unhappy. Sitting in a corner, leaning back on his chair, he appeared half in and half out of the group. He doodled and yawned a lot, and a couple of times he seemed to be sleeping sitting up. When he said something, which was rare, it seemed like a "potshot" disguised as a "disinterested challenge." But even his "potshots" lacked energy. They were more distracting than vindictive; he mostly seemed apathetic.

Although labels are misleading, because you weren't able to see this person in the workshop, allow me to label his behavior for the purposes of this discussion. The clearest picture I can paint for you is to say that he seemed to be "pouting."

When it was his turn to practice in the group, he chose to practice things that were completely safe for him. Things he and everyone else knew he was already very good at doing. It seemed he just wanted to get through the two days and go home without being challenged. His learning ready switch was locked in the "off position."

During the workshop I responded positively to his questions (I think he had two questions in the two days), and at other times invited his participation. When he practiced in front of the group, I "stroked the hell" out of every positive thing he did, and that was a lot. No question this person was an advanced workshop leader.

I took these actions hoping to help him emotionally "let go" of whatever was keeping him stuck and unable to be fully involved in this learning experience. Nothing worked, and because others around him were learning ready, he stood out in the group like a sore thumb.

I heard through the grapevine a few days after the workshop that he felt he had learned something at the workshop, but I heard nothing directly from him. The rather sad ending to this story is that some members of the group later told me he lost his status as "informal leader" during this workshop. His behavior had turned people off. Perhaps it was his very need to preserve his "informal leadership" role that caused him to be so withdrawn and to play it safe for the two days. It now seems it was this behavior that lost him this status. It's uncertain whether over time he'll win back his "informal leader" status in the group.

End

D) Demanding Learning Readiness

What if you try everything to encourage a group to be open to a new way of operating, or to new learning, and nothing works? Do you just give up and quit? The answer is "yes." But do it openly; don't just fold your tent in the night and sneak off. Tell the group what you're doing. Approach the manager, or the person with organizational authority, and let him/her know directly that nothing has worked. It's your only option. It makes absolutely no sense conducting a workshop with people who are not emotionally and intellectually "in the room." As Jim Rohn says, "Refuse to sell to difficult people."[7] Don't waste your time. It's like wrestling with a pig. You both get dirty but the pig likes it!

Unlike workshop and training-program leaders, however, managers often do not have the luxury of leaving. Sometimes managers simply have to command that people learn something, work together a certain way, or do a number of other things that are almost impossible to command. It doesn't work real well, and managers need to follow-up with tough consequences if their commands are ignored (e.g., suspension, firing), but what other choice do they have?

PARTICIPATION READINESS

"Participation readiness" follows from and is related to learning climate and learning readiness. It refers to participants being ready to share their needs, experiences, and stories with others in the workshop.

When people are ready to participate they're willing to *work* in the workshop. For example, they're ready and willing to challenge, to take responsibility for their own needs, to ask questions if they don't understand a point another participant is making, to take part in small group exercises, and to contribute to the group's learning. This is very much the opposite of expecting to be taught, of expecting to be able to just sit there, learn passively, and be entertained to boot.

Like learning readiness, participation readiness is primarily an inside job, although you can certainly do things to influence and encourage participation readiness in a group, for example, contract roles and expectations in the group, model an openness to being challenged and a willingness to learn in front of the group, and set an informal workshop climate of involvement and fun.

This section covers:

A) Why active participation is not a strongly held norm

B) The "Catch-22" of participation readiness

C) Strategies for getting participants active and involved

A) Active Participation Is Not a Strongly Held Norm

Regardless of the circumstances, or mix of education and experience in the group, you can usually expect that the group will *not* be participation ready when you first begin a workshop. This is normal and natural. That's why you must involve participants early and often. Otherwise you're sure to get sucked into traditional teaching (i.e., telling and selling).

> ***Learners have gotten used to the idea that their ability to influence their instruction is close to nil. They subject themselves to their instruction rather than participate in it.***
> ***- Klas Mellander***

Why are some participants often docile and reluctant to challenge and be involved, at least initially in a workshop? Why do so many just sit there without protesting, allowing some stranger to waste their time? The docility that people with otherwise strong personalities display when they first find themselves in the role of workshop participant is amazing.

Understanding the following cultural supports for passivity may help you cope with this phenomenon a little better in your workshops.

- The school system has had an influence. We've been institutionalized into handing over responsibility to the teacher and "being taught." Years of practice have made us good at this game, including knowing just when to execute a "knowledgeable nod" so the teacher will "stay off our back."

- Our organizations have had an influence. For example, the relationship between workshop participants and a workshop leader often parallels how these participants perceive their relationship with their supervisors. Needless to say, sometimes this relationship is one of caution, keeping your mouth shut, and not "rocking the boat."

- TV has played its part. In J.R. Priestley's words, TV has transformed society into a "vast crowd, a permanent audience, waiting to be amused." "We look on more and more and join in less and less."

- Society generally has had an influence. We're just *not* taught to be direct with people in authority. In church, in the boy scouts, and everywhere else in society, our training has consistently been to "be polite," "show respect," "fit in," and "follow the rules."

A story about beginning before the group is ready

Years ago, as a relatively inexperienced workshop leader, I was taking a group through a guided imagery exercise. This was part of some strategy work we were doing. The group consisted of senior finance managers in a large oil and gas exploration company. As an in-house consultant at the time, I knew all the members of this group fairly well. A couple of them were even friends.

Right off the bat, and without getting permission, I told the group I was going to lead them through a visioning exercise. Though I had seen my mentor do this many times, this was my first solo. But knowing how to lead the exercise wasn't my problem; neither was the group. They were all hardworking, intelligent, and well-intentioned managers.

My problem was that the group had never done an exercise like this before, and although they were open to learning, they weren't ready to participate in an exercise like this. They were skeptical. After all, guided imagery is considered a little flaky in conservative management circles. Fifteen years ago, when this happened, it was considered downright "off the wall," at least in this Company.

The group didn't object outright, but they were clearly uncomfortable. I was too busy thinking about what I was doing to notice their discomfort. However, as I was taking them through the exercise, I caught on. They were too polite to say much. They just squirmed a lot.

When their eyes were supposed to be closed, they were open. When they were supposed to be sitting back in their chairs and relaxed, they were sitting forward, bodies rigid. Only a couple of participants succeeded in getting comfortable enough to actually envision anything. The rest of the group tried hard, but envisioned nothing.

Debriefing with the group, we salvaged what we could, and nothing much was said about the exercise flopping. But, as you might expect, I didn't get any repeat business from this group.

Today I would handle this situation differently. First, I wouldn't do the exercise until the group was "participation ready." Second, if I realized the exercise wasn't working, I'd call a "time out." I would debrief with the group and determine why it wasn't working. Then I'd likely laugh at myself a little and move on to something else. Having a lot of different tools in my pocket, I don't have to get "ego invested" in any one of them. I accept that most time the tools work, and sometimes they don't. I have yet to discover even one facilitation method that works all the time, regardless of the circumstances.

End

B) The "Catch-22" of Participation Readiness

Remember Joseph Heller's bestseller, *Catch-22*?[8] It was later made into a movie. It's about the American Air Force flying bombing missions out of Italy in World War II. The airmen in the movie suffered combat fatigue and tried every trick they knew to be relieved of duty. One airman, a lead bombardier named John Yossarian had what seemed like a foolproof approach. He claimed he was crazy. But "Catch-22" in the Air Force policy manual covered this possibility. It stated that anyone who was sane enough to realize they were crazy was sane enough for duty. Thus, claiming you were crazy meant you weren't; "Catch-22" was just bait. Taking this bait meant there was no way out.

There's a "Catch-22" involved in leading workshops. It's usually most at play during the early parts of a workshop. Participants act like they want to be taught as opposed to participating actively in the learning process. Workshop leaders who take this bait begin teaching, allowing participants to move into the traditional "student" role. This has several consequences.

- Participants (now more appropriately called "students") will *not* take responsibility for their own learning or for the success of the workshop. Rather, they pass this over completely to you.

- Workshop success is limited because very little learning results from "passive observation."

- The workshop will now be evaluated based on your performance and on participant enjoyment, rather than on participant learning.

- Adults, even though they may have subtlety encouraged you to teach, will eventually resent you for doing so. (I'm speaking here of teaching in the traditional sense where the teacher pontificates while students listen passively to every golden word that drips from his/her tongue.)

C) Strategies for Getting Participants Active and Involved

You can't teach people to swim by talking about it. Get them in the pool. In a workshop this means get participants doing something, an exercise, simulation, or some other type of small group activity. If you wait too long to get the group active, you set a norm for passive learning. So, take responsibility for keeping the group active and involved throughout the workshop and for getting them active early.

What can you do to help the group get ready to participate?

First, practice the strategies provided here for learning climate and learning readiness (see above). These will go a long way toward getting the group participation ready.

Second, get the group working on something related to workshop outcomes or process (e.g., generating a list of issues and concerns about a topic, developing a product in small groups).

Third, if necessary, you can involve the group in an "ice breaker" or stimulation exercise. These activities are designed for warming-up and energizing groups. They usually don't have a lot to do with the workshop's outcomes, but they do get people up, moving around, and talking to each other. Lots of examples of ice breakers are provided in the University Associates' Annuals and Handbooks. Also see Forbess-Green's book, *The Encyclopedia of Icebreakers* (1983).[9] I'm not adverse to using ice breakers; I just don't use them much. Getting participants working on something directly related to the workshop's outcomes seems like a better use of time. It usually warms up the group just as well as an ice breaker, and you get something relevant done in the process.

Finally, avoid strategies to keep people alert that only make them uncomfortable. For example, don't ask participants to play musical chairs. This is where the workshop or training-program leader has participants move to a different seat every few hours. The idea is to keep people mixing and make sure they don't get bored. Mostly, it just treats adults like children. What is valuable, however, is getting participants to work in different subgroups from time to time versus always having them work with the same subgroup. This helps participants gain fresh perspectives on tasks.

HOW LEARNING CLIMATE, LEARNING READINESS, AND PARTICIPATION READINESS INTERRELATE

A group that's *learning ready* generates its own learning. A group that's *participation ready* generates its own activity and entertainment. A group that's both has fun "on-topic." They mix work and fun. An effective *learning climate* facilitates learning and participation. Participation in turn facilitates learning. Learning in turn generates enthusiasm for participation. This leads to achievement which in turn is very motivating, leading to an increase in learning readiness and so on. Think of this as a "constructive spiral." Needless to say if one or more of these elements is missing, this can also become a "destructive spiral." That is, a poor learning climate can lead to a lack of participation. This in turn can diminish learning readiness and so on.

Obviously all three of these elements influence each other, but which comes first, an effective learning climate, learning readiness, or participants who are ready and eager to be actively involved in the workshop? It's a bit of a "chicken and egg" argument. (Although the definitive answer to that argument is "a chicken is just an egg's way of reproducing itself!") Learning readiness is undoubtedly the most critical of the three, and in most cases will affect participation readiness and learning climate. However, as a workshop leader you can't afford to assume you have any of the three well in hand, so work hard to make these positive factors in your workshops.

CONCLUSION

Summary

Workshop and Learning Climate

Workshop and learning climate refers to whether participants are *feeling* supported, challenged, and energized. This, in turn, supports and encourages learning and participation. You can do a lot to help set a positive learning climate (e.g., practice adult-learning principles, organize the room so participants can talk easily with each other), but whatever you do, avoid traditional teaching and treating participants as students. Rather, hold participants accountable for learning and achieving results. Aim for a strong performance ethic. Model enthusiasm and confidence.

Learning Readiness

Learning readiness refers to the strength of each participant's desire to learn and is a function of their awareness of the need to learn. Just as beauty is in the eye of the beholder, so too "learning readiness" is an internal state. A workshop leader can encourage learning readiness in a group, but individual participants will decide for themselves if and when they are open to new ways of thinking and acting.

Learning climate and learning readiness influence each other, but learning readiness is the ultimate key to workshop success. Any workshop that begins before participants are *learning ready* is doomed to produce marginal results. Thus, you should assess learning readiness prior to introducing new learning material. Ask participants directly and challenge them to prove that they are learning ready (e.g., "Why do you want to hear about the Harvard Negotiation Technique?" "How is this likely to be helpful to you?") Listen actively to their responses and pay attention to their nonverbal signals.

Participation Readiness

Without active and involved participants most workshops fall flat. So, set and maintain a climate of involvement and responsibility. Get participants active early and keep them involved throughout a workshop. It may seem easier at first to "just lecture," but as the workshop or training program progresses you'll discover this is a trap. You will have taken over sole responsibility for the success of the workshop or training program. Participants are now with you "win or tie!" That is, they may be willing to share your success, but you'll fail alone.

Learning Climate, Learning Readiness, and Participation Readiness Interrelate

All three of these elements - learning climate, learning readiness, participation readiness - have a strong influence on each other. For example, participating actively helps create a positive learning climate. A positive learning climate, in turn, supports and encourages one's willingness to participate and learn. Success in learning often leads to more motivation to learn and to achieve and so on.

Checklist

Learning Climate, Learning Readiness, and Participation Readiness	*The Elements of Learning Readiness*
• Learning climate refers to the atmosphere in the workshop (e.g., informal, focused, hardworking, fun, energized) • Learning readiness refers to participants' motivation to learn and to accomplish the workshop or training-program outcomes • Participation readiness refers to participants' willingness to be active and involved in a workshop or training program	• Awareness of problems or opportunities • Awareness of one's role in the situation and of possibilities for improvement • Awareness of personal and organizational benefits • Awareness of the need for learning in order to make improvements • A desire and motivation to learn that exceed the loss of old ways of knowing and working • A supportive and challenging work climate for learning
Strategies for Establishing an Effective Workshop Climate 1) Aim for a strong performance ethic 2) Motivate participants and practice adult-learning principles 3) Establish yourself personally and professionally with participants 4) Clarify purpose and outcomes with participants 5) Show context 6) Start with a bang 7) Start where there is energy 8) Begin at the group's level 9) Work with a clear agenda 10) Make your process visible, discussible, and challengeable	*Strategies for Assessing Learning Readiness* 1) Ask the group directly 2) Have participants talk while you listen 3) Pay attention to tones, nonverbals, and indirect communication 4) Pay attention to rapport 5) Pay attention to little words

11) Involve participants in operating the workshop early on 12) Build participant confidence 13) Lead by example 14) Establish a 50/50 partnership with participants 15) Give participants "permission" (i.e., to challenge, take risks) *Strategies for Getting Participants Active and Involved* 1) Practice strategies for creating an effective learning climate and for encouraging learning readiness 2) Have participants work on something related to workshop outcomes or process 3) Use an ice breaker	*Strategies for Encouraging Learning Readiness* 1) Assess learning readiness 2) State and discuss the benefits 3) Provide expert testimony, senior management support, and/or anecdotal evidence from previous participants 4) Provide hard data 5) Show relevance with stories and examples 6) Give them a taste 7) Demonstrate the need 8) Model confidence and commitment 9) Ask participants to reserve their judgment for now and give the workshop a chance 10) Adapt the workshop when necessary to help participants become learning ready *End*

Exercise

Learning Climate

List five or six key points for each of the following questions:

1) What does an effective learning climate look like?

2) What about a poor learning climate?

3) What can a workshop leader do to establish an effective learning climate?

Exercise

Reading a Group

List five or six points for each of the following questions:

1) What are the signs that a group is "with you" (i.e., learning ready, participation ready)?

2) What are the signs that a group is *not* "learning ready"?

3) What can be done to help a group become "participation ready"?

Notes

[1]de Bono, E. (1985). Six thinking hats. Boston, MA: Little/Brown.
[2]Pfeiffer, J.W., & Jones, J.E. (1978). OD readiness. *The 1978 Annual Handbook for Group Facilitators*. La Jolla, CA: University Associates, pp. 210-225.
[3]1) Rogers, C.A. (1951). Client-centered therapy. Boston, MA: Houghton Mifflin. 2) Rogers, C.A. (1961). On becoming a person. Boston, MA: Houghton Mifflin. 3) Rogers, C.A. (1969). Freedom to learn. Columbus, OH: Merrill. 4) Rogers, C.A. (1980). A way of being. Boston, MA: Houghton Mifflin.
[4]Smith, R.M. (1982). Learning how to learn: Applied theory for adults. Chicago, IL: Follett, p. 88.
[5] Block, P. (1978). Flawless consulting: A guide to getting your expertise used. San Diego, CA: University Associates.
[6] I'd like to thank a friend and colleague, Murray Hiebert, for this perspective on "little words."
[7]This quote taken from a presentation by Jim Rohn, October 25, 1995, in Calgary, Alberta, Canada.
[8]Heller, J. (1961). Catch-22. New York, NY: Laurel.
[9]The University Associates' Handbooks and Annuals date back to 1971. University Associates, Inc. 8517 Production Avenue, San Diego, CA 92121. Also see: Forbess-Green, S., (1983). The encyclopedia of icebreakers. San Diego, CA: University Associates.

Part 4

Getting Underway: Starting Up a Workshop

Chapter 10

First Steps in Starting Up a Workshop

INTRODUCTION

The term "start-up" refers to beginning a workshop or training program, those first few moments or hours (depending on the length of the event) when you get things underway. A half day workshop might involve a start-up of only a few minutes, a few quick introductions and you're off, whereas starting up a week long workshop could involve as much as a half day. The elements of start-up include the *first steps* as outlined in this chapter, *contracting group process* which is detailed in chapter eleven, and developing *learning climate*, *learning readiness*, and *participation readiness*, all of which were discussed in chapter nine.

Starting up is the most difficult part of leading a workshop, but it's also a time of considerable leverage. You can succeed or fail "big time." (I've had the good fortune of both these experiences. Believe me, to err is human, but to really bomb a workshop start-up isn't all that divine.)

A workshop start-up is like being the first comedian on stage for the evening. No matter how funny your first few jokes are, the audience doesn't laugh much, and they certainly don't laugh as a group. They're cold. They need time to make the transition from eating, or drinking, or whatever they've been doing to listening, reflecting, and laughing. So before a comedian can "have 'em rollin' in the aisles," the audience needs to be mentally present and in sync with the delivery, the content, and with the background of the issue. They need to be in the *context*. They need to understand the "set-up" or situation in order to be entertained by the punch line.

Comedians "bomb" when they can't achieve the needed harmony or context with their audience. Jokes out of context just aren't funny. But when a comedian successfully sets the context, the job becomes easy "to get" and a lot of fun. It's the same with starting up a workshop.

The start-up sets the tone for the workshop, generates participant interest, and establishes expectations. It's also a time to demonstrate that you are credible and authentic as a workshop or training-program leader and that you can become a "trusted source" of new learning for participants.

It's only natural that participants make early judgments about you, the workshop, and each other. What makes the start-up particularly challenging is that you haven't yet built a foundation of trust with participants. They are often a little, or even very, skeptical at first. After all, skepticism is how people shelter themselves from quackery.

The start-up is kind of a balancing act. Participants are often anxious to get things done and to get into new learning, yet you, as the workshop leader, have a bunch of organizing and contracting work you need to do before moving too deeply into workshop or training-program content. You need to understand participants' learning needs; assess their learning readiness; identify, create, and manage expectations; contract learning outcomes; and clarify a host of administrative issues, processes, and roles. If you take too long to start up a workshop or training program, participants will feel like you're wasting their time. If you move too quickly through the start-up, you're bound to regret it later, when you realize that participants' expectations are unrealistic or you've misunderstood their learning needs or that participants are holding you accountable for a role you had no intention of playing.

This chapter provides strategies for:

- Leader readiness - Being mentally and emotionally prepared to lead a workshop or training program.
- The first four steps in starting up a workshop or training program.
- The name game - Learning participants' names.

LEADER READINESS - BEING MENTALLY AND EMOTIONALLY PREPARED TO LEAD A WORKSHOP OR TRAINING PROGRAM

The last chapter dealt with learning climate, learning readiness, and participation readiness. Now it's time to talk about leader readiness. Before climbing into the cockpit and starting their engines, pilots walk around their aircraft checking for structural integrity. So, too, must workshop leaders assess their "leadership readiness" prior to starting up a workshop or training program. As a leader, you need to prepare emotionally, intellectually, and physically. Specifically, you need to:

A) Show up prepared, refreshed, and ready to lead.

B) Manage your nervousness and anxiety.

A) Show Up Prepared, Refreshed, and Ready to Lead

You might consider managing your emotions a little more than usual as you mentally prepare to lead a workshop or training program. Do whatever you can to come to the event "authentically positive." Relax and take time to "smell the roses" the evening before the workshop or training program. This doesn't mean watching TV. Rather, take some quiet time. Think about the benefits of the workshop or training program to participants and to their organization. Think about other positive experiences you've had leading workshops and training programs. Think about the growth you have experienced as a result of leading these types of events.

The day of the workshop or training program, just before you begin, stand still for a moment, take a deep breath, and say to yourself in a strong and confident voice, "*Showtime!*" It's kind of like a basketball player putting on his/her game face. Along this same vein Robert Jolles (1993) says, "When it comes to a trainer's attitude toward his curriculum he has no choice; he must fall in love with what he is teaching." (It's important to note that Jolles isn't suggesting the subject, process, or learning content comes first, and that all else is subordinate to these elements. Rather, what he's suggesting is that you need to be enthusiastic and believe in the value of what you have to offer. What comes first, and should never be subordinated to the subject, topic, or process, is always the participants' workshop and learning needs and the outcomes being sought from the workshop or training program.)

My inferiority complexes aren't as good as yours.
- Anonymous

At any rate, this is a time to lock your self-doubts and your critical "inner voice" in their padded cells. You can take them back out later, if you feel they have value, although I recommend a life sentence. Right now you need your power, your ego, and your enthusiasm. Yes, you do need some ego to lead a workshop, but not too big a one. Most people are a little suspicious of perfection, so take the workshop or training program seriously, but don't take yourself or your stories *too* seriously.

It's uncanny how participants will follow your mood, especially at the beginning of a workshop. Your attitude is contagious. If you are low key, serious, and very formal, that's how most participants will act. They'll take your attitude and approach as the desired workshop climate and respond accordingly. If you want participants to bring fun, energy, and enthusiasm to the workshop, then you have to go first: Model the behavior you want to see in the group (e.g., relaxed, informal, open, enthusiastic).

B) Manage Your Nervousness and Anxiety

> ***Security is mostly a superstition. It does not exist in nature, nor do the children of men as a whole experience it. Avoiding danger is no safer in the long run than outright exposure. Life is either a daring adventure or nothing.***
> ***- Helen Keller***

Some nervousness and anxiety are perfectly normal. And there are times, especially when you first begin leading workshops and training programs, when you might feel like a fraud. You might feel like you don't really belong at the front of the room. You tell yourself, "This is a big mistake!" "I'm not really qualified." There's even a term for this feeling. It's called the *impostor syndrome*.

This feeling of being an impostor only happens to people who are stretching and developing themselves. It doesn't happen with people who don't take risks. Of course, if you don't risk, you don't grow either. Thus, the impostor syndrome is a good sign, so don't let it spook you. It means you are learning and growing, and anyway, a little nervousness is always a sign that you're alert and ready for the job. The poem below, about the value of risk, was written by my favorite Greek author, *Anonymous*.

> ***A mistake in judgment isn't fatal, but too much anxiety about judgment is.***
> ***- Pauline Kael***

To laugh is to risk appearing the fool.
To weep is to risk appearing sentimental.
To reach out to another is to risk involvement.
To explore feelings is to risk exposing your true self.
To place your ideas, your dreams before the crowd is to risk loss.
To love is to risk not being loved in return.
To live is to risk dying.
To hope is to risk despair.
To try is to risk failure.
But risk must be taken because the greatest hazard in life is to risk NOTHING.
The person who risks nothing does nothing, has nothing, and amounts to nothing. They may avoid suffering and sorrow, but they simply cannot learn, feel, change, grow, or love.
Chained by certitude, they are slaves; they have forfeited FREEDOM.
Only a person who risks is FREE.

The bottom line with risk and anxiety is this - so few of us are perfect! As a workshop leader, you need to accept that as long as our world is turning and spinning, you're going to be dizzy. As a result, every now and then you're going to make a mistake. Mistakes hurt, but that's life. Apologize and move on. As you make mistakes, and as you're feeling pain from time to time, develop a passion for learning from these experiences. Over time, this learning will help you succeed in all areas of life, not just as a workshop leader.

I'm a great believer in luck, and I find the harder I work the more of it I have
- Thomas Jefferson

The good news: nervousness and anxiety are normal. More good news: there are ways to take some of the pressure off yourself.

In his principles of leadership Masao Nemoto (1987) stresses rehearsal as a key occasion for learning.[1] It's informal, more relaxed, and mistakes are easily corrected. In particular, prepare and rehearse the introduction and other key parts of the workshop start-up. Do this until your approach is smooth and relaxed, but don't overprepare or memorize. Doing so will kill your spontaneity.

Perfect practice makes perfect

Jodie Winquist, a long-time client of mine, herself an experienced workshop and training-program leader, finds it helpful to "talk through" the first few steps of a workshop or training program. She likes to hear how it flows. Sometimes she even does this in the actual training room and walks through the start-up much the way an actor would when rehearsing for a part. She doesn't memorize but she does prepare well. This builds her confidence and doesn't hurt her spontaneity a bit.

Set the room up well before the workshop, perhaps the night before, or at least early that morning. Ensure you're familiar with the AV (audiovisual) equipment that you will be using (e.g., TV, VCR, overhead projector). Don't bother cramming at the last minute. A good rule is to arrive early, double check things, then concentrate on introducing yourself and greeting people as they arrive. There are always a few participants who come early and just want to chat over a cup of coffee. (A little caffeine helps those of us who find it necessary to chemically start our brains in the morning.)

Somehow, meeting a few participants before the workshop relaxes me a little. It's also a great time to pick up a few stories about what people are doing at work, how this workshop fits with their interests, why they came, and a little information about participants' personal lives. (Call me a little snoopy, but I like to know about people.

Are they married, with two kids and a dog? Where are they from? How long have they been with their present employer? I don't just find these things out because it helps me understand their learning needs, although it does. I'm genuinely interested in people. If you're not, leading workshops might be the wrong line of work for you.)

Finally, the best way to get the pressure off yourself during the workshop, and particularly during the workshop start-up, is to keep participants active. Get them talking and doing things early, whether they're introducing themselves, talking about their work, or just laughing and sharing a few stories about what's going on in their company or their community.

Getting into your "resource state"

Genie Laborde (1984) has a wonderful formula for getting into an emotional place where you are feeling powerful, positive, and ready to lead.[2] You establish a state for use in the present, but based on a memory of a time when you were highly successful in a similar situation. I've adapted Laborde four steps for getting your "resource state" as follows.

1) Recall a time when you were very successful, when you did something similar to leading a workshop or training program extremely well, for example, a time when you gave a presentation to your social club, emceed your cousin's wedding, or lead a project team with wildly successful results.

2) Sit quietly for a moment and mentally go back to that time. Pay attention to what you are seeing, feeling, and hearing. Make this memory as vivid as possible.

3) While thinking about this memory, do something to anchor it at an intense (positive, exhilarating) moment. For example, squeeze your left hand with your right hand. This will be your anchor for recalling this intense and powerful experience.

4) Test to ensure you have anchored a "stimulus-response" reaction to the act of squeezing you left hand with your right. You may need to go through steps two and three as many as four times to properly anchor the "resource state."

Now, as you walk down the hallway toward the workshop or training room, squeeze your left hand with your right to recall the experience at a deep emotional level. This will help you get into your "resource state." It's not magic. It's just common sense. The more deeply you recall a similar and successful experience, the more positive and powerful you're likely to feel. It sure beats thinking "black thoughts" before you're expected to be positive, outgoing, and entertaining.

THE FIRST FOUR STEPS IN STARTING UP A WORKSHOP OR TRAINING PROGRAM

No pilot would head down the runway without first warming up the engines. Cold engines are unpredictable and unprepared for the workload ahead of them. The first thing you need to do when the workshop begins is warm participants to you (the workshop leader), to each other, to the idea of participating in the workshop, and to the learning content. This section breaks the warm-up into four steps.

1) A little casual conversation
2) The welcome
3) Introductions
4) The "hook"

1) A Little Casual Conversation

OK, it's time to start the workshop. You've been mingling with people "one on one" and in small groups as they entered the room. You've exchanged greetings, a little ritualistic conversation (e.g., "How about those Chicago Bears?"), and introduced yourself to many in the group, but likely not to everyone. (You get tied up in conversations prior to the workshop and don't get around to say "hi" to everyone.)

The first thing you need to do to officially start up a workshop is to be casual. Don't be "official." Take on the image of a colleague, a coach, or a leader, but not the image of a manager, a teacher, or a boss. Once the group is seated, but before doing anything that looks organized (e.g., formal introductions, reviewing the agenda), just talk casually with them. Introduce yourself, but then get off that subject; you can talk more about yourself later.

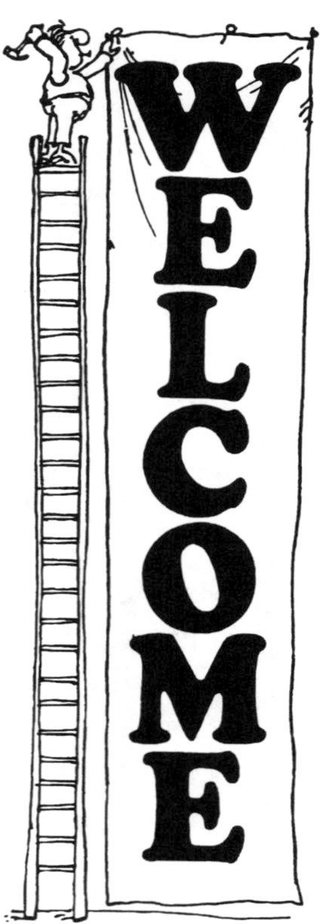

Think of the next few minutes as a kind of "pre-meeting." Sit on the edge of a table or in some other casual position. If you're good at using humor, now's the time. Don't go overboard; just demonstrate that you don't take yourself too seriously. Talk a little with people as *individuals*. Walk over to the people you haven't met yet and shake their hand. There'll always be a couple of participants in the group who say a few things, sometimes wisecracks about each other. That's great. It gets things rolling. Your goal here is simply to establish a bit of human contact. This only takes a few minutes. Spending more than four or five minutes is overdoing it.

Often the perfect time to have this casual conversation is while the group is waiting for one or two stragglers (i.e., people who are late). But even if you're not waiting for stragglers, take the first five minutes to do this anyway. The bottom line here is establishing a little rapport with participants.

2) The Welcome

The "welcome" gets participants' attention. Now they know you're about to lead the workshop. Start the workshop by saying, "welcome," "good morning," or whatever seems appropriate, just so long as it's inviting, positive, and upbeat.

Next, say something like, "I'm delighted to be here this morning." Say this regardless of how you're feeling at the moment (e.g., anxious, nervous, tired). Keep your shoulders back, your head up, and a smile on your face. Even if you'd rather be jogging or reading a book in your backyard hammock, act as if this is the only place in the world you'd like to be at this moment. If this isn't the case, that's OK; just fake it. This is the only time lying is defensible, and anyway, it's only a "white lie." It's not hurting anyone. So "fake it till you make it." One word of caution though: Don't go overboard or you'll come off sounding phony. Simply work extra hard to see the "positives" during the workshop start-up, and remember, it's definitely not a good time to act depressed!

> ***It's not sufficient to know what one ought to say, but one must also know how to say it.***
> ***- Aristotle***

3) Introductions

Ah yes, the dreaded introductions. Dreaded by participants because it's early and they're either tired or relaxed. Right off the bat some participants will say to themselves, "Darn it, I came to watch, to sip on my coffee, to learn, and to be entertained, but not to speak in public, at least not right away!"

Introductions and nerves

What is it about introductions that makes people so nervous? Introductions can even be unsettling to experienced workshop goers. My wife, Cathy, a management employee in a bank, hates introducing herself. Even though she has participated in lots of workshops, she can never concentrate until introductions are over with. And even though I'm practiced at speaking in public, I also know this feeling. As a workshop participant, I've felt anxious about sitting waiting for my turn and then introducing myself. Strangely enough, I no longer get this feeling when I'm leading a workshop.

Introductions are also dreaded by workshop leaders, because they can be rather boring if not managed properly and because they can eat up a lot of valuable time. Yet there's no way around it; you need to do introductions. Even if participants know each other, you should still do introductions, in this case focusing on having them learn a little more about each other and/or discussing their expectations of the workshop (see example below). If nothing else, introducing themselves helps get participants "mentally in the room." It's pretty hard thinking about what's piling up on your desk back at work when you're speaking to a group about yourself.

The questions are: "How can introductions be spiced up a little?" and "How can introductions add value to the workshop?" There are a lot of ways to "skin this cat." For example, ask participants to pair up, interview each other, and then introduce their partner to the group. Or, in larger groups (e.g., twenty-five or more participants), form small groups of five to seven and have participants introduce themselves in these smaller groups. The simplest method of doing introductions is "popcorn" style, where participants simply "jump up" and introduce themselves whenever they feel like it. It breaks the monotony of going around the table in order.

Introduce yourself first to model how you want introductions done. Before introducing yourself, however, give directions verbally and visually (e.g., on a flipchart), noting that participant introductions should be done quickly. Introductions aren't complicated, but without visual directions there will always be someone who goes off track. The problem is that if someone starts telling you their life story, others may follow this example, using up valuable time.

Below are a couple of examples of flipcharts providing directions for introductions. In the first you ask participants to introduce themselves giving their name, their position, and one personal or unique thing about themselves that others might not know. The second is more "down to business" and focuses on the topic of the workshop, in this case "Project XYZ."

Examples of Prepared Flipcharts

Where participants don't know each other (and using a little humor)

Introductions

- Name
- Position (what you do)
- One unique or deeply weird thing about you

Where participants know each other

Introductions

- What is your vision/dream for Project XYZ?
- Where do you fit into Project XYZ?
- What are your feelings about being here today?
- What do you need to call this workshop successful?

The first example (above) may seem innocuous enough, but some participants will be uncomfortable talking about themselves in any personal way. That's why you need to go first. In this way you can "seed" the type of response you're expecting. You might introduce yourself saying, "I like to go backpacking in the mountains with my sons," or "I base my fashion taste on what doesn't itch," or "I have Lhasa apso dogs. One male and one female. They're little house dogs and cute as a button. But what's a little strange is that even though we've had them for a year, they still aren't completely housebroken. By the way, does anybody know where I can rent a good carpet steamer?"

> ***One of the symptoms of an approaching nervous breakdown is the belief that one's work is terribly important.***
> ***- Bertrand Russell***

Relax participants by asking things like, "Who hates introducing themselves?" (Raise your hand to show that you're "polling" the group.) Or say something like, "OK, let's do this quickly because it's important that you have some idea who these strangers are around you." A little humor also helps. For example, ask participants to introduce themselves by telling the group "who you are, what you do, and how you got that way." Then explain more clearly, using a flipchart as shown above.

What do you want participants to tell each other? Ask for a couple of rational things, as in the first example above (name, position), and one thing that's more challenging, personal, or fun (e.g., one unique thing about you). Substitute the latter request for many others, depending on the group involved. For example, you might ask about "your hope for this workshop," or using a little humor, "your most recurring fantasy." It's amazing how people will participate in almost any question, if you make it fun.

After everyone has introduced themselves, go a little further. Ask the group, "What else do you want to ask me that will help you be more comfortable learning in this workshop?" Say, "Ask anything you want. If it's a tough question, I may only pretend to answer, but feel free to ask away." Then pause. Tell the group, "This is a limited time offer. It's only good as long as I'm alive!" The group usually asks one or two questions, getting concerns and suspicions out in the open where they can be dealt with quickly and directly. After the introductions comes the "hook."

4) The "Hook"

The "hook" is a piece of learning content to whet participants' appetites. Use the "hook" immediately after introductions. The other start-up material (e.g., reviewing outcomes, contracting expectations, administrative issues) comes later. However, there's one important piece of contracting you must do before the hook. You need to tell participants "what" you're doing and "why." Otherwise, they'll wonder what happened to the usual discussion around roles, outcomes, agenda, and so on. They'll also wonder how what you're doing, having them do, or telling them fits with the workshop purpose and agenda.

Contracting for the hook isn't difficult. Simply say something like, "We'll be talking about the purpose of the workshop, the agenda, your expectations, and some administrative issues a little later, but for the next half hour I want to ..." Then quickly set the context for the hook, so participants know what's coming and how it fits in the workshop.

I've learned that you can get by on charm for about fifteen minutes. After that, you'd better know something.
- H. Jackson Brown, Jr.

Your hook should only take a half hour to an hour, and it should show participants value quickly, getting them wanting more. Hook participants with one of your best models, exercises, or "sermonettes," just so long as it's relevant, highly involving, and fun.

Once you've got participants hooked, promise more of the same later, but for now bridge back to the workshop start-up. Next comes contracting, which is discussed in detail in chapter eleven.

Examples of "hooks"

- In a training program on communications: Discuss a practical model for giving and receiving feedback. For example, the model provided in the section titled, "Feedback - A Tool for Checking, Maintaining, and Growing," in chapter twelve.
- In a training program on coaching: Ask participants about their best and worst experiences coaching others or being coached by others. Follow up by asking what made these the best or worst experiences. Record responses on flipchart paper for later reference.

- In a training program on negotiations: Use Johnson's (1986) fallout shelter exercise.[3] This exercise involves decision making and compromise, in a group, under time pressures. Once completed the exercise is debriefed in the group. This discussion may influence the emphasis to be placed on various outcomes being sought from the workshop.
- In a team-building workshop: Use the Rath, Kisch, and Miller (1976) exercise dealing with intergroup competition.[4] This exercise gets the group struggling with the effects of both cooperation and competition within their team. As with any simulation, the exercise would be debriefed in the group and conclusions drawn.

End

THE NAME GAME - LEARNING PARTICIPANTS' NAMES

Dr. Barry Gordon (1996) of the Memory Disorders Clinic at Johns Hopkins University in Baltimore says "most of us do perfectly well ... (remembering) the names and faces of at least 1,000 acquaintances."[5] Dr. Gordon goes on to say that "with a reasonable amount of effort, you could probably improve your memory by 30 to 40 per cent." So, don't say you can't remember names, because you've got to, and you can. You can remember at least up to fifteen or twenty names. After that it just takes a little more work.

Here's a good rule of thumb. If group size and workshop duration are such that you should do introductions (e.g., twenty people for a day long workshop), then you should remember first names. If introductions aren't practical (e.g., fifty or sixty people for a half day workshop), then you're off the hook for remembering everyone's name. It this situation you might use name tents or name tags. These are not just for your use but so participants can use each other's names as well. Name tents are usually a good idea when participants don't know each other already. Don't expect them to work as hard at remembering names as you do.

Learning names is important, and it impresses participants when you do this quickly. The first step is preparing a "name chart" as shown below. Either have someone in the group who knows participants' names draw this diagram for you as participants take their seats or draw it for yourself during introductions. Most of us are visual learners, so seeing names in writing is helpful.

Next, do a little "multi-tasking." As participants are introducing themselves or doing some initial exercise, listen with one ear and at the same time go over names in your mind. For example, take a grouping of participants and repeat to yourself, "Shaun, Syd, Jan, Murray" as you look at each person, one at a time. Once you've got this grouping down pat, go to the next grouping and so on. Then, test yourself a little by jumping around and saying a person's name to yourself. It takes a little concentration but it's amazing how quickly this works. Usually within five minutes you've got participants' names in short-term memory. Now all you have to do is glance occasionally at the name chart, just as a check, during the first couple of hours of a workshop.

Remember unfamiliar names or find some way to remember these. For example, you might associate an unfamiliar name with something that will help you remember it. Also find ways to distinguish among similar sounding names.

Remembering an unfamiliar name

I once had a manager in a workshop named "Arun" (pronounced *eh-ruin*). I never forgot his name because I associated it with that old joke about archaeologists - "their careers are in ruins." Thus, "Arun" was easy to remember. (Needless to say Arun is not an archaeologist, nor is his career in ruins. He's a successful finance manager in the public service sector.)

Distinguishing among similar sounding names

Recently I conducted a workshop where Susan and Sandy sat beside each other. Worst yet they had similar features. Luckily Sandy was wearing a brown "sandy looking" sweater. This made it easy. If you try hard enough, you can usually find some way to associate a participant's name with something that will help you remember it (e.g., an object, a song, a phrase).

Don't even listen to last names at first, except where there are two participants with the same first name. You can learn other last names later if need be. And be sure not to get the name wrong the first time, for example, calling Betty Jo, "Betty Lu." This happens most often when you knew a Betty Lu in the past. The problem with getting it wrong the first time is that it sticks in your mind that way. Thereafter it seems to take a little extra effort to make the change to the correct name.

You want to get these names down so well that you can use them casually during the workshop. If you do get a name wrong, apologize and concentrate on not getting it wrong a second time. Or, you can do what one of my mentors, John Jones, does. He just laughs after being corrected by the participant and says, "You just missed an opportunity to be named Betty Lu (or whatever the wrong name was)."

Name Chart

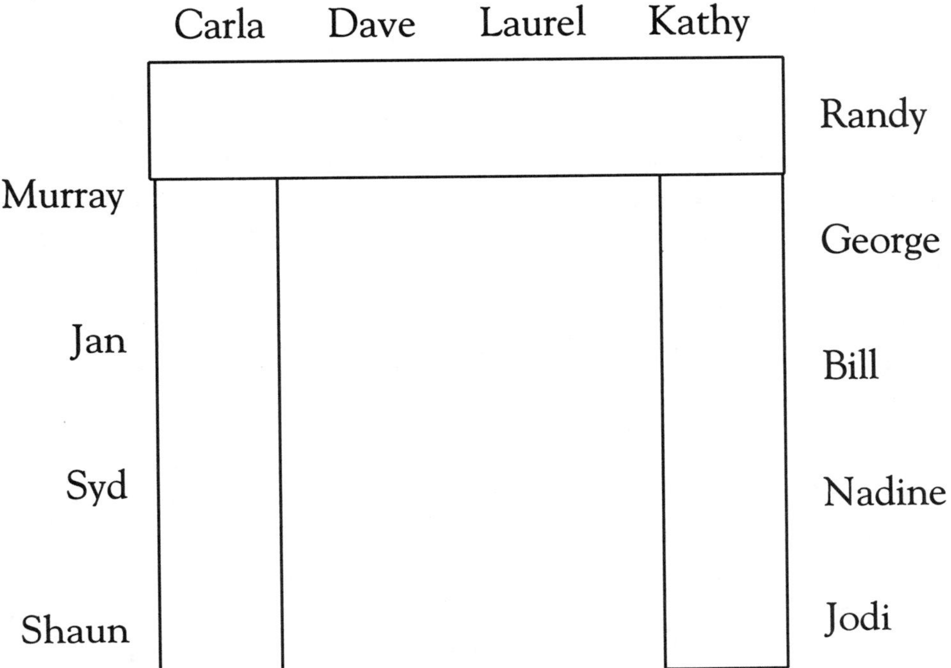

CONCLUSION

Summary

Taking the first few steps in a workshop is a bigger challenge than meets the eye, but when it's done well it propels a workshop forward. A clean take-off conserves energy while reassuring and relaxing everyone on board.

Leader Readiness

Be prepared physically and emotionally for leading the workshop or training program. You owe it to participants to show up relaxed, well rested, enthusiastic, refreshed, organized, confident, and optimistic. Prepare materials at least a day beforehand; then do whatever is necessary the day before to recharge your batteries. For example, take a couple of hours alone in the evening before the workshop or training program just to relax and leisurely review the start-up and your "game plan" for day one. In some cases it will be enough just to "think through" your first steps the day before the workshop or training program. In other cases you'll want to have these well planned and rehearsed. Whatever you do, don't just "wing it."

Have a Game Plan

Have a theory of approach and know what you are trying to accomplish, how you intend to go about it, your options if things don't go as planned, and how to tell when you're off track or have reached a goal.

Establish yourself personally and professionally with participants as soon as possible. Create participation and learning readiness by showing relevancy or context and by setting clear expectations. Your leadership should be clear, confident, and concise. Show you're organized. Demonstrate that you know what you're doing. Model enthusiasm and a flexible belief in your technology. If you make a mistake or two, don't worry. There are countless places to recover. When it's relevant to the workshop's purpose, discuss your "mistakes" with participants, turning them into learning content. Model willingness and openness to learning in front of the group.

Be Sensitive to the Group

Keep your antennae up during a workshop. Be alert and empathetic to the group's needs. Be "up front," direct, and honest. Park your ego and your need to be "right," or "in charge," at the door. You need a bit of an ego to lead workshops, but coupling this with a little humility isn't a bad thing either. Avoid territorial and "role based" attitudes and behavior, for example, playing "I only speak the truth" or "that's the way it's going to be." Don't be defensive or protective of your approach, your role as the workshop leader, or your right to make demands on the group. Share leadership and use your power as a workshop leader wisely. Support, encourage, and challenge, but unless you've tried everything else, avoid demanding, selling, and telling.

The First Four Steps

Four steps are provided for getting started and warming up the group. These are establishing rapport, welcoming participants, doing introductions in a way that models the type of climate you want for the workshop or training program, and "hooking" participants' interest early on.

Welcome participants with an upbeat and positive mood, engaging them in casual conversation to set the tone for the workshop. Make the process for introductions explicit. Use a visual display to clarify each step (e.g., a flipchart or overhead display). Reduce participant anxiety and foster an informal climate by asking participants to share a personal aspect of themselves (e.g., "I enjoy backpacking with my sons").

The Hook

Give participants one piece of learning material (e.g., model, exercise) within the first half hour of a training program just to whet their appetite. Give them something they'll find worth making notes about. Have them saying to themselves, "Wow! I can use this." Build participant confidence and a workshop climate of hard work, joint responsibility, risk taking, informality, and fun. Get them involved and active (e.g., speaking, moving around, providing information, talking with each other). But be sure to start where there's energy and interest, making sure learning material is at the participants' current level of understanding and playing to their strengths and knowledge to bolster confidence. In this way, you "hook" participants' interest early in a training program.

The Name Game

Learn participants' names. It's easy once you get into practice. Demonstrate that each individual participant is important enough to you to be referred to by name.

Checklist

Leader Readiness	*Creating Interest*
• Show up prepared, refreshed, and ready to lead • Manage your nervousness and anxiety	1) A little casual conversation 2) The welcome 3) Introductions 4) The "hook"

Exercise

Assessing Your Experience "Starting Up" Workshops and Training Programs

1) What's the best workshop start-up you ever led?

2) What was it that you did that made this start-up go so well?

3) What's the worst start-up you ever led?

4) Looking back, what could you have done differently to improve this workshop start-up?

5) What two things do you want to do better next time you start up a workshop or training program?

Notes

[1]Nemoto, M. (1987). Total quality control for management: Strategies and tactics from Toyota and Toyoda Gosei. Lu, D. (Ed. and Trans.). Englewood Cliffs, NJ: Prentice-Hall.
[2]Laborde, G.Z. (1984). Influencing with integrity: Management skills for communication and negotiation. Palo Alto, CA: Syntony, pp. 142-143.
[3]Johnson, D.W. (1986). Reaching out: Interpersonal effectiveness and self actualization. Englewood Cliffs, NJ: Prentice-Hall.
[4]Rath, G.J., Kisch, J., & Miller, H.E. (1976) X-Y: A three way intergroup competition. The 1976 annual handbook for group facilitators. San Diego, CA: University Associates, pp. 41-43.
[5]Boyd, R.S. (1996, March 2). Memory. Calgary, Alta: *Calgary Herald*, p. B3.

Chapter 11

Contracting Group Process during Start-Up

INTRODUCTION

The most essential contracting you'll do concerns getting clarity and agreement on the workshop's or training program's purpose and outcomes. This contracting was the focus of Part 2 (chapters three, four, and five). Now, it's time to look at contracting group process. This is done early in the workshop or training program, usually as part of the start-up.

Contracting group processes with participants during the start-up helps the group clarify how they want to work together, and how they want to avoid working together. Inevitably this roots out and corrects faulty assumptions, whether these be about roles, expectations, or any other aspect of the workshop or training program.

Depending on the type of workshop or training program you are leading, there are always some group processes that are absolutely essential for contracting with participants, others that are useful, and still others that aren't needed. This chapter provides a full range of options for you to pick and choose from, depending on what's required in each unique situation.

This chapter covers:

- How to contract workshop process.
- Areas for contracting.

HOW TO CONTRACT WORKSHOP PROCESS DURING START-UP

Before discussing various options for contracting process, it's important to quickly discuss "how" you might go about doing this work, that is, the process you'll use for contracting process.

The first step is data gathering. Find out what participants need, expect, and are prepared to offer each other. For example, participants may expect to be active and highly involved during the workshop. Thus, they expect small group exercises, open and lively discussions, and a decision making role in the workshop process.

Next, communicate what you are willing and able to "provide" and "not provide." For example, you may be OK with participants calling you at home with questions about workshop assignments.

The most common approach to data gathering during the start-up, whether you do this in the group as a whole or in subgroups, is a simple "T" chart. Contrasting statements are presented for group input. In the example below, data would be collected from the group about their hopes for working together and achieving success and about their concerns or fears for the workshop (i.e., what they feel might or could go wrong, if the group wasn't careful).

Hopes & Concerns (An Example)

What I hope does happen in this workshop	*What I hope does not happen in this workshop*

AREAS FOR CONTRACTING

The following list of contracting options is not exhaustive, but does cover the most common areas for contracting workshop and training-program processes with participants. Pick, choose, and adapt these options as you see fit, but don't use more than a few each workshop. That would be "contracting overkill." Your workshop or training program would end up being all contracting and no delivery.

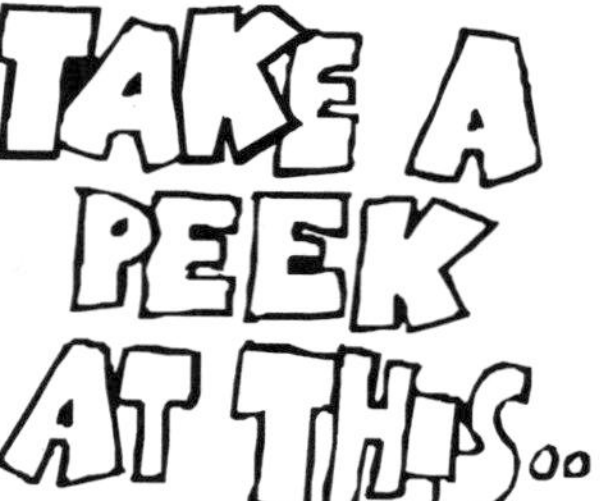

The following fifteen areas for contracting are separated into four categories. The one identified as "essential" needs to be contracted with the group for each and every workshop or training program. Those listed under the category of "basic contracting options" are fairly easy to facilitate and, with a little planning, should not present much difficulty to even the most inexperienced workshop or training-program leader. Intermediate options require a little more finesse to contract with a group. Inexperienced leaders will want to practice these ahead of time. Finally, the options labeled "advanced" are best handled by leaders with a little experience. These options can involve sensitive discussions with the group.

Essential Contracting

1) Revisit and confirm workshop or training-program purpose and outcomes

Basic Contracting Options

2) Contracting administrative issues
3) Contracting the agenda
4) Contracting how decisions will be made
5) Contracting time frames
6) Contracting permission
7) Contracting behavior using ground rules
8) Contracting levels of relating
9) Contracting how digressions will be handled

Intermediate Contracting Options

10) Contracting "ordinary reality"
11) Contracting roles
12) Contracting wants and expectations
13) Contracting for breakdown

Advanced Contracting Options

14) Pre-evaluation
15) Contracting head and heart stuff
16) Contracting with prisoners and vacationers

ESSENTIAL CONTRACTING

1) Purpose and Outcomes

In most cases, *purpose* and *outcomes* will have been contracted prior to the workshop start-up. Nonetheless, it's critical that you revisit and either reconfirm or adjust these, with the group, during the start-up.

BASIC CONTRACTING OPTIONS

2) Contracting Administrative Issues

This isn't complicated, and for the most part it's "informing" not "contracting." Tell participants things like where the washrooms can be found, where the fire exits are, and what the plans are for meals and breaks. And contract with (or inform) the group of start and end times.

There's one important organizing item to contract here: That's evening assignments. Tell participants ahead of time what's expected, and specifically how much time will be required outside of the workshop for completing assignments. (Note: Evening assignments should be anticipated and outlined in the confirming letter to participants. In addition, they should be discussed in the pre-meeting, if there is one.)

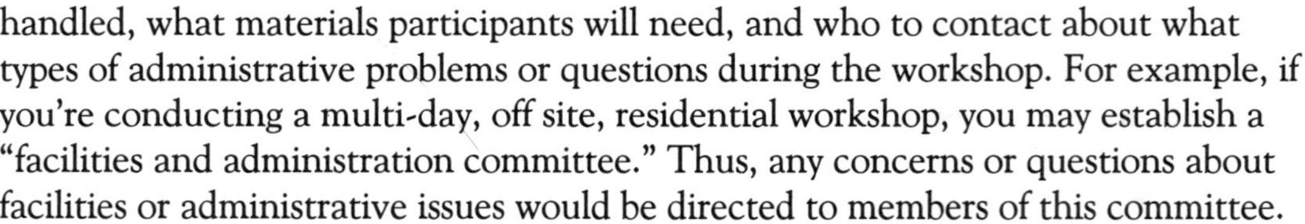

Use a simple checklist to run through administrative issues. It might include things like where the phones are, how messages will be handled, what materials participants will need, and who to contact about what types of administrative problems or questions during the workshop. For example, if you're conducting a multi-day, off site, residential workshop, you may establish a "facilities and administration committee." Thus, any concerns or questions about facilities or administrative issues would be directed to members of this committee.

Sharing responsibility for the functioning and administration of a workshop

For off site, residential workshops where everyone is somewhat isolated from the "real world" for a week or longer, you may want to organize the group into working committees. One committee could be in charge of facilities and equipment; another would have responsibility for recreation; one for morale; another for keeping the group up to date on news, sports, weather, and so on.

I recall being in a dark basement conference room at a mountain resort for a full week. After hearing a lot of complaining about the lack of windows and natural light, the facilities committee took it upon themselves to resolve the matter. Using flipchart pages they drew pictures of windows and posted these around the room. It was good for a laugh the next morning, and a least showed they were "in tune" with the group's concern.

We started each morning at this workshop with a report from the "news, sports, and weather" committee. When we weren't in the workshop, we were either working in subgroups on assigned tasks, on our own doing assignments and readings, taking part in organized recreational activities, or hanging out in the hospitality suite. There wasn't time to keep up with the outside world. Thus, the morning reports from the "news, sports, and weather" committee were a welcome way to start the day. They used a lot of humor, showed a lot of bias, particularly in their sports reporting, and got the group very animated early in the day.

The morale committee could be called on whenever the workshop started to sag a little. They were like firemen, on call, and expected to rush in when needed to pick up participants' spirits. We had a lot of fun challenging them to "make us happy"!

Needless to say the recreation committee did a great job. They organized a cross country ski trip that later turned into one of the most competitive outings I've ever been on. They also talked the hotel's management into giving us exclusive rights to the pool one evening for a game of "Aussie rules water polo."

We even had a committee in charge of the hospitality suite. They didn't get a lot of sleep!

3) Contracting the Agenda

Now for a few words on that most noble of administrative items, the workshop agenda. An agenda is expected, it's traditional, and it's conspicuous by its absence. It doesn't have to be detailed or involved, and you don't have to follow it to the minute, but you do need to have a workshop agenda.

Some people love structure. It's critical for them to see an agenda. Without it they'll assume you're unprepared. And for some, this "illusion of rigor" is even more important than having clearly articulated workshop outcomes. So spend a few minutes reviewing the agenda and timetable with the group during the start-up. But, don't present your agenda as a fait accompli. Rather present it as a "suggested agenda"; then get the group's input, make changes as necessary, and post the agenda where it can be seen and used as a guide.

Finally, remember that an *agenda* outlines activity, whereas *outcomes* speak to results. It's the agreed outcomes, not the agenda, which must be achieved.

4) Contracting How Decisions Will Be Made

Perhaps Victor Vroom and Philip Yetton (1973) were the first to look at how decisions might be made given a range of considerations (e.g., need for employee commitment, urgency, importance or impact of a decision).[1] At any rate, they provide the inspiration for the perspective that not all decisions can or should be made in the same way.

The group might well be advised to decide, ahead of time, how decisions will be made during the workshop. Often groups elect for consensus while reserving the opportunity to use other ways of deciding as the need arises. Contracting how decisions will be made is often more appropriate for workshops (e.g., team building, strategy planning) than for training programs (e.g., learning presentations or interviewing skills).

Decision Making Strategies Worth Considering

Present the following options to groups. These are alternative approaches for making decisions during a workshop or training program.

Command

> The group's manager decides. (Note: This is not the workshop leader.) On occasion command decisions are needed. However, a manager who makes too many decisions this way may, if not careful, become overdrawn in the "relationship bank."

Consensus

> Consensus requires open dialogue. It means most in the group agree, and everyone in the group can "live with" the decision. That is, everyone will go along with the decision even though not all agree with it.

Consultation

The group's manager seeks the group's input, but, because of the importance of the issue, intends to make a command decision. That is, the issue is of such a magnitude that the manager feels he/she cannot abdicate responsibility for the decision. The manager may not follow the group's advice, but promises to consider it before deciding.

Convenience

How this decision is made really doesn't matter. The issue just isn't that significant. For example, someone asks, "Would you like hamburgers or hot dogs on the barbecue?" Answer, "It doesn't matter; you decide."

Voting

Majority rules. People confuse voting with democracy. John Ralston Saul (1994) points out that while voting is a *symbol* of democracy, it's not the *experience* of democracy.[2] That is, people can vote without dialogue or discussion. Voting doesn't even require that people understand the issue being decided. If you must vote, do so only after dialogue and discussion.

Unanimity

Everyone needs to agree, or the default decision is "not to decide." This approach is often a recipe for inaction. Use it only when you require 100% commitment and follow through from all concerned.

Decision Making Strategies to Avoid

Groupthink

Groupthink reminds one on Disney's portrayal of lemmings all jumping off a cliff together. Each has lost his/her capacity to think as an individual. Groupthink has to do with group members' often unspoken need to maintain harmony or at least to avoid conflict. Classic examples cited by Janis (1982) include President Kennedy's bungled "Bay of Pigs" invasion of Cuba and the ironic "domino theory" that took America into war with Vietnam.[3] I say ironic because dominos might be a rather appropriate metaphor for groupthink.

Janis offers the following guidelines for avoiding groupthink.

- Encourage objections.
- Avoid settling, too early, on just one course of action.
- Create subgroups to examine the same problem separately.
- Have group members confer with their subordinates.
- Seek opinions from outside experts.

- Assign a "devil's advocate" within the group.
- Develop alternative scenarios.
- Offer group members a second chance to express their views.

ID (ignore, deny)

Deciding not to decide is itself a decision. It isn't always the wrong decision, but, right or wrong, sooner or later there will be consequences. This approach reminds one of the "Wizard of ID" comic strip by Parker and Hart. The king lives in a world of his own illusions, and conveniently, he has the power to maintain these myths. Ignoring, denying, and downplaying a problem are the ultimate recipe for the status quo. "Nobody moves, nobody gets hurt" is itself a myth.

5) Contracting Time Frames

This contracting is pretty straightforward and really only needed in a strategy development or action planning type of workshop. Here you just help the group get clear on what their "time frame" for planning is. For example, are we planning for a one year period? For a five year period? Don't assume this is clear to the group, because often it's not.

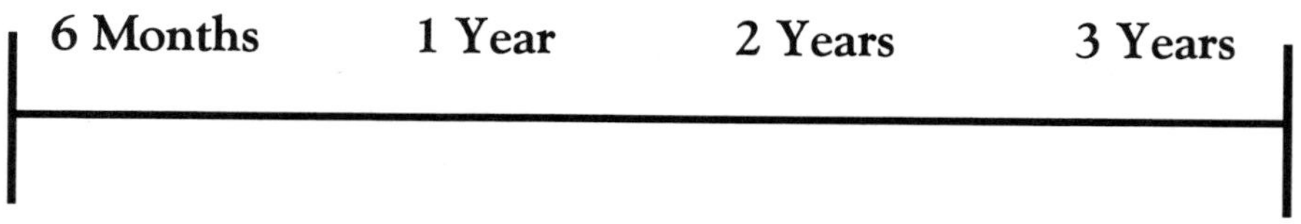

6 Months **1 Year** **2 Years** **3 Years**

6) Contracting Permission

The start-up is a key time for you to clarify your leadership style and to get permission for your idiosyncrasies. Chances are you're not perfect and you have a few quirks, if not annoying little habits. So "fess up." Tell the group about these and get permission to be human. For example, if you have a little asthma and need to cough periodically, tell the group. Let them know you're not infectious. Or if you tend to jump around from topic to topic, let them know. Ask them to challenge you if they get lost.

My flipchart spelling, especially when I'm rushing, is something to behold

I like to get permission ahead of time about my flipchart spelling. It's not that I'm a poor speller, although I do consider spelling to be one of the more minor social conventions. Rather, when I'm thinking of about eight things at once, trying to keep a fast pace to the workshop, and trying to write as fast and as neatly as I can with a marker, well something just happens. Sometimes I just can't spell an everyday word correctly. I get permission from the group to have the spelling errors corrected at the time the flipchart notes are typed.

It's also important to get permission to challenge the group. Aim for a fast paced workshop with lots of challenge and energy. So ask permission to challenge and permission to make slightly outrageous comments from time to time. By making things a little personal, presenting extremes, and by contrasting perspectives, the group gets more stimulated and involved. But take care. This is a technique for experienced facilitators. Always be careful not to go too far and insult the group. And if you do, process this out with the group immediately. Otherwise they might write you off as a "blamer" or someone who's just too antagonistic. (For an example of how I sometimes personalize issues and challenge, see the story in chapter sixteen titled "Being under attack in a training program - A story about dealing with unexpected anger and surfacing indirect communication.")

Make up for your challenges by finding and recognizing people's strengths, and do this a lot. Keep your compliments sincere. Workshop leaders need to be sincere, whether they mean it or not! Seriously, work hard to find the positives. Ken Blanchard (1982) says you need seven or eight positives to balance out one criticism.[4]

Ask permission to wander around during small group exercises and observe. As Casey Stengel once said, "You can see a lot by observing." Looking over participants' shoulders will make some of them a little nervous; that's why telling them ahead of time that you'll be doing this is important. Tell them it's to coach if needed, not to evaluate.

Asking permission for an idiosyncrasy

I have this habit of taking a flipchart over to a corner of the training or workshop room, turning it around so the group can't see the front, and writing notes that I use later with the group. What's a little annoying is that I do this while the group is doing other things. For example, I make these notes while subgroups are working on a task. I use one ear to listen to myself about what I'm writing, leaving the other ear free to listen to what's happening in the subgroups. (Having two ears is great. Thank goodness for redundant systems!) The notes I make on the flipchart are things that occur to me at that moment. I write things I didn't, or couldn't, have predicted I would need on a flipchart.

You might ask, "Why don't you just wait and make these notes after the exercise is finished?" My answer is "time." Making flipchart notes slows things down. By making these notes during the exercise I have them ready to go once the exercise is completed. I can then immediately launch into a sermonette or debrief or whatever it was I was busy writing on the flipchart. This keeps the pace of the workshop fast.

I've found that ninety nine times out of a hundred, participants allow me this little quirk. They accept that I'm human. But every now and then you'll get a perfectionist, someone who's so busy doing my job as the workshop leader they've forgotten they came to learn or accomplish something, not to evaluate every step I take.

It's in these rare cases that I often wish I had gotten permission from the group during the start-up. It only takes a few seconds to tell them about this little quirk. Telling participants ahead of time makes it easier for them to accept when it happens. This way they aren't suspicious or distracted. They simply say to themselves, "Oh yeah, he said he'd be making flipchart notes in the corner."

Asking permission to challenge in the group

Sometimes I'll ask something as simple as, "Can I challenge you on that?" Usually the participant says "yes." Now, I have permission. Asking permission instead of just going ahead and challenging helps prepare the participant and the group as a whole. Without permission, participants may misinterpret your motives in a number of ways. For example, they may see your challenge as an attack on them personally, or they may think you're just "showing off" for the group.

You also need to be very sensitive and empathetic when challenging, so have your antennae all the way out. Pay attention to nonverbals, and always end by thanking the participant for allowing the challenge.

After you've challenged a couple of times and no one has been made "to lose" as a result, participants will "cut you more slack." That is, they now know it's safe to be challenged and to challenge others in the workshop. By asking permission you model a learning climate of challenge coupled with fair-mindedness and empathy.

End

7) Contracting Behavior Using Ground Rules

Ground rules are norms of behavior in a workshop or training program. They need to be developed for and by the group. Only if everyone has a hand in their development will everyone be obliged to follow them.

It takes only fifteen or twenty minutes for the group to brainstorm and agree on a few ground rules. Usually three to seven ground rules are plenty. These should be kept posted on a flipchart during the workshop, referred to, and changed as needed.

Don't write ground rules on everything, and don't write them unless they're really needed. It's like writing a goal about something you're going to do anyway. If you're going to do it anyway, why write a goal? Thus, unless you think punctuality will be a problem in the group, don't write a ground rule about returning on time after breaks.

The best ground rules are written in short, snappy statements. For example:

- Anyone can call "time out"
- Everyone needs to challenge and participate actively
- Don't take feedback personally
- Do your evening work
- No forced disclosure
- It's OK to disagree
- Be open - say what is real
- Listen to what is said and meant
- Push for closure, make agreements, and move on

Ground rules reinforce desired behavior and are a powerful form of contracting. It's not just the group contracting with you (the workshop leader), it's the group contracting with each other. That gives ground rules *value*. They become explicit norms of behavior. When these norms are violated, which isn't often, the group almost always exerts its influence on the participant concerned (and you thought peer pressure ended in grade school).

Dave's ground rule when speaking to a group. This is "yes" and this is "no."

One of my colleagues has a fun way of establishing a "response" ground rule with groups. Among other things Dave is a platform speaker and uses lots of closed and rhetorical questions to test whether the group is "with him" during his talks. If he's not getting much reaction, he contracts for the group to respond "yes" or "no." He does this only after he has first established a little rapport with the group, and inevitably he gets them laughing as he talks about this ground rule. This is important, because as you read on you'll see that it's possible for some members of the audience to misinterpret Dave's approach as an insult. That is, some might think he's being patronizing. In fact he is, but only as a joke. Anyway, he handles it in a casual and humorous way, and no one has yet been insulted. Here's what he does.

Looking up at the unresponsive audience Dave smiles and says,

By the way, I won't ask much of you today, but I need to know that you are awake. I need to establish one ground rule. When I ask you a question, this is yes [Dave says this while nodding his head up and down], *and* [shaking his head from side to side] *this is no. Work with me on this? Let's practice.*

Nodding his head up and down Dave then repeats, "this is yes," and shaking his head from side to side he says, "this is no."

It works! The group laughs and goes along with Dave, practicing their head nodding. They realize they've been unresponsive, and they know he's only kidding. And later when some in the audience (this is a talk, not a workshop) respond by nodding their heads either yes or no, Dave says, "Good, I see some of you learn very quickly." The group laughs again. The group is usually more responsive once Dave has done his "yes-no" routine with them, maybe because they've had a good laugh, and maybe because Dave has drawn their attention to the fact that he needs some response, from time to time, so he knows what to emphasize in his talk.

So how do you know what ground rules are needed when the workshop is just getting started? The answer is "you don't." At least not for sure. But the group will likely know. Simply explain what ground rules are, give an example or two, then ask the group. They usually know what habits or shortcomings ground rules would help them overcome or what strengths ground rules will support. You may also have previous experience with a given group or with people in a particular company. In this way you'll be able to guess about the culture of the group or organization and what ground rules may be useful. Also, you can always go back. Even during the middle of a workshop, when you discover a new ground rule is needed, you can digress for a few minutes and suggest the new ground rule to the group. If agreed, you can add it to those already posted on the wall.

Finally, it's important to use ground rules as guidelines and not interpret them too religiously. As mentioned above, common sense needs to be applied before any model or ground rule will work well.

A story about a ground rule taking on a life of its own

I once co-lead a training program with a colleague where, believing the group to be introverted, we handed out red and green cards to everyone. Green for "go," red for "stop." This was a group of about twenty administrative managers, most at senior levels in very small organizations, and no two from the same organization. They were also a group that met regularly, a few members would join or leave each year, but overall they knew each other fairly well.

We told them to hold up the green card anytime they felt something was particularly valuable and they wanted to hear more and to hold up the red card when they wanted something or someone to stop. Thus, they'd use the red card if someone was going off-topic, taking too long to say something, or offering something they felt wasn't needed or adding value to the workshop.

At first the cards were used sparingly and with respect. Soon, however, they were "red carding" each other with a vengeance. One participant would be trying to make a point and other participants were flashing their red cards. It became a bit of a nightmare. Finally, my co-leader and I had enough and called "a little prayer meetin'." We stopped what we were doing and talked about several problems we were experiencing, one of which was the need for participants to use these cards with more respect, patience, and empathy toward us and toward each other. After that they used their red cards a little more sparingly.

This training program ended up OK, but I would use these cards differently next time. First, I'd make sure the group worked well together. It turned out this group had a history of competitiveness and bickering with each other. Second, I'd consider setting some sort of limit on using the red card (e.g., restrict its use to twice a day), or maybe build in a guideline like Ken Blanchard's seven positives for every negative (referenced above). Thus, the guideline might be something like use the green card four times for every time you use the red card. As I write this it all sounds too complicated. You need to keep ground rules simple. This was my first experience using these cards. I don't think I'll use them again.

8) Contracting Levels of Relating

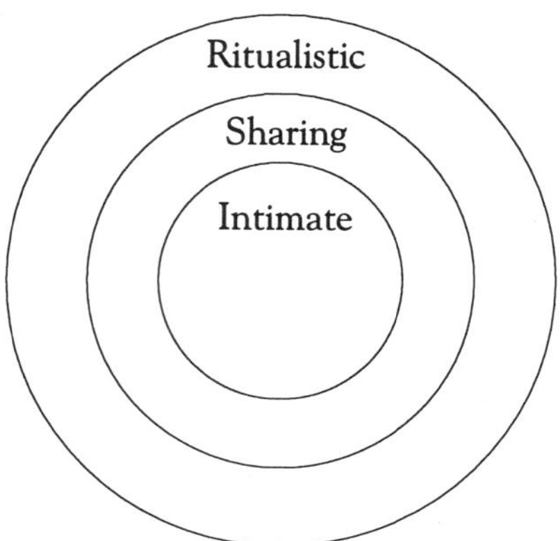

I learned this little strategy from a friend and colleague, David Irvine.[5] At times it helps to position the level at which participants want to relate with each other during a workshop or training program. Draw three circles on a flipchart (see diagram). The outer circle represents the most superficial level of relating. *Ritualistic* behavior is what you see at cocktail parties. People talk about the weather, sports, or about any subject that isn't in any way controversial. A deeper level of relating is *sharing*. Here people may agree, disagree, express different values and beliefs, and challenge each other's views. At the level of *sharing* people are opening up more and taking more risks. *Intimacy* is the deepest of the three levels of relating. This involves discussion of very personal matters (e.g., family problems, social relationships). *Intimacy* goes beyond what is needed, or desired, in most workshops.

These circles are often helpful in that, through contrast, participants understand better what is meant by *sharing*. This is important because in most workshops the aim is to have the group relate at the *sharing* level. *Ritualistic* behavior just doesn't go deep enough for real learning or substantial change. There isn't enough challenge. *Intimacy*, on the other hand, is too risky and almost always unnecessary in a business focused workshop.

Boy, that's a relief!

On occasion, when I've had a room full of very serious business people in a workshop, and after I've explained these three levels of relating, I'll lighten things up a little by asking, "I won't be asking you to be intimate in this workshop. Are you OK with that?" They usually laugh, both in relief and in the knowledge that there's no way on God's green earth they'd ever be intimate with each other anyway!

9) Contracting How Digressions Will Be Handled

Time is money.
- Ben Franklin

Related to the agenda is the issue of workshop time. This is no small matter. You need to think of every hour in a workshop as being three person days (e.g., twenty four participants times one hour). Even if you only have fifteen participants, workshop time is expensive.

Although you'll need to deal with each digression or detour from the agenda as it occurs, get agreement in principle with the group on how digressions will be handled. Chapter sixteen talks about "on-topic" and "off-topic" digressions. On-topic digressions are comments or stories that are related to the purpose of the workshop. Off-topic digressions have no, or very little, relevance to the workshop's purpose and outcomes.

Tell the group if and when you're unable to deal with an "on-topic" digression as it arises (e.g., a relevant issue, question, request, concern, suggestion) and that you will, 1) say so, 2) say why it can't be dealt with at that time, 3) "park" it on a flipchart labeled "Parking Lot," and 4) revisit the request at a more suitable time later in the workshop or training program.

Next, get "permission in principle" to be frank but tactful with "off-topic" requests or digressions. The understanding here is that you'll simply tell the participant that their request won't be covered in the workshop. Of course you owe it to the group to briefly explain "why" the request doesn't fit. This isn't just a matter of saying "no." Where possible you want to say "no," with options. For example, you might suggest where a participant can find an answer to his/her question. You might even offer to help after the workshop session has ended.

Parking Lot

Be ready to go. Post a blank flipchart page labeled "Parking Lot" on the workshop room wall before the workshop begins. As questions, suggestions, or concerns arise that are relevant to the workshop's purpose but unrelated to the immediate discussion (i.e., "on-topic digressions"), "park" them on this flipchart page. If you have no intention of dealing with an issue later in the workshop (i.e., "off-topic digressions"), then don't "park" it. "Parking" an issue equates with a promise to revisit and deal with it later during the workshop.

Parking Lot (for "on-topic digressions" only)

A final note. The section on designing a workshop agenda in chapter six talks to the importance of building flexibility and a cushion of time into the agenda to allow for on-topic digressions. Yet this section talks about how expensive workshop time is and the importance of using this time effectively. On the surface this advice may appear contradictory, but it's not. A flexible agenda is needed not to detour from the workshop's purpose and outcomes, but rather to follow the group's path to these outcomes, that is, a path that's meaningful to the group. For example, some groups may need more practice on a given skill or more time to discuss the value and purpose of a given model, whereas other groups only need to briefly discuss this skill or model and then move immediately to planning application on the job.

INTERMEDIATE CONTRACTING OPTIONS

10) Contracting "Ordinary Reality"

Don't you just love these new-age terms like "ordinary reality." It's to distinguish what goes on in consciousness from the "nonordinary reality" of dreams and the subconscious. Anyway, you need to know whether participants are willing to brainstorm wild and crazy ideas or just want to keep things practical and factual.

This type of contracting is often useful in action planning and decision making types of workshops (e.g., team building, strategy development, leadership transition). It is less useful in structured skills training (e.g., facilitation skills, time management).

Think of the level of discussion in a workshop as being on a continuum. At one end is the very serious, logical, factual, and practical. At the other, the innovative, imaginative, and creative. Thus, discussion can range from the very rational to the sublime and ridiculous. From having your feet planted firmly on the ground to having your head in the clouds.

Presenting these extremes helps groups position their discussion. Very few groups pick either extreme. After all, "extremes" can be dysfunctional. That is, being overly rational limits creativity, while being nothing but wildly imaginary tends to become unrealistic. There's an old joke about highly rational people. "Show me a man with his feet planted firmly on the ground, and I'll show you a man who can't even put his pants on!" At the other extreme, people who have mastered the art of creativity, but only seem to be able to generate wild and absurd ideas, are sometimes called "space cadets."

Draw this continuum on a flipchart and ask the group where they would put a mark. This gets the group thinking about what they want to accomplish and how they want to work together.

Feet on the Ground			Head in the Sky
Practical serious	Some risk taking	Creative innovative	Revolutionary high risk

Yet another way of presenting this discussion is with Mitroff's (1987) continuum of the obvious, the interesting, and the absurd.[6] The "obvious" is what is already known, beyond question, and assumed to be fact. For example, to North Americans and to a lot of other people as well, it's obvious that democracy is the best way to govern a country. Needless to say, what's obvious to one group isn't necessarily obvious to another.

The "interesting" is just the obvious with a twist. Something is interesting if it fits our understanding while expanding our thinking just a little. For example, learning new ways to start a workshop might be interesting to a workshop leader.

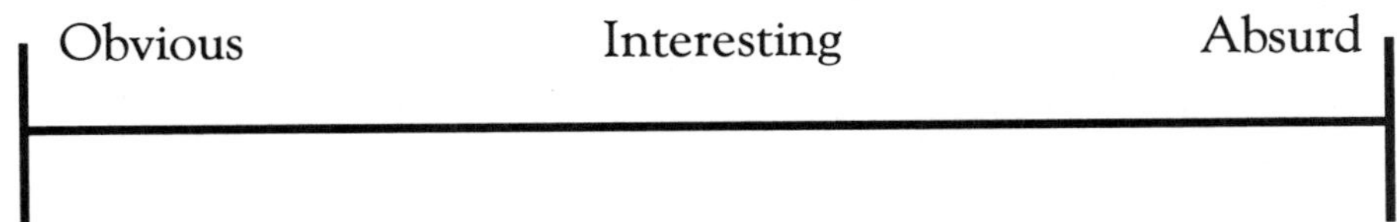

The "absurd" involves an idea that is outside of one's paradigm. Thus, what you're saying doesn't make sense to someone, given their present way of looking at things. For example, suggesting that the earth rotated around the sun was at one time considered absurd, and even heresy. Also, not that many years ago, suggesting that employees be empowered to stop an assembly line was considered absurd. And suggesting that condoms be distributed in high schools was at one time considered absurd. To many people, it still is. It all depends on your paradigm, your way of seeing the world. Your paradigm, in turn, is based on your needs, values, and beliefs.

11) Contracting Roles

Both you and participants have individual and shared responsibilities for workshop or training-program success. Making key roles and responsibilities explicit at the beginning of a workshop or training program leads to improved understanding, clearer expectations, and ultimately to more learning and accomplishment.

The Workshop or Training-Program Leader's Role

As with the concept of learning climate, the nature of your responsibilities as a workshop or training-program leader is discussed throughout this entire book. The following are but a few examples. You need to:

- Have a plan (i.e., an agenda, a clear purpose, outcome statements) and use it flexibly.
- Provide a climate of security, responsibility, sharing, and challenge (e.g., if a participant expresses a minority opinion, it's your job to protect that person so that he/she, and other participants, feel free to express differing views at other times during the workshop).
- Share leadership with participants in an open, encouraging, appreciative, and nondefensive manner.

Participants' Roles

You cannot accept responsibility for participants' learning. This alone is each participant's individual responsibility. Nor can you accept sole credit or ultimate responsibility for workshop or training-program outcomes and accomplishments. This is a shared responsibility with participants.

Participants have the greatest responsibility of all those connected with organizational workshops and training programs. This is the responsibility for learning, accomplishing, and for applying workshop outcomes "on the job." Participants' initial responsibility, however, is to attend, contribute, be open-minded, be actively involved, take a few risks, and learn during the workshop or training program.

Charter of Participants' and the Workshop Leader's Rights and Responsibilities

The participants and your responsibilities and obligations during a workshop or training program are summarized here. For a more detailed overview see Appendix F.

The leader's rights and responsibilities

- To manage the learning climate
- To challenge the group to be learning ready
- To be in charge of group process
- Not to have to tell participants everything
- To be clear about purpose, agenda, context, process, and roles
- To say what outcomes will not be included in the workshop or training-program plan
- To control the schedule and timing
- To use one's own leadership style
- To be human, to make the occasional mistake

Participants' rights and responsibilities

- To express their own feelings, interests, and learning needs
- To be informed and involved in all aspects of the workshop
- To challenge, ask questions, and comment on anything in the workshop
- To share their own thoughts, and not disclose certain information
- To receive a well-organized, worthwhile, and quality learning experience
- To be human, to make mistakes
- To leave a workshop or training program if it is not motivating or appropriate to their needs and interests

12) Contracting Wants and Expectations

It's important to be clear on what you and participants want and expect from each other. This includes what everyone expects to avoid doing as well.

The following examples of "T" chart statements could be used to collect expectations during a workshop start-up. Notice that each is arranged as a dichotomy. When deciding which of these statements may be appropriate for your workshop, consider issues such as the group's familiarity with the training content, their workshop experience, expected resistance, and the type and mix of the group (e.g., management level, technical level). Use only one or two of these dichotomies per group. Any more would be overdoing it.

Two cautions are worth mentioning here. First, give participants lots of permission and encouragement to be "straight" with you, that is, to avoid role playing a process, faking their input, and telling you what they think you want to hear. "Stroke" participant comments, especially comments that seem risky. Remember what seems like a three on the risk scale to you might seem like a ten to a participant who works in a given organization or who works with other participants daily. Second, some of the discussions generated by these dichotomies will require sensitive facilitation (e.g., contributions and sabotage). Others will require that you be nondefensive and nonprotective of special interests, including your own (special interests might include a recent organizational decision or a given manager's style).

Examples of statements that you could "T" chart for data gathering with participants

Give and Take

- One thing I am prepared to give to this workshop.
- One thing I want to take away from this workshop.

Requests and Offers

- What I request of other participants and the workshop leader.
- What I offer other participants and the workshop leader.

Hopes and Concerns

- What I hope happens in this workshop.
- What I'm concerned might happen in this workshop.

Push and Pull

- What's bringing me here today.
- What's pulling me away.

Me and You

- What you need to know about me to help us work together.
- What you want me to know about you to help us work together.

Contributions and Sabotage

- What I can do to make this workshop successful.
- What I can do to sabotage this workshop.

An example - "Me and You"

You might use something similar to the following as a handout during your workshop start-up. This particular example (below) is from a training program titled *Train the Trainer Workshop for Professionals.* It would be possible to flipchart something similar to this, but you'd need to use two flipchart pages. It's a little much for just one page.

Here's how you could use a "T" chart similar to the one below. First, review the left-hand column with participants. As discussed in chapter nine, you need to go first in order to model the process for participants. Once you've reviewed the left-hand column, ask participants if there's any additional information they'd like about you at this time. Once you've answered their questions move to the right-side column. Ask participants to tell you, and each other, what they feel you should know (e.g., about them, their interests, their work) to work with them effectively during the workshop. You might even make a few notes on a flipchart as participants respond. You can post these and use them as a reference throughout the workshop or training program.

Note: You'll see the term "accommodator" in the left column below. This term is from Kolb's learning styles inventory.

Things you should know about me that will help us work together	*Things you think other participants, and the workshop leader, need to know about you to help us work together*
• I think fun comes from achieving and learning. I was a manager in organizations for eighteen years so I have a very practical bent. • I prefer the "accommodator" learning style, so too much structure drives me nuts. • I like to be challenged. Being wrong doesn't cause me much anxiety. • I like to learn. I read, write, and discuss things a lot. • I run to stay fit, but I also eat French fries like they're going out of style. • I'm enthusiastic about leading this workshop. • I like to joke around. I think learning is too important to be taken seriously. • I can't spell "shitt" (a technical term). • I lead workshops by consulting and facilitating rather than by teaching.	

13) Contracting for Breakdown

This contracting has to do with breakdown and changing directions in the middle of a workshop. On occasion these changes are significant, but often they're just a few degrees one way or the other. They're necessary because you're not a magician and you can't read minds, and because you're clients/participants are not perfect either and are not able to fully predict and articulate the exact outcomes they want from a workshop ahead of time.

Here's how it works. Speaking "tongue in cheek" ask that someone in the group interrupt whatever is happening about half way through the first day or early the second day of a workshop. Ask them to use a frustrated tone and say something like, "This isn't getting us anywhere!" This does four things. First, it gets a laugh. Second, it gives participants permission to challenge and help ensure the workshop is focused on their needs. Third, it's a subtle way of letting participants know ahead of time that these breakdowns are OK, and even very positive. Fourth, as you're making this request, it gives you a chance to do a little sermonette on how workshops need to find their own flow and direction, even if this means rethinking some of the original outcomes.

Background Information for Your Sermonette

Regardless of how well you have facilitated the pre-workshop contracting with your clients, rarely will your most successful workshops follow your game plan completely. You still need a game plan, but often after things are started, workshops find their own, sometimes unpredictable, course. You'll be going along at a nice pace and getting things done. The group seems involved and working hard. All of a sudden someone will speak up and say something like, "We've done this before." "This isn't what we need to do." "This isn't getting us where we need to go." or "This is OK but what we really need to do now is ... ." These *breakdowns*, if you facilitate them effectively, will often lead to *breakthroughs* for the group. Initially, when the breakdown happens, you might feel like you've let the group down by not adequately predicting and contracting for their needs. If you've done the necessary pre-workshop contracting, there's no need to feel this way. What's happening is a natural consequence of not being omnipotent.

Why don't clients just tell you during the pre-workshop contracting exactly what they want? In this way you could avoid these breakdowns. The answer is as simple as it is universal: because clients don't know exactly what they want. If they did, they probably wouldn't need your help! Often, when clients ask for a workshop on strategy, for example, they are able to talk only in the vaguest of terms. They aren't even aware that they're being vague when they say things like, "We need to develop a clear focus" or "We need to revisit the business unit's vision." Sometimes this means they want to set a few key high-level goals, other times it means they want to decide several important strategic issues, and still other times it means they need to develop more realistic "strategic assumptions."

It's your job, as their workshop leader, to help clients/participants figure out specifically what they want from a workshop. Some of their needs can be articulated during the pre-workshop contracting, but other needs will evolve as the workshop unfolds and as clients/participants develop their perspective on the issues being discussed. And not infrequently the group just needs time to develop their relationships before the "real" issues can be discussed openly. For example, it might take a group a little time to "come clean" with their boss. Thus, participants may go along "role playing" goal setting, for example, until you ask just the right question. At this point, they find it necessary to either commit to something they don't believe in, or, alternatively, they find the courage to "fess up" with their boss and, as a result, renegotiate a given goal in the workshop. It's your job and your privilege as a workshop leader to value and even encourage these breakdowns, to facilitate subsequent breakthroughs, and, as a result, to move the group to a level of accomplishment they never even thought was possible.

Every workshop needs a Bob Cunes

Bob is a middle manager in a small oil and gas company. He's participated in several workshops that I've run for this company, usually with his peers, his boss, and other senior managers in the room. The following may seem like flattery, but I'm really just making a point. That point is about the value of workshop participants who are willing to share responsibility with other participants and the workshop leader for the success of the workshop. I'll describe just one occasion when Bob spoke up for himself and for the group, resulting in a more effective workshop.

When you're working with a group, especially as an outside consultant, appearances can be deceiving. You can't always be sure that things are going as well as you think. On one occasion, I was leading a strategy planning workshop, believing I was helping the group with meaningful work, when in fact I was not. What I thought was "high value" for the group was actually similar to work they had completed prior to my showing up on the scene. Unfortunately, most of the group just went along, not uninvolved, but not challenging either. They had gone into "dependence" mode and were role playing involvement - being "students" rather than "results minded participants." Then, Bob spoke up. "This is a waste of time," he said. "We've done this before!" Then he asked, "What do others think?"

Bob didn't just object. He worked with me (the workshop leader) and with the group to create a new direction for the workshop. Thanks to his courage and willingness to speak out, the workshop turned out great.

For me, Bob epitomizes the responsible workshop participant. He is both results oriented and sensitive to other participants' needs. Bob's challenges are honest and direct; they aren't "sugar coated," but neither are they vindictive. Most importantly, Bob takes a full share in the responsibility for the success of the workshop. He won't let a workshop leader fail for lack of feedback. I wish I could have a Bob Cunes in all of my workshops.

End

ADVANCED CONTRACTING OPTIONS

14) Pre-Evaluation

Let's say you plan to ask participants to evaluate a workshop or training program using the form titled "Training-Program Evaluation"(see p. 368). They would do this during the workshop or training-program wrap-up. Now, consider the form titled "Training-Program Pre-Evaluation" (see p. 369). The questions on the pre-evaluation form have a one-to-one correspondence with those on the evaluation form, except that on the pre-evaluation the questions are inverted. That's because pre-evaluation is used for contracting with participants during a workshop or training-program start-up.

Here's an example of how pre-evaluation works. If a question on the evaluation form asks, "How involving was the workshop for you?," you would invert this on the pre-evaluation form and ask, "What will you do to ensure the workshop is involving for you?"

Pre-evaluation asks participants to move into their "circle of influence." It conveys the need for participants to exert their influence and to ensure an appropriate focus and a high-quality workshop or training program. Thus, pre-evaluation encourages participants to take responsibility for their own learning needs and to share responsibility - with other participants and the leader - for the success of the workshop or training program.

Have participants work independently during the start-up to complete each question or statement on the pre-evaluation form. Next, discuss each question or statement in the group as a whole. This discussion provides the context for clarifying roles and expectations with participants and for ensuring everyone has a part to play in making the workshop or training program a success.

Everybody wins when you and the participants work together to make the workshop or training-program evaluation - completed during the wrap-up - as positive as possible. Using pre-evaluation as a contracting tool has two key advantages. First, you get information for adapting and adjusting the workshop or training program to meet participant needs. Second, by making participants' roles and obligations explicit and discussible, it's easier to make "midcourse corrections" when needed. The success or failure of the workshop or training program has become a legitimate topic for continued discussion, and anyone can now call "time out" when they feel things have "strayed off course." (Note: Appendix E provides additional examples of pre-evaluation forms.)

Training-Program Evaluation

Name ______________________________ *Date* ____________

Workshop Name ____

Workshop Leader(s) Name ____________________________________

Please circle the appropriate response.

1) Stated outcomes were achieved during the training program.	Not at all			Somewhat				Completely	
	1	2	3	4	5	6	7	8	9
2) Training-program content was relevant and challenging.	Not at all			Somewhat				Completely	
	1	2	3	4	5	6	7	8	9
3) Support materials (e.g., handouts) were helpful.	Not helpful			Somewhat helpful				Very helpful	
	1	2	3	4	5	6	7	8	9
4) The training-program leader was effective.	Not at all			Somewhat				Completely	
	1	2	3	4	5	6	7	8	9
5) This training program has improved my understanding of the topic.	Not at all			Somewhat				Very much	
	1	2	3	4	5	6	7	8	9
6) This training program has equipped me with information and skills that I can use immediately.	Not at all			Somewhat				Very much	
	1	2	3	4	5	6	7	8	9
7) The time allowed for the training program was ...	Too much			About right				Too little	
Overall training-program evaluation	Poor				Fine			Excellent	
	1	2	3	4	5	6	7	8	9

Training-Program Pre-Evaluation

1) I can contribute to helping the group achieve the stated training-program outcomes by ... (e.g., minimizing "off-topic" discussion).

2) I can help ensure training-program content is relevant and challenging by ... (e.g., sharing my experience with the group).

3) I can improve my understanding of training-program materials (e.g., handouts) by ... (e.g., speaking up when I don't fully understand how to use a given handout).

4) I can help the training-program leader and the group to be effective by ... (e.g., participating actively).

5) I can help ensure the training program improves my understanding of the topic by ... (e.g., speaking up if I get lost and can't follow what's being presented).

6) I can challenge to ensure the training program gives me information and skills I can use immediately by ... (e.g., speaking up in the group and making sure the leader and the group understand my learning needs and interests).

7) I can help the leader and the group manage training-program time by ... (e.g., challenging when what we're doing feels like a waste of time).

15) Contracting Head and Heart Stuff

How much does the group want to focus on the "heart stuff" such as emotion, motivation, and commitment? And how much do they want to focus on the "head stuff" such as rational, logical, and tangible outcomes?[7]

You might pass out a handout like the following to give the group an idea of what you mean by "head" and "heart" stuff.

Heart	*Head*	*May involve either*
trust	goals	deciding
respect	planning strategy	making strategy
relationships	role definitions	promising
conflict	action plans	contributing
values	schedules	
vision	problem solving techniques	
feelings	accountability	
commitment	results	
intuition	finances	
compassion	budget	
passion	measures	
caring	agendas	
personal mission	structure	
self-expression	efficiency	
authenticity	details	
process	brainstroming	
uncertainty	clarifying	
turmoil	feedback	

Looking at the diagrams below, keep in mind that the group should be more concerned with direction than with velocity.

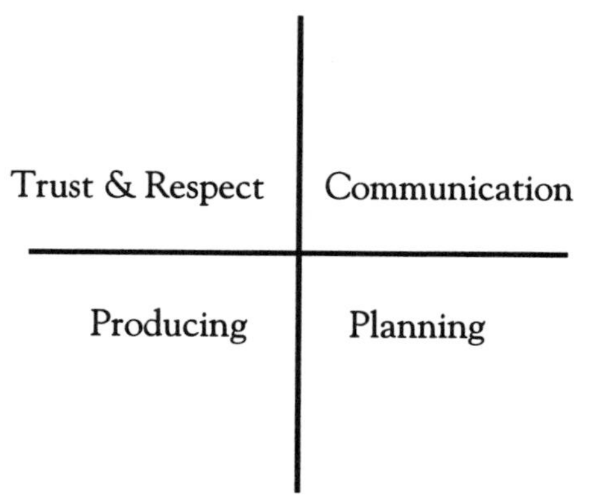

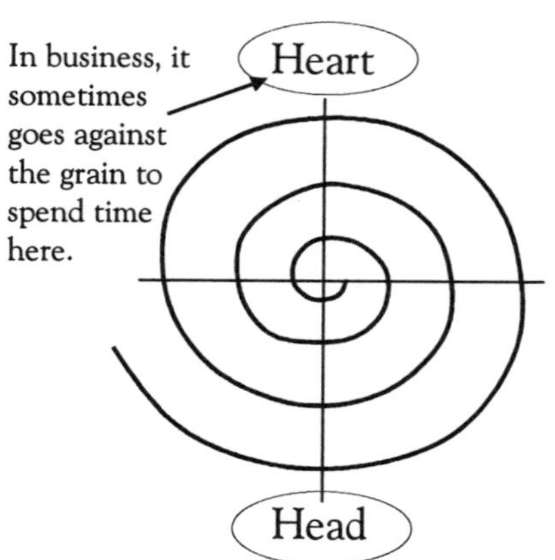

Discuss questions like the following with the group.

- Where is your weak link in these four quadrants?
- Where do you put most of your energy?
- Which of these quadrants represents the group's strength?
- In which direction is your group moving?
- Is the group spending enough time in each quadrant or are some quadrants being ignored? If so, what's this costing the group?
- What happens when one quadrant takes precedence over another? (For example, a great deal of time is spent planning, but trust in the group is "nondiscussible." Or, there is fabulous communication but hardly any results.)
- What happens when you plan and there is no trust?

The heart stuff

Work groups exist in a dynamic of tension. They achieve little without conflict. Although the culture or personality of most work groups suggests how this tension should be managed, it can only be managed where there is trust. However, trust can't be legislated or coerced. You can invite trust but don't demand it.

Trust is the essence of heart stuff. Other elements include goodwill, caring, respect, and a sincere desire to work through tension and differences. These qualities lead to understanding, creative conflict, and support and challenge in work groups.

The following questions help groups assess the group's need to work on "heart stuff."

Trust and Respect

- Are members of the group sincere?
- Are they honest?
- Are they self-aware?
- Do they have the courage to practice their values?
- Do they stand by their values under pressure?
- Do they follow through on promises?

- Do they take responsibility for their own actions?

Communication

- Do group members listen effectively?
- Do they inform and involve others?
- Are they open to feedback?
- Do they give others feedback when appropriate?
- Are they competent (e.g., presenting, questioning, negotiating, discussing, listening)?

The head stuff

Work groups exist to accomplish business results. This takes planning, action, and production. The "head stuff" concerns tangibles such as action plans, work schedules, written contracts, and products.

Use the following questions to help the group assess its need to work on "head stuff."

Planning

- Is the group focused? Are their priorities clear?
- Are they working toward measurable or observable outcomes?
- Are they doing the right things?
- Are their systems and processes efficient?

Producing

- Is the group carrying out their plan?
- Are they involved in the right activities?
- Are they achieving significant business results?
- Are customers pleased with the products and services they receive from the group?
- Are they making enough money for the company?

The group's focus

Presenting a group with this type of contracting decision helps them become conscious of the importance of both head and heart work and of how these two ways of working complement each other.

Focusing exclusively on heart stuff generates heat but very little motion. This approach leads to a kind of country club perspective where groups share and care, talk about process and have fun socially, but don't get a lot done or accomplished.

Focusing exclusively on head stuff can result in a group "role playing" commitment. Thus, a group might generate pages of goals and action plans, but they're mostly to please the boss. If people can't disagree, if they can't dialogue and discuss issues in some depth, then chances of them being committed to action and of following through back on the job are greatly reduced. In knowledge work, to quote Karl Weick (1969), "action without commitment is seldom effective."[8]

16) Contracting with Prisoners and Vacationers

Only rarely do you see prisoners in training programs these days, and that's an improvement. At one time organizations practiced this form of alternative sentencing with vigor. You don't have many options for dealing with prisoners once the workshop begins. However, if and when you discover a person has been sent against their will, offer him/her as many alternatives as you can. Say something like, "How can I help? I'm willing to do what I can as long as it's not dishonest." Offer solutions, for example, "Leave if you wish, but if I'm asked about your attendance, I won't lie and say you were here."

Don't let vacationers "off the hook." Expect them to participate. They came voluntarily to the workshop or training program and therefore have an obligation to other participants, and to you, to contribute to the success of the workshop.

Surprisingly, prisoners and vacationers can often be "turned around." More often than not, after resenting, resisting, and resting for a period of time, and with a little empathy, listening, and gentle challenge, these people decide to participate, contribute, and learn. This is almost always the case if the workshop leader can build trust and rapport with them.

CONCLUSION

Summary

There's no better guarantee of workshop success than having all participants agree on what they're trying to learn and accomplish, what's expected of each of them, and what others have agreed to do and be accountable for during and after the workshop.

Contracting Workshop Process with Participants during the Start-Up

The following list of options is provided for thinking through and deciding what processes need to be contracted with the group

Essential Contracting

1) There's never a good excuse for not contracting *purpose* and *outcomes* with a group. You need to agree on what you're trying to achieve and what success will look like.

Basic Contracting Options

2) *Administrative issues*. This includes everything from the workshop start and end times to smoking policy and the location of fire exits.

3) *The workshop agenda*. Participants need to see some structure. The agenda allows them a glimpse of the "big picture," that is, where the workshop or training program is going, what is covered, and how work is sequenced.

4) *Decision making*. Despite the term "leader," you are not the de facto *dictator* of the workshop or training program. Nor is the workshop necessarily a democracy. You and participants must choose when to use command, consensus, consultation, convenience, voting, and unanimity. "Groupthink" and "ID" are two decision making strategies to avoid.

5) *Time frame*. Is the focus long term or short (e.g., one year or five)?

6) *Permission*. This refers to participants having license to speak up, to challenge, and to disagree. Giving permission is a way of sanctioning disagreement, encouraging confrontation (as opposed to conflict), and valuing marginal perspectives.

7) *Ground rules*. These are simple guidelines for behavior during a workshop or training program (i.e., participants have the right to "pass" on any question).

8) *Levels of relating*. Ritualistic interaction is what takes place at the company Christmas party, where small talk about the local football team or the weather abounds. Most workshops operate at the *sharing* level of interaction. Participants share experiences, stories, and information, helping each other learn. The deepest level of relating, *intimacy*, concerns deeply personal and sensitive issues and feelings and goes beyond what's required in most workshops.

9) *Handling digressions*. Get agreement in principle to "park" on-topic digressions where this is necessary and to be direct, respectful, and tactful in refusing to waste the group's time discussing off-topic digressions.

Intermediate Contracting Options

10) *Ordinary reality*. Contract the level of discussion, be it abstract and focused on theory or pragmatic and practical.

11) *Roles*. Both yourself and participants need to be clear on your roles, obligations to each other, and expectations of each other.

12) *Wants and expectations*. Use a "T" chart to clarify participants' wants, interests, needs, and expectations. And share your own with the group as well.

13) *Breakdown*. Contract for someone in the group to challenge the workshop's focus and direction and to ask the group to rethink the outcomes being sought.

Advanced Contracting Options

14) *Pre-evaluation*. Using the inverse of the questions on the evaluation form, have a serious but informal discussion with participants about specific ways they can contribute to the success of the workshop or training program.

15) *Head and heart stuff*. Determine what priorities participants place on "heart stuff," such as emotion, motivation, and commitment. Do the same for the "heart stuff," such as practical outcomes and action plans.

16) Aim to fully involve *prisoners* and *vacationers*. At the least, minimize their disruptive effect.

Checklist

Decision Making Strategies Worth Considering	*Contracting "Ordinary Reality"*
• Command • Consensus • Consultation • Convenience • Voting • Unanimity	• Head in the clouds, feet on the ground • Obvious, interesting, absurd
Decision Making Strategies to Avoid	*Contracting Wants and Expectations*
• Groupthink • ID (ignore, deny)	• Give and take • Requests and offers • Hopes and concerns • Push and pull • Me and you • Contributions and sabotage
Levels of Relating	*Contracting Head and Heart*
• Ritualistic • Sharing • Intimacy	• Trust and respect • Communication • Planning • Producing

Exercise

Assessing Your Skill at Contracting Process with Groups

1) What types of contracting with groups do you do particularly well?

2) Why are you successful at this contracting?

3) What can you do to continue to build on this success? To get even better at contracting process with groups?

4) What types of contracting with groups do you feel you need to get better at doing?

5) List two specific steps you can take to improve this contracting with groups?

Notes

[1]Vroom, V.H., & Yetton, P.W. (1973). Leadership and decision-making. Pittsburgh, PA: University of Pittsburgh Press.

[2]For a perceptive discussion on voting and referendum see: Saul, J.R. (1994). The doubter's companion: A dictionary of aggressive common sense. Toronto, Ont: Viking, pp. 251-253.

[3]Janis, I. (1982). Victims of groupthink (2nd ed.). Boston, MA: Houghton Mifflin.

[4] Blanchard, K., & Johnson, S. (1982). The one minute manager. New York, NY: William Morrow.

[5] I am grateful to my friend and colleague, Dave Irvine, Cochrane, Alberta, Canada, for these ideas on positioning a workshop.

[6]Mitroff, I.I. (1988). Business not as usual: Rethinking our individual, corporate, and industrial strategies for global competition. San Francisco, CA: Jossey-Bass, p. 29.

[7] I am grateful to my friend and colleague, Dave Irvine, Cochrane, Alberta, Canada, for these ideas on positioning a workshop.

[8]Weick, K.E. (1969). The social psychology of organizing. New York, NY: Random House.

Part 5

Getting It Done: Leading a Workshop

Chapter 12

Moving, Adapting, and Ending a Workshop

INTRODUCTION

Now that the workshop or training program is steaming along, you need tools to keep participants following as the group switches between sessions and between subject areas. The last three chapters looked at how to get a workshop underway. This chapter covers how to keep a workshop responsive to the needs of participants and moving toward agreed outcomes. In particular, it looks at how to bridge from "topic to topic" or "subject to subject" within a workshop session; how to stop and start a workshop session (as opposed to the workshop itself); and how to wrap up and end a workshop.

This chapter covers:

- Moving within and between topics in a workshop session.
- Strategies for getting feedback and staying focused during a workshop.
- Giving and receiving feedback.
- Stopping and restarting workshop sessions.
- Wrapping up and ending a workshop.

CHUGGIN' ALONG - MOVING WITHIN AND BETWEEN TOPICS IN A WORKSHOP SESSION

What's a Session?

It doesn't matter how you define a "workshop session." What is important, however, is distinguishing among a "topic," a "session," and the "workshop" itself. Why this distinction is needed will be made clear below, but right now a few simple definitions.

A "topic" is simply the subject of dialogue and discussion. Workshops and training programs may be specific to one, two, or several topic areas. For example, training topics might include questioning skills, presentation skills, leading small group exercises, and so on. Workshop topics might include a discussion of project leadership, problems with the XYZ product design, or marketing opportunities over the next three years.

A "session" is just a section or part of a workshop. Thus ending a session is not the same as ending the workshop or training program itself. A session could be any period of time, typically includes at least one complete topic but may include several topics, and encompasses a single meeting or series of meetings.

If you choose, organize a workshop by defining sessions. How you define sessions is up to you. It's a matter of convenience, although some logic needs to be involved. For example, you might section a one-day workshop in two sessions, AM for theory and PM for practice, or AM for data gathering and PM for planning. Other times you might simply refer to AM and PM sessions and leave it at that. Yet others times you might define each session to correspond with a given topic. Session one might be one evening a week for six weeks to cover the first topic. Session two might go one evening a week for two weeks to cover the second topic. Session three might be the following Saturday to complete the third topic and wrap up the workshop.

This section focuses on moving from topic to topic within a workshop session. It covers,

A) Reviewing and summarizing within a topic

B) Bridging between topics

A) Reviewing and Summarizing within a Topic

The Value of Reviewing and Summarizing

Today, with "continuous rail," it's all the same smooth sound as a train rolls down the track. Only twenty years ago, however, you'd hear the old rhythmic "clickety-clack, clickety-clack," mile after mile, as the train moved along. The "continuous rail" equivalent in a workshop is "reviewing and summarizing."

Reviewing and summarizing eliminate the bumps, giving the session a seamless feel. As more and more learning material is introduced and experienced, reviewing and summarizing help participants stay focused and minimize their chances of feeling overwhelmed or lost.

When to Review and Summarize

Review and summarize regularly as sessions progress. Mark review and summary times on your workshop plan or agenda to ensure they aren't neglected, but use these times as a guide, not as a rule. As you arrive at these times, check with the group to see if a review and summary are required.

Review and summarize when participants are having trouble digesting material, although ideally, this should be done before participants have difficulty. Review more often in situations where learning material is complex and where participants have limited experience with the topic.

Knowing when to review and summarize comes with practice. Reviewing and summarizing too often frustrate participants. Not doing so often enough frustrates them even more. So keep your antennae up and watch for subtle signals that participants are getting lost.

Finally, a good rule of thumb is if you haven't reviewed and summarized in at least an hour, stop and check just to ensure participants are not falling behind. This check might involve asking the group a few questions or simply checking with your own "reading" of the group as to whether or not they are following the discussion.

How to Review and Summarize

The review and summary are not a lecture but an exercise. Involve participants by asking challenging and stimulating questions. For example, ask participants' for a couple of examples of how they would apply new learning "on the job." Ask participants to answer questions using their own words. Repeating the workshop material verbatim may demonstrate that a participant was attentive during the workshop, but doesn't indicate comprehension or an "application" level of knowledge. Reviewing in their own words also helps participants integrate new learnings with previous experience.

Use visual aids (e.g., flipcharts, handouts) to illustrate key points in the review and summary. For example, the box below is a visual aid that overviews the key points in this section.

A review and summary of "reviewing and summarizing"

The value of

- Eliminates the bumps
- Helps participants stay focused
- Minimizes chances of participants feeling lost
- Gets participants back on track

When to

- Where learning material is complex
- Where participants have limited experience with the topic
- When participants are having trouble digesting the learning material
- Check at least every hour to see if needed

How to

- Involve participants
- Ask questions
- Have participants ask each other questions
- Ask participants to answer in their own words
- Use visual aids

B) Bridging between Topics

The "what" bridge tells participants what's coming next.

The "why" bridge tells participants why a given topic is on the agenda. It explains both "why this" and "why now."

"What" and "Why" Bridges

Remember how Lassie would run back to the farm and warn Gramps that the bridge was out? Usually the humans around Lassie, being of lesser intelligence, took a while to catch on, but when they did, they'd go warn the station agent. The station agent, in turn, would telegraph ahead to warn the oncoming train. All would be saved. Well, unless you've got a real smart dog, and I mean *real smart*, when you miss a bridge in a workshop you won't get any such warning. The bridges referred to here are "what" and "why" bridges.

"What" and "why" bridges are a special type of review and summary. Just as a railway bridge carries a train over a river or canyon, "what" and "why" bridges carry a workshop from one topic to another.

"What" and "why" bridges should be concise and informative. They should contain just enough information to tell participants *what* learning material is coming up next, *why* this material is part of the workshop, and *why* it's up next on the agenda.

An example of "what" and "why" bridges

Introducing a new topic:

Next we need to discuss feedback (the "what" bridge). *Giving and receiving feedback are described in chapter twelve. I want to cover this material now, however, as you will be giving each other feedback during the next exercise. Also, every workshop leader needs to be highly skilled at communicating difficult information so that others will listen, and at receiving feedback well, even when it stings a little* (the "why" bridge).

The Value of "What" and "Why" Bridges

Together, "what" and "why" bridges connect the new topic to learning material that has already been covered and explain how the new topic fits with the workshop's purpose, outcomes, and agenda. Bridges give participants context and help them follow the workshop process.

As a rule, workshop leaders do a pretty good job with "what" bridges, but often they forget about "why" bridges. This is unfortunate because "why" bridges help participants understand context and connections between topics. Most importantly, "why" bridges help create learning readiness. That is, participants are more motivated to learn when they understand how, and why, a new piece of learning material fits with previous learning and how this new material can be of value to them in the "real world" (i.e., on the job).

When Bridges Should Be Minimized or Eliminated Altogether

There are exceptions to the frequent use of "what" and "why" bridges and the clarity they provide. These are times when you want participants to struggle with meaning for themselves and don't want to be particularly clear about *what* participants should be learning. An example is any exercise or simulation where you want participants to come to their own conclusions and arrive at key learnings for themselves. In such a situation a little ambiguity is useful.

Although some participants may experience a little "creative tension," having them struggle to create and discover meaning for themselves is preferable to "spoon-feeding." Struggling is part of the natural learning process and leads to a much deeper level of understanding than "just being told." The value of this deeper learning far outweighs the risks associated with having participants become a little frustrated during an exercise.

Exceptions to the use of "what" and "why" bridges, however, do not include having participants struggle with workshop purpose, outcomes, agenda, or design. These need to be clear each step of the way. Having participants struggle with the relevance of workshop outcomes or design leads more to frustration than to learning.

"What" and "why" bridges - A summary

Defined
- Tells "what" material is coming next and "why."
- Explains "why" the new material is important and how it relates to other material.

When and how to use
- When moving from one topic to another.
- Keep them brief and informative.

The value of
- To provide context.
- To help create learning readiness.
- To model a learning climate of involvement and shared accountability.

When to avoid or minimize
- When you want participants to wrestle with meaning (e.g., a simulation).
- Don't minimize when related to explaining workshop purpose, outcomes, or agenda.

STAYING ON TRACK - STRATEGIES FOR GETTING FEEDBACK AND STAYING FOCUSED DURING A WORKSHOP

It's not enough to get feedback at the end of a workshop or training program; you need to get feedback "on the go." The following methods of gathering feedback are quick, painless, and efficient. Use them often, and use the feedback that results to make small adjustments that, over time, make a big difference to workshop success.

This section scans the following methods of gathering feedback during a workshop.

A) Do temperature checks "on the fly"

B) Talk with participants "one on one" or in small groups during breaks

C) Do "end of the day" verbal feedback sessions with the group

D) Monitor the learning climate as you go

E) Use "quick hit" level-1 evaluation forms to generate instant feedback

F) Co-lead the workshop and ask your co-leader to provide feedback during breaks

A) Do Temperature Checks "on the Fly"

Do periodic "temperature checks" with participants during the workshop to ensure they're getting what they need. Just as the physical temperature in the room needs to be checked every now and then, so too must the emotional temperature be monitored. Every few hours, or when your instincts say the time is right, take anywhere from thirty seconds to a couple of minutes and ask people to answer a question like, "What are you feeling right now?" Next seed a couple of responses like "frustration," "energy." Finally, stay quiet and allow participants time to respond.

Make your process visible. Tell participants what a temperature check is and why you're doing it. Ask clarifying questions where necessary. Don't write any of this down unless absolutely necessary. Finally, summarize and move on. Be sure to act on the feedback, immediately when possible.

B) Talk with Participants "One on One" or in Small Groups during Breaks

Valuable feedback comes from conversations during coffee breaks and lunch hours. It's not so much that participants are reluctant to give you honest feedback in front of the group, but rather that new ideas come to them as you discuss issues and concerns and share stories during breaks. Invariably, participants ask very insightful questions at the breaks. Encourage them to raise these same questions in the group, or failing this, get their permission to raise their questions yourself.

C) Do "End of the Day" Verbal Feedback Sessions with the Group

This is the brainstorming equivalent of a "temperature check." "T" chart a couple of questions on a flipchart. For example,

"T" Chart - Do Differently & Did Well

What could we have done differently today?	*What went well today?*

Do "what" and "why" bridges. That is, tell the group "what" and "why" you're doing this. Say something like,

> *In order to continuously improve the workshop, it's important to do a quick end of the day assessment. Let's take four or five minutes to talk about what we could have done a little better here today, and about what we did well. This isn't just feedback for me; it's for everyone. You need to hear from each other about this day.*

Brainstorm the disapproving or contrary information first (e.g., "What we could have done differently?"). This way you end on a positive note (e.g., "What went well?"). Record responses as you go. Use participants' exact words and phrases. When necessary, force the issue a little by saying something like, "I'd like to hear at least two things that we could have done differently today."

One caveat about getting feedback in public. Follow the principles of receiving feedback outlined below. "Put a pencil in you mouth" while participants are commenting on "what could have been done differently." Anything you say while receiving critical feedback will be seen as defensive.

D) Monitor the Learning Climate As You Go

Needless to say it's your clients, particularly participants, sometimes called the "end-user" clients, who ultimately decide whether a workshop was outstanding, average, or a waste of time. Often this decision, however, is only rendered during the workshop wrap-up or after the workshop has ended. However, a ton of clues are available *during* the workshop to help you assess "how it's going."

Pay attention to what you are seeing, hearing, and feeling. It's difficult to conclude much from just one or two "nonverbals," but taken in numbers and in combination with what participants are saying, they at least alert you to the need to investigate the learning climate a little further.

In addition, the section titled "Comparing Effective and Ineffective Learning Climates" in chapter nine contains a chart comparing what you see, hear, and feel in an outstanding and in a poor workshop. Use this chart to guide your sensitivity to the workshop's climate and to help you "read" what's happening in the room. In particular be conscious of the importance of learning readiness and participation readiness in the group.

E) Use "Quick Hit" Level-1 Evaluation Forms to Generate Instant Feedback

Ask participants to complete a "quick hit" level-1 evaluation form at the end of a workshop session or at the end of a day. Design these forms so they're easy to complete in three or four minutes. Ask participants to post their completed forms in a designated area or hand these in to you. Either way, at the start of the next workshop session (e.g., after lunch, the next day) quickly review these comments with the group, and where possible make adjustments "on the fly."

Following are two examples of "quick hit" level-1 evaluation forms: *one minute feedback* and *session highs and lows*. (See Appendix E for more examples.)

A word of caution. Don't use these forms as substitutes for "face to face" or "face to group" discussion. Rather, use them as supplements to direct dialogue. Thus, you would continue to meet "one on one" or in small groups with participants during breaks, for example.

One Minute Feedback

This form doesn't tell you what specifically might be improved. It does, however, indicate direction. Results will suggest the need for further inquiry or simply to continue "steady as she goes."

One Minute Feedback

So far I'm finding this workshop to be (circle your response)…

Interesting	1	2	3	4	5	Uninteresting
Too fast	1	2	3	4	5	Too slow
Too easy	1	2	3	4	5	Too difficult
Relevant	1	2	3	4	5	Irrelevant
Organized	1	2	3	4	5	Disorganized
Relaxed	1	2	3	4	5	Tense

Please provide a brief comment for improving this workshop.

Participant Name: ________________

Session Highs and Lows

Use a form similar to this one to supplement your feedback at the end of each workshop session.

End of Session Feedback

I was most energized today when …

I was least interested today when …

Suggestions for improving this workshop …

Participant Name: ________________

F) Co-Lead the Workshop and Ask Your Co-Leader to Provide Feedback during Breaks

Where you co-lead a workshop or training program, have your co-leader pay close attention to learning climate, participant nonverbals, and the effectiveness of your facilitation and leadership. Debrief with each other at breaks or between sessions.

Feedback - A Tool for Checking, Maintaining, and Growing

This is the true joy in life: Being used for a purpose recognized by yourself as a mighty one, being a force of nature, instead of a feverish, selfish little clod of ailments and grievances, complaining that the world will not devote itself to making you happy.
- George Bernard Shaw

You need to get and give feedback all through a workshop. This is how a workshop leader stays "plugged into" what's really happening in a workshop. This section looks at the nature and practice of working with feedback including,

A) Assumptions about feedback

B) Types of feedback (description versus evaluation)

C) An actionable framework for feedback

D) Things to avoid when giving and receiving feedback

D) Deciding to give negative feedback to a participant

A) Basic Assumptions Surrounding Feedback

First, understand that "feedback is good!" This isn't as obvious as it sounds. Lots of people, workshop leaders included, shun feedback in very subtle ways (e.g., staying busy, not paying attention to nonverbals, acting defensively). We all need a little feedback every now and then. We need to hear that our singing in the shower sounds differently to others. This helps us decide to keep our day job.

Feedback is the breakfast of champions.
- Ken Blanchard

Second, see feedback as being within what Covey (1989) calls your *circle of influence*.[1] Make feedback a *me*, not a *they*, issue. As a workshop leader, or in any other role, if you're not getting a lot of feedback, it's likely because of how you solicit or receive it, rather than because other people are conspiring to keep things from you. Conversely, if workshop participants or others don't seem to want your feedback, it's likely because of how you present or provide it, rather than because they wouldn't find value in what you have to say.

Understanding Circle of Influence

We don't actually "control" (that is, fully control) much in organizations or workshops, except our own thoughts and behavior. That's why "circle of control" in the diagram below is shown as relatively small.

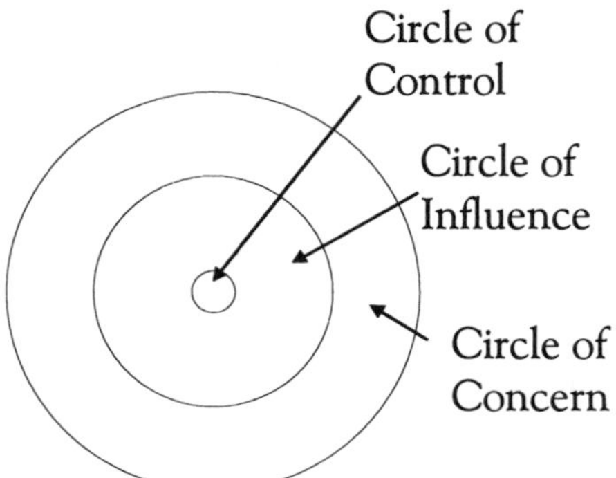

How big our "circle of influence" becomes, however, depends on the choices we make. Make giving and receiving feedback a choice within your circle of influence. For example, rather than complaining that "my boss doesn't give me any feedback," go and ask for feedback. Then, if your boss still won't give you feedback, go and get it somewhere else (e.g., clients, peers, your boss's boss). Expand your circle of influence by letting others know you would appreciate, value, and want their feedback, rather than being dependent and helpless, waiting on others to give you feedback, if and when they so choose.

Seeing yourself as "dependent" on others to give you feedback is placing this important information outside your influence and within your "circle of concern." Feedback now becomes something you can't get when you want it, unless, by lucky coincidence, others are prepared to provide feedback at that time. Seeing feedback this way puts you in a dependent position and keeps you stuck. That is, it keeps you from receiving and understanding important information that you need to make adjustments and develop as a workshop leader.

B) Description Versus Evaluation

Feedback to participants needs to be specific, immediate, and frequent (i.e., provided after every assignment or exercise).

How Much Negative and Positive Feedback Should You Provide to Participants?

Negative feedback hurts. However, feedback that "stings a little" is often the most valuable. It stings because it's true. Follow Blanchard's (1982) guideline of giving six or seven compliments for every piece of negative feedback you give participants.[2]

Remember the concept of the "relationship bank." If you never give anything other than negative feedback, participants will soon avoid you like the plague. Your account will be in the "red." Rather, you need to find value in participants. Don't be stingy with accolades, praise, appreciations, and signs of respect for participants. Ensure these are sincere but also ensure they are plentiful. You need to make deposits in the "relationship bank." Once your account has a large positive balance you can make the odd withdrawal in the form of negative feedback, "constructive criticism" (if there is such a thing), and requests that participants do things differently.

So, feel free to overload participants with positive comments and compliments but never with negative feedback. Participants, like anyone else, can only make so many adjustments to their attitude and behavior at a time. Giving them "the gift of a ton of negative feedback" is not only a waste of energy, it's also harmful to relationships, participant confidence, and workshop climate.

Why Is It Important to Be Descriptive with Your Feedback to Participants?

When giving negative feedback, be descriptive rather than judgmental or evaluative. One way to do this is by using "I" statements and avoiding "you" statements. This isn't foolproof but it helps to keep your comments objective. Thus, you might say something like, "I saw you turn away and walk over to the flipchart when John asked that question," as opposed to, "You ignored John's question." Staying descriptive makes feedback a little easier to swallow, and it has the added benefit of allowing participants to come to their own conclusions. Realizing for themselves what they could have done better has more impact than being told.

Being nonjudgmental is difficult. Try this exercise before reading further. It takes less than a minute.

In a half dozen words or phrases describe Bill Clinton

-
-
-
-
-
-

Once you've written a few words or phrases in the box, put an "E" where your words are judgmental or evaluative. Put a "D" where your words are descriptive. Did you confuse evaluation with description? It's a common mistake.

Evaluating people rather than describing their behavior is the biggest problem people make when giving feedback to others. No one much likes being evaluated or judged. It's subjective and often a matter of perspective. Description, on the other hand, is difficult to argue with. When you state exactly what you heard or saw a participant say or do, the feedback is more acceptable, understandable, and helpful.

C) An Actionable Framework for Feedback

How to Communicate Difficult Information so Others Will Listen	*How to Receive Difficult Information so You Keep Getting Feedback*
Steps 1) Check to see if the receiver is willing to hear the feedback. 2) Focus on, • Actual observations of behavior. • Your reactions to this behavior. • The consequences of this behavior. • Information that the recipient can do something about. 3) State what you want. 4) Thank the receiver for listening.	*Steps* 1) Listen, even if it hurts. • Use eye contact. • Show you're listening by putting the feedback into your own words. • Clarify by asking for examples, but don't defend. 2) Find at least one part of the feedback that's useful. Even if it feels incorrect, find a *kernel of truth*. 3) Thank the giver for the feedback, even if they gave it poorly. 4) Say what you'll do with the feedback, even if it's only to think about it for a while.

D) Things to Avoid When Giving and Receiving Feedback

Things to Avoid When Giving Feedback	*Things to Avoid When Receiving Feedback*
• Describe, don't evaluate. Avoid inferences, labels, and judgments. • Don't repeat yourself. Say it once, then listen. • Don't give advice unless it's asked for. • Avoid raising nonrelated issues from the past. • Don't let things build. Give feedback as soon as possible. • Don't ignore the importance of timing. There are bad times to raise certain issues. • Don't focus on "why." Questioning motives makes people defensive. Anyway, understanding motives is often impossible. • Don't generalize or exaggerate (e.g., you never, you always, this is the hundredth time I've asked you to ...).	• Don't talk, don't explain, just listen. (Put an imaginary pencil in your mouth so you can't talk.) • Know that it's OK to feel defensive; just don't act it. • Don't discount, downplay, deny, or ignore the feedback. • Don't do other activities while receiving feedback (e.g., writing, looking out the window). Even if you're hearing every word, your actions will be misinterpreted. • Avoid overloading yourself. When you've received all the feedback you can deal with, let the giver know. • Be careful about assuming motive, but if you are convinced the other person's intentions are not honorable, then walk away. Don't subject yourself to cheap shots. • Don't expect to be given feedback in a thoughtful, polite, or helpful way. Expecting this would limit your learning. Often helpful feedback comes from people who give it poorly.

E) Deciding to Give Negative Feedback to a Participant

The following filters for deciding to give negative feedback were inspired by Dave Irvine, a friend and colleague, and by Syd Simon (1978, 1991).[3] Ask yourself these questions to decide whether to give a participant difficult or negative feedback about their behavior.

1) Am I in any shape to give direct and honest negative feedback to this participant? Is the participant in any shape to hear it?

   Giving negative feedback is demanding. It requires that you accept participants as they are, not as you would like them to be. It may be wise to delay giving negative feedback, if, at the moment, you're feeling angry or in low self-esteem. Either of these emotional states could cause you to have unrealistically high expectations of the participant, to take the participant's criticisms personally and become defensive, or to ignore your own or the participant's needs and interests.

2) Can the participant, who will be receiving this negative feedback, do anything about it?

   If the participant has no ability to correct the situation, or to change their behavior, then your negative feedback may only damage their self-respect or the trust between you and the participant. For example, the participant's boss may be making demands that prevent the participant from following through on a workshop assignment.

3) Will giving this negative feedback increase my sense of respect for myself and for the participant in question? Am I willing to take my part of the responsibility for improving the situation?

   Negative feedback can be helpful, but not when it's used to control or manipulate others. The litmus test is, "Do I want this relationship to work?" Your commitment to helping this participant must be strong enough that, after providing negative feedback, you are willing to work with him/her to help overcome the problem.

4) Am I positive that none of my own hang-ups are in this negative feedback?

   Ensure your negative feedback is about this participant's behavior, in this situation, at this time. Don't dig up the past or anticipate disaster in the future.

5) Is it just possible that instead of negative feedback, this participant needs more encouragement, validation, or affirmation?

LAYOVERS AND WHISTLE STOPS - STOPPING AND STARTING A WORKSHOP SESSION

The railway has its own jargon (e.g., turn around, shifted load, a meet) and so too do workshop leaders. At this junction it's time to clarify a few simple workshop terms, specifically "stopping," "restarting," and "ending" a workshop.

"Stopping" as it's used here refers to ending a session of a workshop, not to ending the workshop itself. Leaders then need to "restart" a workshop or training program when the group reconvenes following a long break (e.g., overnight, a week later). "Ending" a workshop is probably the most obvious of these terms. When you end a workshop, it's over. The fat lady sings (at least figuratively)!

This section covers

A) Stopping a session

B) Starting a session (or restarting a workshop)

A) Stopping a Session

Review and summarize with the group before ending a session of the workshop (e.g., before ending for the day). Include the following steps:

- Acknowledge the existence of any "loose ends" or unfinished business. Tell the group when, and how, "loose ends" will be dealt with. (More is said about "loose ends" below in the section on ending a workshop.)

- Discuss the "whereas" and the "therefore." The "whereas" looks back. It's a brief summary of what has occurred thus far. The "therefore" looks forward. It involves planning how, when, and under what circumstances new learning will be used.

> ***The "whereas" and the "therefore"***
>
> *The "whereas"*
>
> > *OK, to this point we've covered "feedback" in the workshop. The principles we've discussed apply to giving and receiving feedback in just about any situation, for example, on the job, with friends, and even with mothers-in-law!*
>
> *The "therefore"*
>
> > *Practice these principles regularly and you'll find, over time, that others will be more open to hearing your feedback. As well, you should find that others are giving you more feedback.*
> >
> > *The section on feedback is in chapter twelve of the book. You might want to review this section periodically to ensure you're practicing the principles for giving and receiving feedback.*

- Provide a brief overview of what's coming in the next session and suggest "why" the group will find this valuable. Whet their appetites for more!

- Review assignments for the next session (if any).
- Recognize the group's efforts and successes thus far.
- Gather formal or informal feedback.

End of session feedback

You need to know what the group found useful, a waste of time, and what they feel should be done differently during the next session. Get this feedback from the group as a whole, either informally or formally. Either of these approaches provides direction on what needs to change and stay the same.

The informal way is to brainstorm with the group, for example, "T" chart questions like, "What could we have done differently?" and "What went well?" Or have the group brainstorm what needs to "stop," "start," and "continue" in the workshop.

The formal way is with written "level-1" evaluation forms.

Personally, for end of session feedback, I prefer receiving this in the group (e.g., T charting) over using evaluation forms. Group discussion usually results in more thorough feedback. In addition, you can discuss suggestions for changes "on the spot" with the group.

- Finally, based on participant feedback, contract with the group for adjustments in workshop outcomes, process, content, or style.

Contracting adjustments

Contracting adjustments takes only a couple of minutes and need not be complicated. Simply say something like:

> *Thanks for the feedback. I will take time tonight to look over these lists and think about where I can make adjustments. We can then discuss this briefly tomorrow morning.*

You now have the obligation to complete this planning and report back to the group as promised. Always follow through on any commitment made to a group. If you don't, your credibility will suffer. The next day report back to the group with the changes you are prepared to make. You'll also need to explain *why* other changes can't be made at this time.

End

B) Starting a Session

Your layover has ended; now it's time to get the workshop back in gear and rolling down the rails. Chapters nine, ten, and eleven overviewed starting up a workshop. Now let's talk about restarting a workshop, or starting up a workshop *session*.

You need to restart workshops following long breaks (e.g., overnight, several days, a week). Restarting in a planned way is a good habit to get into, even when you feel a workshop is going well. A structured restart only takes ten or fifteen minutes, yet the benefits are considerable.

The Benefits of a Structured Restart

- It gets participants mentally "in the room." It's hard to worry about problems piling up on your desk when you're talking in a group.
- It gets participants thinking critically about their learning. As participants discuss their learning, they also learn from each other. For example, a participant may have felt a given piece of learning material wasn't all that relevant, until he hears another participant talking about how she has used it successfully on the job.
- It gets participants thinking about what's been learned and accomplished thus far. Taking stock of successes, be they major breakthroughs or small incremental gains, is itself quite motivating.
- Outstanding issues are summarized and agreements are reached about "if and when" these issues will be dealt with in the workshop.
- It's another chance for participants to clarify and ask questions about material already covered. Often very insightful questions are asked in the restart, perhaps because participants had overnight (or a few days) to reflect on their learning.
- Connections are made between what's occurred thus far and the workshop session that's just beginning.

- You get feedback on what participants are finding valuable and on what may still need more emphasis in upcoming sessions.

The Restart Checklist

- Learning review
- Accomplishments thus far
- Outstanding issues
- Agree on adjustments
- Bridge into the new session

Learning Review

Restarting is a great time for summarizing information covered thus far in the workshop (e.g., models discussed, skills practiced) and to check with participants about what they have learned. You might ask participants to write down and tell the rest of the group "two things they have learned." Use a superlative adjective (e.g., best, most, worst) to challenge participants a little. For example, have participants write the two "most" significant learnings they have had thus far and ask them to explain "why" these learnings are important for them (e.g., challenge participants to describe a couple of ways they might use new learnings on the job).

Another option is to ask something like, "What's one thing we talked about in the previous sessions that still doesn't make sense or that you found the 'least' valuable of all the material covered thus far in the workshop?" This sometimes results in a very rewarding conversation because what one participant felt was a waste of time turns out to have been helpful to another. Not surprisingly, by discussing learnings with each other, participants often realize that they've learned more than they thought they had. By way of process, you might get participants working in small groups (e.g., dyads, trios) and coming up with responses to questions about their learning thus far.

Accomplishments to This Point

This step has a little magic in it. Often participants simply forget what they've achieved to a given point in a workshop, likely because they're feeling overwhelmed with what's still ahead of them. Use a common text (e.g., flipchart) to brainstorm what's been accomplished thus far. Examples might include comments like, "We've had a more honest discussion this morning than we've had in a long time." "We now understand where Harry is coming from when he talks about leadership." "We've completed an accurate assessment of project XYZ to date."

You don't have to get unanimity on accomplishments, only consensus. Further, accomplishments don't have to be setting the sun in the eastern sky, just so long as they feel like forward movement to participants. Don't worry about the sequence or magnitude of achievements; just list them, big and small. Then post the flipchart page on a side wall for later reference.

Outstanding Issues

Before bridging to the new session, ask participants what questions they have about work that's been completed or material that's been covered thus far. What concerns do they have? What's not clear as yet? What needs more work? Perhaps new concerns have arisen since the group last met. The idea here is to tie up loose ends and build on what's been learned and accomplished. Next, review items written on the "parking lot" flipchart and decide when these will be dealt with in the workshop.

Agree on Adjustments

Based on the group's last "end of session" evaluation (whether this was a verbal discussion in the group or a formal "written" evaluation) and the results of this structured "restart" (e.g., the learning review, discussion of outstanding issues), some adjustments to the workshop may be required. Whether these are to outcomes, process, or content, you need to inform the group about what adjustments you will be making. In addition, if you're not able to make a specific adjustment, discuss this with the group as well.

Bridge into the New Session

Finally, review the outcomes you're working toward and the agenda for the immediate workshop session. "Bridge in" from the last session, adding context so participants understand how the upcoming new session fits within the entire workshop. ("What" and "why" bridges were discussed earlier in this chapter.) Be sure to talk about the benefits of the upcoming session and make connections to what you know to be the "conscious interests and needs" of participants. (Chapter three makes a distinction between learning needs that participants are fully aware and conscious of and participants' "blind spots." These are areas where participants need to learn, even though they currently have no appreciation of this learning need, and thus little or no interest in working on these "needs.")

THE END OF THE LINE – WRAPPING UP AND ENDING A WORKSHOP

End a workshop by tying up "loose ends" and discussing the "so what" and the "now what." "Loose ends" are issues raised in a workshop that have not yet been dealt with. The "so what" looks at what has taken place, its purpose, and its value. The "now what" concerns what happens next, how learning will be applied, how participants will be supported as they experiment and apply new learnings on the job, and how participants will continue to learn and reinforce their learning.

Wrapping up a workshop effectively takes anywhere from thirty minutes to two hours. The common mistake is to discount the importance of the "wrap-up" and skip over or omit some or all of the following steps. Be sure to build time into the workshop design and agenda for an effective "wrap-up."

Steps to Wrapping Up

a) The "what"

b) The "so what"

c) The "now what"

d) The "what next"

e) Handling loose ends

f) Workshop evaluation

g) Celebration

h) Saying your good-byes

i) Reflecting on the workshop and on what you have learned

a) The "What"

Quickly review and summarize "what" has been completed and achieved in the workshop. Relate this back to the workshop's outcome statements. It helps if you keep flipchart notes posted in some semblance of order on the training room walls. These can be used to review key learnings and accomplishments with the group.

Most of us are visual learners.[4] We learn best by seeing notes, pictures, charts, diagrams, and the like. So have summary points on a handout, flipchart, or overhead transparency. Try a "cartoon summary" of the workshop on overhead transparencies. Use cartoons like The Far Side, Herman, and Dilbert to poke a little fun at the workshop while reinforcing key learning points. (I tell people that Scott Adams' book, "Build a Better Life by Stealing Office Supplies: Dogbert's Big Book of Business," is probably the best management book I've ever read![5] Anyway, using a couple of cartoons without written permission from the publisher shouldn't get you in any trouble. It's common practice. Witness the outside of any university professor's office door!)

b) The "So What"

Don't assume everyone has heard, let alone learned, the same things. Have participants "take stock" of what they have accomplished and learned. Give them "quiet time" to review and make notes to themselves on what they've learned. Have them share what they've written with each other. Hearing what others have learned and found useful stimulates participants to rethink their own learnings.

c) The "Now What"

Next comes action planning. Participants need to plan to apply their learning and to follow through on agreements made in the workshop or training program. Have participants deal with questions like, What happens next? How do we continue our learning? How will our learning be supported and reinforced?

Get participants to make promises about how they're going to apply their new learnings on the job. This may provide incentive to "follow through," or, if nothing else, produce guilt at not having kept their promises. Leon Festinger (1957) coined a term for this. He called it "cognitive dissonance."[6] (Practice saying this enough and you can take the life out of any party!) Cognitive dissonance has to do with the state of consistency between an individual's attitudes and their behavior. Used as suggested here, it has to do with generating a little pressure for practicing new ways of thinking and new behaviors on the job. Thus, by writing application goals and making promises to themselves, to each other, and to you (the workshop leader), participants are made conscious of their commitments and should therefore feel a little "internal" pressure to follow through.

Personally I've never been convinced that "cognitive dissonance" is all that powerful, but like chicken soup, it can't hurt. Anyway, not planning application would be conspicuous by its absence. After all, why are training programs conducted in organizations in the first place? (Hopefully your answer has something to do with behavior change "on the job.")

d) The "What Next"

The follow up needs to be planned. Times need to be scheduled for revisiting learning and for monitoring action planning. Questions like the following need to be answered. How will success be measured? When will action planning be reviewed? How will we celebrate and reward our success and progress?

The "wrap-up" is a good time to either schedule a follow up meeting with the group or at least get "agreement in principle" that the group will meet three or six months down the road to discuss progress and support ongoing application of new learning.

e) Loose Ends

Now is your last chance to deal with promises made or implied and with issues that have been "parked." Hopefully by this time in the workshop, you've been able to deal with most of the issues listed on the "parking lot."

f) Workshop Evaluation

Lots has already been said about the importance of evaluation and feedback. You have a choice about what level you evaluate (e.g., reaction, learning, behavior, results) and about how you go about evaluating, but, for all practical purposes, you have little choice about whether or not to evaluate. Some sort of workshop evaluation needs to take place, and indeed, is often requested by your sponsor client. Often this is simply "level-1 - reaction" evaluation.

The box on page 396 titled "End of Session Feedback" talks about formal or written evaluation and informal evaluation or group discussion. It's suggested you do both during the workshop wrap. In particular, take ten minutes with the group to discuss and evaluate how well the workshop met its stated outcomes or targets. Finally, pass out an evaluation form and ask participants to complete and pass this in to you before they leave the workshop.

g) Celebrate

Thank the group for their hard work, interest, willingness to challenge and experiment, and so on. You may want to acknowledge particular efforts, show appreciation, and help the group celebrate their achievement. This celebration may be as simple as saying a few words at the end of the workshop, a special dinner, or just a beer or coffee with the group.

An important consideration. Participants are often in a hurry to go other places once a workshop ends. As a result, consider holding formal celebrations near, but before the end of a workshop, for example, the evening before the last day of the workshop or at noon hour on the last day of the workshop.

h) Saying Your Good-Byes

Say your "good-byes" and clean up the training room ("administrative clients" appreciate this). Then go home and take a well-deserved rest, especially after a difficult workshop. Reward yourself. Recharge your batteries by "vegging out" in front of what Hughes (1993) calls the "electronic wallpaper" (i.e., your TV).[7] Just relax, lower your IQ about 40 points, and watch a TV sitcom. (Note: You'll need to lower your IQ by 50 points for TV sports and by a full 100 points for the "daytime dysfunctionals.")

i) Reflecting on the Workshop and on What You Have Learned

This step concerns wrapping up your own learnings rather than the workshop itself. After you've rested a little, seek support and challenge from those you trust and respect. Be part of a professional "cuddle group." Talk with close colleagues and clients (a few of my colleagues and clients are also trusted friends). Get feedback about the workshop, discuss your successes and problems, and get their input on what you might consider doing differently during the next workshop. Find ways to learn, grow, and improve with every workshop you operate.

> ***For fast acting relief, try slowing down.***
> ***- Lily Tomlin***

CONCLUSION

Summary

This chapter looked at moving a workshop within and between topics and sessions, at making changes along the way as needed, and at wrapping up and ending a workshop.

Moving from Topic to Topic

Moving within a topic is distinct from moving between topics. A strategy for *reviewing and summarizing* is prescribed for the former; a strategy of *bridging* is provided for the latter. Review and summarize frequently as a session progresses, particularly where learning material is complex and where participants have limited experience with a given topic. Bridges make connections between topics. They're a special type of review and summary that enables participants to journey from topic to topic with a minimum of disruption and a maximum of clarity and purpose. The "what" bridge concerns content; the "why" bridge concerns purpose.

Stopping and Restarting a Workshop

Stopping a workshop session entails reviewing and summarizing, tying up loose ends, discussing the "whereas" and the "therefore," reviewing assignments, getting feedback, and contracting with the group for adjustments to the workshop. Restarting a workshop session involves reviewing learning with participants, dealing with outstanding issues, agreeing on adjustments, and bridging into the next session.

Ending a Workshop

Wrapping up and ending a workshop in a structured way aid clarity, commitment, and follow through. Wrap up in a way that connects learning and accomplishments with action planning. Build in monitoring and follow-up to support this planning, to reinforce learning, and to reward success. The wrap-up includes the "what," the "so what," the "now what," the "what next," handling loose ends, workshop evaluation, celebration, and saying your good-byes.

Checklist

Reviewing and Summarizing	*Feedback*
The value of reviewing and summarizing • Eliminates bumps • Helps participants stay focused • Minimizes chances of participants feeling lost • Gets participants back on track *When to review and summarize* • Where learning material is complex • Where participants have limited experience with the topic • When participants are having trouble digesting the learning material • Check at least every hour to see if needed *How to review and summarize* • Involve participants • Ask questions • Have participants ask each other questions • Ask participants to answer in their own words • Use visual aids *Bridging between Topics* • The "what" bridge • The "why" bridge	*How to receive difficult information so you keep getting feedback* • Listen, even if it hurts • Find the kernel of truth • Thank the giver • Say what you'll do *How to communicate difficult information so others will listen* • Check to see if the receiver is willing to listen • Focus on observations, reactions, consequences, and actionable information • State what you want • Thank the receiver for listening *Things to avoid when giving feedback* • Don't evaluate • Don't repeat yourself • Don't give advice • Avoid nonrelated issues • Don't let things build • Don't ignore the importance of timing • Don't ask "why"

Informal Strategies for Getting Feedback During a Workshop

- Temperature checks
- Talk "one on one" at the breaks
- Get "end of the day" verbal feedback
- Monitor the learning climate
- Use "quick hit" level-1 evaluation forms
- Co-lead the workshop

Review and Summarize with the Group before Ending a Session

- Acknowledge or deal with "loose ends"
- Discuss the "whereas" and the "therefore"
- Overview what's coming next
- Review assignments
- Recognize the group's success
- Get feedback
- Contract with the group for adjustments

The Benefits of a Structured Restart

- Gets participants mentally "in the room"
- Gets participants thinking critically about their learning
- Gets participants taking stock of successes
- Outstanding issues are summarized and agreements are reached
- Another chance for participants to clarify and ask questions
- Connections are made to the previous and to the upcoming session
- You get feedback on what participants are finding valuable

Things to avoid when receiving feedback

- Don't explain
- Don't act defensively
- Don't discount your feedback
- Don't do other activities while receiving feedback
- Avoid overloading yourself
- Don't subject yourself to cheap shots
- Don't expect to be given feedback effectively

The Restart Checklist

- Learning review
- Accomplishments thus far
- Outstanding issues
- Agree on adjustments
- Bridge into the new session

Steps to Wrapping Up a Workshop

- The "what"
- The "so what"
- The "now what"
- The "what next"
- Handling loose ends
- Workshop evaluation
- Celebration
- Saying your good-byes
- Reflect on the workshop and on what you have learned

End

Exercise

When to Review and Summarize

List a couple of key points for each of the following questions:

1) What signs are you good at noticing that indicate that participants may be lost (e.g., confused looks, questions that "miss the mark," requests for information that you have already covered, using a technical term incorrectly)?

2) What signs do you need to get better at picking up that indicate participants are not following the discussion or keeping up with the topic?

3) If you're unable to "read" a group, what things do you typically do to check that they're following the discussion or if it's time to review and summarize (e.g., ask them to explain the learning material in their own words, poll the group with direct and open questions)?

4) What evidence do you typically look for in the group to indicate whether or not your reviewing and summarizing are effective (e.g., participants are involved, participants ask insightful questions)?

Notes

[1]Covey, S.R. (1989). The 7 habits of highly effective people: Powerful lessons in personal change. New York, NY: Simon & Schuster.

[2] Blanchard, K., & Johnson, S. (1982). The one minute manager. New York, NY: William Morrow.

[3]I'd like to thank both Dave Irvine of Calgary, Canada, and Syd Simon for the ideas behind these questions. I heard Syd speak at a workshop in Calgary, Canada, on November 21, 1991. 1) Simon, S.B. (November 21, 1991). Taken from verbal comments by Syd and Suzanne Simon at a workshop they led on the topic of self-esteem. Calgary, Alta. Unpublished. 2) Simon, S.B. (1978). Values clarification: A handbook of practical strategies for teachers and students. New York, NY: Dodd, Mead & Co.

[4] Laborde, G. Z. (1984). Influencing with integrity: Management skills for communication and negotiation. Palo Alto, CA: Syntony.

[5]Adams, S. (1991). Build a better life by stealing office supplies: Dogbert's big book of business. Kansas City, KS: Andrews & McMeel.

[6]Festinger, L. (1957). A theory of cognitive dissonance. Palo Alto, CA: Stanford University Press.

[7]Hughes, R. (1993). Culture of complaint: The fraying of America. New York, NY: Oxford University Press, p. 169.

Chapter 13

Working with Questions

INTRODUCTION

One point that just can't be stressed enough is that motivating participants and keeping them active are essential for workshop success. And the richer the participants' understanding of the context for learning, and the deeper their knowledge of how to apply the learning content, the more successful the workshop or training program.

I keep six honest serving men
They taught me all I knew:
Their names are What and
Why and When
And How and Where and Who.
- Rudyard Kipling

Questions are a valuable tool for taking participants deeper into learning. They focus discussion, stimulate reflection, and encourage sharing. They control and direct conversations much as a water faucet controls the flow of water. That is, questions determine both the type and the amount of information you're likely to receive.

There's more to questions than meets the eye, and once you get good at using them your workshop and training-program leadership will improve markedly. This chapter provides stories, examples, and analogies to help you understand and use questions effectively, but the bottom line is *questioning skills take practice*. Thus, the need to continually experiment with different types of questions and with different methods of directing questions.

Effective questioning doesn't allow participants to sit back and either "tune out" or just listen passively. Rather, it draws their thinking out, requiring them to analyze and evaluate what they're learning. A single question can spark discussion and debate, and get participants asking their own questions and contributing their own perspectives. But questions are a double edged sword. Used improperly, they put participants on the spot and feel more like an interrogation than a positive learning experience.

This chapter covers:

- The function, structure, and orientations of questions.
- Directing, asking, and answering questions.
- Challenging with questions.
- Encouraging and fielding questions and answers.

FUNCTION, STRUCTURE, AND ORIENTATION OF QUESTIONS

The Functions of Questions

Gerard Nierenberg (1973) classifies questions into five categories and argues that while questions appear grammatically structured to *get* information, they have other functions as well.[1] It's useful to understand these functions and to understand that questions are not always what they appear to be. Use questions to:

1) Cause attention (e.g., "How are you?")
2) Give information (e.g., "Did you know he's sixty years old?")
3) Start participants thinking (e.g., "What do you suggest?")
4) Bring to a conclusion (e.g., "Isn't it time to take some action?")
5) Get information (e.g., "How much is it?")

Use these functions alone, or in any combination, in your workshops and training programs.

- To cause attention, start thinking, and get information (e.g., "George, what would you do in this type of situation?")
- To get information and give information (e.g., "How do you spell swimming? With two m's?")
- To cause attention and start thinking (e.g., "By the way, how would you react to that suggestion?")
- To bring to a conclusion and get information (e.g., "What would you do with this assignment?")
- To cause attention and bring to a conclusion (e.g., "I hope you don't mind my asking, but will you be a part of Al's group?")

- To cause attention and give information (e.g., "Have I mentioned before that you need to do it this way?")

The Structure of Questions

Use the following three structures to involve the group, to direct or focus the group, to clarify a participant's response, and to dig deeper for more information.

- Open and closed questions
- Probes and mirrors
- Superlative adjectives and presuppositions

Open and Closed Questions

Open questions expand conversation because participants can answer in a variety of ways. They often start with words like "what," "why," or "how."

- Example of an open question: "What do you think about project A?"

Closed questions serve to focus or narrow conversation. They require a binary answer such as "yes" or "no." Closed questions often start with words like "who," "where," "did," or "do."

- Example of a closed question: "Do you want more information about project A?"

Workshop leaders sometimes ask closed questions without thinking. (Avoid asking individual participants to speak for the entire group.)

- Can everybody hear me?
- Is everybody here?
- Is everybody ready to practice?

Probes and Mirrors

These questions "challenge gently" for more information and keep the conversation going. (For questions that challenge even more, see the section below titled "Challenging with Questions.")

A *probe* asks for more information.

- Example: "What else happened?"

A *mirror* is a casual probe. It reflects back what was said using tones and expressions that imply the need for more information.

- Example: A participant says, "So I said, no way!" You mirror this comment with, "You said, no way?" You then remain silent, implying the need for more information.

Superlative Adjectives and Presuppositions

Questions using *superlative adjectives* use words like "best," "worst," and "last."

- Example: "What's the worst thing that could happen?"

Questions using a presupposition assume participants need more information.

- Example of an open question with a presupposition: "What's not clear?"

- Examples of closed questions with presuppositions: "Who's ready to practice?" or "Who's not ready to practice?"

Orientation of Workshop Questions

The following four orientations were inspired by Robert Jolles (1993).[2] Use them when leading a workshop or training program to help participants assess and integrate their own learning. These questions seek answers that indicate whether participants understand the principles behind their learning. They also get participants thinking about application on the job. The four orientations are:

1) Fact-based questions

2) Opinion-based questions

3) Comparison-based questions

4) Conclusion-based questions

Because *fact-based questions* have a right and wrong answer, they can potentially put participants "on the spot." These questions are often useful in technical, operations, and administrative workshops and training programs.

Examples:
"What's the approved procedure for installing a new operating system on a PC, and why is this procedure important?"
"Who needs to approve purchase orders for Project XYZ?"

Opinion-based questions require subjective answers. There's no right or wrong answer and there's usually a considerable degree of latitude. As such, these questions are less intimidating than fact-based questions. Opinion-based questions allow workshop leaders to get a good "read" on what participants are thinking. They also make good "ice breakers" during workshop start-ups.

Examples:

"What might employees do that indicates they're resisting change?"

"What three things do you want to get from this workshop?"

Comparison-based questions ask participants to discuss similarities and differences between models, methods, processes, and so on.

Example:

"How would you compare the Harvard Negotiation Technique with Gerard Nierenberg's philosophy of negotiating?"

Conclusion-based questions ask participants to respond using learnings from the workshop (e.g., theory, models, steps). They seek participants' views on how they would apply new learnings in a given situation. Conclusion-based questions can be quite challenging and require a supportive workshop environment.

Example:

"How would you use the key principles of the Harvard Negotiation Technique to help you handle a complaint from a team member?"

Directing, Asking, and Answering Questions

Options for Directing Questions in a Workshop or Training Program

Directed Questions

Directed questions target a specific member of the group. They are a simple, if not a subtle, way to hold participants accountable for participating and contributing. They can be used to draw quieter and underparticipating members of the group into the discussion. They can also be used to bypass overparticipating members of the group. The disadvantage is that they put participants on the spot. So, use them with care. For instance, don't use directed questions unless you know a participant is following the discussion, and then use them only to draw out opinions, not to check facts. Embarrassing a participant by catching them off guard, or trying to publicly test their knowledge of the "facts," is manipulative and intimidating. Don't do it.

Example of a directed question:

"What do you think (pause)... Jeff?" or "Jeff, what do you think?"

Group Questions

Group questions are answerable by anyone in the workshop. They don't put anyone on the spot and therefore evoke less anxiety than do directed questions. But this is also their "Achilles' heel." Group questions don't put the onus on any one participant to respond, and therefore, especially with an underparticipating group, you many not get a response. Another disadvantage is that group questions open the door for overparticipating and overaggressive participants to pursue their agendas and monopolize the discussion.

> *Example of a group question*:
> "How would you respond in this situation (pause) ... anyone?"

Relayed Questions

Relayed questions are directed by you (the workshop leader) from one participant to another. By relaying the question you avoid "spoon-feeding" participants. Giving participants an opportunity to answer requires they think about their learning and put it into their own words. This not only reinforces learning, it also provides the group with a different spin or perspective on the learning material.

> *Example of a relayed question:*
> A participant asks you, "Does that fit with the model we've been learning?" You just pass the question along saying something like, "Well, what do others think? Bryan, how about you?"

Reverse Questions

A reverse question is directed by you back to the participant who asked it. Reversing questions spares you from "spoon-feeding" participants, encouraging them to use their learning to answer their own questions. Reversing can also be used to thwart sabotage. Simply turn the participant's question around on him/her. Now, he/she is on the spot.

> *Example of a reverse question*:
> You're asked, "Would the Harvard Negotiation Model work in this situation?" To turn the question back to the participant who asked it, you simply say something such as, "Well, I'd like to hear from you. How might this model fit, and what might its limitations be in this situation?"

> *Example of thwarting overt sabotage*:
> A participant asks, "Does this workshop seem like a waste of time?" You can either reverse or relay the question. To reverse it ask something like, "Well, what makes it seem that way for you?" or "What would make it valuable for you?" To relay the question ask, "What do others think?"

How to Ask Questions

Although it may seem so obvious that it hardly needs mentioning, here's how a workshop leader needs to ask questions. Practice these four steps.

- Ask your question.
- Pause to give participants time to think.
- Listen to the answer.
- Respond or ask other participants to comment on the answer.

It's usually the second step, "pausing," where we panic. Those few seconds seem like such a long time to pause. Try slowly counting to five or six in your mind, even though it's tough as everyone sits there looking at each other and not speaking. Often workshop leaders can't take this silence and they jump in with another question or with their own answer. But keep your cool and wait it out. Jumping in and rescuing participants is the short-term solution that leads to poor long-term results. It's good for the group to feel a little pressure to answer questions. If you don't let participants sweat a little every now and then, your later queries may also meet with blank stares.

Don't assume participants are reluctant to answer. Depending on how complex the question is, it may simply be that they need time to formulate a response. That is, maybe they're just being thoughtful. However, don't wait any longer than five or six seconds. It's rude, especially when the question is directed at a particular participant.

Although you may need to wait longer in special circumstances (such as groups that have little or no knowledge of the topic, or are unfamiliar or uncomfortable with each other), after about six seconds of silence try rephrasing your question. If after asking twice, you still can't get a response, try using the "two good faith replies" method described in chapter sixteen. Thus, after getting no response to two or three questions, deal with the lack of response as an issue in itself. Say something like, "I don't seem to be getting much response to these questions. Have I lost you somehow?" This time wait a little longer (e.g., ten seconds). If you still can't get a response, ask even more directly. For example, "I need your help here. Let's talk about why we're not getting any discussion on this topic." "Is there something I need to do differently?" If you still don't get a response, direct the question to a particular participant. For example, "Steve, what do you think?"

Long silences after a question and hoping not to be called on by name

Participants are just as uncomfortable with long silences as workshop leaders. Many sit there, anxious about being called on by name or feeling guilty because they aren't responding to your question. You'd think that making eye contact with you during these long silences could be fatal. Participants look at the floor or at their notes. But they don't look up.

Watching participants sitting there during these long silences, hoping not to be signaled out by you, often reminds me of my dad flying a bomber during World War II. He flew for Canada in the RCAF and used to tell me how it felt when he was flying through flak sent up by anti-aircraft artillery. He used to make himself as small as possible in his uniform, hoping all that steel flying around wouldn't hit him. I sometimes get the impression that for participants, long pauses after a question are like flying through flak. Making eye contact with the workshop leader is risking a direct hit.

Additional Tips for Asking Questions

Ask questions that require reasoning rather than memory. That is, aim for questions that are challenging and require understanding, but are nonetheless answerable.

Although you usually want to word questions as concisely as possible, sometimes a little ambiguity challenges the group and yields more creative responses.

Workshop leaders often ask a low-yield question like, "Are there any questions?" Then they pause a nanosecond and move on to the next topic. A highly motivated or expert group might respond, but others likely won't. Instead, ask more specifically. Say something like, "OK, let's take five minutes before moving to the next section. I need to hear at least a couple of things from the group. What's still a little unclear? What would help you understand this material a little better?" Then pause for a few seconds. If no response, consider directing the question at a particular participant. If this fails, consider answering questions yourself.

Word questions in simple language and vary accent, innuendo, emphasis, and tone.

When presenting to large groups or when time is pressing, you may want to phrase questions so the answers you want are easy for the group to provide. For example, ask, "Do you want a brief overview of project A next?" rather than, "Do you want a brief overview of Project A or of Project B next?"

It's OK to ask the same question twice. Sometimes you'll get a different answer the second time, because the participant's attitude changed by having been asked the first time.

Wherever possible be "nonforcing" with your questions and lay a foundation as to *why* you're asking a certain question. Participants need to understand the context of your question. They need to understand why they're being asked, why now, and how this discussion fits with the focus of the workshop.

Don't use forced disclosure or risk embarrassing participants. Have a ground rule allowing anyone to say, "I pass."

Ask questions yourself if no one else does.

Don't overdo closed questions. Inexperienced workshop leaders frequently ask too many closed questions and too few open ones. Likely this is because closed questions maintain control, whereas open questions can take a group in unpredictable directions. Whatever the reason, closed questions usually result in the workshop leader talking more, directing more, and taking on more responsibility for the workshop.

Phrase questions casually when dealing with sensitive issues. Sometimes just one word loaded with emotional significance can be disastrous.

CHALLENGING WITH QUESTIONS

Use *forcing questions* with care and empathy and only when you're in rapport with the group. They're powerful tools for seeking additional information and clarification, but they can also backfire. Their principle value is "challenge." Through "challenge" they help participants rethink issues and strongly held opinions. They do this by helping participants surface their assumptions and biases. After all, many of the most important things that ever happened to us, our breakthroughs in life, happened because we had to change our minds.

Use forcing questions when you want to push a participant or group into being specific, into examining their own assumptions, or into seeing possibilities that their *mental blinders* are preventing them from seeing. These questions are like verbal karate. Lawyers use them to rattle witnesses, but you need to use them in a way that shows respect and builds trust with participants.

Remember *Columbo*, the TV series? Lieutenant Columbo was a master at using forcing questions in a firm, respectful, friendly, and emotionally neutral sort of way. Columbo seemed casual, but his questions were very deliberate. He'd ask the toughest questions while "just trying to be helpful" or "just trying to understand." His candid and seemingly naive approach led people to be helpful, even to their own demise! The "demise" you're after as a workshop or training-program leader is the demise of old ways of thinking. That is, you need to use these questions to help participants see an issue differently and become open to new ways of thinking and performing.

Forcing Questions and Examples of Each in Use

The following categories of questions were inspired by Genie Laborde (1984).[3]

All? Always? Never?

This is a way of forcing participants to stop overgeneralizing.

- Example: "Always? Is there ever a time when that isn't the case?"

What Specifically?

Forces participants to be more specific about the "what."

- Example: "What specifically are you referring to?" or "What specifically would you do in this situation?"

How Specifically?

Forces participants to be more specific about the "how."

- Example: "How specifically would you go about doing that?"

What Would Happen "If"?

Forces participants out of their assumptions and challenges them to look at other options for thinking and performing.

- Example: "What would happen if we did this anyway?"

Better?

Forces a specific comparison.

- Example: A participant says, "It would be better if we did it this way." Your reply is, "Better than what?"

Here's how Lieutenant Columbo might ask a "how specifically" question.

"Excuse me Mr. Ford. I hate to bother you again, Sir, but I've got one more question. Oh, is that your horse? Now, that's a beautiful animal, if you don't mind me saying so, Sir. Now my wife's cousin, there's a guy who knows horses. Yes sir, would he ever love to have a horse like that. ... Oh, yeah, one more question Mr. Ford. It's been bothering me. I mean, how could Tony have gotten from the studio all the way across town to Long Beach in under fifteen minutes. It doesn't seem possible. How do you figure he could have done that?"

Using the "What would happen if?" question

I was facilitating the first day of a scheduled two day workshop for a Board of Directors of a large nonprofit organization. They were in the theme park business, and like many Boards of "not for profit organizations" talked as if their role was *governance*, but really spend most of their time dabbling in *operations*. As a result, decision making was slow, senior managers were tied up in endless meetings with Board members, and more attention was needed on the Board's real role of governance and trusteeship.[4]

One of many practices that kept the Board not just dabbling, but wading waste deep in operations and management work, was their volunteer committee structure. They had a committee of volunteers that was chaired by a Board member for just about every aspect of their operation (e.g., finance, HR, marketing, public relations, special functions). They had over ten of these "operating oriented" Board committees, and what made change even more difficult, this structure was well established. It had been in place for almost forty years! Needless to say most of these committees took on a life of their own. Through practice all became *standing* or ongoing committees, even though their purpose was initially only temporary.

I challenged the Board that their *espoused theory* was not consistent with their *theory in use*.[5] That is, they were saying, "We want to focus on governance and Board work and allow management to do their job of running the operation," but they were spending most of their time dealing with operating details and making decisions that were best left to the organization's CEO and senior management group. And one of the biggest reasons for this gap between what they said and what they actually did was the committee structure.

Needless to say, they loved their committees. When I suggested that most of these committees were doing management work, as opposed to Board work, the Board members defended their need for the committees. They argued that without the committees they would have no way of staying involved and informed, in depth, about what was going on in the organization and that their guidance was needed to ensure the proper "care and feeding" of the many volunteers that worked on these committees. I knew any suggestion to move these committees under management would be defeated outright and only build resistance in the group for further discussion of this issue. Yet they had hired me to help them move to becoming more of a governing Board, so I had a mandate to push them a little.

Here's how I used the "What would happen if?" question. I recognized the value these committees were providing to Board members and got their permission to build an alternative scenario. I said, "This isn't committing anyone, and no one has agreed to change the committee structure, but let's at least take a closer look at what a new structure might look like." It's a little like a car salesman suggesting you "take her for a test drive with no obligations." We then constructed a complete picture of what the new committee structure might look like if most of the committees became management committees as opposed to Board committees. And as part of this scenario we listed the losses and risks that would be involved for the Board. These needed to be identified and acknowledged before Board members were prepared to "let go" emotionally of the old committee structure.

Continued

The scenario for change

I'll spare you the details and just show a picture of the change that was discussed.

Old Committee Structure

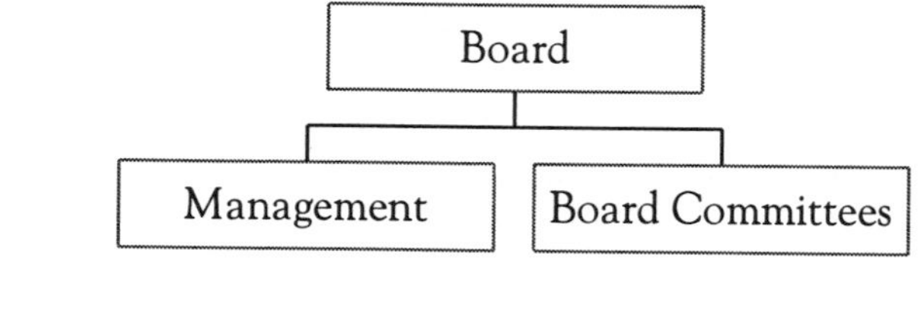

New Committee Structure

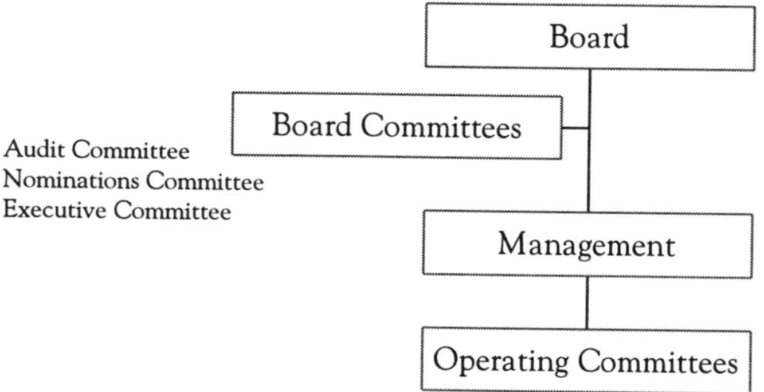

Approximately ten committees each at management's discretion, and each advising management on a specif aspect of the operation.

How it ended

As they talked about the scenario and as their fears were addressed (i.e., ways around their fears were identified), they became more comfortable with the idea that management would be responsible for the committees of volunteers. Within a couple of hours they were able to agree (it turned out they agreed unanimously) to adopt the new structure outlined above. They referred to this agreement as a major breakthrough. We completed our work in one day and decided the next day (which had been scheduled for this workshop) wasn't needed.

The bottom line

Without the "What would happen if?" question, the second day would have been needed, and even with this we might not have arrived at this restructuring agreement. It was the "What would happen if?" question that got us going on the new committee scenario and ultimately lead to the breakthrough agreement.

Finally, because the second day wasn't needed I lost a day's pay. Big harry deal! (During our contracting meeting it seemed like two days would be needed, but as they proved to be unnecessary I couldn't justify charging for the second day.) The way I look at it, I'm in business for the long term, not for a few quick payoffs. What happened at this workshop will almost assuredly get me more work with this client, as well as a few referrals. Indeed, most of my business is repeat business. I have clients that I've worked with regularly, several times a year, for many years.

A digression on sticking to agreed timelines when leading workshops

In the example described above, it was my suggestion, made during the contracting meeting with the Board president and CEO, that two days were needed for this workshop. And it was my suggestion, made near the end of the first day, that the second day was not needed. I learned two things about workshop schedules through years of practice. First, people are rarely upset if the workshop doesn't take as long as estimated. However, going over the scheduled time is not always as well received. Second, people rarely complain about the duration of a workshop as long as it was planned for and something meaningful is getting accomplished, that is, as long as we're making meaning progress in reasonable time. Where people do and should complain, however, is when the workshop outcomes have been achieved yet the workshop continues simply because the time was scheduled. This is when workshops seem to drag. With these two learnings always in mind, I "call" a workshop quickly if it seems there are no further meaningful and agreed outcomes to be achieved. It's always better to end early with people feeling successful than to end as scheduled with people saying, "The first day was great, but the second day didn't seem all that useful." Comments like these don't get you a lot of repeat business.

End

ENCOURAGING AND FIELDING QUESTIONS AND ANSWERS

The following will help you deal with wrong, but sincere, and tricky answers, as well as complex, even obtuse, questions.

Encouraging Questions, Challenge, and Listening

Have a positive attitude toward questions. Welcome them enthusiastically and thank participants for asking. Have a "no questions will be rejected, ignored, downplayed, discounted, or discouraged policy." (If I have strong rapport with the group and I know they'll understand I'm joking, I sometimes say, "There are no dumb questions, ... only dumb people.")

Use participants' words and phrases verbatim, whenever possible, as you respond to their questions. This shows them you value their questions and even legitimizes their way of asking.

- Example: A participant asks, "It seems odd to me, going through all these steps. Particularly step four, confronting. Is confronting really necessary?" You might respond as follows, using the participant's words (these are in italics). "I can see how it *seems odd*, given your situation. But I'd argue *confronting* is *necessary*. Here's why ..."

Recognize that often a question from a participant "rings a bell" with a half dozen other participants. Thus, as soon as the question is asked, other participants are saying to themselves, "Right on, I need to know this."

Comment on, but don't repeat, participant answers for the rest of the group. Encourage participants to listen to each other, rather than relying on you to repeat or rephrase their answers.

Fielding Questions

Misunderstanding the Question

Have you ever heard a participant say, "Great answer, but that wasn't my question?" It's human to hear a question, twist it a little, and jump directly to a point you have been wanting to make. Avoid this. Instead demonstrate effective listening. Unless you're sure you understand the question, repeat it back to the participant and ask her to confirm her intention and the question she's asking. In this way, others in the group also get clear on the question and may even add their perspectives to it. Now you and the other participants are sure what's being asked.

Handling "Off the Wall" Questions

Either relay the questions to the group or say, "Let me get back to you on that." At this point you might "park" the question on the flipchart labeled "parking lot."

Maintaining Your Integrity

Don't feel compelled to answer every question or worry about questions that have no clear-cut answers. And never "make up" an answer. Just say, "I don't know, but I'll check on it."

When asked a question, don't deny what you know. On occasion you might tell the group you have an answer but would like to hear from them first. On other occasions you might simply have to respond that you've heard about the issue but have been asked not to discuss it in the workshop.

The most difficult situations are those where your sponsor client has sworn you to total secrecy. You've been told, in no uncertain terms, to deny any knowledge of an issue. You must not only deny having discussed the situation, you must also deny having heard about it through the grapevine. You're even directed to "deny that you're denying." You want to be authentic, but sometimes this means you'll be shot (i.e., fired). What do you do now? The reality in organizations is that sometimes you can't be authentic unless you're prepared to leave. But at least you don't have to lie to yourself. At least you can be conscious of the fact you're not being authentic. At least you can be authentic "internally." What's definitely out, however, is telling an out and out lie, that is, deliberately misleading the group. Your best response is usually to say, "Sorry, but no comment." You might well follow this up by telling the group that your "no comment" has nothing to do with your caring for or trusting the group.

Acting Nondefensively

This point can't be stressed enough: It's OK to *feel* defensive when answering a question; just don't *act* it. Acting or appearing defensive can cost you *credibility*. At worst you'll get sympathy; at the best, tolerance. Both damage your ability to influence the group.

Fielding Answers

Handling Wrong Answers

If a participant answers your question incorrectly, avoid saying "no," "wrong," or "incorrect." Instead, find some way to thank the participant and then ask someone else to comment on the issue. Failing this, provide a correct answer yourself. And avoid evaluating participants' input, though this is difficult with fact-based questions (i.e., questions where there is a right and wrong answer). Even with correct responses, avoid evaluating with words such as "correct," "better," or "excellent." Instead, say "thanks" or use a combination of nonverbal reinforcers such as smiles, head nods, and eye contact to indicate that the answer was on target. The problem with evaluating responses is that participants may compare your evaluations (e.g., "Why did he say 'great answer' when Ted spoke, and only 'OK' when I spoke?"). Having given this advice I now want to temper it a bit. It's probably overly sensitive. Saying "great answer" to a participant won't likely be the biggest mistake you'll make as a workshop or training-program leader.

Use the "feel, felt, found" technique or something similar for handling wrong answers. The idea is to empathize with and support the participant, but at the same time to correct the wrong answer. Here's an example of how it works. "A lot of people *feel* that way. I *felt* the same way myself when I first started in this field. However, it's been *found* that most managers make better progress when ..."

Humor also works if you're in rapport with the group. For example, say something like, "Well that's a good answer and kind of right, but completely wrong" or "Wrong answer, but thanks for playing." A word of caution here. As with any time you use humor, you need to be confident that participants won't take it the wrong way.

Recognizing "Nonanswers"

There are a variety of ways that participants might "not answer" your question while trying to leave the impression that they have answered it. For example, participants may answer the question incompletely by using a restricted meaning or answer at a lower level than the question was asked. Here are a couple of examples to clarify this point.

> *A small dog growls at Inspector Clouseau as the good Inspector checks into a hotel. Inspector Clouseau asks the hotel owner, "Does your dog bite?" The hotel owner answers "no." The dog then bites Clouseau. Inspector Clouseau, looking puzzled, complains, "I thought you said your dog doesn't bite." The hotel owner replies, "That's not my dog."*

> *Two men ask a fisherman if there are any snakes in the water. The fisherman answers "no." The two men then go swimming. After their swim they ask the fisherman, "Why aren't there any snakes here?" The fisherman replies, "The alligators ate them all."*

Another "nonanswer" technique is to answer the question inaccurately by changing it or rephrasing it slightly. Thus, a participant may be attempting to leave you without the desire to pursue the questioning any further. This is done in a number of ways. For example, a participant might simply state that the question cannot be answered. Other examples include giving "nothing" answers, using disarming praise, stigmatizing your point of view, using humor, counterattacking on an irrelevant point, or causing a distraction instead of answering the question.

CONCLUSION

Summary

Every workshop leader needs to be highly skilled at using questions. They're as important to group involvement as workshop outcome statements are to achieving results. Questions promote interaction and challenge participants to understand

and analyze learning content. This leads to a deeper level of knowing and to a more active and energized workshop.

The Functions of Questions

Use questions not only to obtain information, but also to give information, cause attention, conclude a discussion, and start participants thinking.

The Structure of Questions

Open questions expand conversation, leaving participants with considerable latitude in how they answer. They may begin with, "how" or "what." For example, "How would you handle this situation?" *Closed* questions narrow the focus of the conversation. They might begin with, "who," "where," "when," "can," "will," "did," or "do." They require a succinct or binary answer such as a name, place, time, or yes/no. For example, "What time is it?" "Where can I find him?" "Can I do it this way?"

Probes keep the conversation going and seek additional information. For example, "Then what did you do?" *Mirrors* repeat a statement and rely on tone and inflection to take the form of a question. For example, "You went to Harvard?"

Questions using a *superlative adjective* provide direction and lead participants. For example, "What's the *best* thing that could happen in this situation?" Questions that assume participants need more information contain *presuppositions*. An open question with a presupposition would be, "What else would you like to know?" A closed question with a presupposition would be, "Who wants to go second?"

Orientation of Workshop Questions

Fact-based questions have correct answers. For example, "What's the square root of eight hundred and forty-two?" or "What are the four steps in shutting down a leaky skewer valve, and why is each important?"

Opinion-based questions are subjective and thus less intimidating than fact-based questions. These questions seek opinion and give you a feel for how participants are feeling and thinking. For example, "What options does a supervisor have for handling marginal performers?"

Comparison-based questions force participants to analyze and apply their learning. They require participants to find similarities and contrasts between methods or perspectives. For example, "What are the contradictions between the wave and the particle theory of light?"

Conclusion-based questions ask participants how they would apply new learnings in a specific situation. They require a good understanding of the learning material, its purpose, and its application. For example, "How would you deal with an overly aggressive participant who is also your sponsor client?"

Options for Directing Questions in a Workshop or Training Program

Directed questions target a particular participant. As a result, they put people on the spot and can be unpopular. Directed questions are not answerable by anyone in the group. Thus, they are an effective way of bypassing overparticipating and overaggressive participants and involving underparticipating members of the group.

Group questions are not directed at anyone in particular. They don't put pressure on any one person to respond. However, because there's very little pressure to respond, group questions can go answered, even when several members of the group know the answer.

Relayed questions are passed by you from one participant to another. They help you to avoid "spoon-feeding" the group.

A *reverse* question is directed back to the participant who asked it. It encourages participants to take the responsibility and risk of answering questions for themselves as opposed to being told.

How to Ask Questions

The four steps to asking a question are asking, pausing, listening, and responding. The hardest step is pausing. A few seconds can seem to last forever. Try counting to five or six in your head, giving participants time to formulate their answers, and putting a little pressure on them to answer. Ask questions that require more than memory work, and challenge comprehension and understanding. This takes participants to a deeper level of knowledge than simple awareness. Use innuendo, emphasis, inflection, and accent to vary your questioning style. Provide context with your questions, explaining "why" the question is important and "how" it fits with the subject at hand.

Challenging with Questions

Forcing questions challenge participants and should be used with care. Use them when participants need a little push to see things from a different perspective. Forcing questions require participants to be specific, examine different points of view, and contrast their views and assumptions with others. Examples are, "Has this *always* been the case?" "What would happen *if* you did it anyway?" "*How specifically* would you implement your plan?"

Encouraging Questions

Value and encourage questions; they represent involvement and participation. And ensure that participants know they can "pass" on a question if they don't have an answer. After all, you're conducting a workshop, not an interrogation. With the exception of answers to fact-based questions, avoid saying that a participant's answer is "wrong" or "incorrect." Instead, ask another participant or answer the question yourself.

Fielding Questions and Answers

When fielding participants' questions be sure you understand what's being asked. If you're not clear on the content of the question, ask the participant to repeat or rephrase it.

Off the wall questions can quickly become time wasting digressions, so "park" them on a flipchart. Avoid repeating participants' answers, encouraging them to listen to each other.

> ***Honesty is the best policy but insanity is a better defense.***
> ***- John Jones***

Beware of participants attempting to dodge a question by leaving the impression that they have answered when they really haven't. Answering using a restricted meaning, or answering at a lower level than the question was asked, only gives the illusion of an answer. Other methods of dodging questions include claiming that the question is unanswerable, using humor, or counterattacking on an irrelevant point.

Finally, don't BS your way through or fabricate answers. If you don't know the answer, admit it and promise to find an answer later. Workshop leaders are facilitators of learning, not omniscient gurus.

Checklist

The Functions of Questions • Cause attention • Give information • Start participants thinking • Bring to a conclusion • Get information *The Structure of Questions* • Open and closed questions • Probes and mirrors • Superlative adjectives and presuppositions *Orientation of Workshop Questions* • Fact-based questions • Opinion-based questions • Comparison-based questions • Conclusion-based questions *Options for Directing Questions* • Directed questions • Group questions • Relayed questions • Reverse questions	*How to Ask Questions* • Ask your question • Pause to give participants time to think • Listen to the answer • Respond or ask other participants to comment on the answer *Additional Tips for Asking Questions* • Ask questions that require reasoning • Use a little ambiguity • Use simple language • Phrase questions so the answers you want are easy • It's OK to ask the same question twice • Be "nonforcing" • Ask questions yourself if no one else does • Don't overdo closed questions • Phrase questions casually when dealing with sensitive issues • Don't use forced disclosure *Challenging with Questions* • All? Always? Never? • What specifically? • How specifically? • What would happen "if"? • Better?

Exercise

The Old Nine Dots

Can you connect the nine dots with only four lines and without lifting your pen or going back over a line? Go ahead, you have six chances. Hint: Think, "What would happen if?" Don't look yet, but when you're ready, an answer is on the next page.

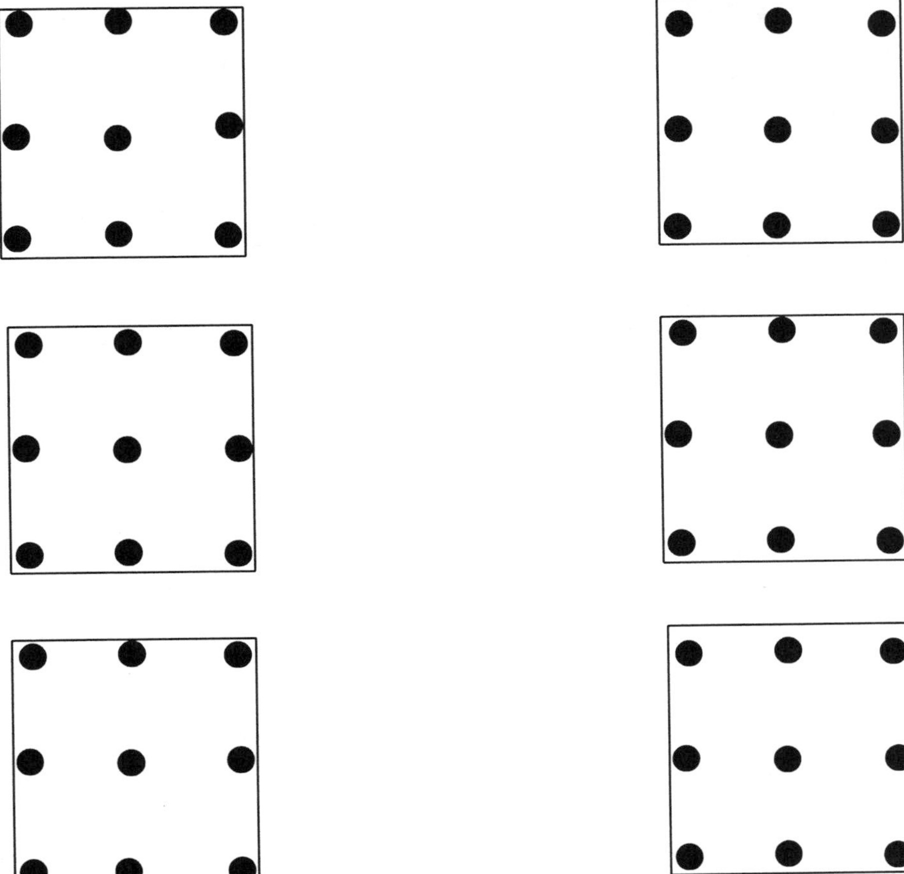

Exercise (continued)

The Old Nine Dots - Answer

One of many possible solutions to the "nine dot" problem is shown here. The trick is to think outside the box. Thus, it's important to ask yourself, "What would happen *if* I was not constrained by the need to keep the four lines inside the box? What would happen if I used a paint brush to draw the lines? What would happen if I cut the dots out and stacked them on top of each other? What would happen if I rolled this page into a cylinder? All these are solutions to the nine dot problem. But to reach these solutions you have to move beyond the usual constraints people tend to put on this sort of problem. Asking, "What would happen if?" is one way of doing this.

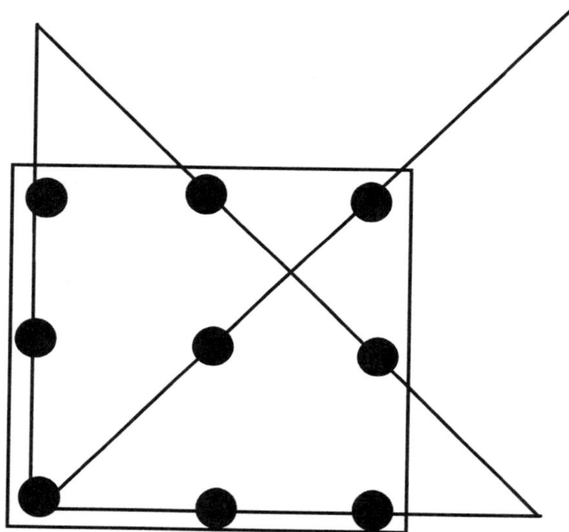

Exercise

Assessing Your Questioning Skills

1) How adept are you at using questions in a group?

2) Are you able to get discussion going, focused, and moving in a productive direction?

3) What specifically are your top three strengths in asking questions?

4) What is one area you need to or could improve about how you use questions in a group?

5) What action will you take to make this improvement?

Notes

[1]Nierenberg, G.I. (1973). Fundamentals of negotiating. New York, NY: Hawthorne Books.
[2]Jolles, R.L. (1993). How to run seminars and workshops: Presentation skills for consultants, trainers, and teachers. New York, NY: John Wiley & Sons, pp. 125-150.
[3]Laborde, G.Z. (1984). Influencing with integrity: Management skills for communication and negotiation. Palo Alto, CA: Syntony.
[4] For an explanation of "policy governance" see: Carver, J. (1991). Boards that make a difference: A new design for leadership in nonprofit and public organizations. San Francisco, CA: Jossey-Bass.
[5]"Espoused theory" and "theory in use" are discussed in depth in: 1) Argyris, C., & Schon, D.A. (1974). Theory in practice: Increasing professional effectiveness. San Francisco, CA: Jossey-Bass. 2) Argyris, C., & Schon, D.A. (1978). Organizational learning: A theory of action perspective. Reading, MA: Addison-Wesley.

Chapter 14

Involving, Motivating, and Maintaining Interest

INTRODUCTION

Chapter nine talked about the importance and interconnectedness of learning climate, learning readiness, and participation readiness. Each of these conditions for success are also closely related to participant involvement and motivation in a workshop or training program. Now it's time to discuss two additional and essential strategies of involving and motivating participants, "exercises and simulations" and "informality, fun, and humor." This chapter provides step-by-step instructions for succeeding at both.

The sections in this chapter discuss:

- Leading exercises, simulations, and subgroup activities.
- Using humor in a workshop.

LEADING EXERCISES, SIMULATIONS, AND SUBGROUP ACTIVITIES

Exercises and small group activities provide an opportunity for participants to "try out" and explore learning content. Use this type of activity often. It adds variety and increases energy and interest, leading to a higher quality of learning, to deeper understanding, and to better application of results "on the job."

Have a clear and relevant purpose for conducting exercises and simulations even though, on occasion, you may not want to spell that purpose out to participants. Sometimes you'll even want to be a little ambiguous with your directions for the exercise. Why all the mystery? Because sometimes it's best to let subgroups struggle, to let them figure out for themselves what they're supposed to be doing, what they should be learning, how the exercise should turn out, and the purpose of the exercise. Struggling leads to deeper learning.

At other times you'll want to be crystal clear on directions as to "how" to do the exercise, but still intentionally vague or completely silent on the purpose of the exercise. The key here is to balance challenge with support. Too much ambiguity and participants may get frustrated and give up; too little and you're robbing participants of the joys of initiating action, inventing options, creating solutions, and discovering meaning on their own.

Finally, if an exercise or simulation feels like a test, let adults score their own answers. Invite them to share their findings or results, but don't force this. And avoid "failure exercises," that is, exercises where you show participants how wrong they are. The object of doing an exercise with adults is not to catch them doing something wrong, but to help them learn, achieve, and gain confidence in their abilities to learn and perform.

A *failure exercise worth forgetting*

I planned and led a "failure exercise." It was years ago. I was only a puppy. My boss made me do it. (So much for accountability!) I won't ever do it again. Mea culpa and all that.

It was dumb but here's what we did. We (that's the royal "we") wanted to teach a number of Human Resources managers how to be better at selecting and screening out candidates for management positions in our organization. I was a very large retail/wholesale organization and we were hiring and moving lots of managers on a regular basis. (In this organization moving from job to job, and town to town, was a way of life.)

Here's what we did. We put together a couple of "typical" resumes and job application forms, but with a few little tricks buried deep within each. My boss and I then roll played the "candidates," and using these resumes and job application forms, we had the participants interview us for various jobs in the organization. In the role played interviews we answered "fairly" honestly, but certainly didn't give any information away.

The whole thing was a "set up," although, if participants asked the right questions, they were able get enough information to be suspicious. If they didn't ask the right questions, however, they would be "hiring a mistake." Needless to say, we managed to make most participants look pretty bad. You can imagine how that opened them up to learning from us! Looking back it reminds me of the game Eric Berne (1964) calls NIGYYSOB (Now I Got You, You SOB).[1] Oh well, even my boss was young then too.

I only have one learning from this experience. Don't use failure exercises. If you intend to test people, that's OK; just tell them it's a test. But if it's an exercise, make it "win-win." Help participants learn without making them look foolish. Practice what Pitman and Bushe (1991) call appreciative inquiry,[2] or, as Ken Blanchard says, "catch people doing things right." We could have easily made this exercise more positive. All we needed to do was alert the participants that they needed to look for a few buried secrets in these resumes and job application forms. Likely, this would have even made the learning fun.

End

This section covers,

A) giving directions

B) your role during the exercise or simulation

C) debriefing the exercise

D) an example of an exercise

A) Giving Directions for an Exercise or Simulation

On occasion you'll be conducting an exercise or simulation for the group as a whole. For purposes of this discussion, however, it's assumed these are conducted in subgroups of two to seven participants. (More than seven participants decreases efficiency because there isn't enough time to actively involve all participants in subgroup activities.)

> ***All this keeping my nose to the grindstone for 25 years has given me is a sore nose.***
> ***- Anonymous***

Use the following principles and steps as guidelines when giving directions for subgroup exercises and simulations.

Principles

- Introduce the exercise with confidence. Act like you know it's going to work. But even if the exercise goes totally awry, there are things to debrief and learnings to discover.

- Give clear "step-by-step" instructions. Be explicit but don't overdirect. The old *KISS* principle applies here (keep it simple stupid).

- Make it fun. Don't take yourself, or the exercise, too seriously. Use a little humor to help open people up to learning. Leading and facilitating adults mean you're also in the entertainment business.

- Keep tight time limits and encourage efficiency. Workshops start to drag if participants have to wait around after they've completed an exercise. *Run 'em hard and put 'em away hot!* That is, work subgroups hard and call them back before they've lost their enthusiasm for discussion and discovery.

Steps

- First give participants two or three minutes to do the physical things (e.g., "take out a blank piece of paper," "form into seven groups with four people in each group"). Don't give further instructions till everyone has this done and the noise settles down.

- Next, review directions and time requirements for the exercise. Read directions aloud as well as displaying them on a flipchart or overhead. Keeping directions visible allows participants the ability to refer back to them later in case they get lost. Tell participants that you'll be debriefing after the exercise. For example, tell participants the exercise will take thirty minutes and that they'll need to appoint a timekeeper to make sure they get everything done on time. Or, alternatively, tell participants that you'll be the timekeeper and that you'll give them feedback on how much time they have left throughout the exercise.

- As discussed in the introduction to this section, there will be times where you want to avoid "bridging" into an exercise or simulation. On other occasions, however, you'll want to do very clear "what" and "why" bridges, emphasizing the benefits of the exercise to participants.

- Tell participants what your role will be during the exercise (e.g., "I'll be around to help if you get stuck." "I'll be going from group to group just to observe." "I'll be the time keeper."). If you intend to be wandering around and looking over people's shoulders, telling them ahead of time gives you "permission" and ensures no one is suspicious or surprised when you show up in their subgroup.

- Ask questions to ensure everyone knows what's expected of them. Open questions work best (e.g., What's not clear? What questions do you have about this assignment?).

- Be alert for and deal with participants' anxieties (e.g., some may be asking themselves, "Is this a test?"). Anticipate and deal openly and directly with possible suspicions and fears participants may have. Say something like, "This is a self-test, but only you and your partner (subgroups of two) will see the results."

- If someone challenges the relevancy of an exercise, simply ask them to reserve their judgment for the time being, promising to explain the importance of the exercise later. This is not uncommon with role playing. Often participants are reluctant to role play but invariably, once it's over, they say something like, "I hate role playing, but that was the most valuable part of the session for me."

- Subgroups occasionally finish exercises and simulations at different times. Leave them with something to do, if they complete an exercise ahead of other subgroups. This prevents the workshop from dragging or becoming disorganized. For example, you might say something like, "If you finish ahead of other subgroups, then use that time to prepare materials for this afternoon's presentation." It's usually wise to avoid giving a subgroup time off for finishing early. For example, avoid saying something like, "If you finish early, you're free to go to lunch early." This kind of direction can split a subgroup between those who are hungry for learning and those who are even hungrier for hamburgers.

- Tell the group confidently and directly exactly when to begin the exercise. Once everyone's in place and you're sure participants know what to do, say something like, "OK, begin." This may feel a little pedagogical, but you need to be very clear and direct with subgroups; otherwise someone is almost always going to be lost.

Designating a "Process Coach" for Each Subgroup

- There will be times when it's useful for each subgroup to designate a "process coach." Process coaches don't participate; rather they observe subgroup performance and give members feedback during the subgroup debrief. Provide a handout with specific guidelines for process coaches. For many participants this will be a new activity.

B) Your Role during an Exercise or Simulation

Principles

- Let subgroups struggle. It yields more creative results. While you may have wanted to be very clear when giving directions, a little ambiguity actually helps when facilitating learning. Let subgroups discover things for themselves. However, there are differences between constructive and nonconstructive suffering, so pay attention to the group's needs. Don't rescue groups too early, but don't let them waste time or flounder either. That is, visit each subgroup to monitor progress and help them overcome roadblocks, but don't spoon-feed or help them too much.

- Leave directions posted during the exercise on a flipchart or overhead.

- Be sensitive to the possibility that some participants experience "performance anxiety" if you hang over their shoulder and watch for too long.

Steps

- Be available during the exercise. This is not a good time for you to take a break. Watch the energy and tension in the room, providing minimal guidance only when absolutely necessary. Once you tell subgroups to begin, don't interrupt with, "And one more thing ..." Interrupt only if you left out a key instruction or if subgroups are really stuck. Otherwise let them struggle.

- Make mental (or written) notes of whatever happens during the exercise, positive or negative. Everything that happens becomes data for the debrief, especially things that go wrong. Often there's as much learning in discussing "why things got off track" as there is in discussing "what went well."

Managing Time

- When there are only a couple of minutes left, give the group a "two minute warning." Yell something like, "Two more minutes," and hold two fingers in the air. This alerts the group of the need to finish what they're working on. Avoid abruptly ending the exercise by running out of time and then telling the group "time's up." This catches people unprepared.

- A useful tip: When you give the "two minute warning" listen to the noise level in the room. If the noise level goes up, the group probably needs more time, so stretch the two minutes or even negotiate with the group for more time. If the noise level goes down, they're probably already finished, so call the group back together for debriefing within another half minute.

- Sometimes, after a two minute warning it becomes obvious that the subgroups need more time. Use a little humor. After another four or five minutes yell out, "Two metric minutes left" or "Two New York minutes left."

- Sometimes you'll need to leave "time" open ended. You simply won't know how much time subgroups will need. Here's how you manage time on these occasions. As you go from subgroup to subgroup you'll get a sense of progress and how much more time they need. Then ask the subgroup that appears the slowest how much more time they need. Be a little directive. Ask, "Will ten more minutes do?" They may answer, "Give us fifteen." That now becomes the standard you work toward. Go around telling the other subgroups, "Fifteen more minutes."

C) Debriefing an Exercise or Simulation

Principles

- Ask open questions.
- Use a common text such as a flipchart or overhead and make information visible (e.g., results, learnings, conclusions).
- Have subgroups report out their results. Have them tell you, and each other, what they learned and how they will use these learnings on the job.
- Treat adults like adults. For example, if you don't want to reveal an answer, then tell participants you're playing "guess what's on my mind." Now, at least they know what you're doing and won't be insulted. Don't tell participants things they can tell themselves. Have them draw their own conclusions and define their own learnings. This builds their confidence. Anyway, they'll listen to themselves better than to you. And this way they'll also see that there's a lot to learn from each other. Only bring in your observations and conclusions if participants miss a key point during the debriefing.

Steps

- Debrief in this order. (Note: You may find participants want to skip about between learnings, answers, feelings, and so on. That's OK. Don't be rigid about this order but know that there's logic here.) Results are the easiest to talk about, followed by what participants actually did. Emotions and conclusions are more difficult to understand and discuss. Needless to say, you want to spend most of the group's "debrief time" discussing learnings, conclusions, and application ideas.
    - Results, answers, and findings. (Ask something like, "What results did you get?")
    - Behavior. (Ask questions like, "What happened?" "How did you go about figuring out the answer?")
    - Feelings. (Ask questions like, "What was this experience like for you?" "How did it feel when that happened?")
    - Learnings, conclusions, and application. Connect the exercise to participants' learning and to what they need to do on the job. (Ask questions like, "What was this about?" "What did you learn?" "How was this exercise relevant for you?" "How was this exercise worthwhile?" "What conclusions have you drawn about using this

skill?" "In what ways was this exercise unrelated to your work?" "How will you use this knowledge?" "When?" "Under what circumstances?")

- Summarize. Review the purpose of the exercise, learnings in the group, and applications discussed. Recognize the group's effort, and thank them for participating.

Debriefing with Large Groups or with Several Subgroups

The larger the group, the more structure you need in the debrief. That is, the more participants, the more data collected. One way to handle this volume is to make several passes around the room asking each participant or subgroup to provide only one piece of information on each pass. During the second pass they can provide a second piece of information or observation and so on. Thus, each participant or subgroup contributes to the conversation. Without this structure, one or two participants or subgroups could monopolize the air time, leaving others to listen passively. Another suggestion is to have subgroups prioritize their data, providing only their top two or three observations during the debrief.

Debriefing with Groups That Are Quiet

Use a discussion guide or list of questions for the group to answer. Use this order. First have individuals write out their own responses and learnings from the exercise. Next have them discuss these in their subgroups. Finally, debrief in the group as a whole.

Having Participants Give Each Other Feedback

On those occasions when participants are role playing or practicing a skill in subgroups, they will need to give each other feedback before the whole group meets together to debrief. Have subgroups provide this feedback in the following order.

Have the person who did the role play or practice, and is receiving the feedback, go first. Ask her to start by giving herself feedback in the subgroup. Ask the participant to say what she did well and, only then, to state what she might have done differently. This forces the participant to recognize that there are things she already does well. It also allows her to demonstrate to others in the subgroup that she is aware of both her own shortcomings and what she could have done differently. Having participants state their own needs for improvement first, before hearing from others, is easier emotionally than hearing someone else give them this feedback.

Next, have those giving feedback to the participant use the same sequence, first telling her what she did well, then suggesting what she might consider doing differently next time.

D) An Example - The Revolutionary Quiz

The following quiz, inspired by Klas Mellander (1993), is about as simple and straightforward as exercises get. Thus, it's a useful example for demonstrating how to lead an exercise.[3] The tools needed for this quiz are the two handouts provided below, two quarters for each participant, and a flipchart or overhead projector for use during the debrief.

A Revolutionary Quiz - Handout #1

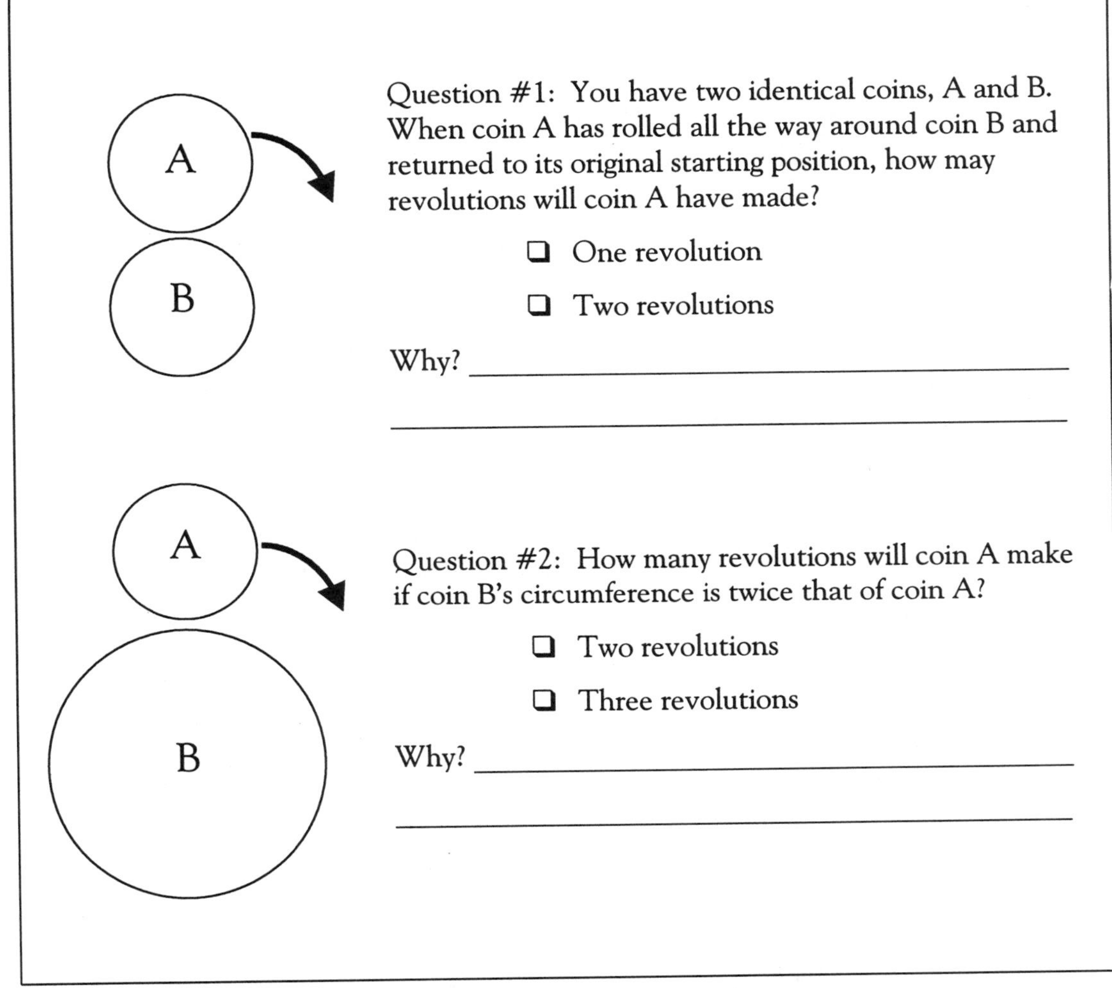

A
B
Question #1: You have two identical coins, A and B. When coin A has rolled all the way around coin B and returned to its original starting position, how may revolutions will coin A have made?
❑ One revolution
❑ Two revolutions
Why?
A
B
Question #2: How many revolutions will coin A make if coin B's circumference is twice that of coin A?
❑ Two revolutions
❑ Three revolutions
Why?

A Revolutionary Quiz - Handout #2

How did you react to this quiz?

How you reacted to this quiz depends on factors such as how much time you had, how interested you were, and your previous experience. These are all factors that normally influence learning.

The following isn't a test of character or attitude toward learning. It's simply a measure of how you felt at the moment doing this particular quiz.

Check the box below that most applies to you (check only one box)

☐ I got through the exercise without difficulty. I had interest and capability.

☐ I had to really work, thinking and checking as I went. I showed interest and energy.

☐ I felt the exercise was meaningless and skipped it. I had neither interest nor any expectations.

☐ I skipped the exercise because I'm not very good at such exercises.

☐ I gave up because the information provided was too ambiguous. I didn't have enough interest to work my way through the ambiguity.

☐ I knew the answer before I started. I lacked interest because I had nothing to gain.

☐ I peaked at other people's answers. I had some curiosity but not enough to do the exercise.

☐ I still don't understand, even though I've been told the answers. I remember the answers but I haven't learned.

☐ Other (please specify):

____

A Context for the "Revolutionary Quiz"

Every exercise, simulation, and subgroup activity you conduct needs to be in context. That is, it needs to have a purpose, and it needs to fit with what's just occurred or is about to happen in a workshop or training program. Without context an exercise doesn't "take." It's like a joke where all you hear is the punch line. It's not funny. There's no basis or context for laughing.

The "revolutionary quiz" is being used here only for the sake of providing an example of how to conduct an exercise. For the purpose of this example, the context is a program for training workshop and training-program leaders. It doesn't matter if you ever lead this type of training program. It is only being used here to provide a context.

Suppose you've introduced the "revolutionary quiz" into this training program for the following reasons.

- To get participants thinking about the concept of learning readiness.
- To demonstrate experiential learning.
- To demonstrate how exercises are conducted and debriefed.

Directing the "Revolutionary Quiz"

As already discussed, when introducing an exercise there will be times when you want to be clear and specific with your directions and bridges ("what" and "why") and times when you want the group to struggle and figure things out on their own.

Here's how you might give a group directions for this exercise.

> *We'll talk about the answers and purpose of this exercise later, but right now I want you to reserve your judgment, and read and complete handout #1. (Don't show them handout #2 at this point.) There are two questions on the handout. Simply check the right answer for each, and fill in your reasons where it asks "why?" Follow the instructions. Work on your own. Be obedient (a little joke). It may take up to five minutes. OK, before you begin, what can I explain a little better? (Now pause for five of six seconds.) If questions come up later, just call me over. I'll be wandering around a little, looking over your shoulder, and trying to make you nervous! OK, begin.*

Now remain silent and let participants do the exercise. Don't make the all too common mistake that workshop leaders make of being constantly interrupting with "and one more thing . . ."

Note: Some may choose to ignore your instructions (e.g., they may talk with their neighbor during the exercise). That's OK; they're adults. But make a few mental notes and discuss this during the debriefing. Compliment participants who "break the rules" when this helps them to learn and get things done.

If the group seems nervous and timid, tell them ahead of time that they'll be the only ones who see their answers (i.e., they won't be required to share their answers with other participants). However, don't rescue participants. Be willing to put them under a little pressure.

Introduce a new element after the group has struggled with this quiz a little (usually for three or four minutes). Give each participant two quarters. Don't tell them what to do with the quarters; instead just place two quarters on the table in front of each participant. Now they can experiment and "try out" their answers for Question #1. (Note: Some may have already done this with change from their pockets or purse.) Using coins (e.g., quarters) takes the quiz from the theoretical to the concrete.

Next, introduce a new rule. "It's now OK to talk with and help others in the room with these questions." If the exercise is going well, it now gets very noisy. Some participants will now change their answers. That's exactly what you want them to do. The object is not to catch participants doing something wrong, but to help them learn by success.

Finally, introduce handout #2 and ask participants to work on their own and quickly check the appropriate box on this handout.

Debriefing the Revolutionary Quiz

Be clear on the points you want to make during the debrief, but keep them to yourself for now. Debrief in the order shown below and challenge the group to draw their own conclusions, asking lots of open ended questions to stimulate conversation.

1) Results

First deal with the participants' results or answers. Ask, "What answers did you get?" In this case there are right and wrong answers. The answer to question #1 is two revolutions. The answer to question #2 is three revolutions.

Next ask, "Why these answers?" "What's the logic behind these answers?" In the case of question #1, coin A makes two revolutions because it does two things at the same time. It makes one full revolution as a result of rolling in a circle along the distance of coin B's circumference (which is also the same distance as coin A's circumference). At the same time it makes a second revolution because as it rolls along coin B's circumference, it makes a

360° turn, because coin B is also a circle. In the case of question #2, coin A makes three revolutions. One because the path it takes is a circle, and two because coin B's circumference is twice that of coin A.

2) Process

Next ask about what participants did. "What did you do with the quarters?" "How did you come up with an answer?" "Did you work with your neighbor to figure this out?"

3) Emotions

Now ask questions about feelings. "What were you feeling as you did this exercise?" "Was this frustrating?" "Why?"

4) Application

Finally, deal with application. This goes directly to the purpose for conducting this exercise in the first place. *Application* is what makes the exercise meaningful for participants. In this example you'll recall the context for using this quiz was a *Train the Trainer workshop* (a workshop for training workshop leaders). You might debrief with questions like, "In completing handout #2 (titled *How did you react to this quiz?*), what box did you tick?" "What was your level of learning readiness during this exercise?" "How could your learning readiness have been improved?" "What does this exercise tell you about the importance of learning readiness?" "Did the quarters help?" "Did it help moving from the abstract to the concrete (i.e., using the quarters)?" "Why were the quarters helpful?"

You might even debrief the steps you took as you directed this exercise. After all, in this example, you're conducting a workshop to train workshop leaders. Ask questions like, "What could I, as the workshop leader, have done to help you more during this exercise?" "What are some other ways you could lead this exercise?"

USING HUMOR IN WORKSHOPS AND TRAINING PROGRAMS

Laughter is the shortest distance between two people.
- Victor Borge

Humor softens our resistance to learning, relaxes participants and builds rapport in a group, and opens us to more risk taking and creative thinking. It also helps diffuse conflict by changing people's perceptions and expectations. Once people are able to reframe and laugh about a problem, they're on their way to resolution. Humor is also a form of shared experience in a group. An old saying conveys this message. "Laugh and the world laughs with you; cry and you cry alone." Finally, humor may be the most powerful part of language in that it helps change people's perspectives. John Ralston Saul (1992) points out that in the days of old, kings and queens feared humor. It was a part of language they could not control.[4]

This section covers

A) Key assumptions about using humor in a workshop

B) Do's and don'ts when using humor

C) Sources of humor

D) Examples of humor in a workshop

My secret source of humor

John Jones usually knows just the right word to use, and his speech is as colorful as speech gets.[5] Colleen Kelley, a senior consultant who also happens to be a close friend of John's, put together a list of his favorite sayings. She titled this list, tongue in cheek, "The Clean Sayings of John Jones." The following is only a sample of this list. John uses these phrases with impeccable timing and only in a good natured way. In addition, because John's sayings have become so much a part of my language over the years, dozens of his phrases are inevitably scattered throughout this book.

- Back in your box
- It's coming back to haunt me
- I could have phoned it in
- That's a big "me-too"
- I have no feelings about that
- When I became a man I gave that up
- It never happens that nothing happens
- I've created a monster
- That's a big DMI (don't mention it)
- I had to dig it out with a dull spoon
- Just one of my services
- If it were a movie, what would it be titled?
- If you were listening, this is what you'd be hearing

A) Key Assumptions about Using Humor in a Workshop or Training Program

- Participants learn better when they enjoy the learning experience. Laughing not only softens people's resistance to learning new information and ways of thinking, it also motivates. It warms us, it connects us, it gets us out of our "serious selves," and it shows us the irony in life. Humor helps create an informal, friendly, and fun learning climate.

- Workshop and training-program leaders are in the entertainment business (at least partly). Of course your primary purpose is not entertainment. No workshop leader wants their workshop to be thought of as "content free entertainment." But, at the same time, "there's no business without show business." Adult learning needs to be informative, involving, motivating, *and* entertaining. Your goal isn't to be hilarious; it's just to communicate with a sense of humor. So make humor a habit. Develop your "funny bone." There's a difference between a person who has a Far Side cartoon on his/her wall and a person who has the company rules posted there. Remember Will Rogers' advice, "An onion can make people cry, but there hasn't been a vegetable invented that can make people laugh."

- You don't have to be Johnny Carson to tell a joke. Humor is a skill that can be learned and developed. All you need is to mix a sense of humor with some basic communication skills and a little "humor plagiarism." Keep a humor file. Collect quips and humorous stories from conferences and after-dinner speeches. Then just relax and be yourself, although, as P.J. O'Rourke says, "Be yourself is about the worst advice you can give some people!"[6] (A little humor here.) Remember, old jokes never die, they live on in workshops.

- Humor only works in context. For example, have you ever listened to someone repeat what they thought was a very funny incident or joke from an earlier experience, and you just didn't get it? Hence the saying, "You had to be there."

- Irrelevant humor is a distraction and is best avoided. Anyway, a quip, story, or humorous quote is much funnier if it's relevant. A joke that doesn't connect in any way to the workshop, or to the group, might still be funny but it's a distraction. It doesn't add to participants' learning.

- Personal anecdotes work better than jokes. Anyway, originality is nothing more than the art of concealing your source. Almost everything you and participants say and do in a workshop is a potential source of humor. Use humor to reframe what someone is saying or to admit your mistakes and laugh at them. Poking fun at yourself creates rapport and helps remove status differences. (But don't put yourself down too much. Somewhere between a "stuffed shirt" and a Woody Allen neurotic type is probably about the right balance.)

> ***The most wasted day of all is that on which we have not laughed.***
> ***- S.R.N. Chamfort***

- Timing is important. Thus a quip like, "Be careful who's toes you step on today, they may be connected to the ass you have to kiss tomorrow" is funny if it's timed right. So, pick your spots. Wait for the right moment (e.g., when discussing topics such as unmotivated employees, politics in the office). Don't force jokes. It they don't fit, leave them out.

- Be careful with anything resembling a vulgar word. If you're not sure the group will respond positively, then soften it up. For example, in the quip above the word "ass" might be considered a "minor taboo violation." If you're not sure how the group will react, you can soften it to "butt" or "behind." It takes a little away from the joke, but that's better than insulting someone. After all, with some groups, the only time it's safe to say "ass" is if Mary's riding it to Bethlehem! A rule for anything resembling a vulgar word is, "When in doubt leave it out." (Don't you just love advice that rhymes?)

- Humor only works when you're in rapport with a group. Without rapport humor is risky. Participants may misinterpret your joke in a personal way, or see you as making fun of something they feel is very serious. Once you're in rapport, however, a group gives you the "benefit of the doubt." Indeed, one sign you are in rapport with a group is that they join in and respond with their own brand of humor.

B) The Do's and Don'ts of Humor

Malcolm Kushner (1990) has a great idea. He suggests you attribute all your jokes to Aristotle. That way, even if no one laughs they will at least think you're smart. Kushner claims he did this while teaching a communications course at the University of Southern California. "To this day," Kushner writes, "the football team thinks it received a classical education." At any rate, most of the following do's and don'ts were inspired by Kushner's book titled, *The Light Touch: How to Use Humor for Business Success.*[7]

> ***Originality is the art of concealing your source.***
> ***- Franklin P. Adams***

Use the following lists to review your humor plan.

The "Do's" When Planning to Use Humor

- Know your audience.

- Have a clear purpose for using humor and be clear on the point you're trying to make with humor.

- Make sure your humor is relevant (e.g., integrate humor into each stage of the workshop).

The "Do's" When Using Humor

> ***You grow up the day you have your first real laugh - at yourself.***
> ***- Ethel Barrymore***
>
> ***A person reveals his character by nothing so clearly as the joke he resents.***
> ***- G.C. Lichtenberg***

- Choose the right word and know your lines.
- Be confident, comfortable, and keep your stories conversational.
- Keep it brief, specific, and put the group in the picture.
- Create an image (e.g., don't say "a car," say "a pink Edsel with flowing fins").
- Always put the punch line right at the end; then wait for the laugh.

The "Don'ts" When Using Humor

- Don't try too hard to be funny, and don't announce you're going to tell a joke. Have some humor planned but use it flexibly or not at all. Don't force jokes or interrupt participants so you can squeeze in planned humor. And never say, "And now I'm going to tell a joke." If participants see you trying too hard, they will resist. They may say something to themselves like, "Oh yeah, you think you're funny. Prove it!" This is the type of challenge professional comedians must face. Your use of humor need not be anything near as formidable.

> ***A diplomat is a person who can tell you to go to hell in such a way that you actually look forward to the trip.***
> ***- Caskie Stinnett***

- Don't worry if some of your humor doesn't "land." It's a matter of "batting average." You want most of your jokes to get a laugh or chuckle, but nobody bats a thousand. Anyway you can't go wrong with humor that's relevant and good natured. Simply work humor into your point. If it's funny, participants will laugh. If it's not funny, you've still made your point.
- Don't take yourself, your stories, or your role too seriously. Do, however, take participants' learning needs seriously. Thus, take your work and the workshop outcomes seriously, but not yourself, your stories, or your role. P.J. O'Rourke says, "People who take themselves too seriously are not just silly, they're dangerous" (1994).[8] Some would say they're also annoying.
- Don't be flippant. For example, when answering a question with humor follow with a serious explanation. Otherwise, you may be seen as treating the question frivolously.

- Don't offend or harass participants with humor. "Humor harassment" is those times when you have to say, "I was only kidding." You see, a lot of humor comes from anger. As a result, a lot of humor is in some way a "put down." Bob Hope has the market cornered on inoffensive humor. Most of his jokes are about himself. He provides a good model for a workshop leader's use of humor.
- Don't finish other people's punch lines. It's rude and insensitive.

A story about using humor without enough forethought

I was leading a *Train the Trainer* program and videotaping each participant's practice session. The sessions were going well, and I had a lot of rapport with the group. The video equipment worked fine for all but one person, a young, bright, and attractive female named Kelly. She was a little disappointed but good natured about this failure. Without thinking, I made a joke of the situation. I said something like, "To make it up to you I'd be willing to go over to your place some Saturday, and videotape you at your convenience." I had this picture of me following Kelly and her family around, videotaping them at the breakfast table, and generally making something of a "Woody Allen" nuisance of myself. However, no sooner had I finished with the words "at your convenience" when the group roared with laughter.

I realized immediately they'd attributed a sexual connotation to my joke. I felt faint. You just don't say things like this in a business environment. I never meant it to be taken this way, but it was too late now. And it was nobody's fault but my own. I carried on with a ten minute session of the workshop that was planned, but then, before bridging to the next session of the workshop, I stopped, got the group's attention, mentioned the joke ten minutes before, and apologized. I never explained that I hadn't intended it the way they took it, and I never tried to justify my actions. That would likely have been seen as defending and rationalizing anyway. I simply turned to Kelly and said, "I'm sorry." She was very gracious and said, "That's OK." Then we got on with the rest of the training program.

No one mentioned it again. When the training-program evaluations were handed in, I looked for problems, but no one held my mistake against me. Even Kelly rated the workshop highly. And I'm still getting repeat business from the organization in question. It was no big deal to anyone but me, but I learned a good lesson. I'm more cautious now before I tell a joke about anything that might be mistaken to have a sexual connotation. I've learned, and I've moved on. As a friend of mine says, "If you get caught up in worrying about past mistakes, you're liable to miss out on the tragedy of the present!"

The other lesson here has to do with the importance of rapport and having something in the "relationship bank" with a group. The same gaff that's laughed off or overlooked when you have strong rapport with a group can be used to bury you when trust is lacking.

End

C) Sources of Humor

Use humorous letters, lists, analogies, definitions, observations, objects (e.g., posters, signs). Use cartoons on the overhead projector to review and summarize learning content and to poke fun at the learning process. The key is ensuring humor and fun are related to the learning content or process.

Read books on humor. These tell you how humor is structured and how and why humor works. Listen to comedians on audiotapes as you commute. Watch comedians on TV. Shows like "A&E's An Evening at the Improv," "Comedy on the Road" with John Byner, and "Richard Jensen's Comedy Hour" all have their share of monotony and vulgarity, but are also potential sources of good material. You can pick up some great "one liners" from these shows. Just be sure you rework them so they aren't offensive in a workshop.

British humor is best. It's subtle and often without the vulgarity becoming so common in North American humor. Jerry Seinfeld says comedians use vulgarity because they can't quite "nail the joke." Vulgarity is a cop out, even on the comedy club circuit. It's not that I'm pompous and strongly against the odd, off-color joke, but rather that these have no place in a workshop.

Finally, there is one type of humor that is highly offensive. That's racist put-downs. Don't use this type of humor. Also, although political correctness has now become so extreme, it's hard not to poke fun at it (e.g., a short person is "vertically challenged," a crook is "morally deficient"), avoid humor relating to women, minorities, or the handicapped. Humor about men, however, is fair game! I have this on good authority from a female colleague of mine.

Examples of John Jones' Humor in a Workshop

Just to show you how easy it is, the following are a few examples of how you might mix "canned humor" with your own style and sense of humor.

Context	*Humor*
If no one volunteers to go first.	"Who'd like to go second?"
While distributing handouts.	"These make nice Christmas gifts." "This makes great bedtime reading." "If you don't want it, you can always give it to a sick friend."
Giving instructions for an exercise.	"When you're done, lay your head on your desk and I'll know you're done. Or, if you want to start an encounter group, lay your head on someone else's desk."
Advising participants on how to receive feedback.	"Just pretend you're not defensive."
Encouraging participants to challenge.	"I'll give you three yes-buts." "If you were talking right now, what would you be saying?"
Encouraging participants to try an exercise.	"Imagine you're competent and go ahead and do it."

Other Examples of Humor in a Workshop

Context	*Humor*
At the end of a break when participants haven't come back at the agreed time.	"Will someone go round up the usual suspects."
In a crowded training room.	"One good thing about middle age spread, it brings people closer together."
When talking about receiving difficult feedback.	"It's a rare person who wants to hear what he doesn't want to hear."
Advising people to "fess up" when they're asked a question that they don't have a good answer for.	"Honesty is the best policy but insanity is a better defense." (John Jones)
Defining knowledge.	"We're all ignorant, just about different things."
Talking about your experience in the education system.	"I myself had a terrible education as a child. I attended a school for emotionally disturbed teachers." (Woody Allen)

CONCLUSION

Summary

The best motivation is intrinsic. That's motivation derived from the work and learning itself, from being involved, from being heard, from sharing your ideas, and from achieving results. You don't have to be a cheerleader to motivate a group, but you do need to lead by example, be enthusiastic, use a little humor, and get participants active and involved.

Exercises, Simulations, and Subgroup Activities

Exercises and small group activities are excellent methods of giving participants "hands on" practice and experience in a workshop. They not only reinforce learning content, they also motivate by helping participants discover for themselves how to apply new learnings. Have a clear purpose for doing an exercise and avoid "failure exercises." You want to develop participant competence *and* confidence, not to sort out winners and losers.

Make the exercise fun and challenging. Tell participants clearly when to begin, keeping an eye on each subgroup to see if interest is waning or if more time is needed. Notify participants beforehand that you'll be wandering around and observing during an exercise and that you're available if they have any questions. Provide minimal assistance and have participants do as much as possible on their own. And make sure participants understand that it's an exercise and not a test. Make mental or actual notes during the exercise of things you see happening, things you want to discuss during the debrief.

Debrief in this order: results, behavior, feelings, and learnings (including conclusions and ideas for application). Write the main points of the debrief or summary using a common text (e.g., flipchart, whiteboard, overhead projector). Only provide your own observations if these are not forthcoming from the group. When working with large groups, more time and structure are needed for debriefing. Try having each subgroup contribute only two or three points to the summary in order to conserve time and allow everyone a chance to have input.

Humor

Workshop leaders need to provide a motivating climate for learning and accomplishing work. There's a huge difference in learning between participants that are half asleep and those that are laughing, energized, and having fun. And the good news is you don't have to be born with a sense of humor; it can be developed. All it takes is good material and a little practice. However, certain conditions must be met for humor to work. First, you need to be in rapport with the group. Second, you need to relax and be conversational. Trying too hard to be funny doesn't work.

Third, humor needs to be relevant. Off-topic jokes are distracting and add little to the workshop.

Checklist

<table>
<tr>
<td>

Giving Directions for an Exercise

Principles
- Introduce the exercise with confidence
- Give "step-by-step" instructions
- Make it fun
- Keep tight time limits

Steps
- First do the physical things
- Review directions
- There will be times to avoid "bridging"
- Explain your role during the exercise
- Ensure everyone knows what's expected
- Ask participants to reserve their judgment for the time being
- Give subgroups something to do if they finish early
- Tell the group to begin

During an Exercise

Principles
- Let subgroups struggle
- Leave directions posted (flipchart, overhead)
- Be sensitive; some participants experience "performance anxiety"

Steps
- Be available during the exercise
- Make mental notes of whatever happens during the exercise

</td>
<td>

Having Participants Give Each Other Feedback

- The person receiving the feedback goes first, saying what he/she did well, then what he/she would do differently
- Those giving feedback go next using the same sequence

Key Assumptions about Using Humor

- Participants learn better when they enjoy the learning experience
- As a workshop leader, you're in the entertainment business
- Humor is a skill that can be learned
- Humor only works in context
- Irrelevant humor is a distraction
- Personal anecdotes work best
- Timing is everything
- Humor only works when you're in rapport

The "Do's" When Planning Humor

- Know your audience
- Have a clear purpose for using humor
- Make sure your humor is relevant

</td>
</tr>
</table>

Debriefing an Exercise *Principles* • Ask open questions • Make results/learnings visible • Have subgroups report out their results • Treat adults like adults *Steps* • Debrief in this order: 1) results, 2) behavior, 3) feelings, 4) learnings, conclusions, application	*The "Do's" When Using Humor* • Choose the right word • Be confident and conversational • Be brief and specific • Create an image • Put the punch line at the end *The "Don'ts" When Using Humor* • Don't try too hard to be funny • Don't worry if some of your humor doesn't "land" • Don't take yourself, your stories, or your role too seriously • Don't be flippant • Don't harass participants with humor • Don't finish other people's jokes (i.e., let them have their punch lines) *End*

Exercise

Using Humor Effectively

1) Name a time when you were able to use humor effectively. It doesn't have to be a workshop situation.

2) What specifically did you do that went over so well?

3) How can you access this strength in a workshop or training program? What two or three things can you do to ensure your sense of humor is available as a resource when you lead workshops or training programs?

Notes

[1]Berne, E. (1964). Games people play: The psychology of human relationships. New York, NY: Ballantine.

[2]Pitman, T., & Bushe, G. (September, 1991). Appreciative process: A method of transformational change. *OD Practitioner*, pp. 1-4.

[3]Mellander, K. (1993). The power of learning: Fostering employee growth. Alexandria, VA: The American Society for Training and Development, pp. 36-39.

[4]Saul, J.R. (1992). Voltaire's bastards: The dictatorship of reason in the West. Toronto, Ont: Penguin Books.

[5]John Jones operates a consulting firm, Organizational Universe Systems, out of San Diego, California.

[6]O'Rourke, P.J. (1994). All the trouble in the world: The lighter side of overpopulation, famine, ecological disaster, ethnic hatred, plague, and poverty. Toronto, Ont: Random House.

[7]Kushner, M.L. (1990). The light touch: How to use humor for business success. New York, NY: Simon & Schuster.

[8] O'Rourke, P.J. (1994). All the trouble in the world: The lighter side of overpopulation, famine, ecological disaster, ethnic hatred, plague, and poverty. Toronto, Ont: Random House.

Chapter 15

Presenting, Facilitating, and Leading

INTRODUCTION

Have you ever had the misfortune of attending a lecture or presentation where the snores of the audience vied with the presenter for your attention? A presentation where you occasionally practice the fine art of astral-projection, sending your conscious mind to Hawaii for a much needed rest on a secluded and sun drenched beach. If you've had this experience, then you understand the importance of excellent presentation skills.

Skilled presenters exert less effort to achieve more results than their less proficient counterparts. They capture and hold people's attention, helping them learn and accomplish more during a workshop or training program. Fortunately presenting is a relatively easy skill to learn. This chapter shows how to improve your presentations by paying attention to structure, the nonverbals of presenting, and how to adjust the presentation to the group's level of experience.

Workshop leaders work with participants to understand problems, identify options, and plan action. A workshop leader doesn't have the answers or the solutions to all of the group's problems but works with the group to develop these. It's a learning process for both the workshop leader and the group. This chapter picks up from chapter one and further explains the facilitation and leadership process. It provides a breadth of wisdom and practical "how to's" to help you improve your facilitation of workshops and training programs.

This chapter covers:

- Presenting.
- The leadership smorgasbord.
- Co-leading a workshop.
- Teaching a specific job or task.

PRESENTING

Henry Boettinger (1969) has a great metaphor for presenting. He writes:

> *When you present an idea to someone (or to a group), it causes effects similar to those produced by casting a baited hook into a pool. The hook causes some fish to scatter, attracts others, and is ignored by the rest, but it rearranges the total pool into new patterns. What happens depends on the place the cast is made, what's on the hook, and the style or skill used in placing it. The temperature, time of day, and season of the year also play a part, as well as how hungry the fish are. Each has its counterpart in the presentation of an idea. Skilled presentation - like skillful fishing - requires a knowledge of what's in the mind, how to attract what you want, and how to reject what you don't. This brings us to the concept of resonance - the most powerful mechanism for transference of an idea from one mind to another. It is the basis for all advice and techniques of ideas communication.* [1]

The "resonance" Boettinger speaks of comes from being in rapport with the group and from being seen as a "trusted source." The only thing I'd change about Boettinger's metaphor is his method of fishing. Presenting to a group is more like fishing with a net than with a single baited hook. You're unlikely to "reach" everybody in the same way, but you do want to make a fairly sizable catch. One or two fish won't do. Anyway, this metaphor has served its purpose and it's time to move on. Participants are not fish to be caught, but people to be valued, challenged, and supported.

Presenting or lecturing is still the most common delivery method in a training program. For starters, it's an efficient way to communicate information, especially to large groups, and it's also a relatively easy skill to learn. In addition, presentations are cost effective, and when done right, they're also involving and concise.

When giving a presentation, remember that you're presenting yourself, not just your information. So, while you need to know your subject, you also need to relax and be yourself (e.g., personal mannerisms are OK). Presentations also need to be well structured. Don't just wing it.

When presenting, ask questions and pay attention to the group's responses. This reduces the time you spend presenting and increases your interaction with the group. Even closed or rhetorical questions will help keep you in touch with the group. Polling is also a good idea (e.g., "By a show of hands, who's seen the XYZ report?"). Smiling and making eye contact help to establish rapport and give the presentation the tone of talking *with* people as opposed to lecturing *at* them. Maintain a brisk pace and vary your voice. Change volume, speed, and tempo, and use pauses and silences to keep the group's attention.

This section covers:

A) Structuring a presentation

B) Nonverbals of presenting

C) Adjusting your presentation to the experience level of the group

D) Twelve ways to involve participants in a lecture

E) Exercise - assessing your skills as a presenter

F) Presenting checklist

A) Structuring a Presentation

Start your presentation with a controversial statement, observation, quotation, or question. A little humor doesn't hurt either. This gets the group's attention fast. Then hold their attention by using examples, anecdotes, analogies, and statistics. Ensure your presentation has a logical flow by using "what" and "why" bridges. Build in reviews and summaries if your presentation is longer than twenty minutes or so, if the content you're presenting is complex, or if your audience is unfamiliar with this content.

Use handouts. These support a presentation in a number of ways. To begin with, most people are visual learners, and when we *see* and *touch* something, we understand and remember more. Handouts help people understand a presentation's flow and can be used as an overview or to emphasize key points. Handouts also provide a place for people to take notes. Because they make information visible, overheads and flipcharts also add structure and flow to your presentation.

> ***If a person wants to exercise influence in a society, a good place to begin is with a proper regard for the techniques of expression.***
> ***- Norman Cousins***

When structuring a presentation, keep in mind that most people's attention spans are only about fifteen or twenty minutes. Don't allow a passive (straight lecture) session to exceed this time. If you must lecture longer, call minibreaks or ask people to stand and stretch often. Ask the group questions to keep them alert and thinking, and provide a variety of activities such as buzz groups, neighbor discussions, and brief assignments. Timing is also important. Avoid passive sessions just before or after lunch or near the end of the day. These are the times during the day when we're likely to feel a little tired or at least not at our most alert.

B) The Nonverbals of Presenting

The *do's* and *don'ts* of body language when presenting are pretty straightforward.

Avoid pacing. To come across as more relaxed, sit on the edge of a table. (An important safety tip from someone who's learned the hard way – check first to ensure the table is sturdy.) Stand when you wish to command attention, and sit when you want to leave the limelight. Move closer to the group and make eye contact (e.g., walk into the "U") to emphasize a point.

Use gestures and noises for variety, such as tapping on a whiteboard or flipchart. But, avoid nervous mannerisms such as jingling change, clicking a pen, throat clearing, putting a hand over your mouth, or swaying. Also avoid overusing phrases such as "uh huh," "OK," or "you know." These distract some people.

C) Adjusting Your Presentation to the Experience Level of the Group

Following are a few key points to help you target your presentation. First, no matter what the group's knowledge level, start with the big picture and not the details. Tell the group "what" your topic is and "why" it will be valuable information for them.

When Group Members Are Relatively Unfamiliar with Your Topic

You'll likely have to help the group become ready to listen. Your topic is foreign territory so don't assume they understand anything, even the basics. Start by showing the context, how your information fits with their unique situation. Explain specifically *why* they should listen to you. Don't assume they'll make this connection on their own. Use clear and uncluttered visuals (e.g., flipcharts, overheads), emphasize key points, speak in plain language, and review and summarize often. Finally, because most of this information is new to the group, take care not to overload them.

When the Group Has Some but Not a Lot of Topic Knowledge

First, check the group's motivation. Are they ready to learn, or do they need something to show them the value of your topic? Second, get an idea of the group's level of knowledge on the topic. Get direction from the group, ask questions, and get feedback. Get the group working with you. Charge them with responsibility for telling you if and when you're giving them information they already have or if they need even more detail than you're providing. Pay a lot of attention to nonverbals and ask clarifying questions (e.g., "Is this new information for you?" "Would you like more detail on this area or is what I've provided about right?"). Ensure you're not telling them things they already know or that you're not talking over their heads. As the group already has some information, your aim is to fill in their information gaps.

When You're Talking to Experts

When talking to experts you don't need to motivate the group to listen, but you do need to recognize the group's expertise. Invite their participation. As with any presentation, start with the "big picture." Next, explain how you're going to cover the material, assuring the group that you recognize their experience. Avoid details unless requested. Finally, with experts you must be brief, and you must involve them. They have a lot to offer and want to participate and contribute.

D) Twelve Ways to Involve Participants When Presenting or Lecturing

*I **hear** and I forget, I **see** and I remember, I **do** and I understand.*
- Chinese proverb

The Chinese proverb opposite gets at the number one problem with presenting - people don't learn well passively.

These twelve points, inspired by Pat Burke Guild (1983), will help you get people more involved and invested in their own learning during your presentations.[2] (Note: Several of the terms used here are defined in chapter six. These include buzz group, brainstorming, neighbor discussion, critical incident, and quiz.)

1) Use visual aids. Show the "big picture" and then map out how your subpoints fit together.

2) Ask the group questions and encourage them to ask you questions. Even rhetorical questions get a group thinking. Regardless of how you intend to handle questions, tell the group before you begin (e.g., "It's OK to interrupt." "I want you to ask lots of questions." "Hold your questions until the end.").

3) Guide note taking. Provide a handout outlining your main points with lots of "white space" beside each point for note taking. When using overheads, give participants a paper copy of your transparencies.

4) Encourage discussion. Use buzz groups and neighbor discussions to involve participants.

5) Ask participants to write out their answer or reaction to a question, idea, or opinion. Allow them time to reflect, struggle with, and clarify their thoughts.

6) Use "are you awake" techniques such as polling (e.g., ask for a show of hands to a question like, "How many of you feel money motivates?").

7) Structure the presentation to solve a specific problem or question, or suggest a specific learning assignment before the presentation begins. This encourages "directed listening." Having a focus helps participants become more active listeners.

8) Take a few minutes occasionally and get the group brainstorming. Get them contributing ideas and examples.

9) Tell stories and provide examples. Ground your information in experience.

10) Use an informal miniquiz to help participants self-assess their understanding.

11) Have participants use "I heard .... and I wonder ..." statements. Thus, "I heard you say.... and I wonder" (e.g., "how this fits with ..., how it's done when ..., would it work if ...").

12) Guide follow up. Offer suggestions for next steps, further thinking, reading, and practice.

E) Presenting Checklist

Use this list when preparing and rehearsing your presentation.

- Structure your message, step by step.
- Speak clearly.
- Use a brisk pace.
- Use simple statements.
- Relax, take a breath, be yourself.
- Don't tell when you can show (e.g., demonstrations, visuals).
- Use visual aids (e.g., a common text such as an overhead transparency or a structured handout).
- Talk with people.
- Check for understanding and keep the group involved (e.g., ask questions, poll the group).
- Watch the group's attention span (e.g., keep lecture time below twenty minutes).
- Review and summarize if the presentation is longer than twenty minutes, if content is complex, or if the group is unfamiliar with the content.
- Make lots of eye contact.
- Use variety in your voice.
- Move around.
- Use your whole body (e.g., arm gestures).
- Be a little controversial.
- Use humor (it's particularly important in long lectures).
- Practice out loud once or twice.

LEADING AND FACILITATING

The activity smorgasbord introduced in chapter seven is the "what to do" or "main course" of a workshop. Now it's time to introduce the facilitation smorgasbord, the "how to do" or the service and management of a workshop. The facilitation smorgasbord lists everything you always wanted to know but were afraid to ask about facilitating and leading a workshop. It's a collection of "one liners," insights, and "rules of thumb" that can be used to guide facilitators as they lead workshops. Most of this material is mentioned elsewhere in the book, so it's only summarized here. Anyway, with a little imagination, all of it should be fairly easy to interpret.

Some of the following may seem trite, only "common sense," basic relating skills, or just "useful reminders," but others might surprise you. Some may even seem contradictory. Indeed, there's plenty of paradox involved in facilitating and leading workshops and training programs. You might want to stop and think about some of these points or discuss them with another workshop leader.

This section organizes facilitation and leadership into the following categories.

A) Focus on action and results

B) Facilitate and lead

C) Contract outcomes, processes, and roles

D) Become a trusted source

E) Practice adult-learning principles

F) Other facilitation tips, tricks, and techniques

A) Focus on Action and Results

Move Quickly to Content and Keep the Focus on Content

- Keep things moving toward a clear purpose and agreed upon outcomes.
- Focus on performance and results, developing action plans as you go.

Aim for Incremental Gain

- Show progress early. (Pick the low-hanging fruit.)
- Defuse big issues by getting groups to achieve small steps. (Anything worth doing is worth doing incrementally.)
- Tackle the emotionally loaded issues (e.g., relationship problems, strongly held differences in goals) after making progress on the more rational issues (e.g., clarifying expectations, sizing up and agreeing on the current situation).

End with Action Steps

- Don't leave issues hanging or incomplete. End with clear next steps. For example, have participants identify when and how they will use new skills and knowledge gained in a training program, or plan how they will apply a decision taken in the workshop. (This also relates back to the potential power of "cognitive dissonance" as discussed in chapter twelve.)

B) Facilitate and Lead

(*Note*: The following summarizes much of the discussion in the section titled "The Basics of Leading Workshops and Training Programs" in chapter one.)

Pure Facilitation Is of Little Value

- The term facilitator comes from the French word *facere*, which means "to do" or "to make easy." Pure facilitation is a *following* role; often it's not enough. Use your knowledge, skill, and personal power to get things done. To paraphrase Geoffrey Bellman (1990), you need to be more than a kind of *WD-40*, or *organizational butler*, whose only role is to help the feature players move smoothly through their lines.[3]

Facilitators Need to Lead

- Move beyond simple process intervention to saying what you know.
- Lead as you facilitate. Add to content and share the facilitation role. With experience you'll be able to be both a process observer and a player (i.e., involved in the content of the workshop).
- Comment on whether this is work that should be done (content) and on how your clients are approaching their work (process). This moves you from pure facilitation to leadership.

Offer Substance and Content

> ***He gives nothing who does not give himself.***
> ***- French proverb***

- Offer substance, substantial alternatives, and recommend action.
- Add content related to changes. You may not be able to add content related to your client's technology (e.g., how to construct floating drilling platforms or how to organize an emergency operating room), but depending on your experience, you can add content relating to such areas as strategy, management systems, and change management.
- Stick to your values. This helps participants avoid action that seems expedient today, but adds to long-term problems.

It's OK to Have Your Own Agenda, but Make It Visible

- Invest in getting something done, something that includes but may even go beyond helping the group do what they presently agree needs to be done.
- Help create work environments in which people respect who they are, what they do, and how they do it. Intervene on behalf of human support, challenge, and growth.
- Express what you think is important, and act on your values. This is how you make a difference.

C) Contract Outcomes, Process, and Roles

Contract Focus and Outcomes

- Contract to work where there is energy and leverage. Start where the group "is," that is, in areas the group feels are important and at the group's level of understanding.
- Deal in the "here and now." Avoid unnecessarily dredging up too much of the past.

> ***The source of all energy, passion, motivation, and an internally generated desire to do good work is our own feeling about what we are doing.***
> ***- Peter Block***

Contract Process

- Contract to observe, audit, and coach subgroups and to be directive when necessary. Don't be bashful about interrupting a subgroup or the group as a whole when it's time to move on.
- Develop simple ground rules with the group (e.g., anyone can call time out).
- Contract time and stay on schedule. Make it "quid pro quo" (e.g., "We'll finish at 5 p.m. if you're all back from lunch at 1 p.m.").
- Contract to keep confidences.
- Contract openness. Don't feel you have to fully disclose everything to the group, but you do need to be honest all the time (e.g., let the group know if there are some things you're not able to talk about openly, and if possible, explain *why*).
- Only open issues if you have time and the skill to close them properly. Like opening a can of worms, you've got to be prepared to deal with what comes out.
- Don't give up control of the process (e.g., don't let people hurt each other, don't abdicate your accountability for time management).

> ***A stiff attitude is one of the phenomena of rigor mortis.***
> ***- Henry S. Haskins***

Continually Solicit Feedback and Recontract If Necessary

- Recontract if it becomes inevitable that you are going to finish after the agreed time.
- Do mid-course corrections. Keep the process flexible. (Ask, "What should we be doing differently?" "What's going well?").
- Listen for cues, watch the emotional thermostat, and do temperature checks. Ask people to respond to, "Right now I'm feeling ..."

Contract Expectations, Roles, and Accountability

- Be clear on roles.
- Ask for what you want and get permission up-front from the group (e.g., "I'll need to push hard to keep us on time today.").
- Hold participants accountable. Usually participants are being paid to attend workshops, so don't let them hide in the group.
- It's OK to put participants on the spot "a little," but when possible, give someone time to prepare before calling on him or her by name.
- Leadership is a shared opportunity. Request and demand joint accountability with the group. Your obligation is to show up refreshed, know the content, have a variety of delivery methods, be authentic, and share accountability for the success of the workshop. You're also responsible for having a clear "theory of approach" versus just "winging it."
- Don't be a spy for the boss (e.g., Don't tell Joe's boss how Joe did at the workshop. Tell the boss to ask Joe.).

- Don't take responsibility for participants' learning. Hold them accountable. Your job is to take them to *the dawn of their own awareness*.
- Refuse to work with hidden agendas.
- Fess up to your own biases. Declare your beliefs and convictions so they don't get in the way (e.g., "I don't believe you can be a team if you can't meet and communicate, at least electronically!).
- Remember, facilitating is a role where substance is form. *What* you do is seen as *how* you work.
- Don't call yourself a teacher. It's a "loaded" word and brings up all sorts of images (e.g., the need for straight rows, distancing, grades, controlling, evaluating, classes not groups, recess, following the rules).

> ***Agree with me now; it will save so much time.***
> ***- Ashleigh Brilliant***

- Don't seek the limelight. Be invisible at times.
- Help people express what they want from each other.
- At times, foster a little *creative tension* in the group.

D) Become a Trusted Source

Be Authentic

- By becoming a trusted source, participants will be more open to your ideas, advice, and to making changes.
- Be a mirror for the group. Reflect back what you see happening.
- Express what you are feeling at the moment in the hope of connecting with the group and of having them "fess up" as well.
- When relevant, talk openly about your inner dilemma. Describe what you're feeling and solicit direction from the group.
- Don't ignore what happens in the room. Acknowledge it by "calling it like you see it"; then move on. For example, the group may be in the habit of downplaying or ignoring when someone has been "put down" or treated badly. Declare what you see happening. Challenge the group to work more effectively. One caveat, however, is "calling it like you see it" is not a license for *you* to treat participants without respect, consideration, or tact. Thus, there may be times when you need to speak with a participant one-on-one at a break rather than challenging them in front of the group.

Avoid Taking Positions

- Focus on interests, not positions. Don't argue. A workshop leader loses *all* arguments with participants. Anyway, arguing is the least effective learning or change inducement technique.
- The best test is, "Is this useful?" Don't intellectualize or try to argue definitions, science, or proofs. For example, if a participant wants to question a survey

result, don't argue the statistical significance of the data; instead discuss the practical utility of interpreting a result one way or another.
- Don't act like "your ticket is being punched," that is, like someone is out to get you. This will only cut off your feedback.
- Stay alive! If you get pushed too hard, take a break and/or recontract.
- Don't "unilaterally" protect others. People resent being treated like they need protection (e.g., support the sponsor client but don't defend him/her).

Deal Directly with Resistance

- Welcome resistance. It's a lot better than apathy, and it means there's energy in the room.
- Don't confuse silence with consent.
- Don't build resistance as you go. Surface "indirect" resistance and defuse resistance. Sometimes people need to "bitch before they build." When someone is being indirect, the best you can do is give two good faith replies, then gently confront. That is, name and recognize the resistance, giving the other person time to "come clean." Maybe they will, maybe they won't. Regardless, at some point the group has to move on.
- Recognize that sometimes it's impossible to have everybody "on board."
- Sometimes the best a workshop leader can do is to ask participants to suspend their judgment for a while. Ask directly, "Would you be willing to … ?" Move people quickly to action versus simply talking about it. Promise to discuss the process and exercise in more detail later.
- Sometimes when someone asks, "Is this test valid?" the best answer is, "It depends." If it feels like a test to them, then it's a test. People's perceptions are their reality.
- If it sounds like a test, don't direct it to a specific person.

Help People Avoid Feeling Defensive

- Don't catch participants off guard. Ask someone ahead of time to go first. For example, ask a particular subgroup if they'd be willing to present their findings first.
- If someone misunderstands your instructions, take the blame yourself. This helps minimize their defensiveness (e.g., "I could have explained that better. Let me try again …"). Be willing to take the blame twice. The third time, confront tactfully and with respect.
- Don't stand over people for too long when they're doing a task. This causes *performance anxiety* in some participants.

Respect People's Boundaries

- Don't play "Mr. Fix It." Get permission before probing in an area not contracted for (e.g., working on a relationship).
- Respect the group's agenda. It's their company.
- Seed ideas. The group will choose where to work. Respect the group's choices.

- Empathize.
- Practice *equifinality*. This term was introduced in chapter three. It means "there's more than one way to skin a cat." (With apologies to cat owners everywhere!)
- Learn about the group's situation. Don't assume you know. Get participants to talk with you and learn as much about their situation as you can before the workshop begins.

Don't Judge or Evaluate

- Don't "mind read" or assume you know a participant's motive.
- Participants, like most people, appreciate being understood and accepted, and they especially appreciate *not* being evaluated. It's rare but very gratifying to be accepted for who you are and not judged by some arbitrary and unspoken standard.

Model the Behavior You Want from a Group

- Behavior gets behavior (e.g., if you want to be listened to, start by listening). In Stephen Covey's words (1989), "Seek first to understand then to be understood."[4]
- Understand that behavior is maintained by its consequences. Look for what is reinforcing undesirable behavior.
- Model openness and flexibility.
- Don't take things personally. It's OK to feel defensive; just don't act it. Or as John Jones says, "Pretend you're not defensive."[5]
- Trust the group and trust your instincts. But don't rely on the group to move things along. Most of the time the group will move things along, but when they don't, that's your job.

Be Confident and Reliable

- Keep commitments and follow through on promises (e.g., if you say you'll send something to participants, do it, and do it promptly).
- Act like the world is going to treat you well. Have a positive outlook.
- Use several positives for every negative. Ken Blanchard recommends seven strokes for every criticism.
- Show up refreshed and ready to work. You owe this to the group and to your sponsor client.

Confront When Necessary but Don't Necessarily Confront

- Recognize and sensitively confront incongruence in the group. Don't allow differences to go unnamed.
- Open agendas. "Peel the onion" slowly and carefully (i.e., take groups to deeper levels of sharing and relating than they traditionally work at). Giving participants a new experience frees them from working in their usual rut.

- Don't let participants get away with acting like teenagers. Support and confront at the same time.
- Be recursive. Ensure your audio matches your video. Walk your talk. Be authentic and act congruently. Be honest about your feelings and your thinking.
- State what you see happening, and use this for learning and challenging the group.
- When something isn't working; call it. Don't apologize or rationalize. Say, "This isn't working, let's try something else." Then move on.
- Confront only when necessary; otherwise spend most your time supporting, challenging, appreciating, and recognizing participants' contributions.

Use Your Power

- Make your commitments personal and hold participants accountable to their commitments as well.
- Follow Argyris and Schon's advice (1974, 1978), by refusing to "deny what you know." That's playing a game.[6] It will also decrease the group's trust in you as a leader. For example, if you have an answer but don't want to divulge it just yet, say so.
- Know your technology. Draw on your own experiences.
- Challenge. Don't be afraid to upset people a little. Take some "calculated risks."

Leading is like being a first time parent. You have to do the right thing before you fully understand the situation. And like effective parents, lovers, teachers, and therapists, good leaders make people hopeful.
- Warren Bennis

Maintain Your Objectivity

- Temporarily, think and act as if you're part of the organization, although this has its dangers. For example, you could "catch the group's disease." That is, you could start thinking the same way and worrying about the same things as the group, blocking your ability to offer a fresh perspective.
- Don't collude with part of the group (e.g., keeping a secret). This neutralizes you as a leader. It ties your hands by making some topics taboo. Be alert for unconscious collusion as well.
- Don't allow yourself to take sides or to be put on one side of an issue.

If you see in any given situation only what everybody else can see, you can be said to be as much a representative of your culture (as) you are a victim of it.
- S.I. Hayakawa

E) Practice Adult-Learning Principles

Motivate Participants

- Focus on what participants see as their learning needs.
- Know that adults will only learn those things they need to learn and do the things they want to do. Help adults understand *why* they should learn something. Show them value.

- Think of your role primarily as one of creating readiness for learning and action versus providing knowledge. What you really want is not so much to teach, but to motivate participants to learn.
- The big job is getting adults learning ready, not teaching them. The real work happens before the teaching begins.
- Hook participants. Get participants in the room "mentally." Get them to invest in their own learning.

Recognize and Reward Participants

- Build relationships in the group. Arrive early. Meet people. Learn names and as much as you can about each individual participant. Have someone make you a seating chart with first names.
- Use participants' actual words on flipcharts (e.g., even if they give you the Gettysburg Address, you can ask, "How can I write that up here?").
- Work hard to understand, finding the "kernel of truth" in what participants say. Rarely is someone completely wrong.
- Be happy with incremental progress and "stroke the hell" out of anything participants do right or approximately right.
- Use the magic words, "I need your help."
- Help groups see the "positives" of what they've been doing. Groups often take themselves for granted.

Build Confidence in Clients

- Avoid jargon and use plain English. If you must use jargon, first clearly define the meaning of each term.
- Follow adult-learning principles (e.g., focus on the "here and now," use participant experiences, share responsibility).
- Avoid failure exercises and trying to catch people doing things wrong. In particular, avoid what Eric Berne (1964) calls NIGYYSOB (this stands for "Now I Got You, You SOB").[7]
- Help groups as little as necessary, but first "stack the deck" so they are sure to succeed. This might involve giving them access and permission to talk with experts in-between sessions, making sure their boss in "on side" with how they are approaching a given project in a workshop, giving them well thought out boundaries for their work, or letting them know what barriers to expect along the way.
- Give a little theory at a time. Don't overwhelm participants.
- Turn questions back to the group.
- Don't teach people things they already know, and don't do things that participants can do for themselves (e.g., don't read to adults). When participants do things for themselves the learning becomes theirs, not yours.

Set the Climate for Learning and Change

- Be willing to experiment. Be a little controversial. Use a little ambiguity.

- Get and give permission to make mistakes.
- Make differences legitimate. Encourage the group to value differences of opinion.
- Provide options and give choice where you can.
- Aim for a climate that is informal, fun, hardworking, involving, challenging, "on time," and results oriented.

Understand That Learning and Change Are Neither Smooth nor Predictable

- Recognize that all learning results from differences and is voluntary. You can't predict what participants will learn.
- Learning is sometimes difficult to define, but *not* in organizations. In organizations learning means behavior change. If behavior doesn't change "on the job," learning is of no consequence.
- Training isn't about changing people or changing organizational cultures. Training is about helping people learn. Only then, and on their own, might they choose to change habits or ways of thinking.
- Real learning is sometimes uncomfortable. Changing habits shouldn't *feel* right. Habits never give up without a fight.
- Learning isn't a straight line forward, but rather a clumsy forward and backward activity.
- People don't learn well passively, yet we've become accustomed to being "passive learners." The first thing the workshop leader must do is "get them active." Get them helping each other (e.g., talking, moving, drawing, writing). Insist on involvement, activity, and joint accountability.

Useful Attitudes, Beliefs, and Outlooks on Facilitating and Leading

- It's OK to feel like an impostor; just don't act it.
- Don't get "hung up" on your expectations. To paraphrase Geoffrey Bellman (1990), one of the best ways to make yourself sick is expecting organizations to be rational.[8]
- You can't get it perfect, so relax and get it approximately right.
- Understand that there are no short cuts to commitment. If people are to commit, they must be allowed to *influence* the purpose, outcomes, and the process.
- Know that communication in a group is more a matter of trust than a matter of technique.
- Accept that you will be leading most of the time because you've chosen to be a workshop leader. Workshop leaders don't get paid to just sit there.
- Enjoy challenge, but don't get carried away with "intellectual jousting."
- Don't be intimidated. You've got a job to do, so do it.
- Be comfortable with a little tension and a little ambiguity. Let things evolve.
- Trust that participants know instinctively about how much a workshop leader can handle. It's unlikely they'll push you beyond your ability.

Practice Adult-Learning Principles When Working with Small Groups

- Use subgroups to divide up the work.
- Get things going, keep them going, and let groups struggle. It's like fishing: "Let them run, reel them back, let them run ..."
- Don't get in the way. Resist the urge to jump in at every opportunity. Don't rescue groups too soon. There are times you need to avoid the limelight.
- Keep a fast pace when working with subgroups. "Run 'em hard and put 'em away hot." Don't let subgroup activities go on too long. But don't end subgroup activities without warning, either. When you sense they've had enough time, or when the agreed time is almost up, yell out "two minutes left." If the noise level goes up, let the group go a little longer. If the noise level goes down, recall the subgroups in less than a minute.

Park Your Ego at the Door

- Give yourself permission to be educated in public. You need to have advanced knowledge in a given field before you can lead others through a workshop, but you don't need to have all the answers in your field or expert knowledge in all fields.
- Feel free to say, "I don't know."
- Don't play "guess what's on my mind" with adults. Be open about your ideas and knowledge. Adults resent being tricked, "techniqued," or made to look foolish.

There never was a horse that couldn't be rode, and there never was a cowboy that couldn't be throwed.
- Samuel Cypert

We're all ignorant, just about different things.
- George Bernard Shaw

The fool doth think he is wise, but the wise man knows himself to be a fool.
- William Shakespeare (As You Like It)

- Roll with the punches. Don't take your process or yourself too seriously. Others will always see things differently.
- Don't tell people how they're feeling (e.g., don't say "I can see the group is highly motivated" or "I can tell you enjoyed that practice session").
- Don't talk too much. Whether you're comfortable or not with silence, wait five or six seconds and allow unresponsive groups time to reflect and answer a question.

F) Other Facilitation Tips, Tricks, and Techniques

Be Organized

- Be organized and keep a "clean stage" (e.g., clean up and organize flipcharts at breaks).
- Poor administration before the workshop can make it difficult to get good results.
- Prepare an outline; don't just wing it. Don't model disorganization.

- Pay attention to room set-up (e.g., a long narrow U shaped table set-up can make it hard to control side conversations).

Use Techniques Sparingly

- Have a "pocketful" of models to draw from.
- Use techniques only when necessary (e.g., going around the room in order, getting everyone's input).
- When normally quiet participants finally speak, thank them for their input and provide encouragement.
- Use pretend techniques (e.g., in a good natured way say something like, "Imagine for a minute that I know what I'm doing ...").
- Float trial balloons, but tell the group what you're doing. Otherwise they may think you're making a recommendation. (*Trail balloons* are "shots in the dark" or "suggestions without prejudice." They sometimes help get groups unstuck. For example, if a group can't agree on how to tackle a difficult problem, you might suggest a few places to start.)
- "Chunk up" to where agreement is obvious, then work back down into disagreements (e.g., "OK we don't agree on the *Strategic Defensive Initiative*, but we do agree on the need for a strong deterrent.").
- Transfer concepts with stories and examples; these help ground and make theory more concrete.
- Use little techniques to get the group active (e.g., polling, buzz groups).

The bravest thing you can do when you are not brave is to profess courage and act accordingly.
- Cora Harris

Give Clear and Simple Directions

- When giving directions, act like you know it's going to work. Be confident in your experiments. If you seem to doubt the outcome, participants will as well.
- Give clear instructions and always explain *why*.
- Make directions visible and in steps (e.g., outline directions in point form on a flipchart).
- Once you give directions, "shut up" and let the group work. Don't interrupt them again unless you've forgotten something important.
- Don't overdirect. Specify only the minimum directions needed for groups to get on with the job.
- Speak simply, directly, and forcefully when giving directions.

Act like you know it's going to work

Whenever I'm introducing a new process or exercise in a group and someone challenges its legitimacy, a little audio recording plays in the back of my head. It's John Jones' voice and he's saying, "Act like you know it's going to work!"

Challenges might sound something like these:

- "Haven't we just done something very similar to this?"
- "I don't see how this is going to get us anywhere?"
- "Isn't this just complicating things?"
- "Isn't this avoiding the real issue?"
- "When are we going to get down to making some decisions?"

Often these challenges come early in a workshop (e.g., the first day), before you've had time to prove yourself to the group. Rarely are they mean spirited. Many possibilities are at play here. Some of those who challenge may be:

- Just naturally skeptical. Tony Robbins (1986) uses the term "direction sort" to indicate how some people just naturally "move away" while others "move toward." That is, some people are, by habit, more negative, seeing the glass as "half empty," while others see it as "half full."
- Wanting a quick fix. These people may just be anxious and wanting to jump to solutions, or they may be having difficulties appreciating the complexities in a given problem or opportunity.
- Wanting to let others know they're there and that their presence is going to be felt.
- Wanting to dabble in process. Some even see themselves as group process experts in their own right and want to try their hand at leading the workshop from the back of the room. They don't really mean any harm, but before you let them do your job, remember that most will share in the workshop success, but you'll fail alone. Back-of-the-room workshop leaders are with you "win or tie!"

An example

I was leading a strategy workshop with a group of senior managers of a manufacturing company. We had just finished a SWOT analysis (this term is explained in chapter six) and I was introducing an exercise to help the group identify the "strategic decisions" that needed to be made over the next few months. At this point a participant challenged the process. "Isn't this the same exercise as what we've just finished?" he asked. Then added, "I don't see how this is getting us anywhere." His tone suggested he might just be wanting others to take notice of his prominence in the group. His motivation, however, is not the issue here. And making it the issue, at this point, would be a big mistake.

I explained how the SWOT exercise we had just completed focused on sizing up the organization's environment, internally and externally. Then I explained that the group needed to get clear on specific actions and decisions needed to meet the challenges of this environment. I knew this participant wasn't convinced, but the rest of the group seemed ready to "push on." So we did. It's a mistake to think you need unanimous agreement every time you introduce a new process or exercise. As it happened, the exercise worked well, the participant who had been challenging the legitimacy of doing the exercise participated fully, and the group got a solid result.

Strategies for handling challenges to a process or exercise

First, accept challenge nondefensively, or, as I've heard John Jones say, tongue in cheek, "Just pretend you're not defensive!" Ask yourself if your "what" and "why" bridges were clear and understandable. The participant doing the challenging may have misunderstood what's coming next and why it's important.

Second, think of the first couple of challenges as being "in good faith." Give the participant the benefit of the doubt. Recognize the challenge may in fact be "indirect." There may be something under the surface that needs to be discussed.

Third, listen actively to the challenge and keep in mind that sometimes the participant challenging is right.

Fourth, "trust the group." Watch for signs of willingness or reluctance to "push on" with an exercise.

Fifth, don't think you need unanimity to proceed. Needing everyone in full agreement, all the time, means nothing happens most of the time!

Sixth, don't get sucked into debating or arguing definitions, process, steps, or the benefits of doing things a certain way. Discuss these briefly if it seems appropriate but don't spend a lot of time doing this.

Seventh, keep the term *equifinality* in mind. Maybe you can get the same result with another process, exercise, or approach.

Eight, if you're feeling really stuck, call a break. Tell the group you need to think about this for ten minutes. You might also ask who would be willing to join you in a corner to help you decide on the next steps.

End

Use Effective Questioning Skills

- Ask open and naive questions (e.g., sometimes a workshop leader can ask a naive question that would be suspect had a member of the group asked it).
- Use presuppositions when asking open questions.
- Use "I" statements and take care not to create defensiveness in the group.

Use Visual Aids

- Use a common text (e.g., flipchart, overhead, whiteboard).
- Use quick and visual methods (T charts, four-box models, sermonettes).

Bring Energy, Fun, and Confidence

- Like a comedian, a facilitator needs "good timing."
- Model spontaneous and productive interaction.
- Push, pull, tease, pontificate, praise, and joke with the group. It helps to produce results.
- Use humor to soften resistance to learning. Enjoy yourself and have fun.

Have a Theory of Approach, Process, and Structure

- Support risk takers.
- Control without dominating.
- Have structure but keep it flexible. Don't always stick to the rules.
- Sometimes you have to manipulate a little. The key is that your intentions are authentic, and respectful, and that you place participants' interests first.
- Watch out for the "felt needs trap."
- Don't make a point too clearly; let the group struggle. Nothing worth much ever comes for free. People remember the little points that they helped to discover and create.
- Be conscious of your process and where it's taking the group.
- Don't cling to tightly to your process or standard methods. If something's not working, call it and make a mid-course adjustment.
- Use lots of "what" and "why" bridges. Summarize and review and continually showing relevancy. Show the whole, then the pieces. Show big frames and simplify for the group.
- Don't lecture more than twenty minutes at any one time. People will go into a trance! Use brief "sermonettes" instead of long lectures, introducing minimum theory at appropriate times.
- Follow principles of giving and receiving good feedback.
- Think in systems terms versus in terms of simple cause and effect.

CO-LEADING A WORKSHOP

Co-leading a workshop (sometimes called team teaching or co-facilitating) takes more work and is sometimes more frustrating than leading on your own, but it can also be more rewarding and more fun. Whether co-leading is very satisfying, or very frustrating, has everything to do with how well you and your co-leader work together. When things work well there's a synergy between you. You and your co-leader add value to each other's work, and this value multiplies for participants. Like a jazz band that gets "jamming," spontaneous and creative approaches emerge, along with a harmony that gives everyone new insights, energy, and enjoyment.

Select a co-leader you can learn from, someone with more experience, different experience, or a different perspective from your own. Pay attention to values, particularly a shared value of caring about participants' learning. Other selection requirements include openness, trust, mutual respect, goodwill, a willingness to experiment, and a willingness to give each other detailed, honest, challenging, timely, and supportive feedback.

Don't try to make your co-leader a Xeroxed copy of yourself or adopt their style "carte blanche." Rather, you'll need to "roll with the punches" and adapt things on the run. So accept the ambiguity and risks associated with co-leading and trust that participants will learn more, your co-leader will learn more, and you'll learn more as a result of working together.

More preparation and coordination are required when co-leading versus working solo. It's comparable to running in a three legged race. It's slower than running on your own, but it's also more challenging, more involving, riskier, and a lot more fun. And if you have one or more of the following reasons for co-leading, it's a race well worth running.

The primary reasons for co-leading a workshop or training program are to:

1) Pool expertise and give participants more than one perspective.

2) Get experienced help.

3) Get feedback and help break your old habits.

4) Continuously upgrade and develop your training program or workshop.

5) Share the workload.

6) Train new workshop leaders.

1) To Pool Expertise and to Give Participants More Than One Perspective

Giving participants more than one perspective is tricky, but can be very rewarding. It's tricky because you and your co-leader don't want to get into or even give the impression that you are into a "who's right?" sort of game. It's rewarding because often there is no objective truth, or one best way, and different perspectives from experts allow participants the opportunity to compare and contrast these perspectives and arrive at their own conclusions.

Co-leaders can also provide "back up" in particularly difficult workshop situations (e.g., where there is a great deal of conflict in a group). And they can help not only with workshop or training-program delivery, but also with planning and design.

Finally, let's recognize that we're not all equally skilled at leading all aspects of a workshop or training program. Thus, you and your co-leader can help each other with your limitations while building on your strengths.

2) To Get Experienced Help

You may want to co-lead a workshop if you're an inexperienced workshop leader or if you've never seen a particular workshop before. Under these circumstances co-leading has obvious advantages, particularly if you co-lead with an experienced workshop leader. By sharing the workload, you only have to learn half as much workshop delivery at any one time. This helps take the pressure off you and increases confidence. In addition, you get guidance and feedback from your co-leader along the way, and you get to learn the workshop as you go. You also get to watch your co-leader in action and learn from his/her style and approach of leading a workshop or training program.

3) To Get Feedback and Help Break Your Old Habits

An experienced workshop leader may want to co-lead to get feedback on his/her habits and style of leading. Your co-leader doesn't even need to have a great deal of experience, as long as you're confident this person is capable of giving you clear, honest, and pointed feedback. Another option is having someone whose opinion you trust audit the workshop rather than co-lead, giving you structured and detailed feedback at the end of each session.

4) To Continuously Upgrade and Develop Your Workshop

Consider selecting your co-leaders carefully, with a view to having them provide you with an ongoing stream of suggestions for revising and improving your workshop.

How Murray developed a "world class" training program by working with co-leaders

Murray Hiebert, a colleague and friend of mine, worked with co-leaders for a couple of reasons: to continuously upgrade and develop his workshop and to share the workload.

Over the course of seven or eight years Murray has worked with dozens of different co-leaders on one particular workshop. If external consultants, his co-leaders are always experienced workshop leaders. If internals (i.e., employees in the organization that the workshop is being offered in) and not experienced as workshop leaders, Murray's co-leaders are nonetheless at senior professional levels in the organization.

Looking through experienced yet fresh eyes provided Murray with a continuous flow of new perspectives, approaches, and thoughts on his workshop structure, process, and materials. As a result, Murray's workshop has been continuously upgraded and today is a major success story, operating in organizations worldwide.

Throughout the many years of working with co-leaders, Murray made sacrifices. For example, he always took the extra time needed to fully inform, coordinate, and support his co-leaders, as they prepared to deliver a portion of the workshop. Murray also sacrificed some immediate income, choosing to compensate his co-leaders far more than necessary. His sacrifices paid off immensely. First, the workshop he created and developed is today helping thousands of people in organizations worldwide. Second, Murray collects much deserved royalties. (Note: The workshop in question is *Consulting Skills for Professionals*, now offered through the Novations Group, Inc. of Provo, Utah.)

5) To Share the Workload

Some workshop designs ask a great deal from workshop leaders. They require you to work with several subgroups at once, while setting up for a new session, while coaching individuals who get stuck, and on and on. In these situations co-leading isn't just a luxury; two people are needed just to get the basic job done.

6) To Train New Workshop Leaders

Co-leading is the best way to coach and train new workshop leaders. It gives them "hands on" experience and immediate and frequent feedback. At the same time, you, as an experienced workshop leader, are providing them with a model of workshop leadership to learn from and adapt to their own style.

A time when working with a co-leader seemed like more of a necessity than a luxury

I had been working with an executive group (vice presidents and their CEO) over the course of a year (something like seven or eight consulting days in total). Over this time I'd tried a number of approaches (e.g., one-on-one coaching, day long workshops, recommending a VP be moved or fired, discussing leadership issues, clarifying accountabilities) to help them manage what was an extreme dysfunction in their group. I can't give you all the details because it would be a book in itself. Suffice it to say that the conflict in this executive group was as bad as it gets. It was more like warfare. Although it was covert and subtle, it had become very personal and was even played out through the middle management ranks in the organization. Not only that, other companies in their industry had "gotten wind of it," and this was hurting the organization's image.

There weren't any villains here. The members of this executive group were all bright, hardworking, dedicated people. As a group, however, they were humorless, and many were full of anger toward other members. Needless to say, anger and stress make people a little stupid. Some of the things these people did to each other were vicious. Little wonder that the tension in this group was like electricity in the air. People would actually be pale at some of our meetings. Two were physically sick. Others were going through problems at home. One had even developed a nervous tick. At least two in the group were actively looking for other employment. Both had approached the CEO asking for severance packages. He said "no."

Finally, out of desperation, and with the CEO's agreement, I asked a colleague of mine to team up with me on this contract. Together we waded back into this work. Over the next six months we logged something like another six or seven consulting days. Finally, things started to happen. One VP was fired. That improved things a little. Next, we (my colleague and I) moved the group toward "fessing up" to their problems. Now, they at least admitted - within their executive group - that these wars were going on, that as a team they were only functioning at about 30% effectiveness, that they weren't willing to share information and consult with each other, that they weren't willing to learn in front of each other, that things had been set up as "win-lose," and so on. A third "minor victory" involved getting the group to agree the situation was untenable and needed to change within a few months at the most. Prior to that, they had wanted to deny or downplay the harm that was being done.

What made this work so difficult (as if you haven't heard enough)

Each time we'd get near a sensitive issue the group seemed to collude, intellectualize, and argue that things were better now, and, as a result, we needed to avoid discussing these sensitive issues (this is known in consulting circles as a "flight into health"). The CEO, although well intentioned, was very much a part of this unspoken and largely unconscious collusion. The one thing they seemed capable of agreeing on as a group was that they didn't want to work the "real" issues. Normally, one of my guiding principles is "trust the group." That is, allow the group to lead and steer the work being done. Trust that they know what needs to be done, how they work best together, and so on. With this group, this guiding principle became a barrier. It kept people safe but it also held progress back.

With this group I needed to take a stand and push hard against their unwillingness to risk, even though, at a point, this becomes an ethical issue. That is, a workshop leader doesn't have the right to demand participants take risks they are unwilling to take (i.e., you don't have the right to demand that people take part in an exercise, let alone one they see as unreasonably risky and threatening).

The value of a co-leader: A specific example

It was early in a planned day-long workshop when one VP spoke up saying, "I have exclusive authority to act in some areas of this organization! The fact that these actions affect other executives, and other departments, doesn't mean I need to consult with them." (This particular VP had a lot of good qualities but emotional maturity wasn't one of them. On occasion he displayed a kind of "peacock-like" behavior, wanting others to admire his magnificent plume. This was one of those occasions.) At that point I challenged the attitude of "exclusivity." My co-leader jumped in and challenged as well. This gave me confidence to pursue things a little further. We digressed briefly to talk about the difference between a problem to be solved and a polarity to be managed. I carry many models around in my head, and I was thinking of Barry Johnson's (1992) model of polarity management at the time.[9] I pointed out that the group needed to see the issue of exclusive/inclusive (i.e., individual/team, me/we) as a polarity to be managed, not a problem to be solved in a linear, dichotomous way. They agreed, but two VP's in the group refused to move off their positions of having "exclusive rights." We then spent ten minutes in our familiar and dysfunctional dance, intellectualizing back and forth. I called a break and was thinking, "It's time to get back to the agenda."

At the break, the CEO came up to me and said, "We're on to something here. I want you to pursue this polarity." I agreed but wasn't sure how to proceed. I knew the group would reject discussing this further. My co-leader, as I knew he would, had several suggestions. We decided on a process that would see each VP receiving feedback from the group about how they saw him/her along the continuum or polarity of "exclusivity/inclusively." We would also insist on specific examples and descriptions, not just evaluation. This would get at some fundamental problems in the group.

Introducing this process after the break got the anticipated rejection from the group. Comments like, "This is too sensitive to discuss" abounded. Here's where my co-leader made all the difference. He kept me from being ganged up on. (I was at the front of the room facilitating at the time.) He was able to articulate the need for the group to take this risk. Finally the group agreed, although reluctantly. One member of the group opted out. We did the exercise. It was stressful for the group, but it worked great! In the debriefing most commented that it "felt like progress." The member who had opted out, having sat through the whole thing taking notes, mostly just criticized the process and how my co-leader and I had carried it out.

Looking back, without my co-leader, I think I would have been "pushed off" this process by the group. I don't believe in forcing people to do things, and we didn't use force. What we did use, however, was pressure, a close cousin of "force." Together, my co-leader and I stood our ground. It resulted in movement forward.

Other benefits of co-leading that I experienced in this particular contract

In addition to the above example, I have experienced a number of "ongoing benefits" by co-leading in this difficult situation. These include:

- Developing strategies together before meeting with the client group.
- Sounding out ideas with each other during workshops with the client group.
- Sharing and building on each other's ideas and models.
- Supporting each other during and after difficult meetings with the client.
- Teaming up to resist client demands to retreat from the "real" problem.
- Giving each other feedback on our workshop leadership behaviors.
- Doing "reality checks" with each other (e.g., "Am I imaging things or was Susan putting Fred down when she ...").
- Modeling teamwork for the client group (i.e., my co-leader and I working together modeled cooperation, trust, and being willing to "learn in public").
- Keeping each other sane during very difficult meetings with the client group.

End

TEACHING A SPECIFIC JOB OR TASK

The following is a little unadvertised feature of this book and will help you teach a specific job or task either "one on one" or to very small groups (e.g., two or three trainees). (Note: The term "trainee" is used in this section to connote on-the-job training as opposed to participation in a workshop or training program.)

This four step process outlines an approach to organizing and teaching a job in a systematic way, ensuring key learning points are emphasized. It's aligned with the natural learning process described in chapter two. It explains both the "why" and the "how" of a task and provides opportunity for practice, feedback, and more practice, until the trainee is capable of doing the job without direct supervision.

Preparing and Beginning

Begin by analyzing each job action and then planning your instruction. First impressions are important. You need to show you're organized and interested in trainees' learning, so have the workplace ready when trainees arrive.

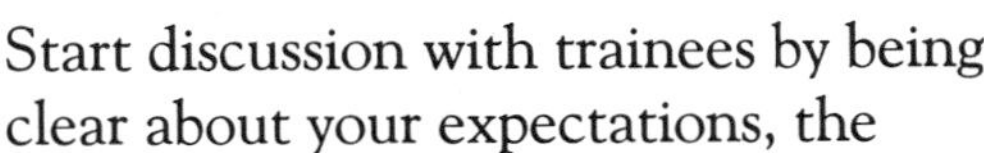

Start discussion with trainees by being clear about your expectations, the learning content, and how your instruction will proceed. Provide context. That is,

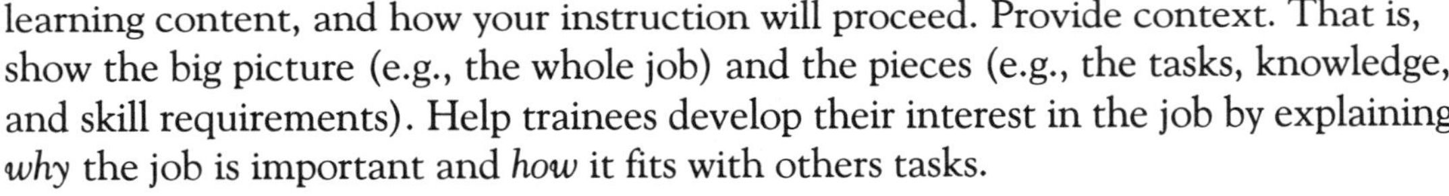

show the big picture (e.g., the whole job) and the pieces (e.g., the tasks, knowledge, and skill requirements). Help trainees develop their interest in the job by explaining *why* the job is important and *how* it fits with others tasks.

Use trainees past experience as a starting point and get them asking questions. You also need to ask questions of them. Ensure trainees are learning ready and understand how their past experience relates to the job they're about to learn.

Demonstrating

Before demonstrating the job, provide trainees with a checklist of steps that allow them to follow your demonstration precisely. As you demonstrate, guide them through the checklist and describe which steps are critical. Ensure trainees understand why each step is important, what it does, and the consequences of not performing it properly.

Only three to five new ideas should be introduced at a time, challenging but not overwhelming trainees. Thus, demonstrations should be long enough to provide a sense of progress, but generally should not exceed twenty or thirty minutes.

When demonstrating, perform the job from the same vantage point or position that the trainee will have when he/she performs. Repeat each action slowly and separately, describing each step while performing. Use simple words in your descriptions, and don't assume trainees know the meaning of technical terms.

To ensure trainees have retained important information, perform the task a second time, having *them* describe the procedure as *you* perform. Trainees should tell you what to do, when to do it, and why it's done. Throughout this process use questions to direct, emphasize, get reactions, and develop interest in the task.

Let Trainees Practice

For the first practice, have each trainee perform the task while you describe it. Next, ask the trainees to perform the task without assistance. Tell them you don't expect perfection the first time around and don't ask too many questions, or help too much, while they're performing the task. Correct any errors immediately. Finally, have trainees perform the task a third time. This time, ask questions of them as they perform. Also, to ensure trainees understand "why" as well as "how" to perform a task have them give you reasons behind each step.

If a trainee is slow to learn, check your training methods in case there is a better way to explain the job. Don't blame; simply describe what you see happening and ask the trainee to explain. If trainees resist, find out why. If their reasons make sense, get them to help develop new methods of completing the task. Trainees will be more receptive to a procedure they helped create.

Be tactful and constructive if trainees make mistakes. Apologize for not explaining the job clearly, particularly for their first couple of mistakes. Putting trainees at ease minimizes the risk of their feeling defensive. If, after explaining a job a couple of times the trainee still hasn't understood, it's time to challenge directly but tactfully. Use the "two good faith replies" method described in chapter sixteen. Thus, after explaining twice, deal with the fact that the trainee is not learning as an issue in itself.

Let Trainees Perform

At this point trainees have gained basic competence and confidence to perform the job or task on their own. However, they may not be able to perform at full speed or handle unique or unpredictable problems efficiently. Before putting them on their own, tell them where they can get help, if needed. Needless to say, where possible, you should continue to coach as trainees develop their new skill. Be generous with praise when they do things right, or even approximately right. And when they make mistakes, help them immediately. Help them to think through what they could be doing differently and to decide on an optimal course of action.

Blanchard and Lorber (1984) have their own way of describing this process. They sum it up in the following five clear steps.[10]

1) Tell the trainee what to do
2) Show him/her how to do it
3) Let him/her try
4) Observe his/her performance
5) When appropriate, praise progress or redirect

CONCLUSION

Summary

Presenting, facilitating, and leading are comprehensive packages of skills essential to conducting workshops and training programs.

Presenting

Three guidelines are suggested for presenting: prepare, relax, and be yourself. Keep presentations brief; any longer than fifteen or twenty minutes and the audience's attention will wane. Start with a "hook." Use humor, stories, or controversial statements to get the group's attention. Most people learn visually, so charts, overheads, and other visuals are essential. Pay attention to participants' nonverbal signals when presenting, and remember that your body language is important, so avoid slouching, pacing, and nervous mannerisms.

Adjust your presentation to the experience level of the group. If the group has little or no experience with a given topic, it's important to "win them over." Help them become learning ready by explaining *why* the information is important. Start with the big picture; then provide the information in small helpings, being careful not to overload participants. Even if the group has some experience with a topic, don't assume they're learning ready. When presenting to experts, acknowledge their expertise and take care not to talk down to them. Experts are usually motivated to learn more about a topic in their field, so learning readiness shouldn't be a problem. Include experts in the discussion as active participants; they have a lot to offer.

Involving participants in a lecture or presentation reduces their boredom and contributes greatly to their learning. Common sense, as well as experience, dictates that active, involved participants learn more than they would by sitting and listening passively. Encourage and ask questions and guide note taking. Miniquizzes, illustrating the presentation with examples and stories, brainstorming, and structuring the presentation to solve a specific problem or question all keep participants active and involved.

Leading and Facilitating

Five areas of facilitating and leading are discussed focusing on action and results, facilitating versus leading, becoming a trusted source, adult-learning principles, and other facilitation tips, tricks, and techniques.

First, focus on action and results. This involves moving quickly and keeping the focus on content. Aim for incremental gain. End the facilitation process with action steps.

Second, facilitators need to lead. The process must accomplish something tangible, and it must meet participants' learning and work needs. Offer the group substance and content and make your own agenda explicit.

Third, contract outcomes, processes, and roles. Recontract if feedback indicates it's necessary, and hold participants accountable for their own learning and accomplishing agreed upon outcomes.

Fourth, become a trusted source. Be authentic and direct with the group, avoid taking positions, deal directly with resistance, and respect people's boundaries (e.g., their right to pass on a question). Don't judge or evaluate. Model behavior you want the group to adopt, use your power to confront participants when necessary, and stay objective.

Finally, practice adult-learning principles. Recognize and reward and build participants' confidence. The leader's attitude is key. Don't let your ego get in your way. Understand that learning and change are a tough, unpredictable road. Participants need to be challenged, but they also need plenty of support.

Co-leading a Workshop

Co-leading a workshop isn't any easier than leading solo, but it offers a multitude of advantages if done properly. A co-leader offers a helping hand, another set of eyes and ears, and another perspective. Co-leaders bring a fresh perspective with them that helps you see what was otherwise invisible or outside your consciousness (i.e., a "blind spot"). When selecting a co-leader, be sure that you can work well together and that the person is trustworthy, competent, and cares about participants' learning.

There are several reasons for co-leading. First is to get a second perspective. Second, if you're relatively inexperienced as a workshop leader, co-leading is an excellent way to get experience and support. Working with another workshop leader takes some of the pressure off and gives you an example to learn from. A third reason for co-leading is to get feedback on your performance and your habits, giving you a better idea of your strengths and weaknesses as a workshop leader. Fourth, co-leading helps you continuously upgrade and develop your workshop.

Fifth, co-leaders share the workload. Some workshops simply have too much going on at once for one workshop leader to handle. Sixth, co-leading is an excellent way to train new workshop leaders.

Teaching a Job

The first step in teaching a specific job or task is preparing and beginning. Be organized and have your instruction planned before trainees arrive. Start discussion by explaining your expectations, what you will be covering, how the job relates to other jobs and tasks, and your leadership and coaching process. Ensure trainees are learning ready before you begin providing information.

The second step involves a brief (twenty to thirty minutes at the most) demonstration of the task. Follow a checklist of steps and explain why each step is important. Demonstrate the job twice. The first time describe the procedure as you demonstrate. The second time have trainees describe the procedure as you demonstrate.

Next, have trainees perform the task. First, have them perform while you describe the steps. Second, have them perform without your guidance. As trainees perform a third time, question them to ensure they understand the *why* as well as the *how* of each step. Take responsibility for each trainee's first couple of mistakes, but if these persist, ask the trainee tactfully and directly what he/she thinks is causing his/her difficulty.

The fourth and final step in teaching a specific job or task is having trainees perform in real time, on the job. Ensure they know how and where they can get help when needed.

Checklist

Structuring a Presentation	*Adjusting Your Presentation to the Experience Level of the Group*
• Start with a controversial statement, observation, quotation, or question • Use a little humor • Get the group's attention fast • Use examples, anecdotes, analogies, and statistics • Have a logical flow • Use "what" and "why" bridges • Build in reviews and summaries • Use handouts • Keep presentations to under twenty minutes • Avoid passive (straight lecture) sessions • Call minibreaks • Ask the group questions • Use buzz groups, neighbor discussions, and brief assignments *The Nonverbals of Presenting* • Avoid pacing • Act relaxed • Stand to command attention; sit to leave the limelight • Use gestures and noises • Avoid nervous mannerisms • Avoid overusing phrases	*When group members are relatively unfamiliar with your topic* • Help the group become ready to listen • Don't assume they understand anything, even the basics • Start by showing the context • Don't assume they'll be able to connect the topic to their needs on their own • Use clear and uncluttered visuals • Emphasize key points • Speak in plain language • Review and summarize often • Take care not to overload the group *When the group has some but not a lot of topic knowledge* • Check the group's motivation • Assess the group's level of knowledge • Get direction from the group • Pay attention to nonverbals • Ask clarifying questions • Ensure you're not telling them things they already know or talking over their heads • The group already has some information; you fill in gaps

Twelve Ways to Involve Participants When Presenting or Lecturing

1) Use visual aids
2) Ask the group questions
3) Guide note taking
4) Encourage discussion
5) Ask participants to write out their answer or reaction
6) Use polling
7) Structure the presentation to solve a specific problem or question
8) Get the group "brainstorming"
9) Tell stories and provide examples
10) Use a "miniquiz"
11) Have participant use *"I heard ... and I wonder ..."* statements
12) Guide follow up

Presenting Checklist

- Structure your message, step by step
- Speak clearly
- Use a brisk pace
- Use simple statements
- Relax, take a breath, be yourself
- Don't tell when you can show (e.g., demonstrations, visuals)
- Use visual aids (e.g., a common text such as an overhead transparency or a structured handout)
- Talk with people
- Check for understanding and keep the group involved (e.g., ask questions, poll the group)
- Watch the group's attention span (e.g., keep lecture time below twenty minutes)

When you're talking to experts

- You don't need to motive the group
- Recognize the group's expertise
- Invite their participation
- Start with the "big picture"
- Explain how you're going to cover the material
- Avoid details
- Be brief, and involve the group

Leading and Facilitating

Focus on action and results

- Move quickly to content and keep the focus on content
- Aim for incremental gain
- End with action steps

Facilitate and lead

- Pure facilitation is of little value
- Facilitators need to lead
- Offer substance and content
- It's OK to have your own agenda

Contract outcomes, process, and roles

- Contract focus and outcomes
- Contract process
- Continually solicit feedback and recontract if necessary
- Contract expectations, roles, and accountability

Become a trusted source

- Be authentic
- Avoid taking positions
- Deal directly with resistance
- Help people avoid feeling defensive
- Respect people's boundaries
- Don't judge or evaluate
- Model the behavior you want
- Be confident and reliable
- Confront when necessary
- Use your power
- Maintain your objectivity

- Review and summarize if the presentation is longer than twenty minutes, if content is complex, or if the group is unfamiliar with the content
- Make lots of eye contact
- Use variety in your voice
- Move around
- Use your whole body (e.g., arm gestures)
- Be a little controversial
- Use humor (it's particularly important in long lectures)
- Practice out loud once or twice

Adult-learning principles

- Motivate participants
- Recognize and reward participants
- Build confidence in clients
- Set the climate for learning and change
- Understand that learning and change are neither smooth nor predictable
- Attitudes, beliefs, and outlooks
- Practice adult-learning principles
- Park your ego at the door

Other facilitation tips, tricks, and techniques

- Be organized
- Use techniques sparingly
- Give clear and simple directions
- Use effective questioning skills
- Use visual aids
- Bring energy, fun, and confidence
- Have a theory of approach

Co-leading a Workshop

1) Offer participants more than one perspective
2) To get experienced help
3) To get feedback and help break your old habits
4) To continuously upgrade and develop your workshop
5) To share the workload
6) To train new workshop leaders

Teaching a Specific Job or Task

- Preparing and beginning
- Demonstrating
- Let trainees practice
- Let trainees perform

End

Exercise

Assessing Your Skills As a Presenter

List two or three key points for each of the following three questions:

1) What are your strengths as a presenter?

2) What are your biggest concerns as a presenter?

3) What things can you do to overcome, or least prepare for and lessen, these concerns?

Exercise

Your Leadership and Facilitation Experience

1) What's the most successful group facilitation or workshop leadership you ever led?

2) What specifically did you do to help the group get results?

3) What are your three strongest attributes as workshop or training-program leader?

4) What's the *least* successful group facilitation or workshop you ever led?

5) In hindsight, what could you have done differently to improve this result?

6) What one or two areas would you like to improve as a workshop and training-program leader?

Notes

[1]Boettinger, H.M. (1969). Moving mountains: The art of letting others see things your way. New York, NY: Macmillan, p. 12.
[2]Burke Guild, P. (April, 1983). How to involve learners in your lectures. *Training*, pp. 43-44.
[3]Bellman, G.M. (1990). The consultant's calling: Bring who you are to what you do. San Francisco, CA: Jossey-Bass.
[4]Covey, S.R. (1989). The 7 habits of highly effective people: Powerful lessons in personal change. New York, NY: Simon & Schuster.
[5]John Jones operates a consulting firm, Organizational Universe Systems, out of San Diego, California.
[6]1) Argyris, C., & Schon, D.A. (1974). Theory in practice: Increasing professional effectiveness. San Francisco, CA: Jossey-Bass. 2) Argyris, C., & Schon, D.A. (1978). Organizational learning: A theory of action perspective. Reading, MA: Addison-Wesley.
[7]Berne, E. (1964). Games people play: The psychology of human relationships. New York, NY: Ballantine.
[8]Bellman, G.M. (1990). The consultant's calling: Bring who you are to what you do. San Francisco, CA: Jossey-Bass.
[9]Johnson, B. (1992). Polarity management: Identifying and managing unsolvable problems. Amherst, MA: HRD Press.
[10]Blanchard, K., & Lorber, R. (1984). Putting the one minute manager to work. New York, NY: William Morrow, p. 36.

Chapter 16

Managing Participation in a Workshop

INTRODUCTION

The railways were one of the first organizations in North America to introduce and formalize management principles and structures. For example, as Alfred Chandler (1988) points out, the first organization charts originated with the railways in the mid-1800's.[1] But no matter how many rules and policies they put in place, they never could run a railway completely by the book. Hard nosed management will likely always have it's place, but a wide range of what are called "soft skills" are also needed. These include leadership skills (e.g., managing conflict, negotiating, coaching) and a range of important human qualities such as caring, empathy, and sensitivity to others.

It's strange that we refer to the old production management skills as *hard* and the more people and leadership oriented skills as *soft*. In fact, practicing production management is fairly straightforward. Mostly it involves following well-established rules and guidelines, although many of these are now badly outdated, particularly in relation to supervising knowledge workers. My point is this: Based on the skill and complexity required in practice, the old production management skills should be called *easy* and the new leadership, relationship, and people oriented skills for managing knowledge workers should be called *hard*.

Active participation is the lifeblood of workshops and training programs, and ensuring it occurs requires both management and leadership, both *hard* and *soft* skills (or, if you buy my arguments above, both *easy* and *hard* skills). Without participation, a workshop is inanimate and dead in the water. This just can't be stressed enough - *participants learn best, and accomplish more, when actively involved.* Passive learning just doesn't cut it. Successful workshop and training-program leaders get groups active, thinking, and emotionally as well as intellectually involved. Involvement allows participants to contribute more of their background and experience to the workshop or training program. This increases learning in training programs and improves results in workshops.

Like anything valuable, participation isn't easy to come by. It must be planned, sought out, and earned. So schedule time for and continually encourage and support participation. But remember, participation needs to be guided and at times even controlled. If completely unchecked, participation can become too much of a good thing, getting out of hand when emotions run high. That is, overly animated participation, discussion, and debate can result in friction, if not open conflict between participants. It's imperative that workshop and training program leaders know how to manage conflict and how to turn disagreement into constructive exchange.

This chapter covers

- The nature of workshop control.
- Managing workshop time.
- Using reinforcement in a workshop.
- Watching for nonverbal cues.
- Valuing and managing differences.
- Models for surfacing and handling participation problems.

The bottom line is that leadership shows up in the inspired action of others. We traditionally have assessed leaders themselves. But maybe we should assess leadership by the degree to which people around leaders are inspired.
- Jack Weber

MANAGING A WORKSHOP - WHO'S AT THE CONTROLS?

Someone needs to be at the controls as a workshop steams down the track. Ultimately someone has to decide when to speed up, slow down, take a spur rail, drop off a couple of boxcars, and so on. This involves the use of power.

What needs to be controlled in a workshop? Certainly not what people learn. You can't control that which can only be perceived by others. But a degree of control can and needs to be exercised around tangibles like workshop or training-program structure, process, behaviors, direction, schedules, and results.

The fundamental concept in social science is power, in the same sense in which energy is the fundamental concept in physics.
- Bertrand Russell

Two diametrically opposed factors come into play when discussing "control."

First, overmanaging a workshop can prevent breakthroughs. Significant accomplishments in workshops can result when a workshop leader shows flexibility, empathy, and sensitivity, as opposed to sticking to his/her workshop plan or agenda. Innovation, in particular, usually results from a mistake or detour rather than from a carefully planned workshop process. Innovation rarely happens according to a plan. Rather it happens when people are learning ready, at ease, and open to novel ideas.

Second, unless resources are unlimited and "time is no object," some control of workshop structure, process, and direction is needed. Somebody has to coordinate and keep the workshop moving toward reasonable and agreed outcomes and make sure this is happening in a cost and time efficient manner. To quote Jim Rohn (1995), "You need to make meaningful progress in reasonable time."[2]

How does one reconcile these two competing needs? The first makes "control" a touchy word with many workshop leaders. The second makes it necessary. But don't get caught up in definitions. Who cares if you call it controlling, managing, coordinating, organizing, influencing, or the exercise of power. The bottom line is that a workshop leader can't abdicate accountability for helping the group achieve a reasonable result in a reasonable period of time.

> ***Men fundamentally can no more get along without direction than they can without eating, drinking, and sleeping.***
> ***- Charles de Gaulle***

What constitutes effective control? What constitutes over- or undercontrol? When, and under what circumstances, should a workshop leader exercise control? How does a workshop leader exercise control without being seen to manipulate or engineer consent? The answer to these questions is "it depends." Like leadership in general, effective control often depends on a number of circumstances at play in each unique situation.

Principles of Control

The group, through their participation, grants the workshop leader the right to influence and control certain aspects of the workshop (e.g., workshop process). The ability of a workshop leader to exercise this control is based on three things: 1) having agreed outcomes in place, 2) maintaining the trust and confidence of the group, and 3) exercising control in a caring, respectful, open, and reasonable manner. This includes making your process visible and consulting participants on issues of timing, structure, and leadership style.

The following six principles help explain the nature of a workshop leader's control.

1) *It's temporary*. Control is neither an entitlement, nor is it forever. It pertains only to a specific process for a particular time and task. Just as a harbor pilot temporarily takes the helm while the captain stands by, a workshop leader, having special knowledge of the waters the group needs to navigate, temporarily takes charge as the group struggles to accomplish a given task. The workshop leader knows this is not his/her ship and that he/she is there to help the captain and crew. He/she also knows he/she needs to maintain their trust to be allowed to help and to be allowed to use his/her special knowledge of these waters.

2) *It's by consent and for a purpose*. Control is not the raison d'être of a workshop leader; it's only an element of workshop leadership. That is, the type of control and structure required to lead a workshop requires moving beyond ego. Control does entail the exercise of power, but this is control with *consent* and for an agreed *purpose*. It's not about exercising a workshop leader's ego.

> ***Leadership is the wise use of power. ... Power is the currency of leaders.***
> ***- Warren Bennis and Burt Nanus***

3) *It's about the ability to influence*. Workshop control isn't binary; it's not something you have or don't have. Rather it's a matter of influence. A high degree of influence is only possible in the context of agreed purpose, participant trust and confidence, and demonstrated caring. Lose any of these and influence declines. Lose enough influence and control breaks down.

4) *It's a power everyone can exert*. Ultimately everybody influences the direction of a workshop. Consensus predominates. That doesn't mean that some decisions won't be by command, voting, or require unanimity. It does mean that, all things being equal, a workshop is about as close to pure democracy as you can get. So how do participants vote in this democracy? In two ways. One, they can either "switch on" or "tune out." After all, learning is voluntary. Thus, they can choose to be active and exert influence, they can go along with whatever the group decides, or they can role play participation. That is, they can quit and stay. Two, although it takes courage, they can vote with their feet. These are adults. Adults can walk out and not come back.

> ***Power is defined ... as the potential ability to influence behavior, to change the course of events, to overcome resistance, and to get people to do things they would not otherwise do. Politics and influence are the processes, the actions, the behaviors through which this potential power is utilized and realized.***
> ***- Jeffrey Pferrer***

5) *It's a duty that can't be abdicated*. The fact that the group disagrees with a workshop leader and demands a different process or structure doesn't excuse the workshop leader from accountability. You have to help organize the group for commitment and action. So, even if the group decides to ignore your suggestions, you're nonetheless accountable for pointing out the consequences of their decision. A workshop leader must ensure that purpose and outcomes are always clear and foremost in participants' minds.

6) *It's possible only when in "sync" with participants' needs and interests*. Rarely do participants reject a workshop leader's exercise of leadership, control, or authority. What they reject is authority and structure that are perceived as arbitrary, unfair, inappropriate, or out of "sync" with their needs and interests. Harrison Owen (1991) writes, "As long as structure provides a useful highway, upon which spirit may travel, all is well and good. But when the spirit is forced to go in unintentional directions, it usually goes off the road."[3]

Note: Control, as discussed above, needs to be understood in the context of several other parts of this book including the nature of leadership and facilitation as discussed in chapter fifteen and in the section titled "Contracting Roles" in chapter eleven. This concerns leader and participant roles, rights, and responsibilities during a workshop or training program.

RUNNING ON TIME - TIME MANAGEMENT

Before the buses and airlines took over their dominant position in the market, travel by rail was considered "the only way to go." Back then the railroads were obsessed with "running on time." Today they mostly handle freight. Freight doesn't get nearly as upset if it's a little late, so "running on time" has lost a lot of its luster. At any rate, this isn't a suggestion that workshop leaders should be obsessed with *time*. Rather, it's a recommendation to be conscious of managing time in a flexible way.

The downside of not managing time well in a workshop is that participants may be deprived of learning content when time runs out. For example, ending a workshop properly requires a review and summary and several other steps that take time. Poor time management can result in a truncated ending, and this can mean a loss of value for participants.

This section covers:

A) Tips for managing workshop time

B) Tips for handling digressions

Time is nature's way of keeping everything from all happening at once.
- Anonymous

A) Tips for Managing Workshop Time

Time management is particularly important for training programs. Not that workshops have all the time in the world, but rather that training programs are usually a little more predictable, have their exercises and content more laid out, and have a greater need to stay close to schedule.

Nothing can make the clock strike for the hours that are passed.
- George Noel Gordon (Lord Byron)

Nothing is so dear and precious as time.
- French proverb

If your clock watching gets too obvious, it tends to distract the group. Our culture has funny norms regarding looking at the time when you're in a group. For example, if someone is talking and sees you looking at the time, they may misinterpret this as not listening, wanting to move on, or disinterest. So, if you don't have a clock at the back of the room where you can see it easily, put your watch on the table in front of you. That way, you can keep track of time at a glance without distracting participants.

Things which matter most must never be at the mercy of things which matter least.
- Goethe

Regardless of time pressures, don't move to a new topic before participants have learned the current one. When in doubt, solicit questions from participants, even if you are behind schedule. You need to know exactly where participants stand with the learning content before moving on. Don't make the mistake of finishing the workshop regardless of whether participants do or not. Be more concerned with achieving agreed upon outcomes than with covering the material or getting through the agenda.

B) Tips for Managing Training-Program and Workshop Time

Managing Time before the Workshop or Training Program Begins

The shortest way to do many things is to do only one thing at a time.
- Richard Cecil

- Come to the workshop or training program with your planning and preparation done. Have times scheduled on your training plan, especially the first few times you deliver a given training program or workshop.
- When you plan the agenda, build in a little extra time as a cushion.
- Pre-write as many flipcharts as you can before the workshop or training program begins.

Managing the "Big Picture"

- Keep the workshop or training-program outcomes posted for easy reference. Make sure you are working on what's important, not just on what seems urgent or has "popped up" in the group. Remember the 80/20 rule. Focus on the 20% of activities that will yield 80% of the outcomes the group is seeking.
- Remind the group, when necessary, that they are spending a extra long time on a given topic. Ask if this is OK, and caution that it may mean giving up another part of the agenda later in the workshop. Recontract "on the spot" if necessary.

- Work with the group to reframe problems when necessary. Be sure the problem has been defined properly before the group dives into the details.

Managing the Details

- "Park" issues if the group gets stuck. Promise to think about solutions between sessions.
- Only use "ice breakers" or "simulation exercises" if they're absolutely necessary.
- Cut off and redirect nonproductive activities as soon as possible (e.g., off-topic digressions).
- Arrange the workshop or training program so that there are no, or very few, interruptions (e.g., no phones, an administrative assistant to take messages and distribute these at the breaks).
- Review and summarize periodically to keep things moving.

Managing Time Around Breaks and Lunches

- Pay attention to the group's habits around starting on time (likely a result of their organization's culture) and make a few adjustments to minimize "time wasters." For example, if participants always come back five minutes late from breaks, then make the breaks five minutes instead of ten minutes long and expect them back in ten minutes anyway. Don't be secretive about this. Tell the group, tongue in cheek, "This is only a five minute break, so I'll see you back here in ten minutes or less, OK!"
- Remind stragglers, and the group as a whole, directly but tactfully, about the importance of being "on time." Make it quid pro quo basis. Promise to finish on time if they arrive back on time after breaks. (Participants tend to throw training-program schedules off first thing in the morning, after breaks, and after lunch.) Say something like, "We'll be able to end on time if we're able to start on time after the breaks." This might well be accepted as a ground rule by the group.
- Call shorter breaks, for example five minutes, as opposed to longer breaks of fifteen minutes. That way participants don't have time to go back to their offices and get involved in something else. (Incidentally, shorter and more frequent breaks help rejuvenate a group in the late afternoons, particularly on about the third or fourth day of an intensive workshop.)
- To ensure everyone is clear, just before calling a break write something like this on a flipchart in large bold letters, *Please be back at 3:15*. Leave this visible during the break.

- If asking the group to be back at a certain time doesn't seem to be working (e.g., "please be back at 3:15"), try asking them to be back in a given time (e.g., ten minutes). It's a long shot, but this might get around participants' watches being set at different times. The point is, if what you're doing isn't working, keep trying different approaches.
- If you know a restaurant is slow and you're in a hurry, talk with the restaurant manager. Ask him/her if it's possible to have the group in and out within an hour.

Managing Time During Subgroup Activities

Learn to pause ... or nothing worthwhile will catch up to you.
- Doug King

- Don't let subgroup exercises go on too long.
- Give subgroups "two minute warnings" before you end an exercise. This way they know to "speed it up."
- Use subgroups to divide tasks and get them done quickly. Subgroup results can later be reviewed quickly with the group as a whole.

Involving Participants to Help Manage Time

- Deputize participants to help you do things to save time. For example, two people may be needed to write on flipcharts during a group brainstorming session.
- When the group gets stuck, ask a participant or small group of participants to take a task as an assignment. Ask them to work the problem between sessions and come back with a recommendation.

Providing Leadership

- Practice the discipline of staying close to the agenda and its allotted times. Model good time management yourself. Be a good influence on the group.

The spoken word perishes; the written word remains.
- Latin proverb

- Manage problem participation quickly and effectively. This can prevent a great deal of wasted time.

C) Tips for Handling Digressions

Digressions can be "on-topic" or "off-topic." The former are often valuable. They build on what's being discussed; the latter pretty much just eat up valuable time.

Workshop and training-program leaders are themselves one of the biggest digressors. They tend to talk too much. So, minimize your talking time and keep *outcomes* in mind. Avoid time consuming details. Don't major in minor things, or as Stephen Covey (1989) says, "Don't let the urgent things drive out the important things."[4]

On-Topic Digressions

On-topic digressions are comments or stories that are related to the purpose of the workshop. They are in addition to the planned agenda. They may arise at the wrong time in a workshop, or alternatively the digression (e.g., a story, a request, a suggestion for an exercise, a contrary opinion) can't be accommodated when it arises for some other reason (e.g., equipment availability, materials need to be prepared beforehand).

Anticipate and build in time for these digressions. They add life to the learning content by way of stories, examples, and analogies. What makes them particularly valuable is that they come from participants. They are a clear indicator that participants are involved, motivated, and sharing responsibility for the workshop. Thus, it's important that you do everything possible to honor participants' stories, process suggestions, examples, requests, and so on.

For those times when it's not possible to immediately act on participants' on-topic digressions, have a single flipchart page hanging on the wall labeled "parking lot." Use this to record, or "park," participant input that is on-topic but best discussed at another time in the workshop. The power of the "parking lot" is that it also parks emotion. Thus, by recording a participant's question or concern on the "parking lot," and promising to deal with it later, a participant can emotionally "let go," knowing that his/her concern has been respected, and will be discussed later in the workshop. Needless to say the participant needs to *trust* that you will indeed deal with his/her suggestion later in the workshop.

It's absolutely essential that you anticipate and build time into the workshop design and agenda for on-topic digressions.

As you go through life you are going to have many opportunities to keep your mouth shut. Take advantage of all of them.
- James Dent

Finally, think of on-topic digressions as clear evidence that the workshop is meaningful and relevant to the group, that participants are integrating the new learning material with their own experiences, and that learning is occurring at a significant level. In other words, on-topic digressions aren't digressions at all. Rather they're the "real meat" of a workshop. So why call them digressions? Answer: for three reasons. First, to emphasize the importance of this type of participant input and involvement.

Second, to stress the importance of anticipating on-topic digressions and building flexibility into the agenda to accommodate them. Third, to distinguish them from off-topic digressions as discussed below.

Off-Topic Digressions

Anticipate and minimize off-topic digressions by letting participants know your "game plan" (e.g., learning outcomes, the process you'll be following, time available, and exactly what *will* and *will not* be covered).

The best way to handle issues that are clearly not in any way relevant to the workshop is to simply, but tactfully, say so as they arise. In this way you have no obligation to deal with them later. Another option is to offer to discuss the participant's issue or concern, one on one, at a break or after the workshop.

> ***A pat on the back is only a few vertebrae removed from a kick in the pants, but it's miles ahead in results.***
> ***- Ella Wheeler Wilcox***

There's one exception to this advice. That's when a bunch of participants have the same or a similar off-topic question or concern. Now you have little choice. You must get permission from the group to "park" the issue or stop what you're doing and deal with it "on the spot."

GREASING THE WHEELS - USING REINFORCEMENT IN WORKSHOPS

Sincere and specific reinforcement, offered with respect, builds rapport and participant confidence. It increases and maintains desirable behavior and discourages undesirable behavior. It can be in the form of social rewards, such as compliments or recognition, or material rewards, such a plaque or tickets to a basketball game.

> ***Most people don't care how much you know until they know how much you care.***
> ***- John Maxwell***

This section looks at

A) Positive reinforcement

B) Other types of reinforcement

A) Positive Reinforcement

Don't equate positive reinforcement too closely with B.F. Skinner's "operant conditioning." Skinner's "carrot and stick" approach to motivating, also known as the great jackass theory of motivation, is far too narrow for working with adults in workshops. His work focused exclusively on behavior. Workshop leaders also need to be concerned with participants' attitudes and motivation.

Ken Blanchard argues that we need seven or eight positive comments for every negative comment or criticism we receive from others.[5] Thus, the importance of recognizing and valuing others, in order to be "psychologically eligible" to offer them difficult feedback at a later time. Stephen Covey talks about this as well. He sees it as making deposits in a "relationship bank."[6] Only once this bank account has a positive balance and has earned a little interest can we make a withdrawal (e.g., a criticism).

Thus, the first rule of reinforcement is "make some deposits." Show people you care. Show you recognize and value participants as individuals and that you see them as important enough to warrant your attention. One of the best ways to do this is to *listen*. The most powerful reinforcement skill available to a workshop leader is the power to listen actively, with understanding, and with empathy, and also to be seen to be listening (i.e., making listening signs like head nods and noises like "uh huhs").

Providing Desirable Consequences

It's a good bet that as long as you're sincere and specific, you can't go wrong giving participants recognition. So, recognize everything participants do that is at least approximately right. For example, when summarizing and reviewing, associate posted comments with the participants who contributed them.

Find value in each participant's contribution and the "kernel of truth" in each participant's answer. With the exception of fact-based questions that have right and wrong answers, an answer is seldom completely wrong. A couple of outrageous examples might make this point. Say one of your more unstable participants stands on his chair and hysterically yells out, "The world is coming to an end!" This is perfectly true. It may be

billions and billions of years from now, but technically it's true. An even more outrageous example, a participant says, "Hitler was a nice guy." OK, he fed his dog. So I can see how his dog might have thought this way.

B) Other Forms of Reinforcement

Positive reinforcement is by far and away the best approach to managing participation. As the old saying goes, you can catch more flies with honey than you can with vinegar. (That is, if you're serious about really building up your fly collection!) In addition to positive reinforcement you might consider some of the following options.

Remove an undesirable consequence

Examples:
- No longer interrupting a participant when he or she is speaking.
- No longer singling out a participant by name with a question.

Remove a desirable consequence

Examples:
- No longer laughing at a participant's off-color jokes.
- No longer giving a participant time to tell his/her long-winded stories.

Provide an undesirable consequence

Examples:
- Confronting a participant tactfully, but firmly, about underparticipating.
- Asking a participant to hold his/her comments and give others a chance to speak.
- Asking an overly aggressive participant to leave a workshop or training program. (Incidentally, I believe this would be an extremely rare event. Indeed, in all the years I've been leading workshops and training programs, I've never once had to ask a participant to leave.)

The latter approach (providing an undesirable consequence) is a form of negative reinforcement. Use it sparingly in a workshop or training program. Whereas the reaction or result you'll get from a participant when using positive reinforcement such as recognition, appreciation, and support is relatively predictable and usually positive. The results you'll get from negative reinforcement are unpredictable and often undesirable, for example, rejection, anger, withdrawal, sabotage. In addition, other participants, who were not directly involved, may also react in unpredictable ways to your use of negative reinforcement. For example, they may resent your treatment of the participant in question.

WATCHING FOR SIGNS AND SIGNALS - NONVERBALS

One thing an engine operator (referred to as "engineers" on the railroad) really catches hell for is missing a signal. For instance, he may get a red light at a meeting place, meaning his train must wait till an oncoming train passes his position. Missing "a meet" could result in a train wreck and loss of life. Workshop leaders also have to watch for signals because participants, being human, aren't always direct about what they're feeling and wanting. The signals referred to here are nonverbal signals. We all give these signals to others, whether we're conscious of them or not.

In a way, we are all experts in "body language." We know instinctively when someone is uncomfortable, agreeable, or upset. Yet, we also misinterpret these cues, and sometimes our misinterpretations can be "way off."

Pay attention to nonverbals, but don't take isolated cues too seriously. Nonverbals, in combination with other cues, can point to success or to potential problems in communicating with participants. However, don't make decisions based on nonverbals alone. This is "mind reading" and always leads to problems. Instead, use nonverbal signals to alert you to the need to investigate, to ask questions, and to invite participants to be direct with you.

As a workshop leader it's helpful to be able to recognize the following body language signals as a way of ensuring participants are "on track." But keep two things in mind. One, nonverbals can be interpreted in a variety of ways. Two, the nonverbal cues outlined below have a distinct "North American" cultural bias.

> ***The face is not the place to look for the speaker's true feelings, because we learn to monitor and control emotional expression in that channel.***
> ***- Arnold Goldstein and Nick Higginbotham***

This section covers

A) Cues indicating potential success as a workshop leader

B) Cues indicating potential problems as a workshop leader

C) What resistance looks like

A) Cues Indicating Potential Success As a Workshop Leader

Participants who are getting value from a workshop will likely be cooperative and agreeable. They'll be anticipating, showing interest, accepting, ready, eager, and wanting to speak. They may be

- sitting forward in their chair
- rubbing their palms together slowly and softly

- taking notes
- nodding their head in a positive manner
- spreading their arms
- gripping the edge of the table

Other participants who are benefiting from the workshop may appear thoughtful and concerned. They'll seem to be assessing and evaluating. Watch for

- pinching the bridge of their nose, eyes closed
- putting their hands on their cheek, leaning forward
- stroking their chin
- squinting

Still others who are benefiting may appear confident and dominant by

- placing their fingers in a steeple position
- leaning back, both their hands behind their head

B) Cues Indicating Potential Problems As a Workshop Leader

Body language cues can also be seen in people who are shutting out, not accepting, rejecting, doubting, or disapproving of your leadership. These participants might express their feelings by

- keeping their eyes downcast with their face turned away from you
- crossing their arms across their chest
- leaning back with their legs crossed
- avoiding eye contact with you
- turning their body sideways

Participants may be suspicious, antagonistic, displeased, guilty, or angry. These feelings may be indicated by

- tightening their jaw muscles, tightening lips, squinting
- keeping hands behind their back
- keeping their hands in a fist-like position
- rubbing their nose with their index finger
- turning their head to one side
- sideways glances at you

Potential problems may also be indicated by participants appearing confused, puzzled, or surprised. They might be:

- frowning
- raising their eyebrows

- tilting their head

Participants looking for reassurance may indicate potential problems. Look for

- putting a pen in their mouth
- pinching their hand
- clenching their hands
- rubbing their hands against each other
- picking at their cuticles

Participants who are frustrated, nervous, or defensive also point to potential problems. These feelings might be signaled by:

- crossing their legs
- leaning away from you
- leaning back with their arms folded and legs crossed
- sitting back from the table with their body sideways and arms and legs crossed
- running their fingers through their hair
- rubbing the back of their neck
- wringing their hands

Participants who are bored may be:

- drumming on the table or tapping their foot
- putting their chin in the palm of their hand
- eyes dropped
- doodling

Participants who are procrastinating or pausing to collect their thoughts might be:

- placing their index finger over their lips
- locking their ankles
- clenching their hands
- cleaning the lenses of their glasses
- putting the ear piece of glasses in their mouth

C) What Resistance Looks Like

Three key points need to be made about resistance. One, it depends on one's frame of reference. Two, it can serve a valuable purpose. Three, it's human.

On the first point, Daryl Conner (1992) draws a vivid

analogy about how a person's perception of a change situation determines whether resistance occurs.[7] He notes that "professional football players go to work every Sunday and endure levels of pain that would put most other people in the hospital." Yet, "from their frame of reference, not going to work due to physical pain would be dodging responsibility."

On the second point, resistance can be a useful tool. Without it, a train would just spin its wheels and go nowhere. It's the resistance between the engine's wheels and the tracks that allows the engine to transform its energy into motion. The same is true with people. Resistance doesn't necessarily mean someone is negative. It can mean quite the opposite. They may feel very strongly and positively about something. It's just that their belief is different than yours. In this way resistance fights off impostors and quacks. It keeps us loyal, committed, and focused on a certain way of thinking and acting. This focus helps us make progress within our paradigm. Thus, resistance needs to be respected; it serves a valuable purpose.

Finally, resistance is natural, especially if you're trying to persuade someone to change a longstanding perspective or habit. It's human and wise to be cautious, to give up old learnings reluctantly, and to move into the unknown with some trepidation.

Needless to say, resistance can also hold us back. A "hot box" on a train - resistance between the axle and wheel causing ball bearings to overheat - can bring trains to a dead stop. In the same way resistance to change can slow or halt our growth as individuals. Habits and outdated ways of thinking and seeing the world hold us back. They keep us from recognizing, reacting, and adapting to change in flexible and innovative ways.

Indirect resistance

The following behaviors may be sincere or they may be forms of "indirect resistance." The only way to find out which is which is to explore with questions.[8]

- Asking for more detail
- Saying more time is needed or no time is available
- Saying "get realistic"
- Acting confused
- Moralizing
- Complying and nothing more
- Questioning methods endlessly
- Debating definitions and concepts (e.g., leadership, politics, control)
- All of a sudden saying, "The problem has gone away" (known as "a flight into health")
- Pressing for solutions too soon
- Saying "I don't want any surprises"
- Attacking you or your position
- Silence
- Intellectualizing
- Continually asserting their agenda

KEEPING IT ON THE RAILS - MANAGING PARTICIPATION PROBLEMS

There are four types of participation problems: underparticipation, overparticipation, overaggressiveness, and apathy. The first three can be handled effectively by a workshop leader, because each embodies a level of energy. This energy may feel negative, but it's energy nonetheless. Trying to deal with apathy, however, is a trap and a waste of time. Don't shoulder the burden for participants' lack of desire or get sucked into leading a workshop when participants couldn't care less. You can't change other people. If the energy is there, as in the case of underparticipation, you can build on it, but if all you find is apathy, it's "game over." As Bruce Springsteen sings, "You can't start a fire without a spark."[9] There's nothing a workshop leader can do to counteract apathy, except end the workshop.

Trains can and do "jump the tracks." Sometimes it's an accident caused by carelessness or a poor maintenance program; sometimes it's sabotage. But when it happens, it creates big problems. It's a lot easier maintaining the railway in good working order than it is repairing the tracks after they've been twisted and tangled from a train wreck and picking up a locomotive and dozens of boxcars from a riverbed.

Although it's rare, workshops can also go off the rails, especially when participants are emotionally or "ego invested" in a given position. Although there are ways to clean up the mess, it's easier, less costly, and less risky to *prevent* participation problems in a workshop than it is to fix them after the fact. As with a railroad, the secret is not just good "clean up" equipment, but good maintenance. Thus, it's necessary to manage participation in a workshop, and to do it in a way that anticipates and handles problems before they become chronic and lead to disaster.

Participation problems can result from apathy or resistance and even from a person's overinterest. (These people are sometimes labeled derisively as "keeners," meaning they are "keen" to learn.) More specifically, participation problems can result from things like a misunderstanding within the group, an oversensitive or defensive stance on your part or by a participant, a lack of tact on the part of a given participant, someone being unwilling to do assignments or try exercises, and even an inappropriate use of humor.

> *In the world that is coming, if you can't navigate difference, you've had it.*
> *- Robert Hughes*

This section looks at how to manage participation and value differences in a workshop,

A) When participants are underparticipating

B) When participants are overparticipating

C) When participants are overly aggressive

A) Managing When Participants Are Underparticipating

Underparticipation is characterized by

- silence
- agreeing all the time
- never or rarely challenging
- arriving late, leaving early
- poor articulation or half answers
- refusing to practice new learning

Possible reasons for underparticipating behaviors are that participants may

- have been required to attend the workshop against their wishes
- be insecure, shy, nervous, or tired
- not be used to working in groups
- be bored or indifferent
- be more knowledgeable on the subject than the rest of the group
- have been "institutionalized" into being passive and dependent learners

People waste more time waiting for someone to take charge of their lives than they do in any other pursuit.
- Gloria Steinem

Steps you can take to manage underparticipation

- Get participants active and talking to each other. Learn participants' names. Then encourage participants by calling on them directly, using their name. Work a little humor and a little controversy into the workshop. Get participants to react and respond. Ask open questions and give them lots of time to answer (i.e., count to ten in your mind).

- Encourage participation by *polling* (e.g., asking for a show of hands) or deferring to the group (i.e., getting participants to answer each others' questions and comment on each others' answers). Ask them to have a brief discussion with a neighbor to formulate questions, think of examples, react to statements, or to rebut an approach or model. Use buzz groups and other small group designs to accomplish this.

- The less you dominate, the more group members will participate. Sit down to take the attention away from yourself. Play "devil's advocate," taking care to ensure the group understands this is what you are doing (i.e., don't allow them to assume you are just being negative).

- When participants do get involved, give lots of verbal and nonverbal reinforcement. Ask for their advice. Build their confidence. For example, thank participants for their input and use minimal encouragements such as, "uh-huhs," head nods, and smiles to encourage participants to continue speaking. Also, remember who said what and quote them later in the workshop (e.g., "as Diane mentioned this morning, ...").

A story about irregular attendance at a training program, and about using humor without enough forethought

Laurel McLean, a friend and colleague, gave me this story about a time when she was leading a training program. As part of the initial contracting during the start-up, the group had discussed the need for prompt and regular attendance. At that point, Tom spoke up saying that he might have a problem being on time over the duration of the two-day training program, but that he would do his best. He then proceeded to duck in and out of the training program, attending three or four business meetings in other parts of the building. Tom was polite about this and told Laurel each time he had to leave. However, as his attendance became so irregular, she then commented to Tom that his coming and going was starting to affect the group. In particular it was disrupting skills-practice exercises. Nonetheless Tom's irregular attendance continued.

Finally, on the last afternoon of the training program, Tom left at two o'clock to attend another meeting that he said was critical. He returned at 3:30 just as the leader was in the middle of giving directions for another skills-practice exercise. Tom had missed most of the theory and demonstrations of the skill that was about to be practiced, so Laurel simply asked him to join one the subgroups as an observer (the skills-practice exercises were done in subgroups). Her thinking was that Tom wouldn't have the background to practice, and she didn't want to put him on the spot when he wasn't prepared. She also felt she couldn't ask the rest of the group to wait while she brought Tom up to speed on the theory and demonstration that he had missed.

There had been a running joke during the training program about the "role playing" and how everyone hated it, even though most also commented that they found it practical and helpful. Anyway, as Laurel asked Tom to join one the subgroups as an observer, she also said in jest, "Talk about rewarding negative behavior." She was referring to the fact that Tom, unlike the others in the group, was not being asked to practice the skill in question. She said the group laughed but Tom didn't seem to react at the time.

Later, Tom really slammed Laurel, and her facilitation practices, on the evaluation form. They worked in the same company so a few days later Laurel talked with Tom about this. It turned out that, even though Laurel had sincerely intended her comment about "rewarding negative behavior" in jest, that's not how Tom had received it. He had taken this personally. In hindsight, Laurel says she would handle this situation differently next time. She would be a lot more careful about joking around in this type of situation.

All for the want of a joke - Why did Laurel's joke backfire?

One thing for sure, this isn't about Laurel's competence as a facilitator or her sense of humor. She's highly skilled in both departments. This doesn't mean she can't make a mistake every now and then, like the rest of us.

Three factors seem to be at play, all resulting from Tom's sporadic attendance at this training program. First, he wasn't "in" on the running joke about role playing. Second, Laurel would have been unable to establish the same level of rapport with him as she would have had with other participants. It's difficult to establish rapport with an empty chair. Third, Tom was probably feeling a little guilty.

When these factors are added together, it's not difficult to see why Laurel's joke backfired. But does that explain why Tom slammed Laurel personally, and her facilitation practices, on the evaluation form? Regardless of whether their perceptions are accurate to start with (i.e., Laurel hadn't intended a "put-down"), when people feel insulted and get angry, logic goes out the window. They shoot in all directions at once. This goes back to attribution theory discussed in chapter one. When someone is upset with you, a lot or all of what you do may be unacceptable to them.

Dealing with irregular attendance

Yogi Berra said, "If they don't want to come to the ball park, you can't stop them." As a workshop leader, however, there are steps you can take to contract and manage attendance.

Five clear steps seem possible.

1) Act early. Nip problems in the bud. When someone starts popping in and out of your workshop or training program as if their attendance and participation don't matter, it's time to confront. This doesn't mean getting into conflict. It does mean, to paraphrase Jones and Biech (1996), requiring the participant to pay attention to something you think is important, in this case the issue of their attendance.[10] You might use an approach like the 5C model described later in this chapter. Do this one-on-one, listen actively, don't assume motive, don't take it personally, and don't take a position too early in the discussion. Rather, focus on interests. (This is a principle of the Harvard Negotiation Technique, also discussed later in this chapter.) Tell the participant what your concern is, and why you feel their full-time participation is important.

2) Make a decision and set clear guidelines. Is the participant's irregular attendance tolerable, even though disagreeable? Or, is it unacceptable? Decide one way or the other. Sitting on the fence only makes things worse. And once you've decided, stick by your decision. Thus, if you decide this irregular attendance is acceptable, "let go" of any frustration you have about this and plan a strategy to make the best of it. Don't say it's OK and then resent the participant for your decision.

3) Communicate your decision and expectations clearly. Tell the participant that their participation matters and tell him/her why. Also tell the participant exactly what you expect from them given the situation. Be supportive but tough minded (e.g., "I understand you can't be here between 10:00 and 11:00 tomorrow morning, but you have agreed to be here for the rest of the day and to participate in that practice session in the afternoon. Is that doable?"). Set clear guidelines (e.g., "If you can't make it after 11:00, then we need to take you off this program and reschedule you for a future training program. Is that OK with you?").

4) Work with the participant and plan a strategy to make it work. For example, if you decide it's OK for the participant to attend irregularly, then make sure the rest of the group understands the situation. Simply say something to the group like, "Just so people know about this ahead of time, Tom will need to be in and out a little over the next two days." Now, as a result of saying this publicly, Tom has "permission" to come and go and not to feel guilty about it. You might even set up a "buddy system" where someone or a small group of people will bring Tom up to speed on what he's missed each time he returns to the training program or workshop. Finally, you might express an appreciation to Tom. See the glass as half full, not half empty. Thank him for agreeing to come at least half time as opposed to dropping out completely.

5) Was it a contracting problem? After the workshop or training program has ended, ask yourself if you could have done something differently during the contracting phase, prior to the workshop or training program start-up, that would have prevented this problem from happening. Could you have said something differently in the pre-meeting, in the letter that went out to participants prior to the workshop or training program, or during the start-up phase of the workshop or training program while you were contracting process with the group? It's probably not possible to completely avoid problems like this in the future. However, it likely is possible to take "preventative measures" so these problems occur less frequently, and so when they do occur, they are easier to manage.

End

B) Managing When Participants Are Overparticipating

Don't assume you understand why some people overparticipate. Don't mind-read. Rather, accept, support, and challenge. Consider these thoughts from Hugh Prather (1970).[11]

> *I talk because I feel, and I talk to you*
> *because I want you to know how I feel.*
> *My statements are requests.*
> *My questions are statements.*
> *My gossip is a plea: Please see me as*
> *incapable of that. Please respect me.*
> *My arguments insist: I want you to show*
> *respect for me by agreeing with me. This*
> *is the way I say it is.*
> *And my criticism informs you: You hurt*
> *my feelings a minute ago.*

Overparticipation is characterized by

- excessive talking
- constantly interrupting
- distracting others
- being off-topic

Reasons for overparticipating might include participants being

- naturally wordy
- well informed
- nervous
- a poor listener
- an "eager beaver"
- needy for recognition

Steps you can take to manage overparticipation

- Acknowledge and show respect for the overparticipating person's authority. It may be that a little recognition is all that is needed. Perhaps this recognition has been earned and is long overdue. I recommend recognizing and appreciating anything participants do that has value, regardless of whether they are overparticipating.

- Check overparticipating by asking closed ended questions. Also ask participants to link what they are saying to the topic under discussion.

- Get participants talking with each other. You might also try interrupting overparticipating members of the group and then summarizing and redirecting their points. For example, "That's interesting. What do others think?"

- Set limits in a *friendly but firm* sort of way and get permission to involve the group. For example, say something like, "Dave and Val are the only people I'm hearing from. I don't want them to hold back because they're making valuable contributions, but I also want others to say more and to be more involved. So I'm going to be asking others directly. Is that OK?"

- Finally, find a way to move on. This could be as simple as saying something like, "Tempus is fugiting; we need to move on." (This is my little Latin joke. *Tempus fugit* in Latin means "time flies." Only the Catholics will laugh.)

C) Managing When Participants Are Overly Aggressive

Overly aggressive participants can be

- argumentative
- constantly playing "devil's advocate"
- challenging excessively
- holding side conversations
- finding fault in everything
- bickering with you or with other participants
- clinging stubbornly to a certain belief or point of view
- constantly asserting their own agenda

Reasons for overaggressiveness may be that participants are

- trying to put you "on the spot"
- upset about the issue being discussed or about personal or job problems
- intolerant of others in general or of someone in particular
- looking for advice
- trying to get you to support a given point of view
- holding an old grudge
- strongly committed to a different point of view

Steps workshop leaders can take to manage aggressive participation

> ***I've learned that we are responsible for what we do, no matter how we feel.***
> ***- H. Jackson Brown, Jr.***

- John Jones says this, tongue in cheek, "When in doubt confront. When all else fails try honesty."[12] This little joke is a powerful way of remembering how easy it is for people to get "sucked into" arguing and defending. When this happens we sometimes take the "expedient" route, even to the point of sacrificing honesty. Stay calm when dealing with overly aggressive participants. Keep your ego and your temper in check and don't argue. A workshop leader loses every argument! Even if you succeed in "showing up" the overly aggressive participant, the other participants who witnessed your counterattack may decide to "hold back and play it safe." Thus, as a workshop leader, you lose because the level of group participation declines. If, on the other hand, the overly aggressive participant succeeds in "showing you up," you also lose. You end up looking incompetent.

Other participants may lose confidence in your knowledge and experience and in your ability to control the workshop process.

- Stephen Covey (1989) says, "seek first to understand, then to be understood."[13] Record the overly aggressive participant's point on a flipchart. Use his/her exact words. This shows that you're listening. Ask for examples. Clarify and try to understand assumptions the participant may be making. Emphasize the points on which you agree.
Acknowledge his/her opinion. This is not the same as agreeing with it. Find the *kernel of truth* in what the overly aggressive participant is saying and let them know what you will do to help. Then keep your promise and take action.

> ***One should forgive one's enemies, but not before they are hanged.***
> ***- Heinrich Heine***

- Sometimes you've got to be very direct. Ask the overly aggressive participant if they will reserve their judgment for now. Or ask if it would be OK to discuss the matter privately, at a break, or at the end of the day.

- Another tactic is to allow the group to deal with the conflict. This can be done by reversing or relaying questions to other participants. However, avoid taking sides yourself or forcing participants onto sides (e.g., we/they, good/bad, right/wrong).

- If none of the above seems to help, direct the participant's attention to the outcomes being sought from the workshop or point out the time limitations and then move on.

- Use humor to help defuse the situation, but use it carefully.

- Use Peter Block's "two good faith replies" method (1978). This is detailed below.[14]

Feeling under attack in a goal setting workshop - A story about dealing with chronic overaggressiveness and very direct communication

If it's true that people with problems have problems with people, then Al and Maurie are people with problems. I remember being "under attack" once by them at an oil refinery. Maurie and Al are senior foremen and known for aggressive behavior (names have been changed to protect the guilty). I knew going in to expect the worst. I also knew they were very upset at the new program (a goal setting process) that I was introducing for their company, and while it felt like I was their target, in reality their target was anyone associated with this new program.

Right off the bat they told me about this poor consultant they had worked with recently, Bill Dovich, (I've changed the name for obvious reasons), and how I reminded them of Bill. They laughed about what a dud Bill was. (By coincidence I knew Bill Dovich, and knew he was anything but a dud.) The one positive was that these two weren't being indirect. I knew exactly what was on their mind (i.e., get the consultant!).

First, because I refused to be naive about the situation (i.e., I realized they wanted to see me fail), I handled my facilitation role carefully. For example, I worded questions to the group so we wouldn't be pulled "off track," and I checked my behavior to be sure I wasn't acting defensively, even though I was certainly feeling this way. I carry the belief that most participants are honest and don't deliberately play games or try to sabotage the workshop. However, if you extend this to believe that there's a little good in every person, under any circumstance, then you probably haven't worked with enough people under enough circumstances.

Second, I also refused to take it personally and was thus able to keep my sense of humor. For example, I made jokes about keeping the motor running on my car, and when one said, "You're exactly like Bill Dovich," I replied, "Oh, he must be *good looking*." The rest of the group laughed, signifying they where enjoying how I was handling these two.

These two were so aggressive that most in the group remained quiet. I made the following comment: "I'm hearing a lot from Maurie and Al, but not from others. I don't want Maurie and Al to stop talking, because they're raising good points, but at the same time I need to hear from others. What opinions do you have about ..." At this point Al hit the roof. He bellowed, "That's it. You're just trying to shut me up. I've got every right to speak, ..." Just then another foreman in the group, one that was supportive of the new program, spoke up. He said, "Al, you didn't listen. Bruce didn't say he wanted you to be quiet. He said he just wanted to hear more from others as well." Most in the group nodded agreement. Others in the group then began to contribute, but cautiously. Not surprisingly, neither Al nor Maurie said much after that.

Finally it came time for participants to draft goal statements. All of the group of about fifteen got right into this, except, of course, Maurie and Al. Rather than direct them, I asked, "I realize you have concerns about this process, but would you be willing to try it out?" As the rest of the group was already hard at work, they would have looked pretty uncooperative if they said "no." When the group finished a first draft of goals we debriefed. Needless to say Maurie's and Al's work was rather shoddy, but I asked permission to review and revise it in the group. In this way I was able to demonstrate the value of the process. Later both Maurie and Al reluctantly commented that the revisions made sense and that the goal setting process had value.

I had lunch later with Al and a couple of others from the workshop. He was still the same obnoxious person as he had been in the workshop. We talked about some noncontroversial topics and exchanged a few light hearted, but subtly serious, barbs. Those with us seemed to enjoy our verbal jousting because we used a lot of humor. For example, he hated modern management methods and derisively commented that he was going to write a book on leadership. I guessed this would be a "very short book." The group laughed.

My satisfaction was proving to myself that I could handle this sort of provocation without overreacting. Also, I later heard that my sponsor client, a senior vice president in a head office a few hundred miles away, was very happy with the results of this workshop.

End

Feeling under attack in a training program - A story about dealing with unexpected anger and surfacing indirect communication

During one particular workshop start-up I was flying along smooth and straight. It seemed like conditions were perfect. Then, all of a sudden, a huge storm cloud came up from nowhere. I wondered if I could fly around it, but it was right in front of me. I had no choice. I had to go right through the middle of it.

That storm cloud came from a participant named John. Moments earlier John had seemed pleasant and "learning ready." Now, all of a sudden, his tone was pure anger. Suddenly something had really "tripped his switch." He wasn't saying directly what made him angry but he wasn't disguising his anger either.

Only on one other occasion had I seen someone express anger this directly in a workshop, and on that occasion I wasn't the target of the anger. But this time I was. At first I felt attacked. Thankfully I know how to act "nondefensively," even when I feel defensive. I stayed calm but was baffled, "What was making John so angry?" Recognizing his anger and using open questions, I asked things like, "You seem pretty upset. Help me understand why. What is it you disagree with?" Right off the bat, John agreed he was upset. That told me his objection was honest. I knew he wasn't trying to sabotage anything.

A couple of other participants in the group tried to rescue me. They tried to answer for me, and one tried to change the topic. Workshop leaders beware! Don't let participants rescue you. They are well intended, but you need to find out what's going on with the upset participant. Why is he/she so angry? You need to explore, ask questions, and listen. What you don't need is well-intentioned rescuing and its ensuing distraction to the group.

So, I explored. I listened to those trying to rescue me, but directed the conversation back to John. I asked more open questions and listened. At first, I couldn't figure out what had gone wrong. Only on about my third or fourth question, and only after not acting defensively and demonstrating that I was really interested in listening, did John "come clean." He was insulted by the way I talked about feedback and had taken my comments personally.

An interlude: How I had talked about feedback

Sometimes, just to "hook" participants' interest, I'll talk about receiving feedback in personal terms. One of the things I'll say is that feedback is within our circle of influence. That is, it's something we can "go out and get," as opposed to having to "wait to be given." Complaining that we don't get enough feedback is akin to saying we are dependent on others for it or that receiving feedback is in our circle of concern.

Here's how I personalized this discussion about feedback. (My premise is that we shut off our own feedback by reacting negatively or defensively.)

> *Employees complain that their boss doesn't give them feedback. But if you think about the last time your boss gave you feedback, and how you reacted, you'll probably understand better why your boss doesn't give you feedback anymore.*

I could protect against participants taking this personally by using myself, instead of them, as the example. So instead of saying "employees say my boss doesn't give me feedback," I could say something like

> *I remember complaining a few years ago that my boss doesn't give me feedback. A friend of mine said, "Think about the last time your boss gave you feedback and how you reacted. Does that tell you why you don't get feedback anymore?" Finally, I realized my friend was right. I was reacting defensively and shutting off my own feedback. Do any of you know people who don't receive feedback well and as a result are rarely offered this gift from others? Giving some people feedback is like pushing on a rope. It just doesn't seem worth the hassle.*

And now, back to our story

John explained that there was a personal and an organizational reason why he got so angry. First, he had a history of being criticized for not receiving feedback well. Second, by coincidence, his department had just received the results of a leadership survey pointing to the need for managers, including John's manager, to provide better and more frequent feedback to employees. No wonder I hit a nerve. John is a bright, responsible, and well-respected man, but like all of us he has his sensitivities.

Conclusion and learnings

Four useful outcomes resulted from John's willingness to challenge how I phrased my comments.

First, it reconfirmed for me how important it is to gather as much information as possible about individual participants and their organization before a workshop or training program. Knowing about the leadership survey results that John's department had received might have changed how I phrased my comments about feedback.

Second, as a result of John's challenge, the group had a lively discussion about feedback. Several participants commented that they had gained a new understanding about giving and receiving feedback as a result of this discussion. I commented that without John pushing the issue, we wouldn't have had this discussion, and therefore, the group had John to thank. This is one of the ways I recognize the value of challenge in a workshop and at the same time encourage and give participants permission to challenge further.

Third, I had a chance to demonstrate how workshop leaders need to handle challenge and anger in a workshop. (This was a *Train the Trainer* workshop so this digression was on-topic.)

Fourth, John, the participant who had challenged me, later commented that this was the best workshop he had ever attended. He didn't say "one of the best," he said "the best." Mind you he said this only a day after the workshop ended, so maybe it has worn off by now! Anyway, it was nice to hear because I have a lot of respect for John.

End

MODEL TRAINS - PREPARING FOR THE REAL WORLD

This section provides six powerful models or frameworks for understanding your own role in a problem, listening to understand rather than to evaluate or compete, surfacing indirect resistance, assessing the level of confrontation and challenge required, being in the right frame of mind for working with participation problems, and for reaching agreements and forming commitments to action.

Like all models, the following are simplifications of the real world. Thus, they have to be practiced in flexible and adaptive ways, and of course, they don't work all the time! When dealing with human motivation and behavior, *nothing works all the time.*

Models are valuable because they provide a simple framework for action. If they were just as complex as reality, they would be just as immobilizing as reality. Thus, models provide a way to see the big picture - the whole forest and not just a few trees. Needless to say if you don't understand anything about trees (i.e., all the factors at play in a workshop including relationships, participants' needs, rapport, trust, roles, outcomes being sought, the nature of learning), then seeing the whole forest isn't going to help anyway.

Mix, match, adapt, and adopt the following models, as needed, when working with workshop participants.

A) *The Three Levels of a Problem* - Moving from analysis and blaming to understanding your own contribution to a problem

B) *Living on the Edge* - Working with problem participants and participant problems

C) *Effective Listening* - Understanding the principles of effective listening and assessing your listening habits

D) *The 5C's for Dealing with Conflict* - A model for deciding what level of action to take with participation problems, and for being fair, direct, and firm in asking for what you want

E) *Two Good Faith Replies* - Surfacing resistance in a workshop

F) *The Harvard Negotiation Technique* - Understanding and agreeing with participants around workshop goals, process, and behavior

Before you start on the road to revenge, dig two graves.
- Chinese proverb

A) The Three Levels of a Problem - Understanding Your Own Role in a Problem

1) The problem in rational terms

The shallowest and safest level for dealing with a problem is simply to discuss it logically and unemotionally, as if it were a math problem. Remember the warden's comment in the old Paul Newman movie, *Cool Hand Luke*, "What we have here is a failure to communicate." The warden's insistence on sounding rational in a very emotionally charged situation turned this comment into a classic "one liner."

2) What others are doing to contribute to the problem

A deeper level of investigating a problem is looking at what others are doing to cause or contribute to the problem. There are dangers here. This can lead to blaming, and blaming keeps us stuck. At this level we express anger, and sometimes that's OK. (Acting out this anger, for example, kicking a garbage can, is never OK. Anger is the only emotion a workshop leader should never act on.) But we also need to influence and confront others, and eventually we need to either take action to correct the situation, or let go emotionally of the problem, so that it no longer drains our energy or takes our time.

3) What I'm doing to contribute to the problem

The third and deepest level of a problem is looking at ourselves. At this level we have control. We can decide, act, let go emotionally, and grow. However, thinking about and discussing a problem at this level takes motivation and courage. It's usually only done when there's pain or opportunity present, that is, when we realize that if we don't change we're going to lose something we don't want to lose or fail to achieve something we really want to achieve. Support from others we trust helps a lot.

Using this model when "under fire" in a workshop

As a workshop leader you won't have the luxury of time for detailed analysis, and you certainly can't afford the loss of trust and rapport that comes with blaming others. Workshop leaders have to regularly hustle directly to the third level of a problem and question what they, not others, need to do differently to improve a situation. Leading workshops can thus be hard on the ego, but great for learning and growing as a person and as a professional.

B) Living on the Edge - Working with Problem Participants and Participant Problems

How involved should a workshop leader be with a participant concern, problem, or conflict? How does the workshop leader stay involved without becoming distant or emotionally detached and without getting "sucked into" or emotionally enmeshed in a participant's problem?

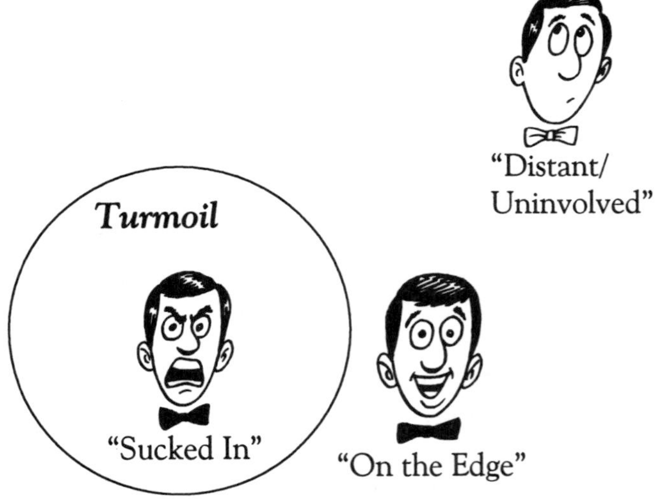

This model is about helping others and self-care when emotions run high. The challenge for workshop leaders, like the challenge for lifeguards at a swimming pool, is to *live on the edge*. From the edge you can help others (e.g., throw them a line) and at the same time make sure you don't get pulled under by a panic stricken swimmer.

Don't get emotionally "sucked into" participant problems or "ego invested" in changing a problem participant. That's jumping into the turmoil where you risk losing "the many" to work with "the few." Or, to put it another way, by jumping into the turmoil you no longer have your eyes on the whole pool, only one problem participant or one participant problem.

Being emotionally or intellectually aloof doesn't help much either. A workshop leader who is too distant from a participant's problem won't demonstrate empathy or caring.

> ***The myth of objectivity, which depends on radical separation of the knower from the known, has been declared bankrupt ... (thus) we never speak of nature without, at the same time, speaking about ourselves.***
> ***- Parker Palmer***

Living on the edge means guiding and influencing without overcontrolling and getting "sucked into" problems, conflicts, and turmoil in the group. It also means staying alert, as objective as possible, and involved. Finally it means coaching, supporting, and challenging, but not ignoring a participant's concern or taking responsibility for others.

Here's how you know when you're getting sucked into participants' problems.

1) You feel powerless or overwhelmed.

2) You blame a participant or some part of the organization.

3) You feel sorry for a participant.

4) You're working very hard as a workshop leader, but feel as though you're getting very little accomplished.

5) You lose sleep over workshop issues.

6) Even a day later you're still tired and haven't recovered from dealing with the participants' problem.

> ***Listening does not mean simply maintaining a polite silence while you are rehearsing, in your mind, the speech you are going to make the next time you can grab a conversational opening. Nor does listening mean waiting alertly for flaws in the other fellow's arguments so that later you can mow him down.***
> ***- S.I. Hayakawa***

C) Effective Listening - Understanding Words and Emotions

Remember that old joke, "A good listener is usually thinking about something else!" Well the following doesn't talk about how to look like a good listener; it talks about how to actually be a good listener. Like any skill, effective listening requires an understanding of basic principles, a few tools, practice, patience, and an awareness of what not to do. Effective listening means being "tuned in" at many levels: the words, the feelings, the underlying message, and the needs that lie below the surface. So listen carefully to the words and phrases a participant is using and also to the tone and feelings behind these words.

Ask yourself, "What's the message in *how* the participant is phrasing this question?" and "What needs might lie beneath the participant's comment?" Next, based on this awareness, check your impression with the participant. Ask directly, don't mind-read or jump to conclusions. And remember, discomfort is a clue to leading, not something to be avoided. It's a clue to start listening harder, exploring, and dialoguing. So if your gut is telling you it's risky to discuss an issue further or to ask probing questions, that's a sure sign you need to bring it up. But, pay attention to timing. Ensure the climate is right and participants are ready to dialogue before raising a sensitive issue.

A closed mouth gathers no feet
- Anonymous

Bore: A person who talks when you want him to listen.
- Ambrose Bierce

Three principles are involved. First, listen and ensure you understand what's being said. Only after you've understood the participant should you seek to be understood yourself. Second, accept that participants don't need to be "fixed," and that even if they did, you can't change them anyway. Third, know that the most effective level of listening comes from looking at what you can change about your own thinking and behavior, not that of others. (For more on this latter point see "The Three Levels of a Problem" outlined above.)

Habits for Effective Listening

We all have established listening practices, ways we've become accustomed to listening, or not listening, when others speak. Some of your listening habits are likely excellent, some mediocre, and unless you've been paying a lot of attention to how you listen, some of your listening habits are likely awful. Use the self-rating form at the end of this chapter to check your listening practices. You might also consider having someone who knows you use this rating form to give you feedback on how they perceive your listening skills and habits.

Active Listening - A Tool for When You're "Really Stuck"

Active listening is rather structured and can be a slow process, but it's also very powerful when you and a participant, or two participants, seem to be continually misunderstanding or misrepresenting what the other is saying.

Here's how to set it up. First, get permission to try this technique. Next, explain the process (see below). Finally, use the technique. Depending on the situation, you may want to conduct this in front of the group or do it in private over the lunch period or at the end of the day.

Three caveats need attention. One, this process can take up to a half hour or even an hour. Two, it takes discipline. There's often a tendency to break out of the process and go back to the old way of communicating. However, it must be remembered this old way is part of the reason why people are feeling misunderstood to begin with. Three, active listening can get a little frustrating, particularly for participants who have trouble expressing themselves or being open and direct about their needs. But this is the very reason active listening is such a powerful tool. It forces clarity, description, specifics, listening, understanding, and empathy.

> ***No siren did ever so charm the ear of the listener as the listening ear has charmed the soul of the siren.***
> ***- Henry Taylor***

The Seven Steps of the Active Listening Process

In the following example, you (the workshop leader) and a participant are having difficulty understanding one another.

1) The participant speaks for herself, using "I" statements, without blaming, and describing rather than evaluating. (e.g., "I feel that you don't take my comments seriously.")

2) You repeat back what you heard the participant say. (e.g., "You feel that I don't take your comments seriously.")

3) The participant fills in any missing pieces. (e.g., "You always get this look on your face when I contribute to the discussion.")

4) Again you repeat back what you heard the participant say until the participant says she feels understood. (e.g., "I seem to raise my eyebrows and look up when you contribute to the discussion.")

5) The participant then expresses a statement of need or expectation from you. (e.g., "I need you to take my comments seriously.")

6) Again you repeat back what you heard until the participant says she feels understood. (e.g., "You need me to listen carefully and to take your comments seriously.")

7) The process is then reversed; you now speak for yourself, using "I" statements, without blaming, and so on.

> ***For some of the large indignities in life the best remedy is direct action. For the smaller indignities, the best remedy is a Charlie Brown movie. The hard part is knowing the difference.***
> ***- Carol Travis***

D) The 5C's - Escalating Conflict One Step at a Time

This model, inspired by William Purkey's 5C's (1992), helps workshop leaders deal with participation problems at the appropriate level.[16] It keeps you focused on a task versus an ego orientation, it helps to be assertive without being punishing, and it provides guidance for "upping the ante" in incremental and logical steps.

It's based on three simple ideas. One, confront "head on" when necessary, but only when necessary. Two, conserve your energy. Only do the minimum amount of work, and evoke the minimum amount of stress required, to get the results desired. Three, escalate confrontation in logical increments or steps. Don't hold your tongue until you're completely fed up and then *blow*, going from "saying nothing" to "taking retribution." That is, don't go directly from a doormat to an atom bomb. This might work sometimes, but most of the time you'll just anger participants and destroy relationships.

There's a good reason for "upping the ante" one step at a time. It gets you asking questions instead of assuming motives. What people do makes sense to them, and usually what might seem like a participation problem is just a misunderstanding or an honest difference of opinion. Most of the time, people aren't trying to sabotage you or the workshop. Even when they're really angry and "acting out," you're likely not their intended target, although it may feel like you are. So, don't assume motive, don't evaluate, and don't act on anger.

1) Concern

"The art of becoming wise is the art of knowing what to overlook."[17] Don't assume you need to do anything about a participant's behavior. First, decide whether the behavior is a "concern" that needs to be dealt with or just a minor annoyance that you are able to overlook and forget.

If it's a concern that you feel you should not overlook, ask yourself if you are able to influence the situation in some way. Is there some action you can take to change or improve the situation?

If not, make the choice to "let go" emotionally. That is, find ways to stop being emotionally affected by this participant's behavior. If you can't emotionally let go, then disengage or in some way minimize your interaction with this participant.

If it is a concern that you feel requires action, move to step 2, "confer."

2) Confer

Raise the concern with the participant, using the following as guidelines.

- Do this "one on one," in private.
- Be clear and direct. Without emotion, describe; don't evaluate. And don't generalize (e.g., don't say "you always ...," when you mean "this has happened twice").
- State how this makes you feel, but don't accuse.
- Give three positives and a request. The positives are things you value about the other person. Your request is exactly what you want the other person to do. Don't say, "I wish you would ..." Rather, ask directly, "Will you ..."

> ***When all other means of communication fail, try words.***
> ***- Ashleigh Brilliant***

An example of conferring

Three positives

"Fred, I'm glad you're participating in this workshop. You bring a lot of experience others can learn from. You also seem willing to share what you know with the group. But I'm having one problem. You're interrupting and criticizing others when they speak. They're less experienced, but you need to give them time to talk and digest the concepts we're dealing with in the workshop."

The request

"Will you hold your comments till others have spoken, and then, when you do comment, will you take care not to criticize others personally?"

Now be quiet. Let the participant think and respond.

3) Consult

If you still haven't achieved the desired result, it's time to raise the stakes one level. Talk with the participant about what you have already discussed. Conferring hasn't worked, so raise it as an issue also. You now discuss two issues. One is the original problem that still exists. The other is that your request, made when conferring, hasn't gotten the desired results.

> ***When in doubt confront; when all else fails try honesty!***
> ***- John Jones***

4) Confront

Still the problem persists. Now you talk about consequences with the participant. Say what you will do if the participant does not comply. Be accurate and specific. Use times, dates, and descriptions, but don't threaten, menace, or bluff. You don't need to take action yet, although you have probably about "reached your limit" with this problem. Just be clear on what will happen next, if the problem is not resolved.

An example of confronting
(Do this face to face and one to one.)

"Fred, we talked about this a couple of times yesterday and you're still interrupting and criticizing other participants. It's causing a lot of disruption in the group, and it's not the kind of workshop climate I'm trying to maintain. If this happens again, I'm going to have to ask you to leave the workshop. I know neither one of us wants this to happen, but there just doesn't seem to be any alternative. I hope it doesn't come to that."

5) Conclude

Still no result. It's time to apply the consequences. You must follow through now or seriously damage your credibility. Don't act angry; just act. It always takes courage to act decisively, but sometimes that's the price we must pay to be successful as a workshop leader. It's why workshop leaders get paid the big bucks!

Important Considerations When Applying the 5C Model

Finally, three important considerations apply when using this model.

First, use the 5C model with three overriding "C's," care, compassion, and consideration. That is, practice the adult-learning principles discussed in chapter two.

Second, there are times you'll need to act quickly, and moving through the 5C's in logical steps won't make any sense. For example, you won't *confer* by saying, "Doug, you're an excellent participant, with lots of energy, and a great sense of humor, but what I really need you to do is stop stealing the other participants' wallets and purses!" There is wisdom in this model. It will guide you to act with integrity and authority. It will help you preserve and build relationships with the group, as well as guide you in standing up for your rights and the rights of all participants in the workshop. However, don't use it as a recipe, or lock-step approach. Rather, adapt it as needed. And remember, no model replaces common sense or the need for good working relationships.

Third, be aware that this model focuses on participant behavior, not on workshop climate. Yet, as a workshop leader you need to pay attention to both climate and participant behavior. Thus, whenever you apply this model (e.g., where participants are underparticipating, overparticipating, or being overly aggressive), you should parallel this focus on participant behavior by also looking at workshop climate. Ask yourself and/or discuss the following types of questions with the group. "Is something in the environment supporting, encouraging, condoning, or even necessitating this behavior from participants?" "Is it something you're doing as the workshop leader?" "Is it something the group is doing?" "Does an approach or process need to change?" "Do the outcomes for the workshop need to be reviewed and revised?" These questions are particularly relevant if the behavior that's causing your *concern* is coming from more than one or two participants, that is, if the problem behavior is common and widespread versus exceptional and isolated.[18]

> ***Thunder is good, thunder is impressive, but it is the lightning that does the work.***
> ***- Mark Twain***

A nonworkshop example of a punishing system that encourages, if not necessitates, behavior problems

My son, Jeff, goes to college and works part time at a huge grocery store. Jeff is a price checker at this store. It's so big that he wears in-line roller skates to get around. Anyway there are probably about two hundred part-time employees there. They have a very punishing "time off" policy. First, if you ask for time off or a change in your schedule, they'll likely say "no." Second, if they do grant time off, you are automatically cut back in your scheduled working hours for the following month. So, guess what employees do when they want a weekend off? They just phone in sick! This way their hours aren't cut back the following month. Phoning in sick has become the standard, common, and informally accepted practice for getting time off.

My point is this. If a supervisor at this store catches an employee claiming sick time to get time off, that supervisor can't just ignore this behavior because it's a common practice. The supervisor needs to take action, perhaps at the level of *confronting* in the above model. But, at the same time, the supervisor is well advised to also look at the system and practices that surround this problem behavior and contribute to the work environment, in this case, the policy of cutting back employees hours for a month if their schedule is revised on request. Thus, one needs to be tough on behavior problems *and also* open to examining one's own leadership systems and practices. This means looking at problems at all three levels. (See the section titled "The Three Levels of a Problem" above for a discussion of these three levels.)

An example of similar systems and leadership problems in workshops and training programs

So what? What workshop practices or leadership approaches encourage behavior problems as in the story above?

An example would be where a workshop leader practices with a combination of faulty assumptions (e.g., assuming silence means consent, assuming participants don't need coaching during a role play).

The workshop leader asks, "Is everyone willing to role play this in trios and report back to the group on your findings?" (First of all, who can answer a question like this? Who can respond for "everyone"?) No one responds. Not hearing any objection the leader then says, "OK, take twenty minutes, then we'll debrief your findings in the group." The workshop leader then leaves the room to make a few phone calls assuming the group will role play as directed. Twenty minutes later he/she attempts to debrief and finds most participants didn't role play, those who did misunderstood what he/she wanted them to focus on, and those that focused as desired weren't able to reach any conclusions as a result of role playing.

Does it make sense to challenge participants on their behavior, perhaps at the level of *conferring* in the above model? You bet it does, as long as this is done with respect, consideration, and caring. But it doesn't make sense to assume motive. And it makes a lot of sense to look at your own assumptions and behavior as a leader. At your own role in this problem (i.e., at level three). At how you directed the group, assumed consent, and disappeared instead of observing and coaching during the role play. Thus, it makes sense to look at participants' behavior and, at the same time, to look beyond their behavior to the workshop climate and the practices, leadership, and process that make up this climate.

E) Two Good Faith Replies - Surfacing Resistance

The "tricky bit" about resistance in workshops is that it can be, and often is, indirect. Indirect resistance is *not* manageable. In order to work with resistance you first have to get it out in the open. Peter Block's "two good faith replies" model will help you do this (1978).[19] (See the section above titled "What Resistance Looks Like" for a discussion and examples of indirect resistance.)

Not everything that is faced can be changed, but nothing can be changed until it is faced.
- James Baldwin

The "Two Good Faith Replies" Model

The first thing to do when you suspect a participant is resisting is "don't assume" and "don't mind-read." That is, even though you suspect a participant is resisting, don't jump to that conclusion. You could be wrong! What looks like resistance could be a genuine request or comment and nothing more.

Treat a participant's comments in good faith and respond accordingly. For example, if a participant asks for more information, provide more information. If he/she asks for more information a second time, then, once again, provide more information. But the third time you might consider responding differently. Now may be the time to recognize and name the resistance.

By giving "two good faith replies" first, before naming the resistance, you invite the participant to be direct with you, while minimizing the risk of driving their resistance further underground. When you finally do name the resistance, do it gently. That is, name it in a way that invites the participant to be open with you, without forcing or threatening. Doing the latter will likely result in further resistance. The example below should help clarify this point.

Finally, recognize that each situation is unique. In some situations you might want to give three or even four good faith responses. In others you might feel that one such response is all that's needed before naming and dealing directly with resistance as an issue in itself.

An example of the "two good faith replies" method in action

A participant tells you she can't complete an assignment because she has "no time," when the *real* reason is that she just doesn't believe completing the assignment will be of value to her. Assume, for now, the participant is being direct with you. Give two good faith replies. If this fails, recognize the resistance and try to surface the *real* reason behind her reluctance to do the assignment.

The conversation might go something like this.

You (the workshop leader), "How about completing only part A of the assignment and leaving the other parts for next week?" This is your first "good faith reply." It takes the participant's concern about not having time at face value and assumes that *time* really is the issue.

The participant responds that she doesn't even have time to complete "part A." So, you try again. "Well, what about if we meet on Wednesday for an hour? I could help you with the assignment then." (Your second "good faith reply.")

Still no agreement. The participant is sticking with her "no time" story. Now it's time to recognize and name the resistance, but sensitively. If you push too hard or blame, the participant will likely get defensive. You'll end up driving her resistance even further underground.

Recognizing the resistance goes something like this, "I hear you saying your time won't allow you to complete this assignment. I've given a couple of options and you've said neither of these will work. Is there some other reason besides not having time available? If there is, maybe I need to hear it. Maybe there's some way I can help."

At this point you've done all you can. The participant will either "come clean" and be direct, telling you that she doesn't believe the assignment has any value for her, or she will become even more heavily invested in her story about time pressures, and her resistance will go even further underground.

Giving two good faith replies and then recognizing the resistance doesn't always work, but at least it gives you a chance of getting at the real issue.

End

F) The Harvard Negotiation Technique - Understanding and Agreeing

The four principles outlined in Fisher and Ury's (1981) Harvard Negotiation Technique hold the secret to understanding interests and different perspectives and to finding ways of agreeing on workshop outcomes, processes, and behaviors.[20]

This is an exceedingly useful tool for dealing with aggressive and overaggressive participation. You might also use it when contracting workshops with sponsor and end-user clients.

This method was originally developed for the "Law of the Seas Conference" in the 70's and 80's. Countries needed to agree on sensitive issues like fishing quotas. They then needed to stick by their agreements, in spite of economic and political pressures at home.

The Harvard Negotiation Technique was thus designed for situations where reaching agreement isn't enough. In these situations, people needed to build on their relationships during the negotiation process itself, and, most importantly, they needed to feel committed to these agreements. Otherwise "follow through" was unlikely.

It's one thing to get agreement. It can be quite another getting a participant or participants to "live by their agreement." Thus, this method is ideally suited for understanding and handling differences in workshops, where you need to build learning readiness and relationships at the same time as contracting for and managing expectations. All the while, you're sharing accountability with participants for workshop success.

The four principles of the Harvard Negotiation Technique

1) *Separate people from the problem*

When negotiating differences, relationships tend to become entangled with the issues or problems under consideration. Take care not to use your fears to deduce participants' intentions. Look for opportunities to act inconsistently with their expectations. Always give them a stake in the outcome by making sure they participate early and frequently in the process.

Acknowledge emotions as legitimate and allow participants to let off steam, if need be. Remember also that whatever you say in a negotiation, you should expect participants almost always to hear something different. Also, listen actively to ensure you are hearing them correctly.

Effective listening includes asking for examples and rephrasing participants' arguments in your own words. It also includes checking with participants to ensure you have understood them correctly.

2) *Focus on interests, not on positions*

Commit to your interests but not to your position. In fact, avoid taking a position altogether. Realize that each side in a negotiation has multiple interests and that you probably share more interests than differences. Communicate your interests while acknowledging participants' interests.

Be hard on the problem and soft on participants, and put the problem before the answer. In other words, don't jump to conclusions. First clarify the problem to everyone's satisfaction.

Finally, look forward, not back. That is, don't dredge up old and unrelated issues. Doing so will just make it more difficult to resolve present issues.

An example of an interest and a position

An example of an *interest* is, "Because I'm in Toronto for two weeks beginning next Wednesday, we need to complete this training module by early next Tuesday. If not, we'll have to leave it till I'm back in two weeks. Are you OK with next Tuesday, or do you have other suggestions?"

A corresponding *position* would be, "You have to be here next Tuesday at 8 AM, so we can finish this training module."

Sticking to your position boxes the participant in and creates unnecessary resistance. By stating an interest rather than a position, more creative solutions are possible.

3) *Invent options for mutual gain*

Separate the act of inventing options from the act of judging them. That is, brainstorm options and then evaluate. As you work, broaden the options on the table rather than looking for a single answer. Keep the word "equifinality" in mind. It means there's more that one way to achieve an outcome.

Invent ways to make agreement easy. Ask about the other person's preferences and what they view as appropriate and inappropriate. People are strongly influenced by *their* notion of legitimacy.

Watch for the following obstacles as you seek to invent and discover options that both of you can agree on.

- Premature judgment
- Searching for a single answer
- Assuming a "fixed pie" (i.e., assuming options can't be expanded)
- Thinking that solving *their* problem or *your* problem is solving *the* problem

4) *Insist on having objective criteria to evaluate proposed options*

Frame each issue as a joint search for objective criteria. Reason, and be open to reason, as to which standards are most appropriate, and how they should be applied. Above all, never yield to pressure, only to principle.

Do's" and "Don'ts"

Following are a few "do's" and "don'ts" when using the Harvard Negotiation Technique.

- However indirect the participant seems to be, don't "mind-read." Don't assume you know what their problem is or what their motive is.

- Don't defend your position. This only "locks you in." Instead, invite criticism. Recast an attack on you as an attack on the problem and focus on the ideas involved, not on personalities. Make perspectives "discussible." Treat emotions as facts, and facts as just one more piece of information.

- Don't reject or attack the participant's position. This only "locks them in." Instead, look behind their position. Try to find out "why" they feel a certain way. Ask questions about their interest instead of about their position; then pause to give them time to respond. Identify where your goals are incompatible with the participant's and then present valid "confirmable" data (i.e., data that can in some way be measured or observed).

- Finally, don't retreat if you believe you're right. If you seem to be at a stalemate, suggest a break to think. Avoid making a premature decision under pressure.

CONCLUSION

Summary

Active participation is one of the most important factors determining workshop success. The key message in this chapter is workshop leaders need to practice preventive medicine, identifying and eliminating participation problems before they spread and ruin the health of the entire workshop. So, be alert to potential participation problems (e.g., pay attention to participants' nonverbal signals, as well as their words). Once participation problems are suspected, you have a variety of treatments at your disposal (e.g., active listening, the Harvard Negotiation Technique, the 5C model).

The Nature of Workshop Control

Naturally you want process and direction to emerge from the group, but when this doesn't happen you have to take charge. Accepting this responsibility is part of being a leader as opposed to a moderator, an observer, or just one of the group. The workshop doesn't necessarily degenerate into chaos if no one is in charge, but if and when it does become disorganized and directionless, who's accountable?

Committeeizing accountability rarely works. Accountability must rest with you, the workshop leader.

There are no clear-cut rules as to how and when you need to exercise control, but there are important principles to keep in mind. These include,

- Never exercise control to suit your own purposes, only to help participants.
- Participants should make many of the workshop's decisions. It's your job to guide these decisions, to point out the consequences of these decisions, and make alternative recommendations when necessary.
- Remember that control is granted by participants. They can also rescind control if it's abused or not used responsibly. Adults can vote with their feet; they can walk out.

Running on Time

Digressions can add a great deal of color and value to a workshop, but they also raise havoc with time schedules. Build in extra time for on-topic digressions. They result in stories, examples, and alternative approaches that add life to theory and help connect participants' experiences to learning content. However, when time is running short, "park" these digressions on a flipchart. You can then deal with them, if and as time permits, later in the workshop.

Off-topic digressions contribute little or nothing to the workshop and are the bane of time-conscious workshop leaders. Deal with these digressions as they arise. Simply, but tactfully, challenge the participant to tell you how their point relates to what's being discussed.

Reinforcement

Don't be stingy with positive reinforcement. Make lots of deposits in the "relationship bank" with participants. When necessary, use negative reinforcement (e.g., confronting). Do this firmly, with respect, and with tact.

Nonverbals

While it's important that you pay attention to participants' words, it's also important to notice nonverbal cues and signals. In conjunction with other cues, these signals provide a host of information about the participants' attention, attitude, and emotions. Pressing for solutions too soon, moralizing, acting confused, and questioning methods endlessly might all indicate resistance. However, keep in mind that resistance is not always negative. More often than not, it's simply that a participant feels strongly about an alternative or contradictory point of view.

Valuing and Managing Differences

Three types of participation that must be managed in a workshop are underparticipation, overparticipation, and overaggressiveness.

Symptoms of *underparticipation* are silence, reluctance to practice new learning, a paucity of challenges, and arriving late and leaving early. Motives behind these behaviors vary. For example, participants may have been forced to attend the workshop or may be uncomfortable working in groups. Get the group active, up, and moving around. Poll participants to get them involved. Minimize your own talking time and encourage members of the group, especially the quiet ones, to express their opinions, ask questions, and to answer each other's questions.

Overparticipating members of the group interrupt and distract others, often asking questions that are off-topic. Sometimes participants are particularly well informed and overparticipate to gain recognition for their knowledge and achievement. Often this recognition is deserved, and granting it solves the problem. Other times, overparticipation is the result of nervousness, enthusiasm, or personality traits such as poor listening or social skills. Regardless of whether it's under- or overparticipation, offer encouragement and support. Deal with overparticipation by asking closed ended questions, redirecting their comments to other members of the group, or summarizing points and moving on. Another approach is to set limits, for example, ask each participant to contribute one comment and then to hold their thoughts until everyone has spoken. This approach ensures the overparticipating member of the group allows others time to speak. It also solicits participation directly from the quieter members of the group.

Overly aggressive participants may be argumentative, hold side conversations, bicker, and challenge incessantly. Strangely enough, sometime they do contribute a valuable perspective even though they are busy asserting their "own agenda." They may be trying to put you on the spot, or maybe they're just upset for personal reasons. Deal with overly aggressive participants by seeking to understand their points and by relaying their points to the group for comment. You might also choose to confront them directly. Use "I" statements, stay descriptive, and avoid arguing. Tactfully point out the workshop's purpose, outcomes, and time constraints. Alternatively, ask the overly aggressive participant to discuss their points later, at a break.

Models for Surfacing and Defusing Resistance

Six complementary and action oriented models are presented for managing participation problems in a workshop.

The Three Levels of a Problem lets workshop leaders quickly ascertain how they're contributing to the problem. Level one involves looking at the problem rationally, without emotion. Level two looks at what others are contributing to the problem.

The third and deepest level is looking at your own contribution to the problem. It's at this level where you have the most power to act.

Living on the Edge focuses on helping participants without getting hopelessly enmeshed in their problems. You need to get close enough to participants and their problems to provide empathy and caring, yet far enough away to avoid being drawn into their problems and losing your objectivity.

Effective Listening helps resolve problems with participants. Without this skill, discussion yields little or no results. Active listening is one strategy for listening effectively. It's highly structured and takes discipline to complete, but, if both parties are willing to work hard and look at their own behavior, active listening can result in remarkable breakthroughs in understanding.

The *Five C Model* guides workshop leaders, step by step, through the always treacherous waters of handling conflict in a workshop. Action required at each step is a little stronger than the last and designed to deal with the problem as it increases in magnitude. This model will help you choose the appropriate response for the appropriate level of conflict. The first "C" is concern. Here, the workshop leader determines whether the problem even needs to be dealt with or should simply be overlooked. The second "C" is confer. Wherever possible, this should be done privately with the participant. Give the participant three compliments and make your request directly. If conferring doesn't resolve the problem, move to the third "C," consult. Now you deal with the original issue as well as the fact that the request made while conferring hasn't worked. The fourth "C" is confrontation. It's time to be firm and talk consequences. Say what will happen if the problem isn't resolved. If the problem persists, move to the fifth and final "C," conclude. Now your choices are limited. You must follow through and apply the consequences. Don't get angry, and don't make it personal; just implement the consequences that were discussed a step four.

The *Two Good Faith Replies Model* helps workshop leaders sort out whether a comment or question is genuine and direct or a form of indirect resistance. This model guides you away from assuming motive and encourages you to take participants' comments or questions at face value, at least initially. First, answer the participant directly, assuming his/her question is open and honest. If that doesn't satisfy the participant, try a second "good faith" response. If the participant raises a third objection or question, it's time to dig a little deeper. Ask if there's something behind his/her concerns. Try to uncover and surface the deeper issue. Gently and tactfully confront the participant, letting him/her know you suspect there may be a concern that he/she is not sharing with you. Don't push too hard; you'll just drive his/her resistance further underground. All you can do is invite openness. And don't get drawn into an argument. At this point the participant will either "fess up" and explain the real reasons behind his/her resistance, or he/she will invest even further in the "original story."

The Harvard Negotiation Technique guides workshop leaders when dealing with strongly held differences. This tool is essential in a workshop where commitment to action and follow through are critical. It's based on four powerful principles. First, separate people from the problem. This means not taking your differences with participants personally, listening actively to ensure you're hearing what participants are saying, and acknowledging participants' concerns and emotions. Second, focus on interests, not on positions. Don't back yourself into a corner by taking a certain stance or commanding participants to act a certain way. Rather, attempt to understand both participants' and your own needs and interests. This leads to the third principle, using your understanding of participants' and your own interests to invent options that will benefit all concerned. Negotiation is a game of give and take, and each party must make sacrifices and contribute something to the other. Fourth, insist on objective criteria for evaluating proposed options. This provides a basis for rational agreement.

Checklist

Principles of a Workshop Leader's Control

- It's temporary
- It's by consent and for a purpose
- It's about the ability to influence
- It's a power everyone can exert
- It's a duty that can't be abdicated
- It's possible only when in "sync" with participants' needs and interests

Positive Reinforcement

- Providing desirable consequences

Other Forms of Reinforcement

- Remove an undesirable consequence
- Remove a desirable consequence
- Provide an undesirable consequence

What Resistance Can Look Like

- Asking for more detail
- Saying more time is needed or no time is available
- Saying "get realistic"
- Acting confused
- Moralizing
- Complying and nothing more
- Questioning methods endlessly
- All of a sudden saying, "The problem has gone away." (This form of indirect resistance is known as a "flight into health.")
- Pressing for solutions too soon
- Saying "I don't want any surprises"
- Attacking you or your position
- Silence
- Intellectualizing

Managing Participation Problems

- Underparticipation
- Overparticipation
- Overly aggressive participation
- Apathy

The Three Levels of a Problem

- The problem in rational terms
- What others are doing to contribute to the problem
- What I'm doing to contribute to the problem

Living on the Edge

- Distant
- Sucked in
- On the edge

The 5C Model

- Concern
- Confer
- Consult
- Confront
- Conclude

The Harvard Negotiation Technique

- Separate people from the problem
- Focus on interests, not on positions
- Invent options for mutual gain
- Insist on having objective criteria to evaluate proposed options

Exercise

Self-Rate Your Listening Practices Note: Take care when completing this rating as some of the following statements are reversed (e.g., I don't ...).	*Scale* **E** = Excellent **O** = OK **M** = Mediocre **A** = Awful

Visible Listening Practices

I pay attention to timing (e.g., I get agreement on the time and place for discussion with participants).	_____
I create a climate for listening. I sit face to face with participants and remove barriers (e.g., getting out from behind a table or podium).	_____
I make eye contact without staring a participant down.	_____
I nod occasionally (i.e., to let participants know I'm conscious).	_____
I don't interrupt or finish a participant's sentences, and I don't change the subject.	_____
I'm comfortable with silence (i.e., I don't rush participants).	_____
I paraphrase the words I'm hearing, in my mind, before responding to a participant (i.e., I aim for understanding, not necessarily agreement).	_____
I reflect back the emotions I'm getting before reacting to a participant's comments or actions (e.g., "I can see that you're really upset about ...").	_____

Exercise (continued)

Self-Rate Your Listening Practices (continued)	*Scale* **E** = Excellent **O** = OK **M** = Mediocre **A** = Awful

Invisible Listening Practices

I assess the level of goodwill and respect in the workshop (e.g., is there a willingness to share information and experiences?).	_____
I give participants my full attention. I don't let my mind wander.	_____
I don't mentally rehearse my response while a participant is speaking.	_____
I respect each participant's style and need for emotional space (e.g., I don't force sharing to a level the group is uncomfortable with).	_____
I look and listen for nonverbal messages in the group (e.g., tone, underlying feelings).	_____
I search for messages lying below participants' words and feelings.	_____
I don't react or pass judgment until I fully understand the participant.	_____

Exercise

Action Planning

Plan improvements to your listening skills based on self-rating your listening practices (above).

1) What are your strongest two or three listening practices? How can you continue to build on these strengths?

2) Which two or three listening practices, if improved, would add a great deal of value to your ability to listen effectively?

3) What steps can you take to improve these listening practices?

Notes

[1] Chandler, A.D. Jr. (March-April, 1988). Origins of the organization chart. Harvard Business Review, pp. 156-157.
[2]Rohn, J. (October 25, 1995). This comment is taken from a presentation by Jim Rohn on the topic of motivation and success. Calgary, Alta. Unpublished.
[3] Owen, H. (1991). Riding the tiger: Doing business in a transforming world. Potomac, MD: Abbott Publishing, p. 142.
[4] Covey, S.R. (1989). The 7 habits of highly effective people: Powerful lessons in personal change. New York, NY: Simon & Schuster.
[5] Blanchard, K., & Johnson, S. (1982). The one minute manager. New York, NY: William Morrow.
[6] Covey, S.R. (1989). The 7 habits of highly effective people: Powerful lessons in personal change. New York, NY: Simon & Schuster.
[7]Conner, D.R. (1992). Managing at the speed of change: How resilient managers succeed and prosper where others fail. New York, NY: Villard, p. 127.
[8]This list was inspired by a friend and colleague, Murray Hiebert, Calgary, Alberta, Canada.
[9]This is from the song "Dancing in the dark" by Bruce Springsteen.
[10]Jones, J.E., & Biech, E. (Eds.). (1996). 1996 HR Handbook. Amherst, MA: HRD Press.
[11]Prather, H. (1970). Notes to myself: My struggle to become a person. Toronto, Ont: Bantam Books.
[12] John Jones operates a consulting firm, Organizational Universe Systems, out of San Diego, California.
[13] Covey, S.R. (1989). The 7 habits of highly effective people: Powerful lessons in personal change. New York, NY: Simon & Schuster.
[14]Block, P. (1978). Flawless consulting: A guide to getting your expertise used. San Diego, CA: University Associates.
[15]I would like to thank a friend and colleague, David Irvine, for this model of "living on the edge." Dave operates his own consulting practice out of Cochrane, Alberta, Canada.
[16]Although the following words are mine, I'm grateful to William Purkey for the idea and names of these five steps. I heard William Purkey give a lecture in Calgary, Alberta, on May 15, 1992. During this lecture he talked about the 5C's. Two sources of his work are, 1) Purkey, W.W. (1970). Self concept and school achievement. Englewood Cliffs, NJ: Prentice-Hall. 2) Purkey, W.W. (1984). Inviting school success: A self concept approach to teaching and learning. Belmont, CA: Wadsworth.
[17]Cypert, S.A. (1994). The power of self-esteem. New York, NY: AMACOM, p. 95.
[18]I'm indebted to Scott Hodge with the city of Winnipeg for challenging a colleague of mine (Dave Irvine) regarding this model. Thanks to Scott's challenges I was able to think through this third application step for the 5C model.
[19]Block, P. (1978). Flawless consulting: A guide to getting your expertise used. San Diego, CA: University Associates.
[20]Fisher, R., & Ury, W. (1981). Getting to yes: Negotiating agreement without giving in. Boston, MA: Houghton Mifflin.

Appendixes

Appendix A

A Process Cycle Definition of Workshops and Training Programs

This definition of workshops and training programs is set out in the format of a process cycle (purpose, outcomes, steps, requirements, feedback). The process cycle is described in chapter three.

Purpose

Workshops

- To help a group think, learn, decide, plan action, solve problems, produce a product, gather information, prepare for a task, or perform a task.

Training Programs

- To help participants gain new knowledge and develop skills.

Outcomes

Workshops

- Quality products (e.g., decisions, action plans, information, feedback).
- Group members own and are committed to the process and its results.
- The group has learned and understood the process.

Training Programs

- Participants integrate new information with existing knowledge.
- Participants learn and practice skills.
- Participants make specific action plans and commit to applying new knowledge and skills on the job.

Steps

Workshops

- Establish a focus (i.e., clear purpose and outcomes).

- Clarify the situation (i.e., work toward a full and common understanding).
- Generate ideas and options.
- Prioritize and select options.
- Summarize and plan action.

Training Programs

- Ensure content relevancy and learning readiness.
- Deliver training with energy and enthusiasm.
- Provide plenty of opportunity for participant dialogue, involvement, and practice.
- Plan application on the job.

Requirements of Participants

Workshops

- A belief that the group has the capability to deal with the issue at hand.
- Self-awareness and the courage to speak directly, openly, and tactfully in the group.
- Sensitivity to issues and concerns not directly expressed.
- Pride in each other's and in the group's success.
- A good background in the topic, issue, or focus area of the workshop.
- Work together as equals.

Training Programs

- Motivation to participate, learn, and practice during the training program.
- Challenge, support, mutual appreciation, and learning from each other during the training program.
- Willingness to commit to, and plan, application of new knowledge and skills on the job.

Feedback (what success looks like)

Workshops

- Issues are understood, options considered, next steps agreed.

- In the future, the group is more able to deal with similar issues without depending as much on an external workshop facilitator.

Training Programs

- Participants participate and practice eagerly during the training program.

Both Workshops and Training Programs

- Lots of noise and energy during the event (workshop or training program), differences shared, good listening, periods of silence.
- Balanced participation, congruent body language.
- People meet their "follow up" commitments after the event.
- The group refers other groups to you, and they ask for help with more challenging issues (be they workshops or training programs).

To Train or to Consult?

Workshop and training-program leaders need to continuously fine-tune their approach to the outcomes being sought and to the group's needs and interests. Some trainers have difficulty operating workshops that demand a consulting perspective, and some consultants have problems meeting the structural demands of training programs.[1]

Issues relating to the two approaches appear on the following pages.

Training Approach	*Consulting /Workshop Approach*	*The group's concern when the leader is training but* ***should be consulting***
Content focus Pre-frames issues and has the answers	*Issue focus* Helps to frame issues and discover answers	"The leader is oversimplifying and avoiding the real issues. He/she has their own agenda and can't seem to adjust to our needs."
Sticks to the plan	Plans and revises on the go	"The leader is preoccupied with staying on time. We're rushing through valuable discussion. He/she needs to be more flexible. It's results, not the agenda, that count."
People focus	Business focus	"The leader lacks a systems perspective. He/she thinks everything is a people or training problem."
Solution focus Directs the group. Uses a roadmap.	*Problem focus* Guides the group. Uses a compass.	"The leader is stuck on his/her personal *truths*. He/she doesn't seem to understand our unique situation. He/she might just as well have mailed us the answers. It's like grade school."

The group's concern when the leader is consulting but ***should be training***	***When a workshop is needed*** *the trainer who has difficulty leading workshops will think...*	***When training is needed*** *the consultant who has difficulty training will think...*
"The leader is complicating the situation and making a mountain out of a molehill. He/she needs to provide direction and a few answers. We're floundering and wasting time."	"The group is too broadly focused and pulling in extraneous factors. It's not that complicated."	"The group is oversimplifying and avoiding the real issues. Why can't they tolerate a little ambiguity? They seem to want to be spoon-fed."
"The leader is too casual about the agenda. If we don't get moving, we won't cover everything."	"The group has trouble staying on track. It's like herding cats. They don't seem to understand the focus. Maybe they're just expecting too much of this material."	"The group is too narrowly focused and seems to want easy answers. If only it were that simple!"
"The leader is too scattered. We need to focus on what knowledge and skills people need to get the job done."	"The group is too scattered. They need to focus on these specific skills if they're serious about meaningful change."	"The group needs to focus more on the business issues. They seem too caught up with simple answers and quick fixes."
"The leader doesn't have the answers, and what he/she does provide causes as many problems as it solves. He/she also needs to show the process. It's not clear how we're going to get this done."	"The group undervalues the material. The steps are clear if they'd just follow them."	"The group is expecting easy answers and seems unable to understanding the complexity and paradox at play here. They need to welcome ambiguity and be willing to struggle a little. We're breaking new ground here. There are no sure-fire recipes."

Notes

[1]This table was inspired by an article by Geoffrey Bellman. Bellman, G. (January, 1983). Untraining the trainer: Steps toward consulting. Training and Development Journal, pp. 70-73.

Appendix C

Examples of Training-Program Outcomes

These examples relate to a specific training-program titled *Train the Trainer*. The first section describes outcomes that can be measured or observed *during* this training program. The second section looks at outcomes several weeks *following completion* of this training program. It's hoped you will be able to adapt some of the ideas in this appendix for your own workshops and training programs.

OUTCOMES - DURING THE TRAINING PROGRAM

The following observations and measurements will be possible during the training program.

Level-1 Evaluation - Reaction during the Training-Program Wrap-Up

- The training program is rated in the top 20% using the client's evaluation form.
- Participants say the training program was relevant to their needs and will be useful to them professionally. They also say it gave them confidence in themselves as leaders and that it provided them with clear direction for designing and delivering their workshops and training programs.
- Participants say they were challenged, worked hard, had fun, and gained a lot for their "two day investment."

Level-2 Evaluation - Learning during the Training Program

There won't be any tests for learning during the training program, but I'll be able to listen to the group. By listening, I'll be able to gather circumstantial evidence that participants are learning.

- Participants ask me and each other questions ranging from the *obvious*, the *interesting*, and the *absurd*. Asking "the obvious" will indicate participants are willing to clarify and "reality check." Asking interesting questions (the obvious with a twist) will demonstrate that participants are thinking and challenging. Absurd questions will indicate participants are willing to explore creative approaches and take risks. It'll also indicate they want to test the limits of their new learning.

- Using their own examples when they discuss learning points during the training program will indicate that participants are integrating new learnings with old knowledge.

Level-3 Evaluation - Behavior during the Training Program

Casey Stengel once said that "you can see a lot by observing." So, I need to keep my eyes open and watch participants' behavior during the training program.

- Participants will be enjoying themselves and working hard. This will be evident in activity levels and nonverbals.
- Watching participants during their "practice delivery sessions," I will observe how well they have prepared and how well they are applying learning points from the training program.
- Participant practice delivery sessions improve from their first to their second (e.g., they make adjustments based on feedback from their first practice session, they show more energy and confidence in their presentation).
- Participants take risks. Being educated in public, that is, learning by performing in front of others, can be stressful. I'll know participants are wanting to become better workshop and training-program leaders if they take a few chances (e.g., they "stretch" themselves by using an unfamiliar training designs in their practice sessions, they challenge me and each other with difficult and probing questions).

Level-4 Evaluation - Results Achieved during the Training Program

Level-4 relates to outcomes achieved as a consequence of a workshop or training program. Thus, level-4 evaluation has no meaning *during* the event itself, because workshops and training programs are not conducted for their own sake. If they were, then the purpose of workshops and training programs is "self-serving." That is, the reason you're conducting a given training program now is so that you can sell even more of these programs in the future. This view would see workshops and training programs as "make work projects," rather than as being in the service of clients and their organizations. I trust that not many people will see workshops and training programs in this way. However, if this is your view, you need to seriously reexamine your philosophy as a workshop or training-program leader.

Outcomes - As a Consequence of the Training Program

The following observations and measurements will be possible several weeks after completion of the training program. (Note: The term "end-user client" is now more appropriate than the term "participant.")

Level-1 Evaluation - Reaction after the Workshop

- On reevaluation, end-user clients rate this program in the top quartile using their organization's evaluation form. This rating is more significant than that completed during the training-program wrap-up. At that time participants were feeling good about their learning, some had just "got religion," and others just wanted to be "nice" on the evaluation form. Now, the reality of just how difficult things are in the real world has returned. Nonetheless, end-user clients still say this program was and continues to be useful to them professionally.
- Most end-user clients say they are using the training-program materials in designing and preparing to deliver their workshops and training programs. Finally, looking back, many say this training program got them started along the road to higher levels of skill and confidence as workshop and training-program leaders.

Level-2 Evaluation - Learning That's Lasted after the Workshop

Learning can quickly wash through a person's mind; in one ear and out the other. Sometimes participants make overgeneralized statements in the training-program wrap-up like, "I enjoyed the training program" or "I learned a few things." However, they must make deliberate attempts at using the training-program material soon after the event. Otherwise, old habits return, and upwards of 95% of new learnings are likely to be forgotten over time.

Below are examples of level-2 training-program outcomes. These could be used to measure or observe whether learning "has taken," that is, whether end-user clients have retained key learnings several weeks after the training program has been completed.

- End-user clients can identify signs of direct and indirect resistance and formulate strategies for dealing with resistance in the training room.
- End-user clients can list ways to establish positive relationships with learners.
- End-user clients can evaluate and discuss the four-step Harvard negotiation technique.
- End-user clients can describe and compare strategies for using small group activities within training programs.

Level-3 Evaluation - Behavior on the Job

Examples of level-3 outcomes for this training program include:

- End-user clients are using the "process cycle" to plan the purpose and outcomes for their workshops and training programs.
- End-user clients are employing adult-learning principles in their workshop and training-program designs. They are also using a variety of design options in order to access all four learning styles.
- End-user clients are demonstrating the principles for giving and receiving effective feedback in their workshops and training programs.
- End-user clients are setting a positive learning climate and getting learners involved quickly at the beginning of their workshops and training programs.
- End-user clients are using "what" and "why" bridges when conducting their workshops and training programs, and they're summarizing and reviewing at the end of each workshop or training-program session.

Level-4 Evaluation - Organizational Results

Level-4 evaluation is the ultimate measure of workshop or training-program success. Given the reality of multiple causality in organizational systems, it's not possible to "portion out" recognition for organization results; however, it may be possible to talk in terms of a workshop or training program contributing to the following types of results.

- A measurable increase in the capacity of the organization to produce
- Decreased employee turnover
- Increased profits
- Improved morale and quality of work life
- Improvements in shareholder value
- Improved levels of customer satisfaction

Appendix

An Assortment of Models for Writing Outcomes

Chapter three provided a detailed approach to writing outcome statements. In addition, you might want to consider any one of the following approaches.

1) SPIRO (a rational approach)

John Jones's SPIRO model (1972) provides the basics for writing outcome statements.[1]

Specify:	Outcomes must be specific. What exactly are you going to do?
Performance:	Outcomes must focus on high value results, not on activities. What do you intend to accomplish?
Involvement:	Participants need to be involved in setting outcomes. What is your part in the outcome?
Realism:	Outcomes need to be realistic and rewarding. If they are too ambitious, they may lead to disappointment. Yet, outcomes must also be challenging or there will be no pride of accomplishment. Can it be done given the resources available?
Observable:	Outcomes need to be measurable or observable. How will you know whether you have been successful?[2]

2) SMART (a rational approach)

Scott and Jaffe (1989) outline an approach similar to that provided above.[3]

Specific:	Outcomes must be specific.
Measurable:	Outcomes need to be measurable or observable.
Attainable:	Outcomes must be "doable."
Realistic:	Outcomes must be attainable and achievable.
Timebound:	Outcomes and steps to achieving these are tied to specific dates so progress can be targeted and measured.

Note: The "T" in SMART could also stand for "trackable" or "truthful." "Trackable" relates to the ability to monitor results (e.g., build milestones into your outcomes and measure incremental gains). "Truthful" suggests you're setting outcomes that you're serious about and committed to achieving.

3) PRICE (a continuous process approach)

Blanchard and Lorber (1984) provide a model that considers ongoing coaching and continuous improvement in performance.[4]

Pinpoint:	Define the performance that's required.
Record:	Graph current performance.
Involve:	Agree on outcomes and steps to accomplish these, including coaching and evaluation.
Coach:	Coach the performer. Provide ongoing support and challenge.
Evaluate:	Track performance graphically. Revise strategies as necessary.

4) The ABC's of Outcomes (a sensory approach)

Genie Laborde (1984) outlines a unique approach to writing outcome statements. She calls it the ABC's of outcomes.[5]

Aim for a specific result	Outcomes must be specific.
Be positive	State your outcomes positively (e.g., "I want...") versus stating what you don't want or what you want to avoid.
see	See, hear, and feel sensory data. Pay attention to what's happening around you.
Dovetail desires	Seek to have "a little something for everyone" in your outcomes.
Entertain the short and long term	Don't just think short term.

5) Task analysis

Task analysis is useful for assessing skill but not knowledge training needs. It involves breaking a job into its logically sequenced subtasks and arranging these in hierarchical order, forming "ends-means chains." This helps organize your thinking and leads to more specific outcomes. For example, if the objective is "the participant will swim across the lake," the participant must first be able to accomplish the following: getting into the water, floating, breathing on alternate strokes, kicking properly, using correct arm strokes, and so on.

Notes

[1]Jones, J.E. (1972). Criteria for effective goal-setting: The SPIRO model. In J.W. Pfeiffer and J.E. Jones (Eds.). The 1972 annual handbook for group facilitators. San Diego, CA: University Associates, pp. 132-133.

[2]These questions accompanying the SPIRO model are taken from a workbook prepared by J.E. Jones and Harry Pollard. This workbook was part of a series of workshops on leadership provided to managers in Dome Petroleum Limited, Calgary, Canada, in the mid 1980's. Unpublished manuscript.

[3]Scott, C.D., & Jaffe, D.T. (1989). Managing organizational change: A practical guide for managers. Menlo Park, CA: Crisp, p. 55.

[4]Blanchard, K., & Lorber, R. (1984). Putting the one minute manager to work. New York, NY: William Morrow.

[5]Laborde, G.Z. (1984). Influencing with integrity: Management skills for communication and negotiation. Palo Alto, CA: Syntony.

Appendix E

Examples of Level-1 Evaluation and Pre-Evaluation Forms

This appendix provides eight examples of level-1, reaction evaluation, and one example of pre-evaluation.

- One minute feedback
- Session highs and lows
- Tailored and quantitative
- Tailored and qualitative
- Critical incident
- Reflections and applications planning
- Mixed
- Categorized
- Pre-evaluation (the inverse of evaluation)

Although the following examples are kept separate and distinct, in practice these should be mixed and matched such that some questions on the evaluation form would be quantitative, others qualitative, and still others seeking information on critical incidents. (*Note*: The "one minute feedback" and "session highs and lows" forms shown below are identical to those provided in chapter twelve. The first page of the "mixed" form shown below is also identical to that provided in chapter eleven.)

ONE MINUTE FEEDBACK

This form is a quick "temperature check." Use it to take the emotional temperature in the workshop or training room.

Workshop Name: ______________________ Date: ____________

One Minute Feedback

So far I'm finding this workshop to be (circle your response)...

Interesting	1	2	3	4	5	Uninteresting
Too fast	1	2	3	4	5	Too slow
Too easy	1	2	3	4	5	Too difficult
Relevant	1	2	3	4	5	Irrelevant
Organized	1	2	3	4	5	Disorganized
Relaxed	1	2	3	4	5	Tense

Please provide a brief comment for improving this workshop.

Participant Name: ____________________

SESSION HIGHS AND LOWS

Use a form similar to this one for gathering feedback at the end of each workshop or training-program session (e.g., half day, day).

Workshop Name: ______________________ Date: ____________

End of Session Feedback

I was most energized today when (please be specific)...

I was least interested today when (please be specific)...

Comments and suggestions for improving this workshop...

Participant Name: ______________________

TAILORED AND QUANTITATIVE

The following example is tailored to a training program aimed at developing workshop and training-program leaders. Quantitative evaluation allows you to compare reactions among participants in a given event and across different workshops or training programs. Asking "why" after each response helps clarify the ratings.

Date: __________

Developing Workshop Leaders

QUANTITATIVE EVALUATION

Rate the following questions on a scale of 1 to 5 (1 low; 5 high) and briefly outline "why" you have circled a particular rating. Please be specific.

1. How would you rate this workshop in terms of its value to you individually?

   1 2 3 4 5

   Why? ____

   ____

2. How would you rate this workshop in terms of its "trickle down" value to your workshop customers (that is, those you will be conducting workshops and training programs for in the future)?

   1 2 3 4 5

   Why? ____

   ____

3. I received useful feedback following my practice sessions.

   1 2 3 4 5

   Why? ____

   ____

4. My confidence as a workshop leader or trainer has improved.

   1 2 3 4 5

   Why? ____

   ____

Page 1

5. I think the workbook will be a useful reference for me in the future.

1 2 3 4 5

Why? ____

____

6. I received valuable insights, models, and suggestions for

Planning workshops 1 2 3 4 5

Why? ____

____

Designing workshops 1 2 3 4 5

Why? ____

____

Organizing workshops 1 2 3 4 5

Why? ____

____

Helping others learn 1 2 3 4 5

Why? ____

____

7. Other comments:

Participant Name: ______________________

Page 2

TAILORED AND QUALITATIVE

The following example is also tailored to a training program aimed at developing workshop and training-program leaders. It uses superlative adjectives (e.g., most, least, worst) to test the boundaries of participant feedback and seeks help for improving the training program. It also solicits participants' suggestions on how they can continue to develop as workshop and training-program leaders.

Date: __________

Developing Workshop Leaders

QUALITATIVE EVALUATION

1. What did you like most about this workshop?

2. What did you like least about this workshop?

3. What are three ways this workshop can be improved?

4. What would you most like to improve about how you lead workshops?

5. What three things are you going to do to further develop your skills as a workshop leader or trainer (e.g., training, practice, reading)?

Participant Name: ____________________

Critical Incident

This approach is designed to gather descriptions of specific incidents where participants felt their strongest reactions during the workshop (e.g., helpful actions, puzzling actions). It encourages description as well as evaluation. Thus, it's an excellent tool for assessing workshop or training-program leader performance and for understanding and appreciating participant emotions, involvement, and learning.

Workshop Name: ______________________ Date: __________

CRITICAL INCIDENT EVALUATION

At what moment during the workshop did you feel most engaged and enthusiastic about what was happening?

At what moment during the workshop did you feel most unresponsive and disinterested in what was happening?

What action (by anyone) during the workshop did you find most affirming and helpful?

What action (by anyone) during the workshop did you find most puzzling and confusing?

What about the workshop surprised you (e.g., your own reactions, what someone did or said)?

Participant Name: ________________

REFLECTIONS AND APPLICATIONS PLANNING

This informal approach mixes reflections about learnings with planning for application of new learnings.

Workshop Name: ______________________ Date: __________

Reflections and Applications Planning

1. What are two learnings that you have gained or strengthened at this workshop?

   a)

   b)

2. What one thing are you going to do differently next week, or sooner, as a result of these new learnings?

3. Name one or two people who you will help and encourage to learn what you've learned in this workshop?

Participant Name: ________________

MIXED

The following requests a mix of quantitative, qualitative, and critical incident evaluation.[1]

Training-Program Evaluation

Name __________________________ *Date* __________

Workshop Name ______________________________________

Workshop Leader(s) Name ________________________________

Please circle the appropriate response.

Stated outcomes were achieved during the training program.	Not at all 1 2 3 Somewhat 4 5 6 7 Completely 8 9
Training-program content was relevant and challenging.	Not at all 1 2 3 Somewhat 4 5 6 7 Completely 8 9
Support materials (e.g., handouts) were helpful.	Not helpful 1 2 3 Somewhat helpful 4 5 6 7 Very helpful 8 9
The training-program leader was effective.	Not at all 1 2 3 Somewhat 4 5 6 7 Completely 8 9
This training program has improved my understanding of the topic.	Not at all 1 2 3 Somewhat 4 5 6 7 Very much 8 9

Page 1

This training program has equipped me with information and skills that I can use immediately.	Not at all Somewhat Very much 1 2 3 4 5 6 7 8 9
The time allowed for the training program was ...	Circle appropriate response. Too much About right Too little
Overall training-program evaluation	Poor Fine Excellent 1 2 3 4 5 6 7 8 9

Highlights - What parts of the training program were *most* interesting and useful for you?

Low Spots - What parts of the training program were of little or no value for you?

Leadership - Comment on the training-program leader's effectiveness (e.g., rapport with group, presentation, methods and models used).

Other comments *Page 2*

Notes

[1]This form is inspired by a similar form at Shell Canada Limited, Calgary, Alberta, Canada. Unpublished document.

Rights and Responsibilities of Participants and the Workshop Leader

Who's in charge of a workshop or training program? Does the workshop leader control anything? Is "control" even the appropriate word? Words like "control" and "leadership" can be ambiguous and emotionally loaded. Clarifying roles in terms of rights and accompanying responsibilities helps determine who needs to do what in a workshop or training program.

In Canada the "Charter of Rights and Freedoms" sets out the rights of every citizen in the country. The idea behind this Charter is protection for the individual from unfair treatment, prejudice, and injustice. The Charter, however, is silent around responsibilities of Canadians. Provided below is a workshop and training-program charter of rights and freedoms. This charter is not silent on the responsibilities that accompany each "right."

Use this charter when contracting roles during a workshop or training-program start-up. It's necessarily incomplete. It would be impossible, and far too wordy, to outline a full charter of rights, freedoms, and responsibilities covering every situation in a workshop or training program. So, use the following as a guideline only. Interpret and adapt it as you see fit to each situation. Use it as a starting place with a group to discuss and develop a charter for a workshop or training program.

You might argue that this charter isn't necessary. The workshop belongs to participants and what they say goes. Something like the old "the customer is king" argument. That argument has some merit insofar as participants are customers. It's their needs which must be met. And after all, the workshop's purpose is that participants learn and accomplish a designated purpose and outcome. But telling workshop leaders to let participants direct the workshop is one of those ideas that works in theory but is too simplistic in practice.

Participants are rarely a unified or homogeneous group. They often have different perspectives on workshop process and even on workshop purpose and outcomes. And it's not just a matter of majority rule either. Your reputation as a workshop leader is at stake with every workshop you operate. A failed workshop can result in a dwindling client list for an external consultant and a loss of credibility for an internal consultant. While the importance of participant input into the workshop process cannot be underestimated, it is you alone who has the expertise, and ultimately the responsibility, for leading the workshop.

The bottom line is that, somehow, someone or some group must decide a range of issues during a workshop (e.g., what to do next, what to emphasize, how to proceed). Asking the group doesn't always produce a single, unified answer. Thus, in practice both you and the participants need to retain some control to make difficult decisions and to be in charge of parts of the workshop. Needless to say this "power to decide" comes with corresponding responsibilities, for both yourself and for participants. That's where the following charters come in. These are far too detailed to be dealt with in depth during a workshop start-up, but as handouts they would provide participants with a sense of direction, roles, expectations, and obligations during a workshop.

As you read the following charters, keep in mind that no model, theory, charter of responsibilities, or any other rational document can replace or make up for a lack of good working relationships, trust, rapport, or common sense in a workshop. These charters are just guidelines to get you and participants thinking about your respective roles during a workshop or training program.

The Workshop Leader's Charter of Rights, Freedoms, and Responsibilities

Workshop leaders have the right	*Workshop leaders have the accompanying responsibilities*
Climate To manage the learning climate (e.g., to organize the training room, to introduce the workshop).	• To involve participants in workshop decisions (e.g., decisions around climate, process, timing). • To ensure the learning climate is practical, useful, stimulating, focused, involving, and about three dozen other things (i.e., that there is a clear context for learning).

Workshop leaders have the right	*Workshop leaders have the accompanying responsibilities*
Learning Readiness To challenge the group to be learning ready (e.g., open to new learning).	• To trust the group unless there is clear evidence to the contrary (e.g., if the group says they are learning ready, if the group says they want to revisit an issue). • To support and respect participants as they struggle with the need to learn new ways of thinking and acting.
Process To be in charge of the process (e.g., to ask participants to be involved in an exercise, to refocus discussion using questions).	• To work toward clear and agreed upon outcomes. • To make your process visible and challengeable (except when there's a specific reason not to).[1] • To respect participants' individual learning needs, pace, and learning styles.
Not to tell participants everything (e.g., what specifically participants are supposed to learn, exactly "why" you've asked a group to do a particular exercise).	• To be a little ambiguous when appropriate (e.g., in small group exercises ambiguity can add struggle and aids the learning process).
To be clear about purpose, agenda, context, process, and roles.	• To work toward clear outcomes and a clear agenda. • To show context (e.g., how and why a given method or model fits into a workshop). • To clarify and summarize learning points. • To ensure participants know what's expected from them and what to expect from you (the workshop leader).

Workshop leaders have the right	*Workshop leaders have the accompanying responsibilities*
Content To say what learning content will not be included in a training program.	• To ensure participants have clear expectations of the workshop (e.g., direct and honest advertising). • To keep promises.
Schedule and Timing To control the schedule and timing (e.g., to start on time, to decide when it's time to move on or when more discussion is needed on a given topic).	• To clearly explain "why" a request can't be met. • To offer alternatives when possible.
Style To one's own leadership style (e.g., to decide whether to use an overhead projector or flipchart, whether to lecture or use small group exercises).	• To care about participant learning (e.g., put the group's interests and learning needs first when deciding on a learning method). • To make the workshop interesting and energizing versus simply presenting learning content (e.g., use a variety of workshop designs). • To be authentic and honest. • To act nondefensively when challenged. • To be self-aware and open about your own biases, preferences, and habits.

Workshop leaders have the right	*Workshop leaders have the accompanying responsibilities*
Mistakes To be human. To make the odd mistake (e.g., to phrase something poorly on occasion, to change your mind about a method or process).	• To minimize mistakes. • To be well organized, informed, and prepared. • To be well intended (e.g., to care about participants' learning).

Participants' Charter of Rights, Freedoms, and Responsibilities

Participants have the right	*Participants have the accompanying responsibilities*
Interests and Needs To their feelings, interests, and learning needs.	• To come to the workshop with a positive attitude, organized and ready to learn. • To be open to new ideas and new ways of thinking. • Take responsibility for their own emotional reactions during the workshop. • To "fess up" to not being learning ready if this is the case (e.g., not to "role-play" involvement or learning).
Information and Involvement To be informed and involved in all aspects of the workshop (e.g., setting outcomes, evaluation).	• To seek ways to be involved versus simply waiting to be asked. • To contribute enthusiastically. • To challenge and ask questions until satisfactory answers are developed or provided.

Participants have the right	*Participants have the accompanying responsibilities*
Challenge To challenge, ask questions, and comment on anything in the workshop. To call "time out" (e.g., when not able to follow the discussion).	• To voice their concerns openly, honestly, and directly. • Not to mislead or distract the group. • To minimize distractions and off-topic discussions. • To give others the benefit of the doubt. • To tolerate a little ambiguity in the workshop (e.g., to be willing to struggle to achieve results and to learn).
Privacy To their own thoughts and not to speak or disclose certain information.	• To reflect on learning content. • To try to integrate new learning with old learning and experience.
Quality To receive a well-organized, worthwhile, and quality learning experience that emphasizes their learning needs.	• To be on time. • To participate actively. • To consider other participants' needs and opinions. • To complete assignments. • To not expect a "free ride" or to be able to learn passively.
Mistakes To be human (e.g., to ask a dumb question, to forget a direction, to lose their concentration).	• To work hard to grasp new learning. • To challenge when bored. • To learn from mistakes.

Participants have the right	*Participants have the accompanying responsibilities*
To Leave To leave a workshop if it is not motivating, energizing, or appropriate to their interests or learning needs.	• To be open minded about their need for new learning and potential benefits of the workshop. • To voice their concerns and be honest about their reasons for leaving. • To not contaminate the workshop with anger or insist that other participants see things their way. • To participate actively if they choose to remain in the workshop.

Notes

[1]An example of a reason for not making your process visible to the group would be when you want to have participants draw their own conclusions from an exercise. Thus, telling them too much about your process beforehand might overdirect participants in the exercise.

Bibliography

Ackoff, R.L. (1981). Creating the corporate future: Plan or be planned for. New York, NY: John Wiley & Sons.

Adams, S. (1991). Build a better life by stealing office supplies: Dogbert's big book of business. Kansas City, KS: Andrews & McMeel.

Argyris, C. (May-June, 1991). Teaching smart people how to learn. *Harvard Business Review*, (pp. 99-109).

Argyris, C., & Schon, D.A. (1974). Theory in practice: Increasing professional effectiveness. San Francisco, CA: Jossey-Bass.

Argyris, C., & Schon, D.A. (1978). Organizational learning: A theory of action perspective. Reading, MA: Addison-Wesley.

Bandler, R., & Grinder, J. (1975). The structure of magic. A book about language and therapy. Palo Alto, CA: Science and Behavior Books.

Bandler, R., & Grinder, J. (1979). Frogs into princes: Neuro-linguistic programming. Ed. J.O. Stevens. Moab, UT: Real People Press.

Bandler, R., & Grinder, J. (1981). Trance-formations: Neuro-linguistic programming and the structure of hypnosis. Ed. C. Andreas. Moab, UT: Real People Press.

Bateson, G. (1972). Steps to an ecology of mind. New York, NY: Ballantine.

Bellman, G. (January, 1983). Untraining the trainer: Steps toward consulting. *Training and Development Journal*, (pp. 70-73).

Bellman, G.M. (1990). The consultant's calling: Bring who you are to what you do. San Francisco, CA: Jossey-Bass.

Bennis, W. (1993). An invented life: Reflections on leadership and change. Reading, MA: Addison-Wesley.

Bennis, W., & Nanus, B. (1985). Leaders: The strategies for taking charge. New York, NY: Harper & Row.

Berne, E. (1964). Games people play: The psychology of human relationships. New York, NY: Ballantine.

Blanchard, K., & Johnson, S. (1982). The one minute manager. New York, NY: William Morrow.

Blanchard, K., & Lorber, R. (1984). Putting the one minute manager to work. New York, NY: William Morrow.

Block, P. (1978). Flawless consulting: A guide to getting your expertise used. San Diego, CA: University Associates.

Block, P. (1987). The empowered manager: Positive political skills at work. San Francisco, CA: Jossey-Bass.

Block, P. (1993). Stewardship: Choosing service over self-interest. San Francisco, CA: Berrett-Koehler.

Boettinger, H.M. (1969). Moving mountains: The art of letting others see things your way. New York, NY: Macmillan.

Boyd, R.S. (March 2, 1996). Memory. Calgary, Alta: Calgary Herald, (p. B3).

Bridges, W. (1994). JobShift: How to prosper in a workplace without jobs. Reading, MA: Addison-Wesley.

Brookfield, S.D. (1987). Developing critical thinkers: Challenging adults to explore alternative ways of thinking and acting. San Francisco, CA: Jossey-Bass.

Brown, H.J., Jr. (1992). Live and learn. Madera, CA: Portal Publications.

Burke Guild, P. (April, 1983). How to involve learners in your lectures. Training, (pp. 43-44).

Burke, W.W. (1987). Organization development: A normative view. Reading, MA: Addison-Wesley.

Burrus, D. (1993). Technotrends: How to use technology to go beyond your competition. New York, NY: HarperBusiness.

Buzan, T. (1983). Using both sides of your brain. New York, NY: Dutton.

Byrum, B. (1989). New age training technologies: The best and the safest. The 1989 annual: Developing human resources. San Diego, CA: University Associates.

Canadian Training and Development Manual. (1994). Program design and development. Toronto, Ont: CCH Canadian Limited, (para. 5001-6051).

Canadian Training and Development Manual. (1994). Training methods. Toronto, Ont: CCH Canadian Limited, (para. 7001-7904).

Carver, J. (1991). Boards that make a difference: A new design for leadership in nonprofit and public organizations. San Francisco, CA: Jossey-Bass.

Chandler, A.D., Jr. (March-April, 1988). Origins of the organization chart. *Harvard Business Review*, (pp. 156-157).

Chaplin, J.P. (1985). Dictionary of psychology. (2nd ed.). New York, NY: Laurel.

Conner, D.R. (1992). Managing at the speed of change: How resilient managers succeed and prosper where others fail. New York, NY: Villard.

Cooperrider & Srivastva. (1987). Appreciative inquiry into organizational life. Research in organization change and development. Vol. 1. New York, NY: JAI Press, (pp. 129-169).

Cousins, N. (1981). Human options. New York, NY: Berkley Books.

Covey, S.R. (1989). The 7 habits of highly effective people: Powerful lessons in personal change. New York, NY: Simon & Schuster.

Cypert, S.A. (1994). The power of self-esteem. New York, NY: AMACOM.

de Bono, E. (1985). Six thinking hats. Boston, MA: Little/Brown.

Deep, S., & Sussman, L. (1995). Smart moves for people in charge: 130 checklists to help you be a better leader. Reading, MA: Addison-Wesley.

Delbecq, A.L., & Vande de Ven, A.H. (1971). A group process model for problem identification and program planning. *Journal of Applied Behavioral Science*, 7, (pp. 466-492).

Delbecq, A.L., Vande de Ven, A.H., & Gustafson, D.H. (1975). Group techniques for program planning: A guide to nominal group and delphi process. Glenview, IL: Scott, Foresman and Company.

Deming, W.E. (1982). Quality, productivity and competitive position. Cambridge, MA: MIT Press.

Doyle, M., & Straus, D. (1976). How to make meetings work. New York, NY: Jove.

Drath, W.H., & Palus, C.H. (1994). Making common sense: Leadership as meaning-making in a community of practice. Greensboro, NC: Center for Creative Leadership.

Drucker, P. (January-February. 1988), The coming of the new organization. *Harvard Business Review*, (pp. 45-53).

Drucker, P.F. (1980). Managing in turbulent times. New York, NY: Harper & Row.

Fahey, L., & Randall, R.M. (Eds.). (1994). The portable MBA in strategy. New York: NY: John Wiley & Sons.

Festinger, L. (1957). A theory of cognitive dissonance. Palo Alto, CA: Stanford University Press.

Fisher, R., & Ury, W. (1981). Getting to yes: Negotiating agreement without giving in. Boston, MA: Houghton Mifflin.

Forbess-Green, S. (1983). The encyclopedia of icebreakers. San Diego, CA: University Associates.

Galbraith, J.K. (1992). The culture of contentment. Boston, MA: Houghton Mifflin.

Glass, G.V. (1975). A paradox about excellence of schools and the people in them. *Educational Researcher*, Vol. 4, (pp. 9-13).

Golden, D. (July, 1994). Building a better brain. *Life*, (pp. 63-70).

Goldenberg, I., & Goldenberg, H. *(1985)*. Family therapy: An overview. (2nd ed.). Pacific Grove, CA: Brooks/Cole.

Goleman, D. (1995). Emotional intelligence. New York, NY: Bantam.

Guba, E.G., & Lincoln, Y. S. (1987). Effective evaluation: Improving the usefulness of evaluation results through responsive and naturalistic approaches. San Francisco, CA: Jossey-Bass.

Hammer, M. & Champy, J. (1993). Reengineering the corporation: A manifesto for business revolution. New York, NY: HarperBusiness.

Handy, C. (1989). The age of unreason. Boston, MA: Harvard Business School Press.

Handy, C. (1995). The age of paradox. Boston, MA: Harvard Business School Press.

Harris, T.A. (1967). I'm OK – You're OK. New York, NY: Avon Books.

Heller, J. (1961). Catch-22. New York, NY: Laurel.

Hersey, P., & Blanchard, K.H. (1982). Management of organizational behavior. Englewood Cliffs, NJ: Prentice-Hall.

Hiam, A. (1990). The vest-pocket CEO: Decision-making tools for executives. Englewood Cliffs, NJ: Prentice-Hall.

Hiebert, M.B., & Smallwood, W.N. (May, 1987). Now for a completely different look at needs analysis: Discover the pragmatic alternatives to traditional methods. *Training and Development Journal*, (p. 77).

Hoffman, L. (1981). Foundations of family therapy. New York, NY: Basic Books.

Hordes, M. (Fall, 1989). Approach to white collar productivity. The Ecology of Work Conference. Toronto, Ont: Audiotape reference no. EC8976.

Hughes, R. (1993). Culture of complaint: The fraying of America. New York, NY: Oxford University Press.

Image Club Graphics Inc. (1994). The digitart clip art collection: Business cartoons. Vol. 22. 729 4th Ave. S.E., Calgary, Alberta, Canada. T2G 5K8. Phone 403-262-8008.

Jacobs, J. (1992). Systems of survival: A dialogue on the moral foundations of commerce and politics. New York, NY: Random House.

Janis, I. (1982). Victims of groupthink. (2nd ed.). Boston, MA: Houghton Mifflin.

Jick, T.D. (1993). Managing change: Cases and concepts. Burr Ridge, IL: Irwin.

Johnson, B. (1992). Polarity management: Identifying and managing unsolvable problems. Amherst, MA: HRD Press.

Johnson, D.W. (1986). Reaching out: Interpersonal effectiveness and self actualization. Englewood Cliffs, NJ: Prentice-Hall.

Johnson, D.W. (1993) Reaching out: Interpersonal effectiveness and self actualization. Boston, MA: Allyn & Bacon.

Jolles, R.L. (1993). How to run seminars and workshops: Presentation skills for consultants, trainers, and teachers. New York, NY: John Wiley & Sons.

Jones, J.E. (1972). Criteria for effective goal-setting: The SPIRO model. In J.W. Pfeiffer & J.E. Jones (Eds.). The 1972 annual handbook for group facilitators. San Diego, CA: University Associates, (pp. 132-133).

Jones, J.E. (December, 1990). Don't smile about smile sheets. *Training and Development Journal.*

Jones, J.E., & Biech, E. (Eds.). (1996). 1996 HR handbook. Amherst, MA: HRD Press.

Kanfer, F.H., & Goldstein, A.P. (Eds.). (1991). Helping people change: A textbook of methods. (4th ed.). New York, NY: Pergamon Press.

Kanter, R.M. (1989). When giants learn to dance: Mastering the challenges of strategy, management, and careers in the 1990's. New York, NY: Simon & Schuster.

Kaplan, A. (1964). The conduct of inquiry. San Francisco, CA: Chandler.

Katzenbach, J.R., & Smith, D.S. (1993). The wisdom of teams: Creating the high-performance organization. New York, NY: HarperBusiness.

Kennedy, P. (1993). Preparing for the twenty first century. Toronto, Ont: HarperCollins.

Kilmann, R. H. (1984). Beyond the quick fix: Managing five tracks to organizational success. San Francisco, CA: Jossey-Bass.

Kirkpatrick, D.L. (1975). Evaluating training programs. Washington, DC: American Society for Training and Development.

Knowles, M.S., & Associates. (1980). Andragogy in action. San Francisco, CA: Jossey-Bass.

Kolb, D.A. (1984). Experiential learning: Experience as the source of learning and development. Englewood Cliffs, NJ: Prentice-Hall.

Kolbe, K. (1993). Pure instinct: Business's untapped resource. Toronto, Ont: Random House.

Kouzes, J.M., & Posner, B.Z. (1987). The leadership challenge: How to get extraordinary things done in organizations. San Francisco, CA: Jossey-Bass.

Krathwohl, D.R., Bloom, B.S., & Masia, B.B. (1964). A taxonomy of educational objectives. New York, NY: David McKay Co.

Kuhn, T.S. (1970). The structure of scientific revolutions. (2nd ed.). Vol. 2. No. 2. International encyclopedia of unified science. Chicago, IL: University of Chicago Press.

Kushner, M.L. (1990). The light touch: How to use humor for business success. New York, NY: Simon & Schuster.

Laborde, G.Z. (1984). Influencing with integrity: Management skills for communication and negotiation. Palo Alto, CA: Syntony.

Larson, E., & Larson-Hegarty, C. (1992). From anger to forgiveness: A practical guide to breaking the negative power of anger and achieving reconciliation. New York, NY: Ballantine.

Larson, E. (1985). Stage II recovery: Life beyond addiction. San Francisco, CA: Harper & Row.

Larson, E. (1987). Stage II relationships: Love beyond addiction. San Francisco, CA: Harper & Row.

Lawler, E.E. (1988). High-involvement management: Participative strategies for improving organizational performance. San Francisco, CA: Jossey-Bass.

LeBoeuf, M. (1987). How to win customers and keep them for life. New York, NY: Berkeley Books.

Leinberger, P. & Tucker, B. (1991). The new individualists: The generation after the organization man. New York, NY: HarperCollins.

Lowy, A., Kelleher, D., & Finestone, P. (June, 1986). Management learning: Beyond program design. *Training and Development Journal*, 40 (6), (pp. 34-37).

Mager, R.F., & Pipe, P. (1984). Analyzing performance problems: Or you really oughta wanna. (2nd ed.). Belmont, CA: David S. Lake Publishers.

Malhotra Bentz, V. (Winter, 1991). Deep learning and group process. Fielding Magazine, (pp. 16-19).

Martin, P.K. (1990). Discovering the WHAT of management. Framington, NJ: Renaissance Educational Services.

McLuhan, E., & Zingrone, F. (Eds.). (1995). Essential McLuhan. Concord, Ont: Anansi.

McWhinney, W. (1992). Paths of change: Strategic choices for organizations and society. Newbury Park, CA: Sage.

McWhinney, W., McCulley, E.S., Weber, J.B., Smith, D.M., & Novokowski, B.J. (1993). Creating paths of change: Revitalization, renaissance and work. Venice, CA: Enthusion.

Mellander, K. (1993). The power of learning: Fostering employee growth. Alexandria, VA: The American Society for Training and Development.

Mintzberg, H. (1994). The rise and fall of strategic planning: Reconceiving roles for planning, plans, and planners. New York, NY: The Free Press.

Mitroff, I.I. (1988). Business not as usual: Rethinking our individual, corporate, and industrial strategies for global competition. San Francisco, CA: Jossey-Bass.

Moyers, B. (1990). A world of ideas II: Public opinions from private citizens. In A. Tucker (Ed.). New York, NY: Doubleday.

Nemoto, M. (1987). Total quality control for management: Strategies and tactics from Toyota and Toyoda Gosei. David Lu (Ed. and Trans.). Englewood Cliffs, NJ: Prentice-Hall.

Nierenberg, G.I. (1973). Fundamentals of negotiating. New York, NY: Hawthorne Books.

O'Rourke, P.J. (1994). All the trouble in the world: The lighter side of overpopulation, famine, ecological disaster, ethnic hatred, plague, and poverty. Toronto, Ont: Random House.

Osbome, D., & Gaebler, T. (1992). Reinventing government: How the entrepreneurial spirit is transforming the public sector. Toronto, Ont: Plume.

Osborn, A.F. (1963). Applied imagination. (3rd ed.). New York, NY: Scribners.

Ouchi, W.G. (1981). Theory Z: How American business can meet the Japanese challenge. New York, NY: Avon.

Owen, H. (1991). Riding the tiger: Doing business in a transforming world. Potomac, MD: Abbott Publishing.

Palmer, P. J. (1993). To know as we are known: Education as a spiritual journey. San Francisco, CA: HarperCollins.

Perry, T.L., Stott, R.G., & Smallwood, W. N. (1993). Real time strategy: Improvising team-based planning for a fast changing world. New York, NY: John Wiley & Sons.

Peters, T. (1994). The Tom Peters seminar. New York, NY: Vintage Books.

Peters, T.J., & Waterman, R.H., Jr. (1981). In search of excellence: Lessons from America's best-run companies. New York, NY: Harper & Row.

Pfeiffer, J.W., & Jones, J.E. (1978). OD readiness. The 1978 annual handbook for group facilitators. La Jolla, CA: University Associates.

Pferrer, J. (1992). Managing with power: Politics and influence in organizations. Boston, MA: Harvard Business School Press.

Pitman, T., & Bushe, G. (September, 1991). Appreciative process: A method of transformational change. OD Practitioner, (pp. 1-4).

Prather, H. (1970). Notes to myself: My struggle to become a person. Toronto, Ont: Bantam Books.

Purkey, W.W. (1970). Self concept and school achievement. Englewood Cliffs, NJ: Prentice-Hall.

Purkey, W.W. (1984). Inviting school success: A self concept approach to teaching and learning. Belmont, CA: Wadsworth.

Rath, G.J., Kisch, J., & Miller, H.E. (1976). X-Y: A three way intergroup competition. The 1976 annual handbook for group facilitators. San Diego, CA: University Associates.

Reich, R. B. (1991). The work of nations: Preparing ourselves for 21st century capitalism. New York, NY: Vintage Books.

Rogers, C.A. (1951). Client-centered therapy. Boston, MA: Houghton Mifflin.

Rogers, C.A. (1961). On becoming a person. Boston, MA: Houghton Mifflin.

Rogers, C.A. (1969). Freedom to learn. Columbus, OH: Merrill.

Rogers, C.A. (1980). A way of being. Boston, MA: Houghton Mifflin.

Rohn, J. (October 25, 1995). A presentation by Jim Rohn on the topic of motivation and success. Calgary, Alta. Unpublished.

Saul, J.R. (1992). Voltaire's bastards: The dictatorship of reason in the West. Toronto, Ont: Penguin Books.

Saul, J.R. (1994). The doubter's companion: A dictionary of aggressive common Sense. Toronto, Ont: Viking.

Saul, J.R. (1995). The unconscious civilization. Concord, Ont: Anansi.

Schermerhorn, J.R., Hunt, J.G., & Osborn, R.N. (1988). Managing organizational behavior. (3rd ed.). New York, NY: John Wiley & Sons.

Scholtes, P.R. (1988). The team handbook: How to use teams to improve quality. Madison, WI: Joiner Associates.

Scott, C.D., & Jaffe, D.T. (1989). Managing organizational change: A practical guide for managers. Menlo Park, CA: Crisp.

Seligman, M.E.P. (1990). Learned optimism: How to change your mind and your life. New York, NY: Pocket Books.

Seligman, M.E.P. (1993). What you can change ... and what you can't: The complete guide to successful self-improvement. New York, NY: Fawcett Columbine.

Senge, P.M. (1990). The fifth discipline: The art and practice of the learning organization. New York, NY: Doubleday.

Senge, P., Ross, R., Smith, B., Roberts, C., & Kiemer, A. (1994). The fifth discipline fieldbook: Strategies and tools for building a learning organization. New York, NY: Currency Doubleday.

Shenson, H.L., & Wilson, J.R. (1993). 138 quick ideas to get more clients. New York, NY: John Wiley & Sons.

Sherman, S. (December, 1993). A master class in radical change. *Fortune*, (p.90).

Simon, S.B. (1978). Values clarification: A handbook of practical strategies for teachers and students. New York, NY: Dodd, Mead & Co.

Simon, S.B. (November 21, 1991). Taken from verbal comments by Syd and Suzanne Simon at a workshop they led on the topic of self-esteem. Calgary, Alta. Unpublished.

Smith, K.K. (1982). Rabbits, lynxes, and organizational transitions. In J. Kimberly & R. Quinn (Eds.) New futures: The challenge of managing corporate transitions. Homewood, IL: Dow Jones-Irwin.

Smith, R.M. (1982) Learning how to learn: Applied theory for adults. Chicago, IL: Follett.

Taylor, R. (1991). "Presenting ... you." Calgary, Alta: Infinite Scope. Unpublished manuscript.

Toffler, A. (1970). Future shock. Toronto, Ont: Bantam Books.

Toffler, A. (1991). Power shift. New York, NY: Bantam Books.

University Associates Handbooks and Annuals. Published each year dating back to 1971. University Associates, Inc., 8517 Production Avenue, San Diego, CA 92121.

Vaill, P.B. (1989). Managing as a performing art: New ideas for a world of chaotic change. San Francisco, CA: Jossey-Bass.

Vroom, V.H., & Yetton, P.W. (1973). Leadership and decision-making. Pittsburgh, PA: University of Pittsburgh Press.

Wagner, A. (1981). The transactional manager: How to solve people problems with transactional analysis. Englewood Cliffs, NJ: Prentice-Hall.

Walton, R.E. (March-April, 1985). From control to commitment in the workplace. *Harvard Business Review*, (pp. 77-84).

Webster's New Collegiate Dictionary. (1981). Toronto, Ont: Thomas Allen & Sons.

Weeks, D., & James, J. (1995). Eccentrics: A study of sanity and strangeness. New York, NY: Villard.

Weick, K.E. (1969). The social psychology of organizing. New York, NY: Random House.

Weisbord, M.R. (1989). Productive workplaces: Organizing and managing for dignity, meaning, and community. San Francisco, CA: Jossey-Bass.

Zukav, G. (1979). The dancing wu li masters: An overview of the new physics. New York, NY: Quill William Morrow.

Non TTT references

Bridges, W. (1980). Transitions: Making sense of life's changes. Reading: MA: Addison-Wesley.

Skynner, R., & Cleese, J. (1993). Life: And how to survive it. London: Methuen.

Index

C

D

E

F

G

H

I

J

K

L

Q

R

S

T

Y

Z

About the Author

A person's philosophy is no small matter. It's your personal guidance system, and it's a major factor in how your life turns out. Part of my philosophy is that work should have "life value." It should be more than just activity and provide more than just economic income. Thus, my consulting practice is a central part of my life, although it's not my entire life. I enjoy my work. As a result, I put a lot of energy into learning. For example, for many years now I've averaged reading a business related book a week. Indeed, I don't just read. I study and mark up my books for future reference. It's gotten so bad my colleagues only allow me to borrow their books if I promise to put my highlighters and pens in a drawer.

I consult within major industrial sectors (e.g., health care, oil and gas, finance, retail/wholesale, manufacturing, education, government, and so on) and focus my practice on strategy and business planning, organization design, change and transition in organizations, team design, coaching leaders, developing boards of directors, and training trainers and workshop leaders. I have a goal of helping organizations be more focused and customer oriented.

This book had its origins in a training program I once operated, and still do occasionally, for workshop and training-program leaders. Today, as a senior consultant to organizations, I rarely conduct training programs, but I still lead workshops two or three times a month. These vary from one to three days in length and are an important tool in my consulting practice, but far from my only tool.

I believe there is opportunity in most organizations for increasing the quality and quantity of output and for improving human potential and the quality of working life. I'm also concerned about accountability and emphasize a practical, plain language approach in my work. I am committed to adding value on behalf of my clients.

As both a staff and line manager in major organizations over eighteen years, and as a consultant over the past six years, I've led more workshops and training programs than I could possibly count. What's made it so much fun over the years is the variety of participants and groups that I've worked with. Some have been so fired up and learning ready that all I had to do was stay out of their way. Others have been skeptical, challenging me to work as hard and as smart as I could to ensure the workshop was successful. On occasion I've even had a few of those rare birds in workshops, who, for whatever reason, devoted all their energy to causing me grief. Perhaps it's from this latter group that we learn the most about ourselves. Thus, even to them I am grateful.

Finally, to give the reader a little further background on my experience related to the subject matter in this book, I've led workshops and training programs of every stripe and color. I've led workshops having to do with creating strategy, goal setting, designing organization structure, forming teams, preparing accountability statements for senior executives, helping groups merge as a result of corporate acquisitions, and on and on. I've led training programs in everything from the very rational (e.g., problem solving and decision making, supervisory practices) to the highly intuitive (e.g., leadership, consulting skills for professionals), with plenty of others in-between (e.g., programs on change and transition, conflict management).

I Would Like to Hear from You

I'm interested in your feedback about this book, what you liked, what you found least helpful, and what you disagree with. I would also like to hear your stories as a workshop or training-program leader and what you learned in the process.

You can write me at:

Bruce Klatt
119 Lake Mead Dr. S.E.
Calgary, Alberta, Canada
T2J 4B2

My e-mail address is:

Klattb@cadvision.com

My fax number is:

403-278-1403

My office phone number is:

403-278-3821